Dear NFT User,

We've seen a lot these last couple of years. There was the Royal Wedding, which cheered up even the most miserable bastards among us. The glorious sight of spitfires and hurricanes flying over the capital was enough to make one feel proud to be British, and a style icon was born when Kate Middleton wore Alexander McQueen up the aisle. Then in 2013 arrival of His Royal Highness Prince George of Cambridge. And in 2015 Princess Charlotte.

Then there was the Olympics: otherwise known as that running-jumping-swimming-cycling-diving event thingummy, the name of which we cannot mention for trademark reasons; luckily it all went smashingly, we were ready (eat it, Mitt Romney!), and Britain's dignity, respectability and credibility remained intact. Well, there was that moment when Boris got stuck on the zip wire…oh, and the mix up with the North and South Korean flags…Russell Brand at the lacklustre closing ceremony. But other than that, all good. Well done everyone, jolly good show.

Elsewhere—specifically, "Sarf of the river"—we have a new Renzo Piano-designed 72-storey glass shard-like pyramid-idoididooby tower. Once destined to be the tallest building in Europe…well, with all that new Russian money we knew that wouldn't last, but we'll always have the view. We could make a joke about the best thing about the view is that it's the one place you can't see The Shard, but that would be a little shabby. Anyway, so that happened.

And to think all this happened amid a backdrop of financial collapse, Mayan nihilism and Danny Boyle's supremely dreary view of the Industrial Revolution. But that's where a stiff upper lip comes in handy. All of which is to say, here it is, a guide to the most delicious, intoxicating, awe-inspiring, groovy destinations in the city. The best places for quaffing, boogying, spending, and caffeinating ourselves silly in one of the best cities in the world. Or just spots that we like—those that become part of our everyday as Londoners and which we've chosen to share with you.

Don't forget to visit us online at www.notfortourists.com for updates and added content. And while we're at it, check out the NFT app—it's a great way to take the little black book on the go. No, we'll never shake the tactile pleasure of the printed page, but that doesn't mean we won't find new ways to reach out and connect. As usual, don't hesitate to let us know how you feel—your comments (and criticism!) are always very much appreciated.

—Jane, Scott, Claire et al.

Table of Contents

Underground Map and Bus Map
foldout, last page

Maps 1–24 · **Central London**

SOMERS TOWN

Regent's Park

REGENT'S PARK

ST. JOHN'S WOOD

ST.

LISSON GREEN ESTATE

EUSTON

Euston Rd

Tavistock Sq

Marylebone Rd

MARYLEBONE

Portland Pl

Great Portland St

Gower St

4

Montague Pl

BLOO

York St

Baker St

Marylebone High St

St James's St

Cavendish St

2

3 FITZROVIA

Goodge St

Tottenham Court Rd

Bloomsbury St

LISSON GROVE

Gloucester Pl

Cavendish Sq Garden

Oxford St

St. Giles

End

PADDINGTON

1

Portman Sq

Seymour St

New Bond St

Soho Square Garden

12

SOHO

LEIG

SO

Marble Arch

11

Shaftesbury Ave

Charing Cross Rd

WEST END

10

T

Hyde Park

Park Ln

MAYFAIR

St James's St

24

Piccadilly

PICCADILLY

Haymarket

Regent St

9

Green Park

Piccadilly

Pall Mall

3

ST. JAMES'S

Kensington Gardens

St. James's Park

Whitehall

Hyde Park Corner

Buckingham Palace Gardens

Grosvenor Pl

KNIGHTSBRIDGE

Strand Sanctuary

Great Smith St

Victoria St

22

SOUTH KENSINGTON

Pont St

Belgrave Pl

Rochester Row

WESTMINSTE

BROMPTON

Sloane St

19 BELGRAVIA

Buckingham Palace Rd

Marsham St

Eaton Sq

20

Vauxhall Bridge Rd

21

Pimlico Rd

Belgrave Rd

SLOANE SQUARE

PIMLICO

Grosvenor Rd

CHELSEA

Map 1 · **Marylebone (West)**

Marylebone (West)

Where the mullah meets the hookah, a stroll down Edgware Road is soundtracked by gurgling shisha pipes and bangin' Arabic pop music. To the east, ostentatiously bejewelled madams patrol Montague Square. They'd turn their noses up at a shawarma at **Beirut Express**, and probably wouldn't deign to shop ≡ **Maroush Deli**. Good, more for the rest of us.

Cinemas

- **Odeon Marble Arch** • 10 Edgware Rd
- **Everyman Baker Street** • 96 Baker St

Coffee

- **Apostrophe** • 19 Baker St
- **Bagel Factory** • 39 Paddington St
- **Borough Barista** • 60 Seymour St
- **Caffe Nero** • 184 Edgware Rd
- **Daisy Green** • 20 Seymour St
- **Eat.** • 400 Oxford St
- **Eat.** • 114 Baker St
- **Kings Cafe** • 177 Edgware Rd
- **Palm Cafe Shisha Bar** • 7 Crawford Pl
- **Pret A Manger** • 556 Oxford St
- **Starbucks** • 29 N Audley St
- **Starbucks** • 34 Edgware Rd

O Landmarks

- **Marble Arch** • Oxford St & Park Ln
- **Speakers Corner** • Cumberland Gate & Park Ln

Nightlife

- **Duke of York** • 45 Harrowby St

Post Offices

- **Baker St** • 111 Baker St
- **Edgware Rd** • 354 Edgware Rd

Restaurants

- **Beirut Express** • 112 Edgware Rd
- **Daisy Green** • 20 Seymour St
- **Locanda Locatelli** • 8 Seymour St
- **Maroush VI Express** • 68 Edgware Rd
- **Twist** • 42 Crawford St

Shopping

- **Maroush Deli** • 45 Edgware Rd
- **Phil Parker** • 106 Crawford St
- **Primark** • 499 Oxford St
- **Spymaster** • 3 Portman Sq
- **Totally Swedish** • 32 Crawford St

Supermarkets

- **Sainsbury's** • 55 Bryanston St

Map 2 · **Marylebone (East)**

Granted the plush boutiques and old moneyisms of Marylebone are far removed from most Londoners' lives, but that's not to say you can't go window-shopping, and with **VV Rouleaux** and **The Button Queen** nearby, you could even craft your own outfit. Don't forget to stop in at **Claridge's** to tell Gordon Ramsay to f*** off, then sedate yourself in the beautiful book haven that is **Daunt**.

Coffee

- **Apostrophe** • 23 Barrett St
- **Back on Track Coffee** • 3 Wimpole St
- **Caffe Nero** • 273 Regent St
- **Caffe Nero** • Marylebone Rd
- **Coffee Republic** • 2 S Molton St
- **Costa** • 19 Wigmore St
- **Eat.** • 9 Avery Row
- **Eat.** • 319 Regent St
- **Eat.** • 25 Hanover Sq
- **Eat.** • 92 Wimpole St
- **Eat.** • 211 Oxford St
- **Paul Rothe & Son** • 35 Marylebone Ln
- **Pret A Manger** • 31 Cavendish
- **Pret A Manger** • 1 Tenterden St
- **Pret A Manger** • 18 Hanover St
- **Starbucks** • 22 Princes St
- **Starbucks** • 14 James St
- **Starbucks** • 63 S Molton St

O Landmarks

- **Hertford House** • Manchester Sq
- **Jimi Hendrix Memorial Blue Plaque** • 23 Brook St
- **St. Christopher's Place** • 23 Barrett St

Libraries

- **Royal College of Nursing Library** • 20 Cavendish Sq

Nightlife

- **Claridges Bar** • 55 Brook St
- **Gunmakers** • 33 Ayrbrook St
- **Inn 1888** • 21 Devonshire St
- **The Phoenix** • 37 Cavendish Sq
- **Purl** • 50-54 Blandford St

Post Offices

- **Marylebone** • 24 Thayer St

Restaurants

- **Casa Becci** • 32 Paddington St
- **Chiltern Firehouse** • 1 Chiltern St
- **Comptoir Libanais** • 65 Wigmore St
- **Diwan** • 31 Thayer St
- **Fischer's** • 50 Marylebone High St
- **The Golden Hind** • 73 Marylebone Ln
- **Galvin Bistrot de Luxe** • 66 Baker St
- **Goodman Mayfair** • 24-26 Maddox St
- **Hush Brasserie** • 8 Lancashire Ct
- **La Galette** • 56 Paddington St
- **Meat Liquor** • 74 Welbeck St
- **No. 5 Cavendish Square** • 5 Cavendish Sq
- **Patisserie Valerie** • 105 Marylebone High St
- **Patty & Bun** • 54 James St
- **Pollen Street Social** • 8 Pollen St
- **The Providores** • 109 Marylebone High St
- **Royal China** • 24-26 Baker St
- **Royal China Club** • 40-42 Baker St
- **Trishna** • 15 Blandford St
- **Zoilo** • 9 Duke St

Shopping

- **Browns** • 24 S Molton St
- **The Button Queen** • 76 Marylebone Ln
- **Content Beauty/Wellbeing** • 14 Bulstrode St
- **Daunt Books** • 83 Marylebone High St
- **Divertimenti** • 33 Marylebone High St
- **The Duffer of St. George** • 268 Oxford St
- **Fenwick** • 63 New Bond St
- **French Sole** • 61 Marylebone Ln
- **Gray's Antique Market** • 58 Davies St
- **John Lewis** • 300 Oxford St
- **La Fromagerie** • 2 Moxon St
- **Monocle** • 2 George St
- **Niketown** • 236 Oxford St
- **Paul Smith** • 38 Marylebone High St
- **Postcard Teas** • 8 Dering St
- **Selfridges & Co.** • 400 Oxford St
- **Skandium** • 86 Marylebone High St
- **VV Rouleaux** • 102 Marylebone Ln
- **The Widescreen Centre** • 47 Dorset St
- **Zara** • 242 Oxford St

Supermarkets

- **Marks & Spencer** • Bond St Station
- **Waitrose** • 98 Marylebone High St

Map 3 · **Fitzrovia**

Fitzrovia

There's a whole recent trend for upmarket Fitzrovians to roam east in return for trendsetting East Enders giving their neighbourhood a bit of cool cred—they're all swapping galleries and premises and god knows what else in some kind of grown-up-exchange programme. Fitzrovia has its own history of cool though; you might be lucky enough to see a star or two at the BBC on Great Portland.

Map 3

Cinemas

- **Odeon Tottenham Court** •
  30 Tottenham Ct Rd

Coffee

- **Apostrope** • 40 Great Castle St
- **Apostrope** • 216 Tottenham Court Rd
- **The Attendant** • 27 Foley St
- **BB's Coffee and Muffins** • 120 Oxford St
- **Ben's House** • 64 Grafton Way
- **Black Sheep Coffee** • 63 Charlotte St
- **Caffe Nero** • 70 Tottenham Ct Rd
- **Caffe Nero** • 187 Tottenham Ct Rd
- **Caffe Nero** • 2 Charlotte St
- **Caffe Nero** • 48 Oxford St
- **Coffee Republic** • 99 Tottenham Ct Rd
- **Eat.** • 44 Goodge St
- **Eat.** • 68 Oxford St
- **Eat.** • 94 Tottenham Ct Rd
- **Kaffeine** • 66 Great Titchfield St
- **Lantana** • 13 Charlotte Pl
- **Mother's Milk** • 12 Little Portland St
- **Pret A Manger** • 298 Regent St
- **Starbucks** • 103 Oxford St
- **Starbucks** • 11 Goodge St
- **Tapped and Packed** •
  114 Tottenham Court Rd

Landmarks

- **BT Tower** • 60 Cleveland St
- **Charlotte Street** • Charlotte St
- **Middlesex Hospital** •
  Mortimer St & Cleveland St
- **Pollock's Toy Museum** • 1 Scala St
- **Sinner Winner Man** • 216 Oxford St
- **Tottenham Court Road** •
  Tottenham Ct Rd

Libraries

- **RIBA British Architectural Library** •
  66 Portland Pl
- **Institute of Contemporary History and
  Wiener Library** • 4 Devonshire St
- **Royal Institute of British Architects** •
  66 Portland Pl

Nightlife

- **100 Club** • 100 Oxford St
- **The Albany** • 240 Great Portland St
- **Bourne & Hollingsworth** •
  28 Rathbone St
- **Bradley's Spanish Bar** • 42 Hanway St
- **Bricklayers Arms** • 31 Gresse St
- **Charlotte Street Hotel** • 15 Charlotte St
- **The Cock** • 27 Great Portland St
- **The Fitzroy Tavern** • 16 Charlotte St
- **The Jerusalem Tavern** • 55 Britton St
- **Market Place** • 11 Market Pl
- **The Northumberland Arms** •
  43 Goodge St
- **The Remedy** • 124 Cleveland St
- **Rising Sun** • 46 Tottenham Ct Rd
- **The Roxy** • 3 Rathbone Pl
- **Shochu Lounge** • 37 Charlotte St
- **The Social** • 5 Little Portland St
- **Yorkshire Grey** • 46 Langham St

Post Offices

- **Great Portland St** • 55 Great Portland St
- **Newman St** • 19 Newman St
- **Oxford Street** • 120 Oxford St

Restaurants

- **Archipelago** • 53 Cleveland St
- **Ask** • 48 Grafton Way
- **Bao** • 31 Windmill St
- **Barnyard** • 18 Charlotte St
- **Barrica** • 62 Goodge St
- **Beard Papa** • 143 Oxford St
- **Berners Tavern** • 10 Berners St
- **Beyond Bread** • 2 Charlotte Pl
- **Bonnie Gull** • 21 Foley St
- **Boopshi's** • 31 Windmill St
- **Brazilian Gourmet** • 70 Cleveland St
- **Carluccio's** • 8 Market Pl
- **Crazy Bear** • 26 Whitfield St
- **Elena's L'Etoile** • 30 Charlotte St
- **Gitane** • 60 Great Titchfield St
- **Govinda's** • 9 Soho St
- **Honey & Co** • 25 Warren St

- **Iberica** • 195 Great Portland St
- **ICCo** • 46 Goodge St
- **Kin Cafe** • 22 Foley St
- **Koba** • 11 Rathbone St
- **Latium** • 21 Berners St
- **Market Place** • 11 Market Pl
- **Navarro's** • 67 Charlotte St
- **Nyonya** • 11 Warren St
- **Picture** • 110 Great Portland St
- **Portland** • 113 Great Portland St
- **Ragam** • 57 Cleveland St
- **The Riding House Cafe** •
  43 Great Titchfield St
- **Roka** • 37 Charlotte St
- **Salt Yard** • 54 Goodge St
- **Sardo** • 45 Grafton Way
- **Stef's** • 3 Berners St
- **Thai Metro** • 38 Charlotte St
- **Villandry** • 170 Great Portland St
- **Yalla Yalla** • 12 Winsley St

Shopping

- **The Aquatic Design Centre** •
  107 Great Portland St
- **Ben's House** • 64 Grafton Way
- **Trimmings** • 14 Great Titchfield St
- **Computer Exchange** • 32 Rathbone Pl
- **Chess & Bridge** • 369 Euston Rd
- **Harmony** • 103 Oxford St
- **Hobgoblin Music** • 24 Rathbone Pl
- **Mango** • 225 Oxford St
- **Maplin** • 218 Tottenham Court Rd
- **Paperchase** • 213 Tottenham Court Rd
- **R.D. Franks** • 5 Winsley St
- **Scandinavian Kitchen** •
  61 Great Titchfield St
- **Stargreen Box Office** • 21 Argyll St
- **Topshop** • 36 Great Castle St
- **Topshop** • 216 Oxford St
- **Urban Outfitters** • 200 Oxford St

Supermarkets

- **Marks & Spencer** • 55 Tottenham Ct Rd
- **Sainsbury's** • 35 Mortimer St
- **Sainsbury's** • 17 Tottenham Ct Rd
- **Sainsbury's** • 145 Tottenham Ct Rd
- **Tesco** • 10 Goodge St

Map 4 · **Bloomsbury (West)**

N

Warren Street
Whitfield St
Road A501
Gower Street A400
Euston Square
Stephenson Way
Euston Square Gardens
Euston Road A501
Church
Euston Street
Euston Road

1

2

78

Beaumont
Place
77
Gower Place
Gower Court
Gower Place
Endsleigh Gardens
Upper Woburn Place A200
Woburn Walk
Flaxman Terrace
Burton Place
Woolf M
Burton Street
Mabledon Pl
Bidborough
Hastings
Sandwick Pl
Leigh

Grafton Way
Tottenham Court Road A400
Hertford Pl
Midford Place
University Street
Mortimer
Mkt
Gower Street A400
Gordon Street
Taviton Street
Endsleigh Street
Endsleigh
Place
Tavistock Square A4200
Gordon Place
Crescent
Cartwright Gdns
Compton Pl
Tavistock

A

Whitfield Pl
Howland Mews E
Huntley Street
Chenies Mews
University
College
London
PAGE 370
Gordon
Square
Gordon Square Park & Gardens
Tavistock Square Gardens
Tavistock
Place
Peabody
DWE
Marchmont Street
Kenton St

Charlotte St
Capper Street
Queens
Yd
Shropshire Pl
Torrington Place
Mallet Place
Byng Pl
Gordon Sq
Woburn Sq
Bedford Way
Coram Street
Herbrand St
Woburn Place A200
Herbrand Street

Chitty St
Scala St
Goodge Street
Alfred Mews
North Crescent
Torrington Square
Torrington Place
Woburn Sq

Tottenham Street
Street B506
Chenies Street
Alfred Place
Ridgmount Gdns
Ridgmount St
Gower Street A400
Malet Street
Bedford Way

Percy Street
3
Ridgmount
Place
Store Street
South Cres
Gower Mews
Senate House
BLOOMSBURY
Thornhaugh St
Russell Square
Russell Square Gardens
5
Bernard Street B502
Russell
Square
Colonnade
Guilford Street
Queen
Square Place

Percy M
Stephen M
Bayley Street
Bedford
Square
Bedford
Square
Montague Place B506
PAGE 470
Russell Square
Southampton Row A200
Queen
Square
Queens
Square Park & Garden

Greisse St
Stephen Street
Evelyn Yd
Morwell Street
Adeline Pl
Bedford
The British Museum
Montague Street
Montague Street Park & Gardens
Bedford Place
Bedford Place Park & Garden
Cosmo
Old Gloucester Street
Grows Ormo
Ormond

B

Hanway St
Tottenham Court Road
Hanway Street
Street A40
Falconberg Mews
Bedford Avenue

Sutton Row
Falconberg Ct
Andrew Borde St
Centre Point
Oxford Street
Goslett
Yd
Bainbridge Street
Dyott St
Streatham St
Bloomsbury Street A400
Coptic Street
Great Russell Street
Gilbert Place
Bury Place
Galen Pl
Little Russell Street
Bloomsbury Square Gardens
Bloomsbury Sq
Bloomsbury
Pl
Boswell Street
Theobald

St Giles High Street
Denmark St
12
Bucknall St
St Giles High Street A400
George
High Bloomsbury Way A40
Barter Street
Vernon Place A40
Southampton Place
Kingsway Tram Tunnel
Fisher Street
Red Lion Sq
Red Lion
Red Lion Square Park & Garden

Charing Cross Road A400
Manette St
Denmark Pl
Grape Buildings
New Oxford Street
Barter Street
Holborn A40
High Holborn A40
Catton Street
Proctor St

13

0.25 mile
0.25 km

Holborn

Bloomsbury (West)

Bloomsbury didn't incite and excite Britain's most prolific set of literature writers—or no good reason. These streets ooze the kind of romanticised idea of London that had Virginia Woolf and E.M Forster zoned in as inspiration. Clever people have lived here in Bloomsbury and cleverer people visit. **The British Museum**'s Age of Illumination collection highlights the world's learners.

Map 4

Cinemas

- **Horse Hospital** • 30 Colonnade
- **Odeon Tottenham Court** • 30 Tottenham Ct Rd

Coffee

- **Café Deco** • 43 Store St
- **Costa** • 44 New Oxford St
- **Costa** • 82 Gower St
- **London Review Cake Shop** • 14 Bury Pl
- **Pret A Manger** • 40 Bernard St
- **Pret A Manger** • 23 Southampton Row
- **Pret A Manger** • 44 New Oxford St
- **Pret A Manger** • 102 Southampton Row
- **Ruskins Café** • 41 Museum St
- **Starbucks** • 24 Southampton Row
- **Starbucks** • 12 New Oxford
- **Starbucks** • 25 Oxford St
- **Store Street Espresso** • 40 Store St

Emergency Rooms

- **University College Hospital** • 235 Euston Rd

Landmarks

- **British Museum** • Great Russell St
- **Centre Point** • 101 New Oxford St
- **Kingsway Tram Tunnel** • Theobald's Rd & Southampton Row
- **Senate House** • Malet St & Torrington Sq
- **SOAS** • Thornhaugh St
- **Student Central** • Malet St
- **Tavistock Square** • Tavistock Sq
- **University College London** • Gower St

Libraries

- **Anthropology Library** • Great Russell St
- **Birkbeck College Library** • Malet St
- **German Historical Institute Library London** • 17 Bloomsbury Sq
- **Institute of Advanced Legal Studies Library** • 17 Russell Sq
- **University of London, Senate House Library** • Malet St

Nightlife

- **All Star Lanes** • Victoria House, Bloomsbury Pl
- **Bloomsbury Bowling Lanes** • Bedford Way
- **Marquis Cornwallis** • 31 Marchmont St
- **The Old Crown Public House** • 33 New Oxford St
- **The Plough** • 27 Museum St
- **The Princess Louise** • 208 High Holborn
- **ULU** • Malet St

Post Offices

- **Marchmont St** • 33 Marchmont St
- **Russell Square** • 9 Russell Sq

Restaurants

- **Alara** • 58 Marchmont St
- **Bi Won** • 24 Coptic St
- **Savoir Faire** • 42 New Oxford St

Shopping

- **Aperture** • 44 Museum St
- **Blade Rubber Stamps** • 12 Bury Pl
- **British Museum shop** • Great Russell St
- **Gosh!** • 1 Berwick St
- **James Smith & Sons** • 53 New Oxford St
- **London Review Bookshop** • 14 Bury Pl
- **Maplin** • 218 Tottenham Ct Rd
- **Paperchase** • 213 Tottenham Ct Rd
- **York Cameras** • 18 Bury Pl

Supermarkets

- **Waitrose** • Brunswick Sq

Map 5 · **Bloomsbury (East)**

Bloomsbury (East)

Map 5

Agog with students, this tract of Bloomsbury is a bustling cultural playground. The brilliant **Renoir Cinema** resides in the belly of the **Brunswick Centre**, a Brutalist masterpiece with some shops thrown in for good measure. For contrast, stroll over to Lamb's Conduit Street and enjoy some boutique shopping. Then indulge in a sit-down cream tea at **Bea's**.

Cinemas

• **Renoir Cinema** • 1 Brunswick Sq

Coffee

• **Café Lumen** • 88 Tavistock Place
• **Continental Stores** • 54 Tavistock Place
• **The Espresso Room** • 31-35 Great Ormond St
• **Knockbox Coffee** • 29 Lambs Conduit St
• **Pret A Manger** • 15 Theobald's Rd
• **Starbucks** • 57 Theobald's Rd
• **T-HQ** • 55 Grays Inn Rd

Landmarks

• **Charles Dickens Museum** • 48 Doughty St
• **Gray's Inn Field** • Theobald's Rd
• **Doughty Street** • Doughty St & Guilford St

Libraries

• **Holborn Library** • 32 Theobald's Rd
• **Royal National Institute of the Blind Research Library** • 105 Judd St
• **St Pancras Library** • Argyle St

Nightlife

• **06 St Chad's Place** • 6 St Chad's Pl
• **The Blue Lion** • 133 Grays Inn Rd
• **Calthorpe Arms** • 252 Gray's Inn Rd
• **The Clerk & Well** • 156 Clerkenwell Rd
• **The Lamb** • 94 Lamb's Conduit St
• **Monto** • 328 Grays Inn Rd
• **The Perseverance** • 63 Lamb's Conduit St
• **Pimp Shuei** • 59 Mount Pleasant
• **Smithy's** • 15 Leeke St

Post Offices

• **Mount Pleasant** • Farringdon Rd & Rosebery Ave

Restaurants

• **Banh Mi Bay** • 4-6 Theobalds Rd
• **Bea's of Bloomsbury** • 44 Theobald's Rd
• **Ciao Bella** • 86 Lamb's Conduit St
• **Cigala** • 54 Lamb's Conduit St
• **The Food Bazaar** • 59 Grays Inn Rd
• **Fryer's Delight** • 19 Theobald's Rd
• **Itadaki Zen** • 139 King's Cross Rd
• **The Lady Ottoline** • 11 Northington St
• **Mary Ward Centre** • 42 Queen Sq
• **Paolina Thai Snack Bar** • 181 King's Cross Rd
• **The Perseverance** • 63 Lamb's Conduit St
• **You Me Sushi** • 180 Grays Inn Rd

Shopping

• **Bibas Hair and Beauty** • 72 Marchmont St
• **The Brunswick** • Hunter St
• **The Flash Centre** • 68 Brunswick Centre
• **Folk** • 49 Lamb's Conduit St
• **Gay's the Word** • 66 Marchmont St
• **International Magic** • 89 Clerkenwell Rd
• **JOY** • 22 Brunswick Centre
• **Magma** • 117 Clerkenwell Rd

Map 6 · **Clerkenwell**

Clerkenwell

Map 6

A villa⬚e in the city provides a perfect contrast of a pretty green square separa⬚ed by only a row of shops from the rest of the corporate world. **The Moder⬚ Pantry** is where suits gather for a business power-breakfast, while lunchtimes centre on Exmouth Market. Potter off the main square for back-alley Be⬚gium beers at **The Dovetail**.

Coffee

- **Ground ⬚ontrol** • 61 Amwell St
- **Worksho⬚ Coffee Co** • 27 Clerkenwell Rd

Libraries

- **Finsbury L⬚brary** • 245 St John St
- **Marx Mem⬚rial Library** • 37 Clerkenwell Green

O Landmarks

- **City Univers⬚ty London** • Northampton Sq
- **The House o⬚ Detention** • St James's Walk

Nightlife

- **1920** • 19 Grea⬚ Sutton St
- **Bandstand Bu⬚king** • Northampton Sq
- **The Betsey Tro⬚wood** • 56 Farringdon Rd
- **Café Kick** • 43 E⬚mouth Market
- **The Dovetail** • ⬚Jerusalem Passage
- **The Harlequin** • 27 Arlington Wy
- **Old Red Lion** • 4⬚8 St John St
- **The Slaughtered Lamb** • 34 Great Sutton St
- **The Three Kings** • 7 Clerkenwell Close
- **Wilmington Arm⬚** • 69 Rosebery Ave

🍴 Restaurants

- **Badabing** • 120 St. John St
- **Caravan** • 11 Exmouth Market
- **Dans Le Noir** • 30 Clerkenwell Green
- **The Eagle** • 159 Farringdon Rd
- **Little Bay** • 171 Farringdon Rd
- **The Modern Pantry** • 47 St. Johns Sq
- **Morito** • 32 Exmouth Market
- **Moro** • 34 Exmouth Market
- **Pham Sushi** • 159 Whitecross St
- **SandwichMan** • 23 Easton St
- **Sushi Tetsu** • 12 Jerusalem Passage

🛍 Shopping

- **EC One Jewellery** • 41 Exmouth Market
- **The Family Business Tattoo Shop** • 58 Exmouth Market
- **London Tattoo** • 332 Goswell Rd
- **M and R Meats** • 399 St. John St
- **Metro Imaging** • 32 Great Sutton St
- **Timorous Beasties** • 46 Amwell St
- **The Wyvern Bindery** • 56 Clerkenwell Rd

Supermarkets

- **Waitrose** • Ayelsbury St & St. John St

Ugly as the brutalist Barbican might be, its surrounds have happily morphed into one of those areas that thrives on its appalling looks and survives on a generation of media peeps. Where the cool crowds flow, top notch hang-outs will follow, Old Street, or Silicon Roundabout, was designed for those who mainline coffee for survival while **Bunhill Fields** provides necessary respite.

Cinemas

• **Barbican Centre Cinema** • Silk St & Whitecross St

Coffee

• **Caffe Nero** • 40 City Rd
• **Coffee Republic** • City Rd
• **Costa** • 68 Goswell Rd
• **Costa** • Ropemaker St
• **Eat.** • 143 Moorgate
• **Fix** • 161 Whitecross St
• **Look Mum No Hands!** • 49 Old St
• **Pitch 42** • Whitecross St Market
• **Popular Cafe** • 85 Lever St
• **Pret A Manger** • 9 Goswell Rd
• **Pret A Manger** • Ropemaker St
• **Shoreditch Grind** • 213 Old St
• **Timberyard** • 61 Old St

O Landmarks

• **Barbican Centre** • Silk St
• **Bunhill Fields Burial Ground** • 38 City Rd
• **Church of St Bartholomew the Great** • Kinghorn St
• **LSO St Luke's** • 161 Old St
• **St. Giles** • Fore St

Libraries

• **Barbican Library** • Silk St
• **Wandsworth Town Library** • 11 Garrett St

Nightlife

• **Nightjar** • 129 City Rd
• **The Two Brewers** • 121 Whitecross St

Post Offices

• **Old Street** • 205 Old St

Restaurants

• **Bavarian Beerhouse** • 190 City Rd
• **Carnevale** • 135 Whitecross St
• **De Santis** • 11 Old St
• **Nusa Kitchen** • 9 Old St
• **Original Bagel Bakery** • 22 Goswell Rd

Shopping

• **Red Dot Cameras** • 68 Old St
• **Whitecross Market** • Whitecross St

Supermarkets

• **Waitrose** • Whitecross St

Map 8 · **Liverpool Street / Broadgate**

N

Cranwood St
Staff St
Old Street A5201
84
Old Street
Cowper Street
Singer St
Great Eastern Street A1202
Rivington
Charlotte Road
Mills Ct
Dereham Pl
Dereham Pl
French
Curtain Road
Shoreditch High Street
Boundary

Willow Ct
Willow Street
Blackall Street
St Paul St
St Paul St
Leonard Street
Ravey Street
Phipp Street
Gatesborough St
Bateman's Row
New Inn Yard
Reliance Sq
Anning St
King John Ct
91

Mallow Street
stone Street
City Road A5201
Kitten St
Mark St
Luke Street
New N Pl
Christina St
Holywell Lane
Fairchild St

A
Olivers Yd
Tabernacle Street
Clere Street
Platina Street
Scrutton Street
Hewett St
Curtain Road
Fairchild Pl
Plough Yard
Dereham
Duval St

Bunhill
Fields
Burial Grounds
Epworth Street
Bonhill Street
Wilson Street Paul
Clifton Street
Holywell Row
Holywell Row
Hearn St
Shoreditch High Street A10

City Road A501
Worship Street
Dysart Street
Clifton St
Vandy S
Norton Folgate A10

Bunhill Fields
Christopher Street
Finsbury St
Wilson Street Paul
Christopher Street
Pindar Street
Sclater
Mkt
Primrose Stree
Spital Sq
Spital Yd

Finsbury Square Garden
Earl Street
Appold Street

swell Street
Finsbury Street
Finsbury Pavement A501
Finsbury Square
Sun Street B100
Broad Ln
Liverpool Street Station
Bishopsgate
18

B
Ropemaker Street
Lackington St
Dominion St
Wilson St
Broadgate Arena
Sun St
PAGE 411
Artiller
Middlese

Moor Lane
New Union Street
Moorfields
S Place
South Place
Finsbury Ave
Eldon Street
Fulcrum at Broadgate
Liverpool Street
Victoria Av
New Street
Davonshire Sq

Moor La
Moorgate A501
Finsbury Circus
Finsbury Circus Garden
Finsbury Circus
Circus Pl
Blomfield Street
Broad Street Avenue
Bishopsgate
cavenshire Row

Fore St
Moorgate
London Wall A1211
Bishopsgate Churchyard
St. Botolph-without-Bishopsgate Gardens
Houndso

all A1211
Basinghall Av
Moorgate A501
Copthall Av
Langthorn P
Gt Winchester St
Telegraph St
Wormwood Street A1211
Union Ct
Car
Dulwich St
17

White Horse Yd
Friars
Austin Friars
Great Winchester St
St
reet
Bevis

| 0.25 mile | 0.25 km |

A grimy maw that spews trendos onto Bishopsgate, Liverpool Street is the gateway to the nowness of Brick Lane and Shoreditch. Its arse-end lets out suits and money into the borders of the City. Avoid a flash-mob in **The Light** after a grease-up in **Damascu Bite**, but c'mon, you know you're really on your way to an all-night rave in Stokey so cut the crap and get on the 149.

Coffee

- **AMT** • Liverpool St & Broadgate Circle
- **Benugo** • 82 City Rd
- **Caffe Nero** • 2 Bishopsgate
- **Caffe Nero** • 40 City Rd
- **Caffe Nero** • 75 London Wall
- **Costa** • 1 Ropemaker St
- **Costa** • 18 Liverpool St
- **Eat.** • 1 City Rd
- **Eat.** • 143 Moorgate
- **Eat.** • 176 Bishopsgate
- **Eat.** • 34 Broadgate Circle
- **Eat.** • 62 London Wall
- **Eat.** • 80 Old Broad St
- **Fab Food Patisserie** • 26 Curtain Rd
- **Salvation Jane** • 55 City Rd
- **Starbucks** • Liverpool St Station
- **Starbucks** • Charterhouse Buildings
- **Starbucks** • 8 Broadgate Circle

O Landmarks

- **Fulcrum** • Broadgate

Libraries

- **Bishopsgate Library** • 230 Bishopsgate

Nightlife

- **The Book Club** • 100 Leonard St
- **Callooh Callay** • 65 Rivington St
- **Casita** • 5 Ravey St
- **Lounge Bohemia** • 1 Great Eastern St
- **Red Lion** • 1 Eldon St
- **Worship Street Whistling Shop** • 63 Worship St
- **XOYO** • 32 Cowper St

Restaurants

- **Damascu Bite** • 21 Shoreditch High St
- **Duck and Waffle** • 110 Bishopsgate
- **Eyre Brothers** • 70 Leonard St
- **Gaucho Broadgate** • 5 Finsbury Ave
- **Hoxton Grill** • 81 Great Eastern St
- **The Princess of Shoreditch** • 76 Paul St

Supermarkets

- **Tesco** • 158 Bishopsgate

Map 9 • **Mayfair / Green Park**

1

2

A

MAYFAIR

50 Berkeley Sq

Grosvenor Square

Grosvenor Square

Grosvenor Street

Broadbent Street

Grosvenor Hill

Mount Row

Berkeley Square

Bruton Place

Bruton Street

Berkeley Square Gardens

Grafton

New Bond St

Old Bond St

Culross Street

Upper Grosvenor St

Reeves Mews

Adams Row

Mount Street

Mount Street

S Audley St

Mount Street Gardens

Farm Street

Hill Street

Hay's Mews

Charles Street

Clarges Mews

Curzon Street

Clarges Street

Bolton Street

Half Moon Street

Stratton Street

Piccadilly A4

Berkeley Street

Dover Street

Stafford Street

Piccadilly

Green Park

10

19

Park Lane

Achilles Way

Apsley House

Hyde Park Corner

Knightsbridge A4

Hyde Park Corner

Apsley Way

Duke of Wellington Place

Hamilton Place

Brick Street

Gratham Pl

Down Street

Brick Street

Yarmouth Place

Shepherd Street

Hertford Street

Pitt's Head Ms

Market Mews

Down St Station

Hard Rock Cafe

Hyde Park

PAGE 342

Curzon Gate

Park Lane A4202

Park Lane A4202

Park Lane A4202

Park Lane

Balfour

Balfour Street

South Audley Street

South Street

Aldford Street

Green Park

PAGE 354

Constitution Hill

Buckingham Palace Gardens

Memorial Gardens

The Mall

Buckingham Palace

St. James's Park

Grosvenor Place A302

Grosvenor Crescent B310

Halkin Street

Chapel Street

Groom Place

Chester Street

Wilton Street

Hobart Place

Lower Grosvenor Place

Buckingham Gate

Buckingham A3214 Gate

Lower Grosvenor Place A3214

Birdcage Walk

Eaton Square

20

23

B

0.25 mile

0.25 km

Three Kings Yard

Brook's Mews

Avery Row

Maddox

Conduit Street

Green Park

St. James's Street

Mayfair / Green Park

A taste of Old Money is a decent enough reason to visit Mayfair; splashing out on High Tea at **The Ritz** is pretty much an investment in one's cultural education. The upside to might-rich neighbourhoods? Art galleries. Ones that give away wine. All the time. Pop down Cork Street on an eve to quaff all the free champagne at a private view then go off somewhere far more interesting.

Map 9

Cinemas

- **Curzon Mayfair** • 38 Curzon St

Coffee

- **Apostrophe** • 10 Grosvenor St
- **Caffe Nero** • 50 Curzon St
- **Caffe Nero** • 70 Piccadilly
- **Costa** • 9 Eton St
- **Eat.** • 8 Berkeley Sq
- **Eat.** • 55 Stratton St
- **Starbucks** • 52 Berkeley St
- **Starbucks** • 84 Piccadilly
- **Taylor St Baristas** • 22 Brook's Mews

O Landmarks

- **50 Berkeley Square** • 50 Berkeley Sq
- **Apsley House** • 149 Piccadilly
- **Buckingham Palace** • The Mall
- **Down Street Station** • Down St & Piccadilly
- **Hard Rock Cafe** • Piccadilly & Old Park Ln

Libraries

- **Mayfair Library** • 25 South Audley St
- **Royal Society of Chemistry Library and Information Centre** • Piccadilly

Nightlife

- **1707 Wine Bar** • 181 Piccadilly
- **bbar** • 43 Buckingham Palace Rd
- **Funky Buddha** • 15 Berkeley St
- **Mahiki** • 1 Dover St
- **Shepherd's Tavern** • 50 Hertford St
- **Whisky Mist** • 35 Hertford St

Post Offices

- **Albemarle St** • 44 Albemarle St
- **Mayfair** • 32 Grosvenor St

Restaurants

- **Alain Ducasse at The Dorchester** • Park Ln
- **Burger & Lobster** • 29 Clarges St
- **Citrus** • 112 Piccadilly
- **Cookbook Cafe** • 1 Hamilton Pl
- **Corrigan's** • 28 Upper Grosvernor St
- **El Pirata of Mayfair** • 5 Down St
- **The English Tea Room at Brown's** • Albemarle St
- **Galvin at Windows** • Park Ln, 28th Floor
- **Gymkhana** • 42 Albemarle St
- **Kitty Fisher's** • 10 Shepherd Market
- **L'Autre** • 5 Shepherd St
- **Momo** • 25 Heddon St
- **Nobu** • 19 Old Park Ln
- **The Ritz** • 150 Piccadilly
- **Theo Randall** • 1 Hamilton Pl

Shopping

- **Diane Von Furstenberg** • 25 Bruton St
- **Dover Street Market** • 17 Dover St
- **Green Valley** • Berkeley St
- **Marc Jacobs** • 24 Mount St
- **Matthew Williamson** • 28 Bruton St
- **Stella McCartney** • 30 Bruton St

Supermarkets

- **Marks & Spencer** • 78 Piccadilly
- **Sainsbury's** • 38 Stratton St

Map 10 · Piccadilly / Soho (West)

Ⓝ

Oxford Street A40

Holles

John Princes St

Great

Castle St

Great Portland

Oxford Street

Oxford St A40

Oxford St A40

lenheim
Street

Dering Street

Tenterden Street

Princes Street

Swallow Place

Market Place

Eastcastle Street

Winsley St

Wells St

Haunch of
Venison Yed

Brook Street

Hanover
Square

Hanover Street

Oxford
Circus

Little
Argyll
Street

Argyll Street

Hills Place

Ramillies

Ramillies Place

Oxford Street A40

▲3

Noel

New Bond Street

Hanover St

Great Marlborough Street

Poland Street

D'Arblay St

A

Maddox Street

Masons
Arms Ms

Pullen St

Foubert's Pl

Newburgh St

Marshall Street

Dufour's Pl

Portland
Ms
(Livonia
Street)

▲2

Mill St

St. George Street

Kingly Court ○

Lowndes Ct

Marlborough
Ct

Broadwick Street

Bloomfield St

B406

Conduit Street

B406

Regent Street A4201

Kingly Street

Hopkins Street

Ingestre Place

on Place

◄9

New Burlington
Place

Lexington Place

Peter St

Bond Street

Barlow Place

on Street

Coach & Horses
Yard

Boyle
St

New Burlington
Street

Beak Street

Upr James St

Bridle Lane

Great Pulteney Street

◄11►

Clifford Street

New Burlington
Mews

Warwick

Upr John St

Lwr James St

Cork Street

Heddon

Regent
Place

Street

Golden
Square

Golden
Square Gardens

Smith's
Court

Albemarle Street

Cork Street
Mews

Old Burlington Street

Saville Row

Street

Lwr John St

Great Windmill Street

Archer Street

Grafton Street

New Bond Street

Burlington Gardens

Vigo Street

Brewer St

Sherwood St

Denman
Pl

Denman Street

B

Royal
Academy

Sackville Street

Regent Street

Air Street

Glasshouse Street

Shaftesbury

Stafford Street

Old Bond Street

Swallow Street

Vine St

A4201

Statue of
Eros

Dover Street

Burlington
Arcade & Piccadilly ○

Albany Ctyd

Carnaby St ○

Piccadilly
Circus Ⓤ

Haymarket

Piccadilly A4

▼23

Piccadilly

A4

Arlington Street

St. James

Bennet
Street

Duke Street

Jermyn Street

Ormond
Yard

Apple Tree
Yard

ames St

St. Albans

Coventr

Ryder

Street

St. James's

Carlton

0.25 mile	0.25 km

Piccadilly / Soho (West)

Map 10

Forget visions of Austin Powers "yeah baby" grooviness, Carnaby Street is a slick study in consumerism with all major streetwear labels present, but the grand dame of department stores, **Liberty**, retains top marks for a unique shopping experience. Have a coffee in Sacred if you can find a seat or else retreat to **Milk & Honey** for a cocktail. **Polpo** restaurant is a winner in the small plate game.

Coffee

- **Caffe Nero** • 62 Brewer St
- **Caffe Nero** • 26 Piccadilly
- **Caffe Nero** • 225 Regent St
- **Costa** • 11 Argyll St
- **Eat.** • 19 Golden Sq
- **Eat.** • 8 Vigo St
- **Fernandez & Wells** • 73 Beak St
- **Pret A Manger** • 298 Regent St
- **Pret A Manger** • 27 Great Marlborough
- **Rapha Cycle Club** • 13 Ganton St
- **Sacred Cafe** • 85 Brewer St
- **Starbucks** • 16 Piccadilly
- **Starbucks** • 71 Piccadily
- **Tonic Coffee Bar** • 15 Sherwood St
- **Yunchaa** • 45 Berwick St

O Landmarks

- **Burlington Arcade** • Piccadilly
- **Carnaby Street** • Carnaby St
- **Kingly Court** • Kingly St & Foubert's Pl
- **Statue of Eros** • Piccadilly Circus

Nightlife

- **5th View** • 203 Piccadilly
- **Ain't Nothing But...** • 20 Kingly St
- **Beyond Retro** • 58 Great Marlborough St
- **The Blind Pig** • 58 Poland St
- **Courthouse Bar** • 19 Great Marlborough St
- **The John Snow** • 39 Broadwick St
- **Milk & Honey** • 61 Poland St
- **The Red Lion** • 14 Kingly St
- **Strawberry Moons** • 15 Heddon St
- **The Windmill** • 6 Mill St

Restaurants

- **Atlantic Bar & Grill** • 20 Glasshouse St
- **Bao** • 53 Lexington St
- **Bob Bob Ricard** • 1 Upper James St
- **Bodean's BBQ** • 10 Poland St
- **Brasserie Zedel** • 20 Sherwood St
- **Cecconi's** • 5 Burlington Gardens
- **Cha Cha Moon** • 15 Ganton St
- **Dehesa** • 25 Ganton St
- **Detox Kitchen** • 10 Kingly St
- **Dishoom** • 22 Kingly St
- **Fernandez & Wells** • 73 Beak St
- **Fernandez & Wells** • 43 Lexington St
- **Kulu Kulu** • 76 Brewer St
- **Le Pain Quotidien** • 18 Great Marlborough St
- **Mildred's** • 45 Lexington St

- **Nordic Bakery** • 14 Golden Sq
- **The Photographers' Gallery** • 16 Ramillies St
- **Ping Pong** • 45 Great Marlborough St
- **Pitt Cue Co.** • 1 Newburgh St
- **Polpo** • 41 Beak St
- **San Carlo Cicchetti** • 215 Piccadilly
- **Sartoria** • 20 Saville Row
- **Sketch** • 9 Conduit St
- **Social Eating House** • 58 Poland St
- **Taro** • 61 Brewer St
- **Ten Ten Tei** • 56 Brewer St
- **Tentazioni Restaurant** • 2 Mill St
- **Tibits** • 12 Heddon St
- **Wagamama** • 10 Lexington St
- **Wild Honey** • 12 St George St
- **Yauatcha** • 15 Broadwick St
- **Yoshino** • 3 Piccadilly Pl

Shopping

- **Abercrombie & Fitch** • 7 Burlington Gardens
- **Anthropologie** • 158 Regent St
- **American Apparel** • 3 Carnaby St
- **Apple Store** • 235 Regent Street
- **b store** • 21 Kingly St
- **Banana Republic** • 224 Regent St
- **Behave** • 48 Lexington Street
- **Beyond Retro** • 58 Great Marlborough St
- **The Black Pearl** • 10 Kingly Ct
- **Burlington Arcade** • Burlington Arcade
- **Cos** • 222 Regent St
- **The European Bookshop** • 5 Warwick St
- **Fortnum & Mason** • 181 Piccadilly
- **Freggo** • 27 Swallow St
- **Hamley's** • 188 Regent St
- **Hatchards Bookshop** • 187 Piccadilly
- **Hoss Intropia** • 211 Regent St
- **Lazy Oaf** • 19 Fouberts Pl
- **Liberty** • 214 Regent St
- **Lillywhites** • 24 Lower Regent St
- **Lucky Voice** • 52 Poland St
- **Mrs. Kibble's Olde Sweet Shoppe** • 57 Brewer St
- **Muji** • 41 Carnaby St
- **Phonica** • 51 Poland St
- **Playlounge** • 19 Beak St
- **Richard James** • 29 Savile Row
- **Rigby & Peller** • 22 Conduit St
- **SKK Lighting** • 34 Lexington St
- **Super Superficial** • 17 Fouberts Pl
- **Twinkled** • 1 Kingly Ct
- **Twosee** • 21 Fouberts
- **The Vin Mag Shop** • 39 Brewer St
- **Whole Foods Market** • 69 Brewer St

Supermarkets

- **Fresh & Wild** • 73 Brewer St
- **Whole Foods Market** • 69 Brewer St

Map 11 · Soho (Central)

By day, th⁻ turning out of London's new favourite caffeine kick—the flat white courtesy of the Aussies—is relentless at **LJ** and **Milk Bar**. All the better to fuel the night⁻ activities: This is still the heart of the red light district, but it's no longer such a sordid affair. Berwick Street is still loved for its record shops and market, and **Madame JoJo's** doesn't miss a trick.

Cinemas

- **Apollo Theatre** • Shaftesbury Ave
- **Cineworld Shaftesbury Avenue** • 13 Coventry St
- **Curzon Soho** • 99 Shaftesbury Ave
- **Empire Leicester Square** • 5 Leicester Sq
- **Prince Charles Cinema** • 7 Leicester Pl

Coffee

- **Coffee Republic** • 7 Coventry St
- **Coffee Republic** • 38 Berwick St
- **Costa** • 62 Shaftesbury Ave
- **Fernandez & Wells Espresso Bar** • 16 St Anne's Ct
- **Foxcroft & Ginger** • 3 Berwick St
- **LJ Coffee House** • 3 Winnett St
- **Milk Bar** • 3 Bateman St
- **Prince Charles Cinema** • 7 Leicester Pl
- **Starbucks** • 60 Wardour St

Landmarks

- **Berwick Street Market** • Berwick St & Rupert St
- **John Snow Water Pump** • Broadwick St
- **Waxy O'Connor's** • 14 Rupert St

Nightlife

- **Blue Posts** • 22 Berwick St
- **The Blue Posts** • 28 Rupert St
- **The Comedy Store** • 1 Oxendon St
- **De Hems** • 11 Macclesfield St
- **Experimental Cocktail Club** • 13 Gerrard St
- **Freedom** • 66 Wardour St
- **The French House** • 49 Dean St
- **The Lyric** • 37 Great Windmill St
- **Old Tom & English** • 187 Wardour St
- **Shadow Lounge** • 5 Brewer St
- **Village** • 81 Wardour St

Restaurants

- **Ba Shan** • 24 Romilly St
- **Balans** • 60 Old Compton St
- **Bar Bruno** • 101 Wardour St
- **Blanchette** • 9 D'Arblay St
- **Bocca di Lupo** • 12 Archer St
- **Bone Daddies** • 31 Peter St
- **Busaba Eathai** • 110 Wardour St
- **Cafe Espana** • 63 Old Compton St
- **Copita** • 27 D'Arblay St
- **Ember Yard** • 60 Berwick St
- **Foxcroft & Ginger** • 3 Berwick St
- **The Full English** • 83 Wardour St
- **Gelupo** • 7 Archer St
- **Grace** • 42 Great Windmill St
- **Honest Burgers** • 4 Meard St
- **Hummus Bros** • 88 Wardour St
- **Imli** • 167 Wardour St
- **Jazz Club** • 10 Dean St
- **Jerk City** • 189 Wardour St
- **Kirazu** • 47 Rupert St
- **Malletti** • 26 Noel St
- **Maoz** • 43 Old Compton St
- **Morada Brindisa Asador** • 18-20 Rupert St
- **The Palomar** • 34 Rupert St
- **Paul** • 49 Old Compton St
- **Princi** • 135 Wardour St
- **Randall & Aubin** • 16 Brewer St
- **Snog** • 9 Brewer St
- **Soho Joe** • 22 Dean St
- **Spuntino** • 61 Rupert St
- **St Moritz** • 161 Wardour St
- **Thai Square** • 27 St Annes Ct
- **Tokyo Diner** • 2 Leicester St
- **Won Kei** • 41 Wardour St
- **Yoshino Delicatessen** • 59 Shaftesbury Ave

Shopping

- **Algerian Coffee Store** • 52 Old Compton St
- **Calumet Photographic** • 175 Wardour St
- **Chappel of Bond Street** • 152 Wardour St
- **Gerry's** • 74 Old Compton St
- **I. Camisa & Son** • 61 Old Compton St
- **Revival Records** • 30 Berwick St
- **Sister Ray** • 34 Berwick St
- **Snog** • 9 Brewer St
- **Sounds of the Universe** • 7 Broadwick St

Map 12 · **Soho (East)**

N

1   2

Soho Street

Streatham Street

Bainbridge Street

Bloomsbury Pl

Soho Street

3

Tottenham Court Road

New   **Oxford**   **Street**   A40

Falconberg Mews

Falconberg Court

Bucknall Street

Earnshaw Street

4

Dyott Street

Street

Carlisle Street

FA Headquarters

A

Soho Square Garden

Sutton Row

St-Giles High

Chapone Pl

Soho Square

Goslett Yard

Denmark Street

Street   A40

Royalty Mews

Orange Yard

A400

Denmark Street

Flitcroft St

New Compton St

Ender

Frith Street

Manette Street

Stacey St

New Compton St

Neal Street

Neal's Yd

Bateman   Street

Greek St

Phoenix St

The Phoenix Garden

St Giles Pas

A401

Monmouth St   B404

Charing   Cross Rd

Old Compton Street

Compton St

Giles Street

Shaftesbury Ave

13

Macclesfield Street

Old

Romilly   Street

Mcor Street

Earlham Street

Earlham Street

Shelton Street

Old Brewer Yard

11

Avenue

A401

West Street

Ching Ct

Mercer Street

Langley Street

B

aftesbury St

ansey Place

Horse & Dolphin Yd

Gerrard Place

Tower Ct

Tower St

Slingsby Place

B402

CHINATOWN

Gerrard   Street

Newport Pl

A400

Litchfield Street

Long   Acre

Lisle Street

Little Newport St

Great Newport St

Greek Yard

Garrick Street

Rose St

King Street

Leicester St

Charing   Cross   Road

24

Leicester Square

's Ln

Leicester Square Garden

| 0.1 mile | 0.1 km |

Soho (East)

While **The Three Greyhounds** (opposite Soho House) might be one of the cheapest pubs in central London, **Jazz After Dark** on Greek Street certainly isn't, but it does have an undeniably attractive ambiance. Blend in with the winos at Soho Square with a shop-bought bottle while **G-A-Y** showcases the more colourful side of Soho.

Map 12

😄 Cinemas

- **Vue West End Cinema** • 3 Cranbourn St

☕ Coffee

- **Caffe Nero** • 32 Cranbourn St
- **Caffe Nero** • 43 Frith St
- **Caffe Nero** • 155 Charing Cross Rd
- **Eat.** • 16 Soho Sq
- **Eat.** • 155 Charing Cross Rd
- **First Out Cafe Bar** • 52 St Giles High St
- **Foyles** • 113 Charing Cross Rd
- **Kaffe Automat** • 62 Frith St
- **Maison Bertaux** • 28 Greek St

O Landmarks

- **Denmark Street** • Denmark St
- **FA Headquarters** • 25 Soho Sq
- **Old Compton Street** • Old Compton St
- **The Phoenix Garden** • 21 Stacey St
- **Soho Square** • Soho Sq

🍸 Nightlife

- **68 and Boston** • 5 Greek St
- **Ape & Bird** • 142 Shaftesbury Ave
- **Bar Termini** • 7 Old Compton St
- **Cafe Boheme** • 13 Old Compton St
- **The Borderline** • Orange Yard
- **Comptons** • 53 Old Compton St
- **The Crobar** • 17 Manette St
- **G-A-Y Bar** • 30 Old Compton St
- **G-A-Y Late** • 5 Goslett Yard
- **Garlic & Shots** • 14 Frith St
- **Green Carnation** • 5 Greek St
- **Jazz After Dark** • 9 Greek St
- **Karaoke Box** • 18 Frith St
- **Ku** • 30 Little St
- **LAB Bar** • 12 Old Compton St
- **The Montagu Pyke** • 105 Charing Cross Rd
- **Ronnie Scott's** • 47 Frith St
- **The Royal George** • 133 Charing Cross Rd
- **The Three Greyhounds** • 25 Greek St
- **The Toucan** • 19 Carlisle St

🍴 Restaurants

- **10 Greek Street** • 10 Greek St
- **Abeno Too** • 17 Great Newport St
- **Arbutus** • 63 Frith St
- **Assa** • 53 St Giles High St
- **Baiwei** • 8 Little Newport St
- **Baozi Inn** • 26 Newport Court
- **Bar Italia** • 22 Frith St
- **Barrafina** • 54 Frith St
- **Barshu** • 28 Frith St
- **Bi Bim Bap** • 11 Greek St
- **Bo Drake** • 6 Greek St
- **Boheme Kitchen and Bar** • 19 Old Compton St
- **Ceviche** • 17 Frith St
- **Corean Chilli** • 51 Charing Cross Rd
- **Ed's Easy Diner** • 12 Moor St
- **Friendly Inn** • 47 Gerrard St
- **Gaby's Deli** • 30 Charing Cross Rd
- **Garlic & Shots** • 14 Frith St
- **Gay Hussar** • 2 Greek St
- **Haozhan** • 8 Gerrard St
- **Imperial China** • 25 Lisle St
- **The Ivy** • 1 West St
- **Koya** • 49 Frith St
- **La Bodega Negra** • 16 Moor St
- **La Porchetta Pollo Bar** • 20 Old Compton St
- **Le Beaujolais** • 25 Litchfield St
- **Maison Bertaux** • 27 Greek St
- **New World** • 1 Gerrard Pl
- **Sartori** • 15 Great Newport St
- **Smoking Goat** • 7 Denmark St
- **Soho's Secret Tea Room** • 29 Greek St
- **The Stockpot** • 18 Old Compton St
- **Taro** • 10 Old Compton St
- **The Three Greyhounds** • 25 Greek Street
- **The Village** • 421 Green Lanes
- **Yang Guang Supermarket** • 28-29 Newport Ct

🛍 Shopping

- **Angels Fancy Dress Shop** • 119 Shaftesbury Ave
- **Fopp** • 1 Earlham St
- **Forbidden Planet** • 179 Shaftesbury Ave
- **Foyles** • 113 Charing Cross Rd
- **Kokon to Zai** • 57 Greek St
- **Macari's** • 92 Charing Cross Rd
- **Porselli Dancewear** • 9 West St
- **Quinto Bookshop** • 72 Charing Cross Rd
- **Rockers** • 5 Denmark St
- **Wunjo Guitars** • 20 Denmark St

Covent Garden

Map 13

Covent Garden is a shopper's delight, especially on Endell Street and Neal Street. However, such activity will not offer a respite from the Piazza and its hordes of spatially unaware folk. Stop for fish and chips at **Rock & Sole Plaice** followed by gelato at **Scoop**. Come the evening, sip cocktails at **Freud** or convene with the ghost of Bernard Shaw at the **Lamb & Flag**.

Coffee

- **AMT** • 14 Neal St
- **Bagariat** • 24 Rose St
- **Bagel Factory** • 18 Endell St
- **The Black Penny** • 34 Great Queen St
- **Café Metro** • 33 Catherine St
- **Caffe Nero** • 30 Monmouth St
- **Caffe Nero** • 83 Long Acre
- **Pret A Manger** • 65 Long Acre
- **Starbucks** • 10 Russell St
- **Starbucks** • 55 Long Acre
- **Timberyard** • 7 Upper St Martin's Ln

O Landmarks

- **Oasis Sports Centre** • 32 Endell St
- **Seven Dials** • Upper St Martin's Ln & Earlham St

Y Nightlife

- **Compagnie Des Vins Surnaturels** • 8-10 Neal's Yard
- **The Cross Keys** • 31 Endell St
- **Freud** • 198 Shaftesbury Ave
- **Guanabara** • Parker St
- **Lamb & Flag** • 33 Rose St
- **The Poetry Cafe** • 22 Betterton St

Post Offices

- **High Holborn** • 181 High Holborn

Restaurants

- **Battersea Pie** • Covent Garden Piazza
- **Belgo Centraal** • 50 Earlham St
- **Café Mode** • 57 Endell St
- **Dishoom** • 12 Upper St Martin's Ln
- **Flesh & Buns** • 41 Earlham St
- **Great Queen Street** • 32 Great Queen St
- **Jar Kitchen** • 176 Drury Ln
- **Kulu Kulu Sushi** • 51 Shelton St
- **Lima Floral** • 14 Garrick St
- **Mon Plaisir** • 21 Monmouth St
- **The Punjab** • 80 Neal St
- **Rock & Sole Plaice** • 47 Endell St
- **Sarastro** • 126 Drury Ln
- **Souk Medina** • 1 Shorts Gardens
- **Wild Food Cafe** • 14 Neal's Yard

Shopping

- **Artbox** • 29 Earlham St
- **The Astrology Shop** • 78 Neal St
- **Beadworks** • 21 Tower St
- **Ben's Cookies** • 13 The Piazza
- **Blackout II** • 51 Endell St
- **Cath Kidston** • 28 Shelton St
- **Coco de Mer** • 23 Monmouth St
- **Cybercandy** • 3 Garrick St
- **David and Goliath** • 4 The Market
- **Ella's Bakehouse** • 20 The Piazza
- **Libidex at Liberation** • 49 Shelton St
- **London Graphic Centre** • 16 Shelton St
- **Neal's Yard Dairy** • 17 Shorts Gardens
- **Nigel Hall** • 18 Floral St
- **Octopus** • 54 Neal St
- **Orla Kiely** • 31 Monmouth St
- **Poetry Cafe** • 22 Betterton St
- **Pop Boutique** • 6 Monmouth St
- **Rokit** • 42 Shelton St
- **Rossopomodoro** • 50 Monmouth St
- **Scoop** • 40 Shorts Gardens
- **Slam City Skates** • 16 Neal's Yard
- **Stanfords** • 12 Long Acre
- **Superdry** • 24 Earlham St
- **Tabio** • 66 Neal St
- **Urban Outfitters** • 42 Earlham St

Supermarkets

- **Sainsbury's** • 129 Kingsway

Map 14 · **Holborn / Temple**

HOLBORN

Queen Square Place
Long Yard
Roger Street
Mount Pleasant
Rosebery
Clerkenwell Road

Theobald's Road A401

Gray's Inn Gardens

Portpool Lane
Portpool Lane
Hatton Wall
Hatton Garden

Gray's Inn Road A5200

Verulam

High

Baldwin's Gardens

Cross Street
Leather Lane

Hatton Garden B521

Greville

Square South

Chancery Lane

High Holborn A40

Holborn A40

Holborn

13

Whetstone Park

Lincoln's Inn Fields

Newman's Row Park & Garden

Sir John Soane's Museum

Lincoln's Inn Fields (Ficketts Fields)

Southampton Buildings

Furnival St

New Fetter Lane A4

15

Great Queen Street B402

Kingsway

The Old Curiosity Shop

Fortugal Street

London School of Economics

Royal Courts of Justice

Carey Street

Bream's Ct

Rolls Bldgs

Site of Sweeney Todd's Barber Shop

Fleet Street

PAGE 368

Aldwych A4

Aldwych A4

Strand A4

BBC Bush House

Strand A4

Strand A4

Somerset House

Aldwych Tube Station
King's College

PAGE 366

Temple

Victoria

Embankment A3211

Inner Temple Gardens

24

Victoria Embankment, New Bridge Street
Victoria Embankment, New Bridge Street
Victoria Embankment, New Bridge Street, Blackfriars Bridge

River Thames

0.25 mile   0.25 km

An essential cog in London's machine, this area is resplendent with curios (**Old Curiosity Shop**, **Sweeney Todd's**), public squares full of depressed lawyers and legions of serious-looking people being integrated into The System. The ghosts of London's past hover around Temple and the Strand, where you'll also find **Aldwych Film** for brunch and a flick.

Cinemas

- **Aldwych Film** • 1 Aldwych

Coffee

- **Caffe Nero** • 333 High Holborn
- **Chancery Coffee** • 90 Chancery Lane
- **Costa** • 15 Chichester Rents
- **Department of Coffee and Social Affairs** • 14 Leather Ln
- **Eat.** • 105 Kingsway
- **Eat.** • 239 High Holborn
- **Eat.** • 34 High Holborn
- **Eat.** • 7 Kingsway
- **Eat.** • 77 Chancery Lane
- **Eat.** • 78 Hatton Garden
- **Fleet Street Press** • 3 Fleet St
- **Pret A Manger** • 10 Leather Ln
- **Pret A Manger** • 240 High Holborn
- **Pret A Manger** • 29 Kingsway
- **Prufrock Coffee** • 23-25 Leather Ln
- **Starbucks** • 10 Kingsway
- **Starbucks** • 99 Kingsway

O Landmarks

- **Aldwych Tube Station** • Strand & Surrey St
- **BBC Bush House** • Aldwych & Kingsway
- **Hatton Garden** • Hatton Garden
- **Inner Temple Garden** • Inner Temple
- **King's College London** • Strand
- **Lincoln's Inn Fields** • Newman's Row
- **London School of Economics and Political Science** • Houghton St
- **The Old Curiosity Shop** • 13 Portsmouth St
- **Royal Courts of Justice** • Strand
- **Sir John Soane's Museum** • 13 Lincoln's Inn Fields
- **Sweeney Todd's Barber Shop** • 186 Fleet St
- **Somerset House** • Somerset House Trust, The Strand

Libraries

- **British Library of Political and Economic Science** • 10 Portugal St

Nightlife

- **Bar Polski** • 11 Little Turnstile
- **Bounce** • 121 Holborn
- **Cittie of Yorke** • 22 High Holborn
- **The Craft Beer Co.** • 82 Leather Ln
- **The Enterprise** • 38 Red Lion St
- **The Seven Stars** • 53 Carey St
- **Volupte** • 9 Norwich St

✉ Post Offices

- **Aldwych** • 95 Aldwych
- **Grays Inn** • 19 High Holborn
- **Holborn Circus** • 124 High Holborn

Restaurants

- **Asadal** • 227 High Holborn
- **Casanova's Treats** • 13 Lamb's Conduit Passage
- **Indigo** • 1 Aldwych
- **MEATmarket** • Jubilee Market Hall, Tavistock St

🛍 Shopping

- **Konditor & Cook** • 46 Grays Inn Rd
- **Topshop** • 60 The Strand

🛒 Supermarkets

- **Sainsbury's** • 129 Kingsway
- **Sainsbury's** • 60 Fetter Ln
- **Sainsbury's** • 71 High Holborn

Map 15 • **Blackfriars / Farringdon**

Ⓝ

Bath St

Bath Place

Aylesbury St

Clerkenwell Close

Great Sutton St

Sutton Lane

B501

A1

Goswell Road A1

Clerkenwell Rd Bri

Summers Street

Back Hill

Eyre St Hill

Ray Street

Ray Street Bridge

Herbal Hill

Vine Hill

Farringdon Lane

St. John's Place

Albe Wy

Clerkenwell Road A5201

Charterhouse Bldgs

Baltic St

Brewhouse Yard

Fann Street

Clerkenwell Road A5201

Hatton Wall

Broad Yard

Turnmill Street

Britton Street

Briset St

St. John's Square

The Green

Rutland Pl

A

St. Cross Street

Saffron Hill

Saffron St

Farringdon Road A201

Lily Pl

Albion Pl

Benjamin St

St. John's Gardens

Eagle Court

Smoke house Yard

Fox & Knot St

Charterhouse Ms

Charterhouse

Rutland St

Carthusian Street

Barbican

Beech B100

Hatton Place

Kirby Street

Hatton Garden B521

Greville Street

Cowcross Street

Farringdon

Street

Greenhill's Rents

Grand Avenue

Charterhouse St

Cloth Fair

Long Lane

Middle St

Newbury St

Half Moon Ct

Cloth Ct

Barth of

Bartholomew Clo

Aldersgate Street A1

St. Cross Street

Dorrington St

Beauchamp St

Brooke St

Chancery Lane

St Leonard's Gardens

Ely Place

Bleeding Heart Yard

Shoe Lane

Charterhouse Street

East Poultry Avenue

West Smithfield

Grand Avenue

Smithfield

Little Britain

Bartholomew Clo

Montague Street

7▸

London

Holborn A40

West Smithfield

Snow Hill

Hosier Lane

Giltspur St

St. Bartholomew's Hospital

Little Britain

Little Britain Park

Brooke's Market

Furnival St

Leather Lane

Printers Inn Ct

Norwich St

Barnard's Inn

Furnival Street

St. Andrew Street A4

New Fetter Lane A4

Plumtree Ct

Shoe Lane

Cock Lane

Snow Hill

Christchurch Greyfriars Gardens

King Edward Street

Angel Street

Corey St

Foster Lane

Bream's Buildings

Plough Place

Fetter Lane

New Thames Ct

Bartlett Ct

St. Bride St

Newcastle Clo

Bear All

Tur. La

Green Arbour Ct

Old Bailey

Bishop's Ct

Newgate Street A40

Paternoster Square

Angel Street

St. Paul's

B

Bream's Buildings

Rolls Bldgs

Harding St

Hind Ct

Pem.

Gough Sq

St. Bride's Pass.

Little New Street

Stone St

St. Bride Street A201

Poppin's Ct

St. Georges Ct

Old Fleet La

Old Seacoal La

Warwick Sq

Warwick La

Amen Corner

Paternoster Square

St. Paul's

St. Paul's Chyd

St. Paul's Cathedral

16▸

Cheapside

New Change

◂14

New Fetter Lane A4

Fleet Street

Daily Express Building

Fleet Street

Shoe Lane

Farringdon Street A201

Old Bailey

Ludgate Circus

Ludgate Hill

Pageant

Ludgate Sq

Ave Maria La

Stationers Hall Ct

Dean's Ct

Paul's Chyd

Festival

Cannon

New Change

Inner Temple Lane

Temple La

Serjeants Inn

St. Dunstan's Court

Whitefriars St

Bouverie Street

Pleydell St

Lombard La

Salisbury Sq

Bridewell Pl

Dorset Buildings

Hutton Street

Bride Lane

New Bridge Street A201

Pilgrim St

Carter Lane

St. Andrew's Hill

Addle Hill

Paul's Bakehouse Ct

Sermon Lane

Carter Lane

Knightrider Street

Distaff

Carter Lane

Churchyard

Wine Office Ct

Crane Ct

Red Lion Ct

Johnson's Ct

Bolt Ct

Hind Ct

Pump Ct

St. Dunstan's

Elm Ct

Middle Temple La

King's Bench Walk

Crown Office Row

Tudor Street

Tudor Street

Temple Avenue

Carmelite Street

John Carpenter St

Bridewell Pl

Kingscote St

Watergate

Tallis St

Black Friars La

Playhouse Yd

Apothecary St

Puddle Dock

Blackfriars

Blackfriars

Queen Victoria Street

Castle Baynard St

Baynard Street

Bennet's Hill

Upper Thames Street

Castle Baynard Street

Lambeth Hill

High Timber St

Inner Temple Gardens

Victoria Embankment

Victoria Embankment

Victoria Embankment A3211

Upper Thames Street

White Lion Hill

Millennium Bridge

Tng

Middle Temple Gardens

| 0.25 mile | | 0.25 km | |

The choices for eating out and drinking in this quarter are myriad, but we recommend getting your chops around a side of cow: **Smith's** and **Gaucho** are two solid options. Get a feel for sixteenth-century London with a potter around the old Livery Halls, then make like a Dickensian Oliver in the gated Charterhouse Square.

Coffee

- **Alchemy Coffee** • 8 Ludgate Broadway
- **Apostrophe** • 3 St Bride St
- **Apostrophe** • 10 St. Pauls Churchyard
- **Café Deco** • Charterhouse St & E Poultry Ave
- **Caffe Nero** • Shoe Lane
- **Caffe Nero** • 30 Newgate St
- **Caffe Nero** • 118 Newgate St
- **Costa** • 13 New Bridge St
- **Costa** • 46 Cowcross St
- **Dose** • 69 Long Ln
- **Eat.** • 88 Cowcross St
- **Farm Collective** • 91 Cowcross St
- **Meze Meze** • 95 Turnmill St
- **Pret A Manger** • 101 Turnmill St
- **Pret A Manger** • 5 St John's Sq
- **Pret A Manger** • 19 Ludgate Hill
- **Pret A Manger** • 10 Paternoster Sq
- **Pret A Manger** • 101 New Bridge St
- **Pret A Manger** • 143 Fleet St
- **Starbucks** • 1 Paternoster Sq
- **Starbucks** • 32 Fleet St
- **Starbucks** • 3 Fleet Pl
- **Starbucks** • 50 New Bridge St
- **Starbucks** • 55 Ludgate Hill
- **Starbucks** • 150 Fleet St
- **The Wren** • 114 Queen Victoria St
- **Workshop Coffee Co.** • 60 Holborn Viaduct

O Landmarks

- **Daily Express Building** • 121 Fleet St
- **Millennium Bridge** • Millennium Bridge
- **Old Bailey** • Old Bailey
- **Postman's Park** • Little Britain

Libraries

- **Shoe Lane Library** • Little New St
- **Society of Genealogists Library** • 14 Charterhouse Buildings

Nightlife

- **The Cocktail Trading Co.** • 50-52 Long Ln
- **Corney & Barrow** • 10 Paternoster Sq
- **The Deux Beers** • 3 Hatton Wall
- **Fabric** • 77 Charterhouse St
- **Fox and Anchor** • 115 Charterhouse St
- **The Hat and Tun** • 3 Hatton Wall
- **Ye Old Mitre** • 1 Ely Pl
- **Ye Olde Cheshire Cheese** • 145 Fleet St
- **Ye Olde London** • 42 Ludgate Hill

Post Offices

- **Farringdon Road** • 89 Farringdon Rd

Restaurants

- **Beppe's Sandwich Bar** • 23 Wt Smithfield
- **Bleeding Heart** • Bleeding Heart Yard
- **Foxlow** • 69-73 St John St
- **Gaucho Smithfield** • 93 Charterhouse St
- **Hix Oyster And Chop House** • 36 Cowcross St
- **Kurz + Lang** • 1 St John St
- **Le Cafe du Marche** • 22 Charterhouse Sq
- **Pho** • 86 St. John St
- **Portal** • 88 St John St
- **Shosharu** • 64 Turnmill St
- **Smiths of Smithfield** • 67 Charterhouse St
- **St. John** • 26 St. John St
- **Tinseltown** • 44 St John St
- **Vivat Bacchus** • 47 Farringdon St
- **Yo! Sushi** • 5 St Paul's Church Yard

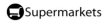Supermarkets

- **Marks & Spencer** • Ave Maria Lane
- **Sainsbury's** • 23 Farringdon Rd

Map 16 · **Square Mile (West)**

Map 16

Aah, the - ity, that faceless square mile at which we direct such disgust and vehemence for the state we're in. Despite meltdowns and protests, the world continues to turn, stocks are traded, and bonuses return. This place has always been empty at the weekends so you can enjoy the caryatids and Doric columns in peace. And of course take in the duomo at San Paulo (so much more romantic sounding, don't you think?)

Coffee

- **Coffee Republic** • 32 Coleman St
- **Costa** • 9 Bow Ln
- **Costa** • 95 Gresham St
- **Eat.** • 15 Basinghall St
- **Eat.** • 88 Wood St
- **Eat.** • 143 Cheapside
- **Fab Food Patisserie** • 19 Watling St
- **Fresco Café Bar** • 21 Masons Ave
- **Pret A Manger** • 30 Gresham St
- **Starbucks** • 1 Poultry
- **Starbucks** • 143 Cheapside

O Landmarks

- **The Guildhall** • Gresham St
- **St Mary le Bow Church** • Cheapside
- **St Paul's Cathedral** • St Paul's Church Yard
- **Temple of Mithras** • Queen Victoria St

Post Offices

- **Southwark** • 136 Southwark Bridge Rd

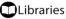

Libraries

- **City Business Library** • Aldermanbury Sq
- **Guildhall Library** • Aldermanbury

Nightlife

- **The Hatchet** • 28 Garlick Hill
- **Planet of the Grapes** • 74 Queen Victoria St
- **The Samuel Pepys** • Stew Ln
- **Ye Olde Watling** • 29 Watling St

Restaurants

- **Barbecoa** • 20 New Change Passage
- **Planet of the Grapes** • 74 Queen Victoria St
- **Pull'd** • 61 Cannon St
- **Sweetings** • 39 Queen Victoria St

Shopping

- **Church's** • 90 Cheapside
- **Space NK Apothecary** • 145 Cheapside

Supermarkets

- **Marks & Spencer** • Cannon St Station

Map 17 • **Square Mile (East)**

N

1 2

London Wall A1211 London Wall Wormwood St

8

Great Winchester St Union Court

Basinghall Ave Coleman Street Moorgate PI Langthorn Court Throgmorton Ave Bishopsgate A10 St. Helens Place

White Horse Yard Great Swan Al Austin Friars Passage Camo

Moorgate Copthall Ave Unde

Telegraph Street

Kings Arms Yd Tokenhouse Yd

A Throgmorton Street Threadneedle St

Gresham Street Lothbury Bartholomew Lane Capel Ct Bank of England White Lion Court 18

Newman's Court Sun

16 Princes St Royal Exchange Ave Finch Lane

Old Jewry Frederick's Place St. Mildred's Court Threadneedle Street Cornhill Corbet Ct A10 Leadenhall Place

Ironmonger Lane Dove Ct Grocer's Hall Ct Birchin Lane Bell Inn Yard

Cheapside **Poultry** Mansion House St **Bank** The Royal Exchange George Yard Gracechurch Street

Queen Street Pancras La Mansion House PI Post Office Ct Lombard Street Brabant

Queen Victoria Street Walbrook Bucklersbury Clements Lane Plough Court St. Benet's Place Talbot Ct Rood Lane

Street Sherbborne La King William Street Abchurch La Nicholas Lane Philpot Lane St. Mary at Hill

Tower Royal Oxford's Ct Salters' Hall Ct St. Swithin's Lane Abchurch Lane Nicholas Lane Martin Lane Monument Eastcheap

Cannon Street London Stone Blush Lane Gophir La Fish Street Hill Puddina La Botolph Lane

B Cloak Lane Laurence Pountney Hill King William St Monument St Pudding Lane

College Hill Dowgate Hill Suffolk La Laurence Pountney La

omas Apostle Cloak Lane College St Laurence Pountney La

ss La College St **Cannon Street Station**

hames **Street A3211** **Upper Thames Street** Angel Pas Swan Lane Lower Thames St 3211

Southwark Bridge Bell Wharf Lane Cousin Lane Allhallows Lane **CITY** London Bridge A3

Bell Wharf Lane London Bridge

0.25 mile 0.25 km

Square Mile (East)

London's most Jekyll-and-Hyde-like hood. By day, the banking district throbs with suits losing fortunes. They still dig steaks at **Gaucho City** though perhaps the Michelin-starred **Rhodes 24** is out of their price range now. Well, probably not. **The Counting House** is for after-work beers, while the possibility of shopping at the Royal Exchange is laughable, but who says you have to buy? By night, well, just don't go there.

Coffee

- **Bagel Factory** • 59 Moorgate
- **Caffe Nero** • 22 Wormwood St
- **Eat.** • 54 Cornhill
- **Eat.** • 123 Cannon St
- **Oi Bagel** • 27 Throgmorton St
- **Pret A Manger** • 43 King William St
- **Starbucks** • 5 Camomile St
- **Starbucks** • 13 Old Broad St
- **Starbucks** • 48 Gracechurch St
- **Starbucks** • 74 Cornhill
- **Starbucks** • 90 Old Broad St

O Landmarks

- **Bank of England** • Threadneedle St
- **London Stone** • 111 Cannon St
- **The Royal Exchange** • Cornhill
- **Threadneedle Street** • Threadneedle St

Nightlife

- **The Counting House** • 50 Cornhill
- **Royal Exchange Grand Cafe** • Royal Exchange

Post Offices

- **Moorgate** | 53 Moorgate

Restaurants

- **Gaucho City** • 1 Bell Inn Yard
- **Jamie's Italian** • 38 Threadneedle St
- **The Mercer** • 34 Threadneedle St
- **Nusa Kitchen** • 2 Adams Ct
- **Simpson's Tavern** • 38 Ball Court Alley, Cornhill
- **Wasabi** • 52 Old Broad St

Shopping

- **Paul A Young Fine Chocolates** • 20 Royal Exchange
- **Pretty Ballerinas** • 30 Royal Exchange

Supermarkets

- **Marks & Spencer** • Cannon St Station
- **Sainsbury's** • 10 Lombard St

Map 18

Tower Hill / Aldgate

Though on the fringe of the financial cesspit, Aldgate is brilliant to walk and gawp around in. **A. Gold**'s British deli (yes...they exist!) is fabulous, as is the atmospheric neighbourhood around Petticoat Lane, where Jack The Ripper used to stalk prozzers. After stodge at Jeff's, head south, past the Erotic **Gherkin** (ahem!), and go siege the **London Wall** alongside the tourists. Alternatively go become one yourself at **Pudding Lane**.

Coffee

- **Cafe Coto** • 12 Mitre St
- **Caffe Nero** • 1 Fenchurch Pl
- **Caffe Nero** • 23 Eastcheap
- **Caffe Nero** • 88 Leadenhall St
- **Curators Coffee** • 9 Cullum St
- **Eat.** • 28 Bushfield St
- **Eat.** • 84 Aldgate High St
- **Eat.** • 2 Eastcheap
- **Eat.** • 155 Fenchurch St
- **Eat.** • 26 Leadenhall St
- **Eat.** • 122 Minories
- **Eat.** • 48 Mark Ln
- **Eat.** • 2 Tower Hill
- **Eat.** • 33 St Mary Axe
- **Market Coffee House** • 52 Brushfield St
- **Pret A Manger** • 3 Cutler St
- **Starbucks** • 8 Brushfield St
- **Starbucks** • 20 Eastcheap
- **Starbucks** • 48 Minories
- **Starbucks** • 66 St Mary Axe

O Landmarks

- **The Gherkin** • 30 St Mary Axe
- **Jewish Soup Kitchen** • Brune St & Tenter Ground
- **The Lloyd's Building** • 1 Lime St
- **Leadenhall Market** • Gracechurch St
- **London Wall** • Cooper's Row & Trinity Sq
- **The Monument** • Monument St
- **Pudding Lane** • Pudding Ln
- **St Dunstan-in-the-East** • St Dunstan's Hill
- **The Ravens** • Tower Hill
- **Thames Clippers** • Tower Pier
- **Tower 42** • 25 Old Broad St
- **Tower of London** • Tower Hill

Libraries

- **Camomile Street** • 15 Camomile St
- **The Women's Library** • 25 Old Castle St

Nightlife

- **Dion** • 52 Leadenhall St
- **Kenza** • 10 Devonshire Sq
- **Mary Janes** • 124 Minories
- **The Minories** • 64 Minories
- **Revolution** • 140 Leadenhall St

Post Offices

- **The City of London BO** • 12 Eastcheap

Restaurants

- **Jeff's Cafe** • 14 Brune St
- **La Pietra** • 54 Commercial St

Shopping

- **A. Gold** • 42 Brushfield St
- **Montezuma's** • 51 Brushfield St
- **Petticoat Lane Market** • Middlesex St
- **Precious** • 16 Artillery Passage

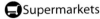 Supermarkets

- **Sainsbury's** • 45 Fenchurch St

Map 19 · **Belgravia**

N

37

46

9

2

20

PAGE 342
PAGE 415

Hyde Park

South Carriage Drive

Hyde Park

Knightsbridge

Knightsbridge A4
Knightsbridge A4

Hyde Park Corner

Hyde Park Corner
Knightsbridge
Piccadilly

Park Lane
Park Lane

Grantham
Hamilton Place
Down St
Hamilton Mews

Apsley Way
Duke of Wellington Place A302

CONSTITUTION HILL

Buckingham Palace Gardens

Seville St
William St
Wilton

Old Barrack Yard
Grosvenor Crescent

Duplex Ride
Studio Pl
Bow Yd
Kin. St
Wilton Place
Wilton Row

Kinnerton St
Ann's Cl
Fre.Ms.
Ki.Pl.S.

Belgrave Square

Belgrave
Square

Grosvenor Crescent B310

Pembroke

Halkin Street

Headfort Pl
Montrose Pl

Chapel St

Grosvenor Place A302

Wilton Cres.
Wilton's Cres.

Belgrave Mews W.

Wagon Cres.

Motcomb Street
Lowndes Street
Kinnerton Street
Belgrave Mews N.

Groom Pl
Chapel Street

Little W.St
Wilton M.

Chester Street

Harriet Walk

Lowndes Square
Lowndes Square
William Street

Harriet Walk

Sloane Street A3216

Basil St
Pavilion Road

Harriet Walk

Lowndes
Square

West Halkin St
Halkin Mews W
Halkin St

Belgrave Square

Chester Close

Grosvenor Place A302
Lower Grosvenor Place

Upper Belgrave St

Chesham
Pl

Belgrave Mews S.

Belgrave Mews S.

Chesham Cl
Lyall

Lyall St
Lyall Mews
Lyall Mews W

Chesham Place
Chesham Street
West Eaton Place Mews

Cadogan Place

Cadogan Lane

Pavilion Road A3216

Sloane Street A3216

Hans Street

Hans Place
Herbert Cres

Hans Crescent

London Pl

Pavilion Road

Sloane Street A3216

B319

Roberts M
Lowndes

Eaton Place

Place Street

Eaton Square

Eaton Mews North

Belgrave Place B310

Eaton Square

Eccleston Square

Eaton Square

Hobart Place

Hobart
Place

Grosvenor Gardens

Beeston Place
Eaton Lane

Gros. Gdns
Gros. Gdns M.E.

Victoria Square

Eaton Mews W.

Eaton
Square

Eaton Square

Eaton

Eaton Mews South

Eaton Square

Eaton Square

Lower Belgrave St

Eaton Row

Buckingham Palace

Terminus Place
Terminus Place

Buckingham Palace Road A3214

Eaton Gate A3217

Cadogan Gate A3216
Ellis Street

D'Oyley St
Cadogan Place

Cliveden
Place

W.Eaton Pl
Colt

Cadogan Gate

Wilbraham Pl
Sloane Terrace

Minera Mews

Boscobel

Eaton Mews W.

Chester Sq
Chester Square

Chester Row

Gerald Road

Ebury
Eaton Terr.

Eccleston Mews

Ebury Mews E.

Church Mews E.

Ebury Mews

Philip's M

Buckingham Palace Road A3214

Victoria
Station

PAGE
415

Sloane Square

Symons Street

Sloane Square

Sloane Gardens

Holbein Mews

Lower Sloane Street A3216

of York Sq

Cadogan Gdns

Cliveden
Place

Eaton Clo
Caroline
Terrace

Chester Terrace
Bourne Street

Chester Row
Chester Square South
Graham

Gerald Road
Eaton Terr.

Chester Row
Eaton Terrace

Whittaker Row

Skinner Pl

Passmore St
Rambardt Clo

Holbein Mews

Graham Terrace
Holbein Place

Bloomfield Ter.

Pimlico Road A3214

BELGRAVIA

Ebury Street

Elizabeth Street

Eccleston
Place

Eccleston Street

Eccleston Bridge

Belgrave
Road A3213

Bessborough

Eccleston
Mews

Cundy Street

Ebury Street

Semley Place
Ebury Bridge

Buckingham Palace Road A3214

Elizabeth Street
Buckingham Palace Road

Ebury Bridge Road

Gillingham

Warwick Way

Ranelagh Grove

Burnhouse
Clo

Avery Farm Row

Bunhouse Pl

Turk's Row

Royal Hospital
Sloane Court E

Dove House
St

St Barnabas St

Rumbold Grove

Bloomfield Ter.

Cambridge Street

Warwick Square

Eccleston
Square

West Warwick Pl
Warwick Way

Westmoreland Ter

Denbigh St

0.25 mile

0.25 km

Ugg and Range Rover fetishists are in a constant state of climax around here. It sure is pretty when the sun isn't being blocked by expensively coiffured bouffants, but one suspects the plummy accents and tasteless richness would dent anyone's enthusiasm for chic dog clothes (**Mungo & Maud**) or curry (**Amaya**).

Coffee
- **Starbucks** • 53 Pimlico Rd
- **Tomtom Coffee House** • 114 Ebury St

Libraries
- **Instituto Cervantes** • 102 Eaton Sq
- **Victoria Library** • 160 Buckingham Palace Rd
- **Westminster Music Library** • 160 Buckingham Palace Rd

Nightlife
- **The Blue Bar** • The Berkeley Hotel • Wilton Pl
- **Nag's Head** • 53 Kinnerton St
- **The Plumbers Arms** • 14 Lower Belgrave St
- **The Wilton Arms** • 71 Kinnerton St

Restaurants
- **Amaya** • Motcomb St
- **Boisdale** • 15 Eccleston St
- **Noura** • 12 William St
- **One-O-One** • 101 Knightsbridge
- **The Pantechnicon** • 10 Motcomb St
- **Yo! Sushi** • 102 Knightsbridge

Shopping
- **Daylesford Organic Farmshop and Cafe** • 44 Pimlico Rd
- **Mungo & Maud** • 79 Elizabeth St
- **Peter Jones** • Sloan Sq

Supermarkets
- **Waitrose** • 27 Motcomb St

Since the Tower of London closed for business, prisoners have been routinely tortured at weekends in Victoria Station. Surrounding the transit hubs is a dignified hood Churchill and Mozart called home. Do a late-night tramp photoshoot on the steps of the magnificent houses of Lupus Street (with a camera from **Grays**) before heading to **The Cask & Glass** for a knees-up with your new pals.

Coffee

- **Bagel Factory** • Victoria Station
- **Bagel Factory** •
  Victoria Place Shopping Centre • Buckingham Palace Rd
- **Caffe Nero** • 31 Warwick Wy
- **Costa** • 3 Cardinal Walk
- **Costa** • 111 Buckingham Palace Rd
- **Eat.** • Cardinal Pl
- **Pret A Manger** • 12 Victoria St
- **Pret A Manger** • 173 Victoria St
- **Pret A Manger** • Unit 36B • Victoria Station
- **Pret A Manger** • 92 Buckingham Palace Rd
- **Starbucks** • 137 Victoria St
- **Starbucks** • Buckingham Palace Rd & Lower Belgrave St

Post Offices

- **Vauxhall Bridge Road** • 167 Vauxhall Bridge Rd

O Landmarks

- **Little Ben** • Victoria St & Vauxhall Bridge Rd
- **Westminster Cathedral** • 42 Francis St

Nightlife

- **The Cask & Glass** • 39 Palace St
- **The Warwick** • 25 Warwick Wy
- **Windsor Castle** • 23 Francis St

Restaurants

- **Grumbles** • 35 Churton St
- **Pimlico Fresh** • 86 Wilton Rd

Shopping

- **Capital Carboot Sale** • Lupus St
- **Grays of Westminster** • 40 Churton St
- **La Bella Sicilia** • 23 Warwick Wy
- **Rippon Cheese Stores** • 26 Upper Tachbrook St
- **Runners Need** • 24 Palace St
- **Topshop** • 18 Victoria St

Supermarkets

- **Marks & Spencer** • Victoria Mainline Station

Map 21 • Pimlico (East)

Howick Place
Howick Place
Artillery Place
Great
Peter
Street
North
Street
Mayfield
Street
Francis
Chadwick
Street
Medway
Street
Monck Street
Tufton
Street
Smith
Square
Dean
Trench
Street
Dearne
Street
Dean
Stanley
Street
Victoria
Tower
Gardens
A3212
Thirlby Road
Greycoat Pl.
Artillery Row
Greycoat Pl.
Rochester Street
Greycoat Street
Horseferry Road
Romney Street
Dean
Bradley
Street

B323 Horseferry Road B323 Horseferry Road

Lambe

22

St. John's
Gardens

Vincent Square
Regency Street
Maunsel Street
Rutherford Street
Fynes
Street
Page Street
Page Street
Thorney Street
Ryle Street
Millbank
A3212

Westminster
School Playing
Fields

Vincent Street
Vincent Street
Vincent Street
Hide Place
Chapter St.
Montaigne
Close
Montaigne
Close
Herrick Street
Marsham
Street
John Islip Street

Millbank Tower ○

Douglas Street
Regency Street
Mont.
Cl.
Erasmus Street
Bul. St.

20

Thorndike
Street
Garden
Terrace
Cureton Street
Herrick
Street
Ponsonby
Place

PAGE 476

Vauxhall Bridge Road A202
Bessborough Gardens Gate

Tate Britain

Atterbury Street B326

Millbank

A3212

St. George's Square
Tachbrook Street
Hampayne Street
Bessborough Gate

Pimlico ⊖

**Chelsea College
of Art & Design**

Ponsonby
Terrace

Millbank A3212

Bessborough
Gardens

Riverside
Gardens

Moreton Place
Moreton Street
Lupus Street
Lupus Street
Chichester Street
Claverton Street
St. George's Square
St. George's Square Garden
Aylesford
Street
St. George's Drive
St. George's Square
Mews
Lindsay Square
Bess-borough Place
Lindsay Square
Bailey
Pl.
Bailey
Gate
Lindsay Square
Balvaird Place
Grosvenor Road
A202 Vauxhall Bridge
A202 Bridgefoot

Grosvenor Road A3212
Pimlico
Gardens

River Thames

A3036 Wandsworth Road
Parry Street

venor Road A3212

| 0.25 mile | 0.25 km |

Pimlico (East)

Hugging the curve of the Thames, this princely patch of Pimlico combines the stately state with imposing embankment architecture and ancient houses. Check out the old-money splendour of Vincent Street before grabbing lunch at the **Regency**, a true gem of a caf. Much fun can be had by pretending you actually live around here, so in this spirit head to the **Morpeth** as your local.

 ## Coffee
• **Starbucks** • 35 Horseferry Rd

 ## Landmarks
• **Millbank Tower** • 21 Millbank

Libraries
• **Pimlico Library** • Rampayne St
• **Royal Horticultural Society Library** • 80 Vincent Sq

 ## Nightlife
• **Morpeth Arms** • 58 Millbank

 ## Restaurants
• **The Regency Cafe** • 17 Regency St
• **The Vincent Rooms** • 76 Vincent Sq

 ## Shopping
• **Black Rose** • 112 Belgrave Rd

Map 22 · **Westminster**

Westminster

Map 22

The long shadow of government falls over these parts, beautiful as they are. Protesters and wannabe Guy Fawkeses head to Parliament Square, where they can harangue whichever bunch of jokers are ensconced in the Houses of Parliament. Get away from tourists at the tiny **St. Stephen's Tavern**, or grab a classy cocktail at **The Cinnamon Club**. If you must shop, head to Victoria Street.

Coffee

- **Caffe Nero** • 1 Bridge St
- **Caffe Nero** • 105 Victoria St
- **Eat.** • 3 Stutton Ground
- **Fresco Cafe Bar** • 11 Tothill St
- **Iris & June** • 1 Howick Pl
- **Pret A Manger** • 75 Victoria St
- **Pret A Manger** • 49 Tothill St
- **Puccino's** • 6 Victoria St
- **Starbucks** • 27 Victoria St

O Landmarks

- **Big Ben** • Bridge St
- **Field of Remembrance** • Victoria St
- **New Scotland Yard Sign** • 8 Broadway
- **St. John's Smith Square** • Smith Sq
- **UK Parliament** • Victoria St & Abingdon St
- **Westminster Tube Station** • Westminster Bridge Rd

 Libraries

- **St James's Library** • 62 Victoria St

Nightlife

- **The Albert** • 52 Victoria St
- **The Cinnamon Club** • 30 Great Smith St
- **The Speaker** • 46 Great Peter St
- **Two Chairmen** • 39 Dartmouth St
- **St. Stephen's Tavern** • 10 Bridge St

Shopping

- **Haelen Centre** • 41 Broadway

Map 23 · **St. James's**

Dignified, decadent, exclusive, Pall Mall and St. James's Street are where the aristobrats come out to play. With stuffy gentlemen's clubs, bespoke tailors, and the stale scent of a cigar-fuelled colonialist past pervading, you'll want to sweeten up with a macaroon at **Laduree**. **Giro** the **Nazi Dog** observes the liberals who get culture fixes at the **ICA**, but he can't come for scraps at **Inn The Park**.

Cinemas

- **Apollo Cinema Piccadilly Circus** • 19 Lower Regent St
- **Cineworld Haymarket** • 63 Haymarket
- **ICA Cinema** • The Mall & Horse Guards Rd
- **Odeon Leicester Square** • 24 Leicester Sq
- **Odeon Panton Street** • 11 Panton St
- **Odeon West End Cinema** • 40 Leicester Sq

Coffee

- **Apostrophe** • 16 Regent St
- **Borough Barista** • 15 Charles II St
- **Caffe Nero** • 35 Jermyn St
- **Coffee Republic** • 63 Haymarket
- **Eat.** • 18 Regent St
- **Eat.** • 3 Duke of York St
- **Eat.** • 9 Crown Passage
- **ICA Cafe** • The Mall
- **Pret A Manger** • 8 King St

O Landmarks

- **Economist Plaza** • 25 St. James's St
- **Giro the Nazi Dog** • 9 Carlton House Terrace
- **Leicester Square** • Leicester Sq
- **TKTS** • Leicester Sq

Libraries

- **London Library** • 14 St James's Sq
- **Westminster Reference Library** • 35 St Martin's St

Nightlife

- **Aura** • 48 St James's St
- **Dukes Hotel** • 35 St James's St
- **Institute of Contemporary Arts** • The Mall

Restaurants

- **Inn The Park** • St James' Park
- **Laduree** • 71 Burlington Arcade
- **The Stockpot** • 38 Panton St

Shopping

- **Partridges Deli** • 2 Duke of York St
- **National Map Centre** • 22-24 Caxton St
- **Richard Caplan** • 60 Pall Mall

Map 24 · **Trafalgar Square / The Strand**

Ⓝ

Aldwych A4

1

2

Wellington Street B401

Montreal Pl

13

Strand

B402

Catherine Street

Russell Street

Earlham Street

Moor St

WestStreet

Tower Street

Monmouth Street

Shelton Street

Langley Street

Brewers Row

Charing Cross Road A401

Gerrard

Newport Pl

Dolphin Yard

Litchfield Street

Upper St. Martin's Lane

Long Acre

Floral Street

B404

Slingsby Pl

12

Garrick Street

Rose Street

King Street

Exeter St

14

Little Newport St

Cranbourn Street

New Rcw

St. Martin's Lane B404

The Actors' Church

Henrietta Street

Southampton Street

Tavistock Street

Burleigh St

Lisle Street

Leicester Square

A400

A

Leicester Square

Irving Street

Charing Cross Rd

St. Martin's Lane B404

Bedfordbury

Chandos Place

Bedford Street

Jane Austen Residence

Maiden Lane

Adam St

Right-hand Drive Street

Strand

Agar St

Savoy St

Carting Lane

Savoy Way

Savoy Hill

Savoy Street

Savoy Pl

Sorrofkll

Whitcomb St

Orange Street

St. Martin's Street

Suffolk Place

Suffolk St

William IV Street

St Martin's Place

Duncannos St

Adelaide

Eleanor Cross

St. Martin-in-the-Fields

Strand A4

Durham He St

William IV Street

John Adam Street

Lower Robert St

York Buildings

Adam Street

Adelphi Terrace

Lower Robert St

Sewer Lamp

Ivybridge Ln

Robert St

Cleopatra's Needle

PAGE 478

National Gallery & National Portrait Gallery

Trafalgar Square

Villiers Street

Corner House Street

Northumberland St

Hungerford Lane

Charing Cross Station

PAGE 410

Embankment

Victoria Embankment Gardens

Pall Mall East

Cockspur Street

Trafalgar Square A4

Craven Street

Embankment Place

Warwick Ho St

Cockspur Court

Spring

Gardens

Northumberland Avenue

Craigs Ct

House Terrace

B

The Mall

Horse Guards Rd

23

Top Secret Tunnels

The Banqueting House

Great Scotland Yard

Scotland Pl

Whitehall Place

Whitehall Court

Whitehall A3212

Whitehall Gdns

Horse Guards Avenue

Victoria Embankment Gardens

Victoria Embankment

River Thames

St. James's Park

Horse Guards Parade

Victoria Embankment Gardens

Jubilee Gardens

10 Downing St

Downing Street

Richmond Terrace

Derby Gate

Parliament Street A3212

King Charles Street

Westminster

A3211

22

| 0.25 mile | 0.25 km |

Trafalgar Square / The Strand

Map 24

The hawkers came and removed the flying rats and lo! the Square was clean and visible. This ain't Mary Poppins—don't feed the birds, you dirty tourists. Instead go to **Terroirs** and pretend you know a lot about wine. Eat at **Wahaca**, one of London's few good Mexicans, then walk it off on **Waterloo Bridge** and watch the sun set over the Thames. Aah. That's why you love London.

Coffee

- **Apostrophe** • 215 Strand
- **Caffe Nero** • 10 Bedford St
- **Caffe Nero** • 181 Strand
- **Caffe Nero** • 125 Strand
- **Caffe Nero** • 36 St Martin's Ln
- **Caffe Nero** • 29 Southampton St
- **Coffee Republic** • 79 Strand
- **Costa** • 17 Embankment Pl
- **Eat.** • 41 Bedford St
- **Eat.** • 39 Villiers St
- **Great American Bagel Factory** • 45 Villiers St
- **Notes** • 31 St Martin's Ln
- **Pret A Manger** • 135 Strand
- **Pret A Manger** • 421 Strand
- **Pret A Manger** • 7 St Martin's Ln
- **Scott's Sandwich Bar** • 10 New Row
- **Starbucks** • 355 Strand
- **Starbucks** • 442 Strand
- **Starbucks** • 4 Villiers St
- **Starbucks** • Villiers St

Landmarks

- **10 Downing Street** • 10 Downing St
- **The Actors' Church** • 29 Bedford St
- **Banqueting House** • Whitehall
- **Cleopatra's Needle** • Embankment
- **Eleanor Cross** • Strand
- **Jane Austen Residence** • 10 Henrietta St
- **Right-Hand Drive Street** • Savoy Ct
- **Sewer Lamp** • Carting Ln & Strand
- **St Martin-in-the-Fields** • Trafalgar Sq
- **Top Secret Tunnels** • 6 Craig's Ct
- **Trafalgar Square** • Trafalgar Sq

Libraries

- **Charing Cross Library** • 4 Charing Cross Rd
- **Royal United Services Institute Library** • Whitehall

Nightlife

- **Asia de Cuba** • 45 St Martin's Ln
- **BYOC** • 28 Bedfordbury
- **The Chandos** • 29 St Martins Ln
- **The Coal Hole** • 91 Strand

- **Covent Garden Comedy Club** • The Arches
- **Gordon's Wine Bar** • 47 Villiers St
- **The Harp** • 47 Chandos Pl
- **Heaven** • The Arches
- **Maple Leaf** • 41 Maiden Ln
- **Punch & Judy** • The Covent Garden Piazza
- **Retro Bar** • 2 George Ct
- **Roadhouse** • 35 The Covent Garden Piazza
- **The Sherlock Holmes** • 10 Northumberland St
- **Terroirs** • 5 William IV St
- **Café Express** • 372 Strand
- **Zoo Bar & Club** • 13 Bear St

Post Offices

- **Trafalgar Square** • 24 William IV St

Restaurants

- **Cafe in the Crypt** • 6 St Martin's Pl
- **Gourmet Burger Kitchen** • 13 Maiden Ln
- **Herman Ze German** • 19 Villiers St
- **India Club** • 143 Strand
- **J Sheekey** • 28 St Martin's Ct
- **Portrait Restaurant & Bar** • St Martin's Pl
- **R.S. Hispaniola** • Victoria Embankment
- **Rules** • 35 Maiden Ln
- **Scott's Sandwich Bar** • 10 New Row
- **Thai Pot** • 1 Bedfordbury
- **Wahaca** • 66 Chandos Pl

Shopping

- **Austin Kaye** • 425 The Strand
- **Australia Shop** • 27 Maiden Ln
- **Gelato Mio** • 45 Villiers St
- **The Italian Bookshop** • 5 Cecil Ct
- **London Camera Exchange** • 98 Strand
- **Motor Books** • 13 Cecil Ct
- **Rohan** • 10 Henrietta St
- **Stanley Gibbons** • 399 Strand

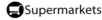Supermarkets

- **Marks & Spencer** • Charing Cross Station

55

KENSAL RISE

WEST KILBURN

KENSAL GREEN

Kensal Green

KENSAL TOWN

25

EALING

Wormwood Scrubs

Westway

NORTH KENSINGTON

Westbourne Pk

Elgin Cres

Kensington

WHITE CITY

Wood Ln

NOTTING HILL

2=

Landbroke Grove

ACTON

EAST ACTON

SHEPHERD'S BUSH

Holland Park Ave

HOLLAND PARK

Acton Park

Uxbridge Rd

32

Shepherds Bush Green

33

Holland Rd

Shepherds Bush Rd

34

Warwick

TURNHAM GREEN

Wendell Park

Goldhawk Rd

Dalling Rd

Ravenscourt Park

40

Hammersmith Rd

WEST KENSINGTON

Bath Rd

Chiswick Common

39

King St

41

Talgarth Rd

HAMMERSMITH

42

CHISWICK

Great West Rd

BARONS COURT

38

Lillie Rd

Hogarth Ln

CASTELNAU

Hammersmith Br

Thames River

Fulham Palace Rd

Dawes R

Chiswick Cemetery

47

Fulham Cemetery

University of Westminster Stadium

Duke's Meadow

BARNES

Putney Park

FULHAM

48

Fulham Palace Gardens

MORTLAKE

Map 25 · **Kensal Town**

Kensal Town

Map 25

The "new Notting Hill" label weighs heavily on the Kensals. They look east for inspiration, ignoring the Harlesden yardies at their backs. **Thai Rice** serves eastern food, while Portobello's Mexican spice shack **Santo** slings some of the best Mexican in the city and grooves to the Latino cool with regular DJ sets. Prepare for Carnival by visiting **What Katie Did** for exhibitionist outfits, while **Trellick Tower** is perfect for real—"I mean it, I'll jump"—attention-seekers.

Coffee

- **Camden Coffee House** • 155 Ladbroke Grove
- **Lisboa Cafe** • 57 Golborne Rd

Landmarks

- **Trellick Tower** • 5 Golborne Rd

Libraries

- **Kensal Library** • 20 Golborne Rd
- **Queen's Park Library** • 666 Harrow Rd

Post Offices

- **Maida Hill** • 37 Harrow Rd
- **Portobello Road** • 325 Portobello Rd

Restaurants

- **Boom Burger** • 272 Portobello Rd
- **Lowry and Baker** • 339 Portobello Rd
- **Santo** • 299 Portobello Rd
- **Snaps + Rye** • 93 Golborne Rd
- **Thai Rice** • 303 Portobello Rd
- **Yum Yum** • 312 Ladbroke Grove

Shopping

- **Honest Jon's** • 278 Portobello Rd
- **Rellik** • 8 Golborne Rd
- **What Katie Did** • 281 Portobello Rd

Supermarkets

- **Iceland** • 512 Harrow Rd

Maida Hill

Map 26

Not as posh as Maida Vale or as cool as Ladbroke Grove, Maida Hill is slightly grubby to the south, not helped by the distinctly unlovely Harrow Road. Things get more upmarket heading north, but the beating heart of the hill can be found Saturdays around Harrow Road's new market. On one of those rare sunny London days get down to the **Union Tavern** and grab a canal side table.

Post Offices
• **Kilburn Park** • 5 Chippenham Gardens

Nightlife
• **Union Tavern** • 45 Woodfield Rd

Restaurants
• **Mosob** • 339 Harrow Rd

Map 27 · **Maida Vale**

MAIDA VALE

Paddington
Recreation
Ground

1

2

Kilburn Park Road

Cambridge Road

Carlton Vale

Kilburn Park Road B411

Malvern M

Malvern Road

Stafford Rd

Stuart

Cambridge Road

Saltram Crescent

Hampton

Close

Malvern Close

Chip. Gdns

Fernleigh

Green Gardens

Randolph Gardens

Andover Place

Greville

Hill

Carlton

B414

A

Essendine
Primary
School

Essendine Road

Widley Road

Wymering Road

Morshead Road

Grantully Road

Randolph Avenue

Lanark Road

Maida Vale A5

St Georges
RC School

Byron
Ct

Byron M

Castleton Road

Oakington Road

Lanhill Road

B414

City of
Westminster
College

Elgin Avenue

Elgin
Mn

68

◄26

Shirland Road B413

Thorngate Rd

Delaware Road

Castellain Rd

Biddulph Road

Ashworth Road

Lauderdale Road

Elgin
Ms

Maida
Vale

Maida Vale A5

Aber

Marylands Road

Sutherdale
Place

St. Peter's
Pl

Paddington
Sports Club

Randolph Avenue

Lanark Road

Vale Close

Abercorn Walk

Sutherland Avenue

Downfield Cl

Braden
St

Warwick Avenue

Pindock M

Sutherland Avenue

Lanark
M
Sutherland Av

Hall

Aldsworth Clo

Clearwell Drive

Barnwood Cl

Elnathan Mews

Castellain Rd

Warrington Crescent

St Josephs
RC Primary
School

Oakington Road

B

Rowington Clo

Formosa Street

Bristol Gdns

Formosa St

Randolph Crescent

Randolph Avenue

Lanark Road

Maida Vale A5

Square

Senior

Street

Lord
Hills Rd

Desb.
Cl

Bourne
Cl

Delamere Terrace

Blomfield Road

Warwick Avenue

Blomfield Villas

Warwick
Avenue

Clifton Villas

Clifton Gardens B413

Clifton Road

31►

St John's Wood

30▼

Bourne Terr

Chichester
Road

Warwick Place

Warwick
Avenue

Clarendon Gardens

Randolph Mews

Blomfield Road

Eliz.
Cl
Brown.
Cl
Robert.
Cl

Clar.
Place
Clar.
Ter.

Lanark

Court

Northwick Ter

North

Aberdeen Place

76►

New Road A404

Westway A40

Westbourne
Green

Blomfield Villas

Randolph Road

Warwick

Ck

Fishert

| 0.25 mile | 0.25 km |

Maida Vale

Map 27

You don't come to Maida Vale for the nightlife, end of story. Though pretty, canal-side walks are a different matter. Away from 'Little Venice' are endless rows of identical-looking Edwardian mansion blocks on peaceful, tree-lined avenues. It's clean, peaceful, and nice (translation: quite dull). Locals frequent the cafés and eateries around the Maida Vale tube station and on Clifton Road. If applicable, head to **The Robert Browning** for cheap Sam Smith's beer by a roaring fire.

Coffee
• **Starbucks** • 68 Randolf Ave

Libraries
• **Maida Vale Library** • Sutherland Ave

Nightlife
• **The Bridge House** • 13 Westbourne Terrace Rd
• **The Warwick Castle** • 6 Warwick Pl
• **The Waterway** • 54 Formosa St

Map 28 • Ladbroke Grove / Notting Hill (West) Ⓝ

NOTTING HILL

Look at the Westway and tell us you can't hear the opening chords of "London Calling." Maybe Rudie didn't fail but he moved up and moved out. This is the quiet, leafy Notting Hill of gated gardens away from the Hugh Grant-hungry tourists scouring Portobello Road. Head to Clarendon Cross or Portland Road for food and stuff. Grab a bite at **Julie's** or wander down to Holland Park Avenue for organic treats at **Jeroboams Deli**.

Coffee

• **Starbucks** • 36 Holland Park Ave

Nightlife

• **Julie's Restaurant & Champagne Bar** • 135 Portland Rd

Shopping

• **Cowshed** • 119 Portland Rd
• **The Cross** • 141 Portland Rd
• **Gelato Mio** • 138 Holland Park Ave
• **Jeroboams** • 96 Holland Park Ave
• **Virginia** • 98 Portland Rd

Map 29 • **Notting Hill Gate**

WESTBOURNE GREEN

WESTBOURNE GREEN SP Complex

NOTTING HILL

KENSINGTON

Kensington Gardens

PAGE 342

Westbourne Park

Ladbroke Grove

Portobello Road Market

Ladbroke Square Gardens

Holland Park

Notting Hill Gate

Bayswater Rd

0.25 mile

0.25 km

It is hard to believe that until relatively recently this now home of the mega-rich was Kensington's rough bad-boy slum. Traces of the Gate's multicultural past are in the wrinkles of the old eccentrics in the **Uxbridge Arms**, the lively Portobello Market, and the buzz of the summer Carnival. To feel old and bitter, go scowl at skinny jeans-clad teenagers in the Notting Hill Arts Club. Pig out on some of London's best gelato at **Dri Dri**, browse the stacks at **Rough Trade Records** and sit back in leather sofa luxury with a Peroni for a flick at the historic **Electric Cinema**.

Cinemas

- **The Electric Cinema** • 191 Portobello Rd
- **Gate Picturehouse** • 87 Notting Hill Gate
- **Notting Hill Coronet** • 103 Notting Hill Gate

Coffee

- **Apostrophe** • 138 Notting Hill Gate
- **Caffe Nero** • 13 Westbourne Grove
- **Caffe Nero** • 3 Notting Hill Gate
- **Caffe Nero** • 68 Portobello Rd
- **Coffee Republic** • 214 Portobello Rd
- **Eat.** • 68 Notting Hill Gate
- **Pret A Manger** • 65 Notting Hill Gate
- **Starbucks** • 5 Westbourne Grove
- **Starbucks** • 27 Portobello Rd
- **Starbucks** • 5 Pembridge Rd
- **Starbucks** • 40 Notting Hill Gate
- **Starbucks** • 61 Notting Hill Gate
- **Talkhouse Coffee** • 275 Portobello Rd

Landmarks

- **Portobello Road Market** • 223 Portobello Rd

Libraries

- **North Kensington Library** • 108 Ladbroke Grove
- **Notting Hill Gate Library** • 1 Pembridge Sq

Nightlife

- **Mau Mau** • 265 Portobello Rd
- **Notting Hill Arts Club** • 21 Notting Hill Gate
- **Sun in Splendour** • 7 Portobello Rd
- **Trailer Happiness** • 177 Portobello Rd
- **Uxbridge Arms** • 13 Uxbridge St
- **Windsor Castle** • 114 Campden Hill Rd

Post Offices

- **Kensington Church St** • 190 Kensington Church St
- **Ladbroke Grove** • 116 Ladbroke Grove

Restaurants

- **Beach Blanket Babylon** • 45 Ledbury Rd
- **Cafe Diana** • 5 Wellington Terrace
- **Crazy Homies** • 125 Westbourne Park Rd
- **Geales** • 2 Farmer St
- **Lucky 7** • 127 Westbourne Park Rd
- **Manzara** • 24 Pembridge Rd
- **Nama** • 110 Talbot Rd
- **Osteria Basilico** • 29 Kensington Park Rd
- **The Shed** • 122 Palace Gardens Terr
- **Taqueria** • 139 Westbourne Grove

Shopping

- **& Clarke's Bread** • 124 Kensington Church St
- **Bodas** • 38 Ledbury Rd
- **Diane von Furstenberg** • 83 Ledbury Rd
- **The Grocer on Elgin** • 6 Elgin Crescent
- **The Hummingbird Bakery** • 133 Portobello Rd
- **Melt** • 59 Ledbury Rd
- **Mr Christian's Delicatessen** • 11 Elgin Crescent
- **Music & Video Exchange** • 38 Notting Hill Gate
- **Negozio Classica** • 283 Westbourne Grove
- **Portobello Road Market** • Portobello Rd
- **R Garcia and Sons** • 248 Portobello Rd
- **Retro Man** • 34 Pembridge Rd
- **Retro Woman** • 32 Pembridge Rd
- **Rough Trade** • 130 Talbot Rd

London's unofficial 'Little Beirut' seems to attract both camera-clad tourists (who have strayed too far from Hyde Park) as well as Londoners (who look for food gems on Westbourne Grove). While the place is bustling, beware of the overpriced, and frankly sh*** tourist traps on Queensway. Instead, chill out with a shisha at **Berdees**, and then be adventurous and try your hand at 1950s-style bowling at **All Star Lanes**. Alternatively do it like the Victorians did and get a rub down at Porchester Gate Spa.

Cinemas
• **Odeon Whiteleys** • Queensway & Porchester Gardens

Coffee
• **Berdees Coffee Shop** • 84 Bishop's Bridge Rd
• **Pret A Manger** • 127 Queensway
• **Starbucks** • 19 Queensway

Libraries
• **Paddington Library** • Porchester Rd

Nightlife
• **All Star Lanes** • Bloomsbury Pl & Southampton Row
• **The Cow** • 89 Westbourne Park Rd

Post Offices
• **Harrow Rd** • 72 Harrow Rd
• **Queensway** • 118 Queensway

Restaurants
• **Al Waha** • 75 Westbourne Grove
• **Berdees Coffee Shop** • 84 Bishop's Bridge Rd
• **The Cow** • 89 Westbourne Park Rd
• **Royal China** • 13 Queensway
• **Tiroler Hut** • 27 Westbourne Grove

Shopping
• **Al Saqi Books** • 26 Westbourne Grove
• **Planet Organic** • 42 Westbourne Grove
• **Porchester Gate Spa** • Queensway & Porchester Rd
• **SCP** • 87 Westbourne Grove
• **Whiteleys Shopping Centre** • Queensway

Supermarkets
• **Sainsbury's** • 88 Westbourne Grove
• **Waitrose** • 38 Porchester Sq

Map 31 · **Paddington**

Paddington Bear may not seem so cuddly if he were one of today's commuters hanging around Paddington Station. This area can seem like zombie land, a mass of tired-looking, harassed faces grabbing food from one of the endless chain eateries. It's not all bad news though. Evening boredom can be banished by listening to famous war correspondents' exotic tales over a meal at the **Frontline Club**. For all other woes solve it with a swift half at **The Victoria**.

Cinemas

• **Frontline Club** • 13 Norfolk Pl

Coffee

• **Caffe Nero** • 14 Spring St
• **Caffe Nero** • Paddington Station
• **Costa** • 254 Edgware Rd
• **Eat.** • Paddington Station
• **Markus Coffee Company** • 13 Connaught St
• **Pret A Manger** • 9 Sheldon Sq
• **Serpentine Bar & Kitchen** • Serpentine Rd

Emergency Rooms

• **St Mary's Hospital** • Praed St & Winsland St

O Landmarks

• **Paddington Bear Statue** • Paddington Station
• **Tony Blair's House** • Connaught Sq & Seymour St
• **Westway Flyover** • Westway

Nightlife

• **Frontline Club** • 13 • Norfolk Pl
• **The Royal Exchange** • 26 Sale Pl
• **The Victoria** • 10 Strathearn Pl

Post Offices

• **Edgware Rd** • 354 Edgware Rd
• **Paddington** • 4 Praed St

Restaurants

• **Bonne Bouche** • 129 Praed St
• **Casa Malevo** • 23 Connaught St
• **Mandalay** • 444 Edgware Rd

Supermarkets

• **Sainsbury's** • Paddington Station
• **Sainsbury's** • 12 Sheldon Sq

Map 32 · Shepherd's Bush (West)

Ⓝ

1 **2**

Pans Gdns

Erica Street

y Road

Gravesend Road

Galloway Road

Bryony Road

Commonwealth Av

Commonwealth

India

Canada Way

Canada

Commonwealth
Avenue

Wormholt Park

Bloemfontein Road

White City Road

Australia Road

Sawley Road

South Africa Road

White City

Ring Road

Dunraven

Ormiston Grove

South Africa Road

Batman Close

Close

White City Road

A

Road

Willow Vale

Adelaide Grove

Hall. Rd

Oaklands Grove

Halsbury Rd

Chase

Loftus Road
Stadium - Queens
Park Rangers F.C.

**PAGE
382**

Close

Batman

Hammersmith
Park

**SHEPHERD'S
BUSH**

33 ▶

Thorpebank

Ellerslie Road

Stanlake Road

Stanlake Road

Ring Road

ingham Mews

Boscombe Road

Oaklands Grove

Bloemfontein Road

Bloemfontein Avenue

Etheldene Road

Ingersoll Road

Arminger Road

Loftus Road

Abdale Road

Tunis Road

Swindon Street

Wood

Macfarlane Road

Uxbridge Road A4020

Bloem
fontein Way

Abdale Road

Tunis Road

Stanlake Road

Stanlake MS

Frithville Gardens

Wood Lane A219

on Road

ville Road

Melina Road

Boscombe Road

Findon Road

Coningham Road

Hetley Road

Godolphin Road

St. Stephens Avenue

Devon
port
Ms

Warbeck Road

Uxbridge Road A4020

Stanlake Villas

Coverdale Road

Stanlake Road

Shepherds
Bush Mkt

**Shepherd's
Bush Market ⊖**

Shepherd's Bush Market

Uxbridge Road

London

Wood Lane A219

Bulwer St

Adine Street

B

Cathnor
Park

Goodwin Road

Stowe

Stowe Road

Godolphin Road

Thornfield Road

Shepherds Bush Market

Lime Grove

Manley Lane

Pennard Road

Shepherds Bush Green A219

Shepherds
Bush Common

Millers Way

Shepherds Bush Road A4020

Eigin Cl

Parnell
Close

venue

Cathnor Road

Coningham Road

Stowe Road

Godolphin Road

Scotts Road

St. Stephens Avenue

Devonport Road

Shaw
Cres

Scotts Road

Gainsborough Court

Melrose Terrace

Poplar
Bamborough
Gardens

Minford Gdns

Westwick

**40
▼**

Brackenbury
Gardens

Gold
hawk
Ms

Titmuss St

Sycamore

Goldhawk Road A402

Richford Street

Smith Grove

Astrop Ter

**Goldhawk
Road ⊖**

Sulgrave Road

Cromwell Grove

Anley R

0.25 mile **0.25 km**

Benbow Road

Shepherd's Bush (West)

Don't be scared. This part of town won't bite … much. Things may look a bit drab, and indeed you wouldn't want to spend your Friday nights in many of the pubs here, but on Uxbridge Road looks truly can be deceiving. While it's nothing special from the outside, **Esarn Kheaw** will blow your head off with authentic Thai green curry and leave you begging for more. Then swoon under the chandeliers to an off-the-radar act at restored dance hall **Bush Hall**.

Nightlife
- **Bush Hall** • 310 Uxbridge Rd
- **The Queen Adelaide** • 412 Uxbridge Rd
- **White Horse** • 31 Uxbridge Rd

Restaurants
- **Abu Zaad** • 29 Uxbridge Rd
- **Esarn Kheaw** • 314 Uxbridge Rd
- **Vine Leaves Taverna** • 71 Uxbridge Rd

Shopping
- **Damas Gate** • 81 Uxbridge Rd
- **Nut Case** • 352 Uxbridge Rd

The Bush has had a bit of a face-lift over the past few years. Once the former grime hub of West London it now sports one of Europe's biggest shopping centres, **Westfield**, and with it comes more traffic and more chain shops. Even the Beeb is on its way out. Fear not though, for Shepherds Bush Market still keeps the place decidedly unpretentious, while the Empire continues to attract the best up-and-coming bands. Experience some in-yer-face theatre at **Bush Theatre** and grab a bonza pie from the Bush's very own Aussie pie shop **Jumbucks**.

Cinemas

- **Vue Shepherds Bush** •
  Shepherds Bush Green & Rockley Rd

Coffee

- **BB's Coffee & Muffins** •
  Richmond Way & Charecroft Way
- **BB's Coffee & Muffins** •
  2117 Westfield London Shopping Center
- **Costa** • 72 Uxbridge Rd
- **Starbucks** • 62 Uxbridge Rd

O Landmarks

- **BBC Television Centre** • Wood Ln & Ring Rd

Libraries

- **Shepherds Bush Library** • 6 Wood Ln

Nightlife

- **Albertine** • 1 Wood Lane
- **Bush Theatre** • 7 Uxbridge Rd
- **The Defectors Weld** • 170 Uxbridge Rd
- **O2 Shepherd's Bush Empire** • Shepherd's Bush Green

Post Offices

- **Shepherds Bush Road** • 146 Shepherd's Bush Rd

Restaurants

- **Busaba Eathai** • Westfield Shopping Centre
- **Jasmine** • 16 Goldhawk Rd
- **Kerbisher & Malt** • 164 Shepherd's Bush Green
- **Mr Falafel** • Units T4-T5, New Shepherd's Bush Market
- **Patio Restaurant** • 5 Goldhawk Rd
- **Piansu** • 39 Bulwer St
- **Popeseye** • 108 Blythe Rd

Shopping

- **Westfield Centre** • Ariel Way

Supermarkets

- **Sainsbury's** • 164 Uxbridge Rd

Map 34 · **West Kensington / Olympia**

N

KENSINGTON

Holland Park

Kyoto Garden

28

29

Campden
Hill Tennis
Club

Holland Park
Lawn Tennis
Club

33

Kensington
(Olympia)

35▶

Kensington High Street

Addison
Cres

Addison Road

Holland Road A3220

Warwick Gardens

Warwick Road A3220

41

Hammersmith Road

North End Road B317

A315

Barons
Court

West
Kensington

42

W Cromwell Road A4

North End Road

EARLS
COURT

0.25 mile   0.25 km

West Kensington / Olympia

West Ken is a Jekyll-and-Hyde kind of place. The calm, village atmosphere around Holland Park soon gives way to an 'in your face' cluster of kebab shops and grime once you go south of High Street Kensington. While the hordes head to Hyde Park, locals in the know make a beeline to the more intimate Holland Park with its peaceful **Kyoto Garden**, sublime in autumn. Olympia Exhibition Centre gets that middle class blood boiling—Erotica Show anyone? Near the tube, **Café Continente** is the place to go for an irresistible stack of blueberry pancakes. The Arab Hall at **Leighton House Museum** is worth a visit alone.

 ## Coffee
• **Cafe Continente** • 62 N End Rd

O Landmarks
• **Kyoto Garden (Holland Park)** • 100 Holland Park Ave

Libraries
• **Barons Court** • North End Crescent

Nightlife
• **The Cumberland Arms** • 29 N End Rd
• **Famous 3 Kings** • 171 North End Rd
• **Society Bar** • 30 Kensington High St

 ## Post Offices
• **Olympia** • 8 North End Rd

 ## Restaurants
• **Belvedere Restaurant** • Abbotsbury Rd

 ## Shopping
• **Homebase** • 195 Warwick Rd

77

Kensington

Kensington is the London of Disney fantasy—Princesses tip-toeing around grand old homes and taking tea at 3 p.m. It's the kind of place where a gentile mews cottage will set you back a cool mill, but if you live here you'll still have some change left over for an SUV and a box of organic veg. You're not going to score any cool points for hanging out here but there's nothing better than frisbee and a picnic (from **Whole Foods**, of course) in Hyde Park on those treasured London summer days. If you've got the cash to splash, High Street Ken has the goods but instead take a detour to **The Builders Arms** for a not-so-posh pint.

Cinemas

- **Odeon Kensington** • Kensington High St & Edwards Sq

Coffee

- **Caffe Nero** • 160 Kensington High St
- **Caffe Nero** • 1 Wrights Ln
- **Costa** • 149 Cromwell Rd
- **Pret A Manger** • 149 Kensington High St
- **Pret A Manger** • 123 Kensington High St
- **Starbucks** • 35 Kensington High St
- **Starbucks** • 97 Kensington High St

O Landmarks

- **Kensington Palace Gardens** •
  Kensington Palace Gardens

Libraries

- **Kensington Central Library** • Phillimore Walk

Nightlife

- **Builders Arms** • 1 Kensington Ct Pl
- **The Devonshire Arms** • 37 Marloes Rd
- **Yashin Sushi** • 1 Argyll Rd

Post Offices

- **Kensington High St** • 257 Kensington High St

Restaurants

- **Bone Daddies** • 63-97 Kensington High St
- **Byron** • 222 Kensington High St
- **Clarke's** • 124 Kensington Church St
- **Kensington Roof Gardens** • 99 Kensington High St
- **Maggie Jones's** • 6 Old Court Pl

Shopping

- **Ben's Cookies** • 12 Kensington High St
- **Notting Hill Housing Trust** • 57 Kensington Church St
- **Trailfinders** • 194 Kensington High St
- **Urban Outfitters** • 36 Kensington High St
- **Whole Foods Market** • 63 Kensington High St

Supermarkets

- **Sainsbury's** • 162 Earl's Ct Rd
- **Tesco** • 100 W Cromwell Rd
- **Waitrose** • 243 Kensington High St

Map 35

Map 35

Map 36 · South Kensington / Gloucester Rd Ⓝ

1 | **2**

Hyde Park

Kensington Gardens

PAGE 342

Albert Memorial

A

South Carriage Drive

Kensington Road

Princes Gate | Princes Gate

gh Street A315

Kensington Road A315

Prince of Wales Terrace

De Vere Gardens

Canning Place Ms

Hyde Park Gate

Park Gate

Queen's Gate

Kensington Gore

Kensington Gore A315

Jay Ms

Jay Ms

Bremner Rd

Kensington Gore

Gore

Princes Gate Court

Low Gdns

Montrose Court

Princes Gate

Kensing ton Ct

Cambridge Pl

Ken sington Ct Ms

Albert Place

Douro Place

De Vere Gardens

Res ton Pl

Hyde Park Gate Ms

Kensington Gate

Kensington Gate

B325

Queen's Gate Mews

Prince Consort Road

Exhibition Road

◀37▶

Royal Albert Hall

Albans Grove

Canning Place

Callendar Road

Princes Gardens

Cottesmore Gardens

◀35

Victoria Road

Launceston Place

Kynance Pl

Gloucester Road

Queen's Gate Terrace

Petersham Place

Gore Street

Queen's Gate

Ayrton Road

Unwin Road

Imperial College PAGE 365

Imperial College

Imperial/College Princes Gate

Eldon Road

Kynance Mews

Elvaston

College Road

Frankland Road

Queen's Gate Place

Queen's Gate Place Mews

B

ngsley

Cornwall

Cornwall Gardens

Cornwall Gnds

Cornwall Gnds

Petersham Mews

Elvaston

Petersham Lane

Queen's Gate

Imperial

Museum Lane

The Science Museum PAGE 474

Victoria & Victoria & Albert Museum PAGE 468

Osten

Cornwall Ms S

SOUTH KENSINGTON

Cornwall Gardens

Grenville Place

Southwell Gardens

Natural History Museum PAGE 472

Exhibition Road

McLeod's Ms

Emperor's Gate

Queen's Gate Gdns

stone Mews

Cromwell Road A4

Cromwell Road

A4

Cromwell

Pl Ms

Cromwell

Cromwell

Thurloe Place

A37

Gaspar Ms

◀43

Gaspar

field Gds

Ashburn Ms

Ashburn Place

Cromwell Road

Gloucester Road

Gloucester Road

Stanhope Mews West

Stanhope Gardens

Queensberry Place

Queensberry Way

Queensberry

Road

Thurloe Place

Road | Thurloe St

South Kensington

Harrington Road

Pelham

◀45

Courtfield

Grenville Place

Stanhope Gardens

Harrington Road

Caslow

Cres

Onslow S

Courtfield Mews

Colbeck Mews

Gloucester Park

Harrington Gardens

Stanhope Ms S

Wetherby Pl

Clareville

Clareville Grove

Manson Place

Summer Pl

44▼

Sumner Mews

Onslow Sq

Sy

Onslow (Mews

Reece Ms

Cranley

Bramley

Place

Onslow Square

Bina Gardens

Rosary Gardens

Hereford

Clareville Street

Old Brompton Road A3218

Summer Place

Wetherby Gardens

Gloucester Road

Brechin Place

Onslow

pton Road

0.25 mile | 0.25 km

Once known as Albertopolis, this place started out as Prince Albert's playground of learning. These days the museums are the carrot that draws the tourists westwards from the buzzing centre. Free entry to museums mean more money for treats, and if it's treats you're after then fresh gelato at **Oddono's** or a good wedge of organic brie at the **South Kensington Farmer's Market** won't fail to disappoint. If your idea of a good night out consists of more than a few quiet shandies then we suggest checking out another 'nabe.

Cinemas
• **Cine Lumiere** • 17 Queensberry Pl

Coffee
• **Café Deco** • 42 Gloucester Rd
• **Pret A Manger** • 99 Gloucester Rd
• **Pret A Manger** • 15 Old Brompton Rd
• **Starbucks** • 7 Gloucester Rd
• **Starbucks** • 8 Gloucester Rd

Landmarks
• **Albert Memorial** • Kensington Gardens
• **Imperial College** • South Kensington Campus
• **Royal Albert Hall** • Kensington Gore

Libraries
• **French Institute Library** • 17 Queensberry Pl
• **National Art Library** • Cromwell Rd
• **Natural History Museum** • Cromwell Rd

Nightlife
• **Boujis** • 43 Thurloe St

Post Offices
• **Gloucester Road** • 118 Gloucester Rd
• **South Kensington Station** • 41 Old Brompton St

Restaurants
• **Cafe Creperie** • 2 Exhibition Rd
• **Caffe Forum** • 145 Gloucester Rd
• **Da Mario** • 15 Gloucester Rd
• **Jakob's** • 20 Gloucester Rd
• **The Kensington Creperie** • 2 Exhibition Rd
• **Oddono's** • 14 Bute St

Shopping
• **Maitre Choux** • 15 Harrington Rd
• **Partridges Deli** • 17 Gloucester Rd
• **Snog** • 32 Thurloe Pl

Supermarkets
• **Sainsbury's** • 158 Cromwell Rd
• **Waitrose** • 128 Gloucester Rd

Map 37 · **Knightsbridge**

Move on over Z-list celebrity, only the truly rich shop here! While you can't move for fur-or tourists, Knightsbridge is still a great place to shop. Window shop, that is **Harrods** and **Harvey Nics** are the big boys here, and if you're after £40 soap you are in the right place. For the rest of us there's the **Victoria & Albert Museum**—free entry, brilliant cafe to escape the crowds, and multiple naked male sculptures to ogle.

 Coffee

- **Bagel Factory** • 102 Brompton Rd
- **Caffe Nero** • 24 Brompton Rd
- **Costa** • 197 Brompton Rd
- **Eat.** • 106 Brompton Rd
- **Pret A Manger** • 132 Brompton Rd
- **Starbucks** • 4 Brompton Rd

 Landmarks

- **Holy Trinity Brompton** •
  Brompton Rd & Knightsbridge
- **Victoria & Albert Museum** • Cromwell Rd & Thurloe Pl

 Libraries

- **Goethe-Institut Library** • 50 Princes Gate

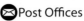 Post Offices

- **Knightsbridge** • 6 Raphael St

 Restaurants

- **Bar Boulud** • 66 Knightsbridge
- **Daquise** • 20 Thurloe Square
- **Ognisko** • 55 Prince's Gate
- **Zuma** • 5 Raphael St

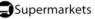 Shopping

- **Burberry** • 2 Brompton Rd
- **Divertimenti** • 227 Brompton Rd
- **Harrods** • 87 Brompton Rd
- **Harvey Nichols** • 109 Knightsbridge
- **Rigby & Peller** • 2 Hans St
- **Skandium** • 247 Brompton Rd
- **Space NK Apothecary** • 307 Brompton Rd

Supermarkets

- **Marks & Spencer** • 179 Brompton Rd
- **Sainsbury's** • 112 Brompton Rd

Map 38 · **Chiswick**

Ⓝ

Hardwicke Road
Acton Green Common
Parade
B409
South Parade
B409
Bath Road
B409
Sta

Mills Row
Essex Road
Bridge Street
Belmont
Alfred Cl
Belmont Grove
Addison Grove
Priory
Gdns
Lullington Road
Gainsborough Road
Roman Road
Melissa Road
Prebend Gardens
Bath Road

Dolman Road
Chiswick High Road
A315
Kirton Close
Clifton Gdns
Holly Rd
Arnott Cl
Fishers Lane
ACTON GREEN
Chiswick Common
Chiswick Lane
Common
Road
Road
⊖ **Turnham Green**
Thornton Avenue
Flanders Road

Chiswick High Road
A3000
Tum
ham
Barley Mow Passage
Bourne Place
Dukes Avenue
Linden Gdns
Lind.
Pas.
Glebe Close
Duke Road
Chiswick High Road A315
Mayfield Road
Turnham Grn
Ter Ms
Chan
Wind
mill
Mews
Turnham Green Terrace
Thornton Avenue
Upham Park Road
Ennismore Avenue
Stamford Brook
Stamford Brook
A315

Prince of Wales Terrace
Glebe Street
Devonshire
Annandale Road
Binns Road
Reckitt Road
Quick Road
Fraser Street
Wood Street
Devonshire Street
St
Swanscombe Road
Brackley Road
Alkerden Road
Swanscombe Rd
Coombe Road
Wilton Avenue
Ashbourne Grove
Balfern Grove
Cornwall Grove
Cranbrook Road
Verona Ct
39▶
CHISWICK
Chiswick High Road
A315
Homefield Road
Airedale Avenue
Merton Avenue
Cleveland Avenue
Ravenscourt Way
Middlesex
Netherwood Road
Beverley Road
Airedale Avenue
Windsor

Wavendon Avenue
Foster Road
Hadley Gdns
Sherlock Avenue
Gardens
Barrowgate Road
Close
Park Road North
Park Road
Park Road
Barrowgate Road
A4
mere Road
A4
Park Road
Dukes Avenue
White Swan Mews

Hogarth Lane
A4
Sutherland Rd
Bennett Street
Nicholas Ms
Shoe
Parrott Paint
Rd
Hogarth Lane
Dorchester Grove A316
Hogarth Roundabout
Great West Road A4
Homefield Recreation Ground
Great West Road
Glebe St
British Grove
British Grove South
Airedale Av
Netheravon Rd South
Flyover
Mawson
Netheravon Rd
Chiswick Lane
Eyot
Gdn
Chiswick Mall

Burlington Lane
A316
Griffin
Pk
Paxton Gdns
Langham
Pl
Church Street
Fuller's Griffin Brewery
Mawson Lane
Chiswick Mall
Chiswick Eyot
River Thames

Chiswick House Grounds
B
Corney Road Cemetery
Dartmouth
Station Road
Malthouse Drive
Chiswick Rd

Alexandra Avenue
A316
Corney Road
Grantham Road
Pumping Reach
Thames Crs
Bedford Road
Latimer Place
Chiswick Sq
Great Ms
Chiswick Mall
Leg of Mutton Nature Reserve
Ferry Lane
Lonsdale Rd
Verdun Road
Howsman

Burlington Lane
Edensor Road
Meadow Place
Promenade Approach
Alexandra Gardens
Market Drive
Edensor Gardens
Alexandra Avenue A316
Riverside
Thames Rd
B350
Harrod's Sports Ground
Barnes Av
Verdun Rd

| 0.25 mile | 0.25 km |

Lean, green and thankfully not so mean. Chiswick's tranquil, leafy, village feel is perhaps what draws families and well-heeled couples with its stacks of laid-back continental style pavement dining and quaint cafes on the High Road. Hit Devonshire Road for boutique shopping, and on sunny days it's all about ice-cream from **Foubert's** and an afternoon chilling out on Acton Green. **The Roebuck** serves up a top-notch Sunday roast but the **High Road Brasserie** still remains the place to be seen.

Coffee

- **Carluccio's** • 342 Chiswick High Rd
- **Starbucks** • 230 Chiswick High Rd

Libraries

- **Chiswick Library** • Duke's Ave

O Landmarks

- **Fuller's Griffin Brewery** • Chiswick Lane South

Nightlife

- **Carvosso's** • 210 Chiswick High Rd
- **George IV** • 185 Chiswick High Rd
- **The Packhorse & Talbot** • 145 Chiswick High Rd
- **The Roebuck** • 122 Chiswick High Rd

Post Offices

- **Chiswick High Road** • 110 Chiswick High Rd

Restaurants

- **Boys Authentic Thai** • 95 Chiswick High Rd
- **Chris' Fish and Chips** • 19 Turnham Green Terrace
- **Foubert's** • 2 Turnham Green Terrace
- **Franco Manca** • 144 Chiswick High Rd
- **High Road Brasserie** • 162 Chiswick High Rd
- **La Trompette** • 5 Devonshire Rd
- **Le Pain Quotidien** • 214 Chiswick High Road
- **Maison Blanc** • 26 Turnham Green Terrace
- **Kalamari** • 4 Chiswick High Rd
- **Union Jack's** • 217 Chiswick High Rd
- **Zizzi** • 231 Chiswick High Rd

Shopping

- **As Nature Intended** • 201 Chiswick High Rd
- **The Bread Shop** • 296 Chiswick Rd
- **Chiswick Health & Wellness Spa** • 300 Chiswick High Rd
- **Gail's Bread** • 282 Chiswick High Rd
- **Mortimer & Bennett** • 33 Turnham Green Terrace
- **Outsider Tart** • 83 Chiswick High Rd
- **Oxfam Books** • 90 Turnham Green Terrace
- **Something Nice** • 40 Turnham Green Terrace
- **Wheelers Garden Centre** • Turnham Green Terrace

Map 39 · **Stamford Brook**

0.25 mile

0.25 km

Stamford Brook

Wedged between Chiswick and Hammersmith, on the surface Stamford Brook may seem like not much more than a tube station and some rather nice, note 'expensive', houses. Brookites, however, know that it's all about that big blue below the A4—The Thames—for a lazy Sunday stroll or long Saturday brunches at **Lola and Simon**. Farther up King Street, **Tosa** serves up some authentic Japanese yakitori while thirsty Brookites head to **The Carpenter's Arms** for oysters and a Guinness in the garden.

Coffee

• **Artisan Coffee** • 372 King St
• **Cafe Ginkgo** • 243 Ravenscourt Park

Nightlife

• **The Raven** • 375 Goldhawk Rd

Restaurants

• **Carpenter's Arms** • 89 Black Lion Ln
• **Lola & Simon** • 278 King St
• **Saigon Saigon** • 313 King St
• **Tosa** • 332 Kings St

Supermarkets

• **Sainsbury's** • 120 Chiswick High Rd
• **Tesco** • 327 King St

Shopping

• **Mac's Cameras** • 262 Kings St
• **Thai Smile** • 287 King St

Map 39

Far enough out on the tube to scare the tourists, this area is a haven for locals who want it all on their doorstep. International flavours colour the Goldhawk Road, Ravenscourt Park offers a calm little slice of green while pretty Thames walks must surely conclude with a visit to the city's most picturesque pub, **The Dove**. Furnival Gardens is the spot to watch the annual Oxbridge boat race.

Cinemas

• **Cineworld Hammersmith** • 207 King St

Coffee

• **Caffe Nero** • 1 King St
• **Camden Coffee House** • 57 78 Goldhawk Rd
• **Coffee Republic** • 207 King St
• **Starbucks** • 3 King St

Nightlife

• **The Dove** • 19 Upper Mall

Post Offices

• **King St** • 168 King St

Restaurants

• **Lowiczanka Polish Cultural Centre** • 238 King St
• **Mahdi** • 215 King St
• **Sagar** • 157 King St
• **Zippy Diner** • 42 Goldhawk Rd

Shopping

• **Bushwacker Wholefoods** • 132 King St
• **Patisserie Sainte-Anne** • 204 King St

Supermarkets

• **Iceland** • 111 King St
• **Tesco** • 327 King St

Hammersmith

Map 41 is in the sidebar.

While the shops and pubs on offer along the main drag (King Street) are all pretty drab, Hammersmith has three great venues for the more culturally inclined. **The Apollo** hosts mainstream bands and big-name comedians; **The Lyric** is an affordable way to indulge in some modern theatre, and **The Riverside Studios** offer a satisfying selection of foreign and art house films. London's vegetarians flock to **The Gate**, with its seriously original and inventive menu.

 ## Cinemas

- **Riverside Studios** • Crisp Rd & Queen Caroline St

 ## Coffee

- **Cafe Brera** • Hammersmith Foyer & Roof Garden
- **Cafe Brera** • King St & Angel Walk
- **Costa** • Butterwick
- **Pret A Manger** • Butterwick
- **Starbucks** • 220 Hammersmith Rd

 ## Emergency Rooms

- **Charing Cross Hospital** •
  Fulham Palace Rd & St Dunstan's Rd

Libraries

- **Hammersmith Library** • Shepherds Bush Rd

 ## Nightlife

- **Brook Green Hotel** • 170 Shepherd's Bush Rd
- **The Distillers** • 64 Fulham Palace Rd
- **Hammersmith Apollo** • 45 Queen Caroline St
- **The Hampshire Hog** • 227 King St
- **Lyric Hammersmith** • King St

 ## Post Offices

- **Hammersmith** • 16 King's Mall

 ## Restaurants

- **The Gate** • 51 Queen Caroline St

 ## Shopping

- **Bakehaus** • 71 King St

 ## Supermarkets

- **Tesco** • 180 Shepherd's Bush Rd
- **Tesco** • 13 Broadway Ctr

Barons Court

Barons Court doesn't have a scene as such, but it is elegantly lovely. Ignore North End Road—a fried chicken blot among Edwardian mansions—and instead get lost in Lille Road's antique stores. **Curtains Up** offers intimate theatre in the pub vaults. If you need a change from polished chic, seek the **Colton Arms** for a jug-pint in its cottage style garden.

 Coffee

- **Café La Cigale** • 353 N End Rd
- **Costa** • 431 North End Rd

O Landmarks

- **Empress State Buidling** • Lillie Rd & North End Rd

 Nightlife

- **Colton Arms** • 187 Greyhound Rd
- **The Curtains Up** • 28 Comeragh Rd
- **The Fulham Mitre** • 81 Dawes Rd
- **The Queen's Arms** • 171 Greyhound Rd

 Post Offices

- **Dawes Road** • 108 Dawes Rd
- **Olympia** • 8 North End Rd

Restaurants

- **Best Mangal** • 104 N End Rd
- **The Malt House** • 17 Vanston Pl

Shopping

- **Curious Science** • 319 Lillie Rd

Supermarkets

- **Co-Op** • 88 N End Rd
- **Iceland** • 290 North End Rd
- **Sainsbury's** • 342 N End Rd

Map 42

93

Map 43 • West Brompton / Fulham Broadway / Earl's Court Ⓝ

0.25 mile

0.25 km

A lively mix of Aussies, Saffas, rich kids, and sweaty Chelsea fans occupy these neighbourhoods. Fulham Broadway is the focus of the action offering heaving bars and clubs. Earl's Court is slightly more sedate while West Brompton is positively sleepy in comparison. On Brompton Road '60s boho café **The Troubadour** is still a happening spot for live music and a coffee while **Vingt-Quatre** is a 24-hour institution serving fry-ups to clubbers in the early hours.

Cinemas

- **Cineworld Fulham Road** • 142 Fulham Rd
- **Vue Fulham** • Fulham Rd & Cedarne Rd

Coffee

- **Caffe Nero** • 430 Fulham Rd
- **Caffe Nero** • 174 Fulham Rd
- **Chairs & Coffee** • 512 Fulham Rd
- **Coffee Republic** • 142 Fulham Rd
- **Pret A Manger** • Fulham Broadway Retail Centre
- **Starbucks** • 29 Old Brompton Rd
- **Starbucks** • 36 Earl's Ct Rd
- **The Troubadour** • 263 Old Brompton Rd

O Landmarks

- **Stamford Bridge** • Fulham Rd & Moore Park Rd

Libraries

- **Brompton Library** • 210 Old Brompton Rd
- **Institute of Cancer Research Library** • 237 Fulham Rd

Nightlife

- **Chairs & Coffee** • 512 Fulham Rd
- **Onboard Karaoke** • 8 Kenway Rd
- **The Blackbird** • 209 Earl's Court Rd
- **The King's Head** • 17 Hogarth Rd

Post Offices

- **Earls Court** • 185 Earl's Court Rd
- **Fulham Road** • 369 Fulham Rd

Restaurants

- **Bodean's** • 4 Broadway Chambers
- **Cafe Brazil** • 511 Fulham Rd
- **Chutney Mary** • 535 King's Rd
- **Harwood Arms** • Walham Grove
- **Vingt Quatre** • 325 Fulham Rd
- **Yo! Sushi** • Fulham Rd

Shopping

- **Fulham Broadway Centre** • Fulham Rd

Supermarkets

- **Sainsbury's** • Fulham Rd
- **Tesco** • 459 Fulham Rd
- **Waitrose** • 380 North End Rd

Map 44 • Chelsea

This area drips old money, 4x4s, and people who own rather large things, like, say, Devon. The only way to do Chelsea is to be seen doing it—and if you're paying all that money at least make it worthwhile. Engage in some (super) star-gazing at **The Bluebird Café**. For a more sedate affair hang out with the locals, property investors 'n all, at local Victorian boozer **The Drayton Arms**.

Coffee

• **Starbucks** • 38–41 King's Rd

Emergency Rooms

• **Chelsea and Westminster Hospital** • 369 Fulham Rd

Nightlife

• **Brinkley's** • 47 Hollywood Rd
• **The Drayton Arms** • 153 Old Brompton Rd
• **The Duke of Clarence** • 148 Old Brompton Rd

Restaurants

• **The Bluebird** • 350 King's Rd
• **Eight Over Eight** • 392 King's Rd
• **Haché** • 329 Fulham Rd

Shopping

• **Furniture Cave** • 533 Kings Rd
• **Richer Sounds** • 258 Fulham Rd
• **The Shop At Bluebird** • 350 King's Rd

Supermarkets

• **Sainsbury's** • 295 Fulham Rd

Map 45 • **Chelsea (East)**

N

36 ▲   37 ▲

Thornwell Gardens A4
Thurloe Place A3218
Thurloe Place
North Terrace
Thurloe
Close
Alexander Place
Thurloe Street
South
Kensington
South Terrace   Alexander Square
Crescent
Place
Pelham Street   Egerton

Stanhope Mews South
Manson Place
Harrington Road
Reece Mews
Bina Gardens
Onslow Crescent
Onslow Square
Sumner Place
Mews
Onslow Place
Pelham
Crescent
Donne Place
Walton Street
Iverna Street
Mossop Street
Draycott Avenue

Clareville Grove
Clareville Street
Manson Mews
Cranley Place
Onslow Gardens
Barkley Place
Onslow Square
Sumner Place
Onslow Square
Sydney
Close
Pelham
Sloane Avenue
Makins Street
Petyward

A3218 Old Brompton Road
Onslow Mews East
Onslow Square
Onslow Mews West
Sydney
Mews
Fulham Road A308
Pond Place
Marlborough
Street
Whitehead's Grove

Cranley Gardens
Roland Gardens
Ensor Mews
Fulls Terrace
Neville Street
Selwood Place
Dudmaston Mews
Sydney Street B304
Burnby Hall
Oratory
Lane
Godfrey
Street
St. Luke's
Gardens
Danube Street
Jubilee Place
Markham Square
Elystan
Place
Bywater Street

A

44 ◄

46 ►

Evelyn Gardens
Elm Place
South Parade
Chelsea
Common
Chelsea Square
Cale Street
Britten Street
Burnsall
St. Luke's Street
Astell Street

Fulham Road A308
Elm Park Gardens
Onslow
Square
Dovehouse Street
Manresa Road
Hemus Place
Dovehouse
Green
King's Road A3217
Fawcett Street
Smith Terrace

Elm Park Lane
The Vale
Mulberry Walk
Carlyle Square
Ramsay Mews
Mallord Street
Elm Park Road

B

Park Gardens
Beaufort Street
King's Road
Old Church Street
Bramerton Street
CHELSEA
Chelsea Manor
Gardens
Flood Walk
Redesdale Street
Tedworth Square
Smith Terrace
Tedworth

Milman's
Street Burial
Ground
Beaufort Street A3320
Paultons Square
Waldron Mews
Ramsay Mews
Margaretta Terrace
B304 Oakley Street
Grove
Cottages
Alpha
Place
Redburn Street
Christchurch Street
Flats

Moravian
Place
Milman's Street
Paultons Street
Upper Cheyne Row
Phene Street
Oakley
Gardens
St. Loo Avenue
Robinson
Street
Caversham Street
Royal Hospital Row

Lavender
Old Chelsea
Petyt
Place
Justice
Walk
Lawrence
Street
Lordship
Place
Cheyne Row
Lordship
Place
Cheyne Walk
Cheyne
Mews
Cheyne
Gardens
Cheyne Walk
Chelsea
Embankment Gardens
Chelsea
Physic
Garden
Physic
Place
Paradise
Walk
Swan Walk
Dilke St

Ropers
Gardens
Cheyne Walk
Chelsea Embankment
Chelsea Embankment
Gardens
Chelsea Embankment A3212

Albert Bridge A3031

River Thames

| 0.25 mile | 0.25 km |

Chelsea East is what Hollywood thinks all of London is like, full of dapper English chaps and potential princesses (who, incidentally, donate their clothes to the **Red Cross shop**; rummage here for London's best bargains). King's Road buzzes as it did when it spawned the Swinging '60s and foodies are spoiled around Cale Street. **Tom's Kitchen** is your place for Sloaney eating without the Sloaney allowance. For a cheaper and sweeter taste of the area get to **The Hummingbird Bakery** for addictive oh-so-good cupcakes.

Cinemas

- **Curzon Chelsea** • 206 King's Rd
- **Cineworld Chelsea** • 279 King's Rd

Coffee

- **Cafe de la Paix** • 159 King's Rd
- **Caffe Nero** • 116 King's Rd
- **Caffe Nero** • 20 King's Rd
- **Caffe Nero** • 66 Old Brompton Rd
- **Starbucks** • 123 King's Rd
- **Starbucks** • 72 Old Brompton Rd

Libraries

- **Chelsea Library** • King's Rd

Post Offices

- **Elm Park** • 66 Elm Park Rd

Nightlife

- **The Anglesea Arms** • 15 Selwood Terrace
- **Chelsea Potter** • 119 Kings Rd
- **The Pig's Ear** • 35 Old Church St

Restaurants

- **Chelsea Kitchen** • 451 Fulham Rd
- **Four o nine** • 409 Clapham Rd
- **Le Columbier** • 145 Dovehouse St
- **The Hummingbird Bakery** • 47 Old Brompton Rd
- **Made In Italy** • 249 King's Rd
- **My Old Dutch Pancake House** • 221 King's Rd
- **The Pig's Ear** • 35 Old Church St
- **Tom's Kitchen** • 27 Cale St

Shopping

- **British Red Cross Chelsea** • 69 Old Church St
- **Frock Me! Vintage Fashion Fair** • Chelsea Town Hall, Kings Rd
- **Nomad Books** • 781 Fulham Rd
- **Sweaty Betty** • 125 King's Rd

Supermarkets

- **Waitrose** • 196 King's Rd

Map 46 · **Sloane Square**

N

1

2

37

19▶

A

Thurloe
Close
Thurloe Square
Alexander Place
South Terrace
Pelham Street
Road A308
Brompton Road A4
Egerton
Crescent Place
Walton Street
Pont Street B319
Chesham Place
Pavilion Street
Shafto Mews
Cadogan Lane
Chesham Place
Lennox Gardens Mews
Lennox Gardens
Pavilion Road
Sloane Street A3216
Cadogan Gate
Milner Street
Ovington Square
First Street
Hasker Street
Moore Street
Cadogan Square
Clabon Mews
Ellis Street
Wilbraham
Place
Sloane Terrace
Cadogan Street
Sedding Street
Grosvenor
Cottages
Eaton Mews
West
Eaton Gate A3
Cliveden Place
Denyer Street
Ixworth Place
Donne Place
Ivey Street
Sloane Avenue
Rawlings Street
Draycott Avenue
Draycott Place
Blacklands Terrace
Draycott Terrace
Culford Gardens
Cadogan Gardens
Symons Street
Sloane A3217
Square
Chester
Cottages
Caroline Terrace
Cheston Row
Eaton
Terrace
Holbein Place
Marlborough
Street
Ixworth Place
Makins Street
Pelward
Whitehead's Grove
Halsey Mews
Elystan Place
Sprimont Place
Bray Place
Coulson
Street
Anderson Street
King's Road A3217
Duke of York Square
Saatchi
Gallery
Lower Sloane Street
Sloane
Gardens
Sloane
Square
Whittaker
Street
St. Michael's
Mews
Graham Terrace
Passmore Street
45◀
St. Luke's Street
Jubilee Place
Markham Street
Markham
Square
Bywater Street
Wellington Square
Chelsea Manor Street
Radnor Walk
Smith Street
Shawfield Street
Smith Terrace
Woodfall Street
St. Leonard's Terrace
Turks Row
Franklin's Row
**SLOANE
SQUARE**
Holbein Mews
Pimlico Road
Bourne Walk
B

Danube Street
Godfrey Street
Burnsall Street
Hemus Place
Redesdale Street
Tedworth
Square
Tedworth
Gardens
Redburn Street
Ormonde
Gate
Christchurch Street
Christchurch
Street
Caversham Street
Dilke Street
Ralston Street
Tite Street
Ormonde Gate
Royal Hospital Road B302
Burton's
Court
Burton's
Court
Chelsea Bridge Road A3216
Ebury Bridge Road A3
Ranelagh Road
Wellington Buildings
20▶

Gardens
Walk
Sloane Manor Place
St. Alpha Place
Cheyne Gardens
St. Loo
Avenue
Cheyne Walk
Chelsea
Embankment Gardens
Robinson
Street
Flood Street
Redburn Street
Cheyne Court
St. Loo Court
Swan Walk
Chelsea
Physic
Garden
Paradise Walk
West Road
East Road
Royal Hospital
Ranelagh
Gardens
Chelsea Grounds
Chelsea Embankment A3212
Embankment Gardens

River
Thames

| 0.25 mile | 0.25 km |

You've got to love a place that spawns an adjective. If you've never met any 'Sloaney' types and are curious as to why the whole of London gets so riled about them, take a walk along the King's Road and observe. **Peter Jones** stands tall over the square and offers everything you didn't know you wanted. This rather beautiful 'nabe also hosts some bank-breaking eateries, such as **Gordon Ramsay** and **Bibendum**, as well as its fare share of cultural fair—the **Saatchi Gallery** being the finest example.

Coffee

- **Eat.** • 82 King's Rd
- **Pret A Manger** • 80 King's Rd
- **Starbucks** • 55 Sloane Ave
- **Starbucks** • 128 King's Rd

O Landmarks

- **Saatchi Gallery** • Duke of York HQ, King's Rd

Post Offices

- **Kings Walk** • 122 King's Rd

Restaurants

- **The Admiral Codrington** • 17 Mossop St
- **Bibendum Restaurant & Oyster Bar** • 81 Fulham Rd
- **Foxtrot Oscar** • 79 Royal Hospital Rd
- **The Good Life Eatery** • 59 Sloane Ave
- **Restaurant Gordon Ramsay** • 68 Royal Hospital Rd

Shopping

- **Partridges** • 2 Duke of York Sq
- **Peter Jones** • Sloane Sq
- **Rigby & Peller** • 13 Kings Rd
- **Space NK Apothecary** • 307 King's Rd

Supermarkets

- **Sainsbury's** • 75 Sloane Ave

This area is an estate agent's wet dream. Leafy, well heeled, on the river, and made for families. Catch the great English game at **Craven Cottage** before making the most of the riverside and grabbing a pint at **The Crabtree Tavern**. Now that you're tipsy, head to **The River Café** where you'll feel less pained shelling out for top-notch, dead-posh grub.

 Coffee

• **Starbucks** • 20 Fulham Palace Rd

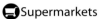 Restaurants

• **The River Café** • Thames Wharf, Rainville Rd

 Nightlife

• **The Crabtree Tavern** • Rainville Rd

 Supermarkets

• **Sainsbury's** • 179 Fulham Palace Rd

Post Offices

• **Fulham Palace Road** • 185 Fulham Palace Rd

Map 48 · **Fulham**

1

2

FULHAM

Dawes Road A3219

▲42

▲43

◄47

49►

Minster Road

Fulham Road A304

Fulham Road A304

Fulham Palace Road
A219

Fulham Palace Road

Fulham High Street A219

Fulham Road A304

New Kings Road A008

Parsons
Green

Parsons
Green

Lillie Road

William Close

Charden Street

Eelbrook Road

Chabot Road

Palace Road

Hickfield Plaza

Pullton

Barclay Road

Cassidy Road

Barclay Close

Munster Road

Harwell Street

Anten Street

Rosaline Road

Sherbrooke Road

Orban Road

St Olaf's Road

Kilmaine Road

Rosaville Road

Parkville Road

Gironde Road

Homestead Road

Burthwaite Road

Lancaster Court

Darlan Road

Shottendale Road

Wheatsheaf
Terrace

Clonmel Road

Kelvedon Road

Fulham Road A304

Bronsart Road

Mablethorpe Road

Rowallan Road

Aliestree Road

Kingwood Road

Wyfold Road

Maryat Square

Dagenhurst Street

Bramber Road

Chesilton Street

Lambrook Terrace

Sidbury Street

Waldo Road

Gowan Avenue

Vera Road

Bowen Avenue

Fernhurst Road

Reporton Road

Bloom Park Road

Marville Road

Brookville Road

Lilyville Road

Radipole Road

Rostrevor Road

Chesilton Road

Filmer Road

Swift Street

Colehill Lane

Winchendon Road

Bridges Place

Epple Road

Purser's Cross Road

St Maur Road

Whittingstall Road

Mimosa Street

Crookham Road

Dancer Road

St Dionis Road

Doria Road

Gastein Road

Heathmans Road

Lettice Street

Novello Street

St Marks Close

Parsons Green Lane

Rockmel Road

Ackmar Road

Horder Road

Colehill Lane

Bishop Road

Kimbell Gardens

Firth
Gardens

Edgeley Terrace

Fulham Park Road

Waldemar Avenue

Hendbridge Road

Heathcote Road

Durrell Road

Dorncliffe Road

Fulham Park Road

The Arches

Munster
Place

Draycott
Mews

Bowindon Road

Ashington Road

Ongar Road

Coniger Road

Alderville Road

Broomhouse

Linver Road

Fulham Park Gardens

Langridge Road

Pentney Avenue

Funqumer Avenue

Eberry Street

Woodlawn Road

Clonmurry Street

Niton Street

Colehill Gardens

Lalor Road

O'berry Avenue

Bishop's Park Road

Bishop's Avenue

Colehill Gardens

Dwight
Court

The Drive

Burlington
Place

Bagwit Road

Fulham Park Gardens

Ellenium
Street

Medrury Mews

Edenhurst Avenue

Ranelagh Avenue

Napier Avenue

Hurlingham Road

Moat
Gardens

Burlington Road

Buer Road

Grimston Road

Ewald Road

Doneraile Street

Foskett Road

Cristowa Road

Fulham
Palace
Meadows Allotment
Gardens

Bishop's
Park

Fulham Palace
Gardens

Steeple
Gate

Church Road

Fulham High Street A219

Putney
Bridge

Putney
Bridge
Station

Approach

Prior
Bank
Gardens

Gonville
Street

Willow
Bank

Hurlingham Gardens

Ranelagh Gardens

○ Putney Bridge
Tube Pill Box

Hurlingham
Stadium

Pitch

Hurlingham
Club Gardens

Hurlingham Club

Bridge A219

This part of town is rather lovely and rather boring in equal measure. Expensive homes belonging to Chelsea FC players sit alongside the often overlooked romantic beauty of Fulham Palace. On the main drag of Fulham High Street is **Hurlingham Books** with its walls stacked high with texts on anything and everything. With not much else going on away from here we suggest contemplating life while staring out at the mighty Thames in Fulham Palace Gardens. When you're done then warm up in their elegant tearoom, **The Drawing Room**.

Coffee

- **Caffe Nero** • 717 Fulham Rd
- **Local Hero** • 640 Fulham Rd
- **Starbucks** • 309 Fulham Rd
- **Tinto Coffee** • 411 Fulham Palace Rd

Landmarks

- **Putney Bridge Tube Pill Box** • Putney Bridge Station

Libraries

- **Fulham Library** • 598 Fulham Rd

Post Offices

- **Fulham** • 815 Fulham Rd

Restaurants

- **Drawing Room Cafe** • Bishop's Ave
- **Fisher's Chips** • 19 Fulham High St
- **Royal China** • 805 Fulham Rd

Shopping

- **Hurlingham Books** • 91 Fulham High St

Map 49 · **Parson's Green**

Parson's Green

Map 49

You know you're in a classy neighbourhood when the kebab house (**Kebab Kid**) gets people travelling across London. This part of town ain't cheap and unless you're looking for a sedate Sunday lunch you'll most likely not find yourself here. If, however, you are looking for a chow down then **The White Horse** (known locally as the 'Sloany Pony') is the place to be, hands down. Otherwise head to charming **Duke On The Green** for a pint in style—they even show the footy!

Coffee

- **Caffe Nero** · 142 Wandsworth Bridge Rd
- **Starbucks** · 95 Wandsworth Bridge Rd

Nightlife

- **Amuse Bouche** · 51 Parsons Green Ln
- **Duke on the Green** · 235 New Kings Rd
- **The White Horse** · 1 Parson's Green Ln

Restaurants

- **Kebab Kid** · 90 New Kings Rd
- **Little H** · 267 New Kings Rd
- **Tendido Cuatro** · 108 New King's Rd

Supermarkets

- **Tesco** · 601 King's Rd

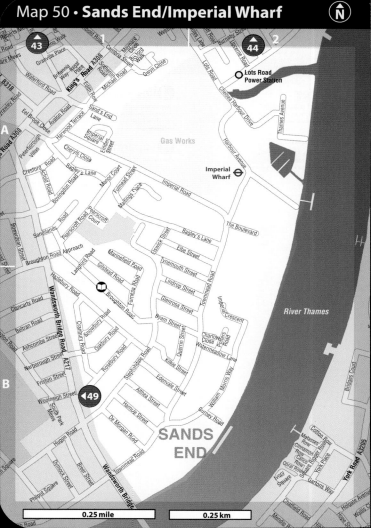

Map 50 · **Sands End/Imperial Wharf**

Sands End/Imperial Wharf

Time was, if you asked any Londoner where Sands End is you'd receive a blank look and a bemused 'you wot?' These days the area sees a lot more foot traffic thanks to a newish London Overground stop and the development of Imperial Wharf. Jazz seems to be a major draw to the area with the autumn Jazz Festival and the **606 Club** on Lots Road. When you're all jazzed out pop into **The Blue Elephant** at its new location for first-class Thai food.

Landmarks

• **Lots Road Power Station** • 27 Lots Rd

Libraries

• **Sands End Library** • 59 Broughton Rd

Nightlife

• **606 Club** • 90 Lots Rd

Restaurants

• **Blue Elephant** • The Boulevard
• **Sands End** • 135 Stephendale Rd

Map 50

Map 51 · **Highgate**

On the cusp of north London you'll find the little suburban gem that is Highgate. Hemmed in by parks, woods and a golf course, the area is an escapist paradise from the chaos of the city, and its well-heeled residents' plush fur is surprisingly—and pleasantly—soft to the touch. Pop into boutique independent shops like **Le Chocolatier** before heading over to Highgate Woods with a bottle to enjoy live jazz during the summer.

Coffee

• **Caffe Nero** • 62 Highgate High St
• **Costa** • 66 Highgate High St

Landmarks

• **Highgate Cemetery** • 1 Swain's Ln
• **Karl Marx's Grave** • Highgate Cemetery

Nightlife

• **The Angel Inn** • 37 Highgate High St
• **The Boogaloo** • 312 Archway Rd
• **The Flask** • 77 Highgate West Hill
• **Prince Of Wales** • 53 Highgate High St
• **The Victoria** • 28 North Hill
• **The Woodman** • 414 Archway Rd
• **The Wrestler** • 98 North Rd

Post Offices

• **Highgate Near Station** • 361 Archway Rd

Restaurants

• **The Bull** • 13 North Hill Ave
• **Cafe Rouge** • 6 South Grove
• **Papa Del's** • 347 Archway Rd
• **The Red Lion & Sun** • 25 North Rd

Shopping

• **The Corner Shop** • 88 Highgate High St
• **Highgate Butchers** • 76 Highgate High St
• **Hops N Pops** • 389 Archway Rd
• **Le Chocolatier** • 78 Highgate High St
• **Mind** • 329 Archway Rd
• **Oxfam** • 80 Highgate High St
• **Walter Castellazzo Design** • 84 Highgate High St
• **Wild Guitars** • 393 Archway Rd

Map 52

Something unexpected is happening here. Designer boutiques keep popping up; fashion labels we've never even heard of—cafés so fashionably quirky they should really be in Shoreditch. But real change takes time and at night this becomes even more obvious. **The Winchester** is still the only decent pub around and **The Caipirinha** still stays open very, very late.

O Landmarks

• **Parkland Walk Nature Reserve** • Parkland Walk
• **Suicide Bridge** • Hornsey Ln & Archway Rd

Libraries

• **London Mennonite Centre Library** •
14 Shepherds Hill Heights

Nightlife

• **Caipirinha Jazz Bar** • 177 Archway Rd
• **The Winchester Pub Hotel** • 206 Archway Rd

Restaurants

• **Bengal Berties** • 172 Archway Rd
• **The Lighthouse** • 179 Archway Rd

Shopping

• **The Green Room** • 192 Archway Rd
• **Pax Guns** • 166 Archway Rd

Map 53 · **Crouch End**

Crouch End

Crouch End gets a bit of a bad rap. It's boring, people say. Just prams and middle-class media types. But, you know, it could be a lot worse. It's safe, with plenty of decent pubs (**The King's Head**), eateries (**Banners**) and a great record shop (**Flashback**). It might be low on the hipster scale, but for plain ol' good livin' it ticks all the boxes.

 Coffee

• **Spiazzo** • 26 The Broadway
• **Starbucks** • 7 The Broadway

O Landmarks

• **Abandoned Warehouse** •
  Parkland Walk & Crouch End Hill

Libraries

• **Highgate Library** • 1 Shepherds Hill
• **Hornsey Library** • Haringey Park

Nightlife

• **Harringay Arms** • 153 Crouch Hill
• **The King's Head** • 2 Tottenham Ln
• **The Queens Pub & Dining Rooms** •
  26 Broadway Parade
• **Stapleton Tavern** • 2 Crouch Hill

 Post Offices

• **Crouch End** • 28 Topsfield Parade

Restaurants

• **Banners** • 21 Park Rd
• **Hot Pepper Jelly** • 11 Broadway Parade
• **Jai Krishna** • 161 Stroud Green Rd
• **Wow Simply Japanese** • 18 Crouch End Hill

Shopping

• **Flashback** • 144 Crouch Hill
• **Haelen Centre** • 41 The Broadway
• **Italian Farmers** • 186 Stroud Green Rd
• **Organic Food** • 196 Stroud Green Rd
• **Soup Dragon** • 27 Topsfield Parade
• **Walter Purkis And Sons** • 17 The Broadway

Map 53

Map 54 • **Hornsey**

Unless you live in Hornsey, if you're in Hornsey, your bus has probably broken down. In this dystopian residential area you'll be lucky to find a tuft of grass let alone a shop. A modicum of life exist up at Tottenham Lane, but that's pretty much Crouch End. **Ridge Cafe** is worth a stop for a cup of coffee and you can watch sport at the unpretentious **Hope & Anchor**.

Libraries

• **Stroud Green Library** • Quernmore Rd

Nightlife

• **The Hope & Anchor** • 128 Tottenham Ln

Restaurants

• **Ridge Cafe** • 97 Tottenham Ln

Shopping

• **Micycle N4** • 8 Ferme Park Rd

Map 55

Green Lanes was once an endless strip of restaurants which although good, meant that the only dinner option was Turkish. The last few years have seen so many new openings, it's becoming a bit (dare we say it?) hip. The spirit of the place remains resolutely the same though and the Turkish grocer **Yasar Halim** stands proud in the middle of it all. Get ribs for dinner at **Autograf** and indulge in some vodka. Or if beer's more your thing, head to **Brouhaha**. Long-standing favourite, **The Salisbury**, is a failsafe choice for a good night and if you need your organic groceries, **Beans and Barley** will keep you happy.

Coffee

- **Beans and Barley** • 595 Green Lanes
- **Cafe Delight** • 31 Green Lanes
- **Mezzo Shisha Lounge** • 64 Grand Parade

Landmarks

- **Railway Fields Nature Reserve** • 381 Green Lanes

Nightlife

- **Brouhaha** • 501 Green Lanes
- **The Beaconsfield** • 359 Green Lanes
- **Jam In A Jar** • 599 Green Lanes
- **The Salisbury** • 1 Grand Parade, Green Lanes

Post Offices

- **Harringay** • 509 Green Lanes

Restaurants

- **Autograf Grill** • 499 Green Lanes
- **Blend** • 587 Green Lanes
- **Bun & Bar** • 553 Green Lanes
- **Devran** • 485 Green Lanes
- **Hala** • 29 Grand Parade

Shopping

- **Beans and Barley** • 595 Green Lanes
- **Harringay Local Stores** • 581 Green Lanes
- **Yasar Halim** • 495 Green Lanes

Supermarkets

- **Sainsbury's** • 4 Williamson Rd

Map 56 · **Hampstead Village**

Templewood Avenue

Heath

West Heath

PAGE 338

1

2

Heath Drive

Redington Road

Templewood Avenue

Birchwood Drive

Grange

Fincre Dr

Gardens

East Heath Road

Heath Brow

North End Way A502

Spaniards Road

Redington Gardens

Heysham Lane

Hampstead Heath

Whitestone Walk

A

hill Avenue

Oak Hill Park

Speden Close

Branch Hill

Upper Terrace

Windmill Hill

Lower Terrace

Judges Wk

Whitestone Lane

East Heath Road

Vale of Heath

Oak Hill Way

Hampstead Observatory

Admiral's Walk

Hampstead Grove

Hampstead Heath

Oak Hill Park

Oak Hill

Park Ms

Lower Terrace

Upper Terrace

Redington Road

Frognal Rise

Windmill Hill

Hampstead Grove

Heath Street A502

Frognal

Mount Vernon

Wind mill Hill

Hampstead Grove

The Mount

Hamp stead Sq

Holford Road

Cannon Place

Mount

Gardens

Church Row

Frognal

Holly Walk

Holly Hill

Holly Mount

Holly Bush Vale

The Mount

New End

Elm Row

Hampstead Sq

New End

Grove Pl

Well Road

Christchurch Hill

Squire's Mount

Cannon Lane

57▶

al Lane

Frognal

Church Row

Oriel Court

Back Lane

Hampstead

Ginsburg Yd

Streatley Place

Boad's Ms

White Bear Place

New End Square

Well Road

Well Walk

Christchurch Hill

Squire's

Well Walk

Ellerdale Close

Perrin's Walk

Ellerdale Road

Perrins Lane

Heath Street A502

Rosslyn Hill A502

Bird in Hand Yd

Spencer Walk

Flask Walk

Gardner Rd

Flask Walk

Gayton Road

Gayton

Crescent

Willow Road

Gainsborough Gardens

Heath Side

al Way

Frognal

TC (Private)

Ellerdale Road

Prince Arthur Ms

Prince Arthur Road

Fitzjohn's Avenue B511

Martys Yd

Greenhill

Hampstead High Street

Willoughby Road

Tudor Close

Crescent

Kemplay Road

Carlingford Road

Denning Road

Vale of Health

B

(Private)

Arkwright Road

Vane Close

Vane Close

Mul berry Close

Pilgrim's Place

Pilgrim's Lane

Netherhall Gardens

Shepherds Walk

Rosslyn Hill A502

67▼

al Road

Fitzjohn's Avenue B511

Lyndhurst Ter

Thurlow Road

Eldon Grove

Downshire Hill

Keats Grove

Willow

East Heath Road

Lyndhurst Road

Tower

Hampstead Hill

PN (Hamp

0.25 mile

0.25 km

Hampstead Village

Map 56

Sure, leafy Hampstead Village defines posh, but there is still some fun to be had. Head to Flask Walk for cute and eccentric local shops and, of course, waffles at **Slice of Ice**. The **Duke of Hamilton** is as good a pub you're likely to find anywhere, and when they kick you out, much like the bankers kicked out the literary-types from the area, there is always **Tinseltown**.

Cinemas
• **Everyman Cinema Club** • 5 Hollybush Vale

Coffee
• **Caffe Nero** • 1 Hampstead High St
• **Ginger & White** • 4 Perrin's Ct

O Landmarks
• **Hampstead Observatory** •
  Lower Terrace & Hampstead Grove

Nightlife
• **The Duke of Hamilton** • 23 New End
• **The Flask** • 14 Flask Walk
• **The Freemasons Arms** • 32 Downshire Hill
• **Holly Bush** • 22 Holly Mount

Restaurants
• **Carluccio's** • 34 Rosslyn Hill
• **La Creperie De Hampstead** • 77 Hampstead High St
• **The Louis Patisserie** • 32 Heath St
• **Tinseltown** • 104 Heath St

Shopping
• **Happy Returns** • 36 Rosslyn Hill
• **Keith Fawkes** • 1 Flask Walk
• **Mystical Fairies** • 12 Flask Walk

Map 57 · **Hampstead Heath**

1

2

Kemplay Road

Willoughby Road

Pilgrim's Place

Pilgrim's Lane

Pilgrim's Lane

Heath
Heath

HAMPSTEAD

Downshire Hill

Hampstead
Ponds

Hampstead
Ponds

Parliament
Hill

Keats Grove

Gardens

Heath Hurst Road

South Hill Park

South Hill Park

Hampstead
Heath

PAGE
338

Rosslyn Hill A502

Pilgrims
Road

Terror Ct

Thurlow Road Close

A

Keats' House

Mayon
Mews

St. Crispins Close

Parliament Hill

The Old
Orchard

Tanza Road

Belsize Ct

Belsize Lane

Lane

Pond Street B518

South End
Road

South End Close

Nessington Road

156

Rowland Hill

Constantine Road
B518

Constantine Road

Children's
Playground
& Paddling Pool

Ornan Road

Fleet Road B518

Byron Mews

Agincourt
Road B518

Mackeson Road

Parliament
Hill Fields
Athletics Track

SIZE Avenue

Ella
Cressy

Fleet Road

Lishurne Road

Roderick Road

Shirlock Road

Savernake Road

Courthope Road

Estelle Road

Rona Road

Adventure
Playground

Aspern Grove

Wood Wlk

Belsize
Place

Aspern Gro

Tennis
Court

Lawn

Garnett Road

Haverstock Hill

Glenloch Road

Lawn
Road
Flats

Howitt Road

Belsize
Park

A502

Downside Cres

Belsize Grove

Lawn Road

Park Road

Dunboyne Rd

Kingsford
Street

Rochford
Street

Mansfield Road B518

Mansfield Road

Elaine Grove

Oak Village

Oak Village

Kiln Village

B

Antrim Grove

Haverstock Hill A502

167

Mews

Fountain

Upper

Parkhill Road

Parkhill Road

Tasker Road

Parkhill Walk

Southampton Road B517

Lismore
Circus

Lamble Street

Wellesley Road

Vicars Road

Barrington
Close

Grafton Road

Kiln Place

58

GOS
OA

Kentish
Town
City Farm

Elizabeth
Mews

Englands Lane

cot Gardens

BELSIZE PARK

Antrim Road

Southampton Road

Quadrant
Grove

Grafton Terrace

Malden Road

Haverstock Road

Wellesley Road

Wellington Road

Dale Rd

Cress

Grafton Road

71

72

Steeles Mews
North

Steeles Road

Eton

Matilda

Park Road

Villas

Herbert St

Gilden

Mansfield

Shirlett

Gardens

Queen's Crescent

Malden Road B517

Olden Road

Ashdown
Cres

Queen's Crescent

Wellington Road

Grafton Road

Woodyard

Arctic St

Place

0.25 mile

0.25 km

Hampstead Heath

Believed to be the inspiration for CS Lewis's Narnia, Hampstead Heath was absorbed into London proper during the Victorian era but still feels more like one of the Home Counties. With the exception of the blight on the landscape that is the **Royal Free Hospital**, the area is charming with boutique shops and restaurants on the South End Road, which cater to a refined and heavy-walleted crowd.

Coffee

• **Starbucks** • 5 South End Rd

Emergency Rooms

• **Royal Free Hospital** • Pond St & Fleet Rd

O Landmarks

• **John Keats House** • 38 Heath Hurst Rd
• **Lawn Road Flats** • Lawn Rd & Garnett Rd

Libraries

• **Heath Library** Keats Grove

Nightlife

• **The Garden Gate** • 14 S End Rd
• **Roebuck** • 15 Pond St

Restaurants

• **Mimo La Buffala** • 45 South End Rd
• **Paradise** • 49 South End Rd
• **Polly's** • 55 South End Rd

Shopping

• **Daunt Books** • 51 South End Rd
• **Giocobazzi's Delicatessen** • 150 Fleet Rd

Map 57

An area you stumble upon by accident, on your way somewhere else, probably Hampstead Heath or Highgate Cemetery. Then you realize how nice it is. Maybe you should try the little restaurants? Soon you find yourself having pizza at **Al Parco** every week and trekking all across London just to find out what new ales they're serving at **The Southampton Arms**. You could live here. You really could.

Nightlife

- **The Bull and Last** • 168 Highgate Rd
- **The Southampton Arms** • 139 Highgate Rd

Restaurants

- **Al Parco** • 2 Highgate West Hill
- **Bistro Laz** • 1 Highgate West Hill
- **Carob Tree** • 15 Highgate Rd
- **Kalendar** • 15 Swains Ln
- **Lalibela** • 137 Fortess Rd
- **Stingray Cafe** • 135 Fortess Rd

Shopping

- **Baba** • 11 Swain's Ln
- **Corks** • 9 Swain's Ln
- **Forks** • 7 Swain's Ln

Map 59 · Tufnell Park

Map 59

Surrounded by the rougher Archway, Kentish Town, and Holloway and immortalised by Simon Pegg in cult comedies *Spaced* and *Shaun of the Dead*, unassuming Tufnell Park has been quietly fashionable for years. Unwind with a book and a coffee at **Rustique**, or hit **Nuraghe Trattoria** for some of the finest Italian food in London. **The Dome** hosts everything from the latest cutting-edge electronica to seasoned indie rock acts.

Emergency Rooms

- **Whittington Hospital** •
  Magdala Ave & Dartmouth Park Hill

Libraries

- **Highgate Library** • Chester Rd

Nightlife

- **Aces And Eights Saloon Bar** • 156 Fortess Rd
- **Boston Arms** • 178 Junction Rd
- **The Dome** • 78 Junction Rd
- **The Hideaway** • 114 Junction Rd
- **The Lord Palmerston** • 33 Dartmouth Park Hill
- **The Star** • 47 Chester Rd

Restaurants

- **Nuraghe Trattoria** • 12 Dartmouth Park Hill
- **Rustique Cafe** • 142 Fortess Rd
- **The Spice** • 161 Fortess Rd

Shopping

- **The Hornsey Trust Charity Shop** • 124 Fortess Rd
- **North London Adoption Centre** • 135 Junction Rd

As grey and gritty as ever, Archway could really do with a fresh lick of paint. For a break from the grime try **La Voute** with their art exhibitions and awesome breakfasts or **RRC Thai** for something spicier. At night, there are enough old man boozers to keep you busy, but bear in mind, nicer places are only a short bus ride away.

Coffee

• **Cafe Metro** • Junction Rd

O Landmarks

• **Banksy's Hitchhiking Charles Manson** • Tally Ho Corner (off Highgate Hill)
• **Dick Whittington's Cat** • 89 Highgate Hill

Libraries

• **Archway Library** • Highgate Hill

Nightlife

• **Mother Red Cap** • 665 Holloway Rd

Restaurants

• **500 Restaurant** • 782 Holloway Rd
• **Il Mio Mosaic** • 24 Junction Rd
• **Junction Café** • 61 Junction Rd
• **Nid Ting** • 533 Holloway Rd
• **St Johns Tavern** • 91 Junction Rd

Shopping

• **Second Chance** • 7 St John's Way
• **Super Persia** • 621 Holloway Rd

Supermarkets

• **Co-Op** • 11 Junction Rd
• **Sainsbury's** • 643 Holloway Rd

Map 61 · **Holloway (North)**

Holloway (North)

Map 61

The borough of Islington, in which North Holloway sits, is supposed to be either a byword for liberal middle-class cosiness or else grim inner-city deprivation, depending on who you talk to. This bit has neither, just lots of dull grey streets. Down on Holloway Road, **El Molino** is a great place for tapas.

Coffee
• **Caffe Nero** • 400 Holloway Rd

Cinemas
• **Odeon Holloway** • 419 Holloway Rd

Libraries
• **North Library** • Manor Gardens

Nightlife
• **The Quays** • 471 Holloway Rd
• **The Swimmer** • 13 Eburne Rd

Restaurants
• **El Molino** • 379 Holloway Rd
• **The Landseer** • 37 Landseer Rd
• **North Nineteen** • 194 Sussex Wy
• **Orexi** • 236 Hornsey Rd
• **Tagine D'Or** • 92 Seven Sisters Rd

Shopping
• **Holloway Car Boot** •
Opposite Odeon Holloway Cinema, Holloway Rd
• **Michael's Fruiterers** • 56 Seven Sisters Rd

Supermarkets
• **Iceland** • 442 Holloway Rd

Finsbury Park used to be somewhere you passed through rather than lingered but with Stroud Green Road slowly being populated with numerous eating and drinking options and £5 million invested in tarting up the park, it really isn't that bad. You could do worse than have a Sunday roast at **The Old Dairy**, prop up the bar at the **Stapleton Tavern** or grab a coffee at **The Deli at 80**. For those who like a bit of culture the **Park Theatre** is saving you a trip to the West End.

Coffee

- **Boulangerie Bon Matin** • 178 Tollington Park
- **The Deli at 80** • 80 Stroud Green Rd
- **Vagabond N5** • 20 Charter Court

O Landmarks

- **North London Central Mosque (Finsbury Park)** •
  7 St Thomas's Rd

Libraries

- **N4 Library** • 25 Blackstock Rd

Nightlife

- **The Faltering Fullback** • 19 Perth Rd
- **The Old Dairy** • 1 Crouch Hill
- **The Silver Bullet** • 5 Station Pl
- **WB Yeats** • 20 Fonthill Rd

Post Offices

- **Stroud Green Rd** • 97 Stroud Green Rd

Restaurants

- **Dudley's Pancake House** • 119 Stroud Green Rd
- **Exeter Street Bakery** • Morris Pl
- **Fassika** • 152 Seven Sisters Rd
- **Girasole** • 150 Seven Sisters Rd
- **Hana Sushi** • 150 Seven Sisters Rd
- **Le Rif** • 172 Seven Sisters Rd
- **Lulu's Caribbean Cuisine** • 84 Stroud Green Rd
- **N4 Street Burger & Burrito** • 8 Clifton Terrace
- **Osteria Tufo** • 67 Fonthill Rd
- **Petek** • 96 Stroud Green Rd
- **Season** • 53 Stroud Green Rd

Shopping

- **The Deli at 80** • 80 Stroud Green Rd
- **Exeter Street Bakery** • Morris Pl
- **The Happening Bagel Bakery** • 284 Seven Sisters Rd
- **Hettie Holland** • 19 Charter Court

Supermarkets

- **Tesco** • 105 Stroud Green Rd

Map 63 · **Manor House**

Don't hang out near the 'scummy round the edges' station as it can get pretty
gruesome at night. You might chance upon a warehouse party round here,
but walk south, dodge the rats around the reservoir, admire the faux turrets of
The Castle Climbing Centre, and head to the **New River Café** for great fry-ups
with views over the leafy oasis of Clissold Park.

Coffee

- **Boulangerie Bon Matin** • 178 Tollington Park
- **Cafe Vintage** • 88 Mountgrove Rd
- **Fink's Salt & Sweet** • 70 Mountgrove Rd
- **Simply Organique** • 316 Green Lanes
- **Vagabond N5** • 20 Charter Court

O Landmarks

- **The Castle Climbing Centre** •
  Green Lanes & Lordship Park

Libraries

- **Woodberry Down Library** • 440 7 Sisters Rd

Nightlife

- **The Brownswood Park Tavern** • 271 Green Lanes
- **The Happy Man** • 89 Woodberry Grove

Post Offices

- **Woodberry Grove** • 107 Woodberry Grove

Restaurants

- **Fink's Salt & Sweet** • 70 Mountgrove Rd
- **Il Bacio** • 178 Blackstock Rd
- **New River Café** • 271 Stoke Newington Church St

Shopping

- **Bennet & Brown** • 84 Mountgrove Rd
- **Cafe Vintage** • 88 Mountgrove Rd
- **Sargent & Co.** • 74 Mountgrove Rd
- **Simply Organique** • 316 Green Lanes
- **Sylvanian Families** • 68 Mountgrove Rd

Stoke Newington

The richer cousin of Dalston and the poorer cousin of Islington, Stoke Newington has an inf-riority complex-cum-swagger which explains why 90% of its inhabitants are creative types. The curvy Church Street is the port of call with its boutique shops (**Metal Crumble**) and aptly Nietzsche stacked bookshops. Great beer and atmosphere (**The Shakespeare**), curry (**Rasa N16**), Sunday roast (**Rose and Crown**) and check out the butterflies and bats at Park Cemetery.

Map 64

O Landmarks

• **Newington Green Church** • 39 Newington Green

Libraries

• **Stoke Newington Library** • Stoke Newington Church St

Nightlife

• **The Auld Shillelagh** • 105 Stoke Newington Church St
• **Londesborough** • 36 Barbauld Rd
• **Rose and Crown** • 199 Stoke Newington Church St
• **Ryan's Bar** • 181 Stoke Newington Church St
• **Ruby's** • 76 Stoke Newington Rd
• **The Shakespeare** • 57 Allen Rd
• **White Hart** • 69 Stoke Newington High St

Post Offices

• **Church Street** • 170 Stoke Newington Church St
• **Stoke Newington** • Stoke Newington High St

Restaurants

• **Anglo Asian** • 60 Stoke Newington Church St
• **Blue Legume** • 101 Stoke Newington Church St
• **Datte Foco** • 10 Stoke Newington Church St
• **Fifty Six** • 56 Newington Green
• **Foxlow** • 71-73 Church St
• **Rasa N16** • 55 Stoke Newington Church St
• **Sariyer Balik** • 56 Green Lanes
• **Yum Yum** • 187 Stoke Newington High St

Shopping

• **Ark** • 161 Stoke Newington Rd
• **The Beaucatcher Salon** •
  44 Stoke Newington Church St
• **Belle Epoque Boulangerie** • 37 Newington Green
• **Bridgewood & Neitzert** • 146 Stoke Newington Church St
• **Church Street Bookshop** •
  142 Stoke Newington Church St
• **Metal Crumble** • 13 Stoke Newington Church St
• **Mind** • 11 Stoke Newington Church St
• **Of Cabbages & Kings** • 34 Kersley Rd
• **Pelicans & Parrots** • 81 Stoke Newington Rd
• **Ribbons and Taylor** • 157 Stoke Newington Church St
• **Rosa Lingerie** • 3 Church Walk
• **Route 73 Kids** • 92 Stoke Newington Church St
• **S'graffiti** • 172 Stoke Newington Church St
• **Sacred Art** • 148 Albion Rd
• **The Spence Bakery** • 161 Stoke Newington Church St
• **Stoke Newington Farmers Market** • Stoke Newington
  Church St & Stoke Newington High St

Supermarkets

• **Whole Foods Market** • 32 Stoke Newington Church St
• **Iceland** • 17 Green Lanes

Map 65 · **West Hampstead**

1

St. Cuthberts Road

Waring Gardens

Exeter Road

Shoot Up Hill A5

Kilburn
Church Avenue

Cavendish
Close

Gladstone
sh Road

A

Garlinge Road

Fordwych Road

Barlow Road

Brassey Road

Brassey
Road

Maygrove Road

Loveridge Road

Loveridge
Mews

Hiel Road

Maygrove Road

Iverson Road B520

Netherwood Street

Dornfell Street

Ravenshaw Street

Glastonbury
Street

Broomsleigh Street

Sumatra
Road

Glenbrook Road

Solent
Road

Narcissus
Road

Holmdale Road

Mill Lane

Metans M6

Aldred Road

en Road B510

Lyncroft Gardens

Denson St

West End

West Cottages

Inglewood Road

66 ▶

Pandora Road

Sumatra Road

Denington Park
Road

Kingdon Road

Sandwell
Cres

West End Lane B510

Lymington Road

Fawley Road

Honeybourne Road

Crediton Hill

Crown
Close

Lymin
Close
Dresden

Liddell Road

Maygrove
Peace Park

Medley
Road

Rown Tree Close

Palmerston
Road

Palmerston Road

Lindsey
Road

Lowfield
Road

Drakes
Court
yd

uckley Road

urton Road

illeseden La

St. Julian's
Road

Brondesbury
Mews

all Road

Kilburn High Road A5

Kilburn Grange
Park

Grange
Park

Messina
Avenue

Gascony
Avenue

Kingsgate
Place

Kings
Gate

Kingsgate Road

Mazenod Avenue

Smyrna
Road

Kitemore Road

Gladys Road

Hemstal Road

Birnham Road

Hilltop
Road

Sherriff Road

Cotleigh Road

West End Lane B510

Woodchurch Road

Blackburn Road

West
Hampstead

Lowfell
West Hampstead Ms

Compayne Gardens

Cleve Road

Canfield Gardens

Broadhurst
Gardens

Priory Road

Broadhurst Gardens

Compayne

Gardens

Fairhazel Gardens

Dunster Gard
ns

Albion
Mews

Road

B

The
Terrace
Road

Victoria Road

Quex Road

Quex
Mews

Matrix Road

Birchington Road

Bransdale
Close

West End Lane

West End
Lane B510

Gosc
yn Rd

Acol Road

Lithos
Mews

Priory Road

Greencroft Gardens

Greencroft Gardens

Canfiel

Fairhazel Gardens

sbury Road B451

rondesbury Villas

Mallard

urn High Road A5

West End
Kilburn Pl

Burn Vale

Priory Terrace

Priory Road

Abbot's Place

St. Mary's
Ms

Abbey Road B507

Aberdare
Gardens

Goldhurst Terrace

Gardens

Goldhurst Terrace

Coleridge
Gardens

Bel-size
Rd

Belsize Road B509

68 ▼

Belsize Road

Abbey

B509

Rowl

0.25 mile

0.25 km

West Hampstead

Map 65

Hampstead's ugly sister, West Hampstead is a leafy suburb that has absorbed some of Kilburn's grittiness. Young urban nomads make up much of the population, as rent is moderate by London standards. Like the rest of London, West Hampstead has its fair share of Caffe Neros and Costa Coffees, but check out **The Good Ship** for music or comedy.

 Coffee

- **Caffe Nero** • 01 Kilburn High Rd
- **Costa** • 203 W End Ln
- **Starbucks** • 01 W End Ln

Libraries

- **West Hampstead Library** • Dennington Park Rd

Nightlife

- **The Black Lion** • 274 Kilburn High Rd
- **The Czech and Slovak Bar** • 74 West End Ln
- **The Good Ship** • 289 Kilburn High Rd

Post Offices

- **West Hampstead** • 128 W End Ln

Restaurants

- **Barraco Cafe** • 10 Kingsgate Pl
- **Small & Beautiful** • 351 Kilburn High Rd

Shopping

- **Party Party** • 206 Kilburn High Rd

Supermarkets

- **Sainsbury's** • 88 Kilburn High Rd
- **Sainsbury's** • 377 Kilburn High Rd

Map 66 · **Finchley Road / Swiss Cottage**

Ⓝ

Mill Lane

Cannon Hill

A41

Greenaway Gardens

Mount Vernon

Frognal

Frognal

West Cottages

Inglewood Road

West End Lane

Park

Frognal

Church Row

Holly

Holly Mt

Holly

Hampstead

Kingdon Road

Dennington

Holmdale Road

West End Lane

B510

Honeybourne Road

Fawley Road

Croediton Hill

Frognal Lane

Langland Gardens

Chesterford Gardens

Church Row

Way

Church Row

Oriel Court

Ellerdale Road

Perrins Wlk

Perrins La

B520

Road

Lymington Road

Cumberland Lawn Tennis Club

A41

Lindfield Gardens

Frognal Close

Ellerdale Road

Prince Arthur Road

Perrins Court

Arthur

B510

Blackburn Road

Sandwell Cres

Crown

Douglas Ms

Dalton Ms

Mint Ms

Worsley

Desden

Lymington Road

Bes Ms

Spode Wlk

Wlk Close

Arkwright Road

WEST HAMPSTEAD

Heath

Prince Arthur Road

West Hampstead

◀**65**

Lithos Road

Rosemont Road

Frognal Way

Netherhall Way

Netherhall Gardens

B511 Fitzjohn's Avenue

Netherhall Gardens

Lyndhurst Road

Lyndhurst

West Hampstead Mews

WesWelr Priory Road

Gardens

Broadhurst

Fairfax Gardens

Broadhurst Gardens

Compayne

Canfield Gardens

Fairfax Gardens

Road

Broadhurst Close

Gardens

Canfield Pl

Frognal Court

Frognal

Gardens

Netherhall

Nutley Terrace

Maresfield Gardens

B511

Avenue

Road

Princess Ms

Belsize Crescent

Lyndhurst

Wedderburn

Belsize

Greencroft Gardens

Finchley Road

⊖

A41

Finchley Road

Pump Peter Close

Fitzjohn's Avenue

67▶

Dalham Mews

Dalham Mews

Bel Pk Ms

Bel Ms

Bel Ms

Burdett Ms

Belsize

Belsize

Belsize

SOUTH HAMPSTEAD

Canfield Gardens

Broadhurst Gardens

Greencroft Gardens

Gardens

Maresfield Gardens

College Crescent

Belsize Lane

Belsize Park

Belsize Square

Belsize

Lancaster Grove

Aberdare Gardens

Goldhurst Terrace

Fairfax Gardens

Goldhurst Terrace

Nasaby

Marston

Harben

Road

College Crescent

Belsize Park

Buckland Crescent

Lancaster Grove

Lancaster

Lancaster Drive

◀**68**

Coleridge Gardens

Fairfax Place

Fairfax Road

Road

Belsize Road

Dobson Close

A41

Adamson Road

BELSIZE PARK

Belsize Road

B509

Rowley Way

Belsize Rd

Hilgrove Rd

Belsize Road

Eton Avenue

Strathray Gdns

Eton Avenue

sworth Way

Boundary Road

Alexandra Place

≷

South Hampstead Rail Station

Alexandra Road

B509

Avenue Road

⊖

Swiss Cottage

Fellows Road

Kings College Road

Lancaster

Manor Mews

Springfield Road

Boundary

Road

Dornan Way

A41

Adelaide Road

Winchester Road

Hornby Circus

A525

69▼

Adelaide Road

| 0.25 mile | | 0.25 km |

Finchley Road/Swiss Cottage

Map 66

With so much promise and surrounded by the likes of West Hampstead, Primrose Hill and Camden, the area is still inexplicably in need of resuscitation. A long list of shops not worth mentioning and a few restaurants whose existence denies dignity should not detract from the fact that **The Camden Arts Centre** and **Freud Museum** are jewels in this battered crown and well worth braving the surrounding boredom to visit.

Cinemas

- **Odeon Swiss Cottage** • 96 Finchley Rd
- **Vue Finchley Road** • Finchley Rd & Blackburn Rd

Coffee

- **Cafe Express** • 25 Finchley Rd
- **Costa** • 149 Finchley Rd
- **Starbucks** • 255 Finchley Rd

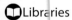

Libraries

- **Swiss Cottage Library** • 88 Avenue Rd

Nightlife

- **Ye Olde Swiss Cottage** • 98 Finchley Rd

Restaurants

- **Bradleys** • 25 Winchester Rd
- **Camden Arts Centre** • Arkwright Rd
- **Singapore Garden** • 83 Fairfax Rd

Supermarkets

- **Sainsbury's** • 255 Finchley Rd
- **Waitrose** • 199 Finchley Rd

Map 67 · **Belsize Park**

Belsize Park

Map 67

There is a reason that Kate Moss, Jude Law, Chris Martin and Noel Gallagher (to name a few) all live here. It's less pretentious than neighbouring banker-filled Hampstead and far enough away from the Primrose set to be artistically elitist. Extraordinarily expensive shops and restaurants reign over the area but in at the celebrity-frequented **Washington** pub there's an excellent atmosphere and foodwise, Belsize Lane never disappoints.

Cinemas

• **Everyman Belsize Park** • 203 Haverstock Hill

Coffee

• **Ginger & White** • 2 England's Ln
• **Starbucks** • 57 England's Ln
• **Starbucks** • 20 Haverstock Hill

O **Landmarks**

• **Freud Statue** •
  Fitzjohn's Ave, opposite Maresfield Gardens Junction
• **St Stephen's** • Rosslyn Hill

**Libraries**

• **Belsize Library** • Antrim Rd

**Nightlife**

• **The Washington** • 50 England's Ln

Restaurants

• **Artigiano** • 12 Belsize Terrace
• **Ginger & White** • 2 England's Ln
• **Paradiso** • 36 England's Ln
• **Retsina** • 48 Belsize Ln
• **Violette Cafe** • 2 England's Ln

Shopping

• **Belsize Village Delicatessen** • 39 Belsize Ln
• **Lotus and Frog** • 32 England's Ln

Map 68 · **Kilburn High Road / Abbey Road** Ⓝ

HAMPSTEAD

abury Rd B451

West End Lane

Priory Road

Goldhurst

Gardens

Fairfax

Abenders

Goldhurst Terrace

Gardens

ury Villas

KilburnVale

Priory Terrace

Belsize

Road

B509

65

Belsize Road B509

Coleridge
Gardens

Belsize Rd

66

Coventry Cl

Kilburn High Road A5

Spring

Langtry Place

Rowley Way

Kilburn Priory

Greville Ms

Mortimer Place

Ainsworth Way

Alexandra
Place

Alexandra Rd

A Road

Maple
Pk Ms

Greville Road

Bolton Road

Boundary Road

Abbey Road B507

Boundary Road

Loudoun Rd

n Park
Road

Maida Vale A5

Boundary Road

Belgrave Gardens

Springfield Road

Boundary Road

Andover Place

Hillgrt Close

Greville Road

Clifton Hill

Clifton Hill

Clifton Hill

Loudoun Road

rlton Vale

Carlton Hill

Carlton Hill

Carlton Hill

Carlton Hill

Finchley Road A41

The
Marlowes

Lanark Road

Blenheim
Passage

Ryders Ter

Marlborough Hill

The Line

B:enheim Terrace

Blenheim Road

Hamilton Terrace

Marlborough Place

Marlborough Place

Queen's Grove

Ross
Mew

Wellgale
Mews

Grey Cl

Violet Hill

Abbey Gardens

Lang

Finchley
Place

Queen's
Terrace

69

Elgin Ms
North

Langford Place

Regents
Ms

Loudoun Road

Waverley Place

Finchley Road A41

St.
John's
Wood

B Avenue

Maida
Vale

Elgin

Avenue

Abercorn Place

Eyre
Ct

Acacia Road

Elgin Ms
South

Abercorn Walk

Abercorn Close

Hill Road

Abbey Road B507

Wellington Rd

tube

St. Ann's Terrace

St. John's

127

Maida Vale A5

Alma Squa:e

Hamilton Gdns

Alma

Grove End Road

ST. JOHN'S WOOD

Cochrane Street

Kingsmill Terrace

St. Ann's Terrace

Southcli
Lodge

Square

Hamilton Gdns

Garden Road

Wellington Court

Circus Road

Aquilar

Cha

Lanark
Mews
Avenue

Grove

Hall Court

Abbey Road
Zebra Crossing

Circus Road

Wellington Place

Gochrane Street

Allitsen
Mews

Denning Cl

Hall Road

B507

Circus Road

Allitsen Road

Bridgeman
Road

Randolph Ro

Maida Vale A5

Hamilton Terrace

Grove End Road

Cavendish Avenue

Wellington Road A41

St. John's Wood High Street

Scot: Ellis

Meling Place

Elm Tree Road

Elm
Tree
Close

Elm Tree Road

76

Cavendish Close

Wellington Place

St. John's

Marylebone Cricket
Club&Middlesex

Middlesex

| 0.25 mile | 0.25 km |

FFS, Let it Be!" Indeed, while the area's main attraction is a crosswalk and a dilapidated recording studio once home to the world's greatest band, the grime and urban decay that surround it hardly make it an "Octopus's Garden." But "Come Together" because "Here Comes the Sun": **The Clifton** is a cool pub and the delightful **Little Bay** does excellent food. Also, don't forget the Art Deco grandeur of the **State Building**.

Coffee

• **Starbucks** • 79 St John's Wood High St

Landmarks

• **Abbey Road Zebra Crossing** • 3 Abbey Rd

Libraries

• **Kilburn Library** • 12 Kilburn High Rd
• **St John's Wood Library** • 20 Circus Rd

Nightlife

• **Love & Liquor** • 34 Kilburn High Rd

Post Offices

• **Kilburn** • 79 Kilburn High Rd
• **St Johns Wood** • 32 Circus Rd

Restaurants

• **Little Bay** • 228 Belsize Rd

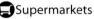Supermarkets

• **Tesco** • 115 Maida Vale

Map 69 · St. John's Wood

Map 69

St. John's Wood

Nouveau riche and bourgeois mix in this leafy salad of a suburb that, you guessed it, reeks of money. Pinned in between Primrose Hill and Regent's Park, there isn't much to do in this mainly residential area, unless you like to gawk at expensive houses. However, the **Swiss Cottage Leisure Centre** on Adelaide Road is pretty swish with its climbing wall and Lord's Cricket Ground is only a stone's throw away.

 ## Nightlife
• **The Star** • 38 St. Johns Wood Terrace

 ## Restaurants
• **Tupelo Honey** • 27 Parkway

Primrose Hill is factory-packed with pretty young things and established actors mixing with models, designers and artistic types in an area that is London's low-key version of Beverly Hills. If you don't stumble across a celebrity or are disinclined to stalk one you can check out the trendy stores, grab a pint in the equally trendy **Lansdowne** or take in the views of London from the Hill itself.

O Landmarks

• **3 Chalcot Square** • 3 Chalcot Sq

Libraries

• **Chalk Farm Library** • 11 Sharples Hall St

Nightlife

• **The Albert** • 11 Princess Rd
• **Cecil Sharp House** • 2 Regent's Park Rd
• **The Lansdowne** • 90 Gloucester Ave
• **Princess of Wales** • 22 Chalcot Rd
• **Sir Richard Steele** • 97 Haverstock Hill

Post Offices

• **Regent's Park Road** • 91 Regent's Park Rd

Restaurants

• **The Hill Bar** • 94 Haverstock Hill
• **J Restaurant** • 148 Regent's Park Rd
• **Legal Cafe** • 81 Haverstock Hill
• **Lemonia** • 89 Regent's Park Rd
• **Manna** • 4 Erskine Rd
• **Melrose and Morgan** • 42 Gloucester Ave
• **Odette's** • 130 Regent's Park Rd
• **Primrose Bakery** • 69 Gloucester Ave
• **Two Brothers** • 297 Regent's Park Rd

Shopping

• **Judith Michael & Daughter** • 73 Regent's Park Rd
• **Miss Lala's Boudoir** • 148 Gloucester Ave
• **Nicolas (off licence)** • 67 Regent's Park Rd
• **Press** • 3 Erskine Rd
• **Primrose Hill Books** • 134 Regent's Park Rd
• **Primrose Newsagent** • 91 Regent's Park Rd
• **Richard Dare** • 93 Regent's Park Rd
• **Shepherd Foods** • 59 Regent's Park Rd
• **Shikasuki** • 67 Gloucester Ave
• **Sweet Pea** • 77 Gloucester Ave
• **Tann Rokka** • 123 Regent's Park Rd

Map 71 • Camden Town / Chalk Farm / Kentish Town (West)

0.25 mile

0.25 km

Camden is still the musical heartbeat of London, and while the ratty-tatty venues of the '80s that solidified its reputation are long gone, or surgically modernized, the pavements still reverberate to a constant beat. The area is crowded during the week and jam-packed during the weekend but the cacophony of wacky stores, bric-a-brac stalls, and an eclectic selection of culinary treats mean London wouldn't be London without it.

Cinemas

- **Odeon Camden Town** • 14 Parkway

Coffee

- **Cafe La Cigale** • 47 Parkway
- **Cafe Metro** • 178 Camden High St
- **Caffe Nero** • 7 Jamestown Rd
- **Caffe Nero** • 11 Parkway
- **Camden Coffee House** • 30 Camden Rd
- **The Coffee Jar** • 83 Parkway
- **Costa** • 181 Camden High St
- **Eat.** • 185 Camden High St
- **Falla and Mocaer** • 82 Parkway
- **Inhabition** • 15 Chalk Farm Rd
- **Pret A Manger** • 152 Camden High St
- **Pret A Manger** • 261 High St
- **Starbucks** • Parkway Camden & Arlington Rd

Landmarks

- **Camden Market** • Camden Lock Pl
- **Grand Regents Canal** • Grand Regents Canal
- **The Roundhouse** • Chalk Farm Rd & Crogsland Rd

Libraries

- **Queen's Crescent Library** • 165 Queen's Crescent

Nightlife

- **Bar Vinyl** • 6 Inverness St
- **Barfly** • 49 Chalk Farm Rd
- **The Constitution** • 42 St Pancras Way
- **Dingwalls** • Middle Yard
- **The Dublin Castle** • 94 Parkway
- **Electric Ballroom** • 184 Camden High St
- **The Enterprise** • 2 Haverstock Hill
- **Fiddlers Elbow** • 1 Malden Rd

- **Good Mixer** • 30 Inverness St
- **The Hawley Arms** • 2 Castlehaven Rd
- **Jazz Cafe** • 5 Parkway
- **Koko** • 1 Camden High St
- **The Lock Tavern** • 35 Chalk Farm Rd
- **Monkey Chews** • 2 Queen's Crescent
- **Oxford Arms** • 265 Camden High St
- **Proud Camden** • Chalk Farm Rd
- **Quinn's** • 65 Kentish Town Rd
- **The Underworld** • 174 Camden High St

Post Offices

- **Camden High Street** • 112 Camden High St
- **Queen's Crescent** • 139 Queen's Crescent

Restaurants

- **Andy's Taverna** • 81 Bayham St
- **Anima e Cuore** • 115 Kentish Town Rd
- **Arancini Factory Cafe** • 115 Kentish Town Rd
- **Bar Gansa** • 2 Inverness St
- **Bento Cafe** • 9 Parkway
- **Cotton's** • 55 Chalk Farm Rd
- **Falla and Mocaer** • 82 Parkway
- **Gilgamesh** • The Stables Market, Chalk Farm Rd
- **Haché** • 24 Inverness St
- **Kim's Vietnamese Food Hut** • Unit D, Camden Lock Palace
- **Marathon Cafe** • 87 Chalk Farm Rd
- **Marine Ices** • 8 Haverstock Hill
- **Market** • 438 Parkway
- **Muang Thai** • 71 Chalk Farm Rd
- **My Village** • 37 Chalk Farm Rd
- **Q Grill** • 29-33 Chalk Farm Rd
- **Thanh Binh** • 14 Chalk Farm Rd
- **Viet-anh Cafe** • 41 Parkway
- **Woody Grill** • 1 Camden Rd
- **Yumchaa Tea Space** • 91 Upper Walkway, West Yard, Camden Lock Market
- **Zorya Imperial Vodka Room** • 48 Chalk Farm Rd

Shopping

- **Acumedic** • 101 Camden High St
- **Aldo Sale Shop** • 231 Camden High St
- **Arckiv Vintage Eyewear** • Chalk Farm Rd & Castlehaven Rd
- **Black Rose** • The Stables Market, Chalk Farm Rd
- **Cyberdog** • Stables Market, Chalk Farm Rd
- **Escapade** • 45 Chalk Farm Rd
- **Eye Contacts** • 10 Chalk Farm Rd
- **Fresh & Wild, Camden** • 49 Parkway
- **General Eyewear** • Chalk Farm Rd & Castlehaven Rd
- **Graham and Green** • 164 Regent's Park Rd
- **Ray Man Music** • 54 Chalk Farm Rd
- **Rokit** • 225 Camden High St
- **Traid** • 154 Camden High St
- **Village Games** • 65 The West Yard
- **Whole Foods Market** • 49 Parkway

Supermarkets

- **Whole Foods Market** • 49 Parkway
- **Sainsbury's** • 77 Chalk Farm Rd
- **Sainsbury's** • 17 Camden Rd
- **Sainsbury's** • 10 Camden Rd

Map 72 · **Kentish Town**

Kentish Town

Map 72

Kentish Town may be Camden's less-interesting and less-affected neighbour but this isn't necessarily a bad thing. The area is on the up and between the grubby, horrible collection of pound shops, charity shops, and industrial stores there are new venues springing forth that offer some of the most welcoming atmospheres in North London. **The Pineapple** is a great little pit-stop pub with an infectious atmosphere.

Coffee

• **Cafe Metro** • 180 Camden High St

Libraries

• **Kentish Town Library** • 262 Kentish Town Rd

Nightlife

• **The Abbey Tavern** • 124 Kentish Town Rd
• **The Assembly House** • 292 Kentish Town Rd
• **The Bull & Gate** • 389 Kentish Town Rd
• **HMV Forum** • 9 Highgate Rd
• **Ladies and Gentlemen** • 2 Highgate Rd
• **The Lion and Unicorn** • 42 Gaisford St
• **The Pineapple** • 51 Leverton St
• **Rio's Health Spa** • 239 Kentish Town Rd

Restaurants

• **The Bengal Lancer** • 253 Kentish Town Rd
• **Cafe Renoir** • 244 Kentish Town Rd
• **Dirty Burger** • 79 Highgate Rd
• **ITTA** • 225 Kentish Town Rd
• **Mario's Cafe** • 6 Kelly St
• **The Oxford** • 256 Kentish Town Rd
• **Pane Vino** • 323 Kentish Town Rd
• **Phoenicia Mediterranean Food Hall** • 186 Kentish Town Rd

Shopping

• **Dots** • 132 St Pancras Way
• **Phoenicia** • 186 Kentish Town Rd
• **Ruby Violet** • 118 Fortress Rd

Supermarkets

• **Co-Op** • 250 Kentish Town Rd
• **EARTH natural foods** • 200 Kentish Town Rd
• **Iceland** • 301 Kentish Town Rd
• **Tesco/Esso** • 196 Camden Rd

Holloway is best known for its women's prison and not much else. To the west of Holloway Road it feels a bit like a sprawling backyard to gentrified Camden, Islington, and King's Cross. Nevertheless, bars like **The Lord Stanley** and **Shillibeer's** have gone all gastro, so it doesn't quite have the gritty vibe that it once had.

Libraries
• **John Barnes Library** • 275 Camden Rd

Nightlife
• **The Lord Stanley** • 51 Camden Park Rd
• **Shillibeer's Bar and Grill** • 1 Carpenter's Mews

Post Offices
• **Brecknock Rd** • 20 Brecknock Rd

Shopping
• **Bumblebee Natural Foods** • 33 Brecknock Rd

Supermarkets
• **Sainsbury's** • 4 Williamson St
• **Tesco/Esso** • 196 Camden Rd

Map 74 · **Holloway Road / Arsenal**

Ⓝ

Seven Sisters Road A503

Tollington Road

Hornsey Road A103

Holloway Road A1

Caledonian Road

Caledonian Road A5203

A

B

62

61

Arsenal

Gillespie Park
Local Nature
Reserve

63

Emirates
Stadium -
Arsenal F.C.

PAGE 376

Queensland Road

Drayton Park Rail

Holloway Road

LOWER HOLLOWAY

Gillespie Park

75

73

Highbury Fields

Paradise Park

Liverpool Road Garden

Liverpool Road B515

79

80

Highbury & Islington

Highbury Corner

St. Paul's

Laycock Street Park

Arundel Square Garden

0.25 mile

0.25 km

Much like the football team the area shares its name with, there is a lot of potential talent here that just needs some time to come to fruition. On match days the streets make a sardine tin look roomy. This area also includes the grotty stretch of Holloway Road. For something different try **Tbilisi** for cheap Eastern European eats.

Coffee

- **Cafe Nero** • 348 Holloway Rd
- **Le Peche Mignon** • 6 Ronalds Rd
- **Vagabond N7** • 105 Holloway Rd

O Landmarks

- **Gillespie Park** • 191 Drayton Park

Libraries

- **Central Library** • 2 Fieldway Crescent

Nightlife

- **The Coronet** • 338 Holloway Rd
- **Hen and Chicken Theatre Bar** • 109 St Paul's Rd
- **The Horatia** • 98 Holloway Rd
- **The Relentless Garage** • 20 Highbury Corner

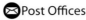 Post Offices

- **Highbury** • 5 Highbury Corner
- **Holloway Rd** • 118 Holloway Rd

Restaurants

- **El Rincon Quiteno** • 235 Holloway Rd
- **Kokeb** • 45 Roman Wy
- **Morgan M** • 489 Liverpool Rd
- **Tbilisi** • 91 Holloway Rd
- **Wolkite Kifto** • 82 Hornsey Rd

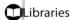 Shopping

- **Vivien of Holloway** • 294 Holloway Rd

Supermarkets

- **Waitrose** • 366 Holloway Rd

Highbury

Map 75

A residential area close enough to Upper Street to keep you entertained and far enough away to keep you grounded, Highbury is blessed with the marvellous Highbury Fields, which during the summer is full of pretty things (in varying states of undress) and a thriving gay bar (**Oak Bar**). Bordered by busy St Paul's Road and bustling Green Lanes, you'll never struggle for something to do here; try the **Snooty Fox** for a quiet drink.

O Landmarks

• **St Paul's Shrubbery** •
St Paul's Rd & Northampton Park

Nightlife

• **Alwyne Castle** • 83 St Pauls Rd
• **The Snooty Fox** • 75 Grosvenor Avenue

Post Offices

• **Grosvenor Avenue** • 91 Grosvenor Ave
• **Highbury Park** • 12 Highbury Park

Restaurants

• **Firezza** • 276 St Paul's Rd
• **Highbury Arts Club** • 73 Highbury Park
• **Prawn on the Lawn** • 220 St Paul's Rd
• **Primeur** • 116 Petherton Rd
• **San Daniele Del Friuli** • 72 Highbury Park
• **Trullo** • 300-302 St Paul's Rd
• **Ustun** • 107 Green Lanes

Shopping

• **Cabbies Delight Auto Parts** • 9 Green Lanes
• **Highbury Vintners** • 71 Highbury Park
• **La Fromagerie** • 30 Highbury Park
• **Mother Earth** • 282 St Paul's Rd
• **Prawn on the Lawn** • 220 St Paul's Rd

Map 76 • **Edgware Road / Marylebone (North)**

1
2

68

Elm Tree Road

Elm
Clos

Elm

Cavendis

Grove

Place

Wellington

Wellington
Place

St. John's
Wood High St

Barr
Mews

Bridgem
Road

Southo
Mews

St. J
W

Newco

Lanark Place

A5

Grove

Scott Ellis
Gdns

Hamilton
Close

Lord's
Cricket
Ground

**PAGE
380**

Lord's, Middlesex
C.C.C.
Practice Ground

St. John's
Wood Church
Gardens

Greenberry Street

Maida Vale

Clifton Road

27

Eliz
Cl
Place

Clar
Cl

Brow
Cl

Blomfield Rd

A5

Maida Avenue

Clifton
Ct

Maida Vale

Northwick
North

Wick Cl

Cunningham Place

St. John's Wood Road A5205

Henderson Dr

Politt Dr

Oak Tree Rd

Lodge Road

North Bank

**Wellington
Road**

Prince Albert Road

A5

69

**LISSON
GROVE**

Reg
Par

**PAGE
348**

Aberdeen Place

Fisherton

Lyons Place

Orchardson

Street

Frampton Street

Fisherton

Street

Street

Lisson Grove B501

Regent's Canal

Jennie

Crescent

Grendon

Jerome St

Swan

Casey Close

Grove
Gdns

Hanover Gate

Outer Circle

Hall Place

mpton Street

Frampton

Street

Hatton Street

Penfold

Luton Street

Boscobel Street

Street

Hatton Street

Bledlow
Close

Hollytwell Close

Capland Street

Cap
lanc

Samford St.

Gandform St

Street

Bernhardt
Crescent

Crescent

Paveley
Street

Lorne
Close

Street

Kent
Terrace

Hanover Terrace

Palgrave Gardens

Cuthbert
St

Adp

St

Church Street

Salisbury St

Mulready St

White
haven St

Ashbridge St

Plympton St

Plympton St

Church Street

Lilestone Street

Mallory
Street

Tresham

Paveley St

Street

Paveley

Alpha
Cl

Hanover Terrace
Mews

**Church Street
Church**

Carlisle Mews

Broadley Street

Broadley Street

Mallory
Street

Rossmore

Tresham

Broadley Terrace

Road

Sussex Place

Outer Circle

Road A404
x Road

31

Miles Pl

Penfold Place

Broadley
Street
Gardens

Corlett
Street

Bell

Ashmill Street

Shroton St

Ranston Street

Daventry Street

Stal
forth
St

Bendall Mews

Harewood Avenue

Portman
Gate

Blandford
Square

Hayes
Place

Harewood

Taunton Pl

Ivor Pl

Balcombe

Ivor Pl

Linhope St

Taunton
Ms

Huntswo
Mews

Street

Dorset

Sussex Place
Mews

Sussex

Outer Circle

2

ed St A4205

**Edgware
Road**

Harrow Road
A404

Harrow Road A404

Burne St

Lisson Street

Cosway Street

Harewood
Row

Harewood Row
Place

**Marylebone
Station**

**PAGE
413**

Boston Place

Gloucester Place A41

Melcombe

Crawford St

Crawford St

Dorset

Sidons Lane

Park Road

Alsop Cl

Alsop
Cl

St A501

haels Street

Street

Junction
M-PI

ssex Gardens
A4209

Chapel Street

Cabbell

Transept St

Shillibeer Place

Old Marylebone Road A501

Marylebone A501

Warren
Place

Daventry
Pl

Marylebone
Road B501

Great Central
Street

Balcombe

Square

Melcombe Street

Dorset
Close

Dorset Square

Gloucester Place

Glentworth

**Sherlock
Holmes'
House**

**Baker
Street**

Ambro
onSale

Crawford Street

Watson's
Ms

Wyndham Street

Enford Street

Knox St

Salisbury Place

Marylebone

A41

Baker

Outer Circle

Alsop

Brendon Street

Cato Street

Place

Seymour Place

York Street

Sq

CSMs

Bickenhall Street

Street

Porter
St

Romney

Place

Norfolk

Bur
wood
PI

Harrow

Crawford
Place

CSMs

Crawford
Beven

York
St

Street

1

Sale
Place

Junction
M-Pl

0.25 mile

0.25 km

Edgware Road/Marylebone (North)

Map 76

Marylebone Road is noisy enough to have you running for the taps of the **twotwentytwo** straight away. Things get calmer (meaning duller) further north, but **Mandalay's** inexpensive Burmese treats save the north end of Edgware Road, while **The Sea Shell of Lisson Grove** does fine fish. And did we mention the great detective? Baker Street, dear Watson, Baker Street.

Coffee
• **Pret A Manger** • 120 Baker St

Emergency Rooms
• **Western Eye Hospital** • 173 Marylebone Rd

O Landmarks
• **Lord's Cricket Ground** • St John's Wood
• **Sherlock Holmes' House** • 221 Baker St

Libraries
• **Church Street Library** • Church St
• **London Business School Library** • 25 Taunton Pl
• **Marylebone Library** • 109 Marylebone Rd

Nightlife
• **twotwentytwo** • 222 Marylebone Rd
• **Volunteer** • 245 Baker St

Post Offices
• **Edgware Rd** • 354 Edgware Rd

Restaurants
• **Mandalay** • 444 Edgware Rd
• **Sea Shell of Lisson Grove** • 49 Lisson Grove

Shopping
• **Alfie's Antiques Market** • 25 Church St
• **Archive Secondhand Books & Music** • 83 Bell St
• **Beatles London Store** • 231 Baker St
• **Lord's Cricket Shop** •
  Lord's Cricket Ground, Lisson Grove

Supermarkets
• **Tesco** • 94 Church St

Map 77 • **Mornington Crescent / Regent's Park** Ⓝ

70

71

London Zoo

Albert Road A205

Outer Circle

Parkway A4201

Delancey Street

Park Village East

Underhill Street

Parkway

Albert Street

Street

Pratt Street

Pratt

St. Martin's Gardens

St. Martins Close

Greenland Street A503

A503

Camden Street A503

Gloucester Gate

Gloucester Gate

St. Kath. pre

Park West

Park Village

Gloucester Gate

A4201

Albany Street A4201

Mornington Terrace

Mornington Street

Mornington Terrace

Mornington Pl.

Arlington Street

Miller Street

Carlow Street

Beatty St.

Camden Road A400

Camden High Street

Symes Ms

Plender Street

Bayham Street

Plender Street

Mornington Crescent ⊖

Hampstead Road

Clarkson Row

Bayham Place

Bayham Place

Crowndale Road B5

Oakley Square A400

Eversholt Street

Oakley Square A4200

REGENT'S PARK

Regent's Park
PAGE 348

Outer Circle

Chester

Chester Pl

Cumb. Pl.

Cumberland Terrace

Cumberland Terrace

Cumb. Ms

Cumb. Pl.

Redhill St

Edward Street

Little Redhill Street

Redhill Street

Park Village East

Augustus Street

Greater London House

Granby Terrace

Lidington Place A4200

Harrington Street

Cranleigh St.

78

Aldenham

Bambury Street

Polygon

Chester Road

Chester Road

Chester Terrace

Nash Street

Market

Cumb. Mkt.

Robert Street

Cumberland Market

Stanhope Street

Mack. Sq.

Varndell Street

Harrington Street

Hampstead Road A400

Hampstead Road

Eversholt Street

A

B

Cambridge Gate

Cambridge Gate

Cambridge Gate Terrace

Ter Ms

Chester Cl. N

Chester Close North

Chester Terrace

Chester Gate

Clarence Gardens

Little Albany Street

Munster Square

Cumberland Market

Robert Street

Clarence Gardens

Everton Bidgs

Netley Street

Cardington St.

Tolmer Sq

St. James's Gardens

⇌ ⊖
Euston Station
PAGE 410

Outer Circle

Cambridge Gate Mews

Albany Street A4201

Little Albany Street

Munster Square

Longford Street

Osnaburgh Ter

Osnaburgh Street

Peto Place

Laxton Place

Wybert Street

Stanhope Street

William Road

Road A400

Drummond Street

George Ms

Starcross St.

N. Gower Street

Drummond St.

Chalton St.

Euston Street

Regnart Bidgs

Stephenson Way

Melton Street

Euston Street

Way

Park Square Gardens

Park Square East

Park Square West

Outer Circle

Regent's Park ⊖
Crescent Gardens

Great Portland Street ⊖

Euston Tower

Hampstead Road A400

Euston Square ⊖

Tolmer's Square

Euston Road A501

Euston Road A501

Euston Rd A400

Colburg Street

Chalton Pl.

Gower Place

Gower Court

Endsleigh Gard

A501

3

4

Park Cres

Marylebone Road A501

Warren Street ⊖

Warren Street

Euston Road A501

0.25 mile

0.25 km

Mornington Crescent/Regent's Park

Map 77

Hemmed in by Regent's Park and Euston, this patch combines pretty streets with tower-block thoroughfares. Skip the din of Euston underpass for Drummond Street, Camden's 'little India'—hit up **Bhel Poori** for decent dosas and visit **Chutneys** for veggies. Wash it all down with mugs of Black Sheep Ale at **The Crown and Anchor** before mingling al fresco with **Edinboro Castle's** yuppie-folk.

O Landmarks

- **Euston Tower** • 286 Euston Rd
- **Greater London House** • Hampstead Rd

Libraries

- **Regents Park Library** • Robert St

Nightlife

- **The Crown & Anchor** • 137 Drummond St
- **Edinboro Castle** • 57 Mornington Terrace
- **Euston Tap** • 190 Euston Rd
- **Queen's Head and Artichoke** • 30 Albany St

Restaurants

- **Chutneys** • 124 Drummond St
- **Diwana Bhel Poori** • 121 Drummond St
- **The Green Note** • 106 Parkway
- **Mestizo** • 103 Hampstead Rd

Shopping

- **Calumet Trading** • 93 Drummond St
- **Chess & Bridge** • 369 Euston Rd

Map 78 · **Euston**

Camden Town

Randolph Street

Agar Grove

St. P...

A503

Camden Road

A503

Camd'n

Kentish

Royal College Street

St. Pancras Way A5202

Baynes Street

Wro'ham

Agar Grove

72

Camden Town Parkway

A5202

Greenland Road

Lyme Street

Camden Street

Georgiana Street

Green View Close

Barker Drive

Bonny Street

St. P...

71

A503

Greenland Street

Greenland Street

Bayham Street

Pratt Mews

Pratt Street

Pratt Place

College Place

Mandela Direct

Royal College Street

Pratt Street

A5202

Castlehaven Road

Hartland

Rossendale Ms

Baynes St

Clarence Way

Camden Town

Camley Way

Cedar Way

CAMDEN TOWN

KING'S CROSS

A

Camden High Street

Pratt St

Street

Pratt Mews

Kelly St

Miller St

King's Terrace

Bayham Street

Plender Street

Bayham Place

Bayham Street

College Place

College Grove

Clarence Way

Plough...

Cloughman

Rea...

Cressfield

Camden St A400

Arlington Road

A503

Camden High St. A400

Carlow St

Beatty St

Mor Cres

Ham

Bayham St

Crowndale Road

St. Pancras Hospital

Granary

Crow...

Camley

Cedar Way

Cedar...

A503

Hampstead Road A400

Harrington Square

Mornington Crescent

Oakley Square

Crowndale Road A400

Crowndale Road B512

St. Pancras Way A5202

St. Pancras Gardens

Camley

Clark

Row

Lid...Place

A400

Oakley Square A400

Chalton Street

Bridgington Cres

Goldington Street

Pancras Road A5202

◀77

79▶

Bambry Road

A400

Cranleigh Street

Bridgeway Street

Werrington Street

Chalton Street

Charrington

Melburn Street

Penny Street

Somers Close

Platt Street

Chenies Pl

Coopers Lane

Purchese Street

Camley Street

Wharf Road

Wharf Road

Aldenham

Street

Polygon

Road

Pancras Road

Goods Way

Weller's Ct

Haul Road

B

Phoenix

Road

Brill Place

Neville Close

Pancras Road A5202

Cheney Rd

Wharfd...

Eversholt Street A4200

Drummond Crescent

Cardington Street

Cardington Street

Cranbourn

Clarendon

Phoenix

Road

Cassidland Road

SOMERS TOWN

Brill Place

York Way A5200

Railway Street

Bidborough Street

AMA

Doric

St. Pancras Station

PAGE 414

A5202

King's Cross Station

PAGE 411

York Way A5200

Wharfd...

≠ ⊖

Euston Station

✉

PAGE 410

Lancing Street

Wellesley Place

Grafton Pl

Doric

Chalton Street

Weirs Pas

The British Library

Platform 9¾

Caledonia Street

Keystone

Omega Place

A501

Euston Road

A501

Euston Road

Upper

Churchway

Chris...Place

Pancras Road A5202

Euston Road A501

Pentonville Road

St. Chad's place

Field...

4

5

Coburg Street

Melton Street

Euston Square

Grafton Place

A501 Euston Road

Bidborough

Argyle Street

Belgrove Street

Crest...

Birkenhead Street

St. Chad's Street

0.25 mile

0.25 km

Euston's the first port of call for thousands of people each day, be it city workers from the Shires or pilgrims to the many erotic bookshops by the railway. Look beyond the station—an ugly grey cube that dominates the area—and you'll find a few gems. Students and bookish types head to the outstanding **library** (British that is) while beer aficionados head to **Euston Tap**.

Coffee

- **Bagel Factory** • Euston Station
- **The Espresso Bar** • 96 Euston Rd
- **Pret a Manger** • 296 Pentonville Rd
- **Pret a Manger** • 117 Euston Rd
- **Starbucks** • 296 Pentonville Rd

O Landmarks

- **The British Library** • 96 Euston Rd
- **Camden High Street** • Camden High St & Delancey St
- **Central Saint Martins** • 1 Granary Square
- **Cheney Road** • Cheney Rd & Weller's Ct
- **Euston Station** • Eversholt St & Doric Wy
- **Platform 9¾** • King's Cross Station
- **St Pancras** • Pancras Rd & Euston Rd
- **St Pancras Hospital** • 4 St Pancras Way

Libraries

- **The British Library** • 96 Euston Rd
- **Camden Town Library** • 218 Eversholt St
- **Wellcome Library** • 183 Euston Rd

Nightlife

- **The Camden Head** • 100 Camden High St
- **The Champagne Bar at St Pancras** • Pancras Rd
- **The Doric Arch** • 1 Eversholt St
- **Lincoln Lounge** • 52 York Wy
- **Purple Turtle** • 61 Crowndale Rd
- **Scala** • 275 Pentonville Rd

Post Offices

- **Kings Cross** • 21 Euston St

Restaurants

- **Asakusa** • 265 Eversholt St
- **Banger Bros.** • Euston Station
- **The Booking Office** • St Pancras Renaissance London Hotel, Euston Rd
- **Camino** • 3 Varnisher's Yard
- **Caravan** • 1 Granary Building
- **Chop Chop Noodle Bar** • 1 Euston Rd
- **Dishoom** • 5 Stable St
- **El Parador** • 245 Eversholt St
- **Grain Store** • 1-3 Stable St
- **Great Nepalese** • 48 Eversholt St
- **Kitchin** • 8 Caledonia St
- **Rodon Live** • 7 Pratt St
- **The Somerstown Coffee House** • 60 Chalton St
- **Tony's Natural Foods** • 10 Caledonian Rd

Shopping

- **All Ages Records** • 27 Pratt St
- **Housmans Bookshop** • 5 Caledonian Rd
- **Peyton & Byrne** • Pancras Rd
- **Transformation** • 52 Eversholt St

Supermarkets

- **Sainsbury's** • 10 Camden High St

King's Cross

No area in North London benefited more from the Olympic games than this crucial commuter hub. The once tawdry Kings Cross Station has a new face and a modern aura while **St Pancras** is as glorious a station as you'll find in Europe. Once London's seediest spot the KC is now full of rakish bars and clubs with excellent live music and some tasty eats up Caledonian Road.

Map 79

Libraries

- **Lewis Carroll Children's Library** • 166 Copenhagen St
- **West Library** • Bridgeman Rd

Nightlife

- **The Big Chill House** • 257 Pentonville Rd
- **Canal 125** • 125 Caledonian Rd
- **Central Station** • 37 Wharfdale Rd
- **Drink, Shop & Do** • 9 Caledonian Rd
- **EGG** • 200 York Wy
- **Hemingford Arms** • 128 Hemingford Rd
- **The Lexington** • 96 Pentonville Rd
- **Lincoln Lounge** • 52 York Wy
- **Simmons** • 32 Caledonian Rd
- **Tarmon** • 270 Caledonian Rd

Post Offices
- **Caledonian Road** • 320 Caledonian Rd

Restaurants

- **Addis** • 42 Caledonian Rd
- **Drink, Shop & Do** • 9 Caledonian Rd
- **Euro Café** • 299 Caledonian Rd
- **Marathon** • 196 Caledonian Rd
- **The New Didar** • 347 Caledonian Rd
- **Oz** • 53 Caledonian Rd
- **Yum Yum** • 48 Caledonian Rd

Shopping
- **Cosmo Cornelio** • 182 Caledonian Rd

Supermarkets

- **Co-Op** • 303 Caledonian Rd
- **Iceland** • 259 Caledonian Rd

169

Map 80 · Angel / Upper St

Ⓝ

74 75 81

Highbury & Islington

Highbury

Corner

St. Paul's Road

John Spencer

Assata Street

Prior Bol.
Street
Hopping
La

Canonbury Rd A1200

Colebeck

St. Mary
Road

Canonbury Road

Wheelwright Street

Offord Road

Roman Way

Atlas
Mews

Bride Street

Farquhar
Close

Cornelia
Street

St Clements
Street

Barnsbury
Grove

Cornelia

Arundel
Square
Garden

Arundel
Square

Arundel
Place

Ellington Street

Offerton Ms.

Crane

Court Gardens

Highbury Station Road

Epping
Place

Laycock
Street Park

Laycock Street

Swan Hamp

Compter

Compton Avenue

Upper Street

Compton
Terrace

Ed.
Cotts

Hydes
Place

Canonbury
Square

Canon
bury Road

A

BARNSBURY

Huntingdon

Thornhill Cres

Thornhill
Square

Bridgeman Rd

Barnsbury
Wood

Belitha Villas

Barnsbury
Terrace

Mount
Cres

Beech
Tree

Belitha
Villas

Barnsbury
Square

Barnsbury Road

Cerfree

Bewdley Street

Barnsbury Street

Ferriby
Cl.

Cobble La

Islington Pk.

Islington Park Street

College
Cross

Cooper's
Yd.

Mews

The
Sut.
Est

Canonbury Lane

Tyndale
Terr.

Tyndale
Lane

Canonbury
Villas

Alwyne Lane

Alwyne Villas

Canonbury Villas

Canon.Vs

Canonbury Road

Lofting
Road

Brayfield

Morland Mews

B515

Haven
Mews

College

Barnsbury Street

Richmond
Grove

Sebbon Street

Florence

Tress
Cl

Canon Path

Canon bury Villas

Braes Street

Halton

79

Ripplevale
Grove

Thornhill Road

Lambert

Lonsdale
Sq.

Albion
Ms

Barnsbury
Park

Milner
Square

Milner
Place

Waterloo Ter

Napier
Street

Battishill
Street

Almeida Street

Hawes
Street

Hay
man
Rd.

Halton
Cross
St.

Essex Road A104

Malvern
Terrace

Box
Grove

Stone
Sq.

Gain. St

Richmond Avenue

Dewey
Street

Gibson Sq

Gibson Square

Thornhill
Cross

St. Mary's
Church
Gardens

Horse
Shoe

Cotden

Elder Wk.

Packer

Popham
Row

Britannia
Row

Essex Road

B

ISLINGTON

Barnard
Park

Charlotte Terrace

Copenhagen
Street

Maygood St

Crane
Grove

Sth
Gro

Cloudesley Road

Cloudesley
Square

Doves Yard

Water
tower

Old Ro.
South

Old Ro.
Free Sq

St. Alban's
Place

Studd St.

Gaskin Street

Collins
Yard

Islington
Green

Arlington
Avenue

Queen's
Row

Croton St.

Dowham
Street

Raleigh

Paul St.

Elystan
Wlk.

Cloudesley Place

Batchelor Street

Barnsbury Road

Earls
Gro.
Dewey Road

Bromfield
Street

Ritchie Street

Berners
Road

Upper Street A104

Islington
Green

Camden
Mews

St. Peters
Street

Camden
Walk

The Bull

83

Deronia Street

Greenhouse Street

Rheidol Street

Alling St.

Tolpuddle Street

Grant
Street

Chapel

White
Conduit

Chapel Market

North
Place

Liverpool Road B515

Upper Street

Charlton Pl.

Camden
St.

Duncan
St.

Gerrard Road

Noel Road

Burgh St.

St. John
Frome St.

Noel Road

Baldwin Terrace

Risinghill
Street

Donegal Street

Penton
Grove

White Lion
Street

Baron Street

Chapel

Angel

Angel
Station Roof

Colebrooke
Row

Vincent Terrace

Graham St.

PENTONVILLE

Cynthia
Street

Hermes
Street

Weston
Rise

Pentonville Road A501

6

Torrens Street

City Road A501

St. John Street

Gaswell Road

Ella
Ms

Colebrooke Row

Ella Street

Ella Mews

Sudeley Street

Rawstorne
St.

Wakley St.

Nelson Pl.

Rheidol Ms

Regent's
Canal

Grand
Junction
Wharf

Wickfords St.

Coombs St.

0.25 mile   0.25 km

Angel / Upper St

Map 80

A purpose-built playground for a twenty-somethings crowd that has to wake up for work in the morning. Whether it's the boutique shops, bars and restaurants that cater to any and all taste preoccupying Upper Street, the antique shops along **Camden Passage**, or an eclectic and vivid live music and theatre scene (Head to the **Kings Head Pub** for both), Angel has it all, and much more.

Cinemas

- **Everyman Screen on the Green** • 83 Islington Green
- **Vue Islington** • 36 Parkfield St

Coffee

- **Brown Bear Coffee & Home** • 41 Cross St
- **Estorick Gallery** • 39 Canonbury Sq
- **Euphorium Bakery** • 202 Upper St
- **Pret A Manger** • 27 Islington High St
- **Starbucks** • 71 Upper St
- **Starbucks** • 30 Upper St
- **Starbucks** • 7 Islington High St
- **Tinderbox** • 21 Upper St

O Landmarks

- **Angel Station Roof**
- **The Bull** • 100 Upper St

Nightlife

- **69 Colebrooke Row** • 69 Colebrooke Row
- **The Angel** • 3 Islington High St
- **The Angelic** • 57 Liverpool Rd
- **Camden Head** • 2 Camden Walk
- **The Castle** • 54 Pentonville Rd
- **Colebrookes** • 69 Colebrooke Row
- **Compton Arms** • 4 Compton Ave
- **The Crown** • 116 Cloudesley Rd
- **Dead Dolls House** • 181 Upper St
- **The Drapers Arms** • 44 Barnsbury St
- **The Garage** • 20 Highbury Corner
- **Hope And Anchor** • 207 Upper St
- **Islington Academy** • 16 Parkfield St
- **King's Head Theatre & Pub** • 115 Upper St
- **Lucky Voice** • 173 Upper St
- **Old Red Lion** • 418 St John St
- **Public House** • 54 Islington Park St
- **The Regent** • 201 Liverpool Rd
- **Round Midnight: Jazz and Blues Bar** • 13 Liverpool Rd
- **Union Chapel** • Compton Terrace

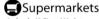 Restaurants

- **Afghan Kitchen** • 35 Islington Green
- **The Albion** • 10 Thornhill Rd
- **Alpino** • 97 Chapel Market
- **The Breakfast Club** • 31 Camden Passage
- **Candid Café** • 3 Torrens St
- **Dead Dolls House** • 181 Upper St
- **Desperados** • 127 Upper St
- **The Elk in the Woods** • 39 Camden Passage
- **Fig and Olive** • 151 Upper St
- **Fredericks** • Camden Passage
- **Gem** • 265 Upper St
- **Indian Veg Bhelpoori House** • 93 Chapel Market
- **Isarn** • 119 Upper St
- **La Forchetta** • 73 Upper St
- **La Porchetta** • 141 Upper St
- **Le Mercury** • 140 Upper St
- **Masala Zone** • 80 Upper St
- **Mem & Laz** • 8 Theberton St
- **Metrogusto** • 13 Theberton St
- **Oldroyd** • 344 Upper St
- **Ottolenghi** • 287 Upper St
- **Pizzeria Oregano** • 19 St Alban's Pl
- **Rodizio Rico** • 77 Upper St
- **The Seagrass** • 74 Chapel Market
- **Tortilla** • 13 Islington High St
- **Zaffrani** • 47 Cross St

Shopping

- **After Noah** • 121 Upper St
- **Annie's Vintage Costume and Textiles** • 12 Camden Passage
- **Camden Passage** • Camden Passage
- **Cass Art** • 66 Colebrooke Row
- **Gill Wing Kitchen Shop** • 194 Upper St
- **Little Paris** • 262 Upper St
- **Micycle N1** • 47 Barnsbury St
- **Monte's Deli** • 23 Canonbury Ln
- **Paul A Young Fine Chocolates** • 33 Camden Passage
- **Twentytwentyone** • 274 Upper St

Supermarkets

- **Iceland** • 62 Chapel Market

Canonbury

Map 81

The Canonbury area is a delicious cocktail of diversity with a heady mix of leafy spacious streets, multi-million-pound mansions, a dollop of tempered hipster abodes and some of London's poorest estates. Essex Road has a Banksy and quirky shops including the notable **Get Stuffed** for all your taxidermy needs. Foodies are well catered for with real butchers (**James Elliot**), bakers (**Raab's**), and great ethnic eateries (**Zigni House** and **Sabor**).

O Landmarks
- **Gladiators Paving Slab** • 10 Canonbury St

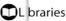

Libraries
- **South Library** • 115 Essex Rd

Nightlife
- **Marquess Tavern** • 32 Canonbury St
- **Myddleton Arms** • 52 Canonbury Rd
- **The Lord Clyde** • 342 Essex Rd

Restaurants
- **Raab's Bakery** • 136 Essex Rd

Shopping
- **Get Stuffed** • 105 Essex Rd
- **HG Lockey & Sons** • 8 Halton Cross St
- **James Elliot Butchers** • 96 Essex Rd
- **Planet Organic** • 64 Essex Rd
- **Sew Fantastic** • 107 Essex Rd
- **Steve Hatt** • 88 Essex Rd

Supermarkets
- **Co-Op** • 132 Essex Rd

Map 82 • **De Beauvoir Town / Kingsland**

N

Ferntower Road

New River Walk

Truman's Rd

Stoke

2

64

A105

Elton Place

Woodville

Green

Arundel

Road

Pyrland Road

Mildmay

Gardens

Road

Hertford

Benyon

Road

Tyssen Rd

Shackwell

Alvinton

Beresford

Terrace

Beresford Road

Queen Margaret's Grove

Mildmay

Place

John Campbell

Road A10

Sandringham Rd

Crossway

Gillett Street

Wilton

Way

Brenthouse Mews

Colve

Grove North

St. Jude Street

Bradbury

Street

Pl

Grosvenor

Avenue

Linden

Mews

Mildmay

Mildmay

St. Paul's

Kingsbury

Ter

Border

Close

Bole

Road

Abbot Street

Hartwell

Heaven Tree

Close

North

Grove South

King Henry's Wk Gdn

Jewish

Burial

Ground

A

Canonbury Rail

Canonbury Park

Oocwra's

Bidgs

Hawthorne

Close

Border

Close

Close Rd

Kingsbury

Kingsland High Street

Dalston Lane

St. Paul's (North) Park

St. Paul's Road A1199

Northampton Pk

St. Paul's Road

Bingham Rd

Mildmay Pk

Border

Road

86

Balls Pond Road

Balls Pond Road A104

Cull

Ms

War C

Eagle

St

Mkt

Pas

Roseberry

Place

Chelmer

Thorndike Road

Dove

Street

Culford Mews

Tottenham

Road

Forest

Richme

CANONBURY

Ramsey Walk

Wakeham

Street

Baxter

Wall

Street

Buckingham

KINGSLAND

Road

Obanna

Mews

Kingsland Road Street Market

Kingsland Road A10

Bee Ho

81

Mitchison Road

Ockendon Road

Culford

Grove

Avenmpell

Road

FreshHold

Ashby Grove

Red Lane

Church Road

Englefield Road

Ufton Grove

Road

Culford Road

Stanford

Road

Hertford Road

Englefield

Middleton

Crowfield

Ter

Oakley Road

Mortimer Road

Rich Pl

Richmond

Northchurch

Ufton Road

De Beauvoir Road

Pl

Elmore Street

Essex Road

Clare Lane

Halford Rd

Orchard

Avenue

Yeats St

con Ms

Dea

Scrungate Gro

Haines

Clo

Crawford Road

North. Ter.

De

Beauvoir

Square

De Beauvoir Square

St. Peter's

Way

Enfield Road

Hoppenson

Rd

Essex Road A104

James

Court

Rumor

Road

Morton

Elizabeth

Road

Orchard

Ms

W. Mill

Mortimer Road

Water

cress

Place

Lan

caster

Place

Arbut

Street

Park

North Road

A1200

Rutherford Street

Downham Road

Park

Place

Benyco

Southgate Road B102

DE BEAUVOIR TOWN

Mulford Road

Hertford

Lee Street

88

Basıra Street

Shepperton Road

Rosemary Gardens

Rose.

St

Balmes Road

De Beauvoir Crescent

Baltic

St

Acton St

Dunston St

83

Wilton

Street

Wilson

St

Baring Street B102

Branch Place

84

Whitmore

Road

Regent's Canal

Canal Path

New North

Whinsha Road

ton St

Penn Street

Hyde Road

Phillipp

Mill Row

Suleymaniye Mosque

Pear Tree

Close

Gopsall St

Hoxton

Clinger

Laburnum

Grange Street

Whiston

Wilmer

New North Road A1200

Shoreditch

Shoreditch

0.25 mile

0.25 km

75

Map 82

De Beauvoir is the buffer zone where swanky Islington meets the self-regard of Dalston. As such it's an ideal place to get a reprieve from either side. To the west are quiet squares and gastropubs. Venture east and you'll be up-'til-dawn boozing, talking to individuals comic book writers couldn't dream up. When you're sick of both, sit in De Beauvoir Square (with its thousands of palm trees) and ponder life.

Coffee

- **2&4** • 4 Southgate Rd
- **Bird Café** • 52 Boleyn Rd
- **Haggerston Espresso Rooms** • 13 Downham Rd
- **Reilly Rocket** • 507 Kingsland Rd
- **Tina, We Salute You** • 47 King Henry's Walk

O Landmarks

- **Suleymaniye Mosque** • 212 Kingsland Rd

Libraries

- **Mildmay Library** • 21 Mildmay Park

Nightlife

- **Dalston Boys Club** • 68 Boleyn Rd
- **Dalston Jazz Bar** • 4 Bradbury St
- **The Duke of Wellington** • 119 Balls Pond Rd
- **The Hunter S** • 194 Southgate Rd
- **The Northgate** • 113 Southgate Rd
- **Rosemary Branch Theatre** • 2 Shepperton Rd
- **The Vortex** • 11 Gillett Sq

Restaurants

- **De La Panza** • 105 Southgate Rd
- **Duke's Brew & Que** • 33 Downham Rd
- **Mother Earth** • 101 Newington Green Rd
- **Peppers and Spice** • 40 Balls Pond Rd
- **Pond** • 3 Gillett St
- **Vietnamese Canteen Huong Viet** • 12 Englefield Rd

Shopping

- **2&4** • 4 Southgate Rd
- **Mother Earth** • 101 Newington Green Rd
- **North One Garden Centre** • 25 Englefield Rd

If you're bored of the bars on Upper Street or the ironic chic of Hoxton, the streets in between (along Essex Road or by the canal) are a better bet, with a more laidback atmosphere. The **Island Queen** (NFT London's official birthplace!) is a cosy local pub and well worth a visit. One day they'll just have to give us one of those blue plaques.

 ## Coffee

• **Food Lab** • 56 Essex Rd

 ## Nightlife

• **Barrio North** • 45 Essex Rd
• **The Charles Lamb** • 16 Elia St
• **The Duke of Cambridge** • 30 St Peter's St
• **Earl of Essex** • 25 Danbury St
• **The Narrow Boat** • 119 St Peters St
• **The Island Queen** • 87 Noel Rd
• **The Mucky Pup** • 39 Queen's Head St
• **The Old Queen's Head** • 44 Essex Rd
• **The Wenlock Arms** • 26 Wenlock Rd

Restaurants

• **The Charles Lamb** • 16 Elia St
• **Shepherdess Cafe** • 221 City Rd
• **William IV** • 7 Shepherdess Walk

Shopping

• **Flashback** • 50 Essex Rd
• **Past Caring** • 54 Essex Rd

Map 84 · **Hoxton**

N

0.25 mile

0.25 km

Map 84

The only constant in Hoxton is change: what passes as monthly rent now was a deposit on a pad a decade earlier. The vibe is special and the pulse of the area radiates out of Hoxton Square and its bedfellow Curtain Road. Shop at **Hoxton Monster Supplies**, check modern art at **White Cube**, drink at **Electricity Showrooms** or **Zigfrid**, and finish on the floor at **Cargo**.

Coffee

- **Apostrophe** • 42 Great Eastern St
- **Cream** • 31 New Inn Yard
- **Eat.** • 59 Great Eastern St
- **Slate** • 9 Curtain Rd
- **Tre Era Cafe** • 30 Whitmore Rd

✚ Emergency Rooms

- **Moorfields Eye Hospital** • 162 City Rd

O Landmarks

- **Hoxton Square** • Hoxton Sq
- **Village Underground** • 54 Holywell Ln
- **White Cube** • 48 Hoxton Sq

Libraries

- **Shoreditch Library** • 80 Hoxton St

Nightlife

- **333 Mother** • 333 Old St
- **Bedroom Bar** • 62 Rivington St
- **Cargo** • 83 Rivington St
- **Charlie Wright's International Bar** • 45 Pitfield St
- **Club Aquarium** • 256 Old St
- **Comedy Cafe** • 66 Rivington St
- **Electricity Showroom** • 39 Hoxton Sq
- **Happiness Forgets** • 9 Hoxton Sq
- **Howl at the Moon** • 178 Hoxton St
- **Hoxton Square Bar and Kitchen** • 2 Hoxton Sq
- **The Macbeth** • 70 Hoxton St
- **The Old Blue Last** • 38 Great Eastern St
- **PortSide Parlour** • 14 Rivington St
- **Red Lion** • 41 Hoxton St
- **The Stag's Head** • 55 Orsman Rd
- **Strongroom** • 120 Curtain Rd
- **Troy Bar** • 10 Hoxton St
- **Zigfrid** • 11 Hoxton Sq

🍴 Restaurants

- **8 Hoxton Square** • 8 Hoxton Sq
- **The Barrel Boulangerie** • 110 Hoxton St
- **Big Apple Hot Dogs** • 239 Old St
- **The Clove Club** • 380 Old St
- **Cream** • 31 New Inn Yard
- **The Diner** • 128 Curtain Rd
- **F. Cooke** • 150 Hoxton St
- **Fifteen** • 15 Westland Pl
- **The Jones Family Project** • 78 Great Eastern St
- **Meat Mission** • 15 Hoxton Market
- **Rivington Bar and Grill** • 28 Rivington St
- **Tramshed** • 32 Rivington St

🛍 Shopping

- **Good Hood** • 41 Coronet St
- **Hoxton Street Monster Supplies** • 159 Hoxton St
- **SCP** • 135 Curtain Rd
- **Shl** • 57 Hoxton Sq
- **Tord Boontje Shop** • 23 Charlotte Rd

🛒 Supermarkets

- **Co-Op** • 136 New North Rd
- **Iceland** • 209 Hoxton St

Map 85 · **Stoke Newington (East)** N

Stamford Grove West

Forburg

Common A107

Jes

Darenth Road

Kyverdale Road

Chardmore Road

Lynmouth Road

Filey Avenue

Gilda Crescent

Lynmouth Road

Oldhill Street

Ossaldeston Road

Chardmore Road

Reizel Close

Lampard Grove

Margaret

Alkham Road

Kyverdale Road

Filey Avenue

Cazenove Road

Geldeston Road

Upper Clap

Margaret Bldgs

Windus Road

Belfast Road

Rossington St

Stoke Newington Rail

Station App

Cazenove Road

Alkham Road

Kyverdale Road

Ossaldeston Road

Fountayne Road

Durlston Road

Hogan Way

Geldeston Road

Cypress Ct

Charmane

Rd

◀64

Gibson Gdns

Briggeford Close

A

Abney Park Cemetery

Northwold Road A10

Abney Gdns

Northwold Road B111

Alconbury Rd

Geldeston Rd

Narford Road

Reighton Road

Wilmer Place

Garnham St

Stoke Newington Common

Benthal Road

Norcott Road

Evering Road

e Newington ch St B104

Lawrence Buildings

Garnham St

Sanford Ter

Jenner Road

Maury Road

Brooke Road

Dynevor Road

B

Manley Court

Smalley Close

Capstone Walk

Brooke Road

Sanford Ter

Brooke Road

87▼

Laundress Ln

Rendlesham Rd

Walsingham

Leswin Road

Stoke Newington High Street A10

Dynevor Rd

Tyssen Road

Darville Road

Oak Park NS

Rectory Road Rail

Evering Road

Benthal Road

Kenninghall Rd

Mu

Hollar Rd

Batley Place

Bayston Rd

Nile Close

Rectory Road A10

Monteagle Way

Victorian Gro

Batley Rd

Glading Ter

Leswin Place

86▼

Evering Road A10

Manse Road

Stellman Clo

Stellman Close

Stellman Close

Rendlesham Road

Monteagle Way

Muir Rd

Nolan Way

ctorian Sq

Coronation Av

Stoke

Sydner Road

Sydney Road

Worsley Ro

| 0.25 mile | 0.25 km |

Stoke Newington (East)

Stokey has turned into something of a Notting Hill of the east with all-terrain buggies taking up the pavement while the MILFs do their organic grocery shopping. It's resplendent in dining options but try **Testi** first. Various abolitionists and Salvation Army veterans are interred at the nineteenth-century **Abney Park Cemetery**, which doubles as an overgrown nature preserve and cruising spot.

O Landmarks

- **Abney Park Cemetery** •
  Stoke Newington High St & Rectory Rd

Libraries

- **Clapton Library** • Northwold Rd

Nightlife

- **Blush** • 8 Cazenove Rd
- **The Jolly Butchers** • 204 Stoke Newington High St
- **Royal Sovereign** • 64 Northwold Rd
- **White Hart** • 69 Stoke Newington High St

✉ Post Offices

- **Stamford Hill** • 82 Stamford Hill
- **Stoke Newington** • 138 Stoke Newington High St

🍴 Restaurants

- **19 Numara Bos Cirrik** • 34 Stoke Newington Rd
- **Bagel House** • 2 Stoke Newington High St
- **Café Z Bar** • 58 Stoke Newington High St
- **Tatreez Cafe** • 188 Stoke Newington High St
- **Testi** • 38 Stoke Newington High St
- **Thai Cafe** • 3 Northwold Rd
- **Three Crowns** • 175 Stoke Newington Church St

🛍 Shopping

- **Bargain Bookshop** • 153 Stoke Newington High St
- **Hamdys** • 167 Stoke Newington High St
- **Stoke Newington Bookshop** •
  159 Stoke Newington High St
- **Rouge** • 158 Stoke Newington High St

The (183) is bottom right.

Stokey has turned into something of a Notting Hill of the east with all-terrain buggies taking up the pavement while the MILFs do their organic grocery shopping. It's resplendent in dining options but try **Testi** first. Various abolitionists and Salvation Army veterans are interred at the nineteenth-century **Abney Park Cemetery**, which doubles as an overgrown nature preserve and cruising spot.

O Landmarks

- **Abney Park Cemetery** •
  Stoke Newington High St & Rectory Rd

Libraries

- **Clapton Library** • Northwold Rd

Nightlife

- **Blush** • 8 Cazenove Rd
- **The Jolly Butchers** • 204 Stoke Newington High St
- **Royal Sovereign** • 64 Northwold Rd
- **White Hart** • 69 Stoke Newington High St

✉ Post Offices

- **Stamford Hill** • 82 Stamford Hill
- **Stoke Newington** • 138 Stoke Newington High St

🍴 Restaurants

- **19 Numara Bos Cirrik** • 34 Stoke Newington Rd
- **Bagel House** • 2 Stoke Newington High St
- **Café Z Bar** • 58 Stoke Newington High St
- **Tatreez Cafe** • 188 Stoke Newington High St
- **Testi** • 38 Stoke Newington High St
- **Thai Cafe** • 3 Northwold Rd
- **Three Crowns** • 175 Stoke Newington Church St

🛍 Shopping

- **Bargain Bookshop** • 153 Stoke Newington High St
- **Hamdys** • 167 Stoke Newington High St
- **Stoke Newington Bookshop** •
  159 Stoke Newington High St
- **Rouge** • 158 Stoke Newington High St

Map 86 · **Dalston / Kingsland**

Dalston / Kingsland

Map 86

Bustling Ridley Road market is still the beating heart of Dalston, while Kingsland Road is like a Vice mag shoot with Nathan Barleys stalking up and down as though it were a catwalk. With hip bars like **Dalston Superstore** and **Ridley Road Bar**, it's no wonder, **Cafe Oto** is the experimental music cafe de jour.

Cinemas

- **Lux** • 18 Shacklewell Ln
- **Rio Cinema** • 107 Kingsland High St

Coffee

- **Betty's Coffee** • 510 Kingsland Rd
- **Coffee@Ridley's** • 91 Dalston Ln
- **Dalston Eastern Curve Garden** • 13 Dalston Ln
- **Metolino Cafe** • 162 Stoke Newington Rd
- **Mouse & De Lotz** • 103 Shackwell Ln
- **To The Jungle** • 6 Dalston Ln

O Landmarks

- **Centreprise** • 136 Kingsland High St
- **Holy Trinity, The Clowns Church** • Beechwood Rd & Kirkland Walk

Libraries

- **CLR James Library** • 30 Dalston Ln

Nightlife

- **Alibi** • 91 Kingsland High St
- **Bar 23** • 23 Stoke Newington Rd
- **Bardens Boudoir** • 38 Stoke Newington Rd
- **Café Oto** • 18 Ashwin St
- **Dalston Superstore** • 117 Kingsland High St
- **Efes Pool Club & Bar** • 17 Stoke Newington Rd
- **The Haggerston** • 438 Kingsland Rd
- **The Moustache Bar** • 58 Stoke Newington Rd
- **Passion** • 251 Amhurst Rd
- **The Prince George** • 40 Parkholme Rd
- **Ridley Road Market Bar** • 9 Ridley Rd
- **The Shacklewell Arms** • 71 Shacklewell Ln
- **Vogue Fabrics** • 66 Stoke Newington Rd

Post Offices

- **Kingsland High Street** • 118 Kingsland High St

Restaurants

- **Arancini Brothers** • 592 Kingsland Rd
- **The Best Turkish Kebab** • 125 Stoke Newington Rd
- **Dalston Eastern Curve Garden** • 13 Dalston Ln
- **Dem Cafe** • 18 Stoke Newington Rd
- **Evin Bar and Café** • 115 Kingsland High St
- **A Little Of What You Fancy** • 464 Kingsland Rd
- **Mangal 1** • 10 Arcola St
- **Mangal 2** • 4 Stoke Newington Rd
- **Peppers and Spice** • 20 Kingsland High St
- **The Russet** • Amhurst Terrace
- **Shanghai** • 41 Kingsland High St
- **Somine** • 131 Kingsland High St
- **Stone Cave** • 111 Kingsland High St
- **The Tea Rooms** • 155 Stoke Newington Rd

Shopping

- **Centre Supermarket** • 588 Kingsland Rd
- **Dalston Mill Fabrics** • 69 Ridley Rd
- **Healthy Stuff** • 168 Dalston Ln
- **LN-CC** • 18 Shacklewell Ln
- **Oxfam** • 514 Kingsland Rd
- **Party Party** • 9 Ridley Rd
- **Ridley Road Food Market** • Ridley Rd
- **St Vincent's** • 484 Kingsland Rd
- **Turkish Food Centre** • 89 Ridley Rd

Map 87 · **Hackney Downs / Lower Clapton** (N)

Cypress Close

85

Duncanford
Bridgeford St
Mount Pleasant Lane
Brampton Close

2

Mt Pleasant
Mundford Rd
Rushton

Alconbury Road
Narford Road
Brighton Road
Hassendean St
Horsenden La

Southwold Road

➡ **Clapton Rail**

Benthal Road
Maury Road
Norcott Road
Evering Road
Ickburgh Road

Gunton Road

Cleveleys Road

Casimir Rd

Lee Valley Park - North Millfields Recreation Ground

Brooke Road
Laura Crescent Ln
Nightingale Road

Prout Road

Upper Clapton A107

Leacroft Road

Lee Valley Park - South Millfields Recreation Ground

A

Evering Road
Walsingham Road

Kenninghall Road

Lea Bridge Road A104

Cotesbach Road
Whiston Road

Stellman Close
Monteagle Way
Mountague Road
Clapton Way

Muir Road
Della Path
Ferron Road

Thistlewaite Road
Cornthwaite Road
Thornby Road

Fletching Rd

Mildenh

Nolan Way
Worsley Gro
Monte Way
Gliddon Drive
Brackenfield
Tiger Way

Charnock Road
Heyworth Road
Napoleon Road

Newick Road

Chatsworth Road
Elderfield Road

Lower Clapton A107

86

Abbey Clo
Downs Road
Queensdown Road

Downs Rd A104

Downs Rd A102

Gaviller Place

Atkinson Rd
Afterden Rd

Millfields Road
Hilsea Street
Elmcroft Street

Colenso Rd
Mayola Road
Lawley St

West Terrace

Hackney Downs

Apprentice Way

Laura Place

Rushmore Road

Rowhill Road

Century Ms

Blurton Road

Mothers Sq

Linscott Road

Glenarm Road
Dunlace Road

Downs Park Road

Tilia Ms
Goulton Road

○ **London Orphan Asylum**

Median Road

Churchwell Walk

Pembury Road A104

Clarence Place
Shelness Rd
Hindrey Road
Tolsford Road
Orchard Place

Amhurst Close
Clarence Mews
Clarence Road
Clapton Square
Clapton Passage

Dean Clo

Ambleside Close
Waterloo Close

Sandringham Road
Andre Street
Aston St
Bodney Road
Pembury Place

Rowe Lane

St. John's Church Road

College Close
Haldon Close

B

Langford Close
Terrace Road
Uxbridge Close

Lushington Terrace
Wayland Avenue
Kreadman Walk

Sigdon Road
Shrubland Road

Dalston Lane ✕ A107

○ **The Strand Building**
Sutton Sq

Lower Clapton Road A107

Urswick Road A102

90

Burnett Close
Stellman

Dalston Ln A104

Hackney Downs Rail

Amhurst Rd A107
Institute Pl
Marcon Place
Poulton Close
Greenwood Rd

Mare St
Kenmure Yard
Kenmure Road
Brett Road

Ashmead Ms
✉

Sutton Place ○ **Sutton House**

Homerton

Fassett Square
Cottrill Gdns
Hartwell Ms

Hackney Central Path
Bohemia Place
Mehetabel Road

Steward St
Terrace

Carriage Mews

89

| 0.25 mile | 0.25 km |

A few years ago you couldn't move for house gigs and secret raves around the Downs, but these days the area is devolving into the moody gangland it used to be whilst breeding the rioters of tomorrow. Lower Clapton, on the other hand, is ever on the up. Shop at **Umit's** for rare films and sweets. Food and coffee can be found at vegan punk paradise **Pacific Social Club**.

Coffee

- **Cooper and Wolf** • 145 Chatsworth Rd
- **Gulluoglu** • 63 Lower Clapton Rd
- **Organic & Natural** • 191 Lower Clapton Rd
- **Pacific Social Club** • 8 Clarence Rd

O Landmarks

- **London Orphan Asylum** •
  Lower Clapton Rd & Linscott Rd
- **The Strand Building** • 29 Urswick Rd
- **Sutton House** • 2 Homerton High St

Nightlife

- **Biddle Brothers** • 88 Lower Clapton Rd
- **The Crooked Billet** • 84 Upper Clapton Rd
- **The Pembury Tavern** • 90 Amhurst Rd
- **Star by Hackney Downs** • 35 Queenstown Rd

Post Offices

- **Dalston Lane** • 244 Dalston Ln
- **Hackney** • 382 Mare St

Restaurants

- **India Gate** • 75 Lower Clapton Rd
- **Mess Café** • 38 Amhurst Rd

Shopping

- **Kate Sheridan** • 112 Lower Clapton Rd
- **Palm 2** • 152 Lower Clapton Rd
- **The Pet Shop** • 40 Amhurst Rd
- **Salvation Army Clapton** • 122 Lower Clapton Rd
- **Umit & Son** • 35 Lower Clapton Rd
- **X Marks The Bokship** • 44 Copperfield Rd

Map 88 · **Haggerston / Queensbridge Rd** Ⓝ

Mayfield Close
86
Grace Jones Close

Hertford Road
Richmond Road
Richmond Road

Englefield Road
Kingsland Road Street Market
Lenthall Road
Gayhurst Road

Mortimer Road
Beehive Close
Busted Road
Holly Street
Lomas Drive

De Beauvoir Square
Glebe Road
Evergreen Square
Mapledene Road

De Beauvoir Square
Avenue
Celandine Dr
Mapledene Road

St. Peter's Way
Freshfield
Evergreen Square
Mulberry Rd
Jacaranda Grove
Lavender Grove

Malvern Road

Oscar Faber Pl
Enfield Road
82
Mayfield Terrace
Albion Terrace
Ropewalk Ms
Middleton Road

A
Lancaster Close
Frederick Terrace
Albion Drive
Albion Square
Albion Drive

Hertford Road
Arbutus Street Park
Livermere Road
Shrubland Road
89

Kingsland Road A10
Arbutus St
Haggerston
Scriven Street
Brownlow Road
Brougham Road

Lee Street
Anna Close
Harriet Close
Byron Close
Marlborough Avenue
Johnson Close
Grand U

Acton Mews
Sstean Street
Loanda Close
Clarissa Street
Wilde Close

Dunston Street
Phoenix Close
Richardson Close
Samuel Close
Aitken Close
Letitia Close
Osborn Close
Magrian Close
Sotheran Close

Baltic Place
Dunston Road
Mary St
Seacole Close
Garden Place
Pownall Road

Stephan Close

Canal Path
Regent's Canal
Denne Terrace
Regents Row

Mill Row
Pear Tree Close
Amber Wharf
Haggerston Road
Regent's Canal
Govan Rd

Phillipp St
Laburnum Street
Gloucester Square
Coster St
Whiston Road
Sportsmans Mews

Wilmer Gdns
Nuttall Street
Nichol Street Mews
Dove Row

84
Hows Street
Kent St
Moye Cl

Kingsland Road A10
Sovereign Mews
Tyler Close
Ormsby St
Appleby Street
Weymouth Street
Thurtle Road
Kent St
Queensbridge Road B108
Haggerston Park
Boston St
Audrey St
Maldon Street
Goldsmith's Sq

B
Hare Walk
Pearson Street
St Mary's Secret Garden
Crabtree Close
Weymouth St
Teale Street

Geffrye Museum Gardens
Hoxton
Dunloe Street
Weymouth Terrace
Dunloe St
Dunloe Street
Torton Street
Hackney City Farm
Kay Street

Shenfield St
Geffrye Museum
Geffrye Street
Fellows Ct
Dawson St
Scawfell St
91
Hackney Road A1208

Cremer Street
Shipton Street

0.25 mile
0.25 km

With the opening of Haggerston Station and the Ginger Line, it seems Shoreditch is merging with Dalston to form one sprawling kingdom of hipdom. Where once **A10** used to be a dodgy little after-hours place, it's now a regular stop-off. Stroll down to the gardens at the **Geffrye Museum** or Haggerston Park for some people-watching with a flat white from **Long White Cloud**.

 Coffee

• **Long White Cloud** • 151 Hackney Rd

 Landmarks

• **Geffrye Museum** • 136 Kingsland Rd
• **St Marys Secret Garden** • 30 Pearson St

 Nightlife

• **The Fox** • 372 Kingsland Rd
• **Passing Clouds** • 440 Kingsland Rd

 **Post Offices**

• **Kingsland Road** • 416 Kingsland Rd

 Restaurants

• **Beagle** • 397 Geffrye St
• **Berber & Q** • Arch 338, Acton Mews
• **Chicks n Sours** • 390 Kingsland Rd
• **Fabrique Bakery** • 385 Geffrye St
• **Faulkner's** • 424 Kingsland Rd
• **Hackney City Farm** • 1 Goldsmiths Row
• **Uludag** • 398 Kingsland Rd
• **Song Que** • 134 Kingsland Rd
• **Viet Hoa Café** • 70 Kingsland Rd

 Shopping

• **KTS The Corner** • 415 Kingsland Rd

189

Map 89 · **London Fields / Hackney Central** Ⓝ

1
2

Madinah R
Carrara

Fassett
Square

Fassett Road

Clifton Grove
ws

Massie Road

Wilton Way

Errington Road
Greenwood Road

St. Philip's Road
To Stamey TS

Marcon Place
Spurstowe Road

Boulton Close

Navarino Road

Navarino Grove

Cottrill Gardens

Amhurst Road A107

Mapal Road

Brett Road

Ware Street
Terrace

Sutton Place

87

Station Path

Bohemia Place

Mehetabel

Churchwell Path

Hackney Central Rail

Nursery Row

Ram CI

B113

86

Graham Road A1207

Dalston
Lane

Durlston Road

Penpoll Road

Horton Road

Eleanor Road

Sylvester Road

Marvin Street

Hillman Street

Morning Lane

Belsham Street

Reading Heath
Fields Path

90

Richmond Road

Blanchard Way

Castleton Street

Eleanor Road

Elsdale St

Reading Lane

Parfitt
Road

Solander
Truth Close

Valette Street

Mare Street

Paragon Road

Chatham Place

Eldda

A

Gayhurst Road

Mapledene Road

Lavender Grove

Middleton Road

Drive

Mens

Appleby Road

London Fields West Side

Wilman Gro

88

O **London Fields Lido**

London
Fields

PAGE
344

Ellingfort Road

Ellington
Road

Martello St

Montrose Terrace

London Lane

Gransden Avenue

Silesia
Bldgs

London Fields Rail

Martello
Terrace

Cyntra Place

Fortescue
Ave

St. Thomas's
St. Thomas
Square
Square

Loddiges Road

Brenthouse Road

Darnley Road

Framppton Park Road

St. Thomas's Place

Well Street A106

Kingshold Rd

B

Lansdowne Drive

Grand Union Crescent

Broxbourne
Road

Dublin Ave

Croston St

Trederwen Road

Welshpool St

London Fields East Side

Lamb Lane

Helmsley Place

Sidworth St

Bayford St

Bayford
Ms

Exmouth Place

Warburton
Road

Warburton
Street

Mare Street A107

Pemberton Pl

Weston
Walk

Ely Road

Tudor Grove

Shore Road

Shore Place

Tudor Road

Tryon Crescent

Templecombe Rd

Clermont Road

Ainsworth Rd

Moulins Road

Cherry Tree Clo

Sharon Gardens

Primro

Kingsland Ave

Johnson Close

Wilde
Close

Magrin
Close

Sotheran Close

Stephan
Close

Regents Row

Benjamin
Close

Broadway Market

Duncan Rd

✉

Jackman St

Ada Street

Westgate Street

Boxing Street

Beck Road

Bush Road

King Edwards Road

Warneford Street

Fremont Street

Helena Road

Leopold
Place

Bluebell
CI

Victoria Park Road A106

St. Agnes
Close

Primro

Govan Street

Dove Row

Moye
Close

Goldsmith's Square

udrey Rd

Wharf Pl

Andrew's Road

Ada
Rd

Darwen Place

Marian
Square

Mariana Place

92

Regent's Canal

Sheep Lane

Booth Cn

Albert
Close

Northiam Street

Elsden
Ms

Pennethorne Clo

Pownall
Road

St. Jude's
Street

Vicars
Close

Corbridge Crescent

Hare

Vyner Street

Park Row

Wadeson Street

Waterlo

Sewardstor

Victoria
Park

93

London Fields/Hackney Central

Map 89

It's quite amusing seeing Chinese tourists waiting at the bus stop opposite Tesco with huge Burberry bags, having been at the **Factory Shop** whilst the rest of us schlep home with our groceries. Skip through London Fields, dip your toes in the **Lido**, and attempt to make your way through the throngs checking out their reflections in the shop windows on Broadway Market.

Coffee

- **Climpson & Sons** • 67 Broadway Market
- **The Corner Deli** • 121 Mare St
- **Donlon Books** • 77 Broadway Market
- **Hackney Bureau** • 3 Mare St
- **Violet** • 47 Wilton Wy
- **Wilton's** • 63 Wilton Way

O Landmarks

- **London Fields Lido** • London Fields Westside

Libraries

- **Hackney Central Library** • 1 Reading Ln

Nightlife

- **Baxter's Court** • 282 Mare St
- **The Dolphin** • 165 Mare St
- **The Dove** • 24 Broadway Market
- **Draughts** • 337 Acton Mews
- **The Old Ship** • 2 Sylvester Path
- **Pub on the Park** • 19 Martello St

Post Offices

- **London Fields** • 39 Broadway Market

Restaurants

- **Buen Ayre** • 50 Broadway Market
- **Cafe Bohemia** • 2 Bohemia Pl
- **Cat and Mutton** • 76 Broadway Market
- **Corner Deli** • 121 Mare St
- **F. Cooke** • 9 Broadway Market
- **Hai Ha** • 206 Mare St
- **Ombra** • 1 Vyner St
- **Pidgin** • 52 Wilton Wy
- **The Spurstowe Arms** • 68 Greenwood Rd

Shopping

- **Broadway Market** • Broadway Market
- **Burberry Factory Shop** • 29 Chatham Pl
- **Candle Factory** • 184 Mare St
- **E5 Bakehouses** • 395 Mentmore Terrace
- **L'eau a la Bouche** • 49 Broadway Market London
- **Viktor Wynd's Shop of Horrors** • 11 Mare St

Supermarkets

- **Iceland** • 150 Mare St
- **Tesco** • 55 Morning Ln

Map 90 · **Homerton / Victoria Park North** Ⓝ

1 **2**

Shellness Rd
Clarence Mews
Clarence Rd
Clapton Square
Redwald Road
Colne Rd
Durrington Road

Pembu
Hindrey Road
Clapton Rd A102
Median Rd
Elderfield Road
Dunlace Rd

Tolsford Road
College
Ambleside
Clifden Road
Clifden Mews

Orchard Place
Lower Clapton Road A107
Haldon Clo
Dean Clo
Walk
Blurton
Walk
Clifden Road
Chelmer Road

Dalston Lane A107
Rowe Ln.
St. John's
Church Rd
Ambleside
Clo
Staveley
Rd
Fisher Clo
Brooksby's Walk
Symington Mews
Coopersale Road
Ashenden Road

Amhurst Road A107
Kenmure Rd
Brett St
Gould
Ter
Mare Street
Urswick Road
Waterloo Close
Barton Clo
Hospital
Road
Homerton Grove
Tranby
Place
Glyn Road
Riding Road

Graham Rd A1207
Station
Path
Bohemia St
Sutton Sq
Sutton Pl
87
Mehetabel Road
Burnett Clo
Fenn Street
Homerton Row
Wardle St
St. Barnabas
Ter
Crozier Terrace
Kenworthy Road

A
Sylvester
Road
Reading
Lane
Morning Ln B113
Churchwell
Nursery
Path
Link Street
Furrow St
Ponsford St
Ryder Ms
Shepherds
Homerton High Street A102
Mackintosh Ln
Sedgwick
✉
Marsh Hill B112
Chevet
Street
Kenl
St
Mare Street A107
Valette St
Bestham St
Ram Place
Woodbine
Pl
Stevens
Avenue
Flanders Way
Digby Rd
Barnabas Rd
Berger Road
Mabl

Reading
Lane
Sidbourne
Train House
Richmond Rd
Paragon Road
Meeting
Fields
Path
Rivaz Pl
Homerton
Ter
Retreat Place
Daley St
Anderson Rd
Oriel Road
Hassett Road
Ballance Road
Homerton Rail
🚇

Darnley Road
Chatham Place
Mead Place
Cresse Road
Brooksbank
Street
Berger
Road
Bentham Road
Wick Road B113
Hebers Gro

89
St. Thomas's
Square
St.
Thomas's
Bldgs
Brenthouse Road
Milborne
Street
Elsdale
Street
Collent Street
Valentine Rd
Queen Anne Rd
Bramley St
Blackstock
Rd
Kenton Road B113
Hartlake Road
Harrowgate Road
Christie Road
Daneside Rd
Glaskin
Ms
King Rd

St. Thomas's Place
Frampton Park Road
Terrace Road
Ickburgh St
Well St
Pickering
Street
Cassland Road A106
Pickering
Close
Meynell Road
Meynell Cres
Meynell Rd
Gascoigne Road

Tudor Grove
Kingshold Road
Ainsworth Road
Holcroft Road
Well Street A106
Meynell
Gardens
Church Crescent
Gerard
Road
Groombridge Road
Elderfield
Road
Lannoy Rd
**Well
Street
Common**
Victoria Park Road A106
Guinness Close

B
Tryon Cres
Clermont Road
Shore Place
Primrose Sq
Clarendon
Close
Alpine Grove
Moulins Rd
Spurstowe Rd
Balcorne Street
Banbury
Road
Penshurst Road
**Victoria
Park**

Templecombe Rd
Blue Bell
Cherry Tree Clo
Sharon Gardens
Moulins Rd
Skipworth Road
Handley Road
Jackson
Close
Southborough Rd
Laurison Rd
Statham St
Minson
Cl
Louisa
St
Parnell
Rd
Providence Cl
**PAGE
356**

St. Agnes
Close
Retreat Pl
Derby
Rd
Victoria Park Road A106
Rutland Road
Connor
St
Ruthven St
Hackney
Cemetery
(Jewish)
Iveagh
Close

**Deer
Park**
Gore Road
Morpeth
Grove
Moopeth Rd
Wetherell Rd
Grove Road
Eastway

| 0.25 mile | 0.25 km |

Homerton/Victoria Park North

Map 90

Aah, Hackney Village: leafy Lauriston Road and its surrounds would make a nice retreat from the madding crowd if everyone else didn't have the same idea. Nevermind, have a Sunday Roast at the **Royal Inn on The Park**. Whereas once one would only be seen in Homerton if one was going to the hospital (or going to the hospital because one was in Homerton), Chatsworth Road (just off map) is now the place du jour.

Coffee

- **Railroad Café** • 120 Morning Ln
- **The Wash** • 206 Well St

Emergency Rooms

- **Homerton University Hospital** • Homerton Row

Libraries

- **Homerton Library** • Homerton High St

Nightlife

- **Chats Palace Arts Centre** • 42 Brooksby's Walk
- **The Kenton** • 38 Kenton Rd
- **The Lauriston** • 162 Victoria Park Rd
- **Royal Inn on the Park** • 111 Lauriston Rd

Post Offices

- **High Street** • 226 Homerton High St
- **Victoria Park** • 112 Lauriston Rd
- **Well Street** • 188 Well St

Restaurants

- **Eat 17** • 64–66 Brooksby's Walk
- **The Empress of India** • 130 Lauriston Rd
- **The Fish House** • 126 Lauriston Rd
- **Machete** • 91 Lauriston Rd
- **Well Street Kitchen** • 203 Well St

Shopping

- **The Ginger Pig** • 99 Lauriston Rd
- **Perlie Rides** • 137 Well St
- **Sublime** • 225 Victoria Park Rd
- **Work Shop** • 77 Lauriston Rd

Supermarkets

- **Tesco** • 180 Well St

(193)

Map 91 • Shoredith / Brick Lane / Spitalfields (N)

Haggerston Park

Hackney City Farm

2

88

Hackney Road

84

Old St A5201

Columbia Road B118

Gosset Street

92

Calvert Ave

A

Bethnal Green Road A1209

St. Matthews Gdns

Dunbridge St B135

8

Shoreditch High Street

Sclater Street

Cheshire Street

Sclater Street Street Market B135

Shoreditch High Street

Truman's Brewery

Sweet Toof Graffiti Alley

Spitalfields City Farm

Dennis Severs' House

Brick Lane

Spitalfields Market

Ten Bells

Brick Lane Mosque

Christ Church Spitalfields

18

B

Commercial Street A1202

96

Whitechapel

Aldgate East

Whitechapel Road A11

95

Aldgate

St. Botolph St

Mount Ter

| 0.25 mile | 0.25 km |

Throbbing with trend-lords on single-speed bikes, great curry houses, and alternative-lifestyle vomit, the trick is to sample Brick Lane and Shoreditch on market days for pure colour and bustle, but to avoid it on weekend eves. Shopping is abundant: **Rough Trade**, **Beyond Retro**, and oodles of great little rag shacks. Head towards **Jaguar Shoes** or **Catch** for booze. For a dash of authenticity, leave your £1000 bike unlocked and see what happens.

Cinemas

- **Rich Mix Centre** • 34 Bethnal Green Rd
- **Short & Sweet** • 91 Brick Ln

Coffee

- **Allpress** • 58 Redchurch St
- **Cafe 100** • 91 Brick Ln
- **Coffee@157** • 157 Brick Ln
- **Esoteria** • 276 Hackney Rd
- **Lanark** • 252 Hackney Rd
- **Leila's Shop** • 17 Calvert Ave
- **Nude Espresso** • 26 Hanbury St
- **Prufrock** • 140 Shoreditch High St
- **Time For Tea** • 110 Shoreditch High St

Landmarks

- **Brick Lane Mosque** • 59 Brick Ln
- **Christ Church Spitalfields** • 2 Fournier St
- **Dennis Severs' House** • 18 Folgate St
- **Spitalfield Market** • 105 Commercial St
- **Sweet Toof Graffiti Alley** • Pedley St & Brick Ln
- **Ten Bells** • 84 Commercial St
- **Truman's Brewery** • Brick Ln

Libraries

- **Dorset Library** • Ravenscroft St

Nightlife

- **93 Feet East** • 150 Brick Ln
- **The Archers** • 42 Osborn St
- **Bar Kick** • 127 Shoreditch High St
- **Bar Music Hall** • 134 Curtain Rd
- **Bedroom Bar** • 62 Rivington St
- **The Birdcage** • 80 Columbia Rd
- **Browns** • 1 Hackney Rd
- **The Big Chill Bar** • Dray Walk off Brick Ln
- **Café 1001** • 91 Brick Ln
- **The Carpenters Arms** • 73 Cheshire St

- **Catch** • 22 Kingsland Rd
- **The Cocktail Trading Co.** • 68 Bethnal Green Rd
- **The Commercial Tavern** • 142 Commercial St • Comedy Cafe • 66 Rivington St
- **The Culpeper** • 40 Commercial St
- **Danger of Death** • 202 Brick Ln
- **The George & Dragon** • Hackney Rd
- **The Golden Heart** • 110 Commercial St
- **Jaguar Shoes** • 32 Kingsland Rd
- **The Love Shake** • 5 Kingsland Rd
- **The Old Shoreditch Station** • 1 Kingsland Rd
- **Owl & Pussycat** • 34 Redchurch St
- **Prague** • 6 Kingsland Rd
- **Pride of Spitalfields** • 3 Heneage St
- **The Redchurch** • 107 Redchurch St
- **The Royal Oak** • 73 Columbia Rd
- **Sager + Wilde** • 193 Hackney Rd
- **Shoreditch House** • Ebor St
- **T Bar** • 18 Houndsditch
- **Vibe Bar** • 91 Brick Ln
- **The Water Poet** • 9 Folgate St
- **Ye Olde Axe** • 69 Hackney Rd

Post Offices

- **Bethnal Green** • 223 Bethnal Green Rd
- **Hackney Road** • 198 Hackney Rd

Restaurants

- **Andina** • 1 Redchurch St
- **Back in 5 Minutes** • 222 Brick Ln
- **Beigel Bakery** • 155 Brick Ln
- **Boundary** • 2 Boundary St
- **Brawn** • 49 Columbia Rd
- **Brick Lane Clipper Restaurant** • 104 Brick Ln
- **Café Bangla** • 128 Brick Ln
- **Chez Elles** • 45 Brick Ln
- **The Culpeper** • 40 Commercial St
- **Dishoom** • 7 Boundary St
- **Drunken Monkey** • 222 Shoreditch High St
- **Ethiopian Food Stall** • Brick Ln
- **Frizzante** • 1 Goldsmith's Row
- **Gourmet San** • 261 Bethnal Green Rd
- **Hanoi Cafe** • 98 Kingsland Rd
- **Hawksmoor** • 157 Commercial St
- **Les Trois Garçons** • 1 Club Row
- **Lyle's** • 56 Shoreditch High St

- **Marksman Public House** • 254 Hackney Rd
- **Mein Tay** • 122 Kingsland Rd
- **Noodle King** • 185 Bethnal Green Rd
- **The Premises** • 209 Hackney Rd
- **Que Viet** • 102 Kingsland Rd
- **Rosa's** • 12 Hanbury St
- **St John Bread and Wine** • 94 Commercial St
- **Taberna do Mercado** • 107 Commercial St
- **Tay Do** • 60 Kingsland Rd
- **Tay Do Cafe** • 65 Kingsland Rd
- **Troy Cafe** • 124 Kingsland Rd
- **Viet Grill** • 58 Kingsland Rd

Shopping

- **Absolute Vintage** • 15 Hanbury St
- **Bangla City** • 86 Brick Ln
- **Bernstock Speirs** • 234 Brick Ln
- **Beyond Retro** • 112 Cheshire St
- **Blackmans** • 44 Cheshire St
- **Blackman's Shoes** • 42 Cheshire St
- **Brick Lane** • Brick Ln
- **Caravan** • 3 Redchurch St
- **A Child of The Jago** • 10 Great Eastern St
- **Columbia Road Flower Market** • Columbia Rd
- **Columbia Road Market** • Columbia Rd
- **Comfort Station** • 22 Cheshire St
- **Duke of Uke** • 22 Hanbury St
- **Dum Dum Donutterie** • 2–4 Bethnal Green Rd
- **FairyGothMother** • 15 Lamb St
- **The Grocery** • 54 Kingsland Rd
- **Hurwundeki** • 98 Commercial St
- **Junky Styling** • 91 Brick Ln
- **The Laden Showroom** • 103 Brick Ln
- **Labour & Wait** • 18 Cheshire St
- **Lily Vanillie** • 6 Ezra St
- **Luna and Curious** • 198 Brick Lne
- **Mast Brothers** • 19 Redchurch St
- **A Portuguese Love Affair** • 142 Columbia Rd
- **Present** • 140 Shoreditch High St
- **Rough Trade East** • 91 Brick Ln
- **Ryantown** • 126 Columbia Rd
- **Sunday (Up)Market** • Brick Ln
- **Taj Stores** • 112 Brick Ln
- **Tatty Devine** • 236 Brick Ln
- **Taylor Taylor** • 12 Cheshire St
- **Taylor Taylor** • 137 Commercial St
- **Treacle** • 110 Columbia Rd

Map 92 · **Bethnal Green**

Queensbridge Road B108

Haggerston Park

Hackney City Farm

Ion Square Gardens

Hackney Road A1208

Warner Place

Squirries Street B108

Bethnal Green Road B108

Vallance Road B108

Dunbridge Street B135

Weavers Fields

Bethnal Green Rail

Three Colts Lane

Brady Street Cemetery (Jewish)

St. Bartholomew Gardens

Westgate Street

Mare Street A107

Victoria Park Road A106

Christchurch Square

Cambridge Heath Rail

Bishops Way

B127

Old Bethnal Green Road B118

Cambridge Heath Road A107

Old Ford Road B118

Museum Gardens

Roman Road

Bethnal Green Tube Station

London Buddhist Centre

Globe Road B119

Bethnal Green Gardens

Cornwall Ave

Cambridge Heath Road A107

Globe Road B120

96

97

Whitechapel Road A11
Mile End Road A11

0.25 mile

0.25 km

Bethnal Green

Map 92

No longer the inner-city ghetto from days of yore, but you can still find some of the gor-blimey-for-love-a-duck cockney cheekiness that one would expect in this hood. **E. Pellicci** is one of the oldest remaining greasy spoons in London, so head in for a Full Monty and a cuppa. If a lager and a burger down the **Sebright Arms** is not your thing, head down to the **Buddhist Centre** for a bit of instant karma.

Coffee

- **Hurwundeki Cafe** • 298 Cambridge Heath Rd

O Landmarks

- **Bethnal Green Tube Station** •
  Bethnal Green Tube Station
- **London Buddhist Centre** • 51 Roman Rd

Libraries

- **Bethnal Green Library** • Cambridge Heath Rd
- **Idea Store Bow** • Roman Rd

Nightlife

- **The Albion** • 94 Goldsmiths Row
- **Bethnal Green's Working Men's Club** • 44 Pollard Row
- **The Florist Arms** • 255 Globe Rd
- **Sebright Arms** • 31 Coate St
- **Satan's Whiskers** • 343 Cambridge Heath Rd
- **The Star Of Bethnal Green** • 359 Bethnal Green Rd

Post Offices

- **Bethnal Green Road** • 365 Bethnal Green Rd
- **Cambridge Heath** • 481 Cambridge Heath Rd

Restaurants

- **Bistrotheque** • 23 Wadeson St
- **E Pellicci** • 332 Bethnal Green Rd
- **The Gallery Cafe** • 21 Old Ford Rd
- **Little Georgia** • 87 Goldsmiths Row
- **Mission** • 250 Paradise Row

Shopping

- **AP Fitzpatrick** • 142 Cambridge Heath Rd

Supermarkets

- **Tesco** • 361 Bethnal Green Rd

Map 93 · **Globe Town / Mile End (North)**

1

2

Pennethorne
Close

Vicars
Close

Vicary's
Street

Lark
Row

Rutland Road

Morpeth
Gro

Morpeth Road

Connor
Street

Lauriston
Road

Hackney
Cemetery
(Jewish)

Wetherall Road

Goss Road

Deer
Park

Victoria
Park

Victoria
Park

PAGE
356

Waterloo Gdns

Sewardstone Road

Bishops Way B127

Bonner Road

Robinson Road

Russia Lane

St. James's Avenue

Approach Road

Sewardstone Road

B127

Lauriston Rd A1205

Old Ford Road B118

Royal Victor Pl

Peachwalk Ms

Nightingale
Mews

Chisenhale Road

Dalling Way

Hewlett Rd

Driffield Road

Eleanor Road

A

◀92

Elsden
Mews

Old Ford Road

B118

Cyprus
Street

Roman
Road

Morgan's
Road

Gawber
St

Walwyn St

Brierly
St

Hartley St

Russian
Road

Cyprus Street
St

Royston St

Mace St

Hartley
St

The
Tent St

Cranbrook
St

Mace St

Gathorne
Street

Tent St

Palmers Road

Wennington
Road

Wennington
Green

Bunsen
St

Kenworthy Road

Vivian Road

Zealand Road

Roman Road B119

Lanfranc Rd

Olga St

Medway

Medway
Blgs

Lyal Road

94▶

Kirkwall Pl

Peary St

Barton St

Butler
St

Knottisford

Morpeth St

Walley St

Digby Street

Bullards Place

Smart
Street

Usk Street

Roman Road

B119

Gernon Road

Thyodon
Road

Medway
St
Ms

Stanfield
Road

Medway Rd

Saxon Road

Mile
End
Park

Arbery Road

Strahan Road

Sapphire Road

Portman Place

Walter St

Meath
Gardens

Haverfield Road

Mile End
Climbing Wall

Grove Road A1205

Antill Road

Cherrywood
Drive

Meath Crescent

Bancroft
Road

Portelet
Road

Roman
Road

Harley Sq

Bradwell Street

Grantley
Street

Longnor Road

Lichfield Rd

Ashcroft
Road

Alloway Rd

Portelet
Mews

Rhondda Grove

B

Cephas
Street

Stafford Cripps
House

Globe Road

Roman Rd

Mace St

Abott St

Dog Row

Leatherdale

Cephas
Street

Massingham Street

Toliet St

Argyle Road

Carlton St

Carlton Sq

Holton St

Colmar Close

Alderney Road

Mile End Place

Carlyle
Mews

Alderney Road
Cemetery
(Jewish)

Bancroft Road

Westfield Way

Mile End Jewish Cemetery

PAGE
346

Mile
End
Park

Art Pavillion

Croft
Road

Morgan St

Aberavon Road

Lawton
Road

Whitman
Road

Eric Street

Burdett Road A1205

Mile
End
Mews

99▶

◀97

Boyton
Clo

Stamer St

Frimley Way

Globe Rd B120

Beaumont Rd

Stepney
Green

Louisa Street

Sundra
Walk

Eastbury Terrace

Ernest Street

Ifor Evans Pl

98

Close

Canal
Union
Drive

Mile End Road A11

Toby Lane

Mile
End

Wentworth
Mews

Mile End
Park

Hamlets Way

| 0.25 mile | 0.25 km |

Map 93

Yeah Victoria Park is nice and all, but it's just a bunch of trees and grass innit? South of all that green sh** is an up-and-coming nabe with so many great little gems. So, **The Palm Tree** is the best pub in Britain. **The Victoria** is becoming a brilliant gig spot. We'd move here if we had the balls, in fact.

Landmarks

- **Art Pavilion** • 221 Grove Rd
- **Mile End Climbing Wall** • Haverfield Rd & Grove Rd

Nightlife

- **The Approach** • 47 Approach Rd
- **Morgan Arms** • 43 Morgan St
- **Palm Tree** • 127 Grove Rd
- **The Victoria** • 110 Grove Rd

Post Offices

- **Roman Road** • 138 Roman Rd

Restaurants

- **Greedy Cow Burgers & Steaks** • 2 Grove Rd
- **Morgan Arms** • 43 Morgan St

Map 94 • **Bow**

Victoria Park
PAGE 356

River Lee or Lea

Jodrell Road
Ollerton Grn

Waterside Close
Candy Street

Parnell Road
Cedar Clo
Ruston Street

East Cross Route A102

Hornbeam Square
Birdsfield
Barge Lane
Gunmakers Lane
Willow
Tree Cl Ln

Old Ford Road
Empire Wharf B118
Old Ford Road
Ruston Road

B118
Ford Road
Rainhill Street
Beale Road
Hawthorn Ave
Sycamore Avenue
Annie Besant Close
Clo
Pulteny

Saw Yard
Swans Bldgs
Chisenhale Rd
St. Stephen's Road
Alice Lane
Crown Close Rd
Arragon Road
Lea Sq
Legion Terrace
Chariot Clo

A
Zealand Road
Ellesmere Road
Daling Way
Ford Street
Allen Road
Wrights Road
Beale Place
McCullum Road
Libra Road
Tamar Clo
Garrison Road
Hadrian Clo

Vivian Road
Drinfield Road
Hewlett Road
Daling Way
Hitchin Sq
Ford Clo
Roman Sq Market
Forum Clo
Tiber Clo

Roman Road
B119
St. Stephen's Road
Ewart Place
Gladstone Place
Roman Road
Usher Road
Hewison Street
Parnell Road B142

93
Lanfranc Road
Medway Bldgs
Medway Road
Lyal Road
Rosa Bank Gdns
Norman Grove
Cardigan Road
Anglo Road
Vernon Road
Usher Road
B142

Barbery Road
Stanfield Road
Selwyn Road
Saxon Road
Stafford Road
Shetland Road
Tredegar Road
Lacey Wk.
Four Seasons Close
Morville Street

Strahan Road
Athelstane Grove
Carlile Road
Orpheus Close
Matilda Gdns
Mews Street
Redwood Close
Primrose Close

Antill Road
Cherrywood Close
Tredegar Road
Hereford Road
Mostyn Grove
Esten Street
Springwood Close

Lichfield Road
Malmesbury Road

B
Alloway Rd
Pembroke Mews
Tredegar Mews
Benworth Street
Lawrence Close
Caxton Grove
Addington Road
Hartington Terrace

Aberavon Road
Rhondda Grove
Morgan Street
Tredegar Terrace
Coborn Road
Coborn Street
Harley Grove
Alfred Street
Denmark Place
Kitcat Terrace

98
A12 05
Mile End
Tredegar Sq
Lyn Mews
Coborn Road
Regal Place
99
Bow Road A11
Bow Road
Bow Church

0.25 mile   0.25 km

What have the Romans ever done for us? Not much, you might think, walking down Roman Road. But look closer and you'll find not only one of the oldest, most authentically East End jellied eels and mash eateries of the city, but also a market so cheap it'll knock even the most die-hard bargain hunters right out of their Centurion sandals. Pint? The haughty-sounding combo of **The Young Prince** or **The Lord Morpeth**.

Nightlife

- **Coborn Arms** • 8 Coborn Rd
- **Lord Morpeth** • 402 Old Ford Rd
- **The Lord Tredegar** • 50 Lichfield Rd
- **Young Prince** • 448 Roman Rd

Post Offices

- **Roman Road (603)** • 603 Roman Rd

Restaurants

- **Chicchi** • 516 Roman Rd
- **G. Kelly Noted Eel & Pie Shop** • 526 Roman Rd
- **Pavilion Victoria Park** • Old Ford Rd

Shopping

- **Roman Road Market** • Roman Rd
- **Sew Amazing** • 80 St Stephens Rd
- **South Molton Drug Store** • 583 Roman Rd

Map 95 • Whitechapel (West) / St Katharine's Dock

Whitechapel Gallery has reclaimed its place as the jewel in the crown of this 'hood since its renovation. Much like a busty Page 3 girl (see if you can spot one titter out of The Sun's nearby offices), the gallery has burst out of its shackles to reveal something quite magnificent. **The Rhythm Factory** is a typically chaotic boozing den—or head to **Wilton's Music Hall** for crumbling decadence and table tennis.

Coffee

- **Black Sheep Coffee** • 2 Leman St
- **Oi Bagel** • Commercial Rd
- **Starbucks** • 45 Whitechapel Rd
- **Vagabond E1** • 59–63 Whitechapel High St
- **White Mulberries** • 3 Ivory House

O Landmarks

- **The Sun HQ** • 1 Virginia St

Nightlife

- **The Dickens Inn** • 1 St Katherine Docks
- **Rhythm Factory** • 16 Whitechapel Rd
- **Simmons** • 61 Mint St
- **Wilton's Music Hall** • Graces Alley & Ensign St

Restaurants

- **Cafe Spice Namaste** • 16 Prescot St
- **The Empress** • 141 Leman St

Supermarkets

- **Waitrose** • Thomas More St & Nesham St

Map 96 • Whitechapel (East) / Shadwell (West) / Wapping

0.25 mile   0.25 km

Ex-dock and Wapping now imports yuppies into its converted warehouses, less-gleaming Shadwell and Whitechapel keep more of the East End spirit alive. Wapping High Street is mainly residential, Whitechapel Road is more lively. Drink at **Indo** if you're boho, stick with **The Captain Kidd** if not. **Tayyab's** is cracking—stick out the queues, or if curry's not your thing head to **Il Bordello**.

Emergency Rooms

• **Royal London Hospital** • Whitechapel Rd & Vallance Rd

O Landmarks

• **Battle of Cable Street Mural, St George's Hall** • 236 Cable St
• **Blind Beggar Pub** • 337 Whitechapel Rd

Libraries

• **Idea Store Whitechapel** • 321 Whitechapel Rd
• **Watney Market Library** • 30 Watney Market

Nightlife

• **Captain Kidd** • 108 Wapping High St
• **Indo** • 133 Whitechapel Rd
• **Town of Ramsgate** • 62 Wapping High St
• **Victualler** • 69 Garnet St

Post Offices

• **Eastern** • 206 Whitechapel Rd
• **Philpot Street** • 12 Philpot St

Restaurants

• **Il Bordello** • 81 Wapping High St
• **Lahore Kebab House** • 2–10 Umberston St
• **Needoo Grill** • 87 New Rd
• **Tayyabs** • 83 Fieldgate St

Supermarkets

• **Iceland** • Watney St & Tarling St
• **Sainsbury's** • 1 Cambridge Heath Rd

Map 97 · **Stepney / Shadwell (East)**

Numbered markers: 1, 92, 2, 93, 96, 98, 3

- Cambridge Heath Road
- Whitechapel Road A11
- Whitechapel Road A11
- Mile End Road A11
- Stepney Green B121
- Commercial Road A13
- Cable Street B126
- The Highway A1203
- The Highway A1203
- White Horse Road
- Belgrave St B121
- Ben Jonson Road
- Branch Rd A101

Areas / landmarks:
- Whitechapel
- Stepney Green
- Stepney Green Park
- Stepping Stones Farm
- Shadwell
- Limehouse
- King Edward VII Memorial Park
- River Thames
- Rotherhithe Tunnel

Street and place names:
Merceron St, Headlam Street, Collingwood St, Nicholas Rd, Durward Street, Winthrop Street, Mount Terrace, Darling Row, Vawdrey Close, Bellevue Place, Adelina Grove, O'Leary Sq, Assembly Pass, Hannibal Rd, Cressy Place, Louisa Street, Maria Ter, Eastbury Ter, More... Court Sq, Shandy Street, Ernest St, Raven Row, Sidney St, Lindley Street, Wolsey St, Smithy Street, Redman's Rd, Jamaica Street, Timsley Rd, Rectory Sq, White Horse Gdns, Trafalgar Gdns, Masters St, Ashfield Street, Varden Street, Newark St, Ford Square, Sidney Square, Ashfield Yard, Stepney Way, Wickham Clo, Ewhurst Close, Garden St, King John St, Clark Street, Clark Street, Jamaica St, Wellesley St, Oglander Rd, Belgrave St, Damien St, Sidney Square, Hungerford St, Hainton Close, Musbury Street, Aylward Street, Seagrave Clo, Head... Aylward, Stepney Way, Walter Terrace, Timberland Road, Corwood Drive, Arbour Sq, Antill Ter, Chudleigh Street, Clichterman Mews, Matlock St, Tarling Street, Morton Close, Aylward, Cleanbrook Way, Summercourt Rd, Marjorie Mews, Old Church Road, Aus St, Westport St, Bromley St, Troon St, Salmon Lane, Martha Street, Long Rydon, Sutton Street, Lukin Street, Commercial Road A13, Ronald St, Havering St, Alpert Gdns, Albert Gdns, Head St, Old Church Rd, Burslem St, Clemsford, Mews, Cornwall St, Juniper Street, King David Lane, Johnson Street, Harding Street, Dropmore Street, Bower St, Lipton Rd, Phila Street, Caroline Street, Ratcliffe Cross St, Ratcliffe La, Flamborough Street, Redcastle Close, Glamis Street, Elf Row, Elf Row, Brodlove Lane, Glasshouse Fields, Schoolhouse La, Bere St, Cranford St, White... Rd, Horseferry Road, Wine Close, Glamis Place, The Highway A1203, Branch Rd A101, Bekesbourne St, Limehouse, Benson Quay, Milk Yard, Jardine Road, Narrow Street, Prospect Place, Wapping Wall

Scale: 0.25 mile / 0.25 km

Cockney geezers run into hipsters and smart new developments sit next to rundown estates. No one quite knows where this area is going. We know where we're going, though—to **The George Tavern**, mainly, for impromptu theatre, blue-collar poetry and other arty madness, or **The Prospect of Whitby**, if we're feeling nostalgic. **Wapping Food**, meanwhile, serves great fare inside a century-old power station.

Cinemas

- **Foxcroft & Ginger** • 69 Mile End Rd
- **Genesis Mile End** • 93 Mile End Rd

Coffee

- **Popular Cafe** • 536 Commercial Rd

Nightlife

- **Cable Street Studios** • 566 Cable St
- **The George Tavern** • 373 Commercial Rd
- **The Prospect of Whitby** • 57 Wapping Wall
- **Troxy** • 490 Commercial Rd

Post Offices

- **Globe Road** • 34 Globe Rd
- **Stepney** • 502 Commercial Rd

Restaurants

- **Dirty Burger** • 27 Mile End Rd
- **Foxcroft & Ginger** • 69 Mile End Rd

Shopping

- **John Lester Wigmakers** • 32 Globe Rd
- **East End Thrift Store** • 1 Assembly Passage

Supermarkets

- **Co-Op** • 193 Mile End Rd

Map 98 · Mile End (South) / Limehouse

Globe Road
Frimley Way
Close Mile End Pl
Rangort Road
Stepney Green
Alderney Road Cemetery (Jewish)
Mile End
Mile End

93 Mile End Road A11

Wentworth Mews
Southern Grove
Eric Street
94

Hayfield
Louisa Street
Maria Terrace
Beaumont Sq
Eastbury Ter
Shandy Street
Toby Lane
Union Drive
Solebay Street
Sandalwood Close
Hamlets Way
Treby Street
Ropery Street
English Street

Stepney Green B121
Beaumont Sq
White Horse Lane
Trafalgar
Ernest Street
Hartord Street
Commodore Street
Entridge Close
Essian Street
Mile End Park
PAGE 346
Bow Common Lane
Portia Way
ViKing Street

Sherard Road
Rectory Sq
Shandy Street
Shandy Park
Bale Road
Bohn Road
Masters Street
Essian Street
White Tower Way
Candle St
Copperfield Road

A

Stepney Green Park
Garden Street
King John Ct
Stepping Stones Farm
Ben Jonson Road
Longola Road
Ragged School Museum
Mile End Stadium
99▶

Walter Terrace
Belgrave Street
◀97
B140
Our House Ben Rd
Rowne Oak Pl
Halley Street
Carr Street
Eastfield Street
Haven Mews
Revolution Karting
St. Pauls Way
Locksley Street
Joseph Street
Baythorne Street

Chudleigh Street
Avis Square
Westport Street
Cyphmarsh Mews
Belgrave Street
Bromley Street
White Horse Road B121
Barnes Street
Aston Street
Maroon Street
Harrisham Street
Repton Street
Dod Street
Turners Road
Clemence Street
Dora Street
Rhodeswell Road
Agnes Street
A1205
Wallwood Street
Thomas

Caroline Street
Ratcliffe Cross Street
Bradlord Street
Wakeling St
Brenton St
Salmon
Yorkshire Road
Farnborough Road
Butcher Row
Ratcliffe Lane
Commercial Road A13
Limehouse
Lowell Street
Dart Street
Salmon Street
Will Pl
Norbiton Road
Southwater
Copenhagen Place
Pixley Street
Burdett Road
A1205

100▶ Limehouse Cut
Dod Street

B

Branch Road A1013
The Highway A1203
Bekesbourne Street
Horseferry Road
Basin Approach
Norway
Wharf Road
Island Row
Mill Place
Newell Street
St. Anne's Pass
Rectory
Three Colt Street
Canton
East India Dock Road
Farrance Street
Old School Sq
Pigott Street

Narrow Street
Geoffart Place
Narrow Street
Nothey
Shoulder of Mutton Alley
Oak Lane
Limehouse Link A1203
Ropemakers Field
Mewell Street
Bredalbane Street
Amoy Place
Grenade Street
Birchfield Street
Stocks Place
West India Dock Road

River Thames

Sovereign
Causeway

0.25 mile   0.25 km

Mile End (South) / Limehouse

Map 98

Scary desolate landscapes and urban decay? Cool! Authenticity and Edge go hand-in-hand 'round here until you get to the water, where it livens up and turns into a Foxtons wank fantasy. Still, **The Grapes**, **The Narrow** and **La Figa** are eats and drinks havens while the **Ragged School Museum** offers a glimpse of what it was like when it was really grim round 'ere.

O Landmarks
• **Ragged School Museum** • 46 Copperfield Rd

Nightlife
• **The Grapes** • 76 Narrow St

Post Offices
• **Ben Jonson Road** • 52 Ben Jonson Rd
• **Mile End** • 1 Burdett Rd
• **Salmon Lane** • 127 Salmon Ln

Restaurants
• **La Figa** • 45 Narrow St
• **The Narrow** • 44 Narrow St
• **The Orange Room** • 63 Burdett Rd

Map 99 · **Bow Common**

N

1

Morgan Street

Tredegar Sq

Coborn Street

Harley Grove

Wilfred Street

2

Bromley High Road

Arrow Road

Rhondda Grove

Lyn Ms

94

Bow Road

Campbell Road

Bow Church

Bruce Road

Abrahams Road

Bow Road A11

Brokesley Street

British Street

Merchant St

Arnold Road

Tomlins Grove

Reeves Road

Devons Road

Talwin

93

Mile End

Went Ms

Southern Grove

Eleanor Street

Archibald Street

Holyhead Road

Wentworth Mews

Eric Street

English Street

Wellington Way

Treloar Street

Hamlets Way

Treby St

Tower Hamlets Cemetery Park

Tidworth Road

Fairfoot Road

Putty

A

Ropery Street

Cantrell Rd

Corby Way

Sweaton Road

Chiltern Road

Bounton Road

Devons Road

Mile End Park

Bow Common Lane

Menmin St

Lockhart St

Ackroyd Dr

Spanby Rd

Knapp Road

Cranwell Close

St. Andrews Way

◄98

Portia Way

Wager Street

Roberson Street

Bow Common Lane

Whitehorn Street

Benton Way

Fern Street

Blackthorn St

B140

Magdalen Street

Morris Grove

Glaucus Street

Violet Road

Mile End Stadium

Joseph Street

Wetherden St

Huddart Street

Selsey Street

Tidey St

Copford Close

Yeo Street

Revolution Karting

Leopold St

Bayrtown Street

Belmaine Ct

Celandine St

Bow Common Lane

Furze Street

Eagle Street

Haven Mews

St. Paul's Way

B140

Booker St

Kilner Street

Locksons Clo

Baxter Road

Rifle Str

Turners Road

Locksley Street

Wallwood Street

Burgess Street

Upper North Street

Broomfield Street

Chisgo Street

Clinton Street

Clemence Street

Burdett Road

Agnes Street

Thomas Road

Brabazon Street

Godalming Road

Cording St

Lango Par

Dora Street

Pixley Street

Cotall Street

Ellesmere Street

Carmen St

Bright

Norbiton Rd

Southwater Cl

Limehouse Cut

Stainsby Road

Arcadia Street

Northumbria St

Augusta Street

Giraud St

Cordelia Street

Hay Curre Street

Copenhagen Pl

A1205

B

Samuel Lane

Dod Street

Bartlett Park

Lindfield Street

Flora Close

Ricardo Street

Chrisp Street

A13

Tile Yard

Farrance Street

Old School Sq

Pigott Street

Hind Grove

Upper North Street

Annabel Close

Cordelia Street

St. Anne Street

Chrisp Street

Willis Street

100

Canton Street

Pekin Street

Grundy Street

Plimsoll Close

Poplar

Three Colt Street

Gill Street

Brackley Street

Saracen Street

Nankin St

Duff Street

Jeremiah Street

Surry Road

101

Oak Lane

Newell Street

Almoy Place

West India Dock

East India Dock Road A13

Granade

Morant Street

Poplar

Westferry

0.25 mile

0.25 km

East India Dock Road A13

All Saints

Desolation Row pretty much. For hardy explorers kitted out with knives and/or chastity belts, the wonderfully overgrown and sh**-your-pants scary **Tower Hamlets Cemetery Park** is great. In fact, keep the afore-mentioned kit on if you intend creeping through the boarded-up council estates and general doom.

Post Offices

• **Poplar** • 22 Market Sq

Map 100 • Poplar (West) / Canary Wharf (West)

Poplar (West) / Canary Wharf (West)

Now that we're officially out of the recession you can wander the wharf marvelling at the 'scrapers without pesky ruined bankers landing on you. Ah yes, the smell of money has resurfaced around finance's engine room and the brilliantly futuristic landscape is once again replete with suits shopping at the bland mall under Cabot Square. They never left of course, they just got used to packed lunches like the rest of us.

Map 100

 ## Cinemas

• **Cineworld West India Quay** • 11 Hertsmere Rd

 ## Coffee

• **Bagel Factory** • 7 Westferry Circus
• **Café Brera** • 45 Bank St
• **Café Brera** • 12 Cabot Sq
• **Café Brera** • 31 Westferry Circus
• **Coffee Republic** • 10 Cabot Sq
• **Coffee Republic** • Hertsmere Rd
• **Fresco Café Bar** • 15 Cabot Sq
• **Fresco Café Bar** • 22 Canada Sq
• **Starbucks** • 1 Canada Sq
• **Starbucks** • 45 Bank St
• **Starbucks** • 8 Westferry Circus

 ## Landmarks

• **Canary Wharf Tower** • 1 Canada Sq
• **Canary Wharf Tube Station** • Canary Wharf

 ## Nightlife

• **Davy's** • 31 Canary Wharf
• **Via Fossa** • 18 Hertsmere Rd

 ## Post Offices

• **Canary Wharf** • 5 Chancellor Passage

 ## Restaurants

• **Browns** • Hertsmere Rd
• **Nicolas** • 480 One Canada Sq
• **Plateau** • Canada Pl
• **Royal China** • 30 Westferry Circus

Supermarkets

• **Tesco** • 15 Cabot Sq
• **Waitrose** • N Colonnade & Canada Sq

213

Map 101 • Poplar (East) / Canary Wharf (East)

One day NFT lay down in the shadow of the Tower after a few in **The Greenwich Pensioner** and gazed up at the 'scraper, admiring its Philip K. Dickian splendour. A small plane buzzed by. Well-heeled bankers stuffed with pub-grub from **The Gun** strode by us. Then we got pulled up by the dreadlocks by a rozzer and got hoofed out for not reading the *Financial Times*. Serves us right.

 ## Libraries

- **Idea Store Canary Wharf** • Churchill Pl
- **Idea Store Chrisp Street** •
  East India Dock Rd • 1 Vesey Path

 ## Nightlife

- **The Greenwich Pensioner** • 28 Bazely Street

 ## Post Offices

- **Churchill Place** • 2 Churchill Pl

 ## Restaurants

- **The Gun** • 27 Coldharbour
- **Jamie's Italian** • 2 Churchill Pl

Map 102 · **Millwall**

Millwall

Though Millwall has award-winning **Docklands Sailing Centre** and decent community venue **The Space** (**Hubbub Café and Bar**), it doesn't really have much else. Bereft of tube, overground, or DLR, it doesn't even have Millwall FC anymore. Despite the potential of Canary Wharf on the doorstep and flush of luxury riverside apartments, it's still tainted with the whiff of BNP and football hooliganism. Buy now.

O Landmarks

• **The Docklands Sailing & Watersport Centre** •
235 Westferry Rd

Nightlife

• **Hubbub** • 269 Westferry Rd

Post Offices

• **Westferry Rd** • 367 Westferry Rd

Map 103 · **Cubitt Town / Mudchute**

🔾Ⓝ

1   **2**

Meridian Place

Marsh Wall

Lawn

Folly Wall

Harbour Exchange Sq

▲101

Limeharbour

Chapel Street

East Ferry Road

Roserton Street

Capstan Sq

River Barge Clse

Oxen Close

Stewart Street

Acre Street

Roffey Street

New Union Close

Launch Street

Pierra Street

Millwall Inner Dock

Pepper Street

◀A Crescent

Crossharbour & London Arena

Stratondale St

Glengall Grove

Marshfield Street

Manchester Road A1206

Amsterdam Road

Deerdon Dr

Rotterdam Drive

Rembrandt Close

Millennium Drive

◀102

Tumberly Quay

Seldon Way

East Ferry Road

Friars Mead

Friars Mead

James Mews

Friars Mead

James St

Ferry golf

Sill golf

Onan Circle

Clippers

Olive Street

Schooner Close

Chichester Way

Sextant Avenue

Mudchute Park

Pier Street

Blyth Close

Plymouth Wharf

Millwall Inner Dock

Telegraph Place

Taeping Street

Taeping Street

Taeping Street

Taeping Street

Spindrift Avenue

Undine Road

Undine Road

Undine Road

Undine Road

Mudchute

Mudchute Farm

Seyssel Street

Kingfield Street

Billson Street

Stebondale Street

Sonage Street

Glengarry St

Storers Quay

Caledonian Wharf

Empire Wharf

Grosvenor Wharf

Saunders Ness Road

Glenaffric Ave

B

Harbinger Road

The Chapel Gate

Macquarie Way

Chapel House Street

Julian Place

Locksfield Place

Millwall Park

Island Gardens

Manchester Road A1206

Cumberland Mills Sq

Lukin St

Westferry Road A1206

Wyman Road

bourne Pl

Lang

Blasker Walk

Ponter Cl

East Ferry Road

Lanchester Grove

Horseshoe Cl

Island Gardens

Saunders Ness Road

Ferry Street

Livingstone Pl

Midland Plwy

St. Davids Square

Felstead Gdns

River Thames

0.25 mile   0.25 km

Though shaded by the skyscrapers of Canary Wharf and a rash of luxury developments, this corner of the Island is blessed by the marvellous **Mudchute Farm and Park** (with the standout **Mudchute Kitchen** and equestrian centre), not one, not two, but three DLR stations, and a number of down-to-earth boozers like **Lord Nelson**. Who let the Isle of Dogs out?

O Landmarks

• **Mudchute Farm** • Pier St

Libraries

• **Cubitt Town Library** • Strattondale St

Nightlife

• **The Ferry House** • 26 Ferry St
• **The Lord Nelson** • 1 Manchester Rd

✉ Post Offices

• **Cubitt Town** • 15 Castalia Sq
• **Isle Of Dogs** • 159 Manchester Rd

🍴 Restaurants

• **Mudchute Kitchen** • Pier St

🛒 Supermarkets

• **ASDA** • 151 E Ferry Rd

THE
STRAND

WAPPING

Tower of
London
Park

SOUTH
BANK

SOUTHWARK

BOROUGH

Tooley St

St. Thomas St

Stamford St

Southwark St

Thrale St

York Rd

The Cut

Union Street

104

Blackfriars Rd

105

Borough Rd

106

Long Ln

Tower Bridge Rd

Druid St

107

Abbey St

Jama

Westminster Br

Waterloo Rd

Bayliss Rd

St. Georges Rd

London Rd

Harper Rd

Great Dover St

BERMONDSEY

108

Grange Rd

Southwark Park

WATERLOO

Kennington Rd

NEWINGTON

ELEPHANT &
CASTLE

New Kent Rd

Old Kent Rd

Dunton Rd

Rolls Rd

LAMBETH

KENNINGTON

VAUXHALL

WALWORTH

Walworth Rd

113

114

115

Peckham Park Rd

Kennington Park Rd

112

Albany Rd

Burgess
Park

Trafalgar Ave

Kennington
Park

CAMBERWELL

Camberwell Rd

Camberwell New Rd

122

PECKHAM

123

Peckham Rd

Hanover Pk

SOUTH
LAMBETH

121

Denmark Hill

Coldharbour Ln

Grove Ln · Dog Kennel Hill

Rye La

STOCKWELL

Hinton Rd

Ruskin
Park

E Dulwich Rd

129

130

BRIXTON

127

Milkwood Rd

Herne Hill Rd

128

Herne Hill

EAST DULWICH

Lordship Ln

Barry Rd

Railton Rd

HERNE HILL

E Dulwich Gro

Dulwich Rd

Half Moon Ln

South Bank / Waterloo / Lambeth North

Map 104

Hug the riverbank and you can culture 'til you puke. But you'll need stamina to survive: with such densely populated institutions your brain will give up long before your body. When it does, head for the cafe by day/bar by night, **Concrete**, tucked away behind the **Southbank Centre**, where the art installation du jour promises to have you wetting your pants in no time.

Cinemas

- **BFI London IMAX** • 1 Charlie Chaplin Walk
- **BFI SouthBank** • Belverdere Rd & Waterloo Rd

Coffee

- **Bagel Factory** • Waterloo Station
- **Benugo Bar & Kitchen** • Belvedere Rd
- **Eat.** • Belvedere Rd
- **Eat.** • Barge House St
- **Four Corners Cafe** • 12 Lower Marsh
- **ScooterCaffe** • 132 Lower Marsh
- **Starbucks** • Belvedere Rd

O Landmarks

- **County Hall** • Westminster Bridge Rd & Belvedere Rd
- **The Hayward Gallery** • Southbank Centre
- **The London Eye** • Westminster Bridge Rd
- **Low Tide at South Bank** • Waterloo Rd & Upper Ground
- **National Theatre** • South Bank
- **The Pier at Oxo Tower** • Barge House St & Upper Ground
- **South Bank Book Market** • Under Waterloo Bridge
- **Waterloo Bridge** • Waterloo Bridge

Libraries

- **Imperial War Museum** • Lambeth Rd
- **Poetry Library** • Royal Festival Hall
- **Waterloo Library** • 114 Lower Marsh

Nightlife

- **The Anchor & Hope** • 36 The Cut
- **Benugo Bar & Kitchen** • Belvedere Rd
- **Concrete** • Southbank Centre
- **Cubana** • 48 Lower Marsh
- **The Cut Bar** • 66 The Cut
- **Da Vinci's** • 6 Baylis Rd
- **The Pit Bar at the Old Vic** • The Cut
- **Royal Festival Hall** • Belvedere Rd
- **Skylon** • Belvedere Rd

Restaurants

- **The Anchor & Hope** • 32 The Cut
- **Canteen** • Royal Festival Hall, Belvedere Rd
- **Concrete** • Southbank Centre
- **The Cut Bar** • 66 The Cut
- **Giraffe** • Riverside Level 1
- **Marie's Cafe** • 90 Lower Marsh
- **Oxo Tower Wharf** • Barge House St
- **RSJ** • 33 Coin St
- **Skylon** • Belvedere Rd
- **Studio 6** • 56 Upper Ground
- **Tas Cut** • 33 The Cut

Shopping

- **Calder Bookshop** • 51 The Cut
- **Calder Bookshop Theatre** • 51 The Cut
- **Greensmiths** • 27 Lower Marsh
- **I Knit London** • 106 Lower Marsh
- **Konditor & Cook** • 22 Cornwall Rd
- **Oasis** • 84 Lower Marsh
- **Radio Days** • 87 Lower Marsh
- **ScooterCaffe** • 132 Lower Marsh
- **Silverprint** • 12 Valentine Pl
- **Southbank Book Market** • Under Waterloo Bridge
- **Top Wind** • 2 Lower Marsh
- **What The Butler Wore** • 131 Lower Marsh

Supermarkets

- **Iceland** • 112 Lower Marsh
- **Marks & Spencer** • Waterloo Station
- **Sainsbury's** • 101 Waterloo Rd

Map 105 • **Southwark / Bankside (West)**

Map 105

The **Tate Modern**, ladies and gents. It deserves all the praise it gets. And next door there's **Shakespeare's Globe**, the modern reconstruction of the Elizabethan playhouse where the Bard of Avon's works were contemporaneously produced. Both make this looked-after stretch of the Thames embankment a treasure for those hungry for culture. For those hungry for something else, you're spoilt with quirky options: Try **Baltic** for Polish Hunters' Stew, **The Table** for award-winning brunches, or **Laughing Gravy** for a restaurant named after Laurel & Hardy's dog.

Coffee

- **Eat.** • Bankside
- **Pret A Manger** • 2 Canvey St
- **Starbucks** • Emerson St (Units 1–3 Benbow House)

O Landmarks

- **Buskers' Archway** • Southbank
- **Elephant & Castle** • Elephant & Castle
- **Michael Faraday Memorial** • Elephant & Castle
- **The Ring** • 72 Blackfriars Rd
- **Shakespeare's Globe** • 21 New Globe Walk
- **Tate Modern** • Bankside

Nightlife

- **Albert Arms** • 1 Gladstone St
- **The Libertine** • 125 Great Suffolk St
- **The Lord Nelson** • 243 Union St
- **Ministry of Sound** • 103 Gaunt St
- **The Prince of Wales** • 51 St George's Rd
- **The Wine Theatre** • 206 Union St

Post Offices

- **Blackfriars Road** • 52 Blackfriars Rd

Restaurants

- **Baltic** • 74 Blackfriars Rd
- **El Vergel** • 132 Webber St
- **Laughing Gravy** • 154 Blackfriars Rd
- **The Table** • 83 Southwark St
- **Tate Modern Restaurant** • Bankside
- **Terry's Cafe** • 158 Great Suffolk St

Shopping

- **Elephant & Castle Market** • Elephant & Castle

Supermarkets

- **Tesco** • Elephant & Castle Station

Map 106

A Shoreditch for grown-ups, these parts have become a bit suitified lately—especially now that it's been reborn as 'London Bridge Quarter' under the Shard. Still, there's plenty of fun to be had. Gourmet-minded **Borough Market** draws the crowds on Saturdays, while the pubs and bars lining Borough High Street keep the party-minded happy throughout the week. Don't miss **The Rake** if you like (unusual) beer, **Brindisa** for Spanish tapas, and **Roast** if meat's your thing.

Coffee

- **Bagel Factory** • 12 Joiner St
- **Caffe Nero** • 3 Cathedral St
- **Costa** • 134 Borough High St
- **Patisserie Lila** • 1 Bedale St
- **Pret A Manger** • 8 London Bridge St
- **Pret A Manger** • 49 Tooley St
- **Starbucks** • Clink Wharf, Clink St

O Landmarks

- **Cross Bones Graveyard** • Red Cross Way & Union St
- **Female Gladiator** • 159 Great Dover St
- **The Golden Hinde** • Clink St & Stoney St
- **The London Tombs** • 2 Tooley St
- **Mint Street Park** •
  Southwark Bridge Rd & Marshalsea Rd
- **Old Operating Theatre Museum** • 9 St Thomas St
- **Roman Cemetery** • 65 Great Dover St
- **The Shard** • 32 London Bridge St
- **Southwark Cathedral** • Cathedral St & Montague Close
- **St George the Martyr** • Borough High St & Tabard St
- **Winchester Palace** • Clink St & Storey St

Libraries

- **John Harvard Library** • 211 Borough High St

Nightlife

- **The Anchor** • 34 Park St
- **Belushi's** • 161 Borough High St
- **The Blue-Eyed Maid** • 173 Borough High St
- **Brew Wharf** • Brew Wharf Yard, Stoney St
- **The George Inn** • 77 Borough High St
- **The Globe** • 8 Bedale St
- **Number 1 Bar** • 1 Duke St Hill
- **The Market Porter** • 9 Stoney St
- **The Rake** • 14 Winchester Walk
- **The Roebuck** • 50 Great Dover St
- **The Rose** • 123 Snowfields
- **Roxy Bar and Screen** • 128 Borough High St
- **The Royal Oak** • 44 Tabard St
- **Southwark Tavern** • 22 Southwark St
- **Wine Wharf** • Stoney St

Post Offices

- **Great Dover Street** • 159 Great Dover St
- **London Bridge** • 19 Borough High St

Restaurants

- **Arabica Bar & Kitchen** • 3 Rochester Walk
- **Boot and Flogger** • 10 Redcross Wy
- **Brew Wharf** • Brew Wharf Yard, Stoney St
- **Champor-Champor** • 62 Weston St
- **Feng Sushi** • 13 Stoney St
- **Fish!** • Cathedral St
- **Hing Loong** • 159 Borough High St
- **Nando's** • 215 Clink St
- **Roast** • The Floral Hall, Stoney St
- **Silka** • Southwark St
- **Tapas Brindisa** • 18 Southwark St
- **Tas Borough High Street** • 72 Borough High St
- **Wright Bros Oyster Bar** • 11 Stoney St

Shopping

- **Borough Market** • 8 Southwark St
- **Brindisa Retail** • Borough Market
- **Paul Smith** • 13 Park St
- **Richer Sounds** • 2 London Bridge Walk
- **Vinopolis** • 1 Bank End

Supermarkets

- **Marks & Spencer** • London Bridge Station
- **Sainsbury's** • 116 Borough High St

Map 107 • **Shad Thames**

The elitist Bermondsey, Shad Thames is home to ultra-hip boutiques, glass balconies, and converted warehouses. No café dares exist without its own gallery. Bermondsey Street blossoms as an epicentre of creatives knocking out their latest best-seller over brunch, while the More London space by the Thames is an invigorating crowd-pleaser. Head to so-new-its-still-burping-formula **Shortwave** for indie flicks, and **The Scoop** for top free events.

Cinemas

• **Shortwave** • 10 Bermondsey Sq

Coffee

• **Caffe Nero** • More Pl
• **Caphe House** • 114 Bermondsey St
• **Coffee @ Bermondsey** • 163 Bermondsey St
• **Hej** • 1 Bermondsey St
• **SoBo** • 83 Tower Bridge Rd
• **Tremors** • 37 Bermondsey St

O Landmarks

• **City Hall** • Queen's Walk, More London Development
• **Design Museum** • Shad Thames
• **Fashion and Textile Museum** • 83 Bermondsey St
• **Floating Gardens** • 31 Mill St
• **HMS Belfast** • Morgan's Lane & Tooley St
• **Stompie** • Mandela Way & Page's Walk
• **Tower Bridge** • Tower Bridge Road

Nightlife

• **Cable** • 33 Bermondsey St
• **The Hide** • 39 Bermondsey St
• **Hilton London Tower Bridge** • 5 Tooley St
• **Village East** • 171-173 Bermondsey St
• **The Woolpack** • 98 Bermondsey St

Restaurants

• **Butlers Wharf Chop House** • 36 Shad Thames
• **Casse-Croute** • 109 Bermondsey St
• **Le Pont de la Tour** • 36 Shad Thames
• **M Manze Pie and Mash** • 87 Tower Bridge Rd
• **Magdalen** • 152 Tooley St
• **Pizarro Tapas** • 104 Bermondsey St
• **Village East** • 171-173 Bermondsey St

Shopping

• **Fine Foods** • 218 Long Ln
• **The Design Museum Shop** • 28 Shad Thames
• **Long Lane Deli** • 218 Long Ln
• **Maltby Street Market** • Maltby St

With its mixed bag of winding cobbled streets, council estates, and posh new builds, you can imagine the awkwardness when the new-to-the-neighbourhood clean shirt steps into the the adamantly local Bermondsey boozer. The old-timers are sticking to their guns, and there is a definite dirty side to this on-the-cusp part of town. For quaint Japanese try **Poppy Hana** on Jamaica Road.

Libraries
• **Blue Anchor Library** • Southwark Park Rd

Post Offices
• **Jamaica Road** • 158 Jamaica Rd
• **Southwark Park Road** • 200 Southwark Park Rd

Restaurants
• **Poppy Hana** • 169 Jamaica Rd

Shopping
• **The Kernel Brewery** • 11 Dockley Road Industrial Estate

Supermarkets
• **Co-Op** • 193 Southwark Park Rd
• **Iceland** • 222 Southwark Park

Map 109 · **Southwark Park**

N

1 **2**

River
Thames

Loftie Street
Bevington Street
Waterside Place
Emba Street
Pottery Street
Bermondsey Wall East
surr 150M

King Stairs Close
Fulford Street
Cathay Street
Paradise Street

Rotherhithe Street
Western Street
Railway Avenue
Kenning Street

St. Mary's Church
Street
Mayflower Street
Elephant Lane
Tunnel Road

Rotherhithe

Adam Street
Swan Road
Brunel Road
Rotherhithe Tunnel
Albion Street

Wilson Grove
Margold Street
Cherry Garden Street
Southwark Park Street
Prospect St

Janeway Place

Bermondsey
Main Rd
Perryn Road
Keetons Road

A
John Roll Way
Tranton Road

Collett Road
Storks Road
Webster Road
Drummond Road
Southwark Park Road
Gataker Street
Slippers Place

Jamaica Road A200

**Albin
Memorial
Garden**

King's
Stairs
Gardens

Lower Road A200

Neptune Street
Moodkee Street
Renforth Street

ROTHERHITH
Canada Wate

Culling Road

Surrey Quays Road
Dial Porters Way

Ca
Wa

Clements Road

Stalham St

◄**108**

Banyard Rd

Layard Square

Layard Street
Frankland Cl

Ann Moss Way
Ann Moss Way

►**110**

Gomm Road

**Gomm
Road**

orange Place
Hothfield Place

Hithe Grove
Gate

Bombay St
Ada Archer Lane

**Southwark Park
Road**

Raymouth Road A2206
Almond Road
Aspinden Road
Nelldale Road
Abbeyfield Road

**Southwark
Park**

►**111**

Canute Gdns
Hadriel Gro

Lower Rd
Rotherhithe Old Road

B
Tasso Rd
Anchor Road
Roseberry Street
Galleywall Road
Lynton Road

Abbeyfield Road

Hawkstone Road

Lucey Road

Rotherhithe New Road A2208

Debnams Road
Corbetts Lane
Corbetts Passage

Shirwood Street
Millender Walk

▼**116**

Weyhill Rd

Rotherhithe New Road

St. Helena Road

Sheppard
Drive
Hyson Rd
Jarrow Road
Alpine Road
Eugenia Road
Concorde Way

Rossetti Road
Stubbs Drive

Island Road
Oldfield Grove

| 0.25 mile | 0.25 km |

Southwark Park

Map 109

Bordered by tower blocks and the unfortunate juxtaposition of a nursing home and undertaker's, you might toy with taking your picnic elsewhere. But step inside, because it's every bit the oasis that local hero Dr Salter hoped it would be. Well-spent investment has given it a boating lake, rose garden, wildlife area, and the inspired Café Gallery Projects. Nip to **The Angel** afterwards for cheap beers and river views.

Nightlife

- **Ancient Foresters** • 282 Southwark Park Rd
- **The Angel** • 101 Bermondsey Wall E

Map 110 · **Rotherhithe (West) / Canada Water**

Rotherhithe (West) / Canada Water

Map 110

If residential flats are your thing, you'll love Rotherhithe West. Not if bars are your thing though. Or shops. Or life. But among the warren of apartments is **The Mayflower**, one of the greatest historical pubs in London, with the grave of the Mayflower ship's captain in the churchyard opposite. Entertain your dad at the **Brunel Museum**, and jog or snog your way along this serene stretch of Thames path.

Coffee
• **Brunel Museum Café** • Railway Ave

O Landmarks
• **Brunel Museum** • Railway Ave & Rotherhithe St

Libraries
• **Rotherhithe Library** • Albion St

Nightlife
• **The Albion** • 20 Albion St
• **The Mayflower** • 117 Rotherhithe St
• **Old Salt Quay** • 63 Rotherhithe St
• **The Ship** • 39 St Marychurch St

Post Offices
• **Lower Road Rotherhithe** • 142 Lower Rd

Restaurants
• **Café Silka** • 30 Albion St
• **Mayflower** • 117 Rotherhithe St
• **The Rainbow** • 33 Brunel Rd
• **Simplicity** • 1 Tunnel Rd

Map 111 · **Rotherhithe (East) / Surrey Quays** Ⓝ

River Thames **1** **2**

Rotherhithe Tunnel

Sovereign Crescent

Rotherhithe Street
Road

Edward Square

Rotherhithe Road

Lavender Road

St. Paul's
Ave

Nugent Crescent

Byfields Rd

St. Paul's Close

St. Paul's
Sports
Ground

Lavender
Pond Nature
Park

Heron Place

Acorn Walk

Rotherhithe Street

Salter Road S205

Globe Pond Road

Staples Close

Buckters Rents

Byfield Pines

Katharine Close

Fisher Athletic
(London)

Foundry
Close

Farrins Rents

Lavado Mews

Football Club
Ground
(Surrey Docks
Stadium)

Timber Pond Road

Stave Yard Road

Brewhouse Walk

Capstan Way

Silver Walk

Dean Road

Midship
Close

Hull Close

Fir Trees
Close

Russia Dock Road

Byfield Close

Surrey
Water

Gunwhale
Close

Mellish
Sports
Ground

Bedwood Road

Rotherhithe Street

Clarence
Mews

Surrey Water Road

Hurley
Close

Teak Close

Salter Road

Brunel Road

Marlow
Way

Cressy
Court

Thame Road

Dock Hill Avenue

Stave Hill
Ecological
Park

Holyoake
Court

Bryan Road

Kinburn St

Schooner
Cl

Barnfield
Close

Trimmerings
Close

Greenacre
Square

Bryan Road

Windrose
Close

Clipper Cl

Poolmans Street

Baltic Ct

Stave
Hill

Downtown Road

Spence
Close

Swan Road

Christopher
Close

Garter Way

Middleton Dr

Archangel Street

Russia Dock
Woodland

Hamilton
Close

Plough Way

Victory Way

O Surrey
Docks Farm

Needleman Street

Steers Way

Vaughan Street

Wyatt Close

Albatross Way

Roberts Close

Shipwright Road

Rediff Est

Surrey Quays Road

◄110

Canada Street

Quebec Way

Lovell Place

Oslo Square

Elgar Street

Canute Gardens

Canada
Water

ROTHERHITHE

Rediff Est

Norway Gate

Bergen
Square

Gulliver Street

Jessop Street

A200

◄109

Teredo Street

Plover Way

Norway Gate

Finland Street

South Sea Street

**Surrey
Quays**

Redriff Road A2202

Omega Gate

Quay
Dock

Helsinki Square

Lower Road A200

Brunswick Quay

Cope Street

◄116

Trundleys Road

Worgan Street

Greenland
Dock

Rope Street

◄118

Hawkstone Rd

Mayflower Street

Greenland Quay

117
▼

Sweden Gate

South
Dock

Plough Way

Trident St

Street B206

Boat Lifter Way

Lighter Close

Neptune Street

Dunnage Crescent

Tissington Close

Plough Way

St. Georges Mews

B206 **PLOUGH WAY**

St. Georges
Square

`0.25 mile` `0.25 km`

It still has some dodgy estates, but Rotherhithe East is blossoming in a clean-cut city-worker kind of way. The docks are delightful and have resisted the chain bars—instead allowing great little independents like **Wibbley Wobbley** and **The Moby Dick** to flourish. Trying to be healthy? Enjoy lunch among the goats at wholesome **Surrey Docks Farm Café**, and visit **Decathlon** for sport equipment paradise.

Cinemas

- **Odeon Surrey Quays** • Redriff Rd & Surrey Quays Rd

Landmarks

- **Surrey Docks Farm** • Rotherhithe St

Nightlife

- **Blacksmith's Arms** • 257 Rotherhithe St
- **Moby Dick** • 6 Russell Place, off Greenland Dock
- **Ship & Whale** • 4 Gulliver St
- **Whelan's** • 11 Rotherhithe Old Rd
- **Wibbley Wobbley** • South Dock Marina, Rope St

Restaurants

- **Café East** • 100 Redriff Rw
- **Café Nabo** • Surrey Docks Farm, Rotherhithe St

Shopping

- **Decathlon** • Surrey Quays Rd

Supermarkets

- **Tesco** • Redriff Rd

Kennington / Elephant and Castle

Map 112

Massive change is being promised in Elephant and Castle, although when and for whom is quite debatable. With masses of social housing lost with the closure of the Heygate Estate, the area could be set to become another drab luxury development a la Docklands. Find out more at **56a Infoshop**, or take your mind off it with a huge pile of potato pancakes at **Mamuska**.

O Landmarks

• **56A** • 56 Crampton St

Libraries

• **Brandon Library** • Cooks Rd
• **Durning Library** • 167 Kennington Ln

Nightlife

• **Brasserie Tolouse Lautrec** • 140 Newington Butts
• **Corsica Studios** • 5 Elephant Rd
• **Dog House** • 293 Kennington Rd
• **The Old Red Lion** • 42 Kennington Park Rd
• **Prince of Wales** • Cleaver Sq
• **South London Pacific** • 340 Kennington Rd

Post Offices

• **Kennington Park** • 410 Kennington Park Rd

Restaurants

• **Brasserie Tolouse Lautrec** • 140 Newington Butts
• **Dragon Castle** • 114 Walworth Rd
• **La Bodeguita** • Elephant & Castle Shopping Centre
• **Lobster Pot** • 3 Kennington Ln
• **Mamuska** • 233 Elephant and Castle Shopping Centre

Shopping

• **Pricebusters Hardware** •
  311 Elephant & Castle Shopping Centre
• **Recycling** • 110 Elephant Rd

Supermarkets

• **Iceland** • 300 Elephant & Castle Shopping Centre

239

Map 113 • Walworth

Map 113 • Walworth

Arch St

Meadow St

Castle St SE1

1

County Street

County Street

Theobald St

Bartholomew St

Brick

Layers

2

Arms A2

Tower

Old Kent Road A2

Aberdour

New Kent Road A201

106

New Kent Road A2

107

New Kent Road A2

Searles

Paragon Ms

Searles Road

Leroy St

Preston

Elephant & Castle Shopping Center

Deacon Way

Rodney Place

Baytree Ms

Munton Road

Worseter Ms

Congreve

Comus Pl

Elephant Road

Deacon Way

NEWINGTON

Deacon Way

Balfour Street

Elba Place

John Maurice Cl

Henshaw Street

Chatham Street

Darwin Street

SE Gerald Road

Mason St

Cross

Townsend Street

A

Wolaston Close

Walworth Road A215

Heygate Street

Brandon Street

Victory Place

Rodney Road

Salisbury Close

Balfour St

Darwin Court Row

Barlow St

Catesby St

Beckway St

Hampton Street

Heygate Estate

Wansey Street

Larcom Street

Larcom St

Larcom St

Club

Wadding Street

Stead Street

Orb Street

Rodney Road

Nursery Row

Elsted

Herring Bells

Halpin Pl

Bath

Tisdall Pl

Flint Street

Tatum St

Congreve St

Dashwood Way

Robert Close

Ethel St

Charleston Street

Colman Street

Brandon Street

Town

Deans

Buildings

Dawes Street

East Street

Sedan Way

112

Cranmore St

Peacock St

Iliffe Yard

Iliffe St

Arment Road

WALWORTH

Occupation Road

Larcom Street

Walworth Commercial Grove

Aspian, Dr

King & Queen Street

Moreshatt Street

Portland Street

East Street

North Church Walk

Merrow Walk

Thurlow Street

114

Manor Place

Penton Place

East Street Market

Pilton Place

Pilton Place

East Street

Blackwood Street

Trafalgar Street

Dawes Street

Merrow Street

Dale St

Merrow Walk

Thurlow Street

Manor Place

Matara Ms

Penrose Grove

Bronti Close

Date Street

Faraday Gardens

Wooler Street

Burton Gro

Aylesbury Road

Villa Street

Browning St

Merrow Street

Inville Road

Inville Road

Beaconsfield Road

B

Surrey Gardens

Manor Close

Barrett Close

Sturgeon Rd

Penrose Street

Sutherland Walk

Beck Pl

Cadiz Street

Liverpool Grove

Liverpool Grove

Urlwin St

Street

Roland Way

Portland Street

Villa Street

Chester Close

Pasley Close

Penrose Street

Sutherland St

Sut Sq

Macleod Street

Merrow Street

Lytham Street

Spectrum Place

Queen's Row

Sondes Street

Phelp Street

Hopwood Road

Carter Close

Eglington St

Fielding Street

Long Lane

Chia St

Empress St

Arnside Street

Hursley

Westmoreland Road

Villa Street

Draco St

Olney Rd

Peller Street

Dartford St

Gateway

Red Lion Close

Boyson Close

Bradenham Close

Beaconsfield Road

B214

Lorrimore Road

Square

John Ruskin Street

Boundary Lane

Albany Ms

Albany Road B214

Canal

122

Burgess Park Kart Track

Olney Road

Hillingdon Street

Harding Close

Denton Court

Grosvenor Terrace

Albany Street

Camberwell

Addington

Albany Road

Wells Way

New Church Road

Burgess Park

121

0.25 mile

0.25 km

Oh, Walworth. With all this about the Elephant and Castle redevelopment, why do we get the funny feeling you will never change? From the excessive amount of Gregg's bakeries along Walworth Road, to the 'who really buys these things?' tat at **East Street Market**, Walworth's lack of motivation is somehow endearing. **La Luna** for pizza is a find, as is **The Beehive** pub.

Coffee
• **Ranya Café** • 314 Walworth Rd

Landmarks
• **East Street Market** • Walworth Rd & East St
• **Heygate Estate** • Deacon Way & Heygate St

Libraries
• **Newington Library** • 157 Walworth Rd

Nightlife
• **Banana's Bar** • 374 Walworth Rd
• **The Beehive** • 60 Carter St
• **Red Lion** • 407 Walworth Rd

Post Offices
• **Walworth Road** • 234 Walworth Rd

Restaurants
• **La Luna** • 380 Walworth Rd

Shopping
• **Threadneedleman Tailors** • 187 Walworth Rd
• **Walworth Surplus Stores** • 211 Walworth Rd

Supermarkets
• **Iceland** • 332 Walworth Rd

Map 114 • **Old Kent Road (West) / Burgess Park** (N)

WALWORTH

Surrey Square Park

Surrey Gro

Burgess Park

Loncroft Road

Burgess Park

Burgess Park Ball Track

Old Kent Road A2

Mandela Way

B203 Dunton Road

Southwark Park Road A2206

Rolls Road

Old Kent Road

Albany Road B214

Trafalgar Avenue B215

Surrey Linear Canal Park

St. Georges Way

Peckham Library

107

108

115

113

122

123

0.25 mile   0.25 km

Now that the 51-acre Burgess Park has been given an £8 million facelift (due to tireless community campaigning), locals have good reason to be smug as they enjoy the 30ft water fountains, 5k running track, or any of the other many new additions on their doorstep. For something different, stroll along the old canal and connect with ghosts of Peckham past.

Coffee
• **Chumleigh Gardens Café** • Chumleigh St

Landmarks
• **The Animatronic Fireman** • Old Kent Rd
• **Peckham Library** • 122 Peckham Hill St

Post Offices
• **Old Kent Road** • 240 Old Kent Rd

Restaurants
• **Shu Castle** • 194-202 Old Kent Rd

Supermarkets
• **Tesco** • 107 Dunton Rd

There must be something to this portion of Old Kent Road, as the Pearly Kings and Queens won't shut up about the whole thing. As far as we can tell, it's not that much more than a giant Asda. Walk along Bird In Bush Road to laugh at its name and over to Peckham Park Road for a damn good fry-up at **Roma Café**.

Libraries
• **East Street Library** • 168 Old Kent Rd

Supermarkets
• **ASDA** • Old Kent Rd & Ossory Rd

Restaurants
• **Roma Café** • 1 Peckham Park Rd

Map 116 · South Bermondsey

(N)

1 2

Southwark Park

Baryard Rd
Fenner Close
Layard Road
Drummond Road
Frankland Close
Park Road
Southwark
Abingdon Road
Frankland Road
Neldale Road

A2206 Raymouth Road A2206

Canute Gdns
Rotherhithe Old Rd A200
Redriff
Surrey Quays
Lower Road
Cope St
Rodney Grove

Harkstone Road
A2208 Rot. New Rd
Rotherhithe New Road A2208
Abbeyfield Rd

A2206 Almond Road

Southwark Park Road
Rosebery Road
Galleywall Road
Rosebery St
Lynton Road

Clements Road
Corbetts Lane
Millender Walk
Luxford St
Wardon St
St. Helena Road
Oldfield Grove
Concorde Way
Island Road
Lambourne Grove
Alpine Road
Enid Street
Goldsworthy Gdns
Reculver Road
Silwood Street
Sketchley Gdns
Somerfield Street

A

Corbetts Passage
Jarrow Road
Rotherhithe New Road A2208

◄108

309

South Bermondsey Rail ⇥

Sheppard Drive
Rossetti Road
Stubbs Drive
Stubbs Drive
Stubbs
Stubbs Drive
Hyson Road

Masters Dr
Masters Dr
Big Drive
Ryder Drive
Kings Arch
Holywell Close
Det Close
Wood Close
Green Close
Cranswick Road
Delaford Road
Creeton
Ablett Street
Brantcome Road
Ildertron Road
Bram Gro

Barkworth Road

Verney Road
Varcoe Road
Varcoe Road
Gerards Ct
Eagle Close

Peckham
Zampa Road
Boleyn Road

○
**Millwall FC
(The Den)**

117►

Stockholm Road

Surrey Canal Rd

◄115

B

Stevenson
Weald
Rollin St
B204
Rotherhithe New Road A2208
Verney Way

Record Street
Hatcham Road
Rollins Road
Ormside Street
Ildertron Road
Rollins Street
Lovelinch Close
Sharratt Street
Lovelinch Close
Sharratt Street
Lovelinch Close
Hornshay Street
Manor Grove

Bridge Meadows
Myers Lane
Mercury Way

Bridge House Meadows

Southlands Road
Ruby Street
Ruby Triangle
Mustock St
Hornshay Street

Old Kent Road A2
Devon Street
Devonshire Grove
Sylvan Grove
Waes

Ethnard Rd
Pencraig Way
Camelot St
Ph Bush Road

124
▼

Hunsdon Road
John Williams
Water Lane
Water Lane
Edric Road
Farrow Lane
Wagner St

0.25 mile   0.25 km

There may be more to this area than we've listed, but the fact is we like you. We want to see you live to enjoy our favourite picks among these pages. If you make the wrong kind of eye contact as you tremble past the Millwall flags fluttering menacingly from the balconies, then we're worried we'll lose a much-loved reader. Swallow your valuables and back slowly away.

O Landmarks

• **Millwall FC Stadium** • Zampa Rd & Bolina Rd

Map 117 · **Deptford (West)**

Apparently, developers have their eye on Deptford West. You've really got to hope so. The Blitz did its best, but the area came back with hastily built and charmless 50s tower blocks. Still, like the rest of Deptford it's going through a gradual regeneration as young buyers move in to make their money stretch.

Map 118 · **Deptford (Central)**

When Christopher Marlowe was murdered in a Deptford tavern, Deptford hit its nightlife peak. That was 1593. Today, while the rest of London turns everything into a pub, Deptford turns its pubs into churches. Without beer, you may want to drown your sorrows in the Thames, but even that is thwarted: here the Thames path breaks to take you through neglected residential areas instead. Escape!

 Nightlife

• **Lord Palmerston** • 81 Childers St

 **Post Offices**

• **Evelyn Street** • 301 Evelyn St

If you're one for a bargain, then this is your place. Browse the charity shops for dresses rumored to be donated by local prostitutes, pick up all manner of junk from the market or visit one of the many fishmongers, who have been known to sell live eels and sharks. And if you want to fit in with the countless old punks drinking cider get yourself a face tattoo on Church Street.

Coffee

• **The Deptford Project** • 121 Deptford High St

Nightlife

• **The Bird's Nest** • 32 Deptford Church St
• **Bunker Club** • 46 Deptford Broadway
• **Dog & Bell** • 116 Prince St

Post Offices

• **New Cross** • 500 New Cross Rd

Restaurants

• **The Big Red Pizza Bus** • 30 Deptford Church St
• **Chaconia Roti** • 26 Deptford High St
• **Manzes** • 204 Deptford High St
• **The Waiting Room** • 142 Deptford High St

Shopping

• **Deptford Market** • Deptford High St

Supermarkets

• **Iceland** • 112 Deptford High St

Greenwich

Map 120

With the **Cutty Sark** magnificently restored and Greenwich's status as an Olympic Borough, the area has been given a new, touristy lease of life recently. There's still plenty of quirky pubs and shops to let you escape the crowds though, from vintage clothes and dusty vinyl at **The Beehive** to artisan beer at **Greenwich Union**. And anyway, if you do want to do some proper sight-seeing, what better place to do it?

Cinemas

• **Greenwich Picturehouse** • 180 Greenwich High Rd

Coffee

• **Rhodes Bakery** • 37 King William Walk
• **Starbucks** • 54 Greenwich Church St

O Landmarks

• **Cutty Sark** • King William Walk & Romney Rd
• **Greenwich Foot Tunnel** •
  Greenwich Church St & Thames St

Libraries

• **West Greenwich Library** • Greenwich High Rd

Nightlife

• **The Beehive** • 60 Carter St
• **The Greenwich Union** • 56 Royal Hill
• **O2** • O2 Arena
• **Up The Creek** • 302 Creek Rd

Post Offices

• **Greenwich** • 261 Greenwich High Rd

Restaurants

• **Craft London** • 1 Greenwich Pl
• **Goddard's Pie Shop Booth** •
  Fountain Court (off Greenwich Church St)
• **Greenwich Park Bar & Grill** • 1 King William Walk
• **The Hill** • 89 Royal Hill
• **Piano Restaurant** • 131 Greenwich High Rd
• **Rivington Grill** • 178 Greenwich High Rd

Shopping

• **Black Vanilla** • 5 College Approach
• **Bullfrogs** • 22 Greenwich Church St
• **Cheeseboard** • 26 Royal Hill
• **Johnny Rocket** • 10 College Approach
• **Meet Bernard** • 23 Nelson Rd
• **Mr Humbug** • Greenwich Market
• **Music & Video Exchange** • 23 Greenwich Church St

Camberwell (West)

This slowly reviving segment of Camberwell brings together a minority of polite arty types in the crumbling-yet-quaint town houses of Camberwell New Road with take-no-prisoners urbanites as seen in the chaos of Denmark Hill and its pointless **Butterfly Walk** (why?). The neighbourhood good stuff includes music bargains (**Rat Records**), killer Indian (**New Dewaniam**), and the unpronounceable Central Asian eatery at the Pasha Hotel: **Kazakh Kyrgyz Restaurant.**

Coffee
• **Kings Cafe** • 120 Denmark Hill

Libraries
• **Minet Library** • 52 Knatchbull Rd

Nightlife
• **The Joiners Arms** • 35 Denmark Hill
• **The Sun of Camberwell** • 61-63 Coldharbour Ln

Post Offices
• **Camberwell Green** • 25 Denmark Hill

Restaurants
• **Kazakh Kyrgyz** • 158 Camberwell Rd
• **New Dewaniam** • 225 Camberwell New Rd
• **Rock Steady Eddie's** • 2 Coldharbour Ln
• **Viet Cafe** • 75 Denmark Hill
• **Zeret Kitchen** • 216 Camberwell Rd

Shopping
• **Butterfly Walk Shopping Centre** • Denmark Hill
• **Men's Traditional Shoes** • 171 Camberwell Rd
• **Rat Records** • 348 New Camberwell Rd

Supermarkets
• **Co-Op** • 177 Camberwell New Rd
• **Iceland** • 120 Camberwell Rd

Map 121

Camberwell (East)

Map 122

Maybe it was Kevin Spacey moving to the Grove, maybe something else entirely, but this area of Camberwell, in particular Church Street, has become something of an eating and drinking mecca in recent years. Work through the mammoth selection of craft beers in **Stormbird** before soaking it up with excellent kebabs from **FM Mangal**, high-end tapas from **Angels & Gypsies**, or regional Chinese from **Silk Road**.

Coffee

- **Daily Goods** • 36 Camberwell Church St
- **Fowlds Café** • 3 Addington Square

Libraries

- **Camberwell Library** • 17 Camberwell Church St

Nightlife

- **Grand Union** • 26 Camberwell Grove
- **The Flying Dutchman** • 156 Wells Wy
- **Hermit's Cave** • 28 Camberwell Church St
- **Stormbird** • 25 Camberwell Church St

Post Offices

- **Southampton Way** • 156 Southampton Wy

Restaurants

- **Angels & Gypsies** • 29 Camberwell Church St
- **Caravaggio** • 47 Camberwell Church St
- **Crooked Well** • 16 Grove Ln
- **Falafel** • 27 Camberwell Church St
- **FM Mangal** • 54 Camberwell Church St
- **Silk Road** • 49 Camberwell Church St
- **Wuli Wuli** • 15 Camberwell Church St

Shopping

- **Architectural Rescue** • 1-3 Southampton Way
- **Cowling and Wilcox** • 8-12 Orpheus St

Map 123 • **Peckham**

Peckham

Map 123

As old pubs, pool halls, telephone boxes, and coal bunkers are converted into galleries faster than you can say 'fixed gear bicycle', it's safe to say Peckham is the epicenter of the new(ish) South London art scene. But don't be scared off—get the cheapest lunch for miles at **Manze's** or pay a visit to the art/music/religion/theatre behemoth that is **The Bussey Building**.

☕ Coffee

- **Cafe Viva** • 44 Choumert Rd
- **Petitou** • 63 Choumert Rd
- **Small White Elephant** • 28 Choumert Rd

📖 Libraries

- **Peckham Library** • 122 Peckham Hill St

🎬 Movie Theaters

- **Peckham Multiplex** • 95 Rye Ln

🍸 Nightlife

- **Bar Story** • 213 Blenheim Grove
- **The Bussey Building** • 133 Rye Ln
- **Canavan's Peckham Pool Club** • 188 Rye Ln
- **Dead Dolls House** • 1 Clayton Rd
- **The Four Quarters** • 187 Rye Ln
- **Frank's Cafe** • 95 Rye Ln
- **The Montpelier** • 43 Chomert Rd

✉ Post Offices

- **Peckham** • 121 Peckham High St
- **Rye Lane** • 199 Rye Ln

🍴 Restaurants

- **Agrobeso African Cuisine** • 139 Peckham High St
- **Dead Dolls House** • 1 Clayton Rd
- **Ganapati** • 38 Holly Grove
- **M. Manze Pie and Mash** • 105 Peckham High St
- **Miss Tapas** • 45 Choumert Road
- **Obalende Suya Express** • 43 Peckham High St
- **Peckham Refreshment Rooms** • 12 Blenheim Grove

🛍 Shopping

- **Curious Science** • 5 Commercial Wy
- **Persepolis** • 30 Peckham High St
- **Primark** • 51 Rye Ln

🛒 Supermarkets

- **Iceland** • 74 Rye Ln

Peckham East (Queen's Road)

Map 124

Although the local halfway house ensures the streets are filled with beggars, and the buses passing through en route to the continent make you wish you were somewhere else, this small pocket of Peckham isn't really so bad. Head for great African food at **805** or take a short walk to the incredible Victorian **Nunhead Cemetery**.

Libraries

• **Nunhead Library** • Gordon Rd

Restaurants

• **805** • 805 Old Kent Rd
• **Tops Carribean Takeaway** • 173 Queens Rd

Map 125 • **New Cross Gate**

N

Rollins Street

1

2

Bridge Meadows

Myers Lane

Juno Way

Rolt Street

Folkeste Garde

Lovelinch Close

Mercury Way

Bridge House Meadows

Samuel Close

Sanford Walk

Knoyle Street

Church Street

Whitche

Lovelinch Close

Cold Blow Lane

Sanford Street

Chipley St

Hornshay Street

John Willia ns Close

Cordwain Lane

118

Cottesbrook Street

Nynehead

A

116

Hunsdon Road

Joseph Hardcastle Close

Sterling Gardens

Bawtree

Water Lane

Avonley Road

Edric Road

Camplin Street

Farrow Lane

Monson Road

Tarragon Close

Southern Way

Pump Lane

Wrigglesworth Street

Leylang Road

Robert Lowe Close

Heathfield Ct

Barlborough Street

Goodwood Road

Wardalls Grove

Reaston Street

Ventnor Road

Auburn Close

Eckington Gardens

Egmont Street

Brocklehurst Street

New Cross Road A2

Hatfield Close

Casella Road

Romney Close

124

Billington Road

Lubbock Street

Pankhurst Close

Kender Street A202

Faulkner Street

Fisher's Court

Briant Street

Hatcham Park Road

126

Nettleton Road

Hatch

B

Kenwood Avenue

Besson Street A202

Hatcham Park Mews

Harts Lane

New Cross Gate

Mylis Close

New Cross Road A2

Godley Close

Lanchester Way

Queens Road A202

Waller Road

Erlanger Road

Pepys Road

Troutbeck Road

Jerningham Road

Drive

| 0.25 mile | 0.25 km |

Since the sad demise of the Montague Arms this strip has become even more of a no man's land—not quite New Cross but not quite Peckham. Apart from a semi-decent junk shop and a not-so-great retail park, there's not much to see. Do yourself a favor and stroll on into one of the aforementioned neighborhoods—or jump on the brilliant London Overground and be in Dalston in no time.

 ## Post Offices

• **New Cross Gate** • 199 New Cross Rd

 ## Restaurants

• **Hong Kong City** • 43 New Cross Rd

Once hailed as the new Shoreditch, this corner of Lewisham has managed to provide us with all the good stuff about hipsterville, while avoiding everything bad. So while there's regularly excellent live music at **New Cross Inn**, you're still guaranteed a smack around the chops off some bloke in the **Hobgoblin** if you try and explain why the blank sheets of paper you stuck on the wall really have a deeper meaning.

O Landmarks

• **Ben Pimlott Building** • University of London, New Cross

Libraries

• **Goldsmiths Library** • Lewisham Wy

Nightlife
• **Amersham Arms** • 388 New Cross Rd
• **Marquis of Granby** • 322 New Cross Rd
• **New Cross Inn** • 323 New Cross Rd

Post Offices
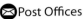
• **Lewisham Way** • 150 Lewisham Wy
• **New Cross Road** • 500 New Cross Rd

Restaurants

• **Birdie Num Nums** • 11 Lewisham Wy
• **The London Peculiar** • 399 New Cross Rd

Supermarkets

• **Iceland** • 277 New Cross Rd
• **Sainsbury's** • 263 New Cross Rd

Map 127 • Coldharbour Lane / Herne Hill (West) Ⓝ

Serenaders Road
Serenaders Road
Peckford Place
Villa Road
Angell Road
Fawley Road
Rupert Edine
Styles Gardens
Major Close
Loughborough Junction
Padfield Road
Luxor Street
Harbour Rd
Bangemouth Road
Northwand Road
Kemerton Road
Cambria Road
Bicknell Road

Max Roach Park
A23
Wiltshire Mews
Peng Freud Road
St. James's Crescent
Sault Place
Stansted Gardens
Ridgeway Road
Ramsar Road
Hinton Road
Herne Hill Road
A2217
Wyck Gardens

Western Rd
Millbrook Road
Barrington Road
Coldharbour Lane A2217
Loughborough Park
Pablo Neruda Close
Langston Hughes Close
Orantside Road
Oakbank Grove
Rush
Par

A

Blacktree Ms
Gresham Road
Valentia Place
Moorland Road
Walt Whitman Close
Codella Close
Dylan Rd
Shakespeare Road
B222
Heron Road
Poplar Rd
Brixton Road
Popes Road
Brixton Station Road
⇆ Ⓣ **Brixton**
Atlantic Road
B223
Electric Lane
◀**145**
Clarewood Walk
Geneva Drive
Corn Drive
Broughton Dr
Caxton Drive
Clifford Drive
Jessop Road
James Joyce Walk
Alice Walker Walk
Louise Bennett Close
Derek Walcott Close
B222
Loughton Road
Farnridale Avenue
Brathwood Road

Rushcroft Road
Saltoun Road
Kellett Road
◀**144**
Marcus Garvey Wy
Railton Road B223
Mervan Road
Tarmit Road
Bankton Rd
Probert Road
Jeff Road
Mantego Close
Jessop Road
Mayall Road
Robert Burns Mews
Gubyon Avenue
Cosbyctot Ave
Osborne Close
Kestrel Avenue
Dorchester Drive

B
St. Matthew's Gardens
Gdns
Effra Road A204
◀**150**
Bailey Mews
Trelawn Road
Morval Road
Chaucer Road
Spenser Road
Effra Parade
Railton Road
Milton Road
Mantord Road
Regent Road
Herne Place
Herne Hill Rail
⇆
Hall Mo

Stockwell Park Road
Crownstone Road
Brixton Water Lane
ay Gardens
Brixton Water Lane
Brixton Water Lane A2214
Tree Hill A204
Josephine Avenue
Aoloch Road
PAGE **328**
Brockwell Park
Dulwich Road A2214
Hurst Street
Romer St.
Cary

⬆**121**
128▶

0.25 mile   0.25 km

Coldharbour Lane / Herne Hill (West)

Map 127

There don't seem to be as many shootings on Coldharbour Lane as there used to be. Maybe the crack dealers are just quietly selling the stuff, as somebody on The Wire once sensibly advised. Or maybe they've all been converted by the pleasant conservatory at **The Florence**, invigorating swims at the **Brockwell Lido**, and handmade jams from the **Blackbird Bakery**. Yes, that's probably it.

Nightlife

- **The Commercial** • 210 Railton Rd
- **The Florence** • 133 Dulwich Rd
- **The Prince Regent** • 69 Dulwich Rd

Restaurants

- **Beanery** • Coldharbour Ln
- **Café Prov** • 2 Half Moon Ln
- **Ichiban Sushi** • 58 Atlantic Rd
- **Naughty Piglets** • 28 Brixton Water Ln
- **New Fujiyama** • 5 Vining St

Shopping

- **Blackbird Bakery** • 208 Railton Rd

Coffee

- **Pullens** • 293 Railton Rd

Map 128 · **Denmark Hill / Herne Hill (East)**

Denmark Hill / Herne Hill (East)

Map 128

There's something quaintly grounded about the leafy Victorian suburb of Herne Hill where funky neo-hippies settle into dreadlocked nuclear families. Denmark Hill sits at its top, with its imposing Salvation Army training grounds, following on to Ruskin Park for ornamental ponds and Edwardian ruins. Half Moon Lane plays main drag----get lost in a book at **Tales on Moon Lane** and lost in a bowl of noodles at **Lombok**.

 Emergency Rooms

- **King's College Hospital •**
  Denmark Hill & Champion Park

 Libraries

- **Carnegie Library •** 188 Herne Hill Rd

 Post Offices

- **Crossthwaite Avenue •** 6 Crossthwaite Ave

 Restaurants

- **Lombok •** 17 Half Moon Ln
- **Number 22 •** 22 Half Moon Ln

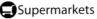 Shopping

- **Tales on Moon Lane •** 25 Half Moon Ln

Supermarkets

- **Sainsbury's •** 132 Herne Hill

East Dulwich is where your ex-flatmate finally settled down and now won't shut up about taramasalata, babies, and how he's only fifteen minutes from London Bridge by train over perfect cocktails. Dodge baguettes, pushchairs, and delis along Lordship Lane, just don't get sucked in. Try **The Sea Cow** for fish & chips and grab a pint at **The Palmerston**.

Coffee
• **Caffe Nero** • Lordship Ln

Libraries
• **Grove Vale library** • 25 Grove Vale

Nightlife
• **East Dulwich Tavern** • 1 Lordship Ln

Restaurants
• **Anderson & Co** • 139 Bellenden Rd
• **The Palmerston** • 91 Lordship Ln

**Supermarkets**
• **Iceland** • 84 Lordship Ln
• **Sainsbury's** • 80 Dog Kennel Hill

Map 130 · **Peckham Rye**

0.25 mile   0.25 km

A noticeboard on Peckham Rye Common alleges that ancient British Queen Boudicca was finally defeated by the Romans here. Anyone suggesting that the very middle class streets around North Cross Road—with its market, twee sweets at **Hope and Greenwood**, and lazy Sunday lunches at **The Rye**—have anything to do with Peckham as we know it might get the same treatment.

## Coffee

- **Blue Mountain Café** • 18 N Cross Rd
- **Old Spike Roastery** • 54 Peckham Rye

Nightlife

- **The Gowlett** • 62 Gowlett Rd
- **The Rye** • 31 Peckham Rye

Restaurants

- **Artusi** • 161 Bellenden Rd
- **Pedler** • 130 Peckham Rye
- **Thai Corner Cafe** • 44 Northcross Rd
- **The Rye** • 31 Peckham Rye

Shopping

- **Flock and Herd** • 155 Bellenden Rd

KENSINGTON

KNIGH

Holland Park

SOUTH
KENSINGTON

BROMP

WEST
KENSINGTON

CHISWICK

EARLS
COURT

WEST
BROMPTON

CHELSEA

HAMMERSMITH

CASTELNAU

Brompton
Cemetery

BARONS
COURT

WALHAM
GREEN

FULHAM

SANDS
END

BARNES

PARSONS GREEN

132

Thames River

MORTLAKE

Putney Bridge Rd

139

136

137

138

WANDSWORTH

PUTNEY

Wandsworth High St.

West Hill

ROEHAMPTON

WEST
HILL

Richmond
Park

146

Wandsworth
Cemetery

EARLSFIELD

Deer Park

SUMMERST

Wimbledon
Park

Wimbledon
Common

WIMBLEDON

Map 131 • **Vauxhall / Albert Embankment** Ⓝ

1 **2**

Westminster Bridge A302
Westminster Bridge Road Westminster Bridge Road A3202

York Road

Lower Marsh

Launcelot Street
Grindal Street
Frazier Street

Waterloo

Cooper Close
Greenham Close
Murphy Street
Burden Street
Emery Street
Webber Street
Gerridge Street

104

LAMBETH

King's College

PAGE 356

Upper Marsh

Newham Terrace

Centaur Street
Carlisle Lane
Hercules Road
McAuley Close

Lambeth North

Cottesloe Mews
Mead Row
St George's Road

St Georges Road

Royal Street
Tenn Cts

Cosser Street
Morton Place

Geraldine Mary
Harmsworth Park

A
Victoria Tower Garden

Abington Street
A3212

River Thames

Lambeth Palace Road A3036

Lambeth Palace Gardens

Sports Grd

Archbishop's Park

Sidford Place

Lambeth Road A3203

Sail Street

Brook Drive

Walcot Square

Walcot Square

St Mary's Gardens

Bishops Terrace

St Mary's Gardens

Lambeth Palace

Norfolk Row

Pratt Walk

Juxon Street

Bedlam Mews
Hornbeam Close
Walnut Tree Walk

Fitzalan Street

Wincott Street

Lambeth Bridge A3203

Thorney Street

A3212

Lambeth Bridge A3203

Nor folk Row
Old Paradise Street

Lambeth High Street

Lambeth Recreation Ground

Ravent Road

Lollard Street
Gibson Road

Saunders Street

112

Lambeth Walk Open Space

Reedworth Street

B

Millbank

River Thames

Albert Embankment A3036

Lambeth High Street

Whitgift Street
Newport Street

Salamanca Place

Salamanca Street

Salamanca Street

Randall Road
Randall Row

Citadel Place

Pedlars Park

Chilc Place

Lambeth Walk

Stoughton Close

Gibson Road

Beaufoy Walk

Lollard Street

Distin Street

Hotspur Street

Chester Row

Denny Street

White Hart

Tinworth Street

Jonathan Street

Iyers Street

Black Prince Road

Sancroft Street

Maude Way

Cleaver Square

Worgan Street
Wickham Street

Vauxhall Street

Orsett Street

Wynyard Terrace

Courtenay Street

Carnigan Street

Stables Way

A23

Bowden Street
Ravensdon Street

Methley Street

Wigtown Street
Windmill Row

Glasshouse Walk

Laud Street

Tyers Terrace

St Oswald's Place

Tyers Street

Dolland Street

Courtenay Square

Kennington Road

Windmill Row

B

A202

Secret Intelligence Service HQ (MI6)

New Spring Gardens Walk

Spring Gardens

Vauxhall City Farm

Spring Gardens

Vauxhall City Farm

Goding Street

Auckland Street

Glyn Street

St Oswald's Place

Durham Street

Dolland Street

Brangton Road
Cottington Street

Fairham Street

Montford Place

Kennington Green

Clayton Street

135

Bridgefoot A202

134

Vauxhall
Rail

Vauxhall

Kennington Lane A3204

Feel like doin' the Lambeth Walk? You can. Right here. On Lambeth Walk, incidentally. Though nowadays 'doing the Lambeth Walk' is likely to have an entirely less innocent connotation if some of the area's kinkier gay clubs are anything to go by. This part of Vauxhall, under the watchful eye of MI6, is slightly less that way inclined, but maintains its share of hot spots like the now popular Hidden (foiled!). If you're after a sausage fest of another kind, get stuffed at Zeitgeist at the Jolly Gardeners.

Emergency Rooms

• **St Thomas' Hospital** •
  Westminster Bridge Rd & Lambeth Palace Rd

O Landmarks

• **Lambeth Palace** • Lambeth Palace Rd & Lambeth Rd
• **Secret Intelligence Service HQ (MI6)** •
  85 Vauxhall Cross
• **Vauxhall City Farm** • 165 Tyers St

Libraries

• **CILT Resources Library** • 111 Vauxhall Bridge Rd
• **Lambeth Palace Library** • Lambeth Palace Rd

Nightlife

• **Area** • 67 Albert Embankment
• **Eagle London** • 349 Kennington Ln
• **The Royal Vauxhall Tavern** • 372 Kennington Ln
• **Zeitgeist at the Jolly Gardeners** •
  49–51 Black Prince Rd

Post Offices

• **Westminster Bridge Road** • 125 Westminster Bridge Rd

Supermarkets

• **Tesco** • Kennington Ln

Battersea (West)

With no tubes or trains to attract the hoi polloi, Battersea West sits smugly hugging the River Thames, happily cut off from the hustle and bustle of the rest of London. However, with the Imperial Wharf Overground not far away, the commute isn't as bad as it used to be (thanks also to **Mr Coffee**) and the masses flock—mostly for the spacious floor-to-ceiling glass apartments with killer river views. Take in a Sunday lunch at **The Prince Albert** or cook your own with meat from **The Butcher & Grill**.

Map 132

Coffee

• **Mr Coffee** • Hester Rd

Nightlife

• **Barrio** • 14 Battersea Sq
• **The Draft House** • 74 Battersea Bridge Road
• **The Greyhound** • 136 Battersea High St
• **Le QuecumBar** • 42 Battersea High St
• **The Prince Albert** • 85 Albert Bridge Rd
• **The Woodman** • 60 Battersea High St

Post Offices

• **Battersea Bridge Road** • 72 Battersea Bridge Rd
• **York Road** • 533 Battersea Park Rd

Restaurants

• **The Greyhound** • 136 Battersea High St
• **Ransom's Dock** • 35 Parkgate Rd

Supermarkets

• **Sainsbury's** • 326 Battersea Park Rd

Battersea (East)

Map 133

An odd slice of post-industrial London dominated by the derelict Battersea Power Station, there's naff-all here until someone decides what to do with the old hulk and its surrounding domain. In the meantime, try registering for a new pooch at the **Dogs' Home** or cycling around nearby Battersea Park. **The Mason's Arms** serves a decent beer.

Landmarks

- **Battersea Dogs' Home** • 4 Battersea Park Rd
- **Battersea Park Gasometers** • Queenstown Rd & Prince of Wales Dr
- **Battersea Power Station** • 188 Kirtling St

Libraries

- **Battersea Park Library** • 309 Battersea Park Rd

Nightlife

- **The Masons Arms** • 169 Battersea Park Rd

Post Offices

- **Battersea Park Road** • 20 Battersea Park Rd

Shopping

- **London Recumbents** • Battersea Park

Supermarkets

- **Sainsbury's** • 326 Queenstown Rd

South Lambeth

Map 134

With an overground, tube, and extensive bus station, Vauxhall's southern counterpart is remarkably well connected. But it offers a mixed bag. Gritty backwater estates intermix with middle class townhouses and no-nonsense gay clubs. For pastel de nata like nobody's business, hit up Little Portugal on South London Road. Get into industrial fetish at **Club Colosseum's** Club Antichrist. Bite into a fois gras toastie at the **Canton Arms** and wash it down with beer and amateur comedy at **The Cavendish Arms**.

Coffee

• **Starbucks** • 2 S Lambeth Rd

Libraries

• **South Lambeth Library** • 180 S Lambeth Rd

Nightlife

• **Bar Estrela** • 113 S Lambeth Rd
• **The Battersea Barge** • Nine Elms Ln
• **The Cavendish Arms** • 128 Hartington Rd
• **Fire** • 38 Parry St
• **The Hoist** • 47 S Lambeth Rd
• **The Priory Arms** • 83 Lansdowne Wy
• **The Vauxhall Griffin** • 8 Wyvil Rd

Post Offices

• **South Lambeth** • 347 Wandsworth Rd

Restaurants

• **A Toca** • 343 Wandsworth Rd
• **Bar Estrela** • 113 S Lambeth Rd
• **Brunswick House** • 30 Wandsworth Rd
• **Canton Arms** • 177 S Lambeth Rd
• **Hot Stuff** • 19 Wilcox Rd
• **O Moinho** • 355 Wandsworth Rd
• **Tia Maria** • 126 S Lambeth Rd

Shopping

• **Fetish Freak** • 76 Bolton Crescent
• **LASSCO** • 30 Wandsworth Rd
• **New Covent Garden Market** • Nine Elms Ln
• **The Nine Elms Sunday Market** • New Covent Garden

Supermarkets

• **Sainsbury's** • 62 Wandsworth Rd

Map 135 • **Oval**

Oval

Posh town houses rub shoulders somewhat uneasily with housing estates here, and there's no denying the walk from Oval Station can be dodgy, but if you're a fan of cricket, the presence of the Oval cricket ground more than makes up for it. When there's a match on, the area fills to the brim, but normally it's a modest and unimposing neighbourhood. Organic foodies delight in the **Oval Farmers' Market** and vegan ex-squat **The Bonnington Café**.

Map 135

O Landmarks

• **The Oval** • Kennington

 Coffee

• **Bonnington Cafe** • 11 Vauxhall Grove

Nightlife

• **The Brown Derby** • 336 Kennington Park Rd
• **The Fentiman Arms** • 64 Fentiman Rd

Post Offices

• **Brixton Road** • 82 Brixton Rd

Restaurants

• **Adulis** • 44 Brixton Rd
• **Bonnington Café** • 11 Vauxhall Grove
• **Oval Kebab** • 32 Clapham Rd

Map 136 · **Putney**

Putney has a bit of a bipolar personality disorder. On the one side, it's suburban middle England with its rugby and rowing types, on the other, it's increasingly vibrant and hip. The High Street's a bit genteel by day and young-and-up-for-it at night. Try **Ma Goa** for authentic Goan cuisine. For fab brunch head to celebrity chef's **Wallace & Co** or **Moomba Kitchen & Bar**.

Coffee

- **Artisan Coffee** • 203 Upper Richmond Rd
- **BB's Coffee and Muffins** • Putney High St & Chelverton Rd
- **Caffe Nero** • 95 Putney High St
- **Caffe Nero** • 112 Upper Richmond Rd
- **Costa** • 132 Putney High St
- **Grind** • 79 Lower Richmond Rd
- **Pret A Manger** • 121 Putney High St
- **Starbucks** • 117 Putney High St

Libraries

- **Putney Library** • 5 Disraeli Rd

Movie Theaters

- **Odeon Putney** • 26 Putney High St

Nightlife

- **The Boathouse** • Brewhouse Ln
- **Duke's Head** • 8 Lower Richmond Rd
- **The Jolly Gardeners** • 61 Lacy Rd
- **Star & Garter** • 4 Lower Richmond Rd

Post Offices

- **Putney** • 214 Upper Richmond Rd

Restaurants

- **Enoteca Turi** • 28 Putney High St
- **Ma Goa** • 242 Upper Richmond Rd
- **Talad Thai** • 320 Upper Richmond Rd

Supermarkets

- **Sainsbury's** • 2 Werter Rd
- **Waitrose** • Putney High St & Lacy Rd

Map 137 · **Wandsworth (West)**

N

1 | 2

River
Thames

Deodar Road

Merivale Road

Oxford Road

Florian Road

Archway Mews

Blade Mews

Blades Court

Alice Court

Wandsworth
Park

138▶

Esmond Street

Winthorpe Road

Wadham Road

Bective Place

Bective Road

Brandlehow Road

Skelgill Road

Putney Bridge Road A3209

Point Pleasant

Northfields

A

Rockland Road

Fawe Park Road

Prospect Cottages

◀136

Grand
Parade
Ms

Woodlands Way

Oakhill Road

Oakhill Place

Pembridge

Upper Richmond Road A205

East
Putney

Ernshaw Place

Keswick Road

Cavalry
Gardens

Burling
ton Ms

St. Stephens
Gardens

Nor. Ct.

Manfred Road

Schubert Road

Galveston Road

Mexfield Road

Cromford Road

Santos Road

Ericson Close

Kendal

Place

Buttermere Drive

Woodlawn
Close

West Hill

Portinscale Road

Lebanon Road

Lebanon Gar

Askill Drive

West Hill A3

Ringford Road

Haldon Road

B

Penrith Close

Laker Place

Everatt Close

Sedleigh Road

Amerland Road

Keswick Road

West Hill A3

Holm Oak Close

Yalonia Gardens

Coldstream Gardens

Sispara Gardens

Upton Grove

Pentitha Road

0.25 mile | 0.25 km

Dissected by the busy Upper and Lower Richmond Roads, this bit of Wandsworth is a bit lifeless though pleasant enough. The pretty, riverside Wandsworth Park is a huge plus and heaves with locals with the first sniff of sunshine.

Restaurants

• **Miraj** • 123 Putney Bridge Rd
• **Putney Fire Bar & Grill** • 40 Upper Richmond Rd

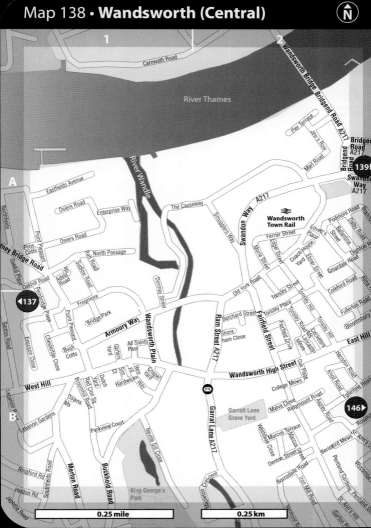

Map 138 · **Wandsworth (Central)**

Wandsworth (Central)

This is East Wandsworth's poorer, uglier cousin—and you've got to feel sorry for it. It's got a drab shopping centre and a four-lane traffic system brings noise and air pollution. On the plus side, plenty of chain stores (Gap, Uniqlo etc.) and a **Cineworld** make life a little easier. To get away from it all, hibernate in the Old York Road. For the best Nepalese food in London, hit **Kathmandu Valley**.

 ## Cinemas

- **Cineworld Wandsworth** • Wandsworth High St & Ram St

 ## Coffee

- **Caffe Nero** • Southside Shopping Centre
- **Coffee Republic** • Wandsworth High St

 ## Nightlife

- **The Cat's Back** • 88 Point Pleasant
- **GJ's** • 89 Garratt Ln
- **The Queen Adelaide** • 35 Putney Bridge Rd

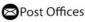 ## Post Offices

- **Wandsworth** • 1 Arndale Walk

 ## Restaurants

- **Brady's** • 513 Old York Rd
- **Kathmandu Valley** • 5 West Hill

Supermarkets

- **Iceland** • Wandsworth High St & Buckhold Rd
- **Sainsbury's** • 45 Garratt Ln
- **Waitrose** • 66 Wandsworth High St

Map 139 · **Wandsworth (East)**

Map 139

Wandsworth (East)

With London's new Overground network and Clapham Junction on its doorstep, this corner of Wandsworth, including what locals call 'the Toast Rack' on East Hill, is becoming more gentrified everyday. You'll hear your share of 'rah's at **Powder Keg Diplomacy**, with its upscale gastro fare and nod to colonial Britain, while yummy mummies stuff their cake holes at **Cake Boy** and practice their French at **Gazette**. Stay true to the neighbourhood's roots with a less than picturesque view of the Thames at **The Waterfront**.

Coffee

- **Birdhouse** • 23 St John's Hill
- **Caffe Nero** • Southside Shopping Centre
- **Coffee Republic** • Wandsworth High St
- **Story Coffee** • 115 St John's Hill

Libraries

- **York Gardens Library** • 34 Lavender Rd

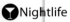Nightlife

- **Powder Keg Diplomacy** • 147 St Johns Hill
- **The Waterfront** • Juniper Dr

Post Offices

- **St Johns Hill** • 7 St John's Hill

Restaurants

- **The Fish Club** • 189 St John's Hill
- **Gazette** • 79 Chatfield Rd

Shopping

- **Cake Boy** • 2 Kingfisher House, Battersea Reach

Map 140 · **Clapham Junction / Northcote Rd**

0.25 mile   0.25 km

Clapham Junction / Northcote Rd

We have a newfound sense of respect for Clapham Junction after it rose like a determined phoenix from the ashes of the summer 2011 riots. Suffering extensive devastation from looters, the neighbourhood dusted itself off with help of volunteers from across the capital and was back in business almost instantly. Seeing the **Party Superstores** open again after nearly burning to the ground is a particular sight for sore eyes. All fancy dress party goers can breathe a sigh of relief.

Coffee

- **Caffe Nero** • 10 St John's Rd
- **Caffe Nero** • 1 Battersea Rise
- **Starbucks** • 3 Northcote Rd

O Landmarks

- **Northcote Road** • Northcote Rd

Libraries

- **Battersea Library** • 265 Lavender Hill
- **Northcote Library** • 155 Northcote Rd

Nightlife

- **Adventure Bar and Lounge** • 91 Battersea Rise
- **B@1 Cocktail Bar** • 85 Battersea Rise
- **Humble Grape** • 2 Battersea Rise

Post Offices

- **Alfriston Road** • 99 Alfriston Rd
- **Battersea** • 202 Lavender Hill

Restaurants

- **Gail's Bread** • 64 Northcote Rd
- **Jack's At The Junction** • 252 Lavender Hill
- **Mien Tay** • 180 Lavender Hill
- **Parisienne** • 225 Lavender Hill
- **Pizza Metro** • 64 Battersea Rise

Shopping

- **Anita's Vintage Fashion Fair** • Battersea Arts Centre, Lavender Hill
- **The Hive Honey Shop** • 93 Northcote Rd
- **Huttons** • 29 Northcote Rd
- **Party Superstores** • 268 Lavender Hill
- **Russ** • 101 Battersea Rise
- **Space NK Apothecary** • 46 Northcote Rd
- **Sweaty Betty** • 136 Northcote Rd
- **TK Maxx** • St John's Rd & Barnard Rd
- **TRAID** • 28 St John's Rd
- **Vintage Market Place** • Battersea Arts Centre
- **Whole Foods Market** • 305 Lavender Hill

Supermarkets

- **ASDA** • 204 Lavender Hill
- **Whole Foods Market** • 305 Lavender Hill
- **Sainsbury's** • Clapham Junction Shopping Centre

Map 140

(297)

Battersea (South)

Apart from the occasional house party, few have reason to go to Battersea South. You either live there, congratulating yourself on your nice Victorian conversion, or you pass through on the way to Clapham or one of the livelier bits of Battersea. The 'action' happens around Lavender Hill. **The Lost Angel** is an eccentrically fabulous boozer that would rather be a mile east or west.

Coffee
• **Captain Corelli** • 132 Battersea Park Rd

Nightlife
• **The Lost Angel** • 339 Battersea Park Rd

Restaurants
• **The Lavender** • 171 Lavender Hill

Shopping
• **Battersea Car Boot Sale** • 401 Battersea Park Rd
• **Comet Miniatures** • 44 Lavender Hill
• **Get A Grip Bicycle Workshop** • 19 Lavender Hill

Map 141

Map 142 · **Clapham Old Town** Ⓝ

1 2

133

St. Philip Sq

Broughton Street

Queenston

Emu Road

Prairie Street

Inglow Road

Stanley Grove

A3216

Queenstown Road

St. Philip Street

Bew'ck Street

Thackeray Road

Tennyson Street

Montefiore Street

Gambetta Street

Heath Road

Dickens Street

Coleridge Close

Silverthorne Road

Frodie Street

Robertson Street

St. Rule Street

Morley Street

Heathbrook Park

Crichop St.

Portslade Road

Westbury Street

Wandsworth Road

B224

Pensbury Place

Pensbury Street

Bradmere Avenue

Netherford Road

Bradmere Avenue

Hesperus

St. Paul's Churchyard

Turret Grove

Stone Close

Iveley Road

A

Robertson Street

Heather Close

Keith Connor Close

Delvino Way

Heather Cl

Ben Cell Close

Daley Thomson

Willard Street

Upcher Mews

Heath Road

Rich Street

Peardon Street

Newby Street

North Street B224

Broadhinton Road

Bobbin Close

Rozel Road

Florys Place

Stephen Place

Charles Barry Close

Smith Terrace

143

Rectory Grove

Fitzwilliam Road

Otterton Road

Liston Road

141

Dunstan Road

Gresham Way

Beaufoy Road

Audley Road

Basnett Road

Cedars Road A3216

Lavender Hill A3036

Turn chapel Mews

Abberley Mews

Garfield Mews

Crosland Place

Freke Road

Taybridge Road

Wix's Lane

Lyncott Crescent

Taybridge Road

Willoughby Mews

Cedars Mews

Victoria Rise

Richmond Mews

Hannington Road

Macaulay Road

Lambourn Road

Lillieshall Road

Orlando Road

Charlotte Row

Lydon Road

Syca more Ms

Scout Lane

Prin Ct

Slater Mews

Grafton Square

Grafton Square

The Polygon

Downers Cottages

CLAPHAM

Wilder ness Mews

Macaulay Square

The Chase

Clapham Common North Side B303

The Pavement B303

Clapham Common

PAGE 330

Cock Pond

B224 The Pavement

Clapham Common

Bromell's Road

Clapham Common North Side A3

Barker Mews

Victoria Mews

Long Road A3

B224

Clapham Common South Side

0.25 mile

0.25 km

Clapham Old Town

The more genteel side of Clapham, Old Town hosts some fine restaurants (**Trinity**), good watering-holes (**The Prince of Wales**, **The Frog**), and one of London's best butchers (**Moen's**), all bordered by the green of Clapham Common. If you need more, head to Queenstown Road for further classy dining establishments.

Coffee

- **The Roaster** • 789 Wandsworth Rd
- **Starbucks** • 40 Old Town

Libraries

- **Clapham Library** • 1 Clapham Common North Side

Nightlife

- **Lost Society** • 697 Wandsworth Rd
- **Prince of Wales** • 38 Clapham Old Town
- **Rose & Crown** • 2 The Polygon
- **The Sun** • 47 Old Town

Restaurants

- **Nardullis Ice Cream** • 29 The Pavement
- **Trinity** • 4 The Polygon

Shopping

- **M. Moen & Sons** • 24 The Pavement
- **Puppet Planet** • 787 Wandsworth Rd

Supermarkets

- **Sainsbury's** • 646 Wandsworth Rd

Map 143 · **Clapham High Street**

Clapham High Street

Clapham is a microcosm of Cath Kidston mummies and their token gay best friends—watch them jog and brunch around the common in all weather. Stock up on al fresco goodies at **Esca**, neck a mojito at **Buena Vista**, and gorge on sushi at **Tsunami** or pizza at **San Marco**. Whatever you do, do not—we repeat, DO NOT—set foot in **Infernos**. We will find out and we will judge you.

Cinemas

- **Clapham Picturehouse** • 76 Venn St

Coffee

- **The Black Lab** • 18 Clapham Common South Side
- **Brickwood** • 16 Clapham Common South Side
- **Café Delight** • 19 Clapham High St
- **Caffe Nero** • 86 Clapham High St

O Landmarks

- **Clapham Common Air-Raid Shelter** • Clapham High St

Nightlife

- **The Alexandra** • 14 Clapham Common South Side
- **Bread & Roses** • 68 Clapham Manor St
- **Buena Vista** • 19 Landor Rd
- **The Clapham North** • 409 Clapham Rd
- **The Coach and Horses** • 173 Clapham Park Rd
- **The Falcon** • 33 Bedford Rd
- **Infernos** • 146 Clapham High St
- **Inn Clapham** • 15 The Pavement
- **The Loft** • 67 Clapham High St
- **The Railway** • 18 Clapham High St
- **Two Brewers** • 114 Clapham High St

Post Offices

- **Clapham Common** • 161 Clapham High St

Restaurants

- **Brickwood** • 16 Clapham Common South Side
- **The Dairy** • 15 The Pavement
- **Gastro** • 67 Venn St
- **The Pepper Tree** • 19 Clapham Common South Side
- **Roti Joupa** • 12 Clapham High St
- **San Marco Pizzeria** • 126 Clapham High St
- **Tsunami** • 5 Voltaire Rd

Shopping

- **Apex Cycles** • 40 Clapham High St
- **Esca** • 160 Clapham High St
- **M. Moen & Sons** • 24 The Pavement
- **Today's Living Health Store** • 92 Clapham High St

Supermarkets

- **Iceland** • 4 The Pavement
- **Sainsbury's** • 133 Clapham High St
- **Sainsbury's** • 33 Clapham High St

Map 143

Map 144 · **Stockwell / Brixton (West)**

Map 144

Stockwell / Brixton (West)

Lift up the roof of **Brixton Market** on Thursday, Friday, and Saturday nights and underneath you will find rows of arcades teaming with all species of hipster. After years of almost being cool, this microcosmic neighbourhood beneath the train tracks has officially earned Brixton the title of hippest place in town. With so much to do, no two nights out are the same. Binge on pizza at **Franco Manca**; dumplings at **Mama Lan**; take in some live music at **Agile Rabbit**; and cocktails at **Seven at Brixton**.

Coffee

- **Federation Coffee** • 77–78 Brixton Village Market
- **Rosie's Deli Cafe** • 14 Market Row

O Landmarks

- **Brixton Market** • Electric Ave & Electric Ln
- **Brixton Village Market** • Coldharbour Ln
- **Electric Avenue** • Electric Ave

Nightlife

- **The Duke of Edinburgh** • 204 Ferndale Rd
- **Marquis of Lorne** • 49 Dalyell Rd
- **Plan B** • 418 Brixton Rd
- **The Prince of Wales** • 469 Brixton Rd
- **The Queen's Head** • 144 Stockwell Rd
- **Seven at Brixton** • 7 Market Row
- **The Swan** • 215 Clapham Rd

Post Offices

- **Stockwell** • 225 Clapham Rd

Restaurants

- **Agile Rabbit** • 24–25 Coldharbour Ln
- **Bellantoni's** • 81 Granville Arcade
- **Breads Etcetera** • 88 Brixton Village Market
- **Brixton Cornercopia** • 65 Coldharbour Ln
- **Casa Morita** • 9 Market Row
- **Falafel Van** • Station Rd
- **Honest Burgers** • 12 Brixton Village
- **Jeff the Chef** • Station Rd
- **Mama Lan** • 18 Brixton Village Market
- **SW9 Bar Cafe** • 11 Dorrell Pl

Shopping

- **A&C Co Continental Grocers** • 3 Atlantic Rd
- **Brixi** • 7 Second Ave
- **Funchal Bakery** • 141–143 Stockwell Rd
- **Lisa Stickley London** • 74 Landor Rd
- **The Old Post Office Bakery** • 76 Landor Rd

Supermarkets

- **Iceland** • 441 Brixton Rd
- **Iceland** • 314 Clapham Rd
- **Sainsbury's** • 425 Brixton Rd
- **Tesco** • 330 Brixton Rd

Map 145 · **Stockwell / Brixton (East)**

1

2

Lansdowne Way

Spencer Mews

South Lambeth Road

Clapham Road A3

Binfield Road

Stockwell Terrace

Stockwell A203

Stockwell Gardens

135

St. Michael's Road

St. Martin's Road

Stockwell Park Crescent

Durand Gardens

Isabel Street

Morat Street

Liberty Street

Hackford Road

Cranworth Gardens

Manston Close

Cowley Way

Gosling Way

Russell Douvil

C'ncell Road

Foxley Square

Fairbairn Green

Eythorne Green

Cromwell

Burnley Road

Crossford Street

Irving Grove

A Fenton Close

Sidney Road

Stockwell Lane

Johnston Close

Penton Close

Hackford Walk

Hillyard Street

Groveway

Lorn Road

Slade Gardens

Park View Mews

Ingleborough Street

Stockwell Park Road

Normandy Road

Melbourne Square

Melbourne Mews

Mostyn Gardens

Mostyn Road

Braganza Green

Fountain Place

Akerman Road

Eythorne Road

Brief Street

St. Lawrence Way

Evesham Walk

Ingleton Street

Burton Road

Robsart Street

Lilford Gardens

Burton Lane

Tavern Lane

Burton Road

Evandale Road

Clapham Road

Broomgrove Road

Stable Yard

Moat Place

Ayton Road

Lidcote Gardens

Thornton Street

Wynne Road

Winans Walk

Loughborough Road

Torrey Drive

Shore Wa

Fir Grove Rd

Morrison Road

Bennett Road

Prideys Road

Loughborough Road

Lilford Road

Fenwick Mews

Argyll Close

Stockwell Green

Stockwell Road A203

Burgoyne Road

Romero Close

Rumsey Road

Knowle Close

Blackmaster Close

BRIXTON

Serenaders Road

Overton Road

Hilda Locket Walk

Commerford Road

Mordaunt Street

Dalyell Road

Stansfield Road

Bennett Road

Stockwell Bowls

Stockwell Park Walk A203

Peckford Place

Villa Road

Max Roach Park

Angell Park Gardens

Mallams Mews

Angell Road

Ferndy Road

Chantrey Road

Gateley Road

St. John's Crescent

Enfield Road

St. James's Crescent

Swinford Gardens

Barrington Road

Hinton Road A222

Rupert Gardens

Stiles Gardens

Pulross Road

Ferndale Road

Bellefields Road

Stockwell Avenue

Solon Road

144

Gresham Road

Canterbury Crescent

Industry Terrace

Beehive Place

St. John's Crescent

Witchne Road

Western Road

Wyck Gardens

Millbrook Road

Ridgeway Road

Belinda Road

B Shannon Grove

Nursery Road

Dorrell Place

Tunstall Road

Barnes Grove

Atlantic Road

Brixton Station Road

Popes Road

Blacktree Mews

Gresham Road

Barrington Road

Somerleyton Road

Trinity Gardens

Brighton Terrace

Dalmain Close

Brixton

Electric Avenue

Electric Lane

B223

Valentia Road

127

Coldharbour Lane A2217

Heritage Close

Acre Lane A2214

Brixton Hill A23

Rushcroft Road

Vining Street

Windrush Square

Salton Road

Clarewood Walk

Geneva Drive

Corry Lane

Hillmead Drive

Loughborough Park

Somerleyton

Moreland Road

Wilkinson Walt Whitman

Porden Road

| 0.25 mile | 0.25 km |

Map 145

Things have changed a bit since The Clash sang 'The Guns of Brixton' in '79 and race riots were a regular occurrence. While the middle classes have infiltrated most parts of Brixton, this neighbourhood still retains a defiant edge. Community spirit and close-knit neighbourhoods take precedence over trendy bars and pricey restaurants. Live music rules here; the legendary **Brixton Academy** still draws the hordes, while **Jamm** offers an eclectic and worthy alternative.

Landmarks

• **Stockwell Bowls** • Stockwell Rd & Stockwell Park Walk

Libraries

• **Anti-Slavery International Library** • Broomgrove Rd

Nightlife

• **Brixton Academy** • 211 Stockwell Rd
• **Jamm** • 261 Brixton Rd

Map 146

Sleepy little Earlsfield tends to mind its own business. It's a pretty sedate kind of place, slightly cut off by the lack of a tube stop. The well-heeled locals seem happy enough and make the most of what's on offer. Try **Amaranth** for great noodles before moving on to **Bar 366** a few doors down for some chilled boozing.

 Coffee

- **Caffe Nero** • 529 Garratt Ln
- **Refuel** • 515 Garratt Ln

Libraries

- **Alvering Library** • 2 Allfarthing Ln
- **Earlsfield Library** • 276 Magdalen Rd

Nightlife

- **Bar 366** • 366 Garratt Ln
- **Halfway House** • 521 Garratt Ln
- **Le Gothique** • Windmill Rd & John Archer Wy

Restaurants

- **Cafe Amaranth** • 346 Garratt Ln
- **Cah Chi** • 394 Garratt Ln
- **Carluccio's** • 537 Garratt Ln

Balham (West)

Map 147

Ensconced between the livelier Clapham and Tooting, this is a gentle slice of residential Southwest London. Bellevue Road offers a number of places to eat and drink overlooking Wandsworth Common, climaxing with the stupendous **Chez Bruce**. Nightingale Lane is terribly twee and hosts a few opportunities to shop organically and **The Hope** serves up a healthy pint of Tribute.

Coffee

• **Caffe Nero** • 37 Balham High Rd

Nightlife

• **The Hope** • Bellevue Rd
• **The Nightingale** • 97 Nightingale Ln

Restaurants

• **Chez Bruce** • 2 Bellevue Rd

Shopping

• **Bon Vivant** • 59 Nightingale Ln

Balham is growing up to become the cooler, decidedly more understated little brother to nearby Clapham. Although it still oozes its own sense of character, evident in quirky mainstays like the **Balham Bowls Club**, the polished wood of **Harrison's** and draw of its **Waitrose** risks losing its hip factor. The happy hour at **Tacuba Bar** soon makes up for it. But if we have to go to another friend's 30th at **The Avalon**, we might have to up sticks and go elsewhere.

Coffee

- **Brickwood** • 11 Hildreth St
- **Camden Coffee House** • 208 Balham High Rd
- **M1LK** • 20 Bedford Hill
- **Starbucks** • 11 Bedford Hill

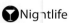

Libraries

- **Balham Library** • 16 Ramsden Rd

Nightlife

- **The Avalon** • 16 Balham Hill
- **Balham Bowls Club** • 7 Ramsden Rd
- **The Bedford** • 77 Bedford Hill
- **The Exhibit** • 12 Balham Station Rd
- **Hagen & Hyde** • 157 Balham High Rd

Post Offices

- **Balham Hill** • 92 Balham Hill
- **Cavendish Road** • 273 Cavendish Rd

Restaurants

- **Brickwood** • 11 Hildreth St
- **The Exhibit** • 12 Balham Station Rd
- **Hagen & Hyde** • 157 Balham High Rd
- **Harrison's** • 15 Bedford Hill

Shopping

- **Moxon's Fishmongers** • Westbury Parade

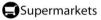

Supermarkets

- **Sainsbury's** • 149 Balham High Rd
- **Sainsbury's** • 21 Balham Hill
- **Waitrose** • Balham High Rd & Ramsden Rd

Clapham Park

This is where all the Claphamites settle down, have kids, move into their dream town house, and one-up their friends with dinner parties and barbecues every other weekend. All this domesticity has left the locals' only restaurant options north on Clapham High Street or south in Balham. Still, you need fodder for your friends, so gourmet food shopping is where it's at at **MacFarlane's**.

Map 149

Coffee
• **Starbucks** • 3 Abbeville Rd

Post Offices
• **Clapham Park** • 49 Poynders Rd

Restaurants
• **Bistro Union** • 40 Abbeville Rd

Shopping
• **MacFarlanes** • 48 Abbeville Rd

Map 150 · **Brixton**

Brixton is where it's at. Shoreditch: old news. Dalston: yawn. Any self-respecting hipster wouldn't be caught dead around these hot spots (too many hipsters) and so they've gravitated south of the river. For Brixton Village's other half, check out Market Row, with its killer kasu (Curry Ono) and flavoured vegan baked goods (**Ms Cupcake**). Stroll to Coldharbour Lane for homemade ginger beer and brunch (**Duck Egg Cafe**). For culture, take in an exhibition at **Photofusion** and a flick at stalwart **The Ritzy.**

Cinemas

• **Ritzy Picturehouse** • Coldharbour Ln & Brixton Oval

Libraries

• **Brixton Library** • Brixton Oval

Nightlife

• **The Dogstar** • 389 Coldharbour Ln
• **The Effra** • 38 Kellet Rd
• **Effra Social** • 89 Kellet Rd
• **Electric Brixton** • Town Hall Parade
• **Grand Union** • 123 Acre Ln
• **Gremio de Brixton** • St Matthew's Rd
• **Hootananny** • 95 Effra Rd
• **Prince Albert** • 418 Coldharbour Ln
• **Satay** • 447 Coldharbour Ln
• **St Matthews Church** • Brixton Hill
• **Upstairs at the Ritzy** •
  Ritzy Picturehouse • Brixton Oval, Coldharbour Ln
• **The Windmill** • 22 Blenheim Gardens

Post Offices

• **Brixton Hill** • 104 Brixton Hill

Restaurants

• **Asmara** • 386 Coldharbour Ln
• **Boqueria** • 192 Acre Ln
• **Curry Ono** • 14 Market Row
• **Duck Egg Cafe** • 424 Coldharbour Ln
• **Elephant** • 55 Granville Arcade
• **Franco Manca** • 4 Market Row
• **KaoSarn** • Coldharbour Ln
• **Khan's of Brixton** • 24 Brixton Water Ln
• **Lounge** • 56 Atlantic Rd
• **Negril** • 132 Brixton Hill
• **Opus Café** • 89 Acre Ln
• **The Phoenix** • 441 Coldharbour Ln
• **Refill** • 500 Brixton Rd
• **Yum-D** • 14 Market Row

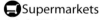## Shopping

• **Bookmongers** • 439 Coldharbour Ln
• **Lab G** • 6 Granville Arcade
• **Ms. Cupcake** • 408 Coldharbour Ln
• **Selectors Music Emporium** • 100 Brixton Hill
• **Supertone Records** • 110 Acre Ln
• **Tasty Rich Bakery** • Brixton Village Market
• **Traid** • 2 Acre Ln

Supermarkets

• **Iceland** • 13 Winslade Rd

Map 151 • **Tooting Bec**

Tooting Bec

Not quite the Bec of beyond, this Tooting is the home of Europe's largest lido and has a plethora of Asian grill bars for post-pub munchies. The best of the curry houses has to be **Al Mirage**, despite a popular following at **Mirch Masala**. For fairy cakes head to **Bertie and Boo** (we boo the name) and cocktails stop at **Smoke**. So what, you say? Sew buttons at the **London Sewing Machine Museum** no less.

Map 151

Coffee

- **Bertie and Boo** • 162 Balham High Rd
- **Caffe Moka** • 23 Balham High Rd
- **Dee Light Bakery** • 14 Ritherdon Rd

Nightlife

- **The Bec Bar** • 5 Tooting Bec Rd
- **The King's Head** • 84 Upper Tooting Rd

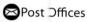Post Offices

- **Upper Tooting** • 63 Trinity Rd

Restaurants

- **Al Mirage** • 215 Upper Tooting Rd
- **The French Cafe** • 16-18 Ritherton Rd
- **Masaledar Kitchen** • 121 Upper Tooting Rd
- **Mirch Masala** • 213 Upper Tooting Rd
- **Spice Village** • 32 Upper Tooting Rd

Shopping

- **Crazy Horse Bike Workshop** • 275 Balham High Rd
- **Russell's Trade & DIY** • 46 Upper Tooting Rd
- **Wandsworth Oasis HIV/AIDS Charity Shop** • 40 Trinity Rd

Map 152 · **Tooting Broadway**

Decent rent, a Northern Line station and a grade one listed bingo hall: there's a lot here to like. Hit the High Street for curries and halal it all. Need anything else? Mitcham Road has the ticket. Local eat treats include **Radha Krishna Bhavan**, **Sette Bello** and **Rick's**, while **Tram & Social** offers proof that trendy pubs can indeed survive this far south.

Coffee

• **Cafee Manal** • 84 Garratt Ln

Landmarks

• **Gala Bingo Hall** • 50 Mitcham Rd

Libraries

• **Tooting Library** • 75 Mitcham Rd

Nightlife

• **The Little Bar** • 145 Mitcham Rd
• **The Ramble Inn** • 223 Mitcham Rd
• **The Secret Bar** • Totterdown St
• **Tooting Tram and Social** • 46 Mitcham Rd
• **Unwined** • 21 Tooting High St

Post Offices

• **London Road** • 47 London Rd
• **Tooting** • 2 Gatton Rd

Restaurants

• **Dosa n Chutny** • 68 Tooting High St
• **Jaffna House** • 90 Tooting High St
• **Radha Krishna Bhavan** • 86 Tooting High St
• **Rick's Restaurant** • 122 Mitcham Rd

## Shopping

• **Tooting Market** • 21 Tooting High St

Supermarkets

• **Iceland** • 27 Tooting High St

General Information

Website: www.alexandrapalace.com
Phone: 020 8365 2121

Overview

If you fancy panoramic London views, exemplary Victorian architecture and an unrelenting stiff breeze to the face, the heights of Alexandra Park could be your cup of tea. With a fraction of the visitors of North London neighbours Hampstead Heath and Primrose Hill, Alexandra Park is nonetheless home to Ally Pally—Alexander Mackenzie's magnificent 1873 exhibition centre once renowned as the home of television after the BBC used it to broadcast the world's first high def transmissions in '36. It also boasts 196 acres of pristine, Green Flag-winning parkland, a two-hectare conservation area, and a fully functioning ice rink to boot.

Parks & Places • Alexandra Palace Park

Practicalities

Alexandra Park is well served by public transport: Alexandra Palace railway station is a short ride from King's Cross and Moorgate and sits directly next to the park's Wood Green entrance. You can also take the underground to Wood Green, catch the W3 direct to Ally Pally from just outside. You could also take advantage of the 2000 free parking spaces in the park itself if driving, though it's only a short walk from Muswell Hill town centre.

Nature

No doubt tempted by the reservoirs, 155 species of birds have been spotted in the park over the last 30 years. Nature fetishists should take in the two-hectare conservation area, which includes a wide array of animals including deer, donkeys, foxes and rabbits. In 1998, there was even a rare water vole sighting. There he was, large as life, like he owned the bloody place.

Architecture

For most Alexandra Park visitors it's all about the Palace, these days a thriving hub for exhibitions, concerts, farmer's markets and, uh, world darts tournaments. The Palace building itself was ravaged by fire in the 80s and has since been restored to its former glory, though nearby banqueting venue Blandford Hall succumbed to the same fate in 1971 and was completely destroyed. No matter: Ally Pally remains an impressive, domineering building well worth a nose-around. For the less active, admiring the view from sedentary perspective from the underrated Phoenix Bar (located in the south wing) is just as good.

Open Spaces

It's safe to say that Alexandra Park has more than enough grass to keep Cheech & Chong happy, being typified by the diverse range of landscaped grounds that can be found within. The Grove Garden actually pre-dates the park itself and there's also a good little café here if you fancy a quick bite. The Rose Garden is to the east side of the Palace and is even more aesthetically pleasing. Many newer small woodlands have been developing over the last few decades owing to the planting of large numbers of trees, producing an environment pleasing to both the rambler and runner.

Performance

The park often plays host to funfairs and circuses, but the Palace itself will usually be used at night for concerts. Its revival over recent years as a gig venue has led to the likes of the Arctic Monkeys and Paul Weller playing there, with its capacity being around 8,500, making it ideal for bands who've outgrown the Brixton Academy. Other parts of the Palace, such as the Great Hall, are used for classical music recitals.

More recently 'The Secret Cinema' took over the Palace for a screening of Lawrence of Arabia, attracting thousands of filmgoers clad in Bedouin attire. Some even brought a camel.

The Palace also houses a theatre, which was dormant for over sixty-five years until a performance took place in 2004. It is still being restored and should be re-opened to the public for performances in the near future.

Check out Ally Pally's informative website (listed above) for a full calendar of upcoming events.

Sports

An indoor ice rink is housed within the Palace with a capacity of 1,250, with all manner of ice sports catered for (you can get further information by ringing 020 8365 4386). There is also a large boating lake with its own islands and fishing area (and even a smaller area for kids to boat on their own), with pedalos and rowing boats available for hire; being a seasonal facility, it's best to ring the operators Bluebird Boats Ltd. (020 7262 1330) beforehand. The boating pond is adjacent to a children's playground as well. For those who like golf with a view, the popular ten-hole pitch and putt course was recently revamped with an injection of Heritage Fund money: for prices and booking info see www.pitchnputt.co.uk or call 01245 257682. Alexandra Palace Park is also popular with cyclists, with the Parkland Walk a particular favourite, being a disused railway line that links up with Finsbury Park. In summertime the park is also a great place to get embroiled in countless spontaneous games of football and Frisbee, or to gawp/hurl insults at joggers

General information

NFT Map: 7

Address: Barbican Centre, Silk St, London, EC2Y 8DS.

Phone: Box Office & Membership: 020 7638 8891 (9 am-8 pm daily); Switchboard: 020 7638 4141

Centre opening times:
Mon-Sat: 9 am-11 pm; Sun & Public Holidays: 12 pm-11 pm (although different parts of the centre may open at different times).

Website: www.barbican.org.uk

Overview

As terrifying as it is impressive, the Barbican Centre is a one-stop shop for all things cultural. At its best, the Barbican is utterly brilliant: a rambling collection of cinemas, galleries, bars, theatres, even a housing estate and a school. But stay after dark, when the culture vultures have left, and you can find yourself alone and lost in this city-within-a-city.

That the centre is brutally ugly makes what's inside even more splendid. The gallery space hosts world-class exhibitions and the cinemas show both mainstream and arthouse films. There's a world, classical and jazz music programme catering for everyone from scruffy backpackers to bearded professors. Most are sensible enough to leave before it gets too spooky. But plan your exit route in advance just in case.

Music

The heart of the Barbican monster is its music hall. A mecca for lovers of cerebral music, the centre's resident band is the London Symphony Orchestra: classical heavyweights who play year-round. The BBC Symphony Orchestra also has a base here, and the stage attracts biggies from around the world, including performances from Yo-Yo Ma, the Vienna Philharmonic and Cesaria Evora. But you don't need a high brow to find something to like: a flick through their listings—which last year included Sufjan Stevens, Sparks,

The Africa Express and Micachu—will soon have you clicking Book Now.

Festivals are another key draw: not the pot-and-portacabin type, but impassioned celebrations. The Mostly Mozart festival reaches sci-fi convention levels of fanaticism; the Great Performers festival is an orgy of some of the world's most spectacular musicians; and the Jazz Festival will have you feeling über hip (then perhaps a bit perplexed. And then, if you're 100% honest, rather wishing it was over). African, Latin, Contemporary and Opera festivals also sell out the near-2000 capacity venue.

Film

The programme has an arty bias but is so diverse that you're bound to find something inviting on one of the three screens. Rule of thumb: silent films, in. J-Lo, out. Subtitles, in. Mighty Duck trilogy, out. But they do offer the screens for private hire, so if you really want you can stick it to 'em and have your own showing of Snakes on a Plane. The Barbican also hosts the annual Australian Film and London Children's Film Festivals, and runs constantly changing series. Recent favourites include the Bad Film Club for fans of the most reviled films, and Second Chance Sunday so you can see on the big screen films which you missed first time around.

Theatre and Dance

Don't be fooled by the Barbican's hulking exterior—the centre dabbles in the more delicate arts rather well. Its two theatres cater for both ends of the performance spectrum. The main room, a shared home for acting and dance, seats over 1,000 punters and attracts some of the biggest names in high culture. Deep in the Barbican's bowels the smaller Pit theatre is home to experimental and new acts. But be warned: with just 200 seats the Pit is small enough for anyone dozing off to be highly visible.

Art

Nowhere else at the Barbican is the idea of making culture accessible for all more apparent than their art spaces. The main gallery hosts temporary exhibitions, mixing all types of art into one cultural hot pot. In 2007, under the umbrella

of Art and Sex from Antiquity to Now, erotic Roman cutlery—that's right: erotic cutlery—shared a stage with impressionist paintings and an 11-minute film of someone's face as she was, ahem, attended to. Every first Thursday of the month the gallery opens for a nocturnal viewing, with talks, performances—burlesque dancers for the art and sex exhibition—and a themed bar. A second space, The Curve, winds its way round the ground floor where the exhibitions are generally free.

The Library

Libraries often get a bad press. They've got stuck with an image of frumpy, middle-aged women peering down their spectacles and telling youths to be quiet. But this couldn't be further removed from the reality of the Barbican Library. Alongside a decent array of books, there's a dazzling collection of live musical recordings. Some of these tracks are so rare that they can't be heard anywhere else in the world. Put some headphones on and rock out. Just don't get carried away and smash up the children's section.

How to Get There

By car: Parking is pricey with two hours costing £6.50 and each hour thereafter costing two or three quid more, though there's a flat weekend fee of £7.50 per day.

By bus: The 153 (which runs from Liverpool Street to Finsbury Park) stops directly outside the Barbican at Silk Street; the following buses run nearby: 8, 11, 23, 26, 35, 42, 43, 47, 48, 55, 56, 76, 78, 100, 133, 141, 149, 172, 214, 242, 243, 271, 344 (seven days a week); 4, (Mon-Sat); 21, 25, 521 (Mon-Fri). If none of these buses can take you home then consider yourself extremely unlucky. By tube: Barbican stations runs on the Circle, District and Hammersmith & City lines. Other stations nearby are Moorgate, St Paul's, Bank, Liverpool Street and Mansion House.

By train: The nearest overland stations are Liverpool Street, Farringdon and Blackfriars. City Thameslink services run through Barbican, Moorgate and Cannon Street.

Practical Information

NFT Map: 132, 133, & 141
Official opening time is 8 am, although the gates are usually unlocked a little earlier than this. The park closes at dusk.
Friends of Battersea Park:
www.batterseapark.org
Zoo: www.batterseaparkzoo.co.uk
Local council: www.wandsworth.gov.uk
(see also for information on the Pump House Gallery)
Cycle hire:
www.londonrecumbents.co.uk
BlueBird boat hire:
www.solarshuttle.co.uk

Overview

Opened in 1858 with the aim of giving the Victorian working classes something to do other than drinking gin, Battersea Park has developed to become one of London's prettiest, most popular and most usable parks. Squeezing a range of gardens, cafes, animals, sports, cultural facilities and even a peace pagoda into its diminutive 200 acres, the park is popular with everyone from hordes of snotty little kids to wandering dog-walkers. It is also centrally located enough to be easy to get to but still far enough from Central London to retain a local feel.

The park is about two miles southwest from Westminster and occupies the spot on the south bank of the Thames between Albert and Chelsea bridges. Originally used for duelling, the Duke of Wellington famously discharged upon the Earl of Winchelsea on the site in 1829. Rather than the vast open and flat spaces that many London parks offer, Battersea is neatly divided into a number of features and sections, making it feel much larger than it is.

Sporting Activities

Battersea has an incredibly good array of sporting facilities. The 'Millennium Arena' is a 400m 8-lane running track situated in the northeast corner of the park; it hosts athletic meets and training sessions and it benefitted from an expensive overhaul in, you guessed it, 1999. Next to the arena are ten tennis courts and an all-weather football pitch whilst there are further all-weather astro-turf pitches in the southeast corner of the park marked for both hockey and football. The park also boasts cricket pitches and practice nets, a bowling green, smooth wide paths for skating and enough open spaces to invite impromptu sessions of pretty much any other sport. If you consider attacking fish a sport, and have a permit and rod licence, the park's lake offers fishing for nine months of the year. Rowing boats and pedaloes can also be taken out on to the lake during July and August (adults £4.50/hour, children £2). Bicycles can be hired from the London Recumbents shop, which is next to the Millennium Arena on the park's East Carriage Drive—but be warned: bikes can only be used in the park itself, and as it takes just 15 minutes for a leisurely pedal around the parameter, an hour's hire can become a little Groundhog Day.

Art

Battersea has fostered a creative relationship with the arts and has a number of sculptures dotted about, its own public gallery and a biannual art fair. Taking pride of place next to the lake are two large Henry Moore and Barbara Hepworth sculptures, both of which are well worth rooting out. The Pumphouse Gallery is a grade II-listed building, originally used to power the park's water works, which has been restored and converted into a gallery and information centre with six exhibitions throughout the year. The Gallery, located northeast of the lake, is also available for private hire and even has a licence to hold civil weddings. The park has hosted the Affordable Art Fair since 1999, which has become a leading showcase for art priced under £3,000.

Performance

In summer music aficionados should head down to La Gondola al Parco, the café by the lake, for free live concerts every Tuesday and Friday from 7 pm. Entrance is free and there's also a BBQ and refreshments aplenty.

Nature and Children's Zoo

Battersea's varied landscapes ensure you stand a decent chance of seeing more than a rat or a pigeon while you saunter round. Squirrels, ducks and Canada geese are all too plentiful. More interesting potential sightings include woodpeckers, cormorants, Peregrine falcons, terrapins and, according to the RSPB, Pochards (whatever they are). If you don't come across any interesting wildlife, your only option is to cheat and visit the park's zoo. A five-minute stroll from the Chelsea Gate entrance, the zoo is aimed at children and has a cool collection of small mammals, including lemurs, as well as small farm animals and some excitingly named birds, such as some 'Peach-faced Love birds'. In case you do fall in love with any of the zoo's inhabitants, most are available for adoption. Mice start at £10 for six months, pay-up and claim it's for your kid. The zoo is open throughout the year and entry costs £8.75 for adults, £6.50 for children.

How to Get There

By tube: Sloane Square (on the Circle and District lines) is the nearest Underground station at just under a mile away. From the station walk down Lower Sloane Street, which becomes Chelsea Bridge Road and leads to the Thames. Walk over Chelsea Bridge and you will see the park on your right. Alternatively take bus no 319.

By bus: From central London, buses run to the park from Liverpool Street (number 344), Notting Hill (452), Oxford Circus (137), Sloane Square (319, 137), Victoria Station (44) and Vauxhall (344).

By train: Battersea Park station is within sight of the park, trains run to both Clapham Junction and Victoria at high frequency. Queenstown Road is around 300m from the park. Trains from this station run to Waterloo and Clapham Junction and depart less often than from Battersea Park.

Chaucer Rd
Spenser Rd
Shakespeare Rd
Milton Rd
Regent Rd
Railton Rd
Gubyon Ave
Woodquest Ave
Millwood Rd

Brixton Water Ln

Herne Pl
Herne Hill

Sport
Pitches

MAP
127

Herne Hill
Railway
Station

Carv

Dulwich Rd

Brailsford Rd

Arlington Rd

Wildflower
Meadows

Sport
Pitches

Pool

Brockwell
Lido

P

Hurst St

Rymer St

Railton Rd

Half M

BMX
Track

Sport
Pitches

Play
Area

Bowing
Pavilion

**Brockwell
Park**

Bascome St

Community
Greenhouses

Walled
Garden

Sport
Pitches

Wildflower
Meadows

Temple

Tulse Hill

Brockwell Park Rd

Wet Play
Area

Café

Brockwell
Hall

Stables

Norwood Rd

Rosendale Rd

Guernsy

Wildflower
Meadows

Norwood
Lodge

Peabody Est

Tulse Hill

Brockwell Park Gdns

Trinity Rise

Norw

llo Cl

General Information

NFT Map: 127
Brockwell Park: www.brockwellpark.com
Brockwell Park Lido: www.brockwelllido.com
020 7274 3088

Overview

Brockwell Park may not be a household name when it comes to London Parks but for many South Londoners—not least residents of neighbouring Herne Hill—it's the pick of the bunch, all the lovelier for its unconventionality, tattiness and relative anonymity. It's eclectic, it's quirky, and it's impossible not to fall in love with.

History

By the end of the 19th century the local population was large, growing and in need of a serious park. Brockwell was secured for use by the public after MP Thomas Bristowe got wind of a private country estate that seemed just the ticket. Still, he might have over-exerted himself in the process: having taken a Bill through Parliament to convert the land, led a committee to negotiate the price, and raised funds from across the community, Bristowe himself promptly collapsed and died on the steps of Brockwell Hall, moments after the opening ceremony in 1892.

Café

If that doesn't put you off your scones, nowadays, the ground floor of Brockwell Hall is a café where refreshments have been served ever since. Located at the top of the hill, it's a great place to stop for inexpensive cake, drinks etc. after some…

Activities!

There's heaps to do. A BMX track, tennis courts, bowling green, football and cricket pitches, basketball courts, outdoor theatre club, a children's play area and a paddling pool. Or you could chill by the ponds, in the walled garden, under the clock tower, at the picnic area, near the flower gardens, etc.

Brockwell Lido and Greenhouses

Built in 1937, Brockwell Lido is essentially an (unattractive) art deco building that replaced an old bathing pond. After experiencing financial difficulty it was restored and reopened in 2007. As well as a large outdoor pool, there is a gym and classes are held in yoga, pilates, tai-chi and meditation. For the under 5s, Whippersnappers have everything from acrobatics to puppets and African drumming. A Miniature Railway runs between Herne Hill Gate and the Lido. Run by a local enthusiast on a not-for-profit basis; it's only £1 for a round trip. May–Sept, Sat–Sun, 11am–5pm.

Brockwell also boasts a superb community greenhouse project open to volunteers. The greenhouses are open Sunday afternoons and give Londoners a rare chance to get green fingers and grow their own produce. Contact the greenhouse secretary on bpcgsecretary@gmail.com to get involved.

Annual Events

July: Lambeth Country Show is always good fun and involves medieval jousting, farm animals, live reggae/dub and rides, and there are homemade cake and jam contests, too. The Alternative Vegetable Animal Competition requires fruit and veg to be crafted into a famous person or building with a very entertaining adult category.
September: The annual Urban Green Fair helps teach London to become more sustainable.
November: The big fireworks show on Guy Fawkes Night is worth braving the cold for.

How to Get There

By rail/tube/foot: The park is a short walk from the following overland and underground stations:

Herne Hill Rail Station—5 mins
Tulse Hill Rail Station—15 mins
Brixton Tube—20 mins
Clapham North Tube—30 mins

By bus: The following all stop at Brockwell Park—2, 3, 37, 68, 196, 322, 468, P15

329

Parks & Places · **Clapham Common**

Overview

Lively and happening; youngish, professional, and trendy (in a safe way). Clapham Common reflects the area well.

Popular all year round, the Common truly comes alive in summer. On a warm weekend you'll find the park overflowing with picnickers sipping champagne and just plain lookin' good. It's a lovely scene made better by the relaxed, friendly atmosphere. And, when the sun finally sets, you're left with a seriously impressive choice of bars close by.

As well as drawing the usual funky sophisticates, the park is also family-friendly with lots of little ones enjoying the space.

Plenty of organised (or not) sport, kite flying, model boating, Ultimate Frisbee, and even fishing happens here too, but while the common is safe as houses during the day, at night time it is best avoided.

History

Clapham began as a Saxon village. Back then it was called Clopp Ham, meaning the village (ham) by the short hill (clopp). The common was used by villagers to graze their livestock and as a source of firewood.

In the late 17th century the population began to grow as refugees arrived from the Great Plague of London (1665) and the fire of 1666. During this time, the rich gentry of London built a number of fine country houses around the common. When the railways were developed there was a sudden influx of commuters, driving the upper class away to somewhere less, um, common.

Today, the surrounding area is one of the more expensive in South London, partly because of its excellent transport links.

Clapham Sect

On the common is the Holy Trinity Church. This was a meeting place of the Clapham Sect, a group of 19th-century Evangelical Anglicans who fought for social reform. "Ugh" you say, but wait…

The Clapham Sect played a significant part in the abolition of slavery in England. They didn't stop there, going on to campaign for the eradication of slavery worldwide. They also fought for reform in the penal system, focusing on unjust sentencing and the dire prison conditions of the time.

Eateries

Cicero's on the Common (vegetarian)
2 Rookery Road, SW49QN, 020 7498 0770

Cafe Des Res (English/ Carribean)
8 The Pavement, SW4 0HY, 020 7622 6602

The Bowling Green Café (sandwiches, pasta etc)
Clapham Common West Side, SW4 9AN, 020 7801 0904

Three ponds

Mount Pond—is a fishing park pond about three acres in size. It contains carp, roach, gudgeon and eels. Suggested baits include pellet, maggot, meat, and boilies, it says here.

Eagle Pond—is a smaller pond with a little island. This one is also fishable. Stocks include carp, tench, bream, roach, rudd, perch, chub and gudgeon. Best baits are bread, pellet, maggot, hemp and castor, it goes without saying.

Long Pond—has a century-old tradition of use for model boating.

Activities

These days there are still some nice leafy pathways lined by mature trees left for the strollers to enjoy.

Sporty types can go for the football, rugby, cricket, softball, tennis, basketball, Aussie rules football, croquet (!) or bowling.

Events

Some of the annual highlights include:

Race For Life—Throughout the year: Race For Life—The girls take on the common in pink to raise awareness of cancer. One of the biggest Race For Life running events.

July: Ben 'n Jerry's Sundae On The Common—also goes down well. If it sounds horribly corporate, it's worth noting that a full restoration of the bandstand in '05/'06 was partly funded by proceeds from this festival. Or, just think of the free ice-cream…

August: The Clapham Common Metro Weekender—Two successful, quality festivals have joined forces. South West Four (progressive house, trance, and breaks) and Get Loaded In the Park (indie/dance) now happen side by side at the end of August.

November: The Bonfire Night Fireworks—it's as good as it gets here.

How to Get There

By train: Wandsworth Road Station (12 minutes), Clapham High Street Station (12 minutes)

By tube: Clapham Common (4 minutes), Clapham South (13 minutes)

By bus: 4, 35, 37, 88, 137, 155, 255, 345, 355, 417, G1

Overview

A lot is packed into this 54-acre park—mostly people. On a sunny day Clissold throngs with Stokenewingtonites; yummy mummies and three-wheeled buggies; gaggles of youths, with or without hoods; lads playing football and assorted dog walkers. Visitors can see deer and goats in the animal enclosure, diamond doves and love birds in the aviary, and coots and moorhens in the nature ponds. Parents take little ones to the paddling pool (summer months only), toddler's group at the One O'clock Club or the well-equipped children's playground. The park hosts the usual hodgepodge of circuses and steam fairs as well as the famous arts festival, StokeFest, in the summer. On grey days, chilly days, or in the early hours, peace can be found—in the rose garden perhaps, or underneath one of the ancient trees.

Clissold House and Café

Phone:	0207 923 9797
Email:	info@clissoldparkcafe.com
Website:	www.hackneyvenues.com/clissold-house
Hours:	Open daily.
Admission:	FREE

Clissold Mansion, the Grade II listed building just visible from Stoke Newington Church Street, is home to a large, child-friendly cafe. Herbal tea drinkers jostle with dripping ice-cream cone lickers on the sun trap front veranda and circular lawn. The large inside rooms are best avoided if you find children's chatter grating, but otherwise a lively spot to tuck into a plate of egg and chips. The building was constructed in the late 18th century on behalf of a Quaker family whose daughter was courted by a local reverend—Augustus Clissold. He wooed, then married her, and swiftly changed the name of the estate to Clissold Place. Where is Catherine Cookson when you need her?

A hundred years later when the land was up for redevelopment, two influential campaigners persuaded the Metropolitan Board of Works to create a public space, and Clissold Park was born on 24 July 1889. Now run by the London Borough of Hackney, Clissold is kept in check by the Clissold Park User Group, who recently secured a multi-million pound lottery bid to spruce the place up a bit and return it to its former 19th century splendour.

Sport in the Park

Year round you can hear the yells of football players churning up mud, the whine of iPods as joggers run in ever decreasing circles, the thwack of cricket ball against cricket bat, and the crunch of misthrown frisbees hitting the litter bins. There is a basketball court and 10 tennis courts (two kiddies' sized) which are bookable by contacting the Park rangers (020 7254 4235) though they are impossible to get your hands on around Wimbledon—and they say TV doesn't affect our behaviour.

But one of the delights of this park is the more unusual sport that takes place. On misty mornings you can watch cotton-clad figures practice tai chi, and on warm weekends you can nearly always spot a group of hotties from the London School of Capoeira circling around each other. Then there is the occasional father/ daughter pair practising Taekwondo, or two dreadlocked crusties slinging up a line to get some tightrope practice in. Most recent addition to watchable sports in the park is run by 'Pushy Mothers'—groups of mums exercising with buggies. The buggy, with child on board, is pushed hither and thither by the panting parent. It's the ultimate in resistance training.

Nature and the Ponds

Hackney is one of the greenest inner-city boroughs and though relatively small, Clissold Park is still an important green, shady and watery spot for local wildlife, particularly waterfowl. The two nature ponds are named Beckmere and the Runtzmere in honour of the two principal founders (Beck and Runtz, in case you were wondering). The third pond in front of the cafe is more of a 'canalette' and actually used to be part of the New River built in the early 1600s to supply drinking water to London.

The animal enclosure with its fuzzy-nosed deer, fluffy rabbits and bearded mini-goats are popular with visitors who stand stuffing chips and handfuls of poisonous leaves from nearby bushes through the fence directly under the signs saying: 'Please don't feed the animals—it will make them ill.'

Note: the paddling pool is not a nature pond and though you still can't let your dog in, hours spent gazing at its inhabitants are not looked on kindly.

How to Get There

By car: Don't. There isn't much in the way of parking. But if you really need to, from Newington Green head north along Green Lanes until you see a large green space with trees on your right. Or from the A10 turn left onto Stoke Newington Church St past all the cute shops and inviting pubs, until you get to the large church on your left. The park is on your right.

By tube: From Manor House, take exit 4 and walk south down Green Lanes for 10 minutes. The park is on your left.

By train: From Stoke Newington station, head south down the High St and turn right up Stoke Newington Church St, walk for 10 minutes until you see the park on your left just past Stoke Newington Town Hall.

By bus: The 341, 141, 73, 393, and 476 all stop at various entrances to the park

Additional Information

London Borough of Hackney
www.hackney.gov.uk/clissold-park.htm

Clissold Park User Group
www.clissoldpark.com

Lothair Rd S.

Cornwallis Rd

Airoy Rd

Endymion Rd

Hermitage Rd

Green Lanes

Vale Rd

Eade Rd

American Football Field

MAP 55

Dagmar Rd

Cornwall Rd

Beatrice Rd

Oakfield Rd

American Gardens Play & Picnic Area

New River

Rowley Gdns

Woodberry Gro

Finsbury Park

Upper Tollington Pk

Scarborough Rd

Carlisle Rd

Bowling Club

Track & Gym

Alpha Dog Club

Manor House Lodge & Garden

Manor House

Basketball Courts

Parkland Walk

Oxford Rd

Boating Pond

Café

McKenzie Flower Gardens

Green Lns

Play & Picnic Area

Princes Cl

Portland Rise

Alexandra Gro

Ursula M

Woodstock Rd

Tennis Courts

Skate Park

Seven Sisters Rd

Adolphus Rd

Henry Rd

MAP 62

MAP 63

Gloucester Dr

Stroud Green Rd

Morris Pl

Wells Ter

Finsbury Park Railway Station

Wilberforce

Queen's Dr

Finsbury Park Rd

Colthurst Cres

Myddleton Ave

General Information

NFT Map: 55, 62, & 63
Website: www.haringey.gov.uk/
finsbury_park_leaflet.pdf

Overview

Sculpted from what was once a large woodland area on the fringes of London, Finsbury Park was baptized officially in the mid 19th century as a green escape for increasingly urbanized North Londoners. Today's Finsbury Park has been revamped to the tune of £5 million in an attempt to shake off the cloak of urban grime which descended during the 1970s. Though it certainly has cleaned up its act, the park is still a barren tundra-esque plain compared to Hyde or Regent's Park. More of a green scab on the city landscape that surrounds it, the sparse shrubbery and token trees are more suitable for football or running away from Staffordshire Terriers. Delve a little deeper, however and there are quaint eccentricities and little gems dotted around.

Practicalities

You can enter this veritable urban Oz at Endymion Road, Seven Sisters Road, Green Lanes and Stroud Green Road. Two tube stops serve Finsbury Park: Manor House and the eponymous Finsbury Park. There are also overland trains at Harringey Green Lanes (grab an opulent Turkish meal on the way) and at Finsbury Park Stroud Green Road. Buses 4, 19, N19, 29, N29, 106, N106, 253, N253, 254, N279, W3 and W7 all touch the park at some point. Bear in mind that if you wish to travel in the area during an Arsenal match day you'd better take a stun gun and a red scarf to navigate the crowds!

Attractions

Quaint Englishness and sweaty sporting pursuits abound within the perimeters of Finsbury Park. There are many activities you can partake in from tennis (seven courts are available on a turn up and play basis) to running in the London Heathside Athletics Club (020 8802 9139). There are even two American Football pitches. For a more twee time stroll up to the tiny boating pond and spend an hour in a beat-up boat circling the aviary island—home to exotic birds like ducks, some swans and, uh, ducks again. The kidz are catered for in the form of a skate park. Best of all is the amazing Parkland Walk, which snakes out from Finsbury Park to Alexandra Palace via Highgate.

Nature

The Arboretum and the Avenue of Mature Trees are the two main spots for tree watching. Granted, experienced botanists may find little to fire them up here, but on a mild Autumn day there are plenty of rich colours and textures that enrich any stroll through the park. There are no real 'wild' areas in the park, unlike Hampstead Heath, but there are some lovely quiet spots in the American Gardens which have been landscaped according to the original 19th century plans, with added kiddie play areas. There are some shrubs planted around the boating pond which Harringey Council calls the 'McKenzie Flower Garden' with capital letters which are barely merited.

Festivals

Recently the vast open spaces of the park have been used for music festivals and various other fairs. The Rise, Fleadh, and FinFest festivals are all fairly regular events. The park is also a popular venue for off special music events—both the Sex Pistols and Morrissey have played controversial shows here. The steam and fun fairs are also worth going to for nostalgic or regressive fun.

Old Woolrich Rd

Romney Rd

Trafalgar Rd

Nelson Rd

National Maritime Museum

Western Hemisphere

Eastern Hemisphere

Greenwich Park Side

Maze Hill

Woodland Cres

Burney St

Park Row

Park Vista

Boating Pond

Maze Hill Railway Station

King George St

Greenwich Meridian 0° Longitude

Herb Garden

Croom's Hill

Conduit House

Flamsteed House

Old Royal Observatory

The Avenue

Queen Elizabeth's Oak

Westcombe Park Rd

Roman Ruins

Woodlands Park Rd

Wellington Gro

Cade Rd

McCartney House

Croom's Hill

Greenwich Park

Café

Great Cross Ave

Blackheath Ave

Maze Hill

Vanbrugh Fields

General Wolfe Rd

Ranger's House

Ranger's Field

Boxer Ave

Flower Garden

Lodge

The Wilderness (Deer Park)

Shooters Hill Rd

Park Office

Charlton Wy

Gaffer's Rd

Long Pond Rd

Shooters Hill Rd

Prince Charles Rd

Maze Hill

Black Heath

Overview

Greenwich Park is the oldest enclosed Royal Park in Britain and has been an integral part of London life for centuries. Saxons built mounds here; Romans worshipped here; King Henry VIII and Anne Boleyn flirted here, and Charles II even built an observatory here. Then the modern day caught up and 2012 brought it to the world as an Olympic venue. It's now a playground for ageing eccentrics escaping London, yuppie families with new puppies, and heaps of tourists trekking up the staggeringly steep hill towards the iconic Royal Observatory.

And it's worth the trek. The sweeping views from the highest point are spectacular and beat the London Eye hands down. London is revealed in all its glory, from the jutting skyline of Canary Wharf, to the sinuous turns of the Thames and the seemed-like-a-good-idea-at-the-time Millennium Dome. All in stark contrast with the neoclassical architecture of the Old Royal Observatory, Royal Naval College, National Maritime Museum and the Queen's House in the immediate foreground.

A well sought-after spot throughout history, the park has belonged to the Royal Family since 1427, and in the early 1600s, under James I, the park was given a makeover in the French style, which gave it its well-groomed tree-lined pathways. He then had Inigo Jones build the missus the stately Queen's House.

The Royal Observatory and Flamsteed House

Address: Greenwich Royal Park, London SE10
Phone: 020 8858 4422
Website: www.rmg.co.uk/royal-observatory
Hours: 10 am-5 pm daily
Admission: Flamsteed House & Meridian Courtyard—£7.00 adults, £2.00 Children

Time begins, rather arbitrarily, here—on the Prime Meridian of the World, or Longitude 0º. Time all over the earth is based on a place's distance east or west from this imaginary line, outlined in metal so throngs of tourists can gawp at it. Thanks to Charles II's interest in science, Sir Christopher Wren was commissioned to build the Royal Observatory and Flamsteed House, the living quarters for the first Royal Astronomer. Time your visit to catch a workshop, talk, exhibition or planetarium show,

which seek to give visitors a richer experience than simply straddling the Meridian with thumbs up.

Also notable is the Camera Obscura, which sits in a small building next to Flamsteed House. A predecessor to the modern camera, this small dark room displays a live image of the distant National Maritime Museum, projected using only a small hole in the roof.

National Maritime Museum

Address: Greenwich, London SE10 9NF
Phone: 020 8858 4422
Website: www.rmg.co.uk/national-maritime-museum
Hours: 10 am-5 pm daily
Admission: Free

Adjacent to the park's boundaries, this is a museum dedicated to all things nautical. It comprises the Royal Observatory, as well as the Queen's House, but its main components are the Maritime Galleries. Highlights include a collection of ships' figureheads, navigational charts, maps, medals, flags and models. They also host relics from Sir John Franklin's ill-fated Northwest Passage expedition (1845-1848) including a pair of his very old-school sunglasses.

Nature

Amongst the well-mowed green are trees of infinite varieties. The scented herb garden is best enjoyed in the summer time. The fallen remains of the 900 year-old Queen Elizabeth Oak can still be viewed and lie as proof of Henry VIII's passion for these grounds, he was said to have danced around the younger tree with Anne Boleyn (before he had her executed, obviously).

How to Get There

The nearest DLR station is Cutty Sark. It's fun too: push the excitable children out the way so you can sit in the front and pretend to be the driver—always a winner with the ladies. By bus, the 53, 177, 180, 188, 199 and 286 will all get you to points of suitable proximity.

You can also take the Greenwich foot tunnel from the Isle of Dogs, which runs beneath the Thames and is open 24 hours a day. Ignore the ominous drips: it's been sturdy for over 110 years, and even if it does at last succumb to the pressure of 50 ft of river above it, then you'll not have time to worry about it. So relax and enjoy!

337

Overview

Hampstead Heath is 791 acres of rambling woods and idyllic meadows worthy of much frolicking. It's the fact that its wilderness seems so, well, wild that makes this London park deceptive. You can be merrily re-enacting the Brothers Grimm, only to be spat out rather rudely onto Parliament Hill and confronted with gob-smacking views of St Paul's and the Gherkin. The Heath is truly nothing short of heaven—until you stumble over George Michael up to no good in the bushes. You can swim naked in its ponds, stroll amongst its tall grasses without seeing another living soul for twenty minutes or more and engage in a little sex scandal amongst the greenery. The park's common theme is one of a hidden countryside retreat right in the middle of it all.

Most likely because it *is* countryside. It's just the rest of London that's gone all urban around it. Long-established hedgerows and ancient trees attest to its lengthy history. The range of wildlife on show is impressive—kingfishers, parakeets, 300 species of fungi and several types of bat, to name a few. All sorts of famous people have enjoyed its leafy company through the years. Boudicca's Mound near the men's bathing pond (hmm... sounds dirty), is said to mark the ancient queen's burial chamber. Karl Marx and his family had a picnic here every Sunday while he lived in London and writer Wilkie Collins used the park as a backdrop for The Woman in White. All in all, the Heath has been a much-loved place of social gathering and strolling for centuries, a place of peace and perspective amongst the greater hustle and bustle of the Big Smoke.

Ponds, Ponds and…Oh Yeah, More Ponds…

It might be argued that losing your Heath virginity consists of swimming in one of its famous outdoor bathing ponds. These are open throughout the year and attract throngs of dedicated swimming fans. On the eastern side—closer to Highgate—are a series of eight 17th and 18th century reservoirs dotted between Parliament Hill Fields and Kenwood House. Amongst these is one swimming pond for guys, another for gals, a toy boat pond, a wildlife reserve pond, and a lake for fishing. On the western side of the Heath are three more, including the 'mixed pond', where you can have some underwater flirtations, should you wish.

Kenwood House

Kenwood House is closed for refurbishment until Autumn 2013. However, the Brewhouse Café remains open and can be visited between 9am-5pm. Kenwood House, a 17th century manor in the middle of the park, adds very nicely to the Heath's countryside effect. Its striking classically white walls and landscaped grounds play backdrop to summer jazz festivals as well as a few scenes in the movie Notting Hill. Purchased by brewing magnate Edward Cecil Guinness in 1925, Kenwood House is more than just a pretty façade. Thanks to Guinness's fortune and interest in art, the manor house is also a very noteworthy art gallery featuring works by the likes of Rembrandt, Turner and Gainsborough.

Golders Hill Park

Golders Hill Park is the younger brother to the bigger Hampstead Heath, adjoining it on the western side. Where the latter is an icon of epic proportions, the former is more of a good ol' neighbourhood park. Its large expanse of grass was created rather suddenly when a house that stood on the grounds was bombed during the Blitz. It has a lot to offer for its size though, with a formal flower garden, a deer park and a small zoo (with alpacas no less). If you're feeling sporty, there are tennis courts, putting greens and plenty of jogging paths.

How to Get There

The closest tube stations are Hampstead, Golder's Green and Archway on the Northern Line. Nearby overland stations include Hampstead Heath and Gospel Oak. Bus numbers running to the park are the 168, 268 and 210, which cuts through on Spaniard's Road (where you may want to stop for a pint at the historic Spaniard's Inn).

Additional Information

City of London
www.cityoflondon.gov.uk
Information and booking tickets for swimming:
020 7485 5757

Heath and Hampstead Society:
www.heathandhampsteadsociety.org.uk

Highgate Cemetery
General Info

NFT Map: 51 & 59
Web: www.highgate-cemetery.org
Phone: 020 8340 1834

West Cemetery

The West Cemetery opened in 1839 and most of the original pathways and structures still exist. This part of the cemetery is a wild wonderland of creeping vines and eerie Victorian tombs. On weekdays, tours take place daily at 1.45 pm from March to November. There's a limit of 15 people so you'll need to book in advance or the number above. The weekends are a free-for-all with tours taking place hourly from 11 am until 4 pm April to November and until 3 pm December to March.

East Cemetery

The newer East Cemetery is located on the opposite side of the road to the West entrance. This side is open daily and for four pounds you get to roam unsupervised for as long as you please. It may not be as impressive as the West side, but it's still a place of breathtaking beauty. Although there are some well-trodden paths and proper walkways, large parts of the cemetery are almost completely overgrown, making it a wonderful place to go for a stroll.

Opening Hours:
1st April to 31st October
Mon-Fri: 10 am-5 pm
Sat-Sun: 11 am-5 pm

1st November to 31st March
Mon-Fri: 10 am-4 pm
Sat-Sun: 11 am-4 pm

Famous Occupants

Quite a few notable people are buried here. The caretakers will be more than willing to inform you of the whereabouts of the following graves and plenty of others.

Douglas Adams, author. Most famous for the *Hitchhiker's Guide To The Galaxy* series of books.

George Eliot, English author and poet; also actually a woman.

Christina Rossetti, English poet.

Karl Marx. Philosopher; considered the father of communism.

Alexander Livinenko, Russian ex-spy, famously murdered by radiation poisoning in a Soho sushi restaurant in 2006.

A whole load of Charles Dickens' clan but not the man himself.

The Highgate Vampire

There have been numerous accounts of shapes, ghosts and supernatural figures seen on the cemetery grounds, and in the early 70s the media picked up on a theory involving a vampire and the legend of The Highgate Vampire. It caused quite a stir and soon mobs of 'vampire hunters' descended on the place (imagine something like the Thriller video, but with flares and tank tops). Finally, Sean Manchester, president

and founder of the Vampire Research Society, claimed to have killed the fiend in 1973, when he tracked it to a nearby house. Manchester was also, in his spare time, patron of the Yorkshire Robin Hood society, and remains, in this publication's estimation, the single most compelling reason not to wander around Highgate Cemetery after dark.

Waterlow Park Overview

Waterlow Park is a beautifully landscaped park located just next to the cemetery, making it a perfect spot for a pre- or post-gravespotting picnic. Often overlooked and overshadowed by nearby Hampstead Heath it is a charming and peaceful alternative. You can feed the ducks in one of the three ponds, hire tennis courts by the hour, admire the awesome view of London, wander in the rose garden, or just go look at the cool hollow tree at the bottom of the park.

Lauderdale House

Address: Highgate Hill, Waterlow Park
          London N6 5HG
Tel: 020 8348 8716
Web: www.lauderdalehouse.co.uk

Lauderdale House operates independently from the park, but is located on its grounds. The original house was built in 1582, but has gone through major alterations and restorations since then. In 1963 a major fire destroyed much of the old building and it was left untouched and unoccupied for 15 years. In 1978 it was finally repaired and reopened in its current incarnation. The house runs classes, concerts and exhibitions by local artists. There's also a small café. The House and the galleries are usually open Tue-Fri 11 am-4 pm, Sat 1.30 pm-5 pm & Sun 12 pm-5 pm, but you can always phone in advance to avoid disappointment.

How to Get There

Nearest tube station is Archway. Exit the station and turn left up Highgate Hill. Waterlow Park is about five minutes walk on your left hand side. To get to the cemetery, cross the park down to the Swain's Lane exit, which is adjacent to the East Cemetery gates.

General Information

Website: http://www.royalparks.org.uk/parks/
hyde-park
parks/hyde_park

Phone: 030 0061 2000

Overview

For over 370 years Hyde Park has been the 'Lungs of London'—the place to go for oxygen-starved Londoners to take a breath of fresh air. This park remains an essential part of the beating heart of London. As the city's grown, so has the desire to preserve this 350-acre mass of parkland and thankfully, Hyde Park has never been in better shape.

Eating

Perambulating through the park is bound to get that metabolism going, so stop off at one of the numerous food stalls to quench your thirst or down a plasticky hot-dog. Yum. For a more civilised affair check out one of the park's seated joints: the **Lido Café** (which also has a paddling pool) or **The Serpentine Bar & Kitchen**.

Nature, Architecture & Sculpture

The Serpentine Lake attracts the usual assortment of ducks as well as some exotic additions, such as Egyptian Geese. **The Lookout Education Centre** holds informative talks about the park's wildlife. **The Grand Entrance** at Hyde Park Corner is an awe-inspiring arched construction of Greek influence, whilst the **Albert Memorial**, erected by Queen Victoria after her husband's death, is a true show of love. The **Diana, Princess of Wales Memorial Fountain**, remains one of the most visited areas in Hyde Park and is worth a look to satisfy curiosity, as is the **Peter Pan Memorial**. And pause to reflect at the heartbreaking 7 July Memorial, which pays tribute to each of the victims of the 2005 London Bombings.

Performance

The park attracts big musical events, and by big we mean Live 8 big. It's only the musical deities that get their own special Hyde Park treatment—Bruce Springsteen, Paul McCartney and Blur, but summer means festival time and the annual Wireless Festival and Hard Rock Calling. Brass band concerts are held throughout the summer at **The Bandstand**. **Speakers' Corner** is guaranteed to entertain. Since 1872 it's been the site of a verbal free-for-all stemming from the activities of the Reform League who marched for manhood suffrage in 1866. These days the topics aren't quite as revolutionary. Heather Mills sounded off here recently…ah, the injustice of having too much cash.

Sports

There are ample jogging paths, designated bike routes (see www.companioncycling.org.uk) and great paths for roller-blading and walking. Even more fun is boating on **The Serpentine Lake** from March to October. Informal games of rugby, football or cricket can be played on the **'Sports Field'** while **Hyde Park Tennis & Sports Centre** does exactly what it says on the tin. There's also a bowling green and horse riding at the **Manege.**

Kensington Gardens

The 111 hectares west of the Western Carriage Drive are known as Kensington Gardens. Annexed from the main park in 1689, the area retains a slightly more formal air, with regular tree-lined avenues to stroll down and less spaces for rambunctious sporting displays. This makes the Gardens an ideal spot for a picnic or a quiet ponder. Kensington Gardens also boasts the **Serpentine Gallery** (in between the Diana Fountain and the Albert Memorial), a toy-sized venue for renowned modern and contemporary art exhibitions, and the rather stunning **Kensington Palace**. Still a royal residence, the palace majestically overlooks some of the most well ordered green spaces London has to offer.

Richmond Rd

Richmond Rd

Tennis Courts

Lido

Playground

Gayhurst Rd

Ellingfort Rd

London Fields West Side

The Pub on the Park

London Ln

Sport Piches

Martello St

Wilman Gro

London Fields Railway Station

Martello Ter

London Fields

Middleton Rd

Lamb Ln

MAP 89

Menmore Ter

Gransden Ave

Lansdowne Dr

Shrubland Rd

Helmsley Pl

Bayford St

Lamb Ln

Sidworth St

Spor Piches

London Fields East Side

Grand Union Cres

Warburton Rd

Exmouth Pl

Dublin Ave

Playground

Triangle Rd

Warburton St

Mare St

Tredervern Rd

Westgate St

Westgate St

Croston St

Denhofe Rd

Broadway Mkt

Mare St

Westgate St

Bocking St

Overview

Best green space of the northeast? Victoria Park might still bag the accolade, but this relaxed, mid-sized park in the middle of Hackney is catching up. And quickly. It's lush and it's spacious and its latest addition, a smashing 50-metres Lido (see below), is hard to beat. Just off busy Mare Street and minutes from Regent's Canal, the park is easily reachable and easily manageable. There are two tennis courts, football, basketball and cricket pitches, and two well-equipped and well-maintained playgrounds, if you have kids in tow. London Fields does a nice job of attracting a pleasantly diverse mix of people, from Hoxton-refugee artists and rollie-smoking would-be philosophers, to pram-pushing mums and East End geezers with no teeth and big dogs. The architecture framing the tree-studded space is just as varied: bland high rises, pretty Victorians, depressing brick estates and fancy new developments, all modern Hackney is there.

The park's own drinking spot, imaginatively called Pub on the Park, is good for a relaxed outside pint, simple pub food or the footie. If you're after a slightly more refined meal, check the gastropub-ish Cat and Mutton at the park's bottom. This is also where Broadway Market begins, a traditional East End market street, now brimming with nice little shops, several pubs and original eateries. If the red wine you shared with your painter friends on their picnic blanket got you into serious party mood, head to the close-by (and late-night) Dolphin on Mare Street. Or just fall asleep in the shadows of those massive oak trees. Chances are, one of the dogs will lick you back to reality.

London Fields Lido

Address:	London Fields Westside, London E8 3EU
Phone:	020 7254 9038
Website:	http://www.hackney.gov.uk/ c-londonfields-lido.htm
Hours:	Mon-Fri 6:30am—8pm
Admission:	£4.50 for adults, £2.70 for kids

You might say that in a city where, essentially, you have the choice between stomach-turningly grotty leisure centre pools and hopelessly overpriced member gym versions, any new public swimming basin would be a winner. Fair enough. But WHAT a winner. Having mouldered closed for almost two decades, a £2.5m effort has restored this art deco gem to its former glory. In fact, it's probably better than ever: the 50-metre basin is nicely heated all year round (25C when we last checked), the changing rooms are modern and clean, admission's okay. Come during the week for a few pre-work lanes, when steam mysteriously hangs over the water, or jump in on the weekend, followed by a Sunday roast in one of the pubs close-by or a picnic in the park. Sounds nice? We know.

Sports

There's no shortage of things to do. The park's two tennis courts can be booked for hourly slots (open 8.30 am-dusk; £6.00/h during peak times, £4.00/h off-peak; call 020 7254 4235 for more info). The Hackney Tennis Club (www.hackneycitytennisclubs.co.uk) also offers classes and joint sessions. The football pitch (just come and play) is located in the middle, the basketball space (ditto) towards the south. Follow the sound of children for the playgrounds, one in the north, one in the south. If cricket is your cup of tea, get in touch with the London Fields Cricket Club (londonfieldscc@gmail.com), who keep the park's long-standing tradition as a cricket pitch alive (which, incidentally, is said to go back to 1800).

How to Get There

By bus: Most buses stop on Mare Street (get off at the London Fields stop), a few minutes walk from the actual park. From Liverpool Street Station, take 48 and 55, from Mile End or Bethnal Green grab the D6. The 106 takes you here from Finsbury Park, the 277 from Highbury & Islington. Two buses stop directly at the bottom of the park: the 236 (connecting to Dalston, Newington Green, Finsbury Park) and the 394 (Hackney Central, Homerton Hospital, Hoxton, Angel).

By train: The train is a great option, since London Fields station is located right next to the park. Train operator National Express East Anglia (formerly known as One Railway) serves the central Liverpool Street Station (via Cambridge Heath and Bethnal Green) and connects the Victoria Line tube stations Seven Sisters and Tottenham Hale further north. You can travel using your Oyster Card, for timetables check www.greateranglia.co.uk.

Victoria Park

Old Ford Rd

Canal

Hertford Union

Grove Rd

Roman Rd

St Stephen's Rd

Cardigan Rd

Vernon Rd

Sheffield Rd

Spilford Rd

Tredegar Rd

Gernon Rd

Vivian Rd

Zealand Rd

Ellesmere Rd

Driffield Rd

Hewlett Rd

Lanfranc Rd

Medway Rd

Lyal Rd

Norman Rd

Saxon Rd

Athelstane Gro

Mace St

Twig Folly Cl

Roman Rd

Grand Union Canal

Grove Rd

Arbery Rd

Strahan Rd

Antill Rd

Cherrywood Cl

Lichfield Rd

Malmesbury Rd

Merchant St

Harley Gro

Morgan St

Tredegar Sq

Coborn Rd

Osborn St

Coborn St

Meath Gardens

Morpeth St

Meath Crescent

Bradwell St

Longnor Rd

Mooby St

MAP 93

Ashcroft Rd

Canton Rd

Lichfield Rd

Alderson Rd

Rhonda Gro

Tredegar Sq

Mile End Rd

British Rd

Lawton Rd

W Field Wy

"The Banana"

Mile End

Southern Grove

Brokesley St

Grantley St

Bancroft Rd

Alderney Rd

Mile End Rd

Solebay St

Eric St

Grove Rd

Hamlets Wy

English St

Eric St

Mansford St

Treby St

Ropery St

Tower Hamlets Cemetery

Stepney Green

Ernest St

Commodore St

Ropery St

Bow Common Ln

Beaumont Sq

White Horse Ln

Shaney St

Hartford Rd

Essian St

Duckett St

Bale Rd

Eohn Rd

Dongola Rd

MAP 98

Ragged School Museum

Copperfield Rd

Mile End Park

Stadium

Burdett Rd

Wager St

Joseph St

Ackroyd Dr

Leopold St

Burdett Rd

Stepney Green

Rectory Sq

Ben Jonson Rd

Halley St

Carr St

Rhodeswell Rd

Rhodeswell

Timothy Rd

St Paul's Wy

Stepney Green

Garden St

Stepney High St

Overview

Bordered at the north by the chain-ridden fake-a-rama, Bow Wharf, to the east and south by rat runs, and to the west by the dank waters of the Regent's Canal, this strange elongated park doesn't appear to have a lot going for it. However, this 32-hectare wiggle of green is more a string of mini parks—divided up by roads and railway lines—and each segment has hidden treasures worth digging for. There is an adventure playground, an arts pavilion with weird orange-and-white sculptural seats by Leona Matuszczak, an ecology park with moths and all sorts, a terraced garden and a sheltered children's playground. Clever landscaping and inventive use of space creates pockets of peace, and when the sun comes out, sparkling on the canal, bouncing off of the reflective jackets of the cyclists bombing past or laying its beams on giggling young couples, the park of many parks comes into its own.

It was created following the Second World War after the area was destroyed in the Blitz. The idea of Lord Abercombie, who envisioned a creepy-sounding 'finger of green' in amongst the rubble, Mile End really came into being in 1999 with Millennium Commission funding providing new areas, strange metal cross signage and an amazing green bridge—known by locals as the Banana. It actually has grass and shrubs taking walkers and cyclists over Mile End Road.

The remains of the Victorian terraces sit on the west side of the park, and one resilient pub, The Palm Tree, squats alone in the middle of a grey car park, a testament to the rows of two-up-two-downs which no longer flank the pub. This great local boozer is filled most nights with a mix of climbers and locals tucking into doorstep sandwiches and draft beer.

For those who want a bit more local history, The Ragged School Museum (www.raggedschoolmuseum.org.uk) on Copperfield St overlooks the southern tip of the park: a canal side slum that was transformed into a school for the local urchins by philanthropist Dr Barnado. It now has a mocked-up Victorian classroom and clunky little cafe. Only open Wednesday and Thursday and the occassional Sunday—check before you go.

Sports in the Park

The southern end of the park is a haven for sporty types with a refurbished stadium and ten all-weather pitches made from recycled car tyres, a go-kart track and the large Ikea-like Mile End Leisure Centre with all the usual sauna, gym, pool and verruca-infested changing rooms. Mile End Climbing Wall is housed in an old pipe engineering works in the middle of the park, and is one of London's 'big three' (The Castle and the Westway are the others). It was opened in the 80s and some of its users seem unaware of time's passage, judging by their fetching leggings.

How to Get There

By tube: Turn left out of Mile End station, cross Grove Rd and you'll find yourself at one of the entrances to the middle section of the park.

By car: The park can be easily accessed from Bow Road, Grove Rd, or Mile End Rd, though according to London Borough of Tower Hamlets, 'The local streets operate a resident's parking permit system and are regularly patrolled by traffic wardens. Limited parking is available at Bow Wharf.'

By bus: The D6, D7, 25, 205, 277, 323, 339 and all take you to various entrances around the park.

Additional Information

London Borough of Tower Hamlets
www.towerhamlets.gov.uk/default.
aspx?page=12599

Mile End Climbing Wall
www.mileendwall.org.uk

General Information

Website: www.royalparks.org.uk/parks/
the-regents-park
Park Tel: 030 0061 2300
London Zoo: www.zsl.org
Open Air Theatre: www.openairtheatre.org

Overview

Whenever your quaint and backward country-dwelling friends are telling you the virtues of rural life, you can silence them with two words: Regent's Park. Let the yokels have their cleaner lungs, their maypoles and their children running barefoot and feral, because London may have its city drawbacks but it knows how to do a good park. When you stroll in Regent's Park, you're strolling on nothing less than Property of the Crown—you can see tigers and gorillas, play on the largest outdoor sports area in London, take in some Shakespeare, or, on a very good day, watch girls playing volleyball in bikinis. With 410 acres of parkland, you will always find a spot away from the (many thousands of) fellow visitors. It is the perfect space to take stock, step back and refresh, to sit in a deckchair with a good book, picnic with friends, breathe better air. Moreover, the same obnoxious people who wouldn't move down the tube to let you on or

who pushed in the sandwich queue, are here relaxing with their families, lazing over a paper in a patch of sun, falling in love, throwing a Frisbee: it can be just what you need to re-bond with London when you're becoming jaded, and to get away from it all without leaving Zone One.

How to Get There

By tube:
Regent's Park—Bakerloo.
Great Portland St—Hammersmith & City, Circle, Metropolitan.
Baker St—Hammersmith & City, Jubilee, Metropolitan, Bakerloo.
St John's Wood—Jubilee.
Camden Town—Northern.

The Park is served by bus routes 2, 13, 18, 27, 30, 74, 82, 113, 139, 189, 274, 453 and C2.

Nature

The Park is a haven for the city's wildlife, thanks to a biodiversity which includes grassland, woodland, wetland, lakes and scrubs, as well as beautifully tended and fragrant gardens. Over 200 species of birds have been spotted in the Park, along with favourite garden mammals such as hedgehogs, squirrels and foxes. But if that's all just a bit too Beatrix Potter, you can get your fix of the more badass species at London Zoo in the Park's north-east end, where in addition to the normal enclosures, visitors can get closer to some of the animals with events like "Meet the Monkeys" or even help as a volunteer.

The Park's size and calm makes it a choice hangout for celebrities (not strictly nature, but dandelion schmandelion: spotting A-Listers doing tai chi in oversized sunglasses will impress more down the pub, and can there be a nobler calling?).

Performances and Events

The Park's permanent outdoor theatre is an absolute treat. The shows have a Shakespearian bias, but the venue also puts on non-bard performances, comedy nights and concerts. It is the experience more than the performance which will likely stay in your memory. Among the atmospheric trees of the park in the evening, with a bottle of wine and a blanket to snuggle up in (it is Britain after all—how many other theatres have an official "weather policy"?), it is a magical way to spend an evening. Outdoor does not mean free however: prices range from £10–£50 (Saturdays are the most expensive), and you pay theatre prices for food and drink. Cheaper to bring a picnic to enjoy in front of the theatre before the performance.

Regent's Park also hosts a number of big outdoor events. Notable regulars include Taste of London and the Frieze Art Fair London. Check the website for one-off listings.

Primrose Hill

To the north of Regent's Park sits Primrose Hill, which is a rather large hill, boasting corking views of much of Central and East London. It's also surrounded by some rather lovely eateries.

The former hunting ground for playboy king Henry VIII has a murky history, becoming the scene of a political feud in 1678, when magistrate Edmund Berry Godfrey was found dead there after being implicated in a plot to kill Charles II. In later generations Primrose Hill became the setting for duels: London lovers fought there over their ladies, while fops found it a good place to settle literary disagreements ("I say Dryden is naught but a one-trick satirist sir!" "Well then I say you are a cad and a scoundrel! Die you maggot!").

Celebrity voyeurs should keep 'em peeled for the likes of Kate Moss, old bumbles himself Mr Boris Johnson, and writer Alan Bennett, while Primrose Hill in winter is the ideal spot to check out panoramic views of fireworks across the city on Guy Fawkes Night (5 November).

Overview

In 1625 Charles I brought his court to Richmond. He subsequently, with quite heroic selfishness, built a wall round a large expanse of open grassland, and created Richmond Park. These days the park is thankfully accessible to the public, opening at 7 am (or 7.30 in the winter) and closing at dusk every day. It's the biggest of the Royal Parks in London, and is an obvious choice for long bike rides, picnics, informal sports and other wholesome pursuits for your golden, happy days of youth. Oh, and there's deer.

Attractions

The park has a number of gardens and wooded areas, the most beautiful of which is probably the Isabella Plantation, an organic woodland garden that blooms with azaleas and rhododendrons. The Pen Ponds is another popular feature, as is Pembroke Lodge, the park's Georgian mansion, which can be rented out for weddings and conferences (www.pembroke-lodge.co.uk or call 020 8940 8207) The adjacent café also does a mean cream team.

Sports

There are three rugby pitches near the Roehampton Gate that are available for rental on weekdays during winter (contact the Rosslyn Park Rugby Club at 020 8948 3209), and two eighteen hole, pay and play golf courses (call 020 8876 1795 for info. and booking). Between 16 June and 14 March you can purchase a fishing permit for the Pen Ponds (call 020 8948 3209 for information). Or for more extreme park-goers there is the option of Power Kiting, whatever the hell that is (www.kitevibe.com), and military-led Boot Camps to shape you up fast and mercilessly.

Kew

The Royal Botanic Gardens, Kew, begun in 1660, is not only easy on the eyes but is an important centre for horticultural research and a UNESCO World Heritage Site. Guaranteed to take place every year are the summer festival 'Kew the Music' (July) and ice-skating (Nov-Feb). Kew is a hugely popular day trip destination for schoolchildren and adults alike and contains such a surplus of sights and attractions that repeat visits are always surprising.

Attractions

Of course the main attractions here are the Gardens themselves. Between the formal gardens, smaller themed collections of plants and wildlife and conservation areas, there is enough walking and cooing to be done to justify any length of cake and sandwich sessions at one of the Gardens' eateries. There are also 39 Grade I and II listed buildings, all of which have some kind of historic significance. The 17th century Kew Palace (www.hrp.org.uk), is one of the most interesting of these, having previously been home to the notoriously 'mad' King George III. Other buildings in the gardens include the Chinese Pagoda of 1762, a traditional Japanese 'Minka' house and a number of museums. Decimus Burton's glasshouses (The Palm House and the Temperate) are iconic examples of this quintessentially Victorian architectural theme, and an essential part of any visit to Kew.

Events

Kew Gardens is run with great enthusiasm and has a packed programme of events throughout the year. These occur and change frequently so it's best to check the Kew website, which has comprehensive listings of everything that is going on in the Gardens, down to the blooming or blossoming of individual plant species: www.kew.org.

Several of the historic buildings, most spectacularly the Temperate Glasshouse, are available to rent for corporate and private parties.

How to Get There

Richmond station (overland trains, District Line) is a 20 minute walk from Richmond Park, or buses 371 and 65 both go from the station to the pedestrian gate at Petersham. Kew Gardens is (surprisingly) the closest station for Kew Gardens, London Overground trains stop here from across North and North West London. Trains from Waterloo stop at Kew Bridge station, a ten- minute walk from the gardens.

A large number of buses go from Hammersmith, Fulham, Clapham Junction, Wandsworth and Ealing to Richmond Park and to Kew Gardens.

Overview

A pedestrianised quarter formed of venues for theatre, music, cinema, art and various other artistically orientated entities, the South Bank is the realisation of a post-war dream of an arts-for-all hub in London. The area has its roots in 1951's Festival of Britain, a technicoloured marvel designed to showcase an optimistic future for Britons used to coal, Spitfires and fake mashed potato. The legacy of the Festival ensured that the surrounding area went on to grow into the playground that it has become today.

The South Bank Centre

The actual 'South Bank Centre' is officially formed of the Royal Festival Hall, the Queen Elizabeth Hall, the Purcell Room, the Hayward Gallery and the Saison Poetry Library, which are all concentrated in the centre of the South Bank. The Royal Festival Hall hosts a variety of musical and dance performances from its auditorium, whilst the Hall's foyer is an enormous and relaxed open-plan area with a bar, performance spaces and shop. The Queen Elizabeth Hall and Purcell Room offer further stages for musical recitals whilst the Saison Poetry Library houses a vast collection of poetry dating from 1912 onwards. The Hayward Gallery has an exterior of frightening ugliness, which shields a surprisingly spacious interior, devoted to exhibitions of the visual arts.

The National Theatre

The National Theatre is next-door to the South Bank Centre complex and is another gaping example of uncompromising architecture. Opened in 1963, it still looks slightly unhinged. The building consists of three theatres and puts on a range of productions from the established to the experimental. It also features an inviting foyer, and in the open spirit of the South Bank, offers back-stage tours, workshops, talks and costume and prop hire to Joe Schmo.

British Film Institute and IMAX

Nestling under Waterloo Bridge, the BFI promotes film and television through its archives, cinema screens, talks and festivals. It's a great alternative to the disgustingly over-priced and sticky-floored chain cinemas of central London and promotes an all-encompassing program from its three screens.

The Film Café and Benugo Bar & Kitchen do good pre- and post-flick munch. The BFI IMAX is the separate, rotund glass building situated around 200m south of the BFI. It shows films on Britain's biggest cinema screen accompanied by sound pumped from a gargantuan 11,600-watt sound system.

Everything Else

Beyond its theatres, music halls, galleries and cinemas, the South Bank has spawned a number of other attractions. The London Eye is an enormous Ferris wheel built in 2000 on the banks of the Thames adjacent to Westminster Bridge, it revolves at a leisurely 0.5 mph and offers brilliant views from its 135m-high peak. The London Aquarium is just opposite but with ticket prices roughly similar to the Eye, seeing big fish in small tanks starts to look a distinctly lame option. Less expensive attractions around South Bank include the open-air book market tucked under Waterloo Bridge and Gabriel's Wharf, a dinky enclave of small shops, bars and restaurants that offer succour to those cultured-out. Or you can ogle at the cool kids doing half pipes at the South Bank Skate Park..

Getting There

By tube: Nearest stations are Waterloo (Northern, Bakerloo, Jubilee and Waterloo & City lines) and Embankment (Circle, District, Northern & Bakerloo lines). From Waterloo, head 50m towards the river. Embankment station is at the northern foot of Hungerford footbridge.

By train: Nearest stations are Waterloo & Charing Cross. For directions from Waterloo, see 'By Tube'. From Charing Cross, walk 100m down Villiers Street towards the river and then walk across the Hungerford footbridge.

By bus: The South Bank is on numerous bus routes. Buses stop on nearby Waterloo Bridge, York Road, Belvedere Road, Stamford Street and Waterloo Station. Most coming from the North get to South Bank via Holborn, The Strand or Victoria. From the South they come via Elephant and Castle or Lambeth North.

By boat: Festival Pier is adjacent to the London Eye. Pleasure boats dock here on cruises, as do riverboat services which sail west as far as Tate Britain and east as far as Woolwich Arsenal.

General Information

NFT Maps: 9 & 23
Website: www.royalparks.org.uk/parks/st-
                jamess-park
                www.royalparks.org.uk/parks/
                green-park
Free guided walks: 020 7930 1793
Inn the Park Café and Restaurant
(St. James's Park): 020 7451 9999

Overview

With Trafalgar Square at one end and Buck Palace at the other, both St. James's and Green Park are slap-bang in the heart of picture-postcard London. When the belching fumes of the Hackney cab and hordes of Oxford Street shoppers threaten both health and sanity, there's only one place to go. Zip past the crowds and pigeons in Trafalgar Square and head under the grand curve of Admiralty Arch into the stately calm of St. James's Park. Stand yourself on the bridge that crosses the lake, take a deep breath and marvel at the history surrounding you in the city's oldest Royal Park, dating back to the days of Henry VIII.

The views: fairytale Buckingham Palace to the west, Downing Street, the seat of Parliament and Big Ben jutting out over Horse Guards' Parade to the east and the towers of Westminster Abbey to the south. There ain't nowhere else in London where you can view the icons of Church, State and Monarchy in one quick spin on your heels. Impressive. And when you're done marvelling, join the families, office workers, joggers and tourists in taking a stroll round the lake, pelican-spotting, duck-feeding, lunching and romancing.

A hop across the Mall and you'll find yourself in the rolling green of, yup, Green Park. Flowerbed free, this 53-acre patch of park with its aged plane trees is the more meditative of the two. A refuge from the noisy thoroughfare of Piccadilly and Hyde Park corner, its grounds soon fill with picnicking office-workers at the slightest suggestion of sun while the tree-lined Mall is the nearest you'll get to a Parisian boulevard.

Nature

The curving lake of St. James's park runs the length of the grounds and is perfect for indulging in some casual bird-spotting. Ever since the days of James I, the park has been home to an exotic menagerie, once including elephants, camels and even crocs.

While the crocs and ellies might be long gone, both Duck Island and the smaller West Island remain home to an impressive array of water birds. Beyond the humble duck and gulls, there are suitably stately black swans, rare golden eyes and the rather less-illustrious sounding shovelers, a close relative of the time-starved office-worker on lunch, we believe. But, with their gentlemanly swagger and mighty beaks, the five resident pelicans unquestionably steal the show. A gift from the Russian Ambassador in 1664, feeding time is worth a gander at 3pm daily. Known for their entertaining antics—like flying to Regent's Park Zoo on fish-stealing sprees—one caused a media storm when, clearly lusting after a menu change, it swallowed a live pigeon whole, flapping feathers 'n' all.

Take some old bread and the park's tame, tubby squirrels will feast from your hand. Hang around 'til dusk and the bats come out to play.

Architecture & Sculpture

As if housing ol' Queenie's Buckingham Palace wasn't enough, the parks are surrounded by two more palaces—Westminster, now the Houses of Parliament, and St. James's. From the Regency elegance of the Mall's Carlton House, home to the Institute of Contemporary Arts (ICA), to the impressive frontage of Horse Guard's Parade, the parks are hemmed in by grandeur.

Once a swampy wasteland for grazing pigs, it's a tale with humble beginnings for London's most royal park. While each passing King and Queen slowly improved St. James's Park, it was Charles II that really put the work in, getting trees planted, lawns laid and then opening it up for the first time to us commoners.

Sobering war memorials in St. James's Park abound, including world war icons Mountbatten and Kitchener in Horse Guards' Parade, and an overblown marble statue of Queen Victoria complete with glitter and gates. Oh, and that grand old Duke of York, best-known for marching his men up and down some hill? He's here too, in bronze atop a mighty pillar by the ICA.

The Parks in Season

St. James's in spring is carpeted with crocuses and daffodils. Come summer, they're quickly replaced with a carpet of sun-starved Tom, Dick and Sallys, laid bare as they dare to catch some rays. For an instant upgrade from the rabble, head to Green Park by the tube and hire a stripy deck-chair at £1.50 a pop from April to September.

Between May and August, add a dash of high-brow culture to your day with free concerts at the bandstand every lunchtime and early evening.

Autumn days might be chilly but clear skies make for impressive sunsets while wintry strolls are all the more head-clearing, especially after a night on the Soho tiles.

Sports

With cycling and ball-games banned—*entirely inappropriate in such stately surrounds!*—jogging, morning tai chi, leisurely strolls and pigeon chasing are as energetic as it gets. Sundays are best for strolling when Constitution Hill is closed to traffic.

The Mall and Constitution Hill are cycle-friendly and make a pleasant cut through the West End. Join the Serpentine running club for regular jaunts through St. James's. (www.serpentine.org.uk).

Enjoy the sedate pace with free lunch-time guided walks twice a month, discussing anything from horticulture to royalty (booking line: 020 7930 1793).

General info

NFT Map: 90, 93, & 94
Website: www.towerhamlets.gov.uk/default.
                aspx?page=12670
Information: 020 7364 2494

Overview

Look at all the joggers, skaters, cricketers and picnickers swarming in Victoria Park on any given weekend, and it seems hard to continue calling this 218-acres green space one of London's best-kept secrets. Yet, to many Londoners not living east, it still is. Lined by Regent's Canal in the south, London's third-largest cultivated green space is a nice blend of Regent's Park's beauty and the wilderness found in Hampstead Heath. It's also far enough off the Central London map to stay virtually tourist-free, while, at the same time, feeling reassuringly inner city urban, with the Gherkin and Canary Wharf's skyscrapers all in sight.

Divided into two handy bits by Grove Road, Victoria Park has much of what makes a park more than just grass and trees: excellent sporting facilities, ranging from athletics to rugby, several lakes, a deer enclosure, a secret garden—and plenty of decent drinking holes

nearby. Designed in the 1840s to bring much needed greenery and breathing space to a soul-destroyingly grim East End, the "people's park" can also look back on an intriguing past of dissent, non-conformist rallying and all sorts of political mischief-making. And it's home to the oldest model boat racing club in the country. Come now, before the Olympics do. Once the squirrels start digging out amphetamines, the secret will be gone forever.

Nature

Ducks, swans, birds and god knows what else live around The Lake in the west, while deer and goats graze slightly further north. You're allowed to fish in the Old Lake, although we're not at all sure that there are really many fish in there. Pretty oak trees and hawthorns stud the whole place; colourful flowers and perfectly-groomed shrubs grow in the Old English Garden. It's a beautifully landscaped gem of a garden and one of this city's most peaceful spots—if you don't mind the odd greying philosopher, mumbling to himself.

Sports

Jogging and skating are popular and, thanks to wide pathways, possible throughout the park. There's a rugby pitch, a large dedicated football area, four tennis courts (call 020 8986 5182) and three all-weather cricket pitches, run by the esteemed Victoria Park Community Cricket League (www.vpccl.co.uk). The children's playgrounds are decent enough, and the athletic field is excellent. Get in touch with the park's own athletics association (www.vphthac.org.uk) for access to changing rooms, showers and its indoor cricket hall.

Architecture & sculpture

Rising in the middle of the park is a Grade-II listed drinking fountain erected by Baroness Angela Burdett-Coutt (England's wealthiest woman at some point, we're told), adorned by several half-naked marble boys, smiling cheekily. The Hackney Wick Great War Memorial, in the east part of the park, is a reminder that this part of London was hit especially hard by the bombings of the Second World War. Close-by, you'll find two alcove-type fragments that survived the demolition of the old London Bridge Station. Fairly unremarkable, but good shelter when it's raining. Let's face it, no one comes here for architecture.

Festivals

The hazy days when The Clash whipped up a beer-can-throwing frenzy in the park—heralding a new era called punk along the way—might be over, but Victoria Park has kept its musical tradition alive. Slightly more tamed and organised, the festivals taking place these days range from the trendy, village-feel Field Day to the indie-and-electro-blending Lovebox Weekender, while big names (Radiohead for one) have also discovered a liking for the park's scenery and music-appreciating attitude.

Eat & Drink

The park's café, next to The Lake, is tiny, but the organic cakes are a tasty lot. That aside, you have to venture to the park's fringes for food and drink, but fear not: a tap is never far. Leave behind the bog-standard, soulless pub that is The Victoria and opt for the East End earthiness of the Top of the Morning instead, near the Cadogan Gate. Good Ales, a real fireplace, and up-marketish pub food make The Royal Inn on the Park, near the Royal Gates, the usually busy favourite. The Fat Cat, a few minutes south of the park along Grove Road, is more restaurant than pub, a bit pricey but a good choice for high-quality pasta, burgers and steaks.

General Information

www.wpcc.org.uk

Overview

If London life starts to get you down, but trekking to the countryside is too much hassle, then Wimbledon Common provides the best of both worlds. Incorporating Putney Heath to the north, Wimbledon Common offers over 1000 acres of wild woodland, scrubland, heathland, ponds and well-tended, mown areas for sports and recreation. Bordered by the urban sprawls of Wimbledon, Putney and Richmond, the common has offered Londoners an escape from city life for centuries. Although thousands visit every weekend, the scale of the place is so vast that you can easily find a private haven for reading a book or a romantic picnic.

Unlike the micro-managed and perfectly structured central London parks, Wimbledon feels much more natural and random. Paths are unpaved and often little more than a muddy track leading off in unlikely directions. The untamed beauty of the common and the lack of traffic noise, or any noise for that matter, make it hard to believe you are still in London.

After a hard day of outdoor activity, or sunbathing, there are plenty of historic pubs to retire to in Wimbledon village. If you prefer your nature tamed or don't want to get your shoes dirty, head to the southeast corner of the common for Cannizaro House and gardens, a grand mansion converted into a boutique hotel and restaurant, with elegantly manicured gardens open to the public. In the summer, the friendly hotel bar opens onto a patio overlooking the grounds and makes a good spot for a sun-downer as you imagine being Lord or Lady of the Manor for the day.

Nature

The common is home to many animals including bats, badgers, and muntjac deer. It's also an important breeding ground for dragonflies and damselflies. For anyone wanting to find out more about the flora and fauna, the London Bat Group organises 'bat walks' while the London Wildlife Trust organises guided walks. You can also take a self-guided wander along The Windmill Nature Trail. 800 metres long, the trail has been created with accessibility in mind and begins right next to the Windmill car park. The visitors' centre behind the Windmill has wildlife exhibits and also tells the history of the common. It also sells maps and booklets giving the low down on the nature on offer.

Recreation

There is loads of space on the common for pick-up games of rugby, football, Frisbee and cricket. If you fancy a 'real game', you can hire tennis courts by the hour, cricket pitches by the day (from as little as £150) or enjoy a round of golf on the two available courses. The common is very popular with runners and steeplechase events have been held here since 1867. Various running clubs such as the South London Harriers and Hercules Wimbledon use the Common. If you've ever fancied trying horse riding, there are a number of stables that make use of the 16 miles of trails—or bring your own nag with you.

Golf
www.wcgc.co.uk
www.londonscottishgolfclub.co.uk

Horse Riding
Wimbledon Village Stables: 020 8946 8579
Ridgway Stables: 020 8946 7400

Rugby, Football and Cricket Pitch Hire
020 8788 7655

How to Get There

By public transport:
The Northern Line goes to South Wimbledon where you can take a bus to central Wimbledon then change or walk to the village and common. Wimbledon station is much closer. Take the District Line from central London or over ground trains from Waterloo or London Bridge. If you are feeling fit, a ten-minute walk up Wimbledon Hill takes you to Wimbledon village and beyond that, the edge of the common. Regular buses serve the village. Alternatively, you can access Putney Heath which joins up with Wimbledon Common. To do this, take the District Line to Putney Bridge or East Putney overground to Putney mainline station and take a bus up Putney Hill.

359

It's likely that at some point during your London residence, you've been seized with the romantic notion of floating your way round a London market—savouring the smells, laughing with a vendor, flirting your way to some freebies. If you have, then your attempts to live that dream almost certainly resulted in you si ently fuming as you crawled among a crowd of thousands, trekking for a cashpoint because you forgot that stalls don't accept cards, and getting crapped on by a pigeon. Don't be put off!

At the markets you can buy some of the most unique, quirky, fresh, stylish, grungy, exquisite, unusual items in London. Sometimes you'll get brilliant bargains, sometimes you'l pay high for something you fall in love with. And sometimes, yes, you'll be driven near to homicidal rampage. But they're one of London's great strengths: use them while you can, because the developers have their evil, dollar-signed eyes on them.

For Groceries

The food in markets isn't necessarily locally grown, but you get a much more tempting choice than in most supermarke s. Expect fruit, veg, breads, cheeses, meats, spices and pastries, as well as stalls concocting irresistible snacks from around the world.

Borough (Map 106)
You don't come here for bargains: you come for ambiance, exquisite international foods, and to impress the person you woke up with. If you're rich and like the finer things in life, then here your weekly shop can consist of some of the freshest vegetables, plumpest fruit, sweetest patisseries and sockiest cheeses in London. If you're poor and just fancy a change from Saturday morning repeats of *Friends*, then head here for a hearty hog roast sandwich and to snaffle some free samples.

Broadway (Map 89)
As gorgeous as Borough, for a third of the price and a fifth of the crowds. It's a pain to get to, stuck in one of the city's remaining quaintly retro spots not closely served by the tube (London Fields), but you'll want to move here by the end of your visit.

Ridley Road (Map 86)
If the gourmet markets are too poncey for you, with their Bavarian organic rye bread and Malaysian honey from breast-fed bees, then get down the Ridley Road. Here, in a market which is bright, chaotic, grubby and bouncing to reggae, you can pick up an incredible array of Jamaican, Turkish, African, Indian and Chinese foodstuffs (and possibly e-coli).

For Market-Chic

You won't necessarily pay less than at the high street, but you will have a choice of original and irresistible items sold with passion and knowledge. Expect to leave these markets with a lighter pocket (though try to make sure it's not because of the pickpockets…).

Spitalfields (Map 91)
Mecca for anyone looking for ethnic-hip and well-priced clothes, bags and jewellery. Here you can often chat to the maker of the clothes you're eyeing up and learn the story behind their designs. Which is all very inspiring, until you try on their beloved creations, realise you're too fat for it, and reject it having slightly stretched it. Because then it's just awkward.

Greenwich (Map 120)
Craft-tastic: a great place to go for beautiful handmade gifts which people love to receive and then put in a cupboard for the rest of their useful life. Here you'll find a gorgeous range of items for home and lifestyle: pictures, antiques, candles, pottery, soft furnishings and clothes, as well as some great food stalls, and an above-average number of beautiful rich people than at most markets.

Portobello Road (Map 29)

Although famed for being the World's Largest Antiques Market, Portobello Road seems to sell *everything*. You'll need patience to work around its sprawling size and the crowds, but just about anything you're looking for is there somewhere or can be sourced by speaking to the right vendor. Stalls include clothes (from classy-vintage to student-cheap), jewellery, fabric, food, as well as 1500 antique stalls selling maps, medals, silverware, and things you never thought you needed (and which, after you've got them home, you realise you didn't).

Camden (Map 71)

Camden is actually home to six markets, though "chic" doesn't do any of them justice. Here you'll find a purse-emptying range of alternative fashions, vintage clothes, accessories, gifts, t-shirts, comedy hot water bottle covers, tie-dyed hippies, teeny-punks and chaps asking if you'd care for a nice bit of crack. Anything goes, and this open, free atmosphere makes it a major and exciting draw. Hit Camden Stables for brilliant international food stalls.

Fer Findin a Bit o' Laaandon Prop'a

If you're a Londoner who "just adores the city! But oh dear *no*, wouldn't *dream* of bringing kids up here", then chances are you don't mingle much with the Prop'a Laandoner. This hardy breed whose family history is a Dickensian yarn of blitzes, TB and chimney sweeps is the core of this city, and the gradual nudging out of their jellied eels and pub sing-songs is tantamount to ethnic cleansing. Find them at London's Propa Markets before they vanish.

Smithfield (Map 15)

Smithfield Market is in full swing at 4 am, which makes it the perfect place to stumble into on your way home from clubbing. Unless you're vegetarian, because while frying bacon may have you yearning for looser morals, the smell of this 800 year old meat market will have you retching over your recycled sandals. It's the best place in London to pick up any meat you could hope for, including, in the 1500s, a barbecued Protestant or a topside of William Wallace, this being the site of hundreds of executions in its time. Some of the local pubs hold special early licenses, so on your way to the office you can swing in for breakfast over a pint with some of the meat porters: they'd just *love* it if you did.

Columbia Road (Map 91)

There's something deeply touching about an exquisite flower market being manned by some of the burliest Cockneys you'll see outside a Guy Ritchie film. Get there first thing on Sundays for the best choice, or in a low-cut top for the best bargains. And if the crowds and cries of the "daffs, dahlin'?" become too much, just slip into the enchanting boutiques lining Columbia Road.

Billingsgate (Map 101)

For the largest selection of fish in London, outside the London Aquarium (where they frown on you if you try to fry the fish. Bloody bureaucracy.), head to Billingsgate. People were buying their fish here long before London went all yuppie, and much the same stock is available—winkles, cockles, potted shrimp and things which smell ungodly. Today you'll find alongside them almost any fish you could hope for (though don't ask for goldfish), as well as poultry, oils and snacks.

General Information

King's Cross Address: Granary Building,
1 Granary Square, London, N1C 4AA

Phone: 020 7514 7000

Website: www.arts.ac.uk/csm
or @CSM_news

Overview

Though hyped to infinity, and often lazily editorialised as the one vital source of all things up-and-coming in London, Central St Martins nevertheless has an undeniable history of producing graduates that tend to rocket to international fame upon leaving. The frequently cited list of alumni reads like a Who's Who of European art-and-design talent, and includes past superstars such as Alexander McQueen, Gilbert and George, and Anthony Gormley, as well as recent fashion darlings Christopher Kane, Gareth Pugh and Kim Jones, to name a few.

Central St Martins is part of the much larger University of the Arts London, made up of CSM, Chelsea College of Art, Camberwell College of Art, London College of Fashion, London College of Communication and Wimbledon College of Art. The school as it is today was formed in 1989 through the amalgamation of two prestigious 19th century institutions, the Central School of Arts and Crafts and St Martins School of Art. Since then it has annexed the Byam Shaw School of Art in Archway, and as a result offers a huge range of courses covering most areas of the visual and performing arts. St Martins has a particularly formidable reputation for fashion design—it is the only university to show student collections as part of London Fashion Week—but it is well respected in all departments for its hyper-progressive ethos (expect to hear words like 'challenging,' and 'risk-taking' liberally thrown around on open days). Whether you find the whole thing pretentious and overrated or are waiting in breathless anticipation for the next St Martins wunderkind, CSM is very difficult to ignore.

Campuses

The swish renovated warehouse building in Kings Cross, opened in 2011, centralises programs and student life in a way that was once difficult. The massive campus anchors the redevelopment of Kings Cross, formerly known for its transport links and general seediness. The facility allows students of art, fashion, design, and drama to be in one location, to interact cross-discipline, and form more of a united front rather than being scattered across the capital. Anyone who has walked the corridors of the old Charing Cross Road building will tell you that however charming the decaying archaic halls of academia may be, a brand spanking new building with technology to match is more than welcome. Occupying the Grade II listed Granary Building, architects Stanton Williams have integrated such wonders as an internal street, the Platform Theatre performance space, and an open-air terrace.

The Byam Shaw School of Art in Archway is a relatively recent addition (2003) to Central St Martins. Devoted solely to fine art, it runs a BA and a more skills-based 2 year FdA as well as a variety of short and post-graduate courses. CSM also has facilities in Richbell Place, Holborn.

College Culture

As is the case with most London institutions, the university community is massively subsumed by the bright lights of the city itself, but this is no bad thing. Though the college puts on frequent exhibitions, talks and events, there is no independent bar or central hub. The Student Union is not particular to Central St Martins but provides services for and represents all the art colleges in London (University of the Arts London) as a whole, and various services and societies (such as sports clubs) are run at this level. As far as the education part goes, it's not always easy being in the midst of the constant search for the next-big-thing, but at the same time the idiosyncratic slant of the teaching makes for a unique experience, and the generally high talent level of the students fosters a fantastic creative and social atmosphere.

Tuition

Fees are £9,000 a year for UK/EU applicants taking an undergraduate or Foundation level degree. Some courses require payment of an additional course fee for materials. International students can expect to pay approximately £16,000 depending upon the type of course taken.

Short Courses

Central St Martins also runs a large number of short courses for all aspirational (and rich) non-students wanting a piece of the action. Prices are high but the courses very popular, partly because of the college's reputation and partly because there are many interesting options to choose from. The courses run in evenings, weekends, or can be taken intensively as a Summer, Easter or Christmas school.

Phone Numbers:

Reception (Granary Building): 020 7514 7444

Drama Centre London: 020 7514 8760

Admissions—Degree Courses: 020 7514 7023

Admissions—Short Courses: 020 7514 7015

International Office: 020 7514 7027

Lethaby Gallery: 020 7514 9897

University of the Arts Students' Union: 020 7514 6270

Press Office: 020 7514 8098

General Info

Address: Northampton Square, London, EC1V 0HB
Phone: 020 7040 5060
Website: www.city.ac.uk or @CityUniLondon

Overview

In London, a place rich with academia, City University often gets overlooked. Unlike King's or LSE it has no grand halls, secret-handshakes or old-boys' networks. Its facilities are modest and its library short on fusty books. But it has carved out a reputation as a supplier of professionals, cementing its place in the top five for graduate employment.

Located on a pretty park on the edge of the City of London—the 'Square Mile' that itself has emerged at the centre of the global economy—the university is overwhelmingly diverse, with many coming from abroad to study at the Cass Business School. It's that section of the university that churns out workers for the finance industry—students who are so hell-bent on business success that they go to school in suits. The other five schools comprising City are the School of Arts & Social Sciences, School of Health Sciences, School of Mathematics, Computer Science & Engineering, School of Informatics, and The City Law School.

The university's first incarnation came in 1894 as an industrial college for the working classes. The on-site swimming pool was used when London hosted the 1908 Olympics, although it wasn't until 1966 that it gained full university status. It has maintained strong links with industry, with alumni including the founding father of budget Euro-travel, easyJet's Stelios (like Sting and Madonna he chooses to use only one name). Students at City may be lined up for good jobs when they graduate, but it comes at the cost of having to explain what their less well-known university is whenever they mention it.

Tuition

Annual undergraduate fees are £9,000. International undergraduate fees can be upward of £15,000.

Student Life

City offers on-campus housing, including a guarantee scheme for first-year undergraduates. The uni hosts some heavyweight lectures. The Students' Union offers limited clubs and societies with all the usual fare—tennis, chess, Christian Union. CitySport is City's state-of-the-art sports and fitness centre. 'Ten' (10 Northampton Square) is where the kids hang out, the social hub of City.

Departments

Cass Business School: 020 7040 8600
Admissions office (undergrad and postgrad): 020 7040 8716
Library: 020 7040 8191
CitySport: 020 7040 5656
Students' Union: 020 7040 5600

1 Gloucester Building
2 Innovation Centre
3 School of Social Sciences
4 College Building
5 Centenary Building
6 Drysdale Building
7 Refectory Building
8 University Building
9 Tait Building
10 Goswell Place
11 Myddelton Building
12 Parkes Building
13 Health Centre
14 Walmsley Building
15 Paramount House
16 Saddlers Sports Centre
17 Finsbury Residence Hall
18 Heyworth Residence Hall
19 Peartree Court Residence Hall

General Information

Address: Imperial College London,
South Kensington Campus, London SW7 2AZ
Phone: 020 7589 5111
Website: www.imperial.ac.uk or @imperialcollege

Overview

Imperial College really did have imperial beginnings with Prince Albert setting up the college as a research and learning centre of science, maths, medicine and engineering to enhance the image of the British Empire in 1847. In the Victorian age, and to this day, the college attracted the most favourite of minds and was the central feature of what was once Prince Albert's successful push to create a centre of culture and learning encompassing the nearby museums, Royal College of Music, Royal Geographical Society and the Royal Albert Hall. The university remains one of the best in the world, and as such remains one of the most selective institutions in the UK with the application to admissions ratio hovering around 7:1. Famous alumni include clever clogs Brian May (Queen), HG Wells and Alexander Fleming. In 2007 Imperial College became independent from the University of London and now awards its own degrees.

Departments

The pride and soul of the college are three faculties, each headed by a principal: engineering, medicine and natural sciences. Imperial also has a business school with Departments of Finance, Innovation & Entrepreneurship, and Management. The main purpose of the Humanities department is to provide elective subjects and language courses for the science students. For medical students Imperial is also associated with various London hospitals including St Mary's Hospital and Charing Cross Hospital.

Campus Culture

Imperial may have a 'heads down' atmosphere but there is still that unwritten rule that if you work hard you play hard. Imperial College Union (www.imperialcollegeunion.org) offers numerous clubs and societies from belly dancing to wakeboarding to backgammon. The Union Bar is also well used, and is particularly lively on an afternoon when a football or rugby match is screened. The free student paper, Felix (felixonline.co.uk), is a popular and useful resource for keeping up to date with campus life and aims to be independent from the College itself. Imperial also has its own student TV station, Stoic, and radio station ICRadio (www.icradio.com). There are also regular public lectures on a variety of subjects.

Facilities

Imperial's main campus in South Kensington is surrounded by many of London's best museums including the Natural History Museum, Science Museum and Victoria & Albert Museum. Being in the thick of it also means a close proximity to the shops and cafes of South Ken and High Street Kensington and being a stone's throw from Hyde Park.

The main campus boats some of the best facilities of the London universities. As well as the usual on-campus shops (including bookshop, cafes, travel agents and bank) there are some impressive sports facilities on offer. The Ethos sports centre contains not only a fully equipped gym but also an inside climbing wall, swimming pool, squash courts, sports hall and a treatment room offering massages and physiotherapy. On top of that there's a boathouse and a 60-acre athletic ground. Naturally, there's a well-stocked central library and various smaller departmental libraries.

Tuition

Home students' (UK/EU) annual fees are £9,000 for undergraduate programmes. International students pay upward of £25,000.

General Information

Address: King's College London, Strand,
London, WC2R 2LS
Phone: 020 7836 5454
Website: www.kcl.ac.uk or @KingsCollegeLon

Overview

Although it grants its own degrees, Kings College is one of the 18 colleges that make up the colossus that is the University of London. King's (or KCL, as otherwise known) has nearly 20,000 students and five campuses—the Strand, Guy's, Waterloo, St. Thomas' and Denmark Hill. In 2011 the school of law moved into the East Wing of the magnificent Somerset House. It has an excellent academic reputation and ranks among the top UK universities. Unlike some of the other University of London colleges, King's is equally well known for its arts and science courses.

Its religious affiliation is now less central, but back in 1829 King's was founded as a Church of England institution to counter University College London, or "the godless college in Gower Street."

The beautifully designed chapel at the Strand campus testifies to its pious beginnings, though few students would consider it a motivation for attending the college. The student body is diverse, as the societies list reflects—it includes a Catholic society, a Christian Union, a Krishna Consciousness group, and a Nomads society, among a myriad of others.

King's boasts a number of famous alumni. Keats studied apothecary there (he didn't like it much), and Florence Nightingale set up the world's first school of nursing at St. Thomas' Hospital, now the Florence Nightingale School of Nursing and Midwifery. In the 1960s, Archbishop Desmond Tutu spent time in its halls.

London prices may take their toll on the student purse, but King's students at least benefit from a prime location. As well as the nightclub, the college has two bars, one at Guy's Campus and one at the Strand. The Waterfront bar at the Strand looks directly onto the Thames, giving a view of everything from Westminster to the OXO Tower. It's also a great gig venue.

Sports

The college's sports facilities are impressive. It caters to almost anything—it has a swimming pool, gym, and even rifle range. Although King's cannot rival the Oxbridge rowing tradition, its sports do have a history—two of the men's rugby clubs, Guy's and St. Thomas', are the oldest in the world. To access the sports grounds students must leave Zone 1; the grounds are in Dulwich, Surrey, and South London.

Culture

Kings has numerous dramatic societies where amateur thespians can hone their skills. More unusually, its classics department stages a play in ancient Greek every year, and is the only classics department in the UK to do so. The college's religious origins are evident in its wonderful choral music. 25 choral scholars uphold this tradition.

Tuition

Annual undergraduate fees are £9,000. International undergraduate fees are upward of £15,000.

Contact Details

Admissions: 020 7848 7000
International Students: 020 7848 3388
Students' Union: 020 7848 1588

Waterloo Campus

MAP 104

Doon St

Cornwall Rd

Franklin-Wilkins Building

Waterloo Bridge Wing

Waterloo Rd

Stamford St

K4 Fitness Centre

Stamford Street Apartments

James Clark Maxwell Building

Secker St

Waterloo Rd

Waterloo Station

Exton St

General Information

Address: Houghton Street,
London WC2A 2AE
Phone: 020 7405 7686
Website: www.lse.ac.uk or @LSEnews

Overview

The London School of Economics and
Political Science, or LSE as it is commonly
known, is a single faculty college focused
on the social sciences, world renowned
for its highly prestigious programmes and
distinguished alumni. Located amidst a hub
of academic activity with UCL, King's College,
SOAS and Birkbeck nearby, the college is
affiliated with the University of London and
stands apart due to its high proportion of
postgraduate students.

LSE was founded in 1895 by the intellectual
socialist movement the Fabian Society with
the aim of bettering society through the
education of Britain's business and political
elite. Today it remains a strongly political
institution, with considerable influence
in government through both its research
programmes and campaigns. Its alumni
are also highly represented in business
and law spheres. While best known for its
economics and politics degrees, the broad
range of social science programmes offered
complements the international ethos of the
school and it remains at the cutting edge in
terms of research.

The college enrolls around 9,500 students from over 140 different countries; over half of these are postgraduates who rarely leave the library unless attending high-brow seminars on globalization and inequality. Its starry alumni includes Nobel laureates, international Heads of State, outstanding academics, and a notable proportion of British MP's. And of course Mick Jagger.

Campus Culture

Despite its reputation for academic excellence, LSE's social activities are mainly fuelled by a lively undergraduate population who also know how to enjoy themselves. With over 170 eclectic student societies ranging from Anime to Beekeeping to Catalan to Philosophy to Swing Dance, the broad international and diverse facets of the student population is encompassed. An atmosphere of work hard/play hard prevails and nightly events lure the undergraduates from the libraries and keep the campus buzzing. The large postgraduate population tends to shuffle by, however, books in hand; the days of cheesy music, luminous drinks in shot glasses and ill-conceived experimental fashions behind them while they actually do some work. LSE also hosts numerous public lectures with acclaimed speakers at the forefront of the subject discussed. Past speakers have included Noam Chomsky, Kofi Annan, David Cameron and architect Richard Rogers.

Sports

Not to be let down by its central, and somewhat geographically limited campus, LSE manages to maintain a thriving sports culture through the Athletics Union. Football and rugby seem to top the bill, with provision for some of the less mainstream athletic pursuits such as capoeira and Ultimate Frisbee. The college makes use of its affiliation with the University of London Union, which broadens the scope for sports participation alongside students of other universities.

Tuition

2015/16 undergraduate fees are £9,000 and international undergraduate fees are upward of £17,040.

Contact

Undergraduate Admissions: 020 7955 7125
Graduate Admissions: 020 7955 7160
Library: 020 7955 7229
Students' Union: 020 7955 7158

General Information

Address: Gower Street, London WC1E 6BT
Phone: 020 7679 2000
Website: www.ucl.ac.uk or @uclnews

Overview

UCL, a constituent college of the University of London, has been a place of diversity from the word go—living very much up to its status as "London's Global University." University College London was founded in 1826 as a progressive alternative to Oxford and Cambridge's social exclusivity and religious restrictions. Thus, it was the first university in England to admit students of any race, class or religion and welcome women on equal standing with men. International students have been a part of the college's fabric since day one and it was the first

English university to offer the systematic teaching of law, architecture and medicine. UCL is strongly associated with philosopher Jeremy Bentham, the university's so-called "spiritual father," perhaps in part because Bentham's clothed skeleton is on display in UCL's South Cloisters.

UCL consistently ranks among the top universities not only in the UK but also worldwide. The science, law and medical departments remain some of its strongest. 29 Nobel prizes have been awarded to UCL academics and students, a large portion of which in Physiology & Medicine. That said, UCL degrees in anthropology, history and the arts are also very highly regarded in their fields.

UCL's many networks of libraries are impressive and an easy place to get lost. The Main Library, designed by William Wilkins, who also designed the similar National Gallery building, focuses on arts and humanities, history, economics, public policy and law. The Special Collections include medieval manuscripts and first editions of works by George Orwell, James Joyce's *Ulysses*, Newton's *Principia* and Darwin's *Origin of the Species*.

There's no such thing as a typical UCL student, as it's such a diverse place. The only thing students have in common is their intelligence and London. Because it's a university with great academics right in the heart of Bloomsbury, it makes for some pretty interesting alums. Where else can you have such diverse graduates as Alexander Graham Bell, Mahatma Gandhi, Ricky Gervais, and all four members of Coldplay?

Tuition

Undergraduate home student (UK/EU) fees are £9,000 per year while International students should expect to pay upward of £15,000 (or upward of £20,000 for science-related programmes).

Sports

UCL's sports are as diverse as its students—everything from hockey, rowing and women's rugby to Kung Fu, skateboarding and water polo. The UCLU (University College London Union) is your one-stop shop for campus sports teams and clubs. If you're looking for football, The 90-acre UCL sports ground at Shenley, Hertfordshire, has very high quality pitches. Watford football club even train there. The Union gym (Bloomsbury Fitness) offers facilities for activities such as basketball and personal fitness programmes.

Culture

Being right in the centre of London means that you're never short of something cultural to do. However, UCL stands up quite well. It even has its own museum—the Petrie Museum of Egyptian Archaeology—accessible from the Science Library. Here you're even given your own torch to explore the collection of over 80,000 rare objects DIY (or Indiana Jones) style. UCL also has its own West End theatre, the Bloomsbury Theatre, wedged into the maze of main buildings. It's a must-stop for top comedian tours. Jimmy Carr and Ricky Gervais have been known to shoot their stand-up DVDs there. The UCL Union has access to the theatre for at least ten weeks a year, where it is dedicated to student drama and music society performances. Although neither drama, music nor dance are formally taught at UCL, this does not stop the Union's drama club from making it to the Edinburgh Fringe Festival. At UCL, despite the fact that students can really go out just about anywhere in London, many stay loyal to the bars within the Union, and it's usually a great place to meet before a bigger night out.

Contact

Admissions: 020 7679 7742
UCL Union: 020 7679 2500 or uclu.org
Bloomsbury Theatre: 020 3108 1000
Petrie Museum: 020 7679 2884

General Information

Address: Thornhaugh Street, Russell Square, London WC1H 0 XG
Phone: 020 7637 2388
Website: www.soas.ac.uk or @SOAS

Overview

School of Oriental and African Studies is a specialist college which focuses on the languages, cultures, law and social studies of Africa, Asia, and the Near and Middle East. SOAS, as it is commonly known, is part of the University of London and is the only institution of ts kind in the United Kingdom. It has an excellent reputation as one of the leading authorities on African and Asian studies in the world and ranks highly in university charts on the strength of its programmes. Originally founded in 1916 to educate and inform British citizens bound for overseas postings, the school began with an Oriental studies' focus and later incorporated African studies. SOAS is nestled in the corner of Russell Square, with another campus up close to King's Cross; its diversity complements the hotbed of academic activity that makes up this part of London.

The college enrolls over 5,000 students, with more than half coming from countries outside of the UK. They are often seen sitting in Russell Square eating their organic lunch, and chatting (in Swahili or Taiwanese) about their UNICEF internships. SOAS's alumni include members of parliament and royalty of a range of countries from Ghana to Burma. The Crown Princess of Norway went here. Well of course she did. The Norwegians are so PC. Except for whale hunting.

Culture On Campus

One thing to be said about SOAS students is they are serious. The Students' Union has a reputation of leaning heavily to the left and is very politically active. SOAS students have been a notable presence at anti-war protests, and they are also now rather concerned with environmental causes—campaigning for the reduction of carbon footprints, among other issues. Societies at the college, unsurprisingly, have a very international, 'right-on' flavour: the Decolonising Our Minds Society, Student Action for Global Internationalist Justice Society, Urdu Conversation Society are just a few.

Tuition

Undergraduate home (UK/EU) fees are £9,000. International undergraduate students can expect to pay £16,090 per year.

Contacts

Undergraduate Admissions: 020 7898 4301
Masters Admissions: 020 7898 4361
Research Admissions: 020 7074 5117
Library: 020 7898 4163
Students' Union: 020 7898 4992
or soasunion.org

General Information

Address: Student Central,
Malet Street, WC1E 7HY
Phone: 020 7664 2000
Website: www.studentcentral.london or @
UoLondonSC

Overview

Students are the same the world over and in London they ain't no different. In amongst the banter over Bronte and misunderstandings about Marx stands beer, boogeying and burgers. Luckily, for over 120,000 of the University of London's students there's a central place to go to make your university years active and sociable—Student Central.

Formerly the student-run University of London Union, or ULU, in 2014 the University of London took over the entity and renamed it Student Central. You will need to be a member of to get into some of the events, although grabbing a cheeky cheap sarnie in the café shouldn't pose too much of a problem for clued-up Londoners. There are 18 University of London colleges that are eligible for membership including Kings College and UCL, as well as ten other smaller institutions.

Practicalities

You cannot really get more central. There is a plethora of tube stations and lines within a five – to ten-minute walk, not to mention Oxford Street. The nearest tube, however, is Russell Square (Piccadilly Line) or Goodge Street (Northern Line).

Clubs & Societies (non-sport)

The range of clubs and societies on offer change more often than Europe's borders. Reason being the turnover of students and the lure from students' own colleges—all the more reason to get down there and sign up now! You've got the usual suspects such as Drama club but it would not be Londontown without a few obscure offerings—Revelation Rock Gospel Choir anyone? Hell, yeah.

Sports

Student Central has to cater to thousands of students, but also attract students away from sports clubs in their particular college. Sports, and the bar afterward, is the place to mix with students from the other colleges. Sportswise there's the usual fare—tennis, football, swimming and martial arts. There's also Energybase which contains a gym and pool. Amongst other things take your pick from salsa, breakdancing, fencing or rifle club. Now there's one for the CV…

Food & Bars

Lunch Box is Student Central's coffee shop, conveniently located on the ground floor for those who want to grab a quick (fair trade) coffee or a bargain meal deal. The Library is the main bar, with a lively atmosphere and live acts. The Gallery Bar is a low-key alternative to The Library, and also serves food. The Venue hosts a club night on Fridays, live music acts (up-and-coming unsigned bands as well as the odd better-known act) and cinema events during the week. For gigs enter Student Central on Byng Place.

Facilities

Copycats Print Centre will resolve all your reprographics and binding troubles. The Student Shop carries everything from lab coats to University of London-branded gear.

Learning in the capital has a long and venerable history. University College London (UCL) was the third university founded in England after Cambridge and Oxford and the first to admit students of any race or religion. Now there are hundreds of universities, colleges and adult education centres offering a mindboggling array of courses.

The first port of call for those with a lust for learning or even an empty Tuesday night to fill is Floodlight (london. floodlight.co.uk), which lists tens of thousands of courses. Fancy brushing up your motorbike maintenance skills at Hackney Community College, getting an NVQ in sugar modelling at the National Bakery School, learning how to create the ultimate kitchen garden at the English Gardening School or studying the nonsense verse of Lear and Carroll at City Lit? The sky is your oyster.

Continuing Education and Professional Development

University College London
Gower Street, WC1E 6BT
020 7679 2000
www.ucl.ac.uk or @uclnews

City University
Northampton Square, EC1V 0HE
020 7040 5060
www.city.ac.uk or @CityUniLondon

London South Bank University
103 Borough Road, SE1 0AA
020 7815 7815
www.lsbu.ac.uk or @LSBU

London Metropolitan University
166-220 Holloway Road, N7 8DB
020 7423 0000
www.londonmet.ac.uk or @
LondonMetUni

University of East London
University Way, E16 2RD
020 8223 3000
www.uel.ac.uk or @UEL_News

University of Greenwich
Park Row, SE10 9LS
020 8331 8000
www.gre.ac.uk or @UniGreenwich

A Little Bit of Everything…

Birkbeck
Malet Street, WC1E 7HX
020 7631 6000
www.bbk.ac.uk or @BirkbeckNews

Open University
0300 303 5303
www.open.ac.uk

Bishopsgate Institute
230 Bishopsgate, EC2M 4QH
020 7392 9200
www.bishopsgate.org.uk or @
BishopsgateInst

Arts and Lifestyle

University of the Arts London
272 High Holborn, WC1V 7EY
020 7514 6000
www.arts.ac.uk or @UniArtsLondon

Leiths School of Food and Wine
16-20 Wendell Road, W12 9RT
020 8749 6400
www.leiths.com or @Leithscooking

The London School of Journalism
126 Shirland Road, W9 2BT
020 7432 8140
www.lsj.org or @LSJournalism

English Gardening School
66 Royal Hospital Road, SW3 4HS
020 7352 4347
www.englishgardeningschool.co.uk

London School Of Beauty & Make-Up
18-19 Long Lane, London EC1A 9PL
020 7776 9767
www.beauty-school.co.uk or @londest

Institute Francais
17 Queensberry Place SW7 2DT
020 7871 3515
www.institut-francais.org.uk or @
ifru_london

London Buddhist Centre
51 Roman Road, E2 0HU
020 8981 1225
www.lbc.org.uk or @LDNBuddhist

The School of Life
70 Marchmont Street, WC1N 1AB
020 7833 10 0
www.theschooloflife.com or @
TheSchoolOfLife

Athletics and Dance

National Centre for Circus Arts
Coronet Street, London, N1 6HD
020 7613 4141
www.nationalcircus.org.uk or @
NationalCircus

Tokei Martial Arts
28 Magdalen Street, SE1 2EN
020 7403 5979
www.tokeicentre.org

The Basement Dance Studio
400 York Way, N7 9LR
020 7700 7722
www.thebasementdancestudio.com or
@basement_studio

Regents Canoe Club
Regents Canal, 6-34 Graham Street, N1
8JX
www.regentscanoeclub.co.uk

**Docklands Sailing & Watersport
Centre**
235a Westferry Road, E14 3QS
020 7537 2626
www.dswc.org or @dswcofficial

London School of Capoeria
1 & 2 Leeds Place, N4 3RF
020 7281 2020
www.londonschoolofcapoeira.com or @
londoncapoeira

General Information

NFT Map: 74
Website: www.arsenal.com or @Arsenal
Phone: 020 7619 5000
Box office: boxoffice@arsenal.co.uk
Location: Highbury House, 75 Drayton Park
London N5 1BU

Overview

Regardless of how many years may have passed since Arsenal last stuffed another piece of silverware into their full trophy cabinet, Arsene Wenger continues to avoid splashing the cash on top names, instead building a young thriving team out of foreign talent and an exciting new crop of home-grown kids. The problem with this is that during the start of every new season at the Emirates it is inevitable that a pundit will proclaim this will be the year Arsenal's young side realize their full potential, but just as equally inevitable, a big money club will breeze in and buy out marquee players adding to the fans dismay and Wenger's greys. However, Arsenal is historically London's greatest club and holds numerous national records with a trophy room packed with more silver than any other, save Manchester United and Liverpool. T'was not always thus of course. From humble beginnings south of the river, Arsenal built themselves up from roots level, with glory years seeming to come in waves. The mid-80s saw the instatement of George Graham, a hugely popular former player, who begat a powerful, muscular side captained by local hero Tony Adams. Wenger brought a continental flavour to the team and an invigorating playing style—the once "boring, boring Arsenal" started playing "sexy football" which reached its zenith with the 2003–04 "Invincibles" who went the entire season without losing a game. Following Arsenal is not always an easy ride. It's surprising that so many people still flock to the Emirates stadium in Holloway given the stupendous ticket prices. If you're lucky enough to have the £1000s needed for a decent season ticket then you get to sit in a huge, soulless stadium named after an airline company to watch what are ostensibly a bunch of bloody foreigners. On the plus side, those bloody foreigners play some of the most dazzling football in Europe and you never know, this just could be the year Arsenal's young team realizes their full potential (groan).

How to Get There

By Car: Unless you have a resident's permit to get around the Event Day Parking Scheme always in effect, it's impossible to park on-street. Which is to say, don't bother bringing a car.

By Public Transport: Arsenal (Piccadilly Line) is the nearest tube station, around three minutes walk from the ground. Finsbury Park (Victoria, Piccadilly Lines and Great Northern rail) and Highbury & Islington (Victoria Line, North London Line and Great Northern rail) stations are around a 10-minute walk—these should be slightly less crowded.

How to Get Tickets

As Arsenal play some damn sexy football, tickets are not easy to come by. However, in the new, swanky Emirates Stadium there is always going to be one or two no-shows or corporate tickets that have slipped into the wrong hands. Members have first dibs on tickets and snap them up but the less scrupulous ones sell them on to make a fast buck. Try Gumtree or matchday touts if you really must. To be honest, it's probably one of the rare instances where it really is worth the hassle.

General Information

Phone: 020 8333 4000
Website: www.cafc.co.uk or @CAFCofficial
Location: The Valley, Floyd Road,
Charlton, London SE7 8BL

Overview

Supporting Charlton is like being a drug addict without a healthy bank balance, the highs are amazing (when they come) but the lows are dark and lonely days. Back in 2007, The Addicks were mixing it with the big boys in the Premier League. But after several seasons in freefall, Charlton found themselves in football's third tier. During the dark days football's ugliest man, Iain Dowie took control and drunkenly drove the team off a bridge. He played a brand of football, which matched his grotesque looks, and got the boot (no, not to his face, that's just how he looks). Inexplicably, Les Reed got the job next—a man with no managerial experience. He lasted a month. That year they went down to the Championship. And guess what? They were relegated again, and finished 13th in League 1 (Third Division). In 2009 Phil Parkinson took over and things remained more or less the same. But during 2010 new ownership meant big changes, the effective but unremarkable Parkinson was given the boot in place of Charlton legend Chris Powell. After the 2010-11 season ended with mixed results the team had a spring clean, literally, Powell bought 19 new players and 2011-12 season ended with Charlton winning the Third Division and earning promotion to the Championship. Subsequent seasons saw the club underperform and under new ownership Powell was sacked. Perhaps coming years should see the darkness lifted from the club and the ground reflect Charlton's reputation as a family club, rather than a stadium full of recovering addicts.

How to Get There

By Car: You can leave the M25 at Junction 2 in order to access the A2, heading towards London. When the A2 becomes the A102 (M), take the right hand exit at the roundabout into the A206 Woolwich Road. After passing the major set of traffic lights at the junction of Anchor and Hope Lane and Charlton Church Lane, turn right at the second roundabout into Charlton Lane. Go over the railway crossing then take the first right into Harvey Gardens, with the road leading to the ground. From central London, travel along the A13 until it becomes the East India Dock Road, then take the A102 through the Blackwall Tunnel. Come off at the second junction and take the first exit at the roundabout, then go along the A206 Woolwich Road into Charlton Lane as detailed above. Thanks to the local residents' parking scheme, you'll be hard pushed to find a parking space; try Westmoor Street, Eastmoor Street, Warspite Road and Ruston Road.

By Public Transport: The ground is within walking distance of Charlton railway station, with the Southeastern line running services from mainline stations Charing Cross and London Bridge and services from Cannon Street on Saturdays. You can also take the Jubilee Line to North Greenwich, and then take a short ride on buses 161, 472 or 486 to get to the Valley. Moderate masochists can walk from the tube station.

How to Get Tickets

For years Charlton couldn't give their tickets away. Now, interest ebbs and flows depending on how close the club is to being relegated, but seeing a match is by no means impossible. Tickets can be ordered by phone from the Box Office, via the internet at the club's website or in person at The Valley.

General Information

NFT Map: 43
Phone: 020 7958 2190
Website: www.chelseafc.com
or @ChelseaFC
Location: Stamford Bridge,
Fulham Road, London, SW6 1HS

Overview

Stamford Bridge, home to one of the Premiership's 'big four' clubs, is now one of Europe's most glamorous stadiums. However, 'The Bridge' was once an unappealing and daunting shit-hole more used to hosting pitch invasions and fighting hooligans than the well-heeled city types and Russian oligarchs of today. In the '70s and '80s, it was the violent 'headhunters' that made the club unpopular, but as 'The Blues' never won anything, no one took much notice. In recent years, Chelsea have succeeded in wrestling the mantle of most-hated team in England away from Manchester United, largely due to winning things with the never-ending supply of money from Roman Abramovich. The hool gans have all but gone, either priced out or grown up, but the antics of Prima Donna players and their sitcom private lives have been placing cement shoes on the club's image of late. While Chelsea's coffers have meant they've been able to import expensive foreign players, leading to back-to-back title wins in 2004–2006, their homegrown players have spent more time on tabloid front covers than on football pitches. John Terry and Ashley Cole's bed-hopping adventures will make a great airport novel one day but they've left a lot of fans disappointed in the meantime. These are troubling times indeed for the Blues; after the departure of celebrated manager Mourinho (his first stint with the club) the top position saw its own share of turbulence. With superstar coach Scolari sacked and the silverware drying up it seems money can't buy you everything. However, after two seasons of relative anonymity and a parade of failed managers, unlikely hero Roberto Di Matteo took over the reins of the club during 2012, managed to win both the FA Cup and the Champions League final (and then was sacked as well). Mourinho returned in 2013 and whatever the club's future, one thing is for sure: money will be thrown to the boys at the bridge, silverware or not.

How to Get There

By Car: It is possible to drive to Stamford Bridge on match days but it's pretty pointless to do so. Traffic snarls up badly and the effects are felt throughout Southwest London. If you do brave the traffic, remember that Fulham Road is closed off on match days. Parking is a nightmare with most zones given over to residents. Gangs of eager traffic wardens are on hand to make your Saturday afternoon miserable.

By Public Transport: Stamford Bridge is a two-minute stroll from Fulham Broadway tube station. Regular district line underground trains deliver the hordes from central London in a matter of minutes. If the idea of a packed train full of sweaty football fans isn't your idea of heaven, many fans descend at Ealing Broadway and take the ten-minute walk to the stadium instead.

How to Get Tickets

With so many competitions and cups, getting tickets is easier than you might think. The 'big' fixtures—London derby's, Man U, Liverpool and the later cup stages are either impossible to get or crazily priced, but tickets for the less glamorous ties can be picked up from the Chelsea website or box office. Otherwise, cheeky geezers will be on hand to fleece you on match day. You will probably end up in the West Stand alongside Japanese and American tourists, but that might be preferable to a fat skinhead in the 'Shed.

General Information

NFT Map: 47
Tickets: 0843 208 1222
Website: www.fulhamfc.com or @FulhamFC
Location: Craven Cottage, Stevenage Road,
London SW6 6HH

Overview

Fulham like to think of themselves as a family club. They have a quaint little stadium by the Thames and they play in Fulham for God's sake. (Now about that "Cottagers" nickname…easily the most off-color in all of football.) When Roy Hodgson took the reins in 2008 they were doomed. But he rescued The Cottagers from relegation and in 2009 guided them into Europe, before taking over football's worst job (England manager) in 2012. Mark Hughes took over the team and inexplicably quit before the season finished which, tossed Fulham into turmoil, until the steady hand of Martin Jol took control and ensured business as usual. The club is owned by Shahid Khan, the Pakistani born embodiment of the American Dream who also owns the NFL Jacksonville Jaguars franchise. (Mohamed Al-Fayed, the club's previous owner, once owned Harrods; he's the father of Dodi Fayed, who died with Princess Diana in Paris in 1997.) The club has been in flux in recent years, and was relegated to the Championship in 2014. All that aside, Craven Cottage is still one of the nicest grounds in London and tickets are relatively easy to come by. Just be wary of that hole in the gents.

How to Get There

By Car: Craven Cottage sits in a leafy, riverside suburb of Fulham. Parking is relatively easy around the ground with plenty of parking meters, although reaching the ground could be difficult as weekend traffic in London is never fun to negotiate.

By Public Transport: Putney Bridge on the District Line is your best bet. Putney also has a mainline station with connections from Clapham Junction and direct trains from Waterloo. Cross the road opposite Putney station and hop on any passing bus. Alternatively, a ten-minute walk down the high street and over the river will get you to the ground.

How to Get Tickets

One of the 'joys' of watching Fulham is that tickets are easy to get your hands on. Many games are available on general sale through the club website. For the biggest matches, priority is given to members but persevere and you should be rewarded. If you can't get a ticket legitimately, you can always take your chance with a tout on match day. Try haggling; due to Fulham's fortunes, you could get lucky.

General Information

NFT Map: 76
Main switchboard: 020 7616 8500
Ticket Office: 020 7432 1000
Lord's website: www.lords.org
or @HomeOfCricket
England Cricket Board:
www.ecb.co.uk or @ECB_cricket
Middlesex County Cricket Club:
www.middlesexccc.com
or @Middlesex_CCC
Location: St John's Wood,
London NW8 8QN.

Overview

Even if you know nothing about cricket, don't be put off coming to Lord's. Yes, some games last for five days, and yes, it can still be a draw at the end of it. But as much as anything else Lord's is a fabulous place to come and have a drink. On a hot day the ground is paradise. The sunburnt crowd get slowly boozed up and by the time the players break for tea—yes, tea—few people are concerned at what's going on in the middle. With the polite hum of chatter building up to full-blown drunken singing, it's worth going to Lord's for the atmosphere alone. But when the rabble have calmed down, Lord's is a very genteel place. It's widely seen as the Home of Cricket, and used to house the international governing body. It hosts a heap of England games every year and it's the home ground of county side Middlesex. There's also a year-round gym—you don't even have to be posh to use it—and an indoor training centre. There's even a museum to amuse you when rain stops play. And, rest assured, at some point rain WILL stop play. At the moment, Lord's holds five Test matches (the marathon international five-dayers) and occasional England one-day games. These are the ground's showpiece events, where the crowd are at their most boisterous. Middlesex games rarely attract many spectators, and unless you're an old man or a dog you may be in a minority.

How to Get There

By Car: There's little parking around Lord's so, as you'll be parked up all day, public transport will always be cheaper. If you must drive, the ground is off the A4, which turns into the M4.

By Public Transport: The nearest station is St John's Wood (Jubilee Line). Marylebone (Bakerloo) and Baker Street (Bakerloo, Jubilee, Hammersmith and City, Metropolitan and Circle) are both nearby. Marylebone mainline station serves the north and west of the country. London Paddington is a short bus ride away. Dozens of buses run to Baker Street, and many of which stop right outside the ground.

How to Get Tickets

Getting your hands on England tickets can be tricky. The first few days of a Test match tend to sell out months in advance, though tickets for the last day never go on pre-sale (as the game could be over by then). Similarly, One Day Internationals are normally sell-outs, so it does take a little planning to get in. Check the website over the preceding winter and you might get lucky. If there are less than ten overs in a day due to rain, or if the game's already over, you can claim the full ticket price back. If the weather limits play to between 10.1–24.5 overs (in English, that's up to 149 balls played) you get a 50 per cent refund. Any more than that and you're deemed to have got your money's worth. Middlesex games rarely sell out, however, so you can just rock up on the day, beers in hand, and enjoy the Lord's village.

General Information

NFT Map: 135
Telephone: 08-4 375 1845
Website: www. iaoval.com or @surreycricket
Location: The Kia Oval,
Kennington, London, SE11 5SS

Overview

What better way to while away a sunny summer's day than at The Oval cricket ground, typically alongside hundreds of other shirkers who also called in sick? The Oval is one of London's twin icons of the game, alongside Lord's in North London, and boasts a rich history stretching all the way back to 1846 when it was converted from cabbage patch to cricket pitch. It now plays host to Surrey County and international test matches, including the biennial England-Australia slugfest "The Ashes." Live international cricket remains a boozy, good natured affair with English fanbase 'The Barmy Army' typically belting out salty chants and cheering occasional streakers. County cricket is a mellower, no less enjoyable event, with readily available tickets and a good portion of the crowd more interested in today's paper than the action in front of them. Taxing it ain't.

How to Get There

By Car: Driving to the Oval is not ideal, because parking is near impossible. Should you be willing to risk it, it's situated on the A202, near the junction with the A3 and A24, south of Vauxhall Bridge. As ever with London driving, you'll need your A to Z and nerves of steel.

By Public Transport: The Oval boasts its own, eponymous tube stop on the Northern Line, from which the stadium is a few hundred yards walk. Determinedly overground travellers should alight at Vauxhall, from which Oval is a ten-minute jaunt, tops. Buses 36, 185 and 436 stop right outside the ground, too.

How to Get Tickets

Tickets for Surrey county matches are relatively easy to get hold of, though seats for some fixtures can only be bought on site on the day of the match. International matches tend to sell out very quickly indeed—touts or online sales sites like eBay and Gumtree are usually the best option, at a price.

General Information

NFT Map: 32
Telephone: 020 8743 0262
Tickets: 0844 477 7007
Website: www.qpr.co.uk
or @QPRFC
Location: Loftus Road Stadium,
South Africa Road,
Shepherd's Bush, W12 7PJ

Overview

Once-itinerant football club Queens Park Rangers have called Loftus Road—based, confusingly, in Shepherd's Bush—home since 1917, give or take a few seasons. Their footballing fortunes have yo-yoed through the decades: once a whisker away from winning Division One in the years before it became the Premiership; they finished the 2011-12 season just above the relegation zone, but gave us what undoubtedly was the game of the season after losing a 2–0 lead in stoppage time to gift moneybags Man City the Premier League title. New ownership, including pint-sized F1 oligarch Bernie Ecclestone, injected some much needed glamour into the club (prior to the takeover, Pete Doherty was the Hoops' most famous fan). But, amid wacky boasts of Euro domination, Bernie was cut down to size; Ecclestone has since sold his stake in the team, and at a healthy profit. The years following the sacking of their Italian boss De Canio has seen the Hoops' top spot resemble a revolving door in a busy brothel. Though different managers and caretakers have come and gone, resulting in turmoil on and off the pitch, the erratic QPR are definitely and defiantly worth watching live.

How to Get There

By Car: Whether you're approaching Loftus Road from the North (from the M1 through the A406 and A40), East (via the A40(M)), South (from the A3 and A219) or West (up the M4 via the A315 and A402 on a wing and a prayer), all routes lead through White City. Once there, turn right off Wood Lane into South Africa Road. Don't even set off without proper navigation tools, or emergency rations.

By Public Transport: The majority of QPR fans are local and rely either on nearby tube stops (White City on the Central Line, Shepherd's Bush on the the Hammersmith and City Line), any of buses 72, 95, or 220 to White City Station, or overground train to Acton Central, followed by a quick bus ride.

How to Get Tickets

Getting tickets for a QPR game is harder than you might expect. The team has a loyal fan base and is quickly becoming a guilty pleasure (due mainly to moments of madness) for casual spectators. However, getting tickets for a run-of-the-mill mid-season game should be a cinch, either via the Rangers' ticket website or by phone. You can also visit the Loftus Road box office on match days.

General Information

Telephone: 0344 499 5000
Ticket: 0344 844 0102
Website: www.tottenhamhotspur.
com or @SpursOfficial
Location: Bill Nicholson Way,
748 High Road, London, N17 0AP

Overview

The times they are a-changin
at Tottenham, the blaggers at
Stamford Bridge robbed them of
a deserved Champion's League
place and the country's favourite
tax dodger Harry Redknapp didn't
get the England job and then, to
add insult to injury, was let go
by the club. The scruffy but (for
some reason) adored century-old
White Hart Lane is on its last legs
as a new mega-development is heading into the
building phase. This isn't a bad thing, because
nostalgia aside, few grounds in the capital are
located further from a tube stop and closer to a
corner of London where even police dogs walk in
pairs. More than most fans, the Spurs faithful have
a tight grasp of history (which could be because
there's been no league title there since 1961).
And it shows at the stadium—supporters even
chant about what a grand old team Spurs are.
But that song only gets sporadic outings. Most
of the chants that ring around White Hart Lane
are about how much the fans hate Arsenal. It's a
rivalry that's as intense as any in football—and as
Arsenal started out in the south of the city, only
moving across the river in 1913, Spurs claim of
being Kings of North London isn't such a wild one.
This division grew deeper during Arsenal's years
of success, their American ownership, snooty
fans, and their new corporate-branded Emirates
Stadium just added fuel to the fire. But Spurs
are contenders now, they have a new stadium
of their own in the pipeline and the days of old
ladies selling bagels inside the ground will soon
be replaced by £400 million hotel-cum-shopping-
centre-cum-football-ground.

How to Get There

By Car: The area's congested at the best of times;
on match days, traffic can grind to a standstill. But
if you don't mind a bit of gridlock, White Hart Lane
is on the Tottenham High Road (A1010) a mile
south of the North Circular (A406). This is easily
accessible from junction 25 of the M25, in itself a
temple to traffic.

By Public Transport: The nearest tube is Seven
Sisters (Victoria Line), which is a 25-minute walk
away. But at least if you work up a hunger from
all that walking there's hundreds of kebab shops
en route. White Hart Lane overland station, which
runs from Liverpool Street through Seven Sisters,
is a five-minute walk from the ground. Bus routes
279, 349, 149, 259 run closest to the stadium, but
many more pass nearby.

How to Get Tickets

Although home games normally sell out, tickets
are fairly easy to get hold of. Club members get
first refusal at tickets, ten days before going on
sale to the public. To get on the season ticket
waiting list, you have to become a One Hotspur
Bronze Member, but as the club's fortunes are on
the rise, the wait could be some time.

383

Sports · **Twickenham**

General Information

Website: www.englandrugby.com/twickenham
Phone: 020 8892 8877
Location: Twickenham Stadium, Whitton Road, Twickenham, TW2 7BA

Overview

The home of English rugby, Twickenham is a behemoth of a stadium. An ugly chunk of concrete seemingly dumped from a great height onto a quiet London suburb, Twickenham lacks the charm and character of Ireland's Landsdowne Road and Scotland's Murrayfield, and has been all but pushed to the sidelines by the magnificent Millennium Stadium in Wales. However, the stadium has largely remained a fortress when it comes to England Internationals. Cheered on by 82,000 well-spoken, white-shirted fans booming out 'Swing Low Sweet Chariot' probably helps. Maybe the England players absorb the unfussy and uncompromising nature of their surroundings into their psyche on match days. Critics would argue that their style of rugby is as ugly and bland as the stadium they play in. This would be harsh if England hadn't consistently underperformed after carrying off the Rugby World Cup in 2003. Twickenham also hosts a series of Rugby tournaments and exhibition matches, including the famous 'Sevens', in addition to the occasional Premiership fixture. Outside the Rugby season, the stadium is given over to rock concerts for international bands like U2, Bon Jovi and Lady Gaga. The World Rugby Museum, located in the East Stand at the stadium, is a collection of over 25,000 items related to the history of the sport. Tours of Twickenham are also available.

By Public Transport: Mainline trains run to Twickenham station from Waterloo and Reading. London Underground runs to Richmond on the District Line where shuttle buses will take fans to the stadium (50p outbound, free return) Hounslow is an alternative Underground station but shuttle buses only run from Twickenham to Hounslow station so you will have to make it to the stadium under your own steam. Bus numbers 281, 267, 481, 681 and H20 all have regular services passing close to the stadium.

How to Get There

By Car: Twickenham is very accessible by road—if you live in the South. The M3 motorway turns into the A316 that passes the stadium, carrying on into central London. Certain roads get closed down on match days so drivers should allow plenty of time. Parking at the stadium is extremely limited and should be booked in advance. Resident permits are helpfully required for all roads bordering the stadium so the best thing to do is park in the general vicinity and walk the rest of the way.

How to Get Tickets

England rugby tickets are hot property, commanding higher prices than top football games. As competition games are relatively infrequent, tickets sell out well in advance so keep checking the website for updates on ticket releases. Premiership tickets and friendly matches are easier to come by but will generally sell out. If you don't get lucky in advance, rugby touts (slightly less aggressive than their football cousins) will happily make your wallet lighter for you. Ticketmaster is the best option for concerts or Gumtree and Craigslist for re-sales and swaps.

General Information

Website: www.whufc.com or @whufc_
official
Telephone: 020 8548 2748
Tickets: www.whufcboxoffice.com or 0871
529 1966
Location: Boleyn Ground, Green Street,
London E13 9AZ

Overview

When bald biscuit king Eggert Magnusson
bought the Hammers everything looked
rosy. But then the world went tits up.
The recession meant Icelander Eggert's
companies were suddenly worth nothing.
He went bankrupt—and West Ham became
a Scandinavian IOU. While boss Gianfranco
Zola was leading a revolution on the pitch—
shepherding a young team to the brinks of
Europe—there were real dangers the club
would fold.

Since the Icelandic money troubles, West
Ham has been owned by an ever-changing
cast of consortiums and moneyed men.
Not really where you want your money
right now. But if they survive, the Irons are
on the way up. If you can find the ground
in deepest East London they're well worth
a look.

Over the years, West Ham has been unfairly
tainted by association with the ICF hooligan
firm. Largely active in the '70s and '80s, a
2005 film, <i>Green Street</i> did its best
to rekindle unwanted memories. The drama
was undermined slightly by giving the lead
role to a hobbit. They finished the 2011
season at the bottom of the Premiership
and were relegated—but during 2012
they proved they were too good for the
Championship and are back with the big
boys. Let's hope they keep doing better,
we don't want to give them any excuse to
get angry.

How to Get There

By Car: Driving in London is a waste of time
even on the best of days, but try it on match
days and you are asking for trouble. East
London is a warren of one way streets, dead
ends and no through roads. You are likely to
either miss kick-off or get a parking ticket
or both.

By Public Transport: The District line will
'whisk' you from central London to Upton
Park in half an hour or so. The Boleyn
Ground is five minutes walk from the
underground station.

How to Get Tickets

Unless you want to pay through the nose for
tickets against the big clubs, you should be
able to find spares for the smaller fixtures.
West Ham is a relatively small ground with
a dedicated, hardcore following. Being
less glamorous than Chelsea, et al. means
that casual fans have a better chance of
watching a game for a decent price.

General Information

Phone: 0800 169 2007
Website: www.wembleystadium.com
or @wembleystadium
Location: Wembley Stadium,
Wembley HA9 0WS

Overview

Wembley Stadium enjoys a strange position in the British psyche. For football fans it's most significant as the scene of England's only World Cup win back in 1966, as well as numerous pitch invasions by angry/jubilant Scottish fans whenever their national team came down to play. Plus, a generation of British bands have

grown up dreaming of the day they'd bellow: "hello Wem-ber-ley, are you ready to r-ck?!!" to tens of thousands of people who've just paid a fiver for a chewy patty of minced spleen 'n' testicles in a dry bun. For these sentimental reasons, then, very few people complained that the National Stadium was a bit of a crap-hole stuck in an inaccessible suburb of West London. By the late '90s the place was looking a bit battered, so they knocked it down and then very, very slowly, and at tremendous, tabloid-scandalising expense, built a replacement on the same site. The result is, just about, worth it. There are none of the blind spots for spectators that the old stadium used to have, plus it has far greater leg-room for 90-thousand-plus people and much more comfortable seating. It also looks fantastically imposing as you walk out of Wembley Park tube with its massive arch curving into the sky. A trip here might not make your knees go "all trembly" as fans used to sing but for football lovers it's one of the world's great venues. They also have a special removable running track for athletics and, to the disgust of "soccer" purists, they've even let American "football" teams play here, too.

How to Get There

By Car: Short of hiring snipers to pick drivers off as they approach the mighty arch, the Stadium could hardly do more to discourage visitors from driving. "Wembley Stadium is a public transport destination. Please leave your car behind," the website primly advises. However, if you are some kind of die-hard, planet-raping petrol-head you'll see signs pointing to the stadium from Great Central Way onwards. There are very few parking spaces at the Stadium itself and these need to be booked in advance. On match days, or when there's anything else happening, the local area becomes residents' parking only, too. Yes, they really don't want you to bring your car.

By Public Transport: The nearest Tube is Wembley Park on the Metropolitan and Jubilee line. Wembley Central (on the Bakerloo line) is about 10–15 minutes walk and there's also Wembley Stadium mainline train station with links all over the country. If you're travelling from outside London there are National Express coaches from 43 different towns and cities.

How to Get Tickets

Easier said than done. 'Club Wembley' have kindly created a 'ten year seat licence'—no doubt to re-coup the massive overspend that accompanied completion of the stadium. These licences give owners access to all major events hosted at Wembley and its worth going on the website to laugh at the ridiculous prices. A 'one-off licence fee' starts at £172 per person per event. Annual season tickets are on top of that. Cloud Cuckoo Land. 'Normal' people can buy tickets to England games through the FA (you need to be a member), for football and rugby cup games through the respective clubs and tickets for one off events and shows through Ticketmaster. It's always worth checking Gumtree.com as you never know who might be flogging off a golden ticket to the highest bidder.

Practice Courts

Aorangi Pavilon

Buses

Aorangi Terrace ("Henman Hill")

No. 1 Court (see right)

Wimbledon Park

Court 18

Court 19

Church Rd

Court 14

Court 15

Court 16

Court 1"

Museum

The Wimbledon Shop

Newstead Wy

Centre Court (see right)

Millennium Building

Long & Lawn Buffet

Somerset Rd

Car Park 3

Covered Courts/ Car Park 2

Court 3

Court 4

Court 5

Court 6

Café Pergola

Car Park 5 →

Court 7

Court 8

Court 9

Court 10

Court 11

Wimbledon Park ⊖ →

Car Park 1

Court 12

No. 2 Court

Maryat Rd

Buses

No. 1 Court

43 1
39 41 36 2 3 5
37 34 4
35 32 6
33 28 30 26 8 9
31 24 A 22 10 11
29 25 12
27 20 18 14 15
23 21 16 17
19

Centre Court

509 510 511
508 309 310 512
308 513
507 307 205 206 207 311 514
206 207 312 515
106 107 108 109 208 315 516
506 306 204 105 111 209 314 517
505 104 112 518
504 103 113 519
503 305 203 102 114 210 315 520 521
502 304 101 115 522
501 303 202 201 212 211 316 523
302 Royal Box 317
301 318

General Information

Telephone: 020 8944 1066
Website: www.wimbledon.com
or @Wimbledon
Location: The All England Lawn Tennis
and Croquet Club, Church Road,
Wimbledon, SW19 5AE

Overview

New balls please! If it's not pissing it
down—which is a big if—Wimbledon's
All England Tennis and Croquet Club is
the place to witness the world's finest
tennis players do battle on rye grass
courts, home as it is to the oldest major
Championship in the game each June/
July. But this is also a place to be seen
and to be merry—sure, it's about the
tennis, but it's also about strawberries
and cream (of which 62,000 pounds
and 1,540 gallons worth are sold each
year respectively), the free-flowing
champagne, the celebrity crowd, and
the Ralph Lauren-designed ballboy
and ballgirl outfits. If you can't actually
get a ticket for the tournament—the
All England Club makes approximately
1,500 of them available each day, and
more importantly, if you're not prepared
to camp out overnight in the queue—
you can always sit yourself on Murray
Mound (formerly Henman Hill) at the
northern end of the complex, where a
vast television screen allows you to watch
British players systematically eliminated
in typically heartbreaking fashion. Really,
we should stick to darts.

How to Get There

By Car: During the tournament, traffic and
parking are nightmarish propositions,
and you're better off using public
transport. Nonetheless, the determined
will need to take the A219 from the A3,
and turn off left onto Church Road once
in Wimbledon itself.

By Public Transport: Wimbledon railway
station is a short journey from both
Waterloo and Clapham Junction, and is
otherwise serviced (Vicar!) by trains from
towns right across the South of England.
From here, board the London General
shuttle bus straight to the grounds; they
depart every five minutes or so during
the tournament. Tube users should head
for Southfields on the District line, from
where a London General shuttle also
operates. Those who prefer to saunter can
mosey on down Wimbledon Park Road
heading south for ten minutes or so, and
you can also walk it from Wimbledon Park
tube station, heading north-west.

How to Get Tickets

You can (legally) come by tickets to
Wimbledon in two ways—one, apply
in advance to the public 'ballot', via the
website, in the hope you are selected
at random to purchase tickets (closing
date end of December). Two, join the
serpentine, overnight queues for on-
the-day tickets, of which five hundred
are usually made available for each of
Centre, Number One and Number Two
Courts. Then, of course, there are all the
other methods of which you're already no
doubt aware.

Any bowling buff will tell you that there are two types of bowling in this country. Ten-pin bowling, the ghastly Americanized import, is by far the most popular among Londoners and the generally disrespectful Youth Of Today. Crown Green Bowling is a far more serene, (elderly) gentlemanly pursuit complete with its own rules and rituals.

London's ten pin bowlers are spoiled rotten. As it's now a trendy pastime shot through with irony, there are plenty of old, large basements converted into pristine bowling alleys designed to look retro. There's no chavs in tracksuits on speed around here: the **All Star Lanes** franchises **(Map 4, 30, 91)** are heaving with immaculately dressed trendos and hen/stag nights drunkenly bowling and singing in the karaoke booths. However, at a peak rate of £8.95 per person per game (your average game is a mere 10 minutes) and an off-peak rate of a laughably similar £6.95 per game, you'll have to access whether it's worth blowing the rent money on one night of fun. **Bloomsbury Bowling Lanes (Map 4)** does the American chic thing a bit better and its lanes are £39 an hour, which works out cheaper in a group. They also host cool gigs and DJs occasionally.

For families and the penniless, London has plenty of more 'traditional' British bowling lanes. By this, of course, we mean cavernous warehouses with pumping chart music, scary underage drinkers and sticky air hockey tables. Try the classic **Rowans (Map 62)** which at its priciest is a mere £5.20 per person per game or **Queens Ice & Bowl (Map 30)** which has also has an ice rink to cool off those skittle blues.

And what of Green Bowling? Well, being an outdoor pursuit in Britain, it's safe to say it is primarily a summer affair. When the sun is out you'll find bowling greens in all the major parks; Hyde Park offers lanes for £7.50 an hour.

After suffering at the hands of boho and cheapo ten-pin bowling facilities you may find that there can be no better way to waste an afternoon than to sit around a bowling green in Finsbury Park with a beer in hand, laughing at your idiot friends' attempts to hit the 'jack.' Maybe those elderly gentlemen are on to something…

Bowling	Address	Phone	Map
All Star Lanes	95 Brick Ln	020 7426 9200	91
All Star Lanes	Victoria House, Bloomsbury Pl	020 7025 2676	4
All Star Lanes	6 Porchester Gardens	020 7313 8363	30
Bloomsbury Bowling Lanes	Bedford Way	020 7183 1979	4
Hyde Park	Hyde Park	020 7262 3474	n/a
Palace Superbowl	First Floor, Elephant &	020 7277 0001	112
Castle Shopping Centre			
Queens	17 Queensway	020 7229 0172	30
Rowans	10 Stroud Green Rd	020 8800 1950	62

Nothing combines relaxation and hypertension quite like golf, nor indeed knee-length socks, spats and flat caps. For golfing Londoners, opportunities to play must be sought towards the outskirts of the capital, where the city shore is lapped once more by greenery and open space. You can, of course, take your one wood out onto London's pavements and practise your fade drive there, but you're odds on to be arrested if you do.

You'll be better received moving clockwise around London from the north, at establishments such as the **Highgate Golf Club** and **Muswell Hill Golf Club**. Both are highbrow member institutions with epic fairways, open nonetheless to the public, as long as that public is wearing a decent shirt. Eighteen holes at each are in the £30-45 range, which is also the case at the **Hampstead Golf Club**, home of one of England's toughest front nines. Nearby **Finchley Golf Club** is similarly priced for visitors but also offers some neat specials such as winter green fees under £30 and knockdown prices for twelve holes of 'twilight golf'. A little farther north, **Mill Hill Golf Club** is a shade cheaper though no less satisfying.

In the south-east, the **Royal Blackheath Golf Club** positions itself as the oldest in the world, which might be why playing eighteen holes as a visitor requires a small trust fund, at £60 during summer. Moving farther

west, the **Central London Golf Centre** is a no-nonsense 'pay-and-play' establishment offering nine full-length holes to golfers of all standards for little more than a tenner. The **Wimbledon Park Golf Club** is another quality members club open to visitors, while nearby **Royal Wimbledon Golf Club** terms itself a 'very private' club—visitors are welcome but will be required to apply in writing, prove handicap and, in all likelihood, undergo some kind of permanently scarring initiation ritual. Access to each of these Wimbledon clubs kicks off at a chokingly high £70 for eighteen holes. You could buy a second-hand Playstation for that. The **London Scottish Golf Club** on Wimbledon Common is much more like it, in the range of £20-30 a round, though a pillar-box red top is compulsory for all. Out west, **Dukes Meadows Golf Club** in Chiswick offers nine three-par holes, a driving range and function rooms, all at a reasonable price.

For golfers who really are determined not to leave Zone One, there is one option after all. **Urban Golf (Map 10)** in Soho and the **Urban Golf (Map 15)** Smithfield location is the last word in golf simulation, with the chance to play, virtual-style, some of the world's top courses. It also boasts well-stocked bars and chic lounge areas. You just know the purists will loathe it.

Golf Club	Address	Phone	Map
Central London Golf Centre	Burntwood Ln	020 8871 2468	n/a
Dukes Meadows Golf Club	Dukes Meadow	020 8995 0537	n/a
Finchley	Frith Ln	020 8346 1133	n/a
Hampstead Golf Club	82 Winnington Rd	020 8455 0203	n/a
Highgate Golf Club	Denewood Rd	020 8340 3745	n/a
Holland Park	Ilchester Pl	020 7602 2226	34
London Scottish Golf Club	Windmill Rd	020 8788 0135	n/a
Mill Hill Golf Club	100 Barnet Way	020 8959 2339	n/a
Muswell Hill Golf Club	Rhodes Ave	020 8888 1764	n/a
Royal Blackheath Golf Club	Court Rd	020 8550 1795	n/a
Urban Golf	33 Great Pulteney St	020 7434 4300	10
Urban Golf	12 Smithfield St	020 7248 8600	15
Wimbledon Park Golf Club	Home Park Rd	020 8946 1250	n/a

Remember the Levi's ad in the pool hall? The one which had The Clash's "Should I Stay Or Should I Go?" as the soundtrack? Yeah, that one. It conjured up a pretty cool image, right? Unfortunately London's pool halls have not had the retro revamp (is that an oxymoron?) that bowling is currently enjoying (**All Star Lanes**, **Bloomsbury Bowling**) so it's rare to actually find a place where you can stand around looking like James Dean, kissing your teeth, chewing on a tooth pick, and generally inviting any hustler to take you on without like, really being taken on by someone from the Russian/Turkish mafia. We also inextricably link shooting some pool with having a drink or two, but it is often the lesser red and yellow-balled "pub" pool table (funnily enough) rather than the greater spotted (and striped) genuine American pool table which is found within the confines of the few remaining non-chain traditional pubs in London. **19:20 (Map 6)** in Clerkenwell has more of a pool hall feel with media types taking their game a little more seriously at the end of the working day. If you do fancy something a little more louche, there are many a pool and snooker hall to be found on the edges of central London which can offer a grittier atmosphere. **Efes (Map 86)** used to be a bit of a no-go for middle-class hipster kids until the owners realised that they were sitting on a goldmine what with having a long-standing late licence and being slap bang in the middle of the action. Now the place hosts gigs and is a regular fixture for anyone doing a Kingsland crawl. Oh yeah, and has pool tables.

Pool & Snooker	Address	Phone	Map
19:20	20 Great Sutton St	020 7253 1920	6
Efes Pool Club & Bar	17 Stoke Newington Rd	020 7249 6040	86
The Elbow Room	97 Curtain Rd	020 7613 1316	84
The Elbow Room	89 Chapel Market	020 7278 3244	80
The Elbow Room	103 Westbourne Grove	020 7221 5211	30
Number 1 Bar	1 Duke Street Hill	020 7407 6420	106
Riley's	638 Wandsworth Rd	020 7498 0432	142
Riley's	16 Semley Pl	020 7824 8261	19
Rowans	10 Stroud Green Rd	020 8800 1950	62
The Westbury	34 Kilburn High Rd	020 7625 7500	68

Tennis

Ah… the other beautiful game, beloved of park fence jumpers and upper class grunters alike. Like many popular sports, tennis may have originated in Britain, but we're pretty consistent in our ineptitude at it. This is not for the lack of trying: the country's capital is packed full of tennis clubs, outdoor park courts and large sports complexes.

Tennis is certainly not as exclusive as it once was, with an hour's playing a lot cheaper than ten-pin bowling, for example. You can mince about amidst leafy surroundings in Hyde Park (Hyde Park Tennis and Sports Centre, 020 7262 3474), fail in the dark depths of Finsbury Park on a turn-up-and-play basis, or in the luxury of the historic Queens Club (www.queensclub.co.uk, 020 7386 3429 for membership information). Also commendable are the Paddington Sports Club (psclondon.com or 020 7286 8448) in Maida Vale and the courts in Regent's Park: go to www.tennisintheparks.co.uk for information on, uh, playing tennis in parks. Indicative of the new equalitarian nature of the game are Tennis London International (www.tennislondon.com) who take pride in being 'the largest gay and lesbian tennis group in the UK.' But it's not all democratic: there's always Wimbledon (www.wimbledon.org, which due to the jaw-dropping ticket prices, still is as exclusive as it's always been. If you still want to get caught up in the annual tennis frenzy, head to Henman Hill, or Murray Mound, or whatever it's called these days. Essentially a hill outside Centre Court, here you can sit on the grass and watch the action on video screens with all the other poor proles who don't have any kidneys left to trade for a ticket.

Squash

Like some weird secret society, squash players spend their time locked indoors, organised into little private clubs and engaged in an activity which will eventually mess them up. Squash is hard—just ask your poor knees. The squash court is a high-octane containment tank swimming in adrenalin, which explains why Londoners have taken to it with such gusto. A court at Sobell Leisure Center (020 7609 2166) in Finsbury Park for example, is near impossible to book at peak times. Be warned—a lot of sports centres don't have squash facilities, but somewhere like the Oasis Sports Centre (020 7831 1804) in Tottenham Court Road is a church to all things sweaty and squashy…and you can go for an outdoor swim afterwards, too. For a quirkier court try Maiden Lane Youth Club (020 7267 9586)—a community centre in a housing estate, which has one beat-up court for an hourly fee. If there isn't a yoga class in progress, that is.

Badminton/Table Tennis

They may be worlds apart in many ways, but badminton and table tennis are usually offered in the same place, and both are 'genteel' sports in which it is almost acceptable to be beaten by the opposite sex (whichever sex you are). Badminton is especially popular across the board, with almost all sizeable sports centres offering courts and equipment. However, if you've any experience in attempting to book a court at most public sports complexes you'll know of the often depressing amount of phone wrangling and frustration that arises from these exchanges. Chief perpetrator is Kings Hall Leisure Centre (020 8985 2158) in Lower Clapton, who will test your patience to inhumane limits. The Brixton Recreation Centre (020 7095 5100) caters to badminton and squash players but always sound like they can't wait to get you off the phone; their rates are £6.25-£8.50 for badminton, which is pretty competitive. The Sobell Centre, as mentioned above, also caters for table tennis (doesn't "ping pong" sound nicer?) and badminton. The best strategy is to phone your local centre to ascertain which racquet sports they cater for and then prepare yourself to be either double-booked, misinformed or given a free session depending on the ability of the desk assistant!

Overview

As the nascent city of 'Londinium' was being named by the Romans in AD 43, in Asia the practice of yoga was entering its third or fourth millennium. Nineteen hundred years on, at last it found its way out west, and London's yoga establishments have flourished ever since. Essentially, the capital's schools can be divided into those concerned primarily with physical fitness—often the larger institutions offering a range of styles—and those with a more spiritual bent. Of the former, Go Yoga in Shepherd's Bush is a fine example, offering yoga and pilates for adults and kids alike, while the popular Triyoga centres in Primrose Hill and Covent Garden are one-stop holistic shops for the upwardly mobile set. More specialised centres include Bikram Yoga College of India in Kentish Town, and its partner Bikram Yoga City—bring water and a towel for hard wearing, specially heated sessions—and the Iyengar Yoga Institute in Maida Vale, which offers a free introductory class. Special mention also goes to Fulham Yogashala, a newish venture offering all sorts including, unnervingly, 'power yoga'. Still, entering the peaceful surroundings of Yogashala is, according to one client, like getting a hug. Those more spiritual schools include the wonderful Sivanada Yoga Centre, an oasis of serenity in the midst of Putney boasting resident yogi teachers, and the Satyananda Yoga Centre in Clapham with its deep focus on yoga-meditation techniques. Shanti Sadam, out west, is also more concerned with inner stillness than downward dogs. And hidden away in Archway, the Kriya Centre runs a series of kundalini yoga classes in humble but hospitable surroundings—Ohm tastic!

There's nothing quite like an obesity epidemic to make a city sporty. We're constantly being told that we're swelling to huge new levels. The message is worrying: buck up fatties or you won't even fit into your own coffin. Unlike the majority of celebrations that take place in the capital, the 2012 Olympic Games didn't leave us dry mouthed and heaving on the floor with a national hangover. Instead the summer games littered our fair city with a legacy of leading sports venues, and lower-level sport has benefited the most with increased involvement citywide. London's sizeable ethnic communities have also brought weird and wonderful games with them (American Football? In London? They keep threatening...). Dozens of leagues, in dozens of sports, gather every evening to try and beat the bulge.

General Tips

A good starting point is the Gumtree website (www. gumtree.com). Their sports and community section is full of ads trying to fills gaps in sports teams. And as it was started by born-to-sweat Aussies, it never lets up in sheer quantity of athletic opportunities. The local press is also a decent bet. All London boroughs have their own newspapers, who cover amateur sports with as much enthusiasm as the professionals. You may never make it in the big leagues, but at least you can be a hero in Camden. But one area where London struggles is with the concept of pick-up games. Perhaps it's part of our reserved nature, but it's unusual to just rock up at a park and challenge whoever's there. By all means try, but you may get rebuked by a stiff upper lip.

Football

Sunday league football in London used to have a reputation of being rough. For many years it was the preserve of hungover builders, who wanted ninety minutes letting off steam by kicking people around. But it's moved on slightly from those days, with a more general acceptance of skill and less emphasis placed on pain. The spiritual home of recreational football is Hackney Marshes. The East London site has a whopping 80-plus pitches—so many leagues and teams play there that it's worth just turning up and asking around. If you draw a blank there, then the FA website (www.thefa. com) has a club locator search. Regardless of where you live, you'll get a mammoth list of clubs. The hardest part of finding a team in London is narrowing down who it is you want to play for. Five-a-side football is also booming in London. In the city centre, where space is at a premium, it's often the only way of getting in a game. Powerleague (www.powerleague.co.uk) organise leagues around the capital, though these can be pricey. A cheaper option is to head to a leisure centre with a five-a-side pitch. They often run leagues and are less profit-driven than the private companies. Lists of leisure centres can be found on specific borough's website (such as Islington's www. islington.gov.uk).

Rugby

Don't mind drinking pints of your team-mates' urine? Enjoy a good eye-gouging? Then you must be a rugby fan! The Rugby in London website (www.rugbyinlondon. co.uk) is a Bible for lovers of casual violence, as it lists hundreds of clubs, contact details and even training venues and times. Female fans of egg chasing are also well represented. Most teams play around Southwest London, though there's a few more dotted around the city. A full list is on the RFU Women's website (www.rfuwlonse.co.uk). If you don't fancy the full-on ear-biting code of the sport there's a flourishing touch rugby scene in London. In this form of the game tackling is represented by tagging your opponent. It's an altogether less bloody type of rugby, although you're still allowed to indulge in the booze-fuelled rituals that the contact players enjoy. In2Touch (www.in2touch.com) lists a few of these leagues.

Cricket

As a sport that takes up plenty of space, you have to head to the leafier parts of London such as Hampstead, Putney, and Dulwich to find cricket clubs at play. But with more green space than any other London borough, Hackney has embraced the gentleman's game, and the thwack of leather on willow can oft be heard on London Fields during the summer months where the North East London Cricket League (nelcl.leaguerepublic.com) has established itself. Victoria Park also has a Community Cricket League (www.vpccl.co.uk). The Play-Cricket website (www.play-cricket.com) has a full rundown on London clubs

Athletics and the London Marathon

Every spring, London's runners dust down their gorilla costumes and tackle the London Marathon. If you feel up to it then you have to plan ahead; places are limited and dished out via a ballot. If you need a helping hand in the run up to the race, consider a jogging and/or roadrunning club associated with British Athletics (www. britishathletics.org.uk): as well as getting you in shape, so you don't die after 20 miles, they can help you get a spot in the starting line-up. And if you catch the bug of competitive athletics, there are six clubs who compete in the London Inter Club Challenge (see London Athletcis at www.londonathletics.org).

Miscellaneous

For fans of all things Irish, there's the London Gaelic Sports Association (www.londongaa.org); American footballers can get their fix with the British American Football League (www.britishamericanfootball.org); and if tight shorts and sleeveless shirts are your thing there's the British Aussie Rules Association (www.aflengland.org; or you could just join the navy).

395

General Information

Address: Gatwick Airport,
West Sussex, RH6 0NP

Airport Code: LGW

General Information: 0844 892 0322

Lost Property: 01293 503162
or gatwick.lostproperty@excess-baggage.com

Website: www.gatwickairport.com
or @Gatwick_Airport

Overview

The UK's second-largest airport (behind Heathrow) and "the most efficient single-runway airport in the world" (seems to repeat the negative, that), Gatwick is not terribly flashy, but not so bad to deal with, and getting better and better. Located 28 miles south of London, Gatwick is not linked by the Tube, but the airport is served by a mostly painless 30-minute train ride from Victoria Station. Gatwick is a much nicer place than it once was ("high-summer sweat-filled free-for-all check-in zones for budget flights to Spain" sounds about right) but after BAA sold the airport to Global Infrastructure Partners (of London City Airport fame), GIP undertook an initial £1.2 billion overhaul of the airport and its services to better position itself as a go-to European hub. And there is even talk of a second runway—good news for Gatwick and especially whichever single-runway airport is the second-most efficient in the world.

Gatwick has two terminals: the South Terminal and the North Terminal. Trains arrive at the South Terminal, and there are more shops there, but if your flight is out of the North Terminal, a free automated train will take you on the five-minute transfer.

As far as amenities go, the usual suspects are all present, with convivial times available at Britain's premier diluting station, J.D. Wetherspoons, and the glamour of Knightsbridge miraculously squeezed into one of those little airport branches of Harrods— just in case you feel the need to inflict one of their god-awful teddy bears on another country. As far as eating's concerned, there are several Jamie Oliver outlets, a Comptoir Libanais and other spots catering to varied tastes and dietary restrictions, including vegetarian and gluten-free options. For shopping there are the usual wide range of shops befitting an airport as destination: Boots but also outlets like Zara, Ray-Ban, and BOSS.

Getting There

The Gatwick Express (www.gatwickexpress.com) runs from Victoria Station in London to the South Terminal at Gatwick in 30 minutes. First trains run at 3:30, 4:30 and then every fifteen minutes thereafter with the last trains at 00:01 and 00:32. If you're near the rail hubs it is by far the most pleasant way to get there—though a single journey is going to set you back around £20. Thameslink (www.thameslinkrailway.com) run trains to Gatwick from Blackfriars, City Thameslink, Farringdon and St Pancras International stations for £19. Easybus (www.easybus.co.uk) coaches offer service to London with prices starting from £2 each way; travel takes about an hour.

To drive to Gatwick from the M25 you need to leave at Junction 7 and carry on southwards along the M23, following the signs. Leave the M23 at Junction 9 and again, follow those handy signs to get to the appropriate terminal.

Parking

Short stay car park rates start at £3 for the first half hour, £6 up to one hour, £10 up to two hours, £12 up to three hours, and climb steadily toward £35 for a 24-hour period. For long stays there are several parks located 5-15 minutes away (via bus transfers) from the airport. These are best booked in advance. For the official Gatwick car park, charges are £20 for the first day and £15 per day thereafter, and may be booked in advance online at www.gatwickparking.com.

Car Hire

The Gatwick on-airport car rental partners are Hertz, Avis, Europcar, Sixt, National, Alamo, Enterprise and Budget. The Gatwick Airport website also offers its own online car rental feature, with special rates.

Hotels

Gatwick has several hotels on site with varying levels of service. Keep in mind that the North and South Terminals are connected via a free five-minute transfer. In the South Terminal there is the 245-room BLOC hotel, the Hilton London Gatwick, and the economical YOTEL, which offers 46 cabins (available for four hour blocks or overnight) in a choice of premium (full-size double bed) or standard (large single). In the North Terminal, there is a Hampton by Hilton close to the airport check-in desks, the Premier Inn directly opposite the main entrance, and a four-star Sofitel. The full-service hotels feature amenities such as salons, restaurants, business facilities, and 24-hour gyms.

Airline/Terminal

Aegean Airlines: South
Aer Lingus: South
Afriqiyah Airways: South
Air Arabia Maroc: South
Air Baltic: South
Air Dolomiti: South
Air Europa: South
Air Malta: South
Air Transat: South
Aurigny: South
Belavia Belarusian: South
British Airways: North
Caribbean Airlines: North
easyJet: North/South
Emirates: North
Flybe: South
Freebird: South
Gambia Bird: South
Garuda Indonesia: North
Germania: South
Icelandair: North
Iraqi Airways: South
Meridiana Airlines: North
Monarch: South
Norwegian: South
Royal Air Maroc: North
Ryanair: South
Swiss International Air Lines: South
TAP Air Portugal: South
Thomas Cook: South
Thomson Airways: North
Titan Airways: South
Tunis Air: South
Turkish Airlines: North
Ukraine International Airlines: South
Vietnam Airlines: North
Virgin Atlantic: South
Vueling: North
WOW Air: South

General Information

Address: Hounslow, Middlesex, TW6
Airport Code: LHR
General Information: 0844 335 1801
Lost Property: 0844 824 3115 or missingx.com
Website: www.heathrowairport.com or @HeathrowAirport

Overview

Ah, Heathrow—London's main link to the outside world, resplendent in all the main airport offenders: infinite queues, bad food, draconian security and the acrid scent of 'the British on holiday.' Or as FM Hugh Grant once noticed, "Whenever I get gloomy with the state of the world, I think about the arrivals gate at Heathrow Airport." Or something like that.

Indeed, ex-London mayor Ken Livingstone once accused Heathrow of keeping people "prisoner" in its "ghastly shopping mall" but there does seem to be slow, gradual improvement. Heathrow has undergone years of seeming perpetual change, resulting in vastly improved transport services and upgraded motorway access. Terminal 1 is a thing of the past and the new Terminal 2 has eclipsed the old Terminal 2 in people's memory. Terminal 5 picked up the baton following a chaotic opening in 2008, taking the annual passenger count to upward of 70 million, and placing the airport in contention for busiest in the world. For years Heathrow has been stretched beyond its capacity, which has resulted in a campaign for a controversial third runway. The local residents might not like it but at least they don't have to suffer an hour on the tube to catch a flight.

Terminals

The terminals are organised around airline networks: Star Alliance, Oneworld, SkyTeam, with the non-aligned airlines wedged in where possible. Terminal 5 is the domain of British Airways.

Departures

Busy and security conscious, Heathrow demands travelers get there early—they suggest three hours before departure for long-haul and El Al flights, two hours for European flights, and a full 90 minutes for flights to the UK and Ireland. Makes you appreciate coach travel. Check-in is on the first floor of Terminal 4, the ground floor in Terminal 3, and the top floor of Terminals 2 and 5. When you arrive look for your check-in zone on the information screens near the entrance; check-in zones are marked by illuminated yellow cubes. If you are travelling through Heathrow, transfers are available between Heathrow Airport's four terminals. Terminals 2 and 3 are a short walk from each other (10–20 minutes) while Terminals 4 and 5 are served by free trains and buses.

Arrivals

As for the romance of the arrivals gate at Heathrow, arrivals areas are located on Level 1 at Terminal 2, the ground level of the Arrivals building at Terminal 3, and the ground levels of both Terminals 4 and 5. Official airport meeting points are marked. There are information screens in the arrivals area with flight status information and status codes: 'Expected' means the flight hasn't landed yet and Heathrow Airport Holdings Limited encourages you to indulge in a spot of shopping, 'Landed' means that you should expect 30–40 minutes for passengers to clear passport control, baggage reclaim and customs (longer at busy periods), and 'Baggage in hall' means that passengers should be in the arrivals area shortly. The Heathrow website also has live flight status information.

Hotels

In addition to the handful of area hotels that cater to Heathrow travellers, there are several hotels at the terminal, accessible by foot. The 605-room luxury Sofitel London Heathrow is located at Terminal 5 and the four-star Hilton London Heathrow Airport is located at Terminal

4. Both hotels offer requisite hotel amenities such as restaurants and business and fitness centres. Terminal 4 also has a YOTEL, the Japanese-style low-budget mini pod cabin that offers sleeping cabins for several hours. The No.1 Traveller Lounge after the security lines in Terminal 3 offers day rooms, both twin bunks and singles.

Getting There

The cheapest option is London Underground's Piccadilly Line, which gets you to central London in less than an hour for £5.70. The wait time for a train is generally no more than 10 minutes. Heathrow has three underground stations; one serving both Terminals 2 and 3, and one each for Terminals 4 and 5.

The fastest option is Heathrow Express (www.heathrowexpress.com), a non-stop train between the airport and Paddington station—in 15 minutes, every 15 minutes. It stops at Heathrow Central Station near Terminals 2 and 3, and also at Terminal 5. On-board fares are £26.50 one way and £40 for a return (£5 less if bought online, from ticket offices or ticket machines). Heathrow Connect follows the same route into west London, but serves intermediate stations making its journey time 25 minutes. At half the price of the Express though, it's probably worth the added minutes. Heathrow Connect trains depart Paddington every 30 minutes from Terminals 2 and 3 (travellers from Terminal 4 and 5 should use the free transfer). Fare is £10.10 one way to Paddington Station, less to intermediate stations. Both these trains run between approx 5 am–12 am.

National Express (www.nationalexpress.com) offers coach service from points around London to Heathrow. Tickets start at £12.

Driving from Central London takes about 45-60 minutes depending on traffic. To Terminals 2 and 3, exit the M4 (Junction 4) or M25 (Junction 15) and follow signs. When leaving Terminals 2 and 3, follow exit signs to the access/exit tunnel. Then follow signs to the M4 motorway, which will eventually bring you into London. Terminals 4 and 5 have separate entrances. If driving, exit M25 at Junction 14 and follow signs (if coming from the M4, leave at Junction 4B and follow the M25 south to Junction 14). A taxi to central London takes 45-60 minutes and costs £35-plus; note that there is no set fare from the airport.

Car Parking

There are short-term and long-term car parks, and both are expensive. Up to 30 minutes at the short stay is £3.50 (£4 for Terminal 4). An hour at the short stay is £6.50 (£7 at Terminal 4), two hours is £10.50 (£11 at Terminal 4), then rising steadily to £56 for 24 hours. The long stay car park is about 10 minutes away by courtesy bus and the standard drive-up price is £26 for the first day, then £20.50 each day thereafter. A peak surcharge is in effect for Easter, Christmas and some summer weeks.

Airline/Terminal

Aegean Airlines: 2
Aer Lingus: 2
Aeroflot: 4
Aeromexico: 4
Air Algerie: 4
Air Astana: 4
Air Canada: 2
Air China: 2
Air France: 4

Air India: 4
Air Malta: 4
Air Mauritius: 4
Air New Zealand: 2
Air Serbia: 4
Alitalia: 4
American Airlines: 3
ANA: 2
Arik Air: 4
Asiana Airlines: 2
Austrian: 2
Avianca: 2
Azerbaijan Airlines: 4
Biman Bangladesh Airlines: 4
British Airways: 5 (some 3)
Brussels Airlines: 2
Bulgaria Air: 4
Cathay Pacific Airways: 3
China Eastern: 4
China Southern: 4
Croatia Airlines: 2
Delta Air Lines: 3 & 4
Egypt Air: 4
El Al: 4
Emirates: 3
Ethiopian Airlines: 2
Etihad Airways: 4
EVA Air: 2
Finnair: 3
Germanwings: 2
Gulf Air: 4
Iberia: 5
Icelandair: 2
Iran Air: 3
Japan Airlines: 3
Jet Airways (India): 4
Kenya Airways: 4
KLM-Royal Dutch Airlines: 4
Korean Air: 4
Kuwait Airways: 4
Libyan Airlines: 4
LOT Polish Airlines: 4
Lufthansa: 2
Malaysia Airlines: 4
MEA: 3
Oman Air: 3
Pakistan International Airlines: 3
Philippine Airlines: 4
Qantas: 3
Qatar Airways: 4
Royal Air Maroc: 4
Royal Brunei Airlines: 4
Royal Jordanian: 3
SAS-Scandinavian Airlines: 2
Saudia: 4
Singapore Airlines: 2
South African Airways: 2
Sri Lankan Airlines: 3
Swiss International Airlines: 2
TAM: 3
TAP Portugal: 2
Tarom: 4
Thai Airways: 2
Transaero: 4
Tunisair: 4
Turkish Airlines: 2
Turkmenistan Airlines: 3
United Airlines: 2
US Airways: 3
Uzbekistan Airlines: 4
Vietnam Airlines: 4
Virgin Atlantic: 3
Virgin Atlantic Little Red: 2
Vueling: 3

General Information

Address: Hartmann Road,
London, E16 2PX

Airport Code: LCY

General Enquiries: 020 7646 0088/0000

Website: www.londoncityairport.com
or @LondonCityAir

Overview

With its one wee runway squeezed over the water between the old George V and Royal Albert Docks, City is London's smallest and most central airport (six miles from the City of London, 22 minutes from Bank station). Where once stevedores ate pie and mash, stockbrokers are now whisked off to lunchtime meetings on dinky short takeoff jets. Primarily used by business types, its small size and short runway means city serves mainly European destinations, with BA's New York service (including a stop off) being the one exception. Still, this means much faster check-in times and fewer delays than at the comparative behemoths of Heathrow and Gatwick.

Amenities at London City Airport include some above-average food options and complimentary WiFi. LCY also has a "silent airport policy," meaning no announcements are made, which also means you definitely shouldn't zone out too far away from your gate (you've been warned).

Getting There

In 2005 someone, somewhere, saw the light and extended the DLR (Docklands Light Railway) to City. The airport now couldn't be simpler to get to by public transport: get on the DLR at Bank; make sure you take a train destined for the King George V branch (these are marked "via City Airport"); and you'll arrive at the airport's station in under 25 minutes. A slightly quicker route is to take the Jubilee Underground line to Canning Town and take the DLR a mere three stops westbound from there. There's a taxi rank directly outside the terminal exit, expect to pay at least £40 for a black cab to go to or from the West End. Don't expect the journey to be much faster than on the DLR/Underground. Pre-booked cabs should be a little cheaper; bookings are available via www.minicabit.com.

If you're driving, given its central location there's no obvious route to City. A useful general rule is to point your wheels at the eastern end of Central London and then keep going that way from Tower Hill on the A1203 (East Smithfield/The Highway). The airport is signposted from this road. If you're getting there from the South East, head through the Blackwall tunnel and follow signs once you emerge into the daylight. If you're near the M25 and like traffic jams, crawl your way to junction 30 and take the Thames Gateway to the airport from there.

Parking

Short stay is directly next to the terminal and rates start at £6 for the first 30 minutes, £11 for one hour, £15 for two hours, and steadily increasing up to £55 for 24 hours. The long stay carpark is a short walk from the terminal and costs £45 per day. Pre-booking long stay parking results in drastically reduced rates; check online for more. All of which is to say, parking is expensive. If you still feel the need to park and can book in advance, get in touch with BCP airport parking for a (slightly) cheaper option at www.parkbcp.co.uk.

Car Hire

On-site car hire desks for Avis, Europcar and Hertz are located next to the terminal. Travellers can book cars through the London City Airport website.

Airlines

Air France
Alitalia
British Airways
Blue Islands
CityJet
Flybe
KLM Royal Dutch Airlines
Lufthansa
Luxair
Sky Work
Sun-Air
Swiss International Airlines (SWISS)

General Information

Address: Navigation House, Airport Way, Luton, Bedfordshire LU2 9LY

Airport Code: LTN

General Enquiries: 01582 405100

Lost Property: 01582 395219 or lostproperty@ltn.aero

Website: www.london-luton.co.uk or @LDNLutonAirport

Overview

You have to admire branding at work: appending "London" to "London Luton Airport" is perhaps slightly wishful thinking, seeing as the facility is located 35 miles north of Central London. That said, it's not impossible to get to the airport and parking is reasonable, but everyone knows why they're flying out of Luton: those ridiculously cheap budget tickets to the Spanish coast.

Luton debuted in 1938, was put to good use during WWII and quickly became a top airport for package holiday travel. Charter trips comprised the majority of flights in and out of Luton until the 1980s, when Ryanair began using Luton for short-haul flights. In the 1990s Luton was reborn as the go-to for no-frills budget air carriers flying in and out of the London area. Thus, the £2.99 flight to the Canary Islands with every other stag or hen party travelling that weekend.

Luton features the requisite airport amenities: Boots, Dixons, et al. plus light meals. For assistance in leaving the airport to wherever it is you're headed, the Onward Travel Centre is located on the main concourse in the terminal building and is open 24 hours a day, seven days a week.

Getting There

Unless you live in North London, getting to and from Luton by public transport isn't quite seamless. It consists of taking a half-hour train service from St Pancras or London Bridge to Luton Parkway. After your train journey you'll be met at Luton Parkway by a shuttle bus. Be sure to purchase your rail tickets with London Luton Airport as your final destination.

Luton is served by rail via the Luton Airport Parkway Station. From there a ten-minute shuttle bus takes you to the terminal. Keep in mind that while rail service from Luton Airport Parkway Station to central London is frequent (and through the night via Thameslink service), the shuttle only operates between 5 a.m. and midnight. Which is to say, if your plane is delayed past midnight—not out of the question with budget carriers—consider coach alternatives.

Coach services, such as the 757 Greenline, easyBus and National Express are good alternatives that will at least get you home if your flight comes in late. Greenline (www.greenline.co.uk/757 or 0844 801 7261) is probably your best bet, and it offers pick-up and drop-off points on Buckingham Palace Road, Marble Arch and Baker Street, as well as free WiFi. Fares to London Victoria are £10 and it takes about an hour, but it runs pretty regularly through the night. The National Express service A1 operates 60 departures a day between Luton and London Victoria, with free WiFi as well.

London Luton Airport is somewhat accessible from both the M1 and M25. If you have a choice, go for the M1, as the airport is only about five minutes from Junction 10. Without traffic, it can take about 45 minutes from central London. This can sometimes be longer when there are extensive road works, which tends to be always. When using Sat Nav systems, use the postcode LU2 9QT.

How to Get There—Really

Seriously. You've paid next to nothing for your airfare, splash out on a private cab. If you book a licensed mini-cab ahead of time, the service is often cheaper than the equivalent black cab fare and definitely easier, as they'll meet you at the arrivals hall. A consistently cheap company is Simply Airports (www.simplyairports.co.uk or 020 7701 4321) which is usually under £55, but you may want to get a quote from your own local company. If you leave it to the last minute, and must take a black cab, get ready to shell out at least £85 (with their meters, this can increase with traffic) plus a meeting fee if you want them to wait for you. Cab rides from central London usually take about an hour.

Parking

Short Term Parking is pricier but situated closest to the terminal, with prices ranging from £4 for 30 minutes or £37 per day drive-up. Mid-term parking is ideal for stays of around five days and is about a five-minute transfer by bus. Mid term is £21 per day drive-up with significant savings if booked well in advance. Long-term parking is about 10 minutes from the terminal by bus, and costs £19 per day, with hefty discounts for booking in advance.

Rental Cars

Car hire desks are located at the Onward Travel Centre on the main concourse in the terminal building. Lots are connected to the airport via free shuttle service. On-site companies are Avis, Europcar/National/Alamo, Hertz and Enterprise.

Hotels

There is no hotel at Luton but there are four hotels near the airport: Ibis Hotel (01582 424488), Holiday Inn Express (01582 589100), Ramada Encore Hotel (01582 218132) and Hampton by Hilton (01582 798477).

Airlines

Air Nostrum
AtlasGlobal
Blue Air
easyJet
El Al
La Compagnie
Monarch
Ryanair
SunExpress
TAROM
Thomson
Wizz Air

General Information

Address: Stansted Airport, Essex CM24 1QW

Airport Code: STN

General Enquiries: 0844 335 1803

Lost Property: 0844 824 3109
or stn.lostproperty@bagport.co.uk

Website: www.stanstedairport.com
or @STN_Airport

Overview

It might be tucked away on a former Roman burial site in the middle of the dull Essex countryside, but Stansted Airport has one thing going for it—it's amazingly simple. One terminal (and quite a nice one too, Norman Foster saluted), one check-in area, one security gate. Take that, Heathrow. Nearly 20 airlines, most of them budget, fly nearly 18 million passengers per year from here to a growing list of mainly domestic and short-haul destinations.

Stansted dates to WWII, and was a base for the RAF and the US Air Force during the war. Post-war Stansted was used for charter flights, then eventually scheduled flights. The Norman Foster-designed main terminal opened in 1991, considered one of the most modern airports at the time. During the 2000s annual passenger traffic doubled from about 12 million to nearly 24 million by 2007 before leveling off to about 17-18 million per year.

A word about amenities. As far as shopping is concerned, Stansted offers Boots and Dixon outlets plus the usual selection of 'small airport shops' more aimed at passing the time than serious purchases. Stansted, like the other area airports, has made efforts to provide nicer dining options (then there's the Burger King); feel free to settle in for a few pints and then grab a sandwich on the run once you hear your name being called for the third time; gingerly avoid screaming children and/or singing hen-night crowds on the way. You could also try the Escape Lounge where, for about the price of an easyJet fare, one can enjoy an open bar, complimentary dishes and free WiFi. Speaking of WiFi travellers get 60 free minutes per device throughout the airport.

Getting There

Stansted might seem a long way from London, but getting there by public transport is surprisingly easy. All you have to do is choose between the train (fast) and the bus (cheap). Several train operators serve the airport from Liverpool Street Station. But before you start struggling with too many timetables for trains that stop at too many stops, opt for the dedicated Stansted Express (www.stanstedexpress.com). The service runs every 15 minutes and takes you to the airport in just over 45 minutes. Tickets start at £19 for a standard single ride between Stansted and London Liverpool Street. Buses will take an hour to take you to the airport, and longer if there's a lot of traffic, but single tickets go for between £8 and £10.50 (potentially even less for easyBus). A number of operators fight for your custom, the main ones are: Terravision (www.terravision.eu), which leaves from Liverpool Street Station and Victoria Station; the slightly more expensive National Express (www.nationalexpress.com) connects to the same stations but some buses also stop in Stratford and Golders Green; and easyBus (www.easybus.co.uk) gives you the intimacy of a small mini-van, stopping in Baker Street and Old Street in the City. If you're traveling during the rush hour, take a book. Whitechapel Road is one of London's most bustling streets, but it will get boring at some point.

Driving

If you're fortunate enough to have a car, or managed to convince your dad-in-law to lend you his, find your way out of the city via Angel and hit the M11. It's a straight drive from here and amid Essex' greenery, the airport is hard to miss. Cab drivers will know how to get you to the airport, but will probably charge you a small fortune for it.

Parking

Short-term parking rates start at £3 for the first 30 minutes and rise in steps to £39 for 24 hours. Long-stay will cost you £19 a day. If you're in for a weekend trip, opt for the mid-stay car park, which is closer to the terminal than the long-stay option and charges £21/day drive-up. Valet parking is available and can be pre-booked. Once there, drop your car at the end of Set Down Lane; the pickup point is next to the Fast Track car park. Book online before you head off for discounts on all Stansted parking options.

Car Rental

Hertz, Avis, Europcar, Budget, National, Alamo, Enterprise and Sixt all have desks at Stansted.

Hotels

There are three hotels either next to or within the perimeter of the airport. The four-star Radisson Blu (01279 661 012) is connected to the airport via a covered walkway. The Premier Inn (0871 527 9352) and Hilton London Stansted Airport (01279 680 800) are both located within the perimeter of the airport and connected by a short shuttle bus ride.

Airlines

Aegean Airlines	FlyBe
Air Berlin	Freebird Airlines
Air Moldova	Germanwings
Atlantic Airways	Pegasus Airlines
Atlasjet	Ryanair
Aurigny	Tangney-Tours
Belle Air	Thomas Cook
Cyprus Airways	Thomson Airways
easyJet	

General Information

TfL Customer Services: 4th Floor,
14 Pier Walk, London SE10 0ES

Phone: 0343 222 1234

Website: www.tfl.gov.uk/modes/tube
or @TfLTravelAlerts

Overview

If the Underground had a motto it wouldn't be "Mind the gap" but "Sorry for any inconvenience caused." But as we grumble and ponder if anyone is ever actually sorry for squeezing you 30m below the surface, in a sweat-box held together by dust, rust and expensive fares, the magnificence of the 'Tube' network should really be appreciated. Across its 250-odd miles of track the Underground will take you to 270 stations spread the length and breadth of London (although with disproportionately few lines reaching into south London). The system is well integrated with the bus and overground train networks which share a common ticketing system with the Oyster card.

When fully functioning, the Underground will get you across town quicker than the bus and without the complicated timetables and schedules of overground trains. When it is struck by signal failures and breakdowns, which is very often, it can be excruciatingly slow and get very overcrowded, very quickly. In conclusion: the Underground won't necessarily get you anywhere on time, in style or in comfort, but it will (eventually) get you pretty much anywhere.

Fares

The vast majority of the network is divided into concentric fare rings or zones (1-6). Zone 1 covers central London, zone 5 covers the outskirts of London. Fares are dependent on how many zones your journey includes and there's a premium for travelling in zone 1. Peak fares (Monday to Friday from 6.30-9.30 am and 4-7 pm) are from 50p to a few pounds more than off-peak, although journeys limited to zone 1 do not benefit from the off-peak discount. Your best bet is to get an Oyster Card—lowest zone 1 single fare is £2.30 instead of £4.80 if you pay by cash. Oyster cards are available for just £5 from vending machines. It's a total no-brainer: the total amount that can be deducted from your Oyster card is also capped over a 24-hour period to match the equivalent cost of a one day travel card. So the fare system is complicated, but if you take £2.30 (which will get you a single journey within zone 1 with an Oyster card) as a base rate, and add to this the further out of zone 1 you travel, things become clearer. If you feel the need to marvel at the full intricacy of the fares and ticketing system, give yourself eye-strain at Transport for London's website.

Frequency and Quality of Service

The vast majority of centrally located stations will have a train at least every three minutes most of the day. At the very beginning and end of the day service frequency tails-off and can get as low as eight minutes between trains. Trains are also much less frequent at the farther reaches of some lines—the Metropolitan line has trains only every 20 minutes from its most north-western stations, even during peak times. Almost all lines have a reduced frequency on Sundays. First trains are 05:00-05:30, last trains are between midnight and 12.30. Last trains are generally safe; expect a slightly raucous mix of pickled after-workers and overly obsequious rough-sleepers rather than any real troublemakers, especially after booze was banned in 2008. The whole network had £5bn thrown at it for the 2012 Olympics, but the only noticeable improvement was increased cleanliness in many of the stations.

Lines

Bakerloo: (Brown coloured on maps) Runs from Harrow & Wealdstone in the north west to Elephant & Castle in the south east.

Central: (Red) Runs from West Ruislip in the west to Epping in the far north east. The central section is buried under Oxford Street and has four stops on the street, the quietest usually being Bond Street.

Circle: (Yellow) Notoriously slow, unreliable, and not strictly a circle—even more so now that a tail reaches down to Hammersmith. For this reason Edgware Road is now the end of the line. Shares almost all of its track and stations with other lines so don't necessarily bother waiting specifically for a dedicated Circle Line train. Look out for the 'Platform for Art' as you pass Gloucester Road station.

District: (Green) One of the few lines to serve deepest south London, branches run into Richmond and Wimbledon in the southwest and also to Ealing. The line continues up to Upminster in the northeast. Almost all of the branches of this fragmented line come together at Earls Court station into an infuriating mess, so plan ahead if changing there.

Hammersmith & City: (Pink) Starts at Hammersmith in the west of the city before heading north to Paddington and continuing east to Barking. Take it to Ladbroke Grove if heading to the Portobello market.

Jubilee: (Silver) Silver coloured as it opened in the year of the Queen's Silver Jubilee in 1977, the line serves northwest, central and east London, including the Canary Wharf business district. The section east of Green Park is the most recent addition to the network (it opened in 1999) and has a number of architecturally exemplary stations.

Metropolitan: (Dark Purple) The oldest of all the lines, this granddaddy of metropolitan underground railways strikes far out in the suburbs and countryside northwest of the city from its central root at Aldgate.

Northern: (Black) Presumably given black as its colour to reflect the dark mood of anyone unlucky enough to have to commute on it, the Northern line is the overcrowded spine of London, covering vast swathes of the city centre, the north and the south.

Piccadilly: (Dark Blue) From Cockfosters in the far northeast this line trundles all the way to Heathrow airport, with some of the most popular tourist spots in between. It's a very cheap way to the airport but is also the slowest. Southgate and Arnos Grove stations are both 1930s modernist brilliance.

Victoria: (Light Blue) Runs from Walthamstow in the north to Brixton in the south. This musty line is currently undergoing refurbishment and will feature new trains and track by 2011. In the meantime, check for early closing and shutdowns, particularly during weekends.

Waterloo & City: (Turquoise) No-one has ever met anyone who has been on this line. Erm, it has two stations, Waterloo and Bank, and is designed for suited and booted commuters coming in by train from Waterloo. No trains on Sundays.

London Overground: (Orange) TfL took over part of the overground rail network, notably the somewhat shabby and North London Line which runs from Richmond to Stratford. This has now been merged with what was the East London Line, which connects East, Southeast and Northeast London. Just think of it as an extension to the tube network.

Bicycles

Bicycles are generally only allowed on the tube outside peak hours and only from stations outside central London. They are not permitted on the Victoria or Waterloo and City lines at all. Folding bicycles can be taken on all sections of the Tube free of charge.

General Info

TfL Customer Services: 4th Floor,
14 Pier Walk, London SE10 0ES

Phone: 0343 222 1234

Website: www.tfl.gov.uk/modes/dlr,
or @LondonDLR

Overview

Not quite a tram, tube or train, it's simply the Docklands Light Railway, a nifty little thing that makes getting to places like Greenwich Village and City Airport easy and cheap. Launched in 1937 with a modest 11 trains and only 15 stations, the regeneration of the Docklands area has seen it grow to seven lines covering 45 stations and counting, serving over 100 million passengers a year. Serving the east and Southeast of the city, it is pretty much as pleasant as London public transport gets. It's reliable, less noisy than the tube, generally less crowded and it's pretty well air-conditioned. The DLR is also fully automated and most of the time there is no driver, meaning that you can take the front seat and pretend that you're actually driving the thing.

The DLR provides a key service for London's suits, with the Bank to Canary Wharf journey taking just over ten minutes. For normal people, Canary Wharf also makes an interesting/unusual weekend destination. Almost completely deserted, a stroll amongst the abandoned skyscrapers is a strangely satisfying way to spend a Sunday afternoon.

Fares

As on the rest of London's public transport you're best off with an Oyster card. One thing to remember is that there are no barriers at DLR stations and instead Oyster readers are located at station exits and entrances. To avoid getting slapped with a fine and to ensure you're charged the right amount, remember to touch in and out correctly. The prices are similar to the tube, so cash works out more expensive (though not as expensive as the tube's cash single).

Hours

The DLR runs 5.30 am–12.30 am (Sundays 7.00 am–11.30 pm), with train frequencies depending on the time of day. On weekdays, trains run as often as every three-and-a-half minutes during peak times, and every five to ten minutes during off-peak times and weekends. The DLR is closed Christmas.

Transport • Overground Trains

General Information

National Rail: www.nationalrail.co.uk
or @nationalrailenq
Eurostar: www.eurostar.com or @Eurostar
TfL London Overground:
www.tfl.gov.uk/modes/london-overground/

Overview

The railways are one of the great British inventions but, unfortunately, the Victorians who built the network in this country did slightly too good a job. Every generation since has taken one look at the massively expensive task of modernising them and scuttled back into their Ford Fiestas. So, while France, Germany and Japan got on with building super-speed bullet trains Britain was stuck with an uneasy compromise between the technologies of 1950 and 1850. This doesn't mean that you shouldn't use trains. It just means that it's probably best to avoid them at peak times. That's when London plays a cruel trick on people who choose to live in places with names like 'Gravesend' and 'Slough' by making them lurch home slowly with less personal space than the legal minimum for cattle. During off-peak times train travel can, in contrast, be positively pleasant. It's a great way to see the countryside, every city and major town in the country is connected, and, if you book far enough in advance and shop around on sites like www.megatrain.com or www.thetrainline.com it can be less expensive than you'd think. In London itself, Transport for London manages four suburban rail routes that use the pay as you go Oyster system.

Stations

Broadly speaking, Euston and King's Cross stations serve the north of the country, Liverpool Street the east, Victoria the south, Paddington and Marylebone the west.

Eurostar

The King's Cross area is also home to the splendid St Pancras—the terminal for the Eurostar train service which connects Britain with the rest of Europe. Since November 2007 it's been possible to get from here to Paris or Brussels in around two hours—with connecting trains to Siberia and beyond.

Charing Cross Station

NFT Map: 24

Address: The Strand, London, WC2N 5HF

Station Code: CHX

General Station Enquiries: 03457 11 41 41

Lost Property: 020 7930 5444

Southeastern: www.southeasternrailway.co.uk
or @Se_Railway

Overview

Perched at the top of the Strand amidst popular tourist attractions such as Trafalgar Square and with the majestic 1865 Charing Cross Hotel being part of the station, you may presume that a cornucopia of ornate delights lies within. Well, it's a dump; the chances of *Brief Encounter* being remade here are pretty slim. But your chances of being barged by a curmudgeonly office worker are very good, what with it being one of the busiest rail terminals in London. Still, can you blame them for wanting to get out of the place so quickly?

Tickets

There is a small ticket office open some 20 hours per day, and three banks of ticket machines on or around the concourse.

Services

If you're in need of a quick bite, there's a decent variety of food outlets to cater for all tastes, from Burger King to a M &S Simply Food outlet. Indulge your Schadenfreude by watching the beleaguered information guy having to dispense a plethora of poor excuses as to why the 17.34 to Margate was cancelled. There is both a Boots and a WHSmith and cash machines can be found on the concourse and in the front entrance.

Public Transport

The station is easily accessible by Charing Cross station (Northern & Bakerloo lines) and also the adjoining Embankment station (Circle & District lines). The nearby Trafalgar Square is a major hub for buses—especially night buses for post-West End madness—which inch their way out to places as far apart as Harrow and Crystal Palace.

Euston Station

NFT Map: 78

Address: Euston Road, London, NW1 2RT

Station Code: EUS

General Station Enquiries: 03457 11 41 41

Lost property: 0207 387 8699

Website: www.networkrail.co.uk/EUS
or @NetworkRailEUS

Overview

Easily the ugliest station in London, Euston creeps up as you nervously edge along Euston Road. The first inter-city terminal built in London, it was originally constructed in 1837, but the lovely original was demolished to make way for the monstrous concrete-and-glass coffin which now squats next to the mail depot. Since privatisation the interior has become an identi-kit British rail station with more chain businesses per head than is morally decent.

It's not all doom and gloom, however. Within this architectural eyesore you'll find a scarily concise summation of human nature. Like most busy stations, there's plenty of eccentricity and electricity here: abandoned Tube tunnels; stressed-out coffee-guzzling power-commuters; fresh-faced backpackers sprawled out on the floor; and the infamous beggar who—to the delight of football lovers everywhere except in Manchester—was arrested for punching Manchester Utd manager Sir Alex Ferguson.

The station is London's gateway to the north west of England and Scotland, and also North Wales. As such it is the point of entry for Scousers, Mancunians, Glaswegians and more. Virgin trains (www.virgintrains.co.uk) to Glasgow can take as little as 4 hrs 10 mins.

Tickets

The ticket cashiers may have the glazed look of Kafka-esque zombies but the cleaning staff are often more helpful. Just use the Fasttrack machines!

Services

There's plenty of eating and drinking options, all of the 'chain' variety. If you're an aficionado and determined to hang around, check out the Doric Arch (1 Eversholt St; 020 7383 3359), a little boozer with train memorabilia lining the walls. The left luggage office is at the top of the ramp to platforms 16–18 and is open between 7 am–11 pm.

Public Transport

As an actual railway station it is adequate. Served by two Tube lines and nine bus routes, it's nothing if not convenient.

King's Cross Station

NFT Map: 78

Address: Euston Rd & Pancras Rd, London, N1 9AL

Station Code: KGX

General Station Enquiries: 03457 11 41 41

Lost property: 020 7278 3310

Website: www.networkrail.co.uk/kingscross

Overview

Previously a dingy playground for prostitutes, drug dealers, and all sorts of similarly bad kids, King's Cross Station scrubbed up a bit, thanks to lots of chin scratching and typically panicked spending on the government's part. Built in 1852 on the site of a former smallpox hospital, it is one of the busiest and most well-connected stations in the country: running trains to Edinburgh; Newcastle; the East coast; as well as six Tube lines. Zany trivia about the station includes the fact that it is supposedly built on top of legendary Fembot-Queen Bouclcea's grave (most probably a total lie) and that it has a tacky little shrine to Harry Potter at what has been designated 'Platform 9 3/4' (oh God).

Nearly all long distance train services leave from the overground platforms under the arches straight ahead of you as you enter from Euston Road. The Tube is also accessible from steps at this entrance and at what used to be the Thameslink station next to the Scala on Pentonville Road. From the main Tube entrance there is a pedestrian subway that comes up on the other side of Euston Road just outside Macdonald's. This is handy for crossing the road at busy times, and of course for getting chips.

Tickets

Tube tickets, including Oyster top ups and season tickets, can be purchased from the machines in front of the Tube entry gates, located just at the bottom of both sets of stairs at the station. For railcard discounts and more specific enquiries you'll have to queue at the manned ticket desks next to the machines. For all other tickets go to the upstairs ticket hall which is to the left of the main Euston Road entrance.

Services

With the renovations, the quality of services has significantly improved. But with the excellent Eat St literally round the corner, ditch the station completely and sample the wares of London's best street food traders. And for the basics, the trusty newspaper kiosk underneath the awning is still going strong.

Public Transport

King's Cross crosses more Tube lines (six) than any other station, and is serviced by at least twice as many buses, many of which run all night.

Liverpool Street Station

NFT Map: 8

Address: Liverpool St, London, EC2M 7PY

Station Code: LST

General Station Enquiries: 03457 11 41 41

Lost property: 020 7247 4297

Website: www.networkrail.co.uk/liverpoolstreet

Overview

It's not that Liverpool Street is particularly ugly, but if it's architectural beauty you're after, you're much better off heading to Paddington or the new, improved St. Pancras International. In comparison to these two icons of British station design, Liverpool Street is extremely modest, boring even. Clean, modern and easy to navigate around, it is simply a good train station. With the markets, bars and restaurants of Spitalfields and Brick Lane just around the corner, the station is the perfect starting point to explore east London. First opened to the public in 1874, it is one of the busiest stations in London. With 18 platforms, the station mainly serves destinations in the east of England, including daytrip favourites such as Cambridge and Southend on Sea.

It is also the home of the Stansted Express, providing easy airport access with departures every 15 minutes. If you're travelling with a group of people a taxi might work out slightly cheaper, but the train is much quicker and more reliable. The Tube station, with its main entrance centrally located on the main concourse, makes all of London easily accessible with the Central, Hammersmith & City, Circle and Metropolitan lines all passing through. Being one of the busiest stations on the underground network, rush hour can get nasty and is best avoided.

Tickets

The ticket office is located on the main concourse, on your left hand side if entering from Bishopsgate. Ticket windows are open during stat on opening hours. There are also several express ticket machines scattered throughout the station. Tickets for the Stansted Express can be purchased from designated ticket machines opposite platforms 5-6. A cluster of cash machines can be found by the stairs leading up to the Old Broad Street exit. There are payphones on both levels and most are located on the Bishopsgate side of the station.

Services

With Brick Lane just around the corner, eating, drinking and shopping here should really be a last resort. The regular big-chain fast food joints are scattered (some of them repeatedly) throughout the station with the usual selection of coffee, burgers, sandwiches and sweets. The main shopping area is on the lower level around the Broadgate and Exchange Square exits, offering everything from toiletries and birthday cards to Italian silk ties and double-glazed windows.

Passengers are invited to wait for their trains in the so-called "food court," which really isn't much more than a few cramped tables near the Burger King. There's a small but nicer waiting lounge located adjacent to platform 10. Here you also find the left luggage, a bureau de change, a less busy cash machine and access to the main taxi rank. Smoking is prohibited at all times throughout the station.

Public Transport

The main bus station is located on the upper level of the station (Broadgate end), and provide a large number of services to destinations throughout London. Plenty of buses also stop on the street just outside the Bishopsgate exit.

London Bridge Station

NFT Map: 106

Address: Station Approach Road, London SE1 9SP

Station Code: LBG

General Station Enquiries: 03457 11 41 4

Lost property: 03451 27 29 20 (Southern Railway)

Website: www.networkrail.co.uk/londonbridge

Overview

Around in one form or other since 1836, when steam trains filled the air with smoke, London Bridge is the city's oldest station. It's a good starting point for weekend trips to Kent's countryside or days on Brighton's beach. Operators Southeastern and Southern cover the south east, while Thameslink operates (little-known) connections to the airports Gatwick and Luton. The station couldn't be better connected to public transport, with two Tube lines and a plethora of buses at the doorstep. The catacombs underneath the station—said to be haunted—have been turned into the museum-cum-gore-fest London Bridge Experience, adding to the spooky entertainment already provided by the London Dungeon next door—just in case a cancelled or delayed train leaves you with too much time on your hands. Does happen, we're told.

Tickets

The main office is located next to the main entrance (London Bridge Street) or there are machines situated throughout the station.

Services

The main concourse is lined with eating and shopping options. Grab Cornish pasties, sandwiches, donuts; and the usual burgers from the usual chains, but Borough Market just over the road though, you'd be mad to waste your money on these. M&S and WH Smith lead the list of practical, but terribly unexciting shop names. The taverns connecting the Underground station with the national trains is teeming with better food options however—some even non-chain.

Public Transport

Connections are excellent. London Bridge Station is served by the Jubilee Line and the Bank branch of the Northern Line. Escalators take you down from the main concourse. Step outside the main entrance for the massive bus station, where buses leave in all directions of the city, except its far western reaches.

Marylebone Train Station

NFT Map: 76

Address: Great Central House,
Melcombe Place, London, NW1 6JJ

Station Code: MYB

Lost Property: 08456 005 165

Overview

Despite Monopoly-board notoriety, Marylebone railway station fell into neglect in the mid – to late-twentieth century, spurned as a rundown piggy-in-the-middle wedged haplessly between neighbours Paddington and Euston. But it's an aimless drifter no more. A refurb' in the 90s and again in 2006 saw Marylebone reinvigorated, with a thorough sprucing up and two new platforms. Servicing the Midlands, it now threads as far as Birmingham, Shakespeare's Stratford-Upon-Avon, Leamington Spa, Aylesbury, and High Wycombe, amongst others. It remains the runt of the London train station litter, but is a popular location for television filming (Doctor Who; Magnum PI; Green Wing; Peep Show) at a fraction of the price of King's Cross. In its bowels, Bakerloo Line trains rumble through an underground station of the same name.

Tickets

Rail ticket windows are to the north of Marylebone's relatively petite concourse and open Monday-Saturday 06.30–22:10 or Sunday 07.30–21.40. As with all mainline train stations, self-service ticket machines are in abundance should ticket offices be closed or queues too long. Sturdy padded-barriers ensure buying tickets on board the train, or getting away without them, is not an option. Underground tickets can be purchased from windows or machines alike within the Tube station itself.

Services

The usual plethora of railway station chains are on hand: newsagent WH Smith, baguette bakers Upper Crust, supermarket Marks & Spencer, and pasty purveyors the West Cornwall Company among them. More individually, Marylebone also hosts AMT Coffee, a cafe with a seating area at the centre of the concourse, the nifty flower stand on the south wall, and The V&A free house in the west passageway—an old man's boozer in the classic, wood panelled style. Cash points and payphones are in this same walkway, and toilets are situated on the south wall.

Public Transport

Marylebone underground station lies directly beneath Marylebone overground, and is serviced (Matron!) by the Bakerloo Line, while buses 2 and 205 stop directly outside the main entrance. A taxi stand is also situated out front. Baker Street and Edgware tube stations are a short walk away.

Paddington Station

NFT Map: 31

Address: Praed Street, London, W2 1HQ

Station Code: PAD

General Station Enquiries: 03457 11 41 41

Lost property: 020 7262 0344

Website: www.networkrail.co.uk/paddington
or @NetworkRailPAD

Overview

If you're in that small minority of people who love stations, then Paddington's paradise. Designed by engineering legend Isambard Kingdom Brunel—his middle name is Kingdom for God's sake, of course his work's going to be magnificent—this barn-like structure harks back to an era when train travel retained a little glamour. If it wasn't for the on-site Burger King you could easily imagine tearful ladies waving silk handkerchiefs at dapper gents.

The station also occupies a unique place in literary heritage. Every British child in the last half-century knows the tales of Paddington Bear. From "deepest darkest Peru", he was left unattended at the station; but a kind family picked him up, took him in, and named him after it. No other station name can inspire such genuine warmth. It certainly wouldn't have worked if he'd been found at Clapham Junction.

Heathrow Express

The super-fast link to Heathrow from Paddington takes just 15 minutes to Terminals 1, 2 and 3. Be warned, though; it's far from cheap (www.heathrowexpress.com).

Tickets

A ticket office and machines are located near platforms 9-10, and there are other machines and an information point near the Eastbourne Terrace entrance and also underneath the mezzanine.

Services

If you have any money left from your ticket—unlikely at today's prices—there are plenty of sharks who can take it off you. Burger King and Upper Crust will overcharge you for burgers or baguettes and there's an 'offie' (off-license) for expensive booze. There are also other ways of staying amused; as it's the main portal for commuters entering London from the west and Wales) there's WiFi, a supermarket, a bookshop and curiously, a lingerie shop. Just what sort of a job do you have if you get to the station and realise: "Bollocks! No suspenders!"? Certainly not one compatible with Paddington's place in children's lit, that's for sure.

Public Transport

The Bakerloo, Circle, District, and Hammersmith & City Tube lines all stop at Paddington. Buses serve west and north west London.

St Pancras International

NFT Map: 78

Address: Euston Road, London, N1C 4QP

Station Reception: 020 7843 7688

Lost Property: 020 7837 4334

Website: stpancras.com or @StPancrasInt

Overview

St Pancras station has been generating waves of breathless excitement ever since its opening ceremony in 2007, which was by all accounts a pretty histrionic affair. This "Cathedral of Transport" situated next door to King's Cross station is now home to the Eurostar international train service and has domestic connections (via Thameslink trains) to Luton Airport, Bedford and Brighton; as well as Midland Mainline connections to places like Leicester and Sheffield. As the first major project of a huge scheme to redevelop the area, St Pancras has been marketed as so-much-more-than-a-station. Alongside its rail platforms it features Europe's longest Champagne bar, a farmers market, and an arcade of pointedly classy shops. All this is housed within beautiful listed buildings dating from 1868, with an extension for the long Eurostar trains designed by British starchitect Norman Foster.

Tickets

The Eurostar ticket office and travel centre is located at the Euston Road end of the long arcade, while self-service machines (for collecting pre-booked tickets) can be found outside the Eurostar departure lounge further along the arcade and to the right. For National Rail services, you will need to buy tickets from machines, or a manned ticket desk at the designated area at the far end of the Arcade, next to that horrific kissing statue.

Services

At St Pancras International there are dozens of places to eat, drink and shop, with a fair number of chain stores as well as some exclusives. Best of all is the Booking Office bar, which serves some of the best cocktails in the city. The station has its own dedicated shopping arcade with branches of classic London stores like Hamleys, as well as a market area and another brace of shops at the north end of the station ('The Circle'). Everything is shiny, new and upmarket, so expect your money to vanish pretty damn quickly. The Betjeman Arms pub—named after the famous poet whose petition saved the listed buildings from the same fate as Euston's arch—hosts beer festivals and music/literature events.

Public Transport

St Pancras can be reached by Tube (via adjacent King's Cross station) on the Victoria, Hammersmith & City, Circle, Piccadilly, Northern and Metropolitan Lines. A large number of buses also stop along Euston Road day and night.

Victoria Station

NFT Map: 20

Address: Buckingham Palace Road, London, SW1E 5ND

Station Code VIC

General Station Enquiries: 03457 11 41 41

Lost property 020 7963 0957

Website: www.networkrail.co.uk/victoria or @NetworkRailVIC

Overview

80 million people use London Victoria per year, making it one of the UK's busiest stations. Hit it at rush hour and it will feel like those 80 million are all there with you. Built a century ago for a less populous, less pushed and less demanding city, it struggles with crowds of commuters who jostle for platform space. It now enforces crowd-control measures at peak times: prepare to be patient. Nevertheless, it is well laid-out with services clearly sign-posted, and a major upgrade is planned to improve its capacity.

Victoria's main train operators are Southeastern, Southern and Gatwick Express, who between them will whisk you to Brighton, Portsmouth,

Hastings and Gatwick, among other Southeastern towns. Or if you're looking for a romantic break and the Victoria route to Bognor Regis is just a little too obvious for you, you can earn yourself brownie points and a hefty overdraft by taking the Orient Express from this station.

The building itself is impressive: look above the modern shop fascias to enjoy century-old architecture. But if that is all a little too high-brow, look up anyway, as the entrance to the South East building sports four caryatids: columns shaped like women, whose tunics saucily hang open so a gratuitous nipple can pop out to cheer the commuters. Rule Britannia!

Tickets

If you haven't booked in advance (why? Why?,) then head for the 24 hour ticket office in the central concourse, where you will queue for anything up to a year to buy your journey for much more money than you'd have paid online a week earlier. If you don't require assistance from a ticket officer, use the automated machines dotted round the concourse: their queues always move faster (unless the person in front of you is a newbie who can't figure out the buttons, which is guaranteed if you have less than five minutes to catch your train). Keep your ticket handy as all platforms are guarded by ticket barriers, and add a few extra minutes to reach platforms 15–19.

Services

All the predictable station fare is available in the main concourse for your journey's usual sandwich, loofah and tie needs. Food options have mercifully diversified so in addition to the obligatory artery-cloggers you can now grab sushi from the Wasabi stand or maintain your body's temple-status at the Camden Food Co. If it's a meal you're after and you must remain at the station, head up to the food court via Victoria Place for a choice of what could charitably be described as restaurants. Victoria Place itself boasts the ubiquitous high street shops to help you kill time or for any last minute gifts (as long as you don't really like the person you're buying for). Station loos are 30p—even up in the food court you can't pee for free—and showers are available if you're getting a bit ripe. Victoria also has a left luggage service, WiFi (charged) and photo booths.

Public Transport

Victoria is on the Victoria, Circle and District lines: entrance to the underground is opposite platform 7. The bus terminus is just outside the main entrance. It is also next door to London's national bus depot for cheapo travel to/from other parts of the UK. The main taxi rank is outside the main entrance, but if it has a heart-sinking queue then head up to the Plaza exit for an alternative rank.

Waterloo Station

NFT Map: 104

Address: Station Approach Road,
London, SE1 8SW

Station Code: WAT

General Station Enquiries: 03457 11 41 41

Lost property: 020 7401 7861

Website: www.networkrail.co.uk/waterloo

Overview

Until 2007, Waterloo was the first port of call for 'Europeans' arriving by train. Thousands of chic foreigners, clutching manbags and sporting huge sunglasses, would arrive at the station every week. But not any more. Nearly 200 years after the British triumphed in the first battle of Waterloo—a town in Belgium—the French got their revenge. Last November Eurostar gave the two fingers to the British Waterloo and promiscuously buggered off to St Pancras. Rumour has it that ex-PM Margaret Thatcher had specifically ordered that Eurostar terminate at a station named after a famous French defeat; but things have moved on a little since the "Iron Lady" left office. We're all Europeans now…

In truth, perhaps it's not that bad a thing. Even though no other British station covers as much space, Waterloo feels like it's at its bursting point. Even without the Eurostar it has a whopping 19 platforms—in almost constant use—and four Tube lines; it's the busiest station in Britain. It's calmed down slightly since the international terminal was put out to stud, but it's still pretty manic.

The station services London's south western suburbs (as can be seen by the swathes of well-dressed commuters) and, farther afield, the towns south west of the capital.

Waterloo East

NFT Map: 104

Address: Sandell St, SE8 8H

General Station Enquiries: 0 800 405 040

Overview

If the south west isn't your bag, you can disappear to England's south east—Kent, Sussex and SE London—from Waterloo East (station code: WAE). There's an escalator next to Burger King opposite platform 12, that makes a trip to the south east look far more alluring than it really is; an elevated walkway over Waterloo Road connects Waterloo East with its larger cousin. The facility, considered its own terminal, is operated by Southeastern. The main entrance is on Sandell St.

Tickets

The main office is opposite platforms 16–17. And it's open 24 hours—so why not charm them into giving you a free ticket after a few drinks? They can't have heard it before, right?

Services

A delay is just unplanned "me time", so make the most of it by buying a newspaper eating your own weight in overpriced pasties and cookies; then wash it down with a few pints of generic football-sponsorlager in the pub before buying your loved-one a novelty tie/'cute' socks to make for up being late. And drunk. And flatulent. And tasteless. There's a left luggage office between platforms 11-12.

Public Transport

Waterloo is served by four underground lines: Bakerloo, Jubilee, Northern, Waterloo & City; and numerous bus routes.

Overview

If there's one thing that screams London, it's big red buses—loads of 'em—preferably passing beneath Big Ben for maximum iconic impact. There was an almighty roar from Londoners when the Routemaster was scrapped: panoramas viewed from the Oxo tower were dotted with fists clutching rolled-up Time Outs shaking at the mayoral offices. The accordion buses which replaced them were met with similar anger but they've now been phased out: one can only guess at the amount of revenue lost by fare dodgers.

Whatever you think of the death of the bendy bus and Boris' reinvention of the Routemaster (also known as the "New Routemaster") one thing is certain: you're going to spend a lot of time on buses, around them, dodging them or moaning about them. Let's have a quick rundown of things to drop in a London bus convo: 'Drivers take pleasure in driving off just as you get to the stop,' 'Why do they always drive so fast/slow?' 'They're earning up to £500 a week? Why are they so grumpy all the time?' ad infinitum. As a Londoner, your list of hobbies and interests now includes transport: deal with it.

There are a variety of different operating companies, but to us they're all the same, all the way out to the frontiers of Zone 6. Get on at the front, get off at the middle. After the old double-decker buses were retired in 2005, Thomas Heatherwick's all-new Routemaster launched in Spring 2012. Just like the classic version there is an open rear platform for hopping on and hopping off. If you do want to live out your 1940s film fantasies, you can still catch the quaint old Routemasters doddering along the Heritage Route 15 during the day, a shorter version of the full route.

Fares

In a further move towards the cashless society, cash is not accepted on buses. A single fare costs £1.50 with an Oyster card, contactless card or one-day paper Travelcard. A bus and tram pass costs £21 per week. The Oyster ("The world's your…"—geddit?) is an electronic swipe card that can be bought at all Tube stations and thousands of other outlets such as newsagents and corner shops. The card can carry a mixture of travel passes (travelcards) and pay-as-you-go cash value. Note that if you choose pay-as-you-go, and you end up making more journeys than you anticipated; once it reaches the equivalent cost of a one-day travelcard, it will cap itself so you don't spend more. When you get on, don't forget to push your card against the scanner by the drivers' window. Sure, you're on camera 300 times per day, and every journey you make is recorded. But if you're paranoid, try another city, because they are watching you here.

24-Hour Services

You'll not hear London referred to as "the other city which never sleeps". Partly because it's unwieldy, but mostly because it's not true. After a hard night's binge-drinking and fighting in taxi ranks, we like our kip. But for those of you that are hardcore no-sleep-till-Brockley types, there is a network of 24-hour services. There are also a large number of night buses. They're just like day buses, except the route number is prefixed by a large 'N' and the view is less interesting.

Information

TfL's website (tfl.gov.uk) is an essential reference. Fare information and travel updates are available, plus PDFs of routes and timetables. As you get closer to central London, many routes operate on a frequency-basis rather than at fixed times. The main reason to visit TfL's site is the useful Journey Planner: enter your start and end points and it will (usually) calculate the best options. A word of warning though, computers are fallible and some route maps are schematics—so do check your own map and use common sense. Like those idiots that follow their GPS even when it tells them to drive into a river, it's frustrating to take three buses in a big circuit then realise you could have walked it in five minutes…

Safety

Like all big cities, London has its fair share of oddballs and criminals. And then a few institution-loads more in case things ever get boring. But CCTV in every bus and the creation of Safer Transport teams is having an effect—and not just on the share price of video camera manufacturers. Also, bus crime is concentrated in particular areas on particular routes. And you'll soon get to know the 'usual suspects' so don't worry. Night buses can get a bit lairy, so follow a few tips to make sure the only stress you suffer is traffic-related. Gangsters may wish to laugh at the following; Mother Theresas may wish to tattoo it on the inside of their eyelids: Avoid top decks where necessary. Sit on the left so the driver can see you (he has a radio link to base). Don't fall asleep. Use the same stop at night and know your surroundings so you can be confident. Keep your belongings close to you and be switched on. Get to know the 'hot spots' so you can be aware.

Overview

Although convenient and cost effective, coaches are traditionally associated with the grimier side of travel. But when it comes to budget travel, grime is in the eye of the beholder. So if your impression of coaches includes cold turkey junkies showering sick on unsuspecting passengers or if you maintain a general aversion to getting within three coach lengths of the portal of hell that is the coach toilet, then perhaps this mode of travel is not for you. That said, coach travel enjoys a long tradition across the UK, and it's much, much better here than many other places.

For years, National Express (www.nationalexpress.com), the UK's biggest coach company, has been trying to shake its image as a purveyor of seedy transport. Having rebranded itself as quick, comfortable and green, their fleet of coaches are shiny and the drivers slightly less grumpy than they used to be. National Express' nemesis is Megabus (www.megabus.co.uk), the £1 people (of course they release only a handful of these tickets for each journey and then the fare rises the closer you get to your preferred date). It hasn't always been this way, but Megabus coaches are now pretty much as good as National Express. Megabus Plus (www.megabusplus.com) combines bus and rail travel for selected destinations. At the same time, National Express started its own super cheap ticket campaign. Eurolines (www.eurolines.co.uk) is National Express' low-cost option to Europe.

Victoria Coach Station (Buckingham Palace Road, London, SW1W 9TP) is the main coach hub is near Victoria train station. You can buy tickets for both Megabus and National Express—the two main operators who run from Victoria Coach Station—from the same booths just inside the station. But, like plane tickets, (only without that last shred of glamour that air travel still has) if you buy in advance, you can get some super-cheap prices. National Express has an office on the road between the train and bus stations. Victoria Coach Station is also a hub for other bus companies serving the continent, some of which can be very cheap.

London's other main hub is Golder's Green. This is the last stop for services heading north (or the first stop for buses coming down into London). If you live in north London, it's worth jumping off here, as it's on the Northern Line and can shave an hour off the trip.

There's also a healthy trade in coaches to Oxford. The Oxford Tube (www.oxfordtube.com) competes with National Express on the route from Victoria; travelling via Marble Arch, Notting Hill and Shepherd's Bush. Tickets normally cost about £15 and you can buy on board. They also run through the night—so if you get drunk and have the urge to go on an impromptu holiday—well, Oxford it is.

Beyond Tooting, Croydon's trams will take you from places like Wimbledon to shop—lemming-like with the locals—at the Ampere Way IKEA. The trams accept Oyster and use a similar charging scale to buses. Once you get back on the map, your flatpacked sideboard will win admiring glances but few friends as you trail home on busy tubes.

General Information

Transport for London: www.tfl.gov.uk

London Cycling Campaign: lcc.org.uk
or @london_cycling

Overview

There's a war going on out there, one with real casualties and collateral damage. When David Cameron was spotted going through a red light on his bicycle, it threw into sharp relief a low-level conflict which has been going on for decades. Bikes v. Cars: with hapless pedestrians caught in the middle.

Cycling around London is not for the faint-hearted, but municipal improvements (especially during Boris Johnson's tenure) and the hard work of the London Cycling Campaign, are encouraging people to drop their Oyster cards and jump on their bikes. London continues to implement its system of Cycle Superhighways providing safer routes (and some dedicated lanes) into Central London and across the city. The city's cyclehire program, Santander Cycles (formerly sponsored by Barclays and also known as 'Boris Bikes'), is a brilliant system based on European models in which users pick up a bike and then drop it off when finished at a suitable point in the city. If you want to explore London this way, note that Transport for London has some fun leisure routes detailed on its website. Transport for London offers great free cycling maps (order via the TfL website); some of the 14 routes have become so popular, cycling along them is like taking part in the Tour de France (albeit slower and with slightly fewer drugs). The maps give colour-coded help; look for the brown routes (separate from the traffic) or even better the green routes (separate from the traffic and passing through parks, beside canals or rivers.)

But cycling does hold some risk. As well as the nightmare of walking around all day with 'helmet hair' you've got accidents and theft. LCC's website has details of road-confidence training and lists local cycling groups who run social events and cycle maintenance classes. They will sometimes cycle your new route to work with you to help you negotiate the difficult bits. Aren't they nice?

For those new to cycling on London's roads, basic rules include: stay a door length (or stride) away from the pavement or parked cars; watch out for distracted office drones leaping into the road and into black cabs; don't undertake bendy-buses or HGVs; don't use your phone while moving; and if in doubt on a tricky junction, transform yourself into a pedestrian—get off and push your bike wherever you need to go.

Bolt-cutting 'tea-leaves' steal thousands of bikes every year. You have three options to reduce this particular risk. One, buy a rubbish bike that no-one would want to steal and lock it with one lock. Two, get a decent bike, carry around a D-lock and two other locks and spend 20 mins each time you stop. Three, get a shit-hot bike and never take it out.

Where to Ride Bikes

There are plenty of great rides around town and a happy cyclist is one who has been able to incorporate one into their commute. Good options are the short but scenic Parkland Walk Nature Reserve, which links Finsbury Park to Highgate via an abandoned railway line; a Saturday morning cycle takes you to one of Highgate's wonderful pubs for lunch and a lazy pint. The City, normally snarled with cabs, buses and kamikaze pedestrians, is a dream on a Sunday morning.

Though not continuous, the path along the Regent's Canal linking Paddington with Canary Wharf takes cyclists away from traffic and along some surprisingly gorgeous stretches of canal (which also sport some top-notch graffiti)—as well as some godawful, festering dumps. A useful section of the canal links the west side of Regent's Park with Paddington via Lisson Grove and Warwick Avenue. Watch out for super-fast cyclists determined to slice a second off their PB, especially where the path narrows under bridges or around ramps.

A jaunt through any of the capital's great parks seems an obvious choice, but beware, some parks (notably Hampstead Heath) ban bikes on almost all paths, thanks to selfish cyclists of the past who went too fast and frightened the jumpy pedestrians.

RideLondon (www.prudentialridelondon. co.uk) is a fun two-day riding festival built on the success of the earlier FreeWheel. Events include a family ride along closed central London roads, a 100-mile ride, and a Grand Prix for pros.

Bike Shops	Address	Phone
Apex Cycles	40-42 Clapham High St, SW4 7UR	020 7622 1334
Archway Cycles	183 Archway Rd	020 8340 9696
Bikefix	48 Lamb's Conduit St, WC1N 3LJ	020 7405 1218
Brick Lane Bikes	118 Bethnal Green Rd, E2 6DG	020 7033 9053
Bobbin Bicycles	397 St John St	020 7837 3370
Brixton Cycles	145 Stockwell Rd, SW9 9TN	020 7733 6055
Cheech Miller	227 Victoria Park Rd	020 8985 9900
Condor Cycles	51 Gray's Inn Rd, WC1X 8PP	020 7269 6320
Decathlon	Surrey Quays Rd	020 7394 2000
Evans (Spitalfields)	The Cavern, 1 Market St, E1 6AA	020 7426 0391
Holloway Cycles	290 Holloway Rd, N7 6NJ	020 7700 6611
London Fields Cycles	281 Mare St, E8 1PJ	020 8525 0077
London Recumbents	Battersea Park	020 7498 6543
Mosquito	123 Essex Rd, N1 2SN	020 7226 8765
ReCycling	110 Elephant Rd, SE17 1LB	020 7703 7001

To consider taking a taxi in London you either need (a) a trust fund, or (b) to be drunk. If you are both, congratulations: prepare to be taken for a ride in more ways than one.

Dating back to the mid-17th Century (kind of), London's 'black cabs', or 'Hackneys', are the world's oldest taxi service and are as representative of London as Routemasters, Big Ben and robbery. They are the most visible, the most iconic and probably the most expensive taxi service in London. While this flag-down option is great (they are the only company licensed to pick up on the street) budgeting for a black cab is tricky. Their prices are designed to confuse passengers into parting with huge wads for what often feels like a round-the-block trip. A whole range of metaphysical problems contribute to that huge sum waiting to be paid at journey's end; all fares start at £2.40 and are based on three types of tariffs—higher tariffs apply on evenings, weekends and late nights. Fares are also affected by traffic. In general, as a very broad guideline, expect to pay around £9 for up to one mile, £14 for up to two miles, and £22 for up to four miles. Fares between Heathrow and Central London are anywhere between £45–£85. A £4 surcharge applies during the days around Christmas and New Year. There's also a 'puke charge' of £40 if you soil the cab and the driver has to take it out of service to clean it; keep it in!

Black cabs are operated by many different companies who are all regulated and licensed by the Public Carriage Office (PCO). Generally speaking, the service you receive doesn't vary much from company to company, though some boast little add-ons to capture your fare. Big, well organized companies like Dial-A-Cab (www.dialacab.co.uk; 020 7253 5000) and Radio Taxis (www.radiotaxis.co.uk; 020 7272 0272) offer online booking, carbon neutral trips, and friendly service. All black cab drivers must pass 'The Knowledge' test to get their license, so every driver will have a labyrinthine understanding of London and most will not be shy in sharing this with you.

Though a cheaper option, going private can be a minefield. Since 2001 all taxi services in London are required by law to be licensed by the PCO: this includes the city's thousands of private-hire minicabs. Private hire companies are everywhere you look and often take the form of nicotine-stained, shoddily built little offices with lots of bored men milling about. Every neighbourhood has plenty of local services and it's really trial and error to find one that doesn't rip you off or drive barely roadworthy chariots of rust. The drivers of these little companies can be pretty eccentric—you can be regaled by tales of times past, given essential life advice or simply receive the discainful silent treatment. The 'private taxi sector' does do upmarket, however. By far the most efficient and elegant service is that offered by Addison Lee, (www.addisonlee.com; 020 7407 9000) who text you twice have huge gleaming six-seaters, and perfectly-manicured drivers. Fares are pretty cheap over longer distances but the minimum is around £10. Transport for London (tfl.gov.uk) has a useful online tool for locating licensed black cabs and minicabs, as well as an app (Cabwise). Another option is Uber (www.uber.com/cities/london), with its handy app and account-based system.

A word of warning: London is awash with rogue taxi-drivers who are not licensed and who will attempt to pick you up from outside a club or theatre. These guys will either charge you more than you agreed upon, not know where they are going, or they will be driving beat-up death-traps. If a ride hasn't been booked with a licensed minicab company, then there is no record of your journey, meaning also that if there is a problem, your driver cannot be traced. There are also many stories of attacks on women, so if in doubt, don't get in!

London Heliport
020 7228 0181
www.londonheliport.co.uk or @LondonHeliport

SW11's very own heliport! Includes aerial tours of London and airport transfers (Heathrow in ten minutes). The nearest tube is Clapham Junction.

EBG Helicopters
0173 7 823 282
www.ebghelicopters.co.uk or @ebgheli

Running helicopter tours of London and charter flights from Redhill Airport in Surrey, 10 minutes by car from Gatwick Airport. £140 will get you 35 minutes over London, the only downside is getting to Surrey. Also offers charters for weddings and corporate events and air taxi service starting from £650 for up to three passengers.

Helicopter Days
0844 815 0952
www.helicopterdays.co.uk or @Helicopterdays

London sightseeing trips starting from £900.

Elstree Aerodrome
www.londonelstreeaerodrome.com

A variety of charters operate out of Elstree offering sky tours, as well as flight academies for those who want to take the wheel. On site is a restaurant, plus it's close to the M1.

Ferries/Boat Tours, Rentals & Charters

London River Services (LRS)
020 7941 2400
www.tfl.gov.uk/gettingaround

Provides commuter river transportation on the Thames. This runs in the East from Masthouse Terrace Pier to Savoy Pier at Embankment. In peak hours services run to Woolwich Arsenal with a further service from Blackfriars Millenium Pier in the City to Putney Pier in the west costing £15 return. WiFi is available on boats serving Woolwich. Services run every 20 minutes. All are wheelchair friendly.

Thames Clippers
0870 7815049
www.thamesclippers.com

London's answer to the NYC water taxis, primarily serving the O2 stadium from Waterloo, Embankment and Tower Bridge. Conveniently runs later than the Tube meaning you can actually stay right to the end of a show

without the worry of being stranded on the south side of the river. Single tickets cost between £3-5 with Oyster Card holders getting 1/3 off. Boats leave every 15 minutes.

Bateux London
020 7695 1800
www.bateuxlondon.com.

Dinner, lunch and charter cruises from Embankment Pier. Yes, there's even a jazz cruise.

Westminster Passenger Services Association
020 7930 2062
www.wpsa.co.uk

One of the only popular charters to offer services upriver to Kew, Richmond and Hampton Court.

City Cruises
020 7488 0344
www.citycruises.com.

Hop on hop off services primarily aimed at tourists and with tourist prices. Tickets start from £11

return for adults from Greenwich to Westminster/Waterloo Pier.

Heritage Boat Charters
01932 224 800
www.heritageboatcharters.com

For something different, try messing about on the river in one of these historic wooden numbers. On offer are skippered cruises down the Thames starting at £825. Formal dinner on board is available.

Silver Fleet Woods River Cruises
020 7759 1900
www.silverfleet.co.uk

Luxury chartered boats. Particularly good at putting on top-notch corporate events.

Thames Cruises
020 7928 9009
www.thamescruises.com

Two words—disco cruise. Hot pants are not required for dinner cruises.

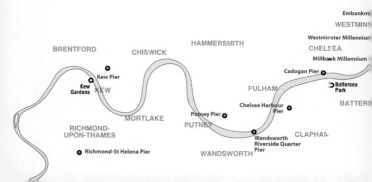

Marinas/Passenger Ship Terminal

Chelsea Marina
07770 542 783
www.chelseaharbourmarina.com

Despite being in upmarket Chelsea, the prices for mooring your boat here are incredibly generous—£2 per metre a night or £300 a year with space for 60 boats. Secure subterranean parking also available.

Chiswick Quay Marina
020 8994 8743
www.chiswickquay.com/marina

Great, secluded spot for West Londoners near Chiswick Bridge. A little far from a tube station, yet Chiswick overland station is within walking distance with services to Waterloo. Prices are on an annual basis at £162 per metre including a resident harbourmaster, shower block, mains water and electricity.

Gallions Point Marina
020 7476 7054
www.gallionspointmarina.co.uk

In London's Docklands and therefore perfect for those working in the city.

St Katharine Haven
020 7264 5312
skdocks.co.uk

One of London's best marinas. Great location by Tower Bridge, close to the quayside bars and restaurants and reasonable London prices—£3.60 per metre, per day.

Welcome Floating Terminal in Greenwich
01474 562 200
www.portoflondon.co.uk

Built in 2004 and believed to be the world's first floating terminal. Welcome has on-site immigration and custom services for cruise ship passengers entering or leaving London.

London Cruise Terminal at Tilbury
01375 852 360
www.londoncruiseterminal.com

The most popular regional departure point for passenger liners is 25 miles from Central London in Essex. Its close proximity to the M25 makes it easy for Londoners to get to. Current destinations from here include Scandinavia and continental Europe.

General Information

TfL Traffic News: tfl.gov.uk/trafficnews
or @TfLTrafficNews

Parking Information for Cars: www.park-up.com

Parking Information for Motorbikes and
Scooters: www.parkingforbikes.com

AA Route Planner:
www.theaa.com/route-planner

Overview

With London's Congestion Charge, Low Emission
Zone, pricey parking, kamikaze bus drivers,
dreaded speed bumps, 20 mph limits, speed
cameras and a road layout that would give Spock
the night terrors—"it's so illogical Captain"—
driving around town is something to be avoided.
Combine this with over 7.5 million people who
just want to get from A to B without anyone
getting in their frickin' way, and you can see
where problems arise.

That said, there are times when a four-wheeler
is the only option, in which case the more you
know… To start, pedestrians can become an
infuriating lot, at least those who love striding
purposefully into the road with nary a thought
for their safety; keep a weather eye out one
foot over the brake and one hand over the horn.
Then there are the cyclists, an ever-increasing
number—give them plenty of space and
remember for the one speedhound jumping
the lights there are hundreds of law abides that
you just don't notice; for your own sanity, try to
focus on them. As for the mechanized obstacles,
remember that motorbikes and scooters are not
all ridden by leather-clad Hells Angels or Jamie
Oliver clones—most just want to get about and
avoid the Congestion Charge; as with cyclists,
give plenty of space and check your blindspots.
A special danger are the black cabs, those roving
London landmarks that have been known, on
occasion, to pull up to the curb, do a 'U-ee' and
even advertise the FT without sufficient warning.
And finally, a word about traffic wardens which
are also known as 'council revenue generating
units': make sure you avoid illegal parking—
unless you are an ambassador. Fines are not
cheap.

Indeed, most of the stress caused by driving in
London, apart from the sheer volume of traffic,
is caused by lack of consideration for others—
usually as drivers are running late. So make sure
you leave PLENTY of time for your journey, try not
to block junctions, and let people out if you have
a chance. And try to avoid rush hour: remember
that morning rush lasts from 7 am to 10.30 am,
lunch rush from 11 am to 2.30 pm, school run
rush from 2.45 pm to 4.15 pm and afternoon rush
from 4.30 pm to 8.45 pm. Bonne chance …

Driving in the Congestion Charge Zone and the Low Emission Zone

The Congestion Charge Zone, introduced in 2003, is a surcharge for driving in Central London between 7 am and 6 pm Monday through Friday (except Bank Holidays). Huge red Cs in circles alert drivers to the start of the zone, if you miss them you should consider a swift visit to your optician. There is ongoing debate over the actual impact of the charge, although it has raised money for public transport.

The charge is £11.50 and there is no extra charge for driving in and out of the zone. Drivers who use the Congestion Charge Auto Pay (CCAP) system receive a £1 discount; Auto Pay keeps a tally of how many days a car was driven and charges your card at the end of the month. Drivers can pay in advance or by midnight on the day of travel. For £14 you have until midnight the following day to pay the charge. Payments are accepted by phone, online, by regular mail, and by text. Exemptions and discounts exist for motorbikes and residents living in or near the charge zone. Penalty charges are steep: £130 penalty charge (reduced to £65 if paid within 14 days).

The Low Emission Zone (LEZ) was introduced in February 2008 to deter everything from pickup trucks and van to buses, coaches and large lorries from dragging their belching exhausts through town. It covers a much larger area than the Congestion Charge: almost all of London within the M25 and applies 24/7. The charge varies between £100 and £200 a day. Best leave your concrete mixer at home.

Red Routes

The red double lines along a roadway indicate a "red route," part of the Transport for London Road Network (TLRN), and amounting to a special enforcement zone patrolled by Transport for London agents. No stopping rules are strictly enforced, as are yellow box junction infractions, banned turns, and unauthorized use of bus lanes. Although only five percent of London's roadways, the TLRN carries 30 percent of the city's traffic. As such the point of the oversight is to keep traffic moving. The rest of the roads are managed by local councils.

Key Roads

A1

Running straight north from St Paul's Cathedral in the City through Islington, Archway, Highgate and beyond, this old Roman Road has some freer stretches allowing the frustrated drive to accelerate to 43 mph for 3 seconds, get a speeding ticket and then slam on the brakes. Ends (eventually) in Princes Street, Edinburgh, Scotland.

North Circular/South Circular (A406)

This is the M25's angrier and twisted little brother. Circling Outer London it has some of the busiest stretches of road in London and even includes a ferry across the river at Woolwich. The way dwindles to one exhausted lane in certain sections, causing great clots of traffic every day in rush hour. See left for rush hour times.

Euston Rd/Marylebone Road (A501)

Running east-west past King's Cross and Euston, this wide road skirts the northern edge of the congestion zone. It gets very crowded, because it's a feeder road to the relatively breezy start of the A40 heading out of London.

Embankment

The view as you drive along the Embankment along the north bank of the Thames is breathtaking. It needs to be to keep you occupied as you inch forward for hours. Runs from Chelsea (A4) to Tower Bridge.

Vauxhall Bridge Rd/Grovesnor Place/Park Lane/Edgware Rd (A5)

Running roughly north-west from Vauxhall Bridge Rd, around Victoria, past Hyde Park Corner and Marble Arch and out to join the A40, this route is a free corridor through the Congestion zone—free from charge rather than free from traffic. Be prepared—it's rammed.

Old Kent Rd/New Cross Rd/Lewisham Way/etc. (A2/A20)

Running south-west from The Bricklayers Arms roundabout and eventually down to Dover, where you catch the ferry to France; the Old Kent Rd, despite being the cheapest Monopoly property, is totally free from traffic at all times. No wait—that can't be right.

A3

Starting at London Bridge, this road eventually ends up in Portsmouth, but you have to struggle past Elephant and Castle, Clapham Common and Wimbledon Common along with everyone else trying to get to Guildford.

Traffic Hot Spots

Angel, Elephant and Castle, Hanger Lane Gyratory, Vauxhall Gyratory, Trafalgar Square, Parliament Square, Hammersmith Gyratory, everywhere else.

Car Share

The great thing about being a Londoner is there's really no need to have a car. Except on those few occasions where you're cursing yourself for hauling a flat-packed Ikea coffee table on the shitty Croydon tram service. This is where joining a membership-based carsharing company, such as such as Zipcar (www.zipcar.co.uk or @ZipcarUK), Enterprise CarShare (www.enterprisecarshare.com or @carshare) or Hertz 24/7 (www.hertz247.com or @Hertz247). When you need to move the band there's also Zipvan (www.zipvan.com)

The membership services are convenient and easy: self-service cars and vans billable by the hour, day, week or month. The vehicles are parked in town, which means you don't have to hike to a car rental centre, stand in a queue or deal with annoying upselling at a counter. Plus, if you get thrown out of your girlfriend's flat at 2 am and need a ride, you're in luck. After signing up for a modest membership fee (less than £100 a year), all you have to do is unlock the car with an entry card or fob, grab the keys from the glovebox and away you go. Cars have hourly rates (in general between £5–10 depending on the plan and type of vehicle) on top of the membership fee. Fuel and insurance are included.

January

- **New Year's Day Parade** · Big Ben to Piccadilly Circus · Marching bands and thousands of kids. How better to cure a hangover?
- **London Boat Show** · ExCel Exhibition Centre · Like we always say: you can never have too many yachts.
- **Russian Winter Festival** · Trafalgar Square · Magical Russian Winterland replaces the normal Pigeon-Crap Land.
- **London Art Fair** · Over 100 galleries and thousands of artists under one roof.
- **The London Bike Show** · ExCel Exhibition Centre · The best of the best of modern cycling equipment pandering to over-indulged cyclists.
- **London International Mime Festival** · Southbank Centre · Even weirder when you see it for real.
- **The London Outdoors Show** · ExCel Exhibition Centre · The country's biggest collection of outdoor goods—ironically hosted indoors.
- **Charles I Commemoration Ceremony** · Trafalgar Sq · St James' Palace · Thousands of uniformed Cavaliers confuse the tourists.
- **TNA Wrestling** · Wembley Arena · Strange men in spandex faux-fighting in front of drunken man-children.
- **Walking with Dinosaurs** · The O2 · Get your prehistoric freak on with twenty life-size dinosaurs (not literally) freaks!

February

- **British Academy Film Awards (BAFTA)** · Royal Opera House · Britain's finest film and television talent take a bow.
- **Chinese New Year** · West End · Party like it's 4707.
- **Destinations: Holiday and Travel Show** · Earls Court Exhibition Centre · Chase away the Winter Blues.
- **Live Tudor Cookery** · Hampton Court Palace · Glutinous Tudor food prepared in classic Tudor fashion. It's OK the New Year's

resolutions will be long dead by now.
- **London Fashion Week** · Somerset House· Far Too Thin.
- **National Wedding Show** · Olympia · Perfect day out for a first date.
- **Professional Beauty** · ExCel Exhibition Centre · Pay to get pretty with the latest developments in modern cosmetics.
- **Lifted** · Harrods · A bizarre annual exhibition inside Harrod's lifts.
- **The Great Spitalfields Pancake Race** · Old Truman Brewery · Pancake race in wacky clothes. No, London. Just, no.
- **Blessing the Throats** · St Ethelreda's Church, Ely Place · Lemsip not working? Sore throats cured by holy candle.
- **Clowns' Service** · Holy Trinity, Dalston · Because God likes clowns too.
- **Kinetica Art Fair** · P3 · Carnivorous lampshades and pole-dancing robots? We're there.
- **BAFTAs** · London Palladium · Ten points per autograph.

March

- **Affordable Art Fair** · The Marquee, Battersea Park · Now even The Great Unwashed can buy art!
- **Affordable Art Fair** · The Marquee, Battersea Park · Now even The Great Unwashed can buy art!
- **Easter Egg Hunt** · Kew Garden's · Delightful Easter affair, perfect for the kids, don't forget to check out the animal farm.
- **Ideal Home Show** · Earls Court Exhibition Centre · Make your home ideal (or a bit less grotty).
- **St Patrick's Day Parade** · Park Lane · Shamrocks, river-dancing, big fluffy Guinness hats: true Irish tradition.
- **London Drinker Beer & Cider Festival** · The Camden Centre · Get rat-arsed on Pressed Rat & Warthog.
- **La Dolce Vita** · Business Design Centre · Get your sampling face on

- **Men's Afternoon Tea** · Mandeville Hotel · Because nothing is manlier than an exclusive tea, champagne and cake afternoon.
- **Move It** · Olympia · Put on your dancing shoes.
- **The International Food & Drink Event** · Olympia · This gorge-fest happens biannually, so start starving yourself now.
- **The Country Living Spring Fair** · Business Design Centre · For those with time for wooden chicken eggs
- **JobServe Live!** · Olympia · Career ideas and thousands of vacancies.

April

- **Cake International** · ExCel Exhibition Centre · Decorate and glutinously devour delicious cakes.
- **Oxford & Cambridge Boat Race** · River Thames · Hole up in a pub by the river and cheer over a beer.
- **Virgin London Marathon** · Greenwich – The Mall · 35,000 pairs of bleeding nipples.
- **London Book Fair** · Earl's Court · The publishing industry's main event. Occasionally stuff for free.
- **Alternative Fashion Week** · Old Spitalfields Market · Huge range of cutting edge fashion. And fetishwear.
- **Queen's Birthday Gun Salute** · Hyde Park · Who said the monarchy is archaic?
- **St George's Day** · Coven Garden / Cenotaph / Shakespeare's Globe · Brush up your Morris dancing skills
- **The Real Food Festival** · Earl's Court Exhibition Centre · Real Food: much nicer than face food.
- **Hot Cross Bun Service** · St Bartholomew-the-Great, Smithfield · Widows get free hot cross bun. Worth losing the husband.
- **London Independent Film Festival** · Various West and Central Cinemas · Cool celebration of cinematographic indieness without The Man. Or something.

General Information · **Calendar of Events**

May

- **Freedom of the City** · Central London · Frequently awesome improv and experimental festival attracting top names.
- **Baisakhi Mela** · Brick Lane · Celebrate the Bengali New Year in the British tradition: vindaloo.
- **Bathing the Buddha** · Leicester Square · Buddha gets a birthday bath.
- **Mind, Body, Spirit Festival** · Royal Horticultural Halls · Make up for all the time in the pub.
- **Camden Crawl** · Throughout Camden · If you're not crawling by the end, you haven't done it right.
- **Chelsea Flower Show** · Royal Hospital Chelsea · You'll go for the flowers. You'll stay for the Pimms.
- **Chelsea Flower Show** · Royal Hospital Chelsea · You'll go for the flowers. You'll stay for the Pimms.
- **Greenwich Beer & Jazz Festival** · Old Royal Naval College · An odd pairing that somehow works.
- **London Pet Show** · Earls Court Two · The cute, odd, scary and weird bring their pets and show them off.
- **Sci-Fi Festival** · London Apollo · The UK's only Sci-Fi Festival. Thank god.
- **Interiors London** · ExCel Centre · For those rich enough to treat their homes like art.
- **The Drag Olympics** · The Way Out Club · Drag Queens are put through their pedicured, high-heeled paces.

June

- **City of London Festival** · The City · Bringing High Culture to a bunch of bankers.
- **Field Day** · Victoria Park · A pseudo hippy music festival with a light hearted vibe.
- **Start of Open Air Theatre season** · Regent's Park · Ignore the climate and take in an outdoor play.
- **Taste of London** · Regent's Park · The best picnic in the world.

- **Wimbledon** · All England Lawn Tennis and Croquet Club · Short skirts and grunting. Marvellous.
- **Trooping the Colour** · Horse Guard's Parade · Hundreds of chaps in uniforms. Ohhhhh yes.
- **Meltdown Festival** · Southbank Centre · Eclectic music festival curated by major musicians.
- **Royal Academy Summer Exhibition** · Royal Academy · Lots and lots and LOTS of art.
- **Arts Festival Chelsea** · Chelsea · The artists formerly known as 'The Chelsea Festival'.
- **Naked Bike Ride** · Hyde Park · Don't think about the bums on seats.
- **Polo in the Park** · Hurlingham Park · Its turbo-rah dahhling, pass the Pimms.
- **Shakespeare Globe Season** · Bankside · To go, or not to go, that is the question.

July

- **Dogget's Coat & Badge Race** · Thames: London Bridge to Chelsea · Intense boat race to win a badge. Hardly seems worth it.
- **Pimms Urban Regatta** · Finsbury Square · People full of Pimms race on land in bottomless boats. Bloody Ozzies.
- **Pride London** · Trafalgar Square · One of Britain's biggest, funnest street parties.
- **The British 10k London Run** · Hyde Park · Whitehall · Work off the pies.
- **Hampton Court Palace Show** · Hampton Court · Stock up your garden / flowerpot / imagination.
- **The Chap Olympiad** · Bedford Square Gardens · Olympics for gentleman—no sportswear please.
- **Uprise Festival** · Islington · Celebrating the best of multicultural London, for free.
- **Swan Upping** · River Thames · Census of swans. For goodness sake.
- **Opening of Buckingham Palace** · Buckingham Palace · The Plebeians allowed in to see how their taxes (and steep entrance fees) are spent.

- **Wireless Festival** · Hyde Park · Big names vibrate the Serpentine.
- **Shoreditch Festival** · Shoreditch · Because you can never have too many local festivals. Apparently.

August

- **Innocent Smoothies Festival** · Regent's Park · You wouldn't think fun could be this wholesome.
- **Great British Beer Festival** · Earls Court Exhibition Centre · A festival that puts the Great in Britain.
- **Trafalgar Square Festival** · Trafalgar Square · 3 weeks of music, theatre, dance and art.
- **Carnaval del Pueblo** · Royal Victoria Docks · Thousands of Latino lovelies. That's all you need to know, right?
- **Camden Fringe** · Camden People's Theatre · Wonderfully weird, hilariously funny and light on the wallet.
- **London Triathlon** · Docklands · Marathons are for pussies.
- **London Mela** · Gunnersbury Park · Partaaaay, Asia-style.
- **Metro Weekender** · Clapham Common · Dance music Saturday, bands on Sunday, chilled all weekend.
- **Notting Hill Carnival** · Ladbroke Grove · Party till your wallet gets nicked.
- **Parliament Tour Season** · Westminster · Go see first hand where it all goes so wrong.
- **Kids Week** · West End · West End shows free for kids. Soooo unfaaaaiiiir.
- **Tiger Beer Singapore Chilli Crab Festival** · Truman Brewery · Cold beer, hot food and cool sounds.

September

- **The Great British Duck Race** · The Thames · Like the Oxbridge boat race. But with 165,000 rubber ducks.
- **Horseman's Sunday** · Hyde Park Crescent · London's horses say their Hail Maries. Yes, really.

- **Oyster & Seafood Fair** · Hays Galleria · The romance of oysters with the unholy stink of kippers.
- **Thames Festival** · Tower Bridge · Westminster · Fireworks, costumes, river races, carnivals. Kids like it.
- **Last Night of the Proms** · Royal Albert Hall · Camp overnight if you want tickets.
- **London Duathlon** · Richmond Park · It's like a triathlon… for people who can't swim.
- **London Tattoo Convention** · Old Truman Brewery · Who cares if it looks crap when you're 80?
- **Spitalfields Show & Green Fair** · Buxton Street · Who has the biggest marrow?
- **Open House Weekend** · Various around London · Over 600 architectural landmarks open for a nosey.
- **Fashion Week** · Summerset House · The September instalment of the famous frockfest.
- **Great Gorilla Run** · Start at London Underwriting Centre · Raise £400 for the Gorilla Organisation and the costume's yours.
- **Vintage Fashion Fair** · Primrose Hill · For those with a passion for vintage fashion.

October

- **The Big Draw** · Museum of Childhood · Pencils, not guns. Unfortunately.
- **Down Under Live** · Olympia · For those contemplating emigrating to warmer climes.
- **'Original Pearly Kings & Queens Association Harvest Festival** · Church of St Martin-in-the-Fields· Affordable Art Fair.
- **International Halloween Festival** · Queen Mary College · Witches, druids and shamans unite for Europe's biggest Pagan festival.
- **Halloween** · London Dungeon · Trick Or Treating is for pussies.
- **Frieze Art Fair** · Regent's Park · Air kisses all round.

- **London Film Festival** · BFI Southbank · Two weeks of the best new films and lectures from A-Listers.
- **Metro Ski & Snowboard Show** · Olympia · London hosts the world's biggest winter sport show. Naturally.
- **Veolia Entertainment Wildlife Photographer of the Year (exhibition opens, for 6mths)** · Natural History Museum Puts your arty market photos to shame.
- **The Yoga Show** · Olympia · Bendy people upon bendy people. Literally.
- **Turner Prize Exhibition** · Tate Britain · Get to know the next Hirst or Emin.

November

- **London's Christmas Ice Rinks** · Venues across London · Much more romantic in your head than in reality.
- **Brighton Veteran Car Run** · Starts Hyde Park · Century-old bangers potter their way to Brighton.
- **Erotica Show** · Olympia · 31,000 horny adults pretend they're just browsing.
- **Barclays ATP World Tour Finals** · O2 Arena · Very rich tennis players make more money at this entertaining but unimportant tournament.
- **Bonfire Night** · Venues across London · Hundreds of thousands of pounds go pop.
- **Country Living Christmas Fair** · Business Design Centre · For those dreaming of a posh Christmas.
- **Royal British Legion Festival of Remembrance** · Royal Albert Hall · Take tissues.
- **Lord Mayor's Show** · Central London · Running for over 800 years and yet still a bit crap.
- **London Jazz Festival** · South Bank Centre · Start practising your jazz hands.
- **Winter Wonderland** · Hyde Park Grottos and Glühweins galore.

December

- **Satan's Grotto** · London Dungeon · Tortured elves and spit-roasting robins.
- **Trafalgar Square Christmas Tree** · Trafalgar Square · The only thing everyone knows about Oslo.
- **Aegon Masters Tennis** · Royal Albert Hall · Former World No.1s wheeze their way through a tournament.
- **Peter Pan Cup** · Serpentine Lido, Hyde Park · Freeze your nipples off on Christmas morning.
- **Great Christmas Pudding Race** · Covent Garden · We're mad, us! What are we like? Crazy!
- **Christmas Carol Sing-along** · Royal Albert Hall · Belt out your favourites and get in the mood.
- **Christmas Carol Sing-along** · Royal Albert Hall · Belt out your favourites and get in the mood.
- **Taste of Christmas** · ExCel Exhibition Centre · Tasty tips for making Christmas that little merrier.
- **Midnight Mass at St Paul's** · St Paul's · Eats the other Midnight Masses for breakfast.
- **New Year's Eve Fireworks** · Jubilee Gardens · Ooooo. And, of course, aaaaaah

Tactics

Finding somewhere to live in London is a ruthless and cutthroat business. Make sure you have plenty of red bull, cigarettes and patience. However, places go in the blink of an eye so it's important to move quick. Take a week off and hire a driver, if you can.

Ok, so these precautions aren't completely necessary, but you will have to work in mysterious and multifarious ways if you don't want to spend the next six months paying through your gullible nose for mice and verrucas. A good place to start by harassing your friends, your friends' friends, and your friends' friends' friends. Send out a group email and hope it gets passed around, and make sure you Tweet like mad about it. Twitter is a great place to get your request passed around. Who knows? Stephen Fry might have a room to let. Estate agents (see below for a list) will invariably try and rip you off but, then again, so will everyone else, so it's worth registering with all the big ones, as well as any whose office you see in the street, or you spot in newspapers, on TV or the internet. After uncovering a fair few completely brazen lies in the property listings on www.gumtree.com you will find that many of the smaller businesses place adverts for (sometimes fake) properties here. Don't be put off by the lies though, because this can be a good way of finding an agent (or getting in direct contact with a landlord) who is keen to make a deal with you, or who will try and match the prices advertised, even if they have nothing that fits the bill at the exact moment of lying. Of course, some of these listings are also genuine, and a good way to find rooms/apartments at lower than usual rates. Just bare in mind that a LOT of people use this site.

General sites

www.gumtree.com
www.craigslist.org
www.rightmove.co.uk
www.roombuddies.com
www.zoopla.co.uk

Estate Agents

There are hundreds of Estate Agents and Letting Agents across the city, some of the larger players (good and bad) include:

www.keatons.com - Offices all over London.
www.keatons.co.uk - Bow, Hackney, Harringey, Kentish Town, Stratford.
www.blackkatz.com - Lettings only agency, numerous offices.
www.fjlord.co.uk - Numerous offices, specialise in uncooperative staff.
www.nelsonslettings.com - South and central London.
www.atkinsonmcleod.com - City and Docklands.

If you do end up using an agent, they will of course want to charge you an additional fee beyond any deposits or advance rent required by the landlord. But, as many of the agents in central London are close together, it's possible that they may be competing with each other to sell/rent the same properties. This will enable you to get a better deal. So shop around, be devious, and backstab as much as possible.

Council Tax

Council Tax is an annoying hidden cost that always comes as a bit of a surprise. It is worked out by your local council and is based on the value of your house/flat, which the council will already have placed in to one of 8 tax bands (bands A–G, G covering the most valuable properties).There are several ways to determine the value of a property, but the easiest is probably to go to the website of the valuation office at www.voa.gov.uk. Having done that, it's possible to weigh up the benefits of different areas by comparing the council tax in equivalent bands charged by different local councils. It's fairly laborious, but worth it in the long run, if you can be bothered.

Because council tax is based on the property, not the people inside it, the rate is

constant no matter how many people live in the house. This means that it's much cheaper to live in a big house with lots of people to split the tax with, than on your own, when you are liable for the full amount. Students do not have to pay council tax at all, but if they are sharing with one or more non-students then there will still be council tax to pay. A single non-student in a house full of students receives a 25% discount on his/her council tax bill, but if there is more than one non-student then all non-students are liable to pay full whack.

Deposit Information

The deposit is the necessary bank drain of every new tendency agreement. Typically deposits range from one – three months rent in advance, but if you pay over a two-month deposit you are entitled to special privileges including the right to sublet your space. If you can't afford the financial outlay there are other options available to you; it is possible to get involved with the Deposit Guarantee Scheme (you will need to contact your local council for more information), or independent agencies offer a similar service for a 10% - 20% fee. While not all landlords in London are Ebenezer Scrooge pre hallucination-esque you'll still hear your fair share of horror stories. Make sure you use the Deposit Protection Scheme (DPS) www.depositprotection.com to protect your cash. For a comprehensive overview on deposit information and your rights visit the Direct Gov website www.direct.gov.uk.

Alternative Options

In a city where house prices have been soaring through the roof for some time now (although it's calmed down somewhat recently), of course people do things like squat, have dreadlocks and go vegan. If you're not willing to go the whole way but fancy an adventure, or simply don't have much money, then it might be worth taking a look at being a guardian for Camelot. This company aims to fill vacant properties with responsible people who prevent them from being abused. You must have good references, a job, and be over eighteen, as well as be ok with sharing with an indeterminate number of strangers, but the benefits are the unusual properties (e.g. schools, disused churches), the often large spaces and the ridiculously cheap rent (£25–60 pw inclusive of all bills). Of course loads of people want to do this and properties in London are not always available but it's nevertheless a good idea to keep an eye on their site if the idea excites you: website: uk.cameloteurope.com.

WAREHOUSES

As with Starbucks and obesity, us Brits have finally caught on to the American craze for warehouse 'live/work' spaces. Okay we may have had the likes of Tracey Emin and other artists living in old carpet factories since the YBA days, but recently a whole crop of established estate agents have been refurbishing lofts and factories for letting at a premium. Any established warehouser will tell you the way to go is independent, through enthusiastic urban explorers who renovate and convert these old buildings for love and enjoyment. Often the only way into this secret brotherhood of the leaky roof is by simply ending up at a huge party at 4am in one of these spaces and asking the residents politely. The freedom of living in these places can be exhilirating if you've spent years toeing the line with grumpy neighbours and grumpier landlords.

CANAL-BOATS

If all this land lubbing is bringing you down, there's always the option of dropping anchor at Little Venice or the Lea Valley Harbour and sampling London's canal networks. More and more skint artsy fartsy folk are squeezing their possessions into canal boats and living a romantic life on the water. A casual stroll down Regent's Canal may convince you this is the way to live, but bare in mind the hidden cons of London nautical life: mooring fees, fuel, unlit walks down leafy paths frequented by degenerates…Don't say we didn't warn you!

The Best of the Best

London is full of interactive children's pursuits, and nothing beats discovering all the joys that the city has to offer to the little ones, so we thought we'd give you some inside tips on what there is!

• **Best Rainy Day Activity:** The Science Museum (Exhibition Road, SW7 2DD, 0870 870 4868) is great fun and one of London's most interactive museums. Don't miss the Launchpad gallery, which is full of hands-on exhibits to tinker with, simulators and a face morphing machine. The museum's occasional Science Nights are activity filled, with overnight camping in the building included. Entry is free. Open 7 days a week from 10am to 6pm.

• **Coolest Cinema:** The BFI London IMAX Cinema (1 Charlie Chaplin Walk, SE1 8XR, 020 7902 1234) has the largest screen (20 metres) in the country, as well as an 11,600-watt digital surround sound system with which to deafen your children. With most of the cinema's 3D programming dedicated to children's films, they'll be spoilt rotten by the whole experience; even the entrance to the place is cool, with futuristic blue lighting paving your way through the tunnels.

• **Goriest Tourist Haunt:** The London Dungeon (28-34 Tooley Street, SE1 2SZ, 020 7403 7221) specialises in the darker side of English history and has a preponderance of gruesome waxworks, theme rides and costumed staff to scare the bejesus out of your children, which they'll love (unless you've brought them up to be soft). Open all week from 11am to 5pm.

• **Best Tour For Budding Media Moguls:** The BBC Television Centre Tour (Wood Lane, W12 7RJ, 0870 603 0304) provides a chance for children 9 and over to take a behind the scenes look at the world of TV as well as a chance to play in an interactive studio. A separate tour (ages 7 and over) entitled "The BBC Experience" is based on the BBC's kids' channel and offers visitors the chance to roam around the Blue Peter garden, amongst other things. Regular tours are conducted every day except Sunday.

• **Best Ice Cream:** It's no secret that kids love ice cream, but the plethora of dodgy "Mr Whippy" vans selling their frozen wares in London can be improved upon. For outstanding homemade gourmet sorbets and exotic ice cream cones,

there is no better place than the kiosk to the side of Golders Hill Park Refreshment House (North End Road, NW3 7HD, 020 8455 8010,; prices are very reasonable and the park is a gorgeous setting within which to consume such tasty delights.

• **Best Inner City Farm:** Hackney City Farm (1a Goldsmiths Row, E2 8QA, 020 7729 6381). You don't want your child to be the one hiding on the bus on their first fieldtrip because they've never seen a cow. Hackney City Farm gives children and adults alike the chance to experience farming first-hand, interact with the animals and understand sustainable living, all of this in the heart of Hackney.

• **Best For Halloween Costumes:** Escapade (45-46 Chalk Farm Road, NW1 8AJ, 020 7485 7384) has been kitting kids out in all manner of costumes since 1982, and offers wigs (maybe one for Dad?), hats, masks, make-up, jokes and magic tricks. Perfect for trick or treat, or for those already bored of their child's ugly face.

• **Best Eatery For Families:** Maxwell's (8-9 James Street, WC2E 8BH) lies deep in the heart of Covent Garden and specialises in burgers (does any child not like burgers?) which won't break parents' banks. A kids' menu is provided, as well as activities and games.

Rainy Day Activities

Especially for when the infamous London weather puts a dampener on outdoor activities…

• **Cartoon Museum** (35 Little Russell Street, WC1A 2HH, 020 7580 8155) This fascinating place archives the development of cartoon art in Britain, from the 18th century through to the present day; best of all, the Young Artists' Gallery lets children try their hands at animation and claymation.

• **London Aquarium** (County Hall, Westminster Bridge Road, SE1 7PB, 020 7967 8000) One of the largest aquariums in the world, over 400 species of aquatic life (including the only zebra sharks in the U.K.) can be found within this building. With three floors, piranhas, and pools where you can prod things, there's more than enough to keep even the most jaded parent happy.

- **London Eye** (Jubilee Gardens, South Bank, SE1 7PB, 0870 500 0600) This 135-metre high riverside Ferris wheel offers breathtaking views of London in up to 25 miles in each direction, all from the vantage point of an air-conditioned glass pod. Book online to beat the queues.

- **Natural History Museum** (Cromwell Road, SW7 5BD, 020 7942 5000) Ever wanted to see a replica skeleton of a 26-metre long Diplodocus dinosaur? It's one of the 70 million items housed within this excellent museum, which also includes the Darwin Centre, a must for any budding paleontologists; non-nerds should love it too.

- **Madame Tussaud's** (Marylebone Road, NW1 5LR, 0870 999 0046) Infamous exhibition of waxworks, with recently introduced interactive exhibits giving you the chance to score a goal for England or sing with Britney Spears (she'll be the one lip-syncing). Worth booking online to avoid the often long queues.

- **Museum Of London** (150 London Wall, EC2Y 5HN, 0870 444 3852, some galleries undergoing renovation and due to re-open late 2009) Explains the history of London in vivid detail; the innovative layout consists of a chain of chronological galleries (no skipping to 1945, OK?) Also has fragments of the old London Wall in the grounds.

- **Peter Harrison Planetarium** (Royal Observatory Greenwich, Greenwich Park, SE10 9NF, 020 8312 8565) Open since 2007 and the only planetarium in London seats 120 and uses the latest technology to take you on an armchair tour of the universe. Children aged 4 and under will not be admitted.

- **Queens Ice And Bowl** (17 Queensway, W2 4QP, 020 7229 0172) An ice rink, ten pin bowling alleys and a pizza restaurant, it's the perfect opportunity for kids to stuff their faces while watching their Dad break a bone on the rink. Children's skating classes available.

- **Topsy Turvy World** (Brent Cross Shopping Centre, Prince Charles Drive, NW4 3FP, 020 8359 9920) A huge indoor playground in the middle of one of London's busiest shopping centres. There's more to this place than just bouncy things and over-excitement, it also offers baking activities (might as well get your children cooking for you early) and various classes.

- **Tower Of London** (Tower Hill, EC3N 4AB, 0870 756 7070) A cornucopia of royal history and English culture lies within the Tower's ancient walls, with royal jewels aplenty. Good for the whole family, and under 5s get in free. Avoid the queues by booking ahead.

- **The V&A Museum Of Childhood** (Cambridge Heath Road, E2 9PA, 020 8983 5200) This lesser known gem of the Victoria & Albert Museum houses the national childhood collection, which basically means it's full of toys, games, dolls, dollhouses, nursery antiques and children's costumes. There's no shortage of activities and events going on here to keep your kids occupied, and it's free.

Classes

A recent resurgence in the amount of out of school programmes being implemented in the capital means that there's more for your kids to do than ever before.

- **Art Club** (Orleans House Gallery, Riverside, TW1 3DJ, 020 8831 6000) A rare opportunity for 5-10 year olds to work with practicing artists and explore new techniques and materials. Every Wednesday and Thursday from 3.45-5pm.

- **Barnsbury One O'Clock Club** (Barnard Park, Hemingford Road, N1 0JU, 020 7278 9494) Fun and games for the under 5s.

- **Brixton Recreation Centre** (27 Brixton Station Road, SW9 8QQ, 020 7926 9779) Recently refurbished, this centre includes The Energy Zone (ages 5-15) for ball games and The Fitness Zone (ages 8-15) with SHOKK fitness equipment specifically designed for the younger body builder/steroid abuser.

- **Camden Square Play Centre** (Camden Square, NW1 9RE, 020 7485 6827) After school (and school holiday) centre with fun activities for children aged 4-12.

- **Camden Swiss Cottage Swimming Club** (Swiss Cottage Leisure Centre, Winchester Road, NW3 3NR, 020 7974 5440) Swimming lessons for children aged 4 and upward.

- **Chang's Hapkido Academy** (Topnotch Health Club, 3 Tudor Street, EC4Y 0AH, 07951 535876) Martial arts school with classes for ages 12 and upward.

- **The Circus Space** (Coronet Street, N1 6HD, 020 7613 4141) Prepare your children for a life in the circus with The Circus Space's variety of classes and workshops for all ages.

- **Crazee Kids** (Jackson Lane Community Centre, Archway Road, N6 5AA, Tuesdays), (Union Church & Community Centre, Weston Park, N8 9TA, Saturdays) 020 8444 5333, Weekly term-time dance, drama and music classes. Summer workshops.

- **Haringey Club** (Hornsey YMCA, 50 Tottenham Lane, N8 7EE, 020 8348 2124) A range of things to do for those aged up to 15, including a pre-school programme, gymnastics, ballet, street dance and kickboxing.

- **The Kids' Cookery School (**107 Gunnersbury Len WE 8HQ, 020 8992 8882) Get your kids cooking at this fine venue which offers classes and workshops for those aged 3 and upwards.

- **Kite Art Studios** (Priory Mews, 2B Bassein Park Road, W12 9RY, 020 8576 6278) Courses and workshops on painting, pottery and jewellery making amongst other fun activities for kids of all ages. Mother and toddler sessions too.

- **London Irish Centre** (50-52 Camden Square, NW1 9XB, 020 7916 7222) Irish dancing classes for beginners upwards, every Monday at 6pm, courtesy of the Barrett Semple-Morris School.

- **The Little Angel Theatre** (14 Dagmar Passage, Cross Street, N1 2DN, 020 7226 1787) Children's theatre offering after-school courses in puppet making, the art of puppetry performance and a Saturday Puppet Club.

- **The Little Gym** (Compass House, Riverside West, Smugglers Way, SW18 1DB, 020 8874 6567) Gymnastics and skills development within a relaxed environment for children aged up to 12.

- **Music House For Children** (Bush Hall, 310 Uxbridge Road, W12 7LJ, 020 8932 2652) Whether it's instrumental or singing lessons, this wonderful place can provide individual and group tuition and even caters for 1 year olds!

- **Painted Earth** (Arch 65, The Catacombs, Stables Market, NW1 8AH, 020 7424 8983) Ceramic arts classes supervised by staff. Children can make their own mugs and plates.

- **Pirate Castle** (Oval Road, NW1 7EA, 020 7267 6600) Kids can canoe or Kayak around Camden's only castle on this outdoor adventure club, which moonlights as a school and youth services centre.

- **Richmond Junior Chess Club** (ETNA Community Centre, 13 Rosslyn Road, TW1 2AR, 07720 716336) Chess classes with a mixture of instruction and play for those up to the age of 18.

- **Sobell Leisure Centre** (Hornsey Road, N7 7NY, 020 7609 2166) No need to book, just turn up for coached sessions in basketball, badminton, football and ice hockey amongst other sports. Children aged 7 and under must be accompanied by an adult.

- **Tricycle Theatre** (269 Kilburn High Road, NW6 7JR, 020 7328 1000) Not just a theatre/cinema/gallery, the Tricycle also runs term-time workshops in drama, storytelling and music.

- **Triyoga** (6 Erskine Road, NW3 3AJ, 020 7483 3344) Let the kids get their Zen on at after school yoga classes for ages 5 and over.

- **Westway Stables** (20 Stable Way, Latimer Road, W11 6QX, 020 8964 2140) Horse riding lessons for the over 5s in the heart of Notting Hill.

Babysitting/Nanny/Services

- **Nannies Unlimited** 11 Chelveton Road, SW15 1RN, 020 8788 9640

- **Nanny Search** 1st Floor, 1 Shepherds Hill, N6 5QJ, 020 8348 4111

- **Sleeptight Nannies** 20 Nursery Road, N14 5QB, 020 8292 2618

- **Top Notch Nannies** 49 Harrington Gardens, SW7 4JU, 020 7259 2626

Where to Go for More Info

www.dayoutwiththekids.co.uk

Shopping Essentials

- **Baby Dior** 6 Harriet Street, SW1X 9JW, 020 7823 2039 – Encourage label envy as soon as possible.

- **Baby Munchkins** 186 Hoxton Street, N1 5LH, 020 7684 5994 – Baby wear.

- **Balloonland** 12 Hale Lane, NW7 3NX, 020 8906 3302 – Balloons and party supplies.

- **Benjamin Pollock's Toyshop** 44 The Piazza, Covent Garden WC2E 8RF, 020 7379 7866 – Toys.

- **Biff** 43 Dulwich Village, SE21 7BN, 020 8299 0911 – Designer and street brands.

- **Boomerang** 69 Blythe Road, W14 0HP, 020 7610 5232 – Clothes and necessities for tots.
- **Bonpoint** Chic clothes.
  17 Victoria Grove, W8 5RW – 020 7584 5131
  197 Westbourne Grove, W11 2SE – 020 7792 2515
  256 Brompton Road, SW3 2AS – 020 3263 5057
  35B Sloane Street, SW1X 9LP – 020 7235 1441
  38 Old Bond Street, W1S 4QW – 020 7495 1680
- **Burberry** 21-23 New Bond Street, W1S 2RE, 020 7839 5222 – Clothes.
- **Caramel** 291 Brompton Road, SW3 2DY, 020 7589 7001 – Cool clothes.
- **Catamini** – Babies and children's clothes. 33C King's Road, SW3 4LX – 020 7824 8897, 52 South Molton Street, W1Y 1HF – 020 7629 8099
- **Cheeky Monkeys** – Mainly wooden toys. 202 Kensington Park Road, W11 1NR – 020 7792 9022, 94 Kings Road, SW6 4UL – 020 7731 3037
- **Children's Book Centre** 237 Kensington High Street, W8 6SA, 020 7937 7497 – Books.
- **Coco Children's Boutique** 27A Devonshire Street, W1G 6PN, 020 7935 3554 – Children's boutique (fancy that!).
- **D2 Leisure** 201-203 Roman Road, E2 0QY, 020 8980 4966 – Bicycle shop.
- **Daisy & Tom** 181 King's Road, SW3 5EB, 020 7352 5000 – Clothes, toys and a carousel.
- **Davenports Magic Shop** 7 Adelaide Street, WC2N 4HZ, 020 7836 0408 – Magic shop.
- **Early Learning Centre** 36 King's Road, SW3 4UD, 020 7581 5764 – Educational toyshop.
- **Disney Store** – Disney merchandise.
  Unit 10, The Piazza, WC2E 8HD – 020 7836 5037
  22A & 26 The Broadway Shopping Centre, W6 9YD – 020 8748 8886
  360-366 Oxford Street, W1N 9HA – 020 7491 9136
- **Eric Snook's Toyshop** 32 Covent Garden Market, WC1 8RE, 020 7379 7681 – Toys and teddies.
- **Escapade** 45-46 Chalk Farm Road, NW1 8AJ, 020 7485 7384 – Costumes and masks.
- **The Farmyard** 63 Barnes High Street, SW13 9LF, 020 8878 7338 – Toys for younger children and babies.
- **GapKids/Baby Gap**
  35 Hampstead High Street, NW3 1QE – 020 7794 9182
  146-148 Regent Street, W1B 5SH – 020 7287 5095

Brent Cross Shopping Centre, NW4 3FB – 020 8203 9696
122 King's Road, SW3 4TR – 020 7823 7272
4 Queens Road, SW19 8YE- 020 8947 9074
101-111 Kensington High Street, W8 5SA – 020 7368 2900
260-262 Chiswick High Road, W4 1PD – 020 8995 3255
47-49 St John's Wood High Street, NW8 7NJ – 020 7586 6123
151 Queensway, W2 4YL – 020 7221 8039
330-340 Cabot Place East, E14 4QT – 020 7513 0241
121-123 Long Acre, WC2E 9PA – 020 7836 0646

- **Green Rabbit** 20 Briston Grove, N8 9EX, 020 8348 3770 – Contemporary kids' wear.
- **Hamley's** 188-196 Regent Street, W1B 5BT, 020 7153 9000 – Toys galore, tourists galore.
- **Happy Returns** 36 Rosslyn Hill, NW3 1NH, 020 7435 2431 – Toys again!
- **Honeyjam** 267 Portobello Road, W11 1LR, 020 7243 0449 – Retro and vintage toys and rocking horses.
- **Igloo Kids** Wide range of kids' clothes. 300 Upper Street, N1 2TU – 020 7354 7300, 80 St John's Wood, NW8 7SH – 020 7483 2332
- **Infantasia Unit 103** Wood Green Shopping City, N22 6YA, 020 8889 1494 – Furniture and bedding.
- **International Magic** 89 Clerkenwell Road, EC1R 5BX, 020 7405 7324 – Magic shop.
- **Joujou & Lucy** 32 Clifton Road, W9 1ST, 020 7289 0866 – Children's boutique.
- **Kent & Carey** 154 Wandsworth Bridge Road, SW6 2UH, 020 7736 5554 – Classic children's clothes.
- **Little Stinkies** 15 Victoria Grove, W8 5RW, 020 7052 0077 – Dolls' houses, toys and puppet theatres.
- **Marie Chantal** 148 Walton Street, SW3 2JJ, 020 7838 1111 – Children's fashion.
- **MIMMO** 602 Fulham Road, SW6 5PA, 020 7731 4706 – Designer duds.
- **Mothercare** – The leading chain for baby stuff in the UK; will sell you everything but the baby.
  Brent Cross Shopping Centre, NW4 3FD – 020 8202 5377
  416 Brixton Road, SW9 7AY – 020 7733 1494
  Unit 7, The Waterglade Centre, 1-8 The Broadway, W5 2ND – 0208 579 6181

Ravenside Retail Park, Angel Road, N18 3HA – 020 8807 5518

14e High Street, SE9 1BJ – 020 8859 7957

4 Palace Gardens, EN2 6SN – 020 8367 1188

31e North End Road, SW6 1NG – 020 7381 6387

Kings Mall Shopping Centre, W6 0PZ – 020 860 2860

44e Holloway Road, N7 6QA – 020 7607 0915

11a High Street, TW3 1NA – 020 8577 1767

Unit 1A, Richmond Retail Park, Mortlake Road, Kew – 020 8878 3758

41 Riverdale High Street, SE13 7EP – 020 8852 21e

52e 528 Oxford Street, W1C 1LW – 0845 365 0515

Uni 2, Aylesham Centre, Rye Lane, SE15 5EW – 020 7358 0093

33-34 The Mall, E15 1XD – 020 8534 5714

BHS Surrey Quays Shopping Centre, Redriff Road, SE1 7LL – 020 7237 2025

Unit 59, Southside Shopping Centre, SW18 4TF – 020 8877 4180

Unit Lsu4, Centre Court, SW19 8YA – 020 8944 529

38-40 High Road, N22 6BX – 020 8888 6920

62 Powis Street, SE18 1LQ – 020 8854 3540

- **Never Never Land** 3 Mildhurst Parade, Fortis Green, N10 3EJ, 020 883 3997 – Toys and dolls.

- **Olive Loves Alfie** 84 Stoke Newington Church Street, N16 0AP, 020 7241 4212 – Children's lifestyle boutique.

- **Patrick's Toys & Models** 107 Lillie Road, SW6 7SX, 020 385 9864 – Outdoor games and equipment.

- **Patrizia Wigan** 19 Walton Street, SW3 2HX, 020 7823 7080 – Clothing boutique.

- **Petit Bateau** 62 South Molton Street, W1K 5SR, 020 7491 4498 – Luxurious baby wear.

- **Petite Ange** 6 Harriet Street, SW1X 9JW, 020 7235 7737 – Exclusive clothing.

- **Please Mum** 85 Knightsbridge, SW1X 7RB, 020 7486 1380 – Expensive clothing.

- **Pom D'Api** 3 Blenheim Crescent, W11 2EE, 020 7243 0535 – Classy shoes.

- **QT Toys** 90 Northcote Road, SW11 6QN, 020 7223 8637 – Toys, games and gifts.

- **Rachel Riley** 14 Pont Street, SW1X 9EN, 020 7935 7007 – Clothes.

- **Rainbow** 253 Archway Road, N6 5BS, 020 8340 9700 – Toys, games and clothes.

- **Showroom** 64 Titchfield Street, W1W 7QH, 020 7636 2501 – Funky children's clothes.

- **Soup Dragon** 27 Topsfield Parade, Tottenham Lane, N8 8PT, 020 8348 0224 – Toys and clothes.

- **The Shoe Station** 3 Station Approach, Kew Gardens, TW9 3QB, 020 8940 9905 – Shoes and footwear.

- **Their Nibs** 214 Kensington Park Road, W11 1NR, 020 7221 4263 – Designer clothes and bedding.

- **Tots** 39 Turnham Green Terrace, W4 1RG, 020 8995 0520 – Clothes boutique.

- **Toys R Us** - Toys, toys, toys.
  Tilling Road (opposite Brent Cross Shopping Centre), NW2 1LW – 020 8209 0019
  Great Cambridge Road, EN1 3RN – 020 8364 6600
  Hayes Road, UB2 5LN – 020 8561 4681
  760 Old Kent Road, SE15 1NJ – 020 7732 7322

- **Traditional Toys** Chelsea Green, 53 Godfrey Street, SW3 3SX, 020 7352 1718 – Timeless toys.

- **The Little White Company** 261 Pavillion Road, SW1X 0BP, 020 7881 0783 – Clothing, bed linen and furniture.

For many, the Internet is *the* key to the city. Before the dawning of the Internet, we Dickensian scamps had to scurry around in the filth foraging for information in 'books' and by talking to actual 'people'. Now that the future is here, Londoners can navigate their city's streets, explore its dark history, organise a debauched weekend in Chiswick or, as is more likely, peer over the shoulder of men in raincoats in Internet Cafes.

Internet Cafes are everywhere. In fact you probably live in one. They can range from the dimly lit 'Money Transfer' shacks that have an air of illegality, to chains that dominated the market before home internet use skyrocketed in the late 90s. To be fair, internet use in these places is usually criminally cheap: as low as 50p per hour in the non-tourist areas. For a large list of London internet cafes check out: www.allinlondon.co.uk/directory/1166.php.

London was one crowned WiFi capital of the world, owing to its astronomical rate of increase in WiFi networks in 2007. Today, it is difficult to move in your local cafe without catching the edge of a laptop. **The Apostrophe Cafe** chain is efficient, expensive and has WiFi as standard, but if you wish to cook your internal organs with your MacBook you can do so in hundreds of cafes across London. An alternative to those of you who have joined the growing legion of smartphone users and don't want the commitment of a long-term contract try **Gigaff** (www.giffgaff.com). For £10 you can get 250 minutes, unlimited texts and unlimited data for a month with no additional cost incurred. They offer a best in business rate for the Internet addicts among you.

Useful and/or Fun London Links

www.notfortourists.com/London.aspx
www.fedbybirds.com
www.royalparks.org.uk
www.tfl.gov.uk
www.londonist.com
www.londonfreelist.com
www.davehill.typepad.com
www.shadyoldlady.com
www.derelictlondon.com
www.walk-london.blogspot.com
www.hiddenlondon.com
www.londonbloggers.iamcal.com
www.london-underground.blogspot.com
www.fancyapint.com
www.dailycandy.com/london
www.gumtree.com
www.timeout.com
www.brickads.blogspot.com
www.wildinlondon.blogspot.com
www.westlondonblogger.blogspot.com
www.dalstonoxfamshop.blogspot.com
www.viewlondon.co.uk
www.lecool.com/cities/london
www.deadcafesociety.org.uk
www.londonreviewofbreakfasts.blogspot.com
www.beerintheevening.com
www.london-se1.co.uk
www.talkonthetube.com
www.london.thewayweseeit.org
londoncabby.blogspot.com

The doom-sayers have less cause to complain about the decline of Gayhood in London recently, what with **Heaven** (London's self-proclaimed most famous gay club) hanging on and new nights popping up everywhere. Yes, popular indie discos **Popstarz** and **Rebel Rebel** have relocated and **Girl's Action** at Ghetto promises great things and we are so in love with 'polysexual' club **Dalston Supermarket** at the moment. Of course every time one door (read: gay club) closes another one opens, and let's face it, the latter will probably open later and sell you even cheaper Red Bull and vodka.

One of the most exciting developments in the past few years has been the advent of what has been dubbed London's new 'Gay Village'—the cluster of clubs, saunas and after-hours hangover incubators that have sprung up in Vauxhall. Now it's possible, though still just as inadvisable, to party from Thursday through to Tuesday without stopping to reapply deodorant, or think about the consequences of what you're doing—hooray. The small outcrop of gay and 'polysexual' nights in the East End, is still thriving, and offers another refreshing alternative to Soho for those in search of an aggressive fashion consciousness and a less cruisy atmosphere. This said, if you can handle bright lights, pop music, tight t-shirts and a lot of hair gel, you'll still have massive amounts of fun around Soho and Old Compton Street, the traditional central London gay epicentre. This area is always buzzing, day and night, and is a great place to sit back and do some people watching as well as to go out and, y'know, go crazy.

For girls there is still room for improvement, with options fewer and less centralised, but **The Minories'** new Girls' night is a blast and the continuing women-only nights at **Village** and **Element** are cause for celebration. Many mixed and polysexual nights (such as Motherfucker at **Barden's Boudoir**) also draw large female crowds, and though dedicated lesbian bars and clubs are few and far between, there is enough going on in the city to make any day of the week a possible night out.

Websites

www.dirtydirtydancing.com - Super-airbrushed photos from many of the trendier Soho and east London nights.

http://scene-out.com - Comprehensive mainstream scene guide.
www.gingerbeer.co.uk - Lesbian guide to London.
www.girlguidelondon.co.uk - Does what it says on the tin.
www.gmfa.org.uk - Gay men's health charity.
www.patroc.com/london/clubs.html-Great source for upcoming gay events.
www.pinkdate.com - Speed dating events for gay men and women in central London.

Publications

The following are all free listings/scene magazines that can be found in most gay shops and venues (anywhere on Old Compton Street should have some copies lying around):

Boyz Magazine - Weekly scene news and listings, out Thursdays. www.boyz.co.uk

G3 Magazine - Lesbian scene, monthly. www.g3mag.co.uk

Out in the City Mag - Monthly London lifestyle magazine for gay men. www.outmag.co.uk

Qx Magazine - Gay men's mag. www.qxmagazine.com

Shops

Gay's the Word, 66 Marchmont Street, WC1N 1AB, 020 7278 7654, http://freespace.virgin.net/gays. theword/, The only dedicated Gay and Lesbian Bookshop in London, recently threatened by rising rent. Visit whilst it's still there!

Prowler, 5–7 Brewer Street, W1F 0RF, 020 7734 4031, The ultimate gay men's shop, stocking everything from (skimpy) clothes to sex toys plus mountains of lube, pornography, and the other usual suspects.

Sh! Women's Erotic Emporium, 57 Hoxton Square N1 6PD, 020 7697 9072, http://www.sh-womenstore. com/, London's only female-orientated sex shop, run by women, for women.

Sexual Health

A comprehensive list of London clinics that offer same day HIV testing and PEP treatments for gay/ bisexual men is available at www.gmfa.org.uk/ londonservices/clinics. CLASH, below, is particularly recommended.

441

CLASH (Central London Action on Street Health), 11 Warwick Street, W1B 5NA, 020 7734 1794, Friday night clinic for gay men, with incredibly friendly staff who will offer comfort and advice. Same day (often instant) HIV testing, PEP treatment. Fridays, 5 - 8.30pm, call for an appointment.

Support Organizations

Again, a more comprehensive list can be found at the GMFA website: www.gmfa.org.uk/londonservices/support-groups/index

Stonewall, Tower Building, York Road, SE1 7NX, www.stonewall.org.uk, Gay rights charity and lobbying group.

PACE Youthwork Service, 34 Hartham Road, N7 9LJ, 020 7700 1323, www.outzone.org, Support organization for gay and lesbian youths under 25. Organizes regular social events and offers one to one consultations with advisors: phone or visit the website to get involved.

London Friend, 86 Caledonian Road, N1 9DN, 020 7833 1674, www.londonfriend.org.uk, Voluntary organization which runs several helplines, group workshops and social events, as well as offering advice on reporting hate crime.

London Lesbian and Gay Switchboard, 0300 330 0630, www.llgs.org.uk, Counselling and information service.

Kairos in Soho, Unit 10, 10-11 Archer Street, W1D 7AZ, 020 7437 6063, www.kairosinsoho.org.uk, Gay and lesbian charity which organises a variety of recreational events to promote the health, well being and development of the LGBT community.

Naz Project London, Palingswick House, 241 King Street, W6 9LP, 020 8741 1879 www.naz.org.uk, Charity that organizes support and sexual health services for black and ethnic minority communities in London. Various services, including free one-on-one counselling and support groups are available, phone or check website for details.

GALOP, PO Box 32810, N1 3ZD, 020 7704 6767, www.galop.org.uk, Charity specialising in advice about reporting hate crime.

Annual Events

Pride London, www.pridelondon.org, Large pride festival, takes place every July.

GFEST – www.gaywisefestival.org.uk, London's premier cross-party festival, GFEST features a variety of established and new LBG&T artists. The festival promotes the queer arts scene while keeping LBGT human rights the underlying focus of proceedings.

London Lesbian and Gay Film Festival, www.bfi.org.uk/llgff, Film festival at the BFI on South Bank, March–April.

London LGBT History Month, www.lgbthistorymonth.co.uk, Nationwide awareness month, with various talks and events staged in London, every February.

Gay/Mixed Venues

Soho:

79CXR, 79 Charing Cross Road, WC2H 0NE, 020 7734 0769, Dingy bar with middle aged crowd.

The Admiral Duncan, 54 Old Compton Street, W1D 4UB, 020 7437 5300

Barcode Soho, 3-4 Archer Street W1D 7AT, 020 7734 3342

Box, 32–34 Monmouth Street, WC2H 9HA, 020 7240 5828, Civilised bar and eatery.

Comptons, 53–57 Old Compton Street, W1D 6HN, 020 7479 7961, Crammed gay pub.

Duke of Wellington, 77 Wardour Street, W1D 6QA

The Edge, 11 Soho Square, W1D 3QF, 020 7439 1313

G-A-Y Bar, 30 Old Compton Street, W1D 5JX, 020 7494 2756, Poptastic bunker. Video walls and cheap drinks.

G-A-Y Late, 5 Goslett Yard, WC2H 0ER, 020 7734 9858, Cheap drinks and pop videos wipe out brain functions 'til 3am.

Ghetto, Falconberg Court, W1D 3AB, 020 7287 3726, Loud electro at this busy gay club. Thursday is ladies night.

Halfway to Heaven, 7 Duncannon Street, WC2N 4JF, 020 7321 2791.

Heaven, Under the Arches, Villiers Street, WC2N 6NG, 020 7930 2020, Legendary gay club. An institution.

Ku Bar, 30 Lisle Street, WC2H 7BA, 020 7437 4303, Newly relocated bar for the young and clueless.

Kudos, 10 Adelaide Street, WC2N 4HZ, 020 7379 4573

Profile, 56–57 Frith Street, W1D 3JG, 020 7734 8300

Shadow Lounge, 5 Brewer Street, W1F, 020 7439 4089, Supposed to be a shi-shi cocktail lounge. Hmmmm.

Soho Revue Bar, 11 Walkers Court, Brewer Street, W1F 0ED, Cabaret acts followed by dancing 'til late.

The Village, 81 Wardour Street, W1D 6QD, 020 7437 2124 Tacky, flirtatious bar spread across two floors.

Trash Palace, 11 Wardour Street, W1D 6PG, 020 7734 0522, Bratty queer indie bar.

North:

Cosmo Lounge, 43 Essex Road, N1 2SF, 020 7688 0051 Subdued bar, normally full of regulars.

Central Station, 37 Wharfdale Road, N1 9SD, 020 7278 3294. Pub/club with ominously blacked out windows.

The Green, 74 Upper Street N1 0NY, 0871 971 4097, Innocuous gay bar/restaurant frequented by many unsuspecting straight couples.

King Edward VI Pub, 25 Bromfield Street, N1 0PZ

The Black Cap, 171 Camden High Street, NW1 7JY, 020 7428 2721, Slightly crummy gay pub.

East:

Bistrotheque, 23–27 Wadeson Street, E2 9DR, Jonny Woo's restaurant, great food and drag acts.

The Black Horse, 168 Mile End Road, E1 4LJ, 020 7790 1584

George and Dragon, 2 Hackney Road, E2 7NS, Small, atmospheric pub full of trendy boys and girls.

Joiners Arms, 116–118, Hackney Road, E2 7Q, Late opening free-for-all with a wonderfully mixed crowd ('til 2/3am most nights)

South

Area, 67–68 Albert Embankment, SE1 7TP

Barcode Vauxhall, 69 Albert Embankment, 020 7582 4 80

The Two Brewers, 114 Clapham High Street, SW4 7UJ, 020 7498 4971

Depot, 56 Albert Embankment, SE11 7TP, Sister club of Area with a more cruisy vibe.

Fire, South Lambeth Road, SW8 1RT, 020 7434 1113, The quintessential Vauxhall club. Open pretty much forever, bulging muscles everywhere.

The Foot, 131 Grange Road, Bermondsey, SE1 3AL - Themed cruising/fetish/sex bar.

Kazbar Clapham, 50 Clapham High Street, SW4 7UL, 020 7622 0070

Little Apple Bar, 98 Kennington Lane, SE11 4XD Mixed/lesbian bar.

The Powder Monkey, 22 King William Walk, SE10 PHU, 020 8293 5928, thepowdermonkey.net

Royal Vauxhall Tavern, 372 Kennington Lane, SE11 5HY, 020 7820 1222

South Central, 349 Kennington Lane, SE11 5QY, 020 7793 0903

Substation South, 9 Brighton Terrace, SW9 8DJ, 020 7737 2095

XXL, 51–53 Southwark Street, SE1 1TE, www.fatsandsmalls.com, Busy bear club.

West:

Bromptons, 294 Old Brompton Road, SW5 9JF, 020 7370 1344

The Coleherne, 261 Old Brompton Road, SW5 9JA020 7244 5951

Recommended Nights

Club Motherfucker, second Saturdays @ Barden's Boudoir, 38 Stoke Newington Road, Dalston, N16 7XJ, Polysexual band night. Sweaty, noisy, very much about the music.

Circus, Fridays @ Soho Revue Bar, 11 Walkers Court, Brewer Street, W1F 0ED, Drag Queen Jodie Harsh's long running night attracts its fair share of celebrities from both on and off the scene. Get there early or be prepared to queue.

DTPM, www.myspace.com/dtpm, Legendary event, no longer with a fixed location. See site for details of upcoming parties.

For3ign, Saturdays @ Bar Music Hall, 134 Curtain Road, EC2A 3AR, 020 7613 5951, Outlandish costumes and, of course, thumping electro.

Horsemeat Disco, Sundays @ South Central, Italo and 70s Disco bring all sorts to this fantastic night, originally a bear love club.

Icon, Sundays @ Essence, 562a Mile End Road, E3 4PH, 0208 980 6427, mob 07843 440 443 (weekly), New night in the East End. Yet to prove itself.

Issue, monthly (check site for details) @ Electricity Showrooms, 39a Hoxton Square, N1 6NN, issueclub.blogspot.com, Polysexual parties to coincide with the launch of this scene/fashion magazine.

Matinee, monthly (check site) @ Fabric, 77a Charterhouse Street, EC1M 3HN, 020 7335 8898, www.matineelondon.com, Irregular gay night at this enormous club in Farringdon.

Popstarz, Fridays @ Sin, 144 Charing Cross Road, WC2H 0LB, 020 7240 1900, Gay indie institution, recently relocated.

Trailer Trash, Fridays @ On the Rocks, 25 Kingsland Road, E2 8AA, 020 7688 0339, The dirtiest electro and the drunkest you've ever been. Crammed with sweating fashionistas.

Wet Yourself, Sundays @ Aquarium, 256–264 Old Street, EC1V 9DD, 020 7251 6136, This used to be the place to be after Boombox. It's lost only a little of its charm since (mixed polysexual crowd).

Lesbian Venues

Blush Bar, 8 Cazenove Road, Stoke Newington N16, 020 7923 9202, www.blushbar.co.uk

Candy Bar, 23-24 Bateman Street, W1V 5HR, 020 7437 1977, The reluctant epicentre of the Lesbian scene in this.

First Out Café Bar, Soho - 52 St Giles High St, WC2H 8LH, 020 7240 8042, Cafe with nightly events. All girls on Friday.

Oak Bar, 79 Green Lanes, N16, www.oakbar.co.uk, 020 7354 2791,

The Star At Night, 22 Great Chapel Street, Soho, W1 8FR, 020 7434 3749, Mixed cocktail bar with a predominantly female crowd.

Recommended Nights

100% Babe, Bank Holiday Sundays @ The Roxy, 3 Rathbone Place, W1P 1DA, 020 7636 1598, Irregular party for fans of funky house, R&B, old skool and electropop.

Blue Light, last Saturdays @ Bar Med, Triton Court, 14 Finsbury Square, EC2, 020 7588 3056

Club Wotever, first Saturday of the month @ The Masters Club, 12 Denman Street, Piccadilly, W1D 7HH, 020 7734 4243, Draggy night with a large 'King' quota.

Code, irregular night @ the Enclave, 25–27 Brewer Street, W1F 0RR, www.club-code.net - check website for details.

Girls on Girls, Wednesdays @ Village, 81 Wardour Street, W1D 6QD, 020 7434 2124

Lounge, second Thursdays @ Vertigo, 1 Leicester Square, WC2H 7NA, 020 7734 0900, Relaxed cocktail night at this swish Leicester Square club.

Miss Shapes, Thursdays @ Ghetto, Falconberg Court, W1D 3AB, 020 7287 3726, Popular girls-only indie night.

Pink, Wednesdays @ Element, 4-5 Greek Street, W1D 4DD, 020 7434 3323.

Play, irregular night @ Bar Rumba, 35 Shaftesbury Ave, W1F 7EP, 020 7287 2715, www.myspace.com/_clubplay

Rumours, last Saturday of the month @ 64–73 Minories, EC3, 07949 477 804

Smack, irregular night @ various venues, check website, www.myspace.com/smackclub

Wish, first Saturdays @ Gramophone, 60–62 Commercial Street, E1 6LT, Style conscious night for young techno-heads and indie girls.

Women's Anarchist Nuisance Cafe, Penultimate wednesdays @ the RampART Creative Centre and Social Space, Rampart St, Aldgate, E1 2LA, Social group and cooperative vegan women's cafe.

Stickier Options

Club Fukk, second Fridays @ Central Station, 37 Wharfdale Road, N1 9SD, 020 7278 3294, www.centralstation.co.uk or www.woteverworld.com/id12.html, Predominantly Lesbian fetish/play club. One of many sex/cruising nights at the venue – check site for details.

Chariots, www.gaysauna.co.uk, Popular chain of gay saunas, with branches at the following locations: *Shoreditch*: 1 Fairchild Street, EC2A 3NS, *Waterloo*: 101 Lower Marsh, SE1 7AB, 020 7401 8484, *Limehouse*: 574 Commercial Road, E14 7JD, 020 7791 2808, *Streatham*: 292 [rear of] Streatham High Road, SW16 6HG, 020 8696 0929, *Farringdon*: 57 Cowcross Street, EC1M 6BX, 020 7251 5553, *Vauxhall*: 63-64 Albert Embankment, SE1, 020 7247 5333

The Fort, 131 Grange Road, Bermondsey, SE1 3AL , Themed cruising/fetish/sex bar.

Hard On, monthly @ Hidden, 100 Tinworth Street, SE11 5EQ, www.hardonclub.co.uk, Rubber and fetish sex club for gay and bisexual men and women.

The Hoist, Arch 47b & 47c, South Lambeth Road, SW8 1RH, 020 7735 9972, www.thehoist.co.uk, Fetish sex club with strict dress codes, check website for details.

Nudity, first Fridays @ Hidden, 100 Tinworth Street, SE11 5EQ, Nude men's dance/play club.

Purrrr, 87 Fortess Road, Kentish Town NW5, www.purrrr.co.uk, Monthly S&M play club for Lesbians.

London Timeline

A timeline of significant events in London's history.

50: The Romans found Londinium, building the first London Bridge.

61: Queen Boudicca burns Londinium down.

100: Londinium becomes the capital of Roman Britain.

200: The Romans build the London Wall.

410: Roman occupation ends and Londinium is largely abandoned for many years.

604: King Aethelbert of Kent completes the first St Paul's Cathedral.

700: The Saxons build Lundenwic a mile to the west of old Londinium.

851: The Vikings burn Lundenwic down (starting to see a pattern, here?)

878: Alfred The Great defeats the Vikings and establishes a new settlement within the Roman Walls.

1013: The Viking King Canute besieges London.

1066: William The Conqueror becomes the first king to be crowned at Westminster Abbey.

1088: William The Conqueror builds the Tower Of London.

1097: William Rufus builds Westminster Hall—later part of the Houses Of Parliament.

1176: The wooden London Bridge is replaced by a stone structure.

1343: 'The Canterbury Tales' author Geoffrey Chaucer is born in London.

1348: The Black Death wipes out between a third and half of London's population in 18 months.

1381: Peasants revolt, storming the Tower Of London.

1599: William Shakespeare's theatre company The Chamberlain's Men build the Globe Theatre.

1605: Guy Fawkes' Gunpowder Plot fails to blow up the Palace Of Westminster.

1635: Hyde Park opens to the public.

1649: King Charles I is beheaded at Whitehall.

1665: The Great Plague kills a fifth of London's population (starting to see another pattern, here?)

1666: The Fire of London destroys 60% of the city, including St Paul's Cathedral, but wipes out the plague. This really must have been a great year.

1708: The new St Paul's Cathedral is completed by Sir Christopher Wren.

1732: Downing Street becomes the home of the Prime Minister.

1750: Westminster Bridge is built.

1814: Lord's Cricket Ground is opened.

1829: Robert Peel establishes the Metropolitan Police force, policemen known as 'Bobbies' or 'Peelers'.

1831: London becomes the world's biggest city.

1834: The Houses Of Parliament are built.

1843: Nelson's Column is completed in Trafalgar Square.

1851: Six million people gawp at newfangled technology and design at The Great Exhibition.

1858: The Great Stink inspires the 19th century's biggest civil engineering project—London's sewerage system.

London Timeline

1863: The first London Underground line is built.

1876: The Albert Memorial to Queen Victoria's husband Prince Albert is completed.

1877: The first Wimbledon Championship takes place. A Brit wins, but only Brit's are playing.

1884: An imaginary line through Greenwich Royal Observatory is internationally accepted as the Prime Meridian. Except by the French.

1887: Arthur Conan Doyle publishes the first Sherlock Holmes story 'A Study In Scarlet.'

1888: Jack The Ripper's first victim, Mary Ann Nichols, is murdered.

1908: London hosts the Olympics for the first time.

1915: German Zeppelin airships launch first air raids on London, ultimately killing over 700 people.

1923: Wembley Stadium is built in 300 days, costing £750,000.

1940: The Blitz begins—German bombs kill over 30,000 Londoners by the end of WW2 and destroy large areas of the city.

1946: Heathrow Airport opens for commercial flights.

1948: The second London Olympics is held.

1951: The Royal Festival Hall is built as part of the Festival Of Britain.

1952: The Great Smog, caused by a combination of fog and coal smoke, kills 4000 people in five days.

1956: The Clean Air Act puts an end to London's smog problems.

1965: The Notting Hill Carnival is established by West London's Caribbean community

1966: England win the FIFA World Cup at Wembley stadium, better still, against Germany.

1969: The Beatles play their last ever gig on the roof of the Apple building.

1976: The Sex Pistols play at the first 'International Punk Festival' at the 100 Club on Oxford Street.

1981: The first London Marathon.

1983: Six people are killed when the IRA bombs Harrods.

1991: London's tallest building, One Canada Square (better known as Canary Wharf), is completed.

2000: Ken Livingstone becomes London's first directly-elected Mayor.

2005: 52 people are killed by four suicide bombers on Underground trains and a bus.

2007: The rebuilt Wembley Stadium is completed after four years, costing £778 million.

2008: Boris Johnson defeats Red Ken in the London Mayoral Election with a promise to re-instate the Routemaster.

2011: Royal Wedding mania.

2012: London's third Olympics held; Danny Boyle adapts NHS as West End spectacular.

2012: Queen Elizabeth II celebrates her Diamond Jubilee with a rainy-day boat show.

2013: Prince George of Cambridge born.

London is an egotist—it just *loves* to talk about itself. As you might expect, there's a vast array of print and online publications, not to mention radio stations, designed to let the city do exactly that. Single-handedly forcing the environmental movement back twenty years are freebie dailies **The Metro** and the more fiscally orientated **City A.M.** Free weeklies to look out for include **Stylist** on Wednesday's for girls, **ShortList** on Thursday's for boys and **Sport** on Friday's for, well, sports enthusiast. The Aussies are pushing **TNT** at tube stations on Monday, but it lacks the wider appeal. A newer addition to the freesheet line-up is the substantial **Evening Standard**, which went free in January 2009, and is the preferred news-roundup du jour of suburbanites and city types alike, if only for the sudoku and quick crossword puzzles. Online, **www.thisislocallondon.co.uk** condenses forty local newspapers into 'one online voice." On the wireless, **Capital Radio** broadcasts an irksome parade of popular hits and frenetic DJs, whilst **Heart** and **Magic** corner the market on lip-trembling power ballads, mid-paced chart rock and wacky quizzes. All of the British Broadcasting Corporation's national radio stations—including the snazzy, young(ish) **Radio 1** and ovaltine-drinkers' choice **Radio 2**—are based in London, as is (surprisingly) **BBC London**, a decent option for weekend sports coverage. Cooler, urban types are more likely to be tuning into **Kiss FM** (dance, hip hop), **Smooth FM** (jazz, soul) or **Choice** (dancehall, roots), while alternative rockers tune their dials anguishedly to **XFM**, and the talkative indulge in unreserved subjectivity over at **LBC**. Of course the undisputed king of alternative London broadcasting is Resonance FM, a 'community run' station. Expect everything from 'Calling All Pensioners' to live psycho-geographic wanders around city's warped dark streets. Un-licensed and illegal pirate radio stations offer a slightly un-hinged ear into the fringes of London's musical society. Twiddle your dials around the extreme ends of the FM spectrum for pirate stalwarts **Rude FM** and **Kool FM**. On the telly-box, the latest news is spoon-fed to you on ITV's **London Tonight** show and delivered in short slots at the end of the BBC and ITV national news programs. For those actually risking going outside, **Time Out** remains the socialite's sacred text.'

Print

The Evening Standard Northcliffe House, 2 Derry Street, W8 5TT, 020 7938 6000, Newly reinstated as a freesheet, it continues to be London's favourite journey home read.

Metro Northcliffe House, 2 Derry Street, W8 5TT, 020 7651 5200, Free underground daily from same stable.

City AM New London Bridge House, 25 London Bridge St, SE1 9SG, 020 7015 1200, Free morning business bulletin for city-goers.

Sport Third Floor, Courtyard Building, 11 Curtain Road, EC2A 3LT, 0207 375 3175 Free sports overview every Friday.

TimeOut London 251-255 Tottenham Court Road, Universal House, W1T 7AB, 0207 813 3000, Listings & reviews across the city. Pretty damned comprehensive.

Literary Review 44 Lexington Street, W1 0LW, 020 7437 9392, Fortnightly publication for the bookish.

London Gazette PO Box 7923, SE1 5ZH, 020 7394 4517, Capital's oldest paper—official journals record of the government.

The London Magazine 32 Addison Grove, W4 1ER, 020 8400 5882, Bi-monthly Arts reviews.

TNT London 14-15 Childs Place, Earls Court, SW5 9RX, 020 7373 3377, Info and opinion for the antipodean set.

Loot 31 John Street, WC1N 2AT, 0871 222 5000, Classifieds: flats, bought/sold and lonely hearts.

The Voice GV Media Group Ltd, Northern & Shell Tower, 6th Floor, 4 Selsdon Way, E14 9GL, 020 7510 0340, African-British national.

Polish Express 603 Cumberland House, 80 Scrubs Lane, NW10 6RF, 020 8964 4488 , News and info for the Polish community.

Live Listings Magazine Keith Villa (House), 102 Mallinson Rd, SW11 1BN, 020 7207 2734 Guide to what's on in multicultural London.

ShortList 6 Emerald Street, London, WC1N 3QA, 020 7242 5873, A Thursday freebie for metrosexuals.

Sport 18 Hatfields, London SE1 8DJ, 020 7959 7800, A free Friday magazine dedicated to, you guessed it, sports.

Stylist 6 Emerald Street, London, WC1N 3QA, 020 7242 5873, London's first free women's glossy. Handed out on Wednesdays.

General Information • **Media**

Public Radio

FM

89.1 BBC Radio Two: Middle-aged music and chat.
91.3 BBC Radio Three: Classical.
93.5 BBC Radio Four: Current affairs, comfort listening.
94.9 BBC London: Chat, sport.
95.8 Capital FM: Capers.
96.9 Choice FM: Hip Hop, R&B.
97.3 LBC: Phone in, chat.
98.8 BBC Radio 1: Pop, rock, more pop.
100.0 Kiss FM: Dance, urban.
100.9 Classic FM: Classical.
102.2 Smooth FM: Jazz, soul.
102.6 Essex FM: Audible in East London.
103.3 London Greek Radio: Um, Greek.
103.5 BBC Essex: Audible out East.
104.4 Resonance FM: Always bizzare, always brilliant.
104.9 Xfm: Alternative, rock.
105.4 Magic: Pop, slush.
105.8 Virgin Radio: Pop, rock.
106.2 Heart: Chart, pop.
106.6 Time: West London only.
107.3 Time: South East London only.

AM

252 Atlantic: Rock.
558 Spectrum International: Multi-ethnic.
648 BBC World Service: Global.
720 BBC Radio Four: Spoken word.
909 BBC Radio Five Live: Sport, phone in.
963 Liberty Radio: 70s, 80s pop.
1035 Ritz: Country.
1089 talkSPORT: Sports phone in.
1152 LBC News: News, weather.
1215 Virgin Radio: Pop, rock.
1305 Premier Radio: Christian.
1458 Sunrise: Asian.
1548 Capital Gold: Rock 'gold', sport.
1584 London Turkish Radio: Turkish community.

Essential London Books

The Diary of Samuel Pepys (1825): Samuel Pepys: eyewitness accounts of the Restoration, Great Plague and Fire of London from noted sixteenth century scribbler.

Oliver Twist; Hard Times; Great Expectations (1837, 1854, 1860): Charles Dickens: any Dickens novel paints Victorian London at its most exacting.

The Strange Case of Dr. Jekyll and Mr. Hyde (1886): Robert Louis Stevenson: the book that enthralled a city unnerved by Jack the Ripper.

The Adventures of Sherlock Holmes; The Hound of the Baskervilles (1892): Arthur Conan Doyle: classic whodunits featuring Holmes and Watson.

The Inimitable Jeeves (1923): P.G. Wodehouse: prewar upper-class tomfoolery in London Town.

Mrs Dalloway (1925): Virginia Woolf If you know London, you can follow Clarissa Dalloway every step of the way – in real time.

Londinium: London in the Roman Empire, John Morris (1982): London's rise from a Roman outpost into a debauched medieval mecca.

V For Vendetta (1982-1989): Alan Moore, The world's greatest comic writer blows up London in a fit of Anarchist fantasies.

London Fields (1989): Martin Amis: post-modern jaunt through London at the end of the millennium.

London – The Biography, and **Illustrated London** (2000): Peter Ackroyd: definitive, eight hundred page mother lode of remarkable city history, and lavish pictorial version.

London's Disused Underground Stations (2001): JE Connor: documenting forgotten, ghostly tube stations beneath the pavements.

London Orbital and Hackney That Rose Red Empire (2002): Iain Sinclair: London's premier scribe continues to fill our brains with joy despite being ripped off by devotee Peter Ackroyd.

The Clerkenwell Tales (2003): Peter Ackroyd: corking murder mystery set in the time of Chaucer.

Brick Lane (2003): Monica Ali: award winning coming-of-age tale centred on Brick Lane's Muslim community.

Art Deco London (2003): Colin Michael Hines: Wistful but enjoyable stroll around London's Art Deco heritage.

Intimate Adventures of a London Call Girl (2005): Belle de Jour: steamy, real-life shenanigans ahoy.

From Here to Here (2005): Simmons, Taylor, Lynham, Rich: 31 top notch short stories about Circle Line destinations, includes Simon Armitage.

Secret London: Exploring the Hidden City, with Original Walks and Unusual Places to Visit (2006): Andrew Duncan: an explorer's dream.

The London Bombings: An Independent Inquiry (2006): Nafeez Mosaddeq Ahmed: balanced, subtle overview of 2005 Underground bombings.

Around London with Kids – 68 Great Things to See and Do (3rd edition; 2006): Eugene Fodor: should keep the little rascals from breaking into cars.

I Never Knew That About London (2007): Christopher Winn: Well, did you?

The London Encyclopaedia (2008): Ben Weinreb and Christopher Hibbert: London's history and culture documented in minutest detail

Derelict London (2008): Paul Talling: The urban explorers' bible!

Essential London Songs

Lambeth Walk, Noel Gay/Douglas Furber (1937): All together! Doing the Lambeth Walk! Oi!

A Nightingale Sang in Berkeley Square, Judy Campbell (1940): Wartime cheer made famous by Vera Lynn.

London Pride, Sir Noel Coward (1941): Written during the Blitz, this sentimental ballad gave comfort to Londoners being bombed nightly.

Maybe It's Because I'm a Londoner, Hubert Gregg (1944): Pearly Queen favourite crammed with WWII spirit.

A Foggy Day (In London Town), Ella Fitzgerald (1956): Definitive recording of Gershwin classic.

Waterloo Sunset, The Kinks (1967): Timeless paean to the nation's capital.

Consider Yourself, Lionel Bart (1968): Oliver Twist hoodwinked into a life of crime by the Artful Dodger, the rascal.

Primrose Hill, John and Beverly Martyn (1970). Folk rock's second couple never had to deal with Katie Frost and Kate Moss when they were watching the sun set, did they?

Streets Of London, Ralph McTell (1974). Cool folk dude destroys credibility forever with international monster hit.

Baker Street, Gerry Rafferty (1978): Feel that sax line, air that guitar.

London Calling, The Clash (1979): Joe Strummer paints an apocalyptic vision of a city in post-punk transition.

Electric Avenue, Eddy Grant (1983): Roots-rock champion name checks 80s Brixton scene.

London, The Smiths (1983): Morrissey lugubriously debates a trip south. Miserable dude.

West End Girls, Pet Shop Boys (1986): East London working class meets West London affluence in electro-pop classic.

Pump Up London, Mr. Lee (1988). Squelchy Chicago House dude makes London sound amazing whilst name checking every British town he can think of: Leeds! Manchester! Scatland!

Parklife, Blur (1994): Home counties-boys get cockney makeover while eyeing London's jogging scene.

Sunny Goodge Street, Donovan (2002). Folk crooner sings of a hippy London goneby.

The London Underground Song, Amateur Transplants (2005): Sweary, infectiously catchy and a comical ballad to the tube, rings painfully true.

Sheila, Jamie T (2006): Mr. T delivers an excellent poetic diatribe on what being young and hopeless in London is like.

Hometown Glory, Adele (2007): This song will make you fall in love with the city all over again.

Essential London Films

The 39 Steps (1935): Hitchcock adaptation of John Buchan novel.

Pygmalion (1938): Leslie Howard as Henry Higgins and Wendy Hiller as Eliza Doolittle prove Shaw's classic comedy does very well without music.

Great Expectations (1946): Rare Richard Attenborough acting outing in classic Dickens adaptation.

The Ladykillers (1955): Superb black comedy from the Ealing canon, with pre-Obi Wan Alec Guinness.

One Hundred and One Dalmations (1961): Innocent pelt-seeker tortured by 101 belligerent pups. For shame.

Mary Poppins (1964): Notable for Dick Van Dyke's confounding, lanky turn as cockney chimney sweep.

A Hard Day's Night (1964): Classic, swinging 60s' comedy from the Fab Four.

Alfie (1966): Caine in much-lauded role as audience-addressing lothario.

Carry On Doctor (1967): Critically-panned, guilty-pleasure raunchfest from Pinewood Studios.

The London Nobody Knows (1967): The greatest film about London ever. Period.

Oliver! (1968): Sprightly musical adaptation of Dickens classic.

A Clockwork Orange (1971) Kubrick's dystopian masterpiece was set in Thamesmead, which is still, "Feeling a bit shagged and fagged and fashed."

The Elephant Man (1980): John Merrick 'accepted' by London's polite Victorian-era society in David Lynch masterpiece.

An American Werewolf in London (1981): US student attacked on moors; gets haunted; romps with Jenny Agutter; becomes werewolf; slaughters innocents; is shot in alley; credits roll.

My Beautiful Launderette (1985): Hanif Kureishi's controversial depiction of cross-culture, same-gender love in the Thatcher-era.

Muppet Christmas Carol (1992): That Michael Caine, he sure can act. But he sure can't sing.

London (1994): Patrick Kellier's abstract ramble through 'the most unsociable and reactionary of cities.'

Lock, Stock and Two Smoking Barrels (1998): East End crime capers from Madonna's (not from the East End) husband.

Notting Hill (1999): Hugh Grant as mumbling, bumbling, lovesick fop.

Bridget Jones's Diary (2001): Rene Zellweger goes Sloane in adaptation of Helen Fielding novel.

28 Days Later (2002): Us Londoners finally erupt in pandemic rage at how slow tourists are on the tube.

Love Actually (2003): Expansive Richard Curtis romcom with Grant in slightly-less mumbly, slightly-more bumbly form

Shaun of the Dead (2003): Fighting off zombies at the local pub. Hilarious.

The Kings Speech (2010): A stuttering King finds his voice and wins a few Academy Awards for his efforts.

There can't be anything worse than the inconvenience of trying to find a convenience when nature takes an unexpected hold of your nether regions; you may choose to follow the lead of many a Saturday evening reveller and use a public doorway, but is it really worth the £80 fine that will be levied if caught in the act (and let's face it, it's hard to conceal the evidence)?

Unfortunately, London has seen a recent decline in the provision of public toilet facilities, as local councils seem to have decided that they are under no obligation to provide such a service; you'll also be hard pushed to find a toilet attendant manning a lavatory these days, and the dubious goings-on in some loos may not be quite what you had in mind, unless your name has a "Michael" in it. Most surviving public toilets seem also to emit their own particular aroma of…well, you don't really have to use your imagination. But don't get down in the dumps!

The most obvious place to go to when in need is McDonald's. Despite what some may say about their food, their outlets are the place to go when caught short and not wishing to pay to pee. Usually maintained and cleaned throughout opening hours, they can also be used inconspicuously and without purchasing anything; and let's face it, you can't move without the glow of those golden arches following you across London. It's also a safe bet to visit Starbucks, Caffe Nero and Costa Coffee bars, although they often have a policy of access to toilets by key only, which can be a bit of a bummer (groan).

It may seem like a good idea to visit pubs or bars solely for their toilets, but you might find yourself being hauled out by an irked landlord mid-act. Furthermore, don't expect luxury; pub toilets are usually fairly scummy and often not furnished with toilet paper. It's also unlikely to find a men's cubicle that will have a working lock in it; do you really wish to have an unwanted visitor whilst on the throne? Exceptions are the Wetherspoon's chain, which prides itself on having toilets cleaned on the hour, and the nicest of gastro pubs, which can offer commodious and clean facilities (at least during the day). Otherwise, if desperate, at least go for a pub or bar that's busy.

Also bear in mind that if you find yourself in need in the City of Westminster, you can use a toilet text service from your mobile phone! Known as SatLav, texting the word 'Toilet' to 80097 will result in a message being sent to your phone informing you of the nearest public convenience. It may prove to be the most relieving 25p you'll ever spend in London…

A good and extensive list of London public toilets can be found at www.lastrounds.co.uk/public_toilets.html.

If none of the afore-mentioned places are available, there are other options:

Other street public toilets—yes, those bizarre futuristic looking structures on some of London's central streets are toilets. Known as sanisettes or "superloos", there is a charge to use them and once in, you've got 15 minutes before the door automatically opens (don't get extended stage-fright). They're self-cleaning, which usually means that they're in a right state, and are also quite popular with junkies and prostitutes, so best saved for when extremely desperate.

There are also a few pop up toilettes which, although intended for the right use, unfortunately stink like hell and fortunately return back there during the day. These are only suitable for (drunk) men and rise to the challenge of channelling away an evening's excesses from 7pm to 6am. Located at notorious 'wet spots' in the West End, they are linked to the main sewerage system; taking the piss, indeed…

Stations—including almost all large railway stations and a few central London tube stations. There will usually be a cost for these facilities though (around 30p).

Department Stores—All the large ones, including John Lewis, Selfridges, Debenhams and Harrods. Smaller shops rarely have toilets for public use.

Supermarkets—many larger branches of Sainsbury's and Marks & Spencer.

Museums—the majority of London's large museums and galleries are free to enter (erm, and have toilets).

Libraries—most libraries will have an area of salvation for the needy.

Universities and Colleges—and you get to pass yourself off as a student or lecturer (in need of the loo).

Hospitals—you can also drop in on that relative that you always meant to visit, or maybe leave a stool sample; just try not to leave with a superbug.

Parks—not on the grass, please.

Hotels—larger hotels shouldn't pose a problem.

London has some of the finest hospitals in the world attracting top-notch specialists who carry-out state-of-the-art procedures—the trick is, getting in to see one of them. An appointment at a specific hospital, or with a specialist, requires a referral from your GP and plenty of patience. In an emergency go to your nearest A&E—bring a book and some earplugs. On the weekends after eleven, waiting times for non-urgent problems can be measured in aeons, but rest assured, if something is seriously wrong you'll be seen very quickly—lucky ol' you. For non serious injuries or illnesses, find your nearest Minor Injuries Unit or

Walk-in Centre on www.nhs.uk. You'll spend less time hanging around and free up A&E for critical cases and over-cidered teens needing stomach pumps. The ever-friendly 24 hr NHS Direct 0845 4647 is also always available for advice.

If you have the money, numerous private sector hospitals and clinics are available to cure what ails you, or to pander to your hypochondriacal needs. You won't necessarily get better treatment, but there'll be less waiting, more pampering and more grapes by your bedside. For information, start at www.privatehealth.co.uk.

A & E	Address	Phone	Map
Charing Cross Hospital	Fulham Palace Rd & St Dunstan's Rd	020 3311 1234	41
Chelsea and Westminster Hospital	369 Fulham Rd	020 8746 8000	43
Homerton University Hospital	Homerton Row	020 8510 5555	90
King's College Hospital	Denmark Hill & Champion Park	020 3299 9000	128
Moorfields Eye Hospital	162 City Rd	020 7253 3411	84
Royal Free Hospital	Pond St & Fleet Rd	020 7794 0500	57
Royal London Hospital	Whitechapel Rd & Vallance Rd	020 7377 7000	96
St Mary's Hospital	Praed St & Winsland St	020 3312 6666	31
St Thomas' Hospital	Westminster Bridge Rd & Lambeth Palace Rd	020 7188 7188	131
University College Hospital	235 Euston Rd	0845 155 5000	4
Western Eye Hospital	173 Marylebone Rd	020 7886 6666	2
Whittington Hospital	Magdala Ave	020 7272 3070	59

Other Hospitals	Address	Phone	Map
Bupa Cromwell Hospital	162 Cromwell Rd	020 7460 2000	35
Capio Nightingale Hospital	11 Lisson Grove	020 7535 7700	76
Charing Cross Hospital	Fulham Palace Rd & St Dunstan's Rd	020 3311 1234	41
Chelsea and Westminster Hospital	369 Fulham Rd	020 8746 8000	43
City Medical	17 St Helen's Pl	0845 123 5380	17
Dove Clinic	19 Wimpole St	020 7580 8886	2
Eastman Dental Hospital	256 Gray's Inn Rd	020 7915 1000	5
Elizabeth Garrett Anderson Hospital	Huntley St	0845 155 5000	4
Fitzroy Square Hospital	14 Fitzroy Sq	020 7388 4954	3
Gordon Hospital	Bloomburg St & Vauxhall Bridge Rd	020 8746 8733	21
Great Ormond St Children's Hospital	34 Great Ormond St	020 7405 9200	5
Guy's Hospital	Great Maze Pond & St Thomas St	020 7188 7188	106
Heart Hospital	16 Westmoreland St	020 7573 8888	2
Highgate Private Hospital	17 View Rd	020 8341 4182	51
Homerton University Hospital	Homerton Row	020 8510 5555	90

Other Hospitals	Address	Phone	Map
Hospital For Tropical Diseases	Martimer Market & Capper St	0845 155 5000	4
Hospital of St John and St Elizabeth	60 Grove End Rd	020 7806 4000	68
King Edward VII Hospital For Officers	5 Beaumont St	020 7486 4411	2
King's College Hospital	Denmark Hill & Champion Park	020 3299 9000	128
Lambeth Hospital	108 Landor Rd	020 3228 6000	144
Lister Hospital	Chelsea Bridge Rd	020 7730 7733	20
London Bridge Hospital	27 Tooley St	020 7407 3100	106
London Chest Hospital	Bonner Rd & Approach Rd	020 7377 7000	93
London Independent Hospital	1 Beaumont Sq	020 7780 2400	97
London Welbeck Hospital	25 Welbeck St	020 7224 2242	2
Marylebone Consulting Rooms	10 Bulstrode Pl	020 8872 3838	2
Maudsley Hospital	Denmark Hill & Champion Park	020 3228 6000	104
Mile End Hospital	Bancroft Rd & Alderney Rd	020 7377 7000	93
Moorfields Eye Hospital	162 City Rd	020 7253 3411	84
National Hospital for Neorology and Neurosciences	Queen Sq & Great Ormond St	0845 155 5000	5
Portland Hospital For women and Children	209 Great Portland St	020 7580 4400	3
Princess Grace Hospital	42 Nottingham Pl	020 7486 1234	2
The Rosenheim Building	25 Grafton Way	0845 155 5000	4
Royal Brompton Hospital	Sydney St & Cale St	020 7352 8121	45
Royal Free Hospital	Pond St & Fleet Rd	020 7794 0500	57
Royal London Homeopathic Hospital	60 Great Ormond St	020 7391 8888	5
Royal London Hospital	Whitechapel Rd & Vallance Rd	020 7377 7000	96
Royal Marsden Hospital	Fulham Rd & Sydney Close	020 7352 8171	45
Royal National Orthopaedic Hospital	51 Bolsover St	020 8954 2300	3
Royal National Throat, Nose and Ear Hospital	330 Gray's Inn Rd	020 7915 1300	5
St Bartholomew's	West Smithfield & Hosier Ln	020 7377 7000	15
St George's at St John's Therapy Center	162 St John's Hill	020 8812 5385	139
St Mary's Hospital	Praed St & Winsland St	020 3312 6666	31
St Pancras Hospital	4 St Pancras Way	020 7530 3500	78
St Thomas' Hospital	Westminster Bridge Rd & Lambeth Palace Rd	020 7188 7188	131
University College Hospital	235 Euston Rd	0845 155 5000	4
Wellington Hospital	8 Wellington Pl	020 7586 5959	76
Western Eye Hospital	173 Marylebone Rd	020 3312 6666	2
Whittington Hospital	Magdala Ave & Dartmouth Park Hill	020 7272 3070	59

Overview

Librarians love nothing more than a warm cardigan and a complex cataloguing system, nevertheless, they've done themselves proud with London's libraries. London boasts an enormous, if somewhat eccentric and confusing, network of over 360 libraries. In 2009 the Chief Librarians initiative passed and 3,000 libraries in England, Wales and Northern Ireland can now be easily accessed and used for all library services including checking out books, as long as you have an existing library card and proof of address. This excludes the elite British institutions (see below) and all books must be returned to a library in the same area.

London's libraries vary enormously in subject, range and facilities, with some accessible for free, some for a fee, some with an appointment and some only if you are very very nice and give the curator a chocolate digestive. But the treat of such a large network, apart from the world-class breadth, depth and quality of collections, is that many of the libraries have a unique personality to make them a treasured part of London. For example, £10 will get you a day's membership to the **London Library (Map 23)**, an atmospheric labyrinth where you can browse alongside ghosts of past members including Dickens, Tennyson and Darwin, and feel several IQ points higher than before you went in. In Tower Hamlets, libraries are now **"Ideas Stores" (Map 92, 101, 96)**, because Tower Hamlets is, like, cool. In addition to the books, magazines, music and internet facilities which are available at most public libraries, these superb spaces also offer activities such as free PopLaw legal advice clinics, homework clubs and jazz classes. The borough has built four of these wonders; find them in Bow, Whitechapel, Canary Wharf and on East India Dock Road. London linguists are spoiled with the excellent **French Institute (Map 36)**, **Instituto Cervantes (Map 19)** and the **Goethe Institut (Map 37)**, while more cunning linguists may prefer the eye-opening gynaecological collection among the 2.5 million medical-related works in the **Wellcome Library (Map 4)**. Poets should meander their way to the **Saison Poetry Library (Map 104)**, ensconced within the South Bank Centre, for a little inspiration. Artists will enjoy the **National Art Library (Map 36)**, which nestles within the V&A Museum. You can use many of London's academic and specialist libraries through the Inspire London scheme, which grants one-day reference access to collections throughout London; ask your local library to refer you.

However, the Daddy of them all is the **British Library (Map 78)**. This behemoth receives a copy of every publication printed in the UK and Ireland, and requires 625km of shelving space to accommodate its 150million items. But it's just such a tease. You cannot borrow books, and to even access the collections you need to obtain a Reader Pass, via an introductory discussion to establish why you need it and whether you're likely to doodle on the books. This requires two forms of ID, no compromise: refer to www.bl.uk for the latest guidelines. Once you have your pass you can access the Reading Rooms, albeit with your personal belongings in a clear plastic bag (or stored in a locker). But if you just fancy seeing the Magna Carta, Shakespeare in Quarto or some Beatles manuscripts, you can access the book-free visitor areas without appointment and still gain an impressive look at one of the world's greatest information resources.

General Information

Important phone numbers:
All emergencies: 999
Non-emergencies: 101
Anti-terrorism hotline: 0800 789 321
Crime Stoppers: 0800 555 111
Neighbourhood Watch: 020 79934709
Missing Persons: 0500 700 700
Complaints: 08453 002 002

Websites:
www.met.police.uk
www.cityoflondon.police.uk (Separate police force specifically covering the Square Mile).
www.btp.police.uk (Separate police force specifically covering public transport).

Statistics* (Greater London)

	2008/09	2009/10	2010/2011
Murder	146	113	124
Rapes	2,177	2,839	3279
GBH	11,212	10,525	8374
Burglary (res)	59,176	60,909	60803

* all sourced from the MPS Crime Website http://content.met.police.uk

Police Stations

	Address	Phone	Map
Albany Street Police Station	60 Albany St	030 0123 1212	77
Battersea Police Station	112 Battersea Bridge	030 0123 1212	132
Belgravia Police Station	202 Buckingham Palace Rd	030 0123 1212	20
Bethnal Green Police Station	Cambridge Heath Rd & Roman Rd	030 0123 1212	92
Bow Road Police Station	111 Bow Rd	030 0123 1212	94
Brick Lane Police Station	25 Brick Ln	030 0123 1212	91
Brixton Police Station	367 Brixton Rd	030 0123 1212	144
Camberwell Police Station	22 Camberwell Church St	030 0123 1212	122
Cavendish Road Police Station	47 Cavendish Parade	030 0123 1212	149
Charing Cross Police Station	Agar St & Strand	030 0123 1212	24
Chelsea Police Station	2 Lucan Pl	030 0123 1212	46
Chiswick Police Station	209 Chiswick High Rd	030 0123 1212	38
Clapham Police Station	51 Union Grove	030 0123 1212	51
Deptford Police Station	114 Amersham Vale	020 8297 1212	126
East Dulwich Police Station	173 Lordship Ln	030 0123 1212	129
Fulham Police Station	Fulham Rd & Heckfield Pl	030 0123 1212	42
Greenwich Police Station	31 Royal Hill	030 0123 1212	120
Hackney Police Station	2 Lower Clapton Rd	030 0123 1212	87
Hammersmith Police Station	226 Shepards Bush Rd	030 0123 1212	33
Hampstead Police Station	26 Rosslyn Hill	030 0123 1212	56
Harrow Road Police Station	325 Harrow Rd	030 0123 1212	26
Holborn Police Station	10 Lamb's Conduit St	030 0123 1212	5
Holloway Police Station	284 Hornsey Rd	030 0123 1212	61
Hornsey Police Station	98 Tottenham Ln	030 0123 1212	54
Isle of Dogs Police Station	165 Manchester Rd	030 0123 1212	103
Islington Police Station	2 Tolpuddle St	030 0123 1212	80
Kennington Police Station	49 Kennington Rd	030 0123 1212	104
Kensington Police Station	72 Earl's Court Rd	030 0123 1212	35
Kentish Town Police	12 Holmes Rd	030 0123 1212	72
Lavender Hill Police Station	176 Lavender Hill	030 0123 1212	140
Limehouse Police Station	29 West India Dock Rd	030 0123 1212	100
Marylebone Police Station	1 Seymour St	030 0123 1212	1
Notting Hill Police Station	100 Ladbroke Grove	030 0123 1212	28
Paddington Green Police Station	2 Harrow Rd	030 0123 1212	31
Peckham Police Station	177 Peckham High St	030 0123 1212	123
Rotherhithe Police Station	99 Lower Rd	020 7378 1212	110
Shoreditch Police Station	4 Shepherdess Walk	030 0123 1212	83
Southwark Police Station	323 Borough High St	030 0123 1212	106
St John's Wood Police Station	20 Newcourt St	030 0123 1212	69
Stoke Newington Police Station	33 Stoke Newington High St	030 0123 1212	64
Tooting Police Station	251 Mitcham Rd	030 0123 1212	152
Walworth Police Station	12 Manor Pl	030 0123 1212	113
Wandsworth Police Station	146 Wandsworth High St	030 0123 1212	138
West End Central Police Station	27 Savile Row	030 0123 1212	10

Overview

London hotels can be sources of hopelessly romantic creativity. In 1899 Claude Monet painted the Houses of Parliament from his balcony at the Savoy hotel. About 100 years later, Fay Weldon moved in with her typewriter as writer in residence. If you've got visitors in town, fancy giving Claude a run for his money, or just can't face going back to your dump of a flat, you'll need the services of a hotel. When choosing your hotel, think carefully about what kind of London you're looking to experience and whom the room is for. We've identified a few of the usual suspects for whom you may find yourself booking a hotel room, and heartily offer you our best suggestions for each. Just don't expect to emerge from any of them clutching a masterpiece penned overnight.

Only the Best, Daah-ling

So you need to find a hotel for a VIP client who will accept nothing but the best. Where to start? Since you don't have to cover the bill yourself, here is where you can really dig into London hospitality at its most deluxe. Start by trying to book **The Ritz (Map 9)**, with its amazing views of Green Park, Rococo detailing and killer high tea. **Brown's (Map 9)** is a stunning five-star and was the first hotel in London to have a lift. There is also the **Dorchester (Map 9)**, and its neighbour the **Hilton Park Lane (Map 9)**, where you may see a celebrity stumbling back to their quarters at four in the morning, if you're very, very lucky. **The Landmark (Map 76)** is a wonderfully Victorian retreat in the centre of ritzy Marylebone and has a rather fine atrium. But the granddaddy of luxury London must be the **Savoy (Map 24)**. This elegant old-timer stunk of old money until its temporary closure in 2007 for a £100 million spruce-up. It was built on the location of the Savoy Palace, which burned down during the Peasants' Revolt in 1381. We say let them eat cake (and tea).

A Dirty Weekend

This can be any weekend where a Londoner decides booze-goggled sex and/or quick-to-bed access after a night of clubbing is worthy of dishing out the dosh on an über-chic central hotel. It's one (giant) step up from splurging on a taxi and is the realm of the London boutique hotel where location is everything. **Hazlitt's (Map 12)** is right in the middle of Soho yet still wonderfully intimate. **Andaz Hotel (Map 8) (formerly Great Eastern Hotel)** is in the heart of the City, with funky Shoreditch on its doorstep, whilst the 'modern English' style of the **Charlotte Street Hotel (Map 3)** is painfully hip and sophisticated.

The Tea-and-Crumpet Tourist

Then there's the hotel for your sweetly naïve cousin that sees London through rose-tinted Ray Bans: full of scones, Mary Poppins and the chimes of Big Ben. You wouldn't want to burst her cute little bubble, would you? Not to worry, there are plenty of hotels to satisfy the Harrods tourist. **San Domenico House London (Map 46)** is a Chelsea boutique hotel that is about as warm and cuddly as a cup of sugary tea. **The Rookery (Map 15)**, built amongst a row of once derelict Georgian townhouses in Clerkenwell, is cluttered with museum-worthy furniture, open fires and ye oldey worldey frippery. Or, if she can't bear to be too far away from Buckingham Palace, there's the nearby **Windermere (Map 20)**.

Parents in Town?

If your parents have spent their nest egg on bailing you out of your London-induced debt, they will probably want to get the most out of London for the least money possible. But if the hotel you pick for their stay is anything short of perfect, you'll never hear the end of it. If they have loyalty cards with any of the bigger hotel chains, now is a good time to use them. **The London Bridge Hotel (Map 22)** is an independent four-star that usually has good deals and is conveniently close to Borough Market and London Bridge station. Gower Street has a wealth of small family-run hotels at reasonable prices, including the **Cavendish (Map 23)**, within stumbling distance of the British Museum. There's also the nearby **Crescent Hotel (Map 4)**, next to Russell Square. If you miss home cooking, get your 'rents a serviced apartment with a kitchenette. Marlin Apartments and Think London have a few different properties, often ripe for the celeb sighting as pop stars are known to hitch up their wagons there during drawn-out tours.

In Lieu of a Couch to Crash On

Then you get your university friend still in strong denial of the real world, who refuses to get a real job. The amount of times this sponger has crashed on your sofa has been enough to send your might-be-the-one girl/boyfriend packing. Instead of blaming him/her for your future life of loneliness, banish them from the flat and call in the services of one of London's cheapies. They do exist; you just have to look hard. The **Hoxton Hotel (Map 84)**, an urban cheap boutique founded by the owner of Pret a Manger, is famous for its £1 hotel room sales. Cheap but cheerful chain Premier Inn (multiple locations) boasts rooms from £29 a night. Sometimes short-term rental companies, like **Airbnb** (www.airbnb.com), offer shared facility flats at very cheap prices. This is perfect if a guest is wishing to stay for a week or more. Airbnb has over 9,000 listings in London, which start as low as £10 a night. This can be a necessary and friendly alternative to endless weeks of friends imposing on your hospitality.

Where to Stick Your Best Friend From School
(And Her Husband, Two Perfect Kids and a Dog)

Unfortunately, for some people visiting London, a dodgy guesthouse isn't going to cut it. You want to show them how your city can be just as perfect as their countryside home and how not jealous you are of them! Of course, they don't see the point in paying tons either. This is where the few and far between bed and breakfasts come out of the woodwork. Most of these are small, so book in advance. London's best is the warm and welcoming **Bay Tree House and Annex B&B (Out of coverage)**. Great for families or singletons alike, it's in New Southgate (about 25 minutes by tube from central London) but can be a relaxing retreat. **Barclay House (Map 43)** is a hidden gem in Fulham Broadway (make sure you write down the address as it's not signposted and can blend in). **Aster House (Map 45)** is a bit pricier but close enough to posh High Street Kensington to give a glimpse of how the other half live.

With all these hotels, compare prices online, ask for their best rate and/or call for last minute deals, you may be surprised at the reductions available. Good offers mean you can pay less than you'd think for the best, and London does really have the best.

As you might expect from a site constantly inhabited since the Roman invasion of Britain, and probably before, London has managed to assemble a vast array of good, bad and ugly landmarks. The city is, in fact, stuffed with them, and the following is a slightly subjective rumination on a small proportion of some of the most noteworthy.

Historical

London gracefully bears a massive weight of history, and many of its landmarks reflect this. One of the oldest is the remains of the **Temple of Mithras (Map 16)** on Walbrook, built by the Romans when London was Londinium. Parts of the **London Wall (Map 18)**, also originally built by the Romans, still exist, the best fragments are around Tower Hill station. In Medieval times London became a bustling place; celebrate one of its most beautiful churches by visiting the oddly named **St Giles' Cripplegate (Map 7)**, which is ensconced within the brutal **Barbican Centre (Map 7)**, a landmark itself. By the 1600s, London was bustling so hard it got the plague and then some idiot burnt the entire city down in 1666. Celebrate three days of the Great Fire by climbing to the top of the 202 feet high **Monument (Map 18)**, before visiting post-fire architect Christopher Wren's masterpiece, **St Paul's Cathedral (Map 16)**. Into the 18th century, things became a little more sophisticated and some of London's prettiest domestic architecture bloomed. Stroll down Bloomsbury's **Doughty Street (Map 5)**, stopping at Charles Dickens' House, for perfectly proportioned Georgian elegance. The Victorians had a huge impact on London, with whole tracts of the city bearing the stamp of the starched times of chimney sweeps and empire bashing. For the lighter side of Victorian London, poke about the museums quarter from the **Victoria & Albert Museum (Map 37)** up to the **Albert Memorial (Map 36)**. For the darker, dodge the elderly at the **St Pancras Hospital (Map 78)**, an ex-workhouse.

Tourist Bait

London has a host of over-exposed landmarks that are honey to the swarms of tourist worker-bees but over-rated in the eyes of many Londoners. We don't necessarily share this view, but if you want to venture beyond the crowds at **Big Ben (Map 22)**, try some of the following. The aforementioned **St Paul's Cathedral (Map 16)** is an absolute wonder, although try the smaller **Southwark Cathedral (Map 106)** for a more intimate option. **The British Museum (Map 4)** is a beauty made fairer by its recent courtyard renovation; peruse the library to see where Marx pondered upon 'Das Kapital'. **The Burlington Arcade (Map 10)** is how shopping should be. The crypt under **St Mary-le-Bow Church (Map 16)** is 11th century weirdness complete with its own vegetarian restaurant. The Thames is long enough to provide you with your own spot of riverside tranquillity. If you're scared of bridges, burrow under the river at the **Greenwich Foot Tunnel (Map 120)**, or chug across it on the free Woolwich Ferry. For a weekend mooch, try the **Grand Regent's Canal (Map 71)**.

Modern Landmarks

The 20th century blessed the city with some opinion splitting contributions. **The Hayward Gallery (Map 104)** and **National Theatre (Map 104)** are both concrete frighteners which we are learning to love. Despite originally housing a power station, **Tate Modern (Map 105)** has been more graciously received. Meanwhile, further down the river, long abandoned **Battersea Power Station (Map 133)** will be undergoing major developments in 2013 and will be replaced by some form of flashy money-without-substance monstrosity. The **BT Tower (Map 3)** is like a 1960s lighthouse for central London drunks. **The Lloyds Building (Map 18)** and **Tower 42 (Map 18)** are both absorbing odes to the banker and glare menacingly at new rival **One Canada Square (or Canary Wharf Tower) (Map 100)**. A more recent contribution to the city is the **Canary Wharf Underground Station (Map 100)**. Until at least 2014 the 150-year squabble over what to put in **Trafalgar Square's (Map 24)** fourth and only empty plinth rages on. Expect modern, classic and performance art in this space for the time being, at least, until they add a statue of Britain's future supreme commander Rupert Murdoch strangling Lady Justice in 2014.

Lowbrow

In these clean times of starchitects, steel and glass, a few minutes spent gawping at **Elephant and Castle (Map 105)** shopping centre is enough to remind anyone how awry a landmark can go. Even a quick squizz at the nearby **Faraday Memorial (Map 105)** may not lift your gloom, largely as it now forms the body of a clogged roundabout. However, London can do lowbrow with the best of them, starting with the **Westway Flyover (Map 31)**: a noisy, dusty shard of concrete to remind you that the car is still king. The disused **Kingsway Tram Tunnel (Map 4)** is a forgotten piece of prime underground real estate and **Centre Point (Map 4)** and **Millbank Tower (Map 21)** are good examples of dodgy skyscrapers that no-one needed. **Battersea Park Gasometers (Map 133)** are imposing monsters, whereas **Lots Road Power Station (Map 50)** is fast becoming London's trendiest disused power station. If you must jump upon band wagons, keep your eyes peeled around east London for art left on walls by Banksy. Mobile lowbrow starts with a trip on a Routemaster, despite the buses being withdrawn in 2005, two heritage routes are still running. Lowbrow (along with logic, aesthetic quality and planning) finishes with **Euston Station (Map 78)**, which is, simply, disgusting.

General Information · **Landmarks**

Map 1 · Marylebone (West)

Marble Arch	Oxford St & Park Ln	Randomly plonked gateway to nowhere.
Speakers' Corner	Cumberland Gate & Park Ln	It's easy—stand on the corner and listen to the 'speeches.'

Map 2 · Marylebone (East)

Hertford House	Manchester Sq & Hinde St	Terribly twee home of the Wallace Collection.
Jimi Hendrix Memorial Blue Plaque	23 Brook St	Jimi lived here. Some bloke called Handel lived next door.

Map 3 · Fitzrovia

BT Tower	60 Cleveland St	A 574 foot tall official government secret until 1993.
Charlotte Street	Charlotte St	Restaurant strip for the advertising in-crowd.
Middlesex Hospital	Mortimer St & Cleveland St	Closed-down and spooky-looking.
Pollock's Toy Museum	1 Scala St	Brimming with delightful, traditional toys and Dickensian atmosphere.
Sinner Winner Man	216 Oxford St	Are you a sinner? Or a winner? London's top preacher's patch.
Tottenham Court Road	Tottenham Ct Rd	Buy your electronics 'ere, innit?

Map 4 · Bloomsbury (West)

The British Museum	Great Russell St & Museum St	Newly-covered Great Court is architectural manna.
Centre Point	101 New Oxford St	Ugly skyscraper looking kinda out of place.
Kingsway Tram Tunnel	Theobalds Rd & Southampton Row	Spooky remnant of London's defunct Tram network.
SOAS	Thornhaugh St	University focused on Africa, Asia and the Middle East.
Senate House	Malet St & Torrington Sq	Ominous art deco building; Orwell's Ministry of Truth.
Student Central	Malet St	University of London's giant students' union.
Tavistock Square	Tavistock Sq	Has a statue of Gandhi looking as cool as ever.
University College London	Gower St	London's "Global University," upholding progressive ideals since 1826.

Map 5 · Bloomsbury (East)

The Dickens House Museum	48 Doughty St	Unassuming from the outside, mecca for Dickens' fans on the inside.
Doughty Street	Doughty St & Guilford St	Exquisite Georgian street in heart of literary land.
Gray's Inn Field	Theobald's Rd	Holborn Hideaway.

Map 7 · Barbican / City Road (South)

Barbican Centre	Silk St & Whitecross St	An architectural eyesore. Bloody good events though.
Bunhill Fields	38 City Rd	120 thousand dead people, including William Blake. All buried, luckily.
Church of Saint Bartholomew the Great	6 Kinghorn St	Stroll in for your daily dose of frankincense and choir song.
LSO St Luke's	161 Old St	Home to the London Symphony Orchestra. Peaceful gardens for relaxation.
St. Giles-without-Cripplegate	Fore St & Wood St	Medieval church which defied the Blitz. Catch an organ recital.

Map 8 · Liverpool Street / Broadgate

Fulcrum at Broadgate	Broadgate	Richard Serra's overwhelming steel megalith.

Map 9 · Mayfair / Green Park

50 Berkeley Square	50 Berkeley Sq	The most haunted house in all of London town!
Apsley House	149 Piccadilly	"Number One, London"—former hip address of Duke of Wellington.
Buckingham Palace	The Mall	Unofficial HQ for Fathers For Justice.
Down Street Station	Down St & Piccadilly	Bricked-up Underground station.
Hard Rock Cafe	150 Old Park Ln	The Turtles didn't live here. Original location; check out free Vault memorabilia collection downstairs.

Map 10 · Piccadilly / Soho (West)

Burlington Arcade	Burlington Arcade & Piccadilly	Welcoming shoppers since 1819.
Carnaby Street	Carnaby St	Will anything innovative ever come from here again?
Kingly Court	Kingly St & Foubert's Pl	Flash the cash to cut a dash.
Statue of Eros	Piccadilly Circus	God of Love, smothered in pigeon crap: a cautionary tale.

General Information · **Landmarks**

Map 11 · Soho (Central)

Huge Tree In Pub (Waxy O'Connor's)	14 Rupert St	No, you're not drunk, it really is a tree.
John Snow Water Pump	Broadwick St	Source of 1854 Cholera outbreak identified by Snow.
Berwick Street Market	Berwick Street & Rupert St	Arrive early for traditional Cockney trader songs / off-duty hookers.

Map 12 · Soho (East)

Denmark Street	Denmark St & Charing Cross Rd	Guitar land. 'Enter Sandman' forbidden in most stores.
FA Headquarters	25 Soho Sq	Home of English football's top brass.
Old Compton Street	Old Compton St	Dubious gay hub.
The Phoenix Garden	21 Stacey St	A beautiful green mini-oasis in the middle of the city.
Soho Square	Soho Sq	Great atmosphere on hot summer days.

Map 13 · Covent Garden

Oasis Lido	32 Endell St	A lido in central London! In a 50s housing estate!
Seven Dials	Upper St Martin's Ln & Earlham St	Slum area in the past. Now great for shopping!

Map 14 · Holborn / Temple

Aldwych tube station	Strand & Surrey St	Creepy abandoned tube station. With a photo booth... of doom?
BBC Bush House	Aldwych & Kingsway	London calling the world, since 1940.
Hatton Garden	Hatton Garden	Historic jewelry and diamond district
Inner Temple Garden	Inner Temple	So peaceful even the lawyers look relaxed.
Lincoln's Inn Fields	High Holborn & Chancery Ln	Largest public square in London.
The Old Curiosity Shop	13 Portsmouth St	The oldest shop in London is truly Dickensesque.
Royal Courts of Justice	Strand & Bell Yard	Witness justice meted out to all, even the McCartneys.
Sir John Soane's Museum	13 Lincoln's Inn Fields	Spooky museum dedicated to the great 18th century architect.
Site of Sweeny Todd's Barber Shop	186 Fleet St	Swing by for a demon haircut and lovely pie.
Somerset House	Strand	18th century palace, beautiful fountains; has various modern functions.

Map 15 · Blackfriars / Farringdon

Daily Express Building	121 Fleet St	Art Deco sleeper.
Millennium Bridge	Millennium Bridge	Footbridge famous for wobbling alarmingly when it was opened.
Postman's Park	King Edward St & Little Britain	Tile memorial for 'average' people who did really cool things.

Map 16 · Square Mile (West)

The Guildhall	Gresham St & Basinghall St	Big, posh, old... Like Prince Phillip but less entertaining.
St Mary le Bow Church	Cheapside & Bow Ln	A historic place for City tycoons to save their souls.
St Paul's Cathedral	St. Paul's Church Yard & Cannon St	Magnificence since 604AD.
Temple of Mithras	Queen Victoria St & Queen St	3rd century Roman temple foundations. Discovered 1954 and moved here.

Map 17 · Square Mile (East)

Bank of England	Threadneedle St	The 'Old Lady' still churns out the pounds.
London Stone	111 Cannon St	Possibly used by Romans to measure all distances in Britannia.
Threadneedle Street	Threadneedle St & Prince's St	London's original Grope Cunt Lane. Seriously, it's a true story.

Map 18 · Tower Hill / Aldgate

The Gherkin	30 St Mary Axe	Phwoar.
Leadenhall Market	Leadenhall Market	Designed by Horace Jones (Billingsgate and Smithfield Markets)
The Lloyds Building	1 Lime St	Dystopia's nicer side.
London Wall	Cooper's Row & Trinity Sq	Ruins, should be re-built to keep Northerners out.
The Monument	Monument St & Fish St Hill	Climb 311 coronary-inducing steps for unique, unsung London views.
Pudding Lane	Pudding Ln	Starting point for Great Fire of 1666. No smoking.
Royal Raven Lodgings	Wakefield Tower	Want to upgrade your pokey flat? Become a raven.

Soup Kitchen for the Jewish Poor	Brune St & Tenter Ground	The kitchen's gone; the stunning ornate façade is still there.
Thames Clipper	Tower Pier	
Tower 42 (Natwest Tower)	25 Old Broad St	One of London's skyscrapers. Great view (and restaurant) at top.
Tower of London	The Tower of London	Kings and Queens. Surprisingly insightful, annoyingly expensive.

Map 20 • Victoria / Pimlico (West)

| Little Ben | Victoria St & Vauxhall Bridge Rd | Big Ben's runty kid brother. |
| Westminster Cathedral | 42 Francis St | Yep, impressive. |

Map 21 • Pimlico (East)

| Millbank Tower | 21 Millbank | Ugly sore thumb. And Labour Party HQ! |

Map 22 • Westminster

Big Ben	House of Commons	The world's most famous clock and pretty damn cool.
Bolan Rock Shrine	Queen's Ride, Putney	Memorial shrine where 70s rock star Marc Bolan died.
Field of Remembrance	Victoria St & Dean's Yard	Sea of crosses and poppies to honour veterans.
New Scotland Yard Sign	8 Broadway	It spins!! Just like on the telly!!
Smith Square	Smith Sq	Square with great concert venue—watch out for MPs.
UK Parliament	Victoria St & Abingdon St	Parliament buildings where you can watch government debates.
Westminster Tube Station	Bridge St & Victoria Embankment	A daunting, soulless, engineering playground. Good and bad both extinct here...

Map 23 • St. James's

Economist Plaza	25 St James's St	Rotating sculpture installations from bratty young artists.
Giro the Nazi Dog	9 Carlton House Terrace	London's sole Nazi memorial. You'd think there'd be more…
Leicester Square	Leicester Sq	Tragic, tacky, always inexplicably heaving. Avoid.
TKTS	Leicester Square & St Martin's St	Cheapo tickets to sometimes worth-seeing shows.

Map 24 • Trafalgar Square / The Strand

10 Downing Street	10 Downing St	The Prime Minister's house.
The Actors' Church	29 Bedford St	Somewhat hidden and unique church long-associated with thesps.
The Banqueting House	Whitehall & Horse Guards Ave	Unsullied Renaissance cum-shot. Still does private parties.
Cleopatra's Needle	Embankment	Ancient-Egyptian Empire esoterica, with additional Luftwaffe-era 'distressed' styling.
Eleanor Cross	Charing Cross Station, The Strand	A mourning King's tribute to his expired Queen.
Jane Austen Residence	10 Henrietta St	The first Bridget Jones' bachelorette crashed here for a time.
Right-hand Drive Street	Savoy Ct	Britain's only right-hand-drive street. Like being on holiday! (Ish)
Sewer Lamp	Carting Lane & Strand	Lit by the power of your bowels.
St Martin-in-the-Fields	St Martin's Pl & Duncannon St	Was indeed surrounded by fields once. Just TRY to imagine!
Top Secret Tunnels	6 Craig's Ct	Government's WWII tunnels, 100ft below London. But shhh: top secret.
Trafalgar Square	Trafalgar Sq	Hardly an oasis but space to sit, look and think.

Map 25 • Kensal Town

| Trellick Tower | 5 Golborne Rd | Grade II listed 1960s council estate inspiring love/hate reactions. |

Map 29 • Notting Hill Gate

| Portobello Road Market | 223 Portobello Rd | Antiques, clothes, food and more. A London institution. |

Map 31 • Paddington

Paddington Bear Statue	Paddington Station	The statue's pleasant. But they're milking it with the crap shop.
Tony Blair's house	Connaught Square & Seymour St	Promise not to do anything naughty now.
Westway Flyover		Coolest car route into London

Map 33 · Shepherd's Bush

BBC Television Centre	Wood Ln & Ring Rd	Treasure it before the BBC moves out in 2013.

Map 34 · West Kensington / Olympia

Kyoto Garden (Holland Park)	100 Holland Park Ave	Traditional Japanese Garden in Holland Park offering peace and tranquility.

Map 35 · Kensington

Kensington Palace Gardens	Kensington Palace Gardens	Billionaire's Row. Stunning street to amble down and gawp at the mansions.

Map 36 · South Kensington / Gloucester Rd

Albert Memorial	Kensington Gardens	The shiniest balding head in town.
Royal Albert Hall	Kensington Gore	One stunner of a music hall, inside and out.

Map 37 · Knightsbridge

Holy Trinity Brompton	Brompton Rd & Knightsbridge	Historic HTB is home to the Alpha course. Even Guy Ritchie's been!
Victoria & Albert Museum	Cromwell Rd & Thurloe Pl	Victorian treasure trove, building a beauty itself.

Map 42 · Baron's Court

Empress State Buidling	Lillie Rd & North End Rd	Awesome Art Deco building now a scary cult center.

Map 43 · West Brompton / Fulham Broadway / Earl's Court

Stamford Bridge	Fulham Road & Moore Park Rd	That's not sweat you smell but money at Chelsea FC's HQ.

Map 46 · Sloane Square

Saatchi Gallery	Duke of York HQ, King's Rd	See rich dude's great art collection, for free.

Map 48 · Fulham

Putney Bridge Tube Pill Box	Putney Bridge Station	"We will fight them on the platforms!"

Map 50 · Sand's End

Lots Road Power Station	27 Lots Rd	Pint-sized power station, now disused.

Map 51 · Highgate

Highgate Cemetery	1 Swain's Ln	Eerily gothic home to Karl Marx and The Highgate Vampire.
Karl Marx's grave	Highgate Cemetry	Exactly what it says on the tin.

Map 52 · Archway (North)

Parkland Walk Nature Reserve	Parkland Walk	Hedgehogs and graffiti to be spotted along this abandoned railway.
Suicide Bridge	Hornsey Ln & Archway Rd	Former London entry point, now very much an exit point.

Map 53 · Crouch End

Abandoned Warehouse	Parkland Walk & Crouch End Hill	Dereliction galore along one of the best walks in London.

Map 55 · Harringay

Railway Fields Nature Reserve	381 Green Lanes	Calm oasis at former railway depot near Green Lanes station.

Map 56 · Hampstead Village

Hampstead Observatory	Lower Terrace & Hampstead Grove	The highest point in London, and open to the public!

Map 57 · Hampstead Heath

John Keats House	38 Heath Hurst Rd	Here lived a writer whose name was writ with water.
Lawn Road Flats	Lawn Rd & Garnett Rd	c.1934 modern living. Learn to love concrete.

General Information · **Landmarks**

Map 60 · Archway

Banksy's Hitchhiking Charles Manson	Tally Ho Corner (off Highgate Hill)	Early stencil by internationally renowned graff artist.
Dick Whittington's Cat	89 Highgate Hill	Small stone statue of obscure Mayor's cat.

Map 62 · Finsbury Park

North London Central Mosque (Finsbury Park)	7 St Thomas's Rd	New name, ethos for once controversial, now myth-dispelling, mosque.

Map 63 · Manor House

The Castle Climbing Centre	Green Lanes & Lordship Park	Fake castle, real climbers.

Map 64 · Stoke Newington

Newington Green Church	39 Newington Green	'ERECTED 1708, ENLARGED 1860'...well, it made us laugh.

Map 67 · Belsize Park

Freud Statue	Fitzjohn's Ave, opposite Maresfield Gardens Junction	Statue by Oscar Nemon near the psychoanalyst's Hampstead home.
St Stephen's	Rosslyn Hill	Gothic awesomeness. Currently being restored to its former glory.

Map 68 · Kilburn High Road / Abbey Road

Abbey Road Zebra Crossing	3 Abbey Rd	Go on. Take THAT photo. You know you want to.

Map 70 · Primrose Hill

3 Chalcot Square	3 Chalcot Sq	Home of poet Sylvia Plath, 1960-61.

Map 71 · Camden Town / Chalk Farm / Kentish Town (West)

Camden Market	Camden Lock Pl	Shop, hang, drink, listen, pose, watch, chill, rock, laugh.
Grand Regents Canal	Grand Regents Canal	London's best bike lane. Or canoe to Birmingham.
The Roundhouse	Chalk Farm Rd & Crogsland Rd	Prominent round building and historic performance venue.

Map 74 · Holloway Road / Arsenal

Gillespie Park	191 Drayton Park	Weird and wonderful nature park along the train tracks.

Map 75 · Highbury

St Paul's Shrubbery	St Paul's Rd & Northampton Park	All Monty Python jokes welcome, in fact, positively encouraged.

Map 76 · Edgeware Road / Marylebone (North)

Sherlock Holmes' House	221 Baker St	It's elementary my dear Watson!

Map 77 · Mornington Crescent / Regent's Park

Euston Tower	286 Euston Rd	Quite an impressive erection.
Greater London House	180 Hampstead Rd	Crazy Art Deco building.

Map 78 · Euston

The British Library	96 Euston Rd	Prestigious research library with unmatched collection.
Camden High Street	Camden High St & Delancey St	'Alternative' tourist mecca.
Cheney Road	Cheney Rd & Weller's Ct	"Chaplin, "Alfie" and many more were filmed on these cobbles.
Euston Station	Eversholt St & Doric Way	So ugly it's oogly.
Platform 9¾	King's Cross Station	This Harry Potter thing has gone way too f'ing far.
St Pancras Station	St Pancras Way	Listed Gothic frontage, massive modern Eurostar hangar behind.
St Pancras	Pancras Rd & Euston Rd	Ex-Victorian workhouse turned superbug den.

Map 80 · Angel / Upper St

Angel Station Roof	Angel	You can get on the roof here, you epic teens.
The Bull	100 Upper St	Hands up: who loves beer?

Map 81 · Canonbury

Gladiators Paving Slab	10 Canonbury St	Logo of fighty telly show built into pavement. Me neither.

Map 82 · De Beauvoir Town / Kingsland

Suleymaniye Mosque	212 Kingsland Rd	Striking minaret silhouetted against Shoreditch Church spire and Broadgate Tower.

Map 84 · Hoxton

Hoxton Square	Hoxton Sq	Great in summer. Buy some cans and join the hipsters.
Village Underground	54 Holywell Ln	How did they get the trains up there?
White Cube	48 Hoxton Sq	Jay Jopling's homage to modern art

Map 85 · Stoke Newington (East)

Abney Park Cemetery	Stoke Newington High St & Rectory Rd	Egyptian revival-style, spooky nature reserve.

Map 86 · Dalston / Kingsland

Centreprise	136 Kingsland High St	Multi-cultural art centre, cafe, bookshop and venue.
Holy Trinity, The Clowns Church	Beechwood Rd & Kirkland Walk	Every Feb, clowns mourn Grimaldi. In full costume.

Map 87 · Hackney Downs / Lower Clapton

London Orphan Asylum	Lower Clapton Rd & Linscott Rd	Grandiose remains of historic site now beloved of enviornmental artists.
The Strand Building	29 Urswick Rd	Beautiful Art Deco building, NOT the subject of Roxy Music song.
Sutton House	2 Homerton High St	Music and arts in the oldest house in East London.

Map 88 · Haggerston / Queensbridge Rd

Geffrye Museum	136 Kingsland Rd	English interior design from 1600 to today.
St Mary's Secret Garden	50 Pearson St	A bit calm amongst the bees and the butterflies.

Map 89 · London Fields / Hackney Central

London Fields Lido	London Fields Westside	Open-air swimming for hardy Hackney folk.

Map 91 · Shoreditch / Brick Lane / Spitalfields

Brick Lane Mosque	59 Brick Ln	The area's changes reflect on the building – once a synagogue, now a mosque.
Christ Church Spitalfields	2 Fournier St	Star architect Nicholas Hawksmoor's pretty masterpiece.
Dennis Severs' House	18 Folgate St	Candle-lit cellar, parlour, smoking room – step 300 years back in time.
Spitalfields Market	105 Commercial St	No bargains but certainly one-of-a-kind fashions.
Sweet Toof Graffiti Alley	Pedley St & Brick Ln	Signature sweeties and skulls – just off Brick Lane.
Ten Bells	84 Commercial St	Where Jack the Ripper got his victims.
Truman's Brewery	91 Brick Lane	Beautiful old building now a hip weekend market. That's progress...

Map 92 · Bethnal Green

Bethnal Green Tube Station	Bethnal Green Tube Station	Scene of the worst civilian loss of the Second World War.
London Buddhist Centre	51 Roman Rd	Get your freak on.

Map 93 · Globe Town / Mile End (North)

Art Pavillion	221 Grove Rd	Arts center seemingly designed by the Teletubbies.
Mile End Climbing Wall	Haverfield Rd & Grove Rd	Classic climbing centre - one of London's big three.

Map 95 · De Beauvoir Town / Kingsland

The Sun Ho	1 Virginia Street	It's probably not legal to stake out Page 3 girls.

Map 96 · Whitechapel (East) / Shadwell (West) / Wapping

Battle of Cable Street Mural, St George's Hall	236 Cable St	Celebrating an almighty multi-faith bashing of a 1930s fascist march.
Blind Beggar Pub	337 Whitechapel Rd	A killing here finally led to Ronnie Kray doing porridge.

Map 98 · Mile End (South) / Limehouse

Ragged School Museum	46 Copperfield Rd	Barnado's school 'for the deserving poor' turned East End museum.

General Information · **Landmarks**

Map 100 · Poplar (West) / Canary Wharf (West)

Canary Wharf Tower	1 Canada Sq	You can smell the money yards away. Look, don't touch.
Canary Wharf Tube Station	Canary Wharf	Norman Foster's Jewel in the Jubilee Line Extension.

Map 102 · Millwall

The Docklands Sailing & Watersport Centre	235 Westferry Rd	Award-winning sailing centre.

Map 104 · South Bank / Waterloo / Lambeth North

County Hall	Westminster Bridge Rd & Belvedere Rd	One of London's most historical and vast buildings.
The Hayward Gallery	Southbank Centre	Revered and reviled bruiser.
The London Eye	Westminster Bridge Rd	Two words: Tourist. Trap. Nice view though.
Low Tide at South Bank	South Bank	Go for a walk on the exposed riverbed.
National Theatre	Waterloo Rd & Upper Ground	South Bank centre-piece, looked like it was from 2050 in 1960.
The Pier at OXO Tower	Barge House St & Upper Ground	Screw OXO! Have a picnic on the pier instead.
South Bank Book Market	Under Waterloo Bridge	Little-known outdoor market; heaps of vintage and second-hand reads.
Waterloo Bridge	Waterloo Bridge	When tired with London, come here and watch the sunset.

Map 105 · Southwark / Bankside (West)

Buskers' Archway	Southbank	Excellent acoustics make the decorated tunnel a coveted buskers' spot.
Elephant & Castle	Elephant & Castle	Everything that was wrong with 60s town planning. Concrete hell.
Michael Faraday Memorial	Elephant & Castle	He gave us electromagnetism, we gave him a roundabout.
The Ring	72 Blackfriars Rd	London's first boxing ring was here; now a characterful pub.
Shakespeare's Globe	21 New Globe Walk	The Bard's famous playhouse reconstructed.
Tate Modern	Bankside	Herzog and de Meuron dazzler.

Map 106 · Bankside (East) / Borough / Newington

Borough Market	8 Southwark St	London's best food market. Enjoy the free samples.
Cross Bones Graveyard	Redcross Way & Union St	Medieval resting place for London's ladies of the night.
Female Gladiator	159 Great Dover St	1st centruy AD grave of London's very own Xena.
The Golden Hinde	Clink St & Stoney St	Amazing replica of Francis Drake's Tudor war ship.
The London Tombs	2 Tooley St	Lesser known Tower experience—beware the plague pits.
Mint Street Park	Southwark Bridge Rd & Marshalsea Rd	Open space on the site of the old Evelina Children's Hospital.
Old Operating Theatre Museum	9 St Thomas St	Macabre ancient operating theatre, with gallery for eager spectators.
The Shard	32 London Bridge St	72-storey Renzo Piano glass pyramid along the river.
Southwark Cathedral	Cathedral St & Montague Close	Worth the diversion to see Chaucer and Shakespeare's stomping grounds.
St George the Martyr	Borough High St & Tabard St	Look for the homage to Dickens.
Winchester Palace	Clink St & Storey St	Random 13th century ruins with remarkable rose window.

Map 107 · Shad Thames

City Hall	Queen's Walk, More London	Dubbed 'The Testicle' by Mayor Ken Livingston. Nice.
Design Museum	Shad Thames	Fairly unsatisfying shows - drool-worthy bookshop.
Fashion and Textile Museum	83 Bermondsey St	DAH-ling, it's just fabulous!
Floating Gardens	31 Mill St	Gardens. Mad tramps. On Boats. What else do you want?
HMS Belfast	Morgan's Lane & Tooley St	Floating WW2 killing machine, much beloved of children.
Stompie	Mandela Way & Page's Walk	Sounds like a baby elephant. But it's a Soviet tank.
Tower Bridge	Tower Bridge Road	Messing about on the water.

Map 110 · Rotherhithe (West) / Canada Water

Brunel Museum	Railway Ave & Rotherhithe St	Where engineering geeks can seek refuge from being picked on.

General Information • **Landmarks**

Map 111 • Rotherhithe (East) Surrey Quays

Surrey Docks Farm	Rotherhithe St & Salter Rd	Show the kids what their bacon used to look like.

Map 113 • Walworth

East Street Market	Walworth Rd & East St	Gloriously useless stuff.
Heygate Estate	Deacon Way & Heygate St	A testament to urban planning gone horribly wrong.

Map 114 • Old Kent Road (West) / Burgess Park

The Animatronic Fireman	Old Kent Rd	Be afraid. Be very afraid.
Peckham Library	122 Peckham Hill St	Groundbreaking modern architecture or huge, carelessly dropped Tetris block?

Map 116 • South Bermondsey

Millwall FC Stadium	Zampa Road & Bolina Rd	A football mecca for somebody?

Map 120 • Greenwich

Cutty Sark Gardens	King William Walk & Romney Rd	Where the Archbishop of Canterbury was murdered in 1012.
Greenwich Foot Tunnel	Greenwich Church St & Thames St	Walk/crawl/skip/limp under the Thames.

Map 126 • New Cross

Ben Pimlott Building	University of London, New Cross	A building of cheerful, dreary, warped, modern fascist fun.

Map 131 • Vauxhall / Albert Embankment

Lambeth Palace	Lambeth Palace Rd & Lambeth Rd	Where the Archbishop of Canterbury lives; no, not in Canterbury, stupid.
Secret Intelligence Service HQ (MI6)	85 Vauxhall Cross	Real life James Bonds in a not-so-secret location.
Vauxhall City Farm	165 Tyers St	So that's where an egg comes from.

Map 133 • Battersea (East)

Battersea Dogs' Home	4 Battersea Park Rd	Re-house a pooch. Now does cats too.
Battersea Park Gasometers	Queenstown Rd & Prince of Wales Dr	Rusting monsters.
Battersea Power Station	188 Kirtling St	The world's most beautiful power station, surely.

Map 140 • Clapham Junction / Northcote Rd

Northcote Road	Northcote Rd	Middle-class marketing-types mecca.

Map 143 • Clapham High Street

Clapham Common Air-Raid Shelter	Clapham High St	The depths of government paranoia.

Map 144 • Stockwell / Brixton (West)

Brixton Market	Electric Ave & Electric Ln	Caribbean flavours, smells and sounds.
Electric Avenue	Electric Ave & Brixton Rd	First shopping area in Britain lit by electricity, in 1880.

Map 145 • Stockwell / Brixton (East)

Stockwell Bowls	Stockwell Rd & Stockwell Park Walk	70's concrete skatepark, take quads and get beaten-up.

Map 152 • Tooting Broadway

Gala Bingo Hall	50 Mitcham Rd	Bingo hall with Grade One listed interior.

MAP
37

Level 6

137 138 139 140 141 142 143 144 145

118 118a
119
120
22d 22c 22a 125c 25
121 122 123 125

level 4

128a
127 128 129 131

Europe
Asia
Modern
Materials & Techniques
Special Exhibitions

81 87 94 95
82 88 96
70a 65 66 67 68 69 89 88a 97
98
70 90 90a 102 99
71 83 100
72 84 101
73
level 3
74 National Art Library 85 109 107 108
111
40a
113 114a 114b 114c 114d 114e
116 117 112

52 52b
52a
52a
53 53a
54
54a 54a 56a 56b
55 56 57 58

level 2

151 156

Level 0
1
2
3
4 5 6 7 8 9

11 16a
Special
Exhibitions
17 27
18
19 26 Shop 38a
20
51 25 32 33
21 21a 22 23 24
40 41 42 44 45 46a 46 46b
47a 47b 47c 47d 47e 47f 47g
48a 49 50a 50b

Level 1

General Information

NFT Map:	37
Address:	Cromwell Road
	London SW7 2RL
Phone:	020 7942 2000
Website:	www.vam.ac.uk
Hours:	10am – 5.45pm daily. Select areas open until 10pm every Friday. National Art Library open 10am – 5.30pm daily and 6.30 on Fridays. Check website for areas/ activities that require booking. Closed 24th, 25th and 26th of December.

Admission: Free to the permanent collection. There is a charge for temporary exhibitions. Tickets have an allotted time slot and although they can be purchased on the day, it is recommended you book ahead of time by phone or online, especially with the more popular exhibitions.

Overview

The Victoria and Albert Museum, or the V&A, calls itself the world's greatest museum of art and design and nowhere has there ever been such an eclectic collection of objects inducing so many 'oooooohs', 'aaaaahs' and 'holy shits!'. With a permanent collection of over 4.5 million objects, pretty much all on display in the 145 galleries, you can go everyday for a lifetime and be blown over by something you hadn't noticed before. For the tourist and non-tourist alike, the V&A is a wonderful maze of cultural ramblings. You'll get lost, overwhelmed and flustered, but we promise you won't get bored.

The V&A is a cabinet of curiosities of gargantuan proportions, boasting 5000 years of art and design, in every medium imaginable (from wax dioramas to a little black dress made of bras), spread over seven levels and organised by five themes—Asia, Europe, Materials & Techniques, Modern and Exhibitions. The trouble is where to start. You'll no doubt spend the first 10 minutes mesmerised by the glass Chihuly chandelier over the information booth, but what you do afterwards depends on how much time you have. Got hours? Avoid structure and just wander. Got an hour? Take a look at the map, see what strikes your fancy and head straight there. Just don't forget to hit up the gift shop afterwards—it's killer.

The Greatest Hits

There's no real method to the V&A's madness. Despite their best efforts to categorise everything, Vivienne Westwood gowns are just a stumble away from 1000 year-old Buddhas. But this is a great thing. The best advice is really to ditch the guidebook and go with your instincts. To make sure you take in the best stuff, start in the basement (having arrived through the Tunnel Entrance from the tube station), where you'll find the 17th century **Cabinet of Curiosities**— predecessors to the modern museum—which will get you in the right mind set. Weaving past bits and pieces of **Versailles**, you emerge onto the ground floor (Level 1) which covers fashion, Asia and both Medieval and Renaissance Europe. Highlights of which include the **cast courts**, which boast a life-size replica of **Trajan's Column** in plaster, then onto ancient **samurai swords** and spectacular **kimonos** in Asia, the **Ardabil Carpet**—the largest and most amazing Islamic carpets in existence dating from 1539 (lit up on the hour and half-hour), an extensive costume room covering everything from **18th century crinolines** to **Juicy Couture** worthy of Paris Hilton, and lastly, **Raphael's cartoons**— massive sketches for a 1515 commission of tapestries that now hang in the Vatican. Before heading on, stop for a tea in the **Morris, Gamble & Poynter Rooms** café for teacakes in 1860s arts and crafts surroundings. Level 2 consists of the tucked away **British Galleries**, including the **Great Bed of Ware** as well as the endearing **Lord and Lady Clapham** dolls bedecked in miniature turn-of-the-18th century outfits. Up again on Level 3, you'll find the Materials & Techniques rooms, with its vast collections of **silver, ironwork and musical instruments**, as well as some dynamite paintings. Don't miss **Rossetti's The Daydream** and then **Ron Arad's Chair** in the modern rooms. This floor also houses the **National Art Library**—an art history student's research dream (you have to get a reading pass to study here though). Level 4 has a wonderfully tactile display of **glasswork**, as well as **architecture** and more **British Galleries from 1760-1900**. If you've made it this far, you deserve a knighthood.

MAP 4

Upper Floors

Restaurant

Main Floor

Montague Place Entrance

Reading Room

Great Court

Paul Hamlyn Library

Restaurant

Main Entrance
Great Russell Street

Lower Floor

Clore Education Centre

Ford Centre for Young Visitors

Ancient Greece & Rome
Middle East
Asia
Egypt
Enlightenment
North & Central America
Africa
Exhibitions and changing displays
Europe
⊠ Lift
||| Stairs

General Information

NFT Map: 4

Address: Great Russell Street, WC1B 3DG

Phone: 020 7323 8299 (information) or
020 7323 8181 (exhibition tickets)

Website: www.britishmuseum.org

Hours: The galleries open daily 10am
– 5.30pm and until 8.30pm on
Fridays. The Great Court is open
9am – 6pm and 8.30pm on
Fridays. Check website for planned
maintenance causing gallery
closures. Closed 1st of January and
24th, 25th and 26th of December.

Admission: Free, with a charge for some
special exhibitions.

Overview

Unless you're Indiana Jones, combining archaeological expertise with the swashbuckling energy to defeat obnoxious school groups, then do not attempt to cover the British Museum in a day. With 13 million items covering two million years of human history in almost 100 permanent and temporary galleries, you are better off treating yourself to different sections when the mood takes you—a perk of having one of the world's largest museums on your doorstep and open for free.

At 250 years, it is also the oldest museum in the world, but forget preconceptions of dusty urns and endless Roman coins—they're there if that's your bag, but this is a very modern organisation. The permanent displays include some of the world's most fascinating treasures, while the temporary exhibitions bring London a chance to break and loan artefacts which have seen some of the greatest moments of history, such as the recent display of drawings by Michelangelo, Raphael, Leonardo, and some other Renaissance scribblers who didn't make Ninja Turtle status.

However, while preserving artefacts to inspire its visitors, the Museum can also be seen as a testament to the great British pastime of looting. Some of the shining lights of its collection were acquired under the shadiest of circumstances, and the countries which were plundered so that snotty kids could chortle at the genitalia of their sculptures are increasingly vocal about getting the items back. For example the Elgin Marbles,

rechristened with their pleasantly playful English name after the earl who helped himself to them, are huge slabs hacked from the 2500 year old Athenian Parthenon (albeit Elgin's entire nose later rotted off due to syphilis: a gratifying example of one-upmanship by nature). The legality of this move is hotly debated, but apart from the damage to the Parthenon, the Marbles undeniably suffered when they were cut into smaller pieces for transport to Britain, and when rowdy schoolboys bopped the leg off a centaur in 1961. The Museum holds firm that returning debated items would empty the museums of the world, but it has extended the occasional olive branch to ease the controversy; compensation was paid for the display of drawings stolen by Nazis, and they returned the Tasmanian Ashes (aboriginal human remains) to Australia after a 20-year battle.

The Greatest Hits

The **Great Court** is not just a Greatest Hit of the Museum, but of London as a whole. Being "the world's largest covered public square" may sound too niche an accolade to be impressive, but it really is stunning. The 150 year old **Reading Room** at its centre is a delight, both for the excellent library and for the wall-mounted list of major historical figures who have sought inspiration within its round walls. Whatever your ethics on plunder, some of the most morally-dubious exhibits are among the absolute must-sees: the **Elgin Marbles** in Room 18 are remarkable, while the **Rosetta Stone** in Room 4 gives you the irresistible buzz of seeing something so legendary up close, or as close at the backpacked hordes will allow, in your own town. A whole **Moai Statue** from Easter Island is in Room 24, the **Lewis Chessmen** set is in Room 42, and the **Mausoleum of Halikarnassos** exhibition displays some of the last remaining fragments of one of the Seven Wonders of the World. However, it is the stories of heartache, adventure, mystery and passion behind the items which bring them to life. Asking the steward of Rooms 62-3 how the **mummies** came to be in the museum, or seeing the pages from **The Book of the Dead** which recorded lives of the deceased, is a fascinating way to gain insight into people around the world and throughout time. And if that's a bit too deep, just head to one of the four **shops** for a mummy-shaped pencil case or replica Rosetta Stone.

General Information

NFT Map:	36
Address:	Cromwell Road, SW7 5BD
Phone:	020 7942 5000
Website:	www.nhm.ac.uk
Hours:	Daily 10 am–17.50 pm (Last admission 17.30) "After Hours" events run on the last Friday of each month during Nov–Apr. 24–26 Dec: closed.
Admission:	Free access to most of the Museum. Fee charged for some special exhibitions (free to Members).

Overview

Visiting the Natural History Museum is like reading National Geographic, if it was edited by JK Rowling. As imagination-tingling to adults as it is to kids, you can mull over serious questions about genetic modification and the environmental cost of modern life, while walking inside a termite mound or knocking on a petrified tree.

With more than 70 million specimens in their collection, you simply won't see it all at once, or for most of us—ever. But with free entry, regularly refreshed exhibits and unforgettable special exhibitions, it's worth dropping in when you have the opportunity. Grab a free map at the entrance to work

out your route, which is colour-coded for a (slghtly) easier life: Red Zone for the planet and forces of nature; Green for ecology and the environment; Blue for dinosaurs, mmmals and biology; and Orange for the Wldlife Garden and behind-the-scenes peks.

Weekends are inevitably heaving with hyeractive button-pressing families, spellbound tourists and Londoners trying to reuild the brain cells they killed off with the niht before's drinking; weekdays are amok wh school groups. But don't let this put yc off. If there's a queue outside the main ertrance on Cromwell Road, and you don't facy killing time by spotting all the different cratures carved around the entrance arch, pc 'round the side to Exhibition Road ertrance and you'll fast-track yourself in. Yc can go early or late for fewer crowds, or stck with the permanent exhibitions, which ar superb but not as sexy as the world-clss special exhibitions which draw in the msses. Or, if all else fails, just shove the kids out the way: they're smaller than you and the buttons are *so much fun* to press.

The Greatest Hits

Ayone who didn't see the **Dinosaur Exhibition** as a child really missed out: run hre and rectify the situation immediately if you haven't been, or revisit and enjoy th modernised exhibits if you have. Th **Mammals Exhibition** will get you wndering exactly *how* someone stuffs a giraffe, and gives you a chance to get clse to the gaping jaws of a hippo. For a dfferent perspective on this room, go up tc the balcony around it: watching people stre agog at the brilliantly-displayed **blue wale** is as entertaining as the exhibits thmselves. For proof that even history geks can make the earth move for you,

visit the **Power Within** exhibition which recreates an earthquake (thoug don't expect a Universal Studios experience. The will is there, bless, but the buget just isn't…). Watch blushing parents introduce their kids to the birds and the bees in the **Human Biology** section, where an B-times-life sized model of a **foetus** will put you off pregnancy forever. The **Wildlife Garden** is an oasis of serenity open from April–October, or you can impress a date (or not, depending on your coordination) by **ice-skating** next to the stunning Victorian building from November–January.

The Museum's Special Exhibitions are superb—check the website for current information. The annual **Veolia Wildlife Photographer of the Year**, October–April, is utterly inspirational, while a varying daily programme of events includes **lectures, behind the scenes tours** of the botany department, and **fossil workshops** for kids. Due to the success of the children's version, the museum is now running Dino Snores sleepovers for adults, which includes a three course meal, life drawing classes and an all night monster movie marathon. So if you fancy yourself as Ben Stiller in Night at The Museum start saving, as the stay will cost you a whopping £175.

Like the creatures it displays (except for the Dodo—you'll find one in the Green Zone), the museum keeps evolving. Aptly, the latest major development is the Darwin Centre, where you can stoke your nightmares by checking out the giant tarantulas, experience life in a cocoon (like life in a London flat, but more spacious), and watch scientists at work. You might not think that watching scientists analysing and cataloguing bits of plant would be much of a spectator sport, but an hour in the centre will whiz by and leave you bursting with new knowledge to irritate your mates with.

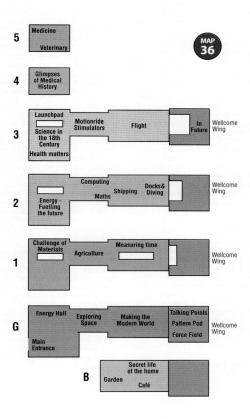

MAP 36

5 Medicine
Veterinary

4 Glimpses of Medical History

3 Launchpad
Science in the 18th Century
Health matters
Motionride Stimulators
Flight
In Future
Wellcome Wing

2 Computing
Maths
Energy - Fuelling the future
Shipping
Docks & Diving
Wellcome Wing

1 Challenge of Materials
Agriculture
Measuring time
Wellcome Wing

G Energy Hall
Main Entrance
Exploring Space
Making the Modern World
Talking Points
Pattern Pod
Force Field
Wellcome Wing

B Secret life of the home
Garden
Café

General Information

NFT Map: 36

Address: Exhibition Road, South Kensington, London SW7 2DD.

Phone: 0870 870 4868

Website: www.sciencemuseum.org.uk

Hours: Open 10 am–6 pm every day except 24 to 26 December. check website for special school holiday and summer opening hours.

Admission: Free, but charges apply to IMAX 3D Cinema, simulators & a few special exhibitions.

Overview

Museum and Science. Two words known to strike fear into the heart of many a child. And many a grown-up, come to that. But the Science Museum is one of the most visited museums in London. How so? Perhaps its the heady mix of mildly erotic pistons and shafts; 60s room-sized computers and Bakelite ashtrays; special effects simulators and the mighty IMAX theatre? Or maybe it is the multitude of buttons; red and blue and green actual buttons, as well as Minority Report-style touch screens? We know they're aimed at kids, but we like. Oh and levers, did we mention levers?

The museum has its origins in the popular Great Exhibition of 1851. Prince Albert (no laughing in the back please) suggested the extra cash made by the Exhibition be used to found a number of educational establishments. Following a number of building moves and expansions the Science Museum as we know and love it opened in 1385.

The Greatest Hits

The museum's 300,000 gidgets, gadgets and gizmos attract 2.5 million visitors a minute or something, but venture above the third floor, to the **medical floors**, and you will have the place almost to yourself. The most popular area is the main drag along the ground floor which includes **Exploring Space** hung with real life space probes and other relics that look like they've come from the Doctor Who costume and props department, and **Making of the Modern World** featuring **Stephenson's Rocket**, to titillate your dormant trainspotter.

The third floor's **Launchpad** area has as many interactive displays as an 8-year-old could ever want. Parents hope their little darlings are actually learning something as they race from exhibit to exhibit whirling wheels, spinning liquids in plastic tubes and grimacing through head-sized lenses till tiredness or RSI sets in. For younger kids the tactile **Pattern Pod** on the ground floor makes up for its lack of buttons by its immensely pleasing shape.

The museum has its own Imax to impress the grown-ups and to make whimpering children cower as 3D Rexes loom into their faces. Don't even think about going in with a hangover. A huge silver hoop joins the **Energy exhibition** on the second to the ground floor. Answer a question on a nearby monitor, (don't worry they are easy) and watch your initials and age whiz around the inside of the ring. But what's that BUZZ? Like a huge electric fly killer? It's the inspired **'don't touch' display**— irresistible for the naughtiest in the class, one small electric shock later, the rest of the lemmings race over for a turn. Hilarious.

Tate Modern

7
Bar | East Room

6
Members Room

5
8 | 9 | 10 | 11 | 12 | 11 | 10 | 9 | 8
7 | 2 | 3 | 2
6 | 5 | 4 | 3 | 2 | 1 | 1 | 2 | 4 | 5 | 6

4
Espresso Bar

3
6 | 7 | 2 | 9 | 10 | Scale | 9 | 8 | 7
8 | 3 | 6
5 | 3 | 2 | 1 | 1 | 2 | 3 | 4 | 5

2
Café | Seminar Room | River Entrance | Gallery
Starr Auditorium

1
Shop | Gallery
Main Entrance

MAP 105

Tate Britain

5 | 4
6 | 3
2 | 1 | Duveen Galleries
7
8 | 28 | 27
9 | Octagon | Art Now | 26
10 | 11 | 12 | 23 | 24 | 25
14 | 13 | 18 | 22 | 21 | T1 | T4 | T5 | T7 | T8
15 | 19 | 20 | T2 | T3 | T6 | T9
16 | 17

T10

Millbank Entrance

Manton Entrance (Atterbury St)

Restaurant | Cafe

Auditorium

Sculpture Court

Clore Entrance

MAP 21

Level 5
States of Flux
Energy and Process
Conceptual Models

Level 4
Exhibitions

Level 3
Poetry and Dream
Material Gestures

|||| Stairs
Escalators

Level 3
Level 2
Level 1

General Information

Tate Britain:

NFT Map:	21
Address:	London SW1P 4RG
Phone:	020 7887 8888
Website:	www.tate.org.uk/britain
Hours:	Open 10am – 6pm Saturday to Thursday, and until 10pm on Fridays. Last admission to special exhibitions is 45 minutes before closing time.

Tate Modern:

NFT Map:	105
Address:	London SE1 9TG
Phone:	020 7887 8888
Website:	www.tate.org.uk/modern
Hours:	Open 10am—6pm daily. Last admission to special exhibitions is 45 minutes before closing time.

Overview

In a city renowned for its galleries and museums, London's Tate galleries shine from the banks of the Thames. The first Tate was founded in 1897 as the National Gallery of British Art, but was renamed soon afterwards after its main patron Henry Tate—he of Tate and Lyle and the sugar cube. Originally on the site of the former Millbank Prison (where Tate Britain remains), the gallery gradually expanded and divided its collection over the four sites, two in London, one in Liverpool and the last in St Ives. In London, Tate Britain houses British art going from 1500 to the present day, while Tate Modern was created to house—yes you've guessed it—more modern work from 1900 to the present day, and is reportedly the most visited modern art gallery in the world.

The two Tates carry the same trendy Tate logo and the shops contain much of the same avant-garde merchandise with a great range of children's stuff available in both. But while the more traditional Tate Britain more closely resembles the National Gallery in architectural and artistic flavour, Tate Modern has a very hip feel and draws a slightly broader audience, in part due to its location in the increasingly buzzy South Bank.

Both museums have popular restaurants and cafes, but to encourage those without a membership to sign up, each offers an exclusive members' room. These provide the best views, nicest toilets, designated staff and ever so slightly self-important customers, and are always a safe bet to impress a date.

Tate Modern

Based in the former Bankside Power Station, Tate Modern has proved to be an extremely popular attraction for tourists and Londoners alike since its opening in 2000. It houses the national collection of modern art, so expect plenty of inspirational and challenging works alongside works that look like your cat sicked them up. The temporary art installations of the five-storey tall Turbine Hall provide much of the draw to the gallery. This huge space displays specially commissioned works from October to April of each year—a programme which was intended to run for only five years, but was extended due to its popularity. Quirky exhibitions fill the vast Turbine Hall, like Olafur Eliasson's 'Weather Project' which encouraged visitors to lie back on the floor in their thousands, gazing at the shadows cast by the artificial sun. Ai Wei Wei's Sunflower Seeds, in 2010/11, was probably his most ambitious and attention-grabbing work before going MIA—ironically and probably due to the unwanted exposure it brought to the Chinese government. That and the fact punters had to be forbidden from walking on the seeds due to the fine dust the porcelain they were made from produced which could have been inhaled and damage the lungs. Again, ironically. As always, we await with baited breath who will fill the Turbine Hall and with what. If it all seems like you could have created better art yourself, then try one of the gallery's excellent workshops or courses and give it a go.

Tate Britain

The Tate Britain boasts the most comprehensive collection of British art in the world, and is home to the annual and unmissable Turner Prize show. Stone steps lead up to the portico and once inside, the Duveen Galleries' ethereal sculptures lie straight ahead, giving the first taste of a breathtaking collection of artwork. Tate Britain's collection is divided chronologically and dedicates space exclusively to notable artists, such as Turner, Blake and Constable. The gallery also includes significant works by William Hogarth, Stanley Spencer and Francis Bacon. Look out for the themed guides to suit your mood, such as "The I've Just Split Up", "The I'm In A Hurry" and "The I Haven't Been Here For Ages" collections: a highly endearing way ease you through the 500 years of exhibits.

General Information

NFT Map: 24
Address: Trafalgar Square
London WC2N 5DN
Phone: 020 7747 2885
Website: www.nationalgallery.org.uk
Hours: 10 am–6 pm daily,
Fridays until 9 pm.

Admission: Free to the permanent collection and temporary exhibitions in the Sunley Room, Room 1 and The Space on Level 2. There is a charge for temporary exhibitions held on Level 2 in the Sainsbury Wing. Tickets have an allotted time slot and although they can be purchased on the day, it is recommended you book them ahead of time online, especially with the more popular exhibitions.

Overview

The National Gallery is home to one of the best and largest collections of Western European painting in the world, coming in at around 2100 paintings on display at any one time. An emphasis on *Western* and *painting* is needed. If you're looking for Roman antiquities or Persian miniatures, head for the British Musuem or the V&A—this is not where you're going to get it. Furthermore, if you're into anything post-Impressionist, make an about face for the Tate Britain. This is a celebration of the arts of Europe in all their old-school occidental glory. Taking the surprisingly manageable tour around the galleries (most of which are on one floor) will leave you wowed by how many works of art you will recognise. This is a collection that has been branded deep into your subconscious—with its oh-yeah-that-one Turners, Hogarths, Rembrandts and Leonardos. Bring a date and even the most culturally challenged will be able to impress.

The collection came into being in 1824 when the House of Commons paid £57,000 for 38 paintings belonging to a banker, using his Pall Mall home as the exhibition space. Compared to the Louvre, calling a few paintings in some guy's house the National Gallery was a little too embarrassing for the British public. So the great and the good demanded the Government pull their finger out and get to work on a purpose-built gallery worthy of a national art collection. In 1832, architect William Wilkins was given the job, constructing the recognisable porticoed façade in an up-and-coming area known as Trafalgar Square, called by one trustee 'the very gangway of London'. The most recent addition to the gallery is the Sainsbury Wing, designed in 1991 by leading contemporary architects Robert Venturi and Scott Brown after much controversy. Prince Charles, notoriously fussy when it comes to architecture, dismissed one suggested design as "a monstrous carbuncle on the face of a much-loved and elegant friend".

The National Gallery can be tackled in one exhausting afternoon, if you put your mind to it. Take advantage of the fancy benches, as many of the more epic paintings are best viewed from a distance. Be sure to get lost in the many smaller galleries, which house some dynamite, lesser-known, works. If you're feeling hungry, the National Dining Rooms is a critically acclaimed (read: expensive) restaurant, serving up the best in British fare. If you're feeling like a little culinary nationalism, the more casual National Café serves a very good cream tea.

The Greatest Hits

Starting with the Sainsbury Wing, the collection snakes around, covering European painting in chronological order from 1250 to 1900. There are a lot of paintings and it can get slightly overwhelming, so if you're pressed for time and want to make sure you've 'done' the National Gallery, try one of their 60 minute taster tours or pick up their guide to the must-see paintings. Don't miss the **Arnolfini Portrait** (signed with 'Van Eyck was here' above the mirror—hilarious), **Botticelli's Venus and Mars**, **The Wilton Diptych**, and **Uccello's The Battle of San Romano**. Moving onto the 1500-1600 range, you'll recognise **Leonardo's cartoon** of The Virgin and Child with St Anne and St John the Baptist, **'The Ambassadors'** by Hans Holbein the younger (the one where you have to crouch to see the skull), the still-hilarious portrait of **A Grotesque Old Woman** by Quinten Massys (a 1664 example of the classic conundrum—a 64 year-old trying desperately to look 16) and **Titian's Bacchus and Ariadne**. Moving on, the collection houses a rather large collection of Dutch masters, including **Rembrandt, Rubens and van Dyck**. If you're sick of 2-D, a rather cool contraption is **Samuel von Hoogstraten's peepshow**. Peer through the peep hole in this painted box for an eye-popping view of the interior of a Dutch house. Very cool. A trip to the museum is never complete without viewing a **Gainsborough, Turner and Hogarth**, all of which are housed in the 1700-1900 galleries. Do not miss Hogarth's **Marriage a la Mode** a comical rendition of an 18th century arranged marriage—in a series of six paintings. Last but not least, onto the juxtaposition of three epic 19th century history paintings depicting corporal punishment with chilling realism—**Manet's Execution of Maximillian, Delaroche's Lady Jane Gray and Puvis de Chavanne's Beheading of St John the Baptist.** What a way to end it all, quite literally.

479

General Information

Address: Peninsula Square,
London, SE10 0DX
Website: www.theO2.co.uk
General Information: 020 8463 2000
Tickets: 0871 984 0002

Overview

Exactly how the Millennium Dome transformed itself from national embarrassment and vortex for millions of taxpayers' money to the slick new home of groovy events is a bit of a mystery. Or maybe it's blindingly obvious—suits are better than politicians at this kind of thing. Anyway, on the outside it looks the same— the oversized lovechild of a jellyfish and hedgehog. Inside, gone are the attractions and concepts of 1999, aimed at celebrating all things British, that visionary that visitors stayed away in droves. Instead, the contents of an above-average high street have been stuffed inside—generic bistro food and wine bars, a multi-screen cinema. Whoopee-doo you might think. But hold on—people come for the music. No really, they do.

Enter the O2 Arena or its little sis, the IndigO2 (see what they did there?) and be very impressed. The Arena has been engineered to provide sight lines that older venues can only dream of. The air conditioning—usually a rarity at London gigs, actually works. The acoustics have to be heard to be believed. It might not be a destination venue for mosh-loving purists and those who like the sweat and beer to fly, but if you like your music with a bit of comfort and luxury, you know, like toilets that work and don't stink of piss (548 of them!) then the 02 is well worth a look. Wheelchair users are catered for with fully accessible facilities. London seems to have its first venue that feels like some real thought has gone into its creation. If the organisers get their act together and diversify the bands appearing, including more that veer away from mainstream bands then it could become unstoppable.

How to Get There—Driving

Driving to the O2 isn't as daft as it might sound considering its location—previously un-chartered industrial wastelands of south east London. 2,000 parking spaces can be reserved in advance. With decent road links, traveling after rush hour should be bearable. The A102 linking north and south London runs through the Blackwall Tunnel, right next to the venue.

How to Get There—Mass Transit

In theory, the O2 has excellent transport links no matter how you travel. In practice, there's a good chance that your gig coincides with engineers digging up the precise bit of track you need to travel on. Check www.tfl.gov.uk before you travel. But when everything is working, then the Jubilee line at nearby North Greenwich connects directly with Waterloo and London Bridge. The Docklands Light Railway is one stop away and several bus routes drop off right outside. But the best way to arrive has to be by boat— the high speed Thames Clipper runs every 20-30 minutes. from several piers including Greenwich, Embankment and Waterloo. It's not only relaxing, but you get to see London at its best on the trip.

How to Get Tickets

Ticketmaster. Naturally. Try Gumtree and Craigslist for swaps, unwanted tickets and scum-of-the-earth touts.

Life in London can sometimes seem like one continuous, eventful film, but if you like your plots to take place on screen then the city has a lot to offer. Going to catch a flick in London can often unravel like some kind of Indiana Jones-esque adventure—the Holy Grail being a reasonably-priced ticket in a clean, comfortable theatre, that can only be sought after battling hundreds of tourists and fellow Londoners all with the same thought. Every year 164 million people visit London's cinemas; now that's a fair few ticket stubs. Thankfully, by leaving The Twilight Zone (a.k.a. the tourist trap of the West End) there are plenty of cinematic treasures to be plundered. Whatever genre of film takes your fancy, whatever time of night and whether you want a velour seat and popcorn or a leather chair and glass of champagne, you are sure to find it in the nation's capital.

For those who are desperate to catch Spielberg's latest offering, and are crazy enough to stick it out in the West End, chain cinemas abound. You'll find **Odeon** (Maps 1, 4, 23, 30, 35, 61, 66, 71, 131 & 136), **Vue** (Maps 12, 33, 43, 66 & 80) and **Cineworld** (Maps 11, 23, 40, 43, 45, 100 & 138) theatres all over London. If you're brave, or just fancy seeing a star or two at one of the regular premiers, **Odeon Leicester Square** (Map 23) (made up of two separate theatres) could be for you. Another monster on the square is the historic **Empire** (Map 11), seating an impressive 1,300 patrons is a landmark in itself, although she is a slightly faded leading lady these days. Beware though. While the price of a cinema ticket in the big smoke is normally enough to make you choke on your Butterkist, wandering into any of the theatres in Leicester Square may force you to re-mortgage with prices as high as £22.50 a ticket at peak times. **Apollo West End Multiplex (Map 23)** on Lower Regent Street was formerly the home of Paramount Pictures in the UK but now houses five small, luxurious theatres showing the latest flicks on general release.

It's not hard to find cinemas offering art house and independent films in London. Finding a good one, however, can be more of a challenge. **The Barbican** (Map 7) is always a good bet, and you can take in an exhibition before your film to really beef up your grey matter. We highly recommend the **Curzon Soho (Map 11)** offering not only a wide range of cinematic

gems but also a plush bar to loosen you up for that three hour Kurasawa number. Remember if the queue is snaking along the pavement, tickets can be bought at the bar downstairs too. Check out the cinema's cousin in **Mayfair (Map 9)** as well as the slightly shabby **Renoir (Map 5)** in Brunswick Square. **Cineworld Chelsea (Map 45)** on the lustrous King's Road is one of London's premier art houses with two-seaters available for the perfect smooching experience. **The Gate (Map 29)** in Notting Hill was created from a restaurant in 1911 and now offers independent releases in a luxurious setting. **BFI Southbank (Map 104)** specializes in film through the ages as well as hosting frequent events. Who would have thought old Charlie would help us save our pennies? **The Prince Charles Cinema (Map 11)** off Leicester Square sits in a perfect location and offers revivals, cult and foreign language films for as low as £1.50. Now that's a bloody bargain. For those with a penchant for 'le cine' courtesy of our French neighbours visit **Cine Lumiere (Map 36)** in South Kensington. Uber-cool Clapham has an equally trendy art house cinema, the **Clapham Picturehouse (Map 143)**, Dalston's Art Deco gem the **Rio Cinema (Map 86)** is worth a look, while Bloomsbury offers up **The Horse Hospital (Map 4)**—the name's almost as avant-garde as the films they show. Just leave Dobbin behind.

There are some wonderful cinematic experiences to be had too. **BFI IMAX (Map 104)** is housed in a curious circular building, south of Waterloo Bridge, with the biggest screen in the UK—the size of five double-decker buses. Then there are those three magic words—**The Electric Cinema (Map 29)** on Portobello Road. Grab a Pinot Grigio, rest your derriere on a soft leather seat and munch away at home-made ice cream all the way from sunny Hampshire while catching the latest Polish release. We now have the first British cinema to be opened in the 21st century: **Shortwave (Map 107)**, popped up in 2009 in the stylish Bermondsey Square, and among its 50 seats are some which were shrewdly rehoused from the Electric Cinema. And treat your mates to another round and a packet of crisps, because there are increasing numbers of mini-cinemas in pubs and bars such as **The Garrison** (Map 107) and **The Roxy (Map 106)**.

Cinemas	Address	Phone	Map
Aldwych Film	1 Aldwych	020 7300 1000	14
Apollo Cinema Piccadilly Circus	19 Lower Regent St	0871 2233 444	23
Barbican Centre Cinema	Silk St & Whitecross St	020 7638 4141	7
BFI London IMAX	1 Charlie Chaplin Walk	0870 787 2525	104
BFI Southbank	Belverdere Rd & Waterloo Rd	020 7928 3232	104
Cine Lumiere	17 Queensberry Pl	020 7073 1350	36
Cineworld Chelsea	279 King's Rd	0871 200 2000	45
Cineworld Fulham Road	142 Fulham Rd	0871 200 2000	43
Cineworld Hammersmith	207 King St	0871 200 2000	40
Cineworld Haymarket	63 Haymarket	0871 200 2000	23
Cineworld Shaftesbury Avenue	13 Coventry St	0871 200 2000	11
Cineworld Wandsworth	Wandsworth High St & Ram St	0871 220 8000	138
Cineworld West India Quay	11 Hertsmere Rd	0871 200 2000	100
Clapham Picturehouse	76 Venn St	020 7498 2242	143
Curzon Chelsea	206 King's Rd	020 7351 3742	45
Curzon Mayfair	38 Curzon St	020 7495 0501	9
Curzon Renoir	1 Brunswick Sq	033 0500 1331	5
Curzon Soho	99 Shaftesbury Ave	020 7292 1686	11
The Electric Cinema	191 Portobello Rd	020 7908 9696	29
Empire Leicester Square	5 Leicester Sq	020 7437 9011	11
Everyman Baker Street	96 Baker St	020 3145 0565	1
Everyman Belsize Park	203 Haverstock Hill	020 3145 0520	67
Everyman Hampstead	5 Hollybush Vale	0870 066 4777	56
Everyman Screen on the Green	83 Islington Green	020 3145 0525	80
The Exhibit	12 Balham Station Rd	020 8772 6556	148
Frontline Club	13 Norfolk Pl	020 7479 8950	31
Gate Picturehouse	87 Notting Hill Gate	020 7727 4043	29
Genesis Mile End	93 Mile End Rd	020 7780 2000	97
Greenwich Picturehouse	180 Greenwich High Rd	087 0755 0065	120
Hackney Picturehouse	270 Mare St	0871 90 25 734	89
ICA Cinema	The Mall & Horse Guards Rd	020 7930 3647	23
Lux	18 Shacklewell Ln	020 7503 3980	86
Notting Hill Coronet	103 Notting Hill Gate	020 7727 6705	29
Odeon Camden Town	14 Parkway	020 7482 4576	71
Odeon Holloway	419 Holloway Rd	0871 22 44 007	61
Odeon Kensington	Kensington High St & Edwards Sq	0871 22 44 007	35
Odeon Leicester Square	24 Leicester Sq	0871 22 44 007	23
Odeon Marble Arch	10 Edgware Rd	0871 22 44 007	1
Odeon Panton Street	11 Panton St	0871 22 44 007	23
Odeon Putney	26 Putney High St	0871 22 44 007	136
Odeon Surrey Quays	Redriff Rd & Surrey Quays Rd	0871 22 44 007	111
Odeon Swiss Cottage	96 Finchley Rd	0871 22 44 007	66
Odeon Tottenham Court	30 Tottenham Ct Rd	0871 22 44 007	4
Odeon West End Cinema	40 Leicester Sq	0871 22 44 007	23
Odeon Whiteleys	Queensway & Porchester Gardens	0871 22 44 007	30
Peckham Multiplex	95 Rye Ln	0870 0420 299	123
Phoenix Cinema	52 High Rd	020 8444 6789	na
Prince Charles Cinema	7 Leicester Pl	020 7494 3654	11
Renoir Cinema	1 Brunswick Sq	0870 0420 299	5
Rich Mix Centre	34 Bethnal Green Rd	020 7613 7490	91
Rio Cinema	107 Kingsland High St	020 7241 9410	82
Ritzy Picturehouse	Coldharbour Ln & Brixton Oval	020 7733 2229	150
Riverside Studios	Crisp Rd & Queen Caroline St	020 8237 1111	41
Shortwave	10 Bermondsey Square	0207 357 6845	107
Vue Finchley Road	Finchley Rd & Blackburn Rd	08712 240 240	66
Vue Fulham	Fulham Rd & Cedarne Rd	08712 240240	43
Vue Islington	36 Parkfield St	08712 240240	80
Vue Piccadilly Circus	19 Regent St	087 1224 0240	23
Vue Shepherds Bush	Shepherds Bush Green & Rockley Rd	08712 240 240	33
Vue West End Cinema	3 Cranbourn St	08712 240 240	12

It seems that every pub, bench and bridge in London has a tale to tell of past literary greats mulling over their troubles, weeping over lovers lost or launching themselves into the Thames. Ours is a city saturated in literary history and literature-lovers, with an abundance of bookshops and diversity of readers. While so many other retailers are homogenising, our independent bookshops—with their knowledgeable staffs and their often narrow focus—remain as eclectic and enthusiastic as ever. As well as a great selection of specialist independent stores, London is also home to dozens of second-hand bookshops, book markets, a literature festival, a major international book trade fair, and Europe's largest bookshop.

General

The **Foyles** flagship store on Charing Cross Road **(Map 12)** is a London institution, with a history as eccentric as its stock. Along with mainstream books and best-sellers, it offers a good range of second hand and out-of-print books, as well as a specialist Antiquarian department and a chilled jazz café. Venerable **Hatchard's (Map 10)** has been hawking books for over 200 years, making it London's oldest bookstore. The **London Review Bookshop (Map 4)** offers a huge range of constantly updated books with an intellectual bent and intellectual staff. **Metropolitan Books (Map 6)** is small but perfectly stocked, and Phil the owner makes time for any customer seeking advice or a friendly chat. Kids can find a bookshop wonderland in **Tales on Moon Lane (Map 128)** while parents can find the books they grew up with at **Ripping Yarns (Map 51)**. The excellence of the independent stores has meant the chains have had to up their game—and loath though we are to say it, some, such as academic specialists **Blackwells (Maps 4, 12 & 71)** has gotten it very right indeed. In particular, **Waterstone's** in Piccadilly **(Map 23)** attracts all sorts of excitable superlatives, being the largest bookshop in Europe, running a range of literary activities to complement their stock, and even hosting a bar with some of the finest views of London.

Second Hand

Sadly, the world-renowned status Charing Cross Road used to command as the Mecca of second-hand bookstores is fading, and those who go looking for the genteel expertise immortalised in Helene Hanff's bestseller *84 Charing Cross Road* will find a "Med Kitchen" (shudder) at number 84. Many shops still cling to their ideals however, such as **Any Amount of Books (Map 12)** selling titles from as little £1 and offering a leather-binding service so your books can furnish your room as well as your mind. Good places to start if you are scouting for quality second-hand bookshops are: the tardis-like **The Bookshop (Map 129)** staffed by bookworms who have read *everything* (or so it seems) and can always help you find a gem; **John Sandoe (Map 46)** for true bookshop charm (rickety staircases, passionate staff, enchanting atmosphere); and the **Trinity Hospice (Map 136)** and **Oxfam Bookshops (Maps 38, 51, 86)**—not only an astonishingly cheap and broad collection of works, but all for charidee.

Specialist

Finding a bookshop devoted to your passion is like finding a club of old friends, and London caters for all tastes. Bored of cheese toasties? **Books for Cooks (Map 29)** smells as good as the recipes look, as they're tested in their kitchen first, while in-store cooking workshops teach new skills to avid customers. Sci-Fi nerds will be in their element at **Forbidden Planet (Map 179)**. **Gekoski (Map 4)** stocks a good range of modern first editions, or for older and rarer first editions try **Henry Sotheran (Map 10)**: a unique, but pricey, treat for any enthusiast. Head to **Atlantis (Map 4)** for all your occult needs (though no doubt the Spirits had already tipped you off on that one). Arty types are extensively catered for: **The Photographers' Gallery (Map 3)**, a treat in itself, has a substantial shop stocking photography titles, artists' monographs and unusual cameras; the **ICA Bookshop (Map 23)** is a great destination for art and film fans, and you can take in an exhibition while you're there; **Travis & Emery (Map 24)** stocks a vast range of music books and scores; comic geeks can get their fix at **Gosh! (Map 4)**. And for those with a passion for passion, pop along to the book section of **Coco de Mer (Map 13)**. Head

to **Artwords (Map 84)** for books on—nope, I'll see if you can guess. Or to **Chappell (Map 11)** to supplement your Abba Hits keyboard book with some of their 50,000 music titles. **Motor Books (Map 24)**, surprisingly London's only shop dedicated to motoring, rail, aviation and military books, is the ideal repository for your menfolk when you need some peace.

Travel

Feeling lethargic? Head to one of the city's superb travel bookshops to have your energy restored. **Stanford's (Map 13)** has been inspiring London for 150 years, with its enormous collection of travel books and maps. A bookshop for travellers who like to read, **Daunt Books (Maps 2, 28, 57 & 67)** arranges all its books by geographical location, so even its fiction, cookbooks and history are shelved by country. Or to learn any of over 150 languages, head to **Grant & Cutler (Map 10)**, the UK's largest foreign-language specialist.

Politics

Bookmarks (Map 4) stocks left-leaning works on a huge range of issues and takes a lively role in political activism, giving it a real and infectious sense of purpose. Also hugely right-on, both representing and driving several lefty

social movements, is **Housmans (Map 78)**. Or for a more balanced approach with political works across the parties and even the odd Minister browsing for ideas, try **Westminster Bookshop (Map 22)**.

Talks and Events

Publishing is a cut-throat business, and many writers have to sell their soul to get noticed. For them, it means an endless round of book signings and talks; for us, it means a fabulous chance to hobnob with our favourite authors. Most bookshops host occasional signings, but for regular events from the most celebrated authors, the big boys predictably have all the clout. **Foyles (Maps 12, 33, 78, 104)** and **Waterstone's (see p.489)** attract huge names: recent guests have included JK Rowling, Louis de Bernières, Salman Rushdie and AS Byatt. **Stanford's (Map 13)** offers opportunities to hear well-known travel editors, writers and photographers for an inspirational and sometimes career-changing evening. For intellectually stimulating debates and literary discussions, check out the **London Review Bookshop (Map 4)** and **Bookmarks (Map 4)**. Some events are free, some as much as a theatre ticket, but all should be booked in advance to ensure a place.

Bookshops	Address	Phone	Map
Any Amount of Books	56 Charing Cross Rd	020 7836 3697	12
Artwords	65 Rivington St	020 7729 2000	84
Atlantis	49 Museum St	020 7405 2120	4
Bargain Bookshop	153 Stoke Newington High Street	020 7249 8983	85
Bertram Rota	31 Long Acre	020 7836 0723	13
Blackwell Business + Law Bookshop	243 High Holborn	020 7831 9501	14
Blackwell Medical Bookshop	St Thomas Street	020 7403 5259	106
Blackwells	183 Euston Road	020 7611 2160	4
Blackwells	100 Charing Cross Rd	020 7292 5100	12
Bookmarks	1 Bloomsbury St	020 7637 1848	4
Books for Cooks	4 Blenheim Crescent	020 7221 1992	29
The Bookshop	1 Calton Ave	020 8693 2808	129
Chappell of Bond St	152 Wardour St	020 7432 4400	11
Coco de Mer	23 Monmouth St	020 7836 8882	13
Daunt Books	83 Marylebone High St	020 7224 2295	2
Daunt Books	193 Haverstock Hill	020 7794 4006	67
Daunt Books	51 S End Rd	020 7794 8206	57
Daunt Books	112 Holland Park Ave	020 7727 7022	28
Donlon Books	77 Broadway Market	020 7684 5698	89
The Dover Bookshop	18 Earlham St	020 7836 2111	12

Bookshops	Address	Phone	Map
Forbidden Planet	179 Shaftesbury Ave	020 7420 3666	12
Foyles	113 Charing Cross Rd	020 7437 5660	12
Foyles	Upper Ground	020 7440 3212	104
Foyles	Pancras Road	020 3206 2650	78
Foyles	Westfield	020 3206 2656	33
Gay's the Word	66 Marchmont St	020 7278 7654	5
Gosh! Comics	39 Great Russell St	020 7636 1011	4
Hatchard's	187 Piccadilly	020 7439 9921	10
Henry Sotheran	2 Sackville St	020 7439 6151	10
Housmans Bookshop	5 Caledonian Rd	020 7837 4473	78
ICA Bookshop	The Mall	020 7766 1452	23
John Sandoe	10 Blacklands Terrace	020 7589 9473	46
Librairie La Page	7 Harrington Rd	020 7589 5991	7
The Lion and Unicorn Bookshop	19 King Street	020 8940 0483	n/a
London Review Bookshop	14 Bury Pl	020 7269 9030	4
Ma ma	8 Earlham St	020 7240 8498	12
Magor Books	13 Cecil Court	020 7836 5376	24
Oxfam	80 Highgate High St	020 8340 3888	51
Owl Books	209 Kentish Town Rd	020 7485 7793	72
Pages of Hackney	70 Lower Clapton Rd	020 8525 1452	87
The Photographers' Gallery	16 Ramillies St	020 7831 1772	10
Quinto	72 Charing Cross Rd	020 7379 7669	12
R. A. Gekoski	15 Bloomsbury Square	020 7706 2735	4
Ripping Yarns	355 Archway Rd	020 8341 6111	51
Southbank Book Market	Under Waterloo Bridge	0871 663 2501	104
Stanford's	Long Acre	020 7836 1321	13
Stoke Newington Bookshop	159 Stoke Newington High Street	020 7249 2808	85
Tales on Moon Lane	25 Half Moon Ln	020 7274 5759	128
Travis & Emery	17 Cecil Ct	020 7240 2129	24
Trinity Hospice Bookshop	208 Upper Richmond Rd	020 8780 0737	136
Village Books	1 Calton Ave	020 8693 2808	129
Waterstone's	421 Oxford St	020 7495 8507	2
Waterstone's	82 Gower St	020 7636 1577	4
Waterstone's	Spencer Street	020 7608 0706	6
Waterstone's	9 Garrick St	020 7836 6757	13
Waterstone's	176 Fleet St	020 7353 5939	14
Waterstone's	Ludgate Circus	020 7236 5858	15
Waterstone's	54 London Wall	020 7628 9708	17
Waterstone's	1 Whittington Ave	020 7220 7882	18
Waterstone's	206 Piccadilly	020 7851 2400	23
Waterstone's	Trafalgar Square	020 7839 4411	24
Waterstone's	151 King's Rd	020 7351 2023	45
Waterstone's	255 Finchley Road	020 7433 3299	56
Waterstone's	128 Camden High Street	020 7284 4948	78
Waterstone's	45 Bank Street	020 7719 0688	100
Waterstone's Economists' Bookshop	Clare Market	020 7405 5531	14
Westminster Bookshop	8 Artillery Row	020 7802 0018	22
WHSmith	124 High Holborn	020 7242 0535	14
WHSmith	Fenchurch Street Station	020 7480 7295	18
WHSmith	Surrey Quays Shopping Centre	020 7237 5235	111
WHSmith	Elephant and Castle Shopping Centre	020 7703 8525	112

Yep you've heard the news. Theatre in the capital is all commercial. Predictable. Repetitive. Uncontroversial. If you believe the whingers, it's all boring stuff. Don't, because it's not. Yes, the West End, that heartland of commercial theatre around Shaftesbury Avenue, is filled with tourist-grabbing, crowd-pleasing musicals. Yes, there are more star-dominated, tried-and-tested plays than ever. Yes, the Mousetrap is still taking up the space at St Martin's after 58 years of we-bloody-well-know-whodunit.

But all that's only half the story. To find the other half, look beyond the glittering billboard signs to find the daring, small West End theatres, such as the **Donmar Warehouse (Map 13)**, bringing the innovative and unusual to Theatreland. There are the Off-West End theatres that proudly fly the flag for new writers, unafraid of being political, controversial and in-yer-face: **The Royal Court (Map 19)**, **The Soho (Map 11)**, **The Bush (Map 33)**. There are the unconventional, anarchic ensemble companies, such as PunchDrunk, shaking up things all the way from the fringe to the West End, while innovative short-play evenings are popping up at pubs across the city (see below).

But let's not forget the cracking double-whammy of the **National Theatre (Map 104)** and **The Old Vic (Map 104)**, two artistic powerhouses currently going from strength to strength. At the National, the unstoppable Nicholas Hytner brings original works to this Southbank concrete colossus (coupled with a £10-tickets offer), while down the road, Hollywood-star-turned-theatre-connoisseur Kevin Spacey is returning the Old Vic into its former glory. The refurbished **Young Vic (Map 104)**, meanwhile, is one of the best places to see fresh, new theatre (and get drunk afterwards). And, whatever you do, you're never far from a good Shakespeare production.

Keeping It Real in the West End

The Donmar Warehouse (Map 13), the West End's smallest theatre, has gained a reputation for being one of Theatreland's most innovative, yet still crowd-pleasing houses. It's quite common for good new plays that have successfully kicked off at a fringe or Off-West End venue to transfer to the West End, such as Tom Stoppard's guitars-meet-politics cracker

Rock'n'Roll. **Dean Street's Soho Theatre (Map 11)** hunts out some of the most original, fearless or hilarious theatre around, while the **Comedy Theatre (Map 23)** may play it a little more safe but packs its shows with jaw-dropping casts. The West End is also a great place to catch up on those classics you always wanted to see but never got round to: from Beckett to Shakespeare.

Off-West End & The Fringe—The Best

The underground-led, breakneck guerrilla heyday might· be over, but theatre outside the West End is in rude health. Head to rough-around-the-edges Dalston, where the **Arcola Theatre (Map 86)** continues to thrive in its scruffy ex-factory home, thanks to eclectic programming, an early-fringe-days feel and heaps of creative energy. The tiny **Bush Theatre (Map 33)** has long been a fierce champion of new work, and after being rescued by a star-studded tantrum in the face of funding cuts in 2008 it will doubtless continue to discover exciting new talent. So will **The Royal Court (Map 19)** on Sloane Square, which is one of London's finest. For new, innovative work, also keep your eyes on the **Battersea Arts Centre (Map 140)**, to watch what others will pay £50 to see next year (such as its premiere of Jerry Springer The Opera while other theatres nervously wrung their hands).

Theatre can't change society? Try telling that to the conviction-led crew of Kilburn's **The Tricycle (Map 65)**—easily London's most radical and most dedicated, political theatre. Islington's **Almeida (Map 80)** is far more conventional, but pretty—and that's got to count for something. If you're up for a laugh, check **The Hackney Empire (Map 87)**, a turn-of-the-century music hall, hosting some of London's best variety shows. **The Old Red Lion (Map 80)**, home inside an Islington pub, stubbornly clings to its unconventional, ale-fuelled fringe attitude, while **Battersea's Theatre 503 (Map 132)** is as provocative as ever. Be surprised.

If the thought of being in a theatre at all is too bourgeois for you, then you're still well catered for. London thesps it up wherever it can so you're never too far from a performance and its sometimes unwitting audience. Recent outings

have included an opera about domesticity and flatpack furniture in the Wembley Ikea, and a thriller performed in an office while the audience watch with binoculars and audiophones from the terrace opposite. Or if it's sunny, squeeze among the crowds and their bottles of rosé for the occasional performances at **The Scoop**.

Tickets

If you know what you're after, check the theatre's website—they will either have their own system, a link to a ticket selling site, or provide a phone number. If not, check www.officiallondontheatre. co.uk, which lists shows by name, theatre and genre. The site also displays shows that are just opening, or just closing, and links straight to the appropriate ticketing website, once you have made your mind up. There's a handy map of all West End venues, too.

Fancy a bargain? The iconic TKTS ticket booth on Leicester Square sells on-the-day tickets for most big shows, half-price. The queue can be mind-boggling, so go early. There's a £2.50 booking fee, but it's included in the price shown. Many theatres also have their own discount schemes. If you don't mind standing, you can get Royal Court tickets for as little as 50p. Yes, that's 50p. Just show up between 6 pm and 6.30 pm on the day of the performance. The National has £5 standing tickets for all shows, but the view ain't always great.

Exciting & New

Enter the ensemble. They are multi-skilled, imaginative and are shaking the cosy, venue-obsessed Theatreland with a vengeance. Ensemble companies like PunchDrunk and Kneehigh are touring their way through London's venues in vigorously anarchic fashion. The result is increasingly physical, increasingly unconventional—and increasingly exciting theatre, which you'd be mad to miss.

PunchDrunk (punchdrunk.com) have gained a reputation for site-specific productions, inviting the audience to walk around and follow actors and themes as they please. Their 2006 treatment of Goethe's Faust at the National Theatre was widely hailed as one of the best things to have happened to British theatre in

years. Kneehigh (www.kneehigh.co.uk) enjoy setting their nightmarish productions in outside mystical locations, but aren't afraid of West End constraints either. The award-winning Cheek by Jowl (www.cheekbyjowl.com), which have been producing Shakespeare and European classics since 1982, keep discovering hot talent—and ways to innovate.

If that's not grassroots enough, visit one of the themed short-play evenings that are popping up across town. Bringing together writers, actors and directors for twenty-minutes-or-so mini-shows, they have become a popular theatre alternative. Take your pick: Established organisers Nabokov (www.nabokov-online.com) have found a West End home at the **Trafalgar Studios (Map 24)** and relative newcomers DryWrite have made Whitechapel's **The George Tavern (Map 97)** their own. The message is spreading. What you thought was a boozer, really is a stage. The possibilities are endless.

Contemporary Dance

From small company shows to big stage spectacles, contemporary dance is having one hell of a ride. **Sadler's Wells (Map 6)** (www.sadlerswells.com), the grand old lady of dance venues, is still doing a fine job bringing some of the world's best dance to London. Check their Sadler's Wells Sampled programme, showcasing dazzling future talent for as little as £10. **The Barbican (Map 7)** (www.barbican.org.uk) has established itself as a reliable source of powerful dance performances, while the **Royal Festival Hall (Map 104)** attracts increasingly bold and interesting works to its refurbished riverside location. For London's most innovative dance performances, check **The Place (Map 4)**, a stylish venue that combines performance, training and dance education (www.theplace.org.uk).

Theatres	Address	Phone	Type	Map
Adelphi Theatre	The Strand	020 3725 7060	West End	24
The Albany	Douglas Way	020 8692 4446	Performing Arts	119
Aldwych Theatre	49 Aldwych	0870 4000 805	West End	14
Almeida Theatre	Almeida St	020 7359 4404	Fringe	80
Ambassadors Theatre	West St	084 4811 2334	West End	12
Apollo Theatre	Shaftesbury Ave	084 4579 1971	West End	11
Apollo Victoria Theatre	17 Wilton Rd	020 7834 6318	West End	20
Arcola Theatre	27 Arcola St	020 7503 1646	Fringe	86
ArtHouse	159 Tottenham Ln	020 8245 3099	Performing Arts	54
Arts Theatre	6 Great Newport St	084 5017 5584	West End	12
Barbican Centre	Silk St & Whitecross St	020 7638 4141	Performing Arts	7
Barons Court Theatre	28 Comeragh Rd	020 8932 4747	Fringe	42
Battersea Arts Centre	Lavender Hill & Theatre St	020 7223 2223	Fringe	140
Bloomsbury Theatre	15 Gordon St	020 7388 8822	Fringe	4
Brixton Academy	211 Stockwell Rd	020 7771 3000	Performing Arts	145
Bush Theatre	2 Shepherd's Bush Rd	020 8743 3584	Fringe	33
Cadogan Hall	5 Sloane Terrace	020 7730 4500	Performing Arts	19
Cambridge Theatre	Earlham St	084 4412 4652	West End	13
Chats Palace Arts Centre	42 Brooksby's Walk	020 8533 0227	Performing Arts	90
Comedy Theatre	Panton St	087 1297 5454	West End	23
Criterion Theatre	218 Piccadilly	087 0060 2313	West End	10
The Dogstar	389 Coldharbour Ln	020 7733 7515	Fringe	150
Dominion Theatre	268 Tottenham Court Rd	020 7413 3546	West End	4
Donmar Warehouse Theatre	41 Earlham St	020 7438 9200	West End	13
The Drill Hall	16 Chenies St	020 7307 5060	Fringe	4
Duchess Theatre	Catherine St	084 5434 9290	West End	14
Duke of York's Theatre	St Martin's Ln	087 0060 6623	West End	24
Etcetera	265 Camden High St	020 7482 4857	Fringe	71
Fortune Theatre	Russell St	020 7369 1737	West End	13
Garrick Theatre	Charing Cross Rd	020 7520 5690	West End	24
Gate Theatre	11 Pembridge Rd	020 7229 0706	Fringe	29
The George Tavern	373 Commercial Rd	020 7790 7335	Fringe	97
Gielgud Theatre	Shaftesbury Ave	084 4482 5130	West End	11
Greenwich Theatre	Crooms Hill & Nevada St	020 8858 7755	Fringe	120
Hackney Empire	291 Mare St	020 8985 2424	Fringe	89
Hampstead Theatre	Eton Ave	020 7722 9301	Fringe	66
Hammersmith Apollo Theatre	Queen Caroline St	020 8563 3800	West End	41
The Hen & Chickens Theatre Bar	109 St Paul's Rd	020 7354 8246		109
Her Majesty's Theatre	Haymarket	0844 412 2707	West End	23
Indigo2	Millenium Way	020 8463 2000	Performing Arts	na
Jermyn Street Theatre	16 Jermyn St	020 7287 2875	Fringe	23
King's Head Theatre & Pub	115 Upper St	020 7226 1916	Fringe	80
Koko	1 Camden High St	087 0432 5527	Performing Arts	71
Leicester Square Theatre	5 Leicester Pl	020 7534 1740	West End	11
Little Angel Theatre	14 Dagmar Passage	020 7226 1787	Performing Arts	80
London Palladium	Argyll St	020 7494 5020	West End	10
Lyceum Theatre	21 Wellington St	020 7432 4220	West End	14
Lyric Theatre	29 Shaftesbury Ave	020 7494 5045	West End	11
National Theatre	South Bank	020 7452 3400	West End	104

Theatres	Address	Phone	Type	Map
New London Theatre	Drury Ln	0870 890 0141	West End	13
Noël Coward Theatre	St Martin's Ln	084 4482 5140	West End	24
Novello Theatre	Aldwych	084 4482 5170	West End	14
Old Red Lion	418 St John St	020 7837 7816	Fringe	6
The Old Vic Theatre	103 The Cut	084 4871 7628	West End	104
Palace Theatre	Shaftesbury Ave	020 7870 6876	West End	12
Pan Theatre	Clifton Terrace	087 0890 0142	Fringe	62
Phoenix Theatre	Charing Cross Rd	087 0060 6629	West End	12
Piccadilly Theatre	16 Denman St	020 7478 8800	West End	10
The Place	17 Duke's Rd	020 7121 1000	Performing Arts	4
Playhouse Theatre	Northumberland Ave	084 4871 7631	West End	24
Prince Edward Theatre	28 Old Compton St	084 4482 5151	West End	12
Prince of Wales Theatre	Coventry St	084 4482 5115	West End	11
Queen Elizabeth Hall	South Bank Centre	020 7960 4200	Performing Arts	104
Queen's Theatre	Shaftesbury Ave	084 4482 5160	West End	11
Riverside Studios	Crisp Rd & Queen Caroline St	020 8237 1111	Fringe	41
Ronnie Scott's	47 Frith St	020 7439 0747	Performing Arts	12
The Roundhouse	Chalk Farm Rd & Crogsland Rd	020 7424 9991	Performing Arts	71
Royal Albert Hall	Kensington Gore	020 7589 8212	Performing Arts	36
Royal Court Theatre	Sloane Sq	020 7565 5000	West End	19
Royal Festival Hall	Belvedere Rd	084 4875 0073	Performing Arts	104
Royal Opera House	Bow St	020 7304 4000	Performing Arts	13
Sadler's Wells	Rosebery Ave	084 4412 4300	Performing Arts	6
Savoy Theatre	The Strand	0870 164 8787	West End	24
Scala	275 Pentonville Rd	020 7833 2022	Performing Arts	78
The Scoop	The Queen's Walk	020 7403 4866	Performing Arts	107
Shaftesbury Theatre	210 Shaftesbury Ave	020 7379 5399	West End	13
Shakespeare's Globe	21 New Globe Walk	020 7902 1400	West End	105
Shepherd's Bush Empire	56 Shepherd's Bush Green	084 4477 2000	Performing Arts	33
Soho Theatre	21 Dean St	020 7478 0100	Fringe	11
Southwark Playhouse	77 Newington Causeway	020 7407 0234	Fringe	106
The Space	269 Westferry Rd	020 7515 7799	Fringe, Performing Arts	na
St John's	Smith Square	020 7222 1061	Performing Arts	22
St Martin's Theatre	West St	020 7836 1443	West End	12
Sutton House	2 Homerton High St	020 8986 2264	Performing Arts	87
Theatre 503	503 Battersea Park Rd	020 7978 7040	Fringe	132
Theatre Royal Drury Lane	Catherine St	087 0890 6002	West End	13
Theatre Royal Haymarket	Haymarket	020 7930 8890	West End	23
Toynbee Studios	28 Commercial St	020 7650 2350	Fringe	91
Trafalgar Studios	14 Whitehall	087 0060 6632	West End	24
The Tricycle Theatre	259 Kilburn High Rd	020 7372 6611	Fringe	65
Vaudeville Theatre	404 Strand	087 0890 0511	West End	24
Victoria Palace Theatre	Victoria St	084 4248 5000	West End	20
Wembley Stadium	Wembley Hill Rd	0800 169 2007	Performing Arts	na
Wigmore Hall	36 Wigmore St	020 7935 2141	Performing Arts	2
Wilton's Music Hall	Graces Alley & Ensign St	020 7702 2789	Fringe	95
Wyndham's Theatre	32 Charing Cross Rd	084 4482 5120	West End	12
The Young Vic Theatre	66 The Cut	020 7922 2922	West End	104

There are many great things about London's vibrant art world. The best? It's free. Granted, if you want to see some of the big show-stopping exhibitions that pass through the **Tates (Maps 21 & 105)**, **British Museum (Map 4)**, **National Gallery (Map 23)** and **Royal Academy (Map 2)** you'll have to pay quite a hefty sum, but overall, you can experience visual arts throughout the capital without coughing up much dough. This might be a contributing factor to London's sprawling art scene, as it is so easy to duck in and out of the capital's 300+ museums and galleries on a lunch break.

Of course, there are concentrations of art in locations around Piccadilly and Bond Street (check out Cork Street for its galleries, such as **Messum (Map 10)** and the **Adam Gallery (Map 10)**, running parallel with Savile Row), the East End (funkier affair and an artistic hipster breeding ground—check out Vyner Street in Bethnal Green). South Kensington/Chelsea (a major culture scene as a result of the Great Exhibition of 1851) and various institutions dotted along the Thames (as seen from the Tate to Tate boat service). If you're feeling really adventurous/ bored pretend you're really in the know and head to the New Cross, Peckham and Camberwell areas of South London where artists and galleries are pushing new boundaries in creativity/ pretentiousness. Great art is all over this city, so get your Oyster Card, and get ready to cover a lot of ground.

Starting with London's modern art, the **Tate Modern (Map 105)**, with its massive smoke stack, has become a major London landmark. This is despite it only existing as a separate entity from the **Tate Britain (Map 21)** since 2000. Check out its spacious Turbine Hall, with often spectacular installations.

It's not surprising that the Tate Modern is often the London tourist's first stop these days, as the city has become well-known for contemporary art. Due in part to the too-cool-for-school London art scene of the 1990s, which saw the establishment of Turner Prizers Tracy Emin, Rachel Whiteread and Damien Hirst, and made a major mark under Saatchi's guiding light. This light has faded somewhat, as the movement's personalities have slowly sold out a little (Emin signing for Longchamp is a case and point). But certain London galleries remain as monuments to this explosion of counter-culture, and, in addition to the **Saatchi Gallery (Map 46)**, these include the **Serpentine Gallery (Map 30)**, **Haunch of Venison (Map 10)**, and **Victoria Miro (Map 31)**. Other inspiring alternatives include the **Riflemaker (Map 10)**, **South London Gallery (Map 122)**, **Camden Arts Centre (Map 66)**, the **White Cube** at Mason's Yard **(Map 23)**, Hoxton Square **(Map 84)**, and Bermondsey **(Map 107)**.

London is a city with a lot on offer, and if you're looking for something a bit more traditional, start with the **National Gallery (Map 24)** in Trafalgar

Square, moving onto the **National Portrait Gallery (Map 24)** next door, which presents you with a who's who of British culture past and present. Stroll up Charing Cross Road to the awesome **British Museum (Map 4)** with its jaw-dropping two acre roof over the Great Court (yet another example of Norman Foster's obsession with glass and geometry). Be sure to take in the Parthenon Marbles, aka Elgin Marbles, before the Greek government makes any attempt to get them back. Then over to the not-nearly-praised-enough **Wallace Collection (Map 2)** behind Selfridge's for some tea and Watteau action. A traditional art-lover's tour of London is not over without a trip to the **Royal Academy (Map 2)** with its epic exhibitions and finally to the **Tate Britain (Map 21)**, where the Pre-Raphaelites reign supreme.

Feeling a little non-conformist? London has a brilliant array of cultural institutions that offer more than just marble and canvas. From ceramics to dolls houses, kimonos to plaster casts of just about every great sculpture in the world—the V&A has it all (not to mention an awesome gift shop). Other alternatives to the mainstream include **The Photographers' Gallery (Map 13)** by Leicester Square, which not only squeezes in the best photographic exhibitions in town, but also boasts the best bookshop on the subject. Odd in its own way is the **Museum of London (Map 7)**, which walks you through the history of the city from prehistoric times to the present day. Recent London museum gems also include the newly renovated **London Transport Museum (Map 24)**, **Fashion and Textile Museum (Map 107)**, **Museum of Brands, Packaging and Advertising (Map 29)** and the **Design Museum (Map 107)**, with cars and video games in case you're stuck entertaining your nephew. Or check out one of London's hidden glories, from the The Vault at The Hard Rock Café **(Map 9)** by Hyde Park, or the mind blowing **Hunterian Museum (Map 14)** for fans of fetuses in jars and other macabre wonders (although be warned, do not go suffering from a weak stomach). The Horniman (*snigger*) Museum is a legacy of Victorian curiosity, starring an overstuffed walrus whose taxidermist didn't realise that walruses are supposed to have wrinkles.

The **Geffrye Museum (Map 88)** is a good one to check out when you're in Shoreditch and tired of being hip. Just up Kingsland Road from **Flowers (Map 91)** (a good British contemporary art gallery), this museum of domestic interiors runs through the history of Britain one living room at a time. Somewhat forgotten are the weird and wonderful **Sir John Soane's Museum (Map 14)**, **Leighton House (Map 35)** and **Dennis Severs' House (Map 91)**—but we'll let you discover these gems for yourself.

So forget Pret a Manger—feed your soul in one of London's many museums and galleries. They certainly have more to offer than one of those crappy no bread sandwiches, anyway.

Museums & Galleries	Address	Phone	Map
2 Willow Road	2 Willow Road	020 7435 6166	56
19 Princelet Street—Museum of Immigration and Diversity	19 Princelet St	020 7247 5352	91
7 Hammersmith Terrace	7 Hammersmith Terrace	0208 741 4104	39
Adam Gallery	24 Cork St	020 7439 6633	10
Apsley House	149 Piccadilly	020 7499 5676	9
Arsenal Museum and Stadium Tour	Drayton Park	020 7704 4504	74
Bank of England Museum	Threadneedle Street	020 7601 5545	17
The Banqueting House	Whitehall & Horse Guards Ave	020 3166 6000	24
Benjamin Franklin House	36 Craven St	020 7839 2006	24
The Bramah Museum of Tea and Coffee	40 Southwark Street	020 7403 5650	106
Britain At War Experience	66 Tooley Street	020 7403 3171	107
The British Library	96 Euston Rd	084 3208 1144	78
The British Museum	Great Russell St & Museum St	020 7323 8299	4
Brunel Museum	Railway Ave & Rotherhithe St	020 7231 3840	110
Brunswick House	30 Wandsworth Rd	020 7394 2100	134
Camden Arts Centre	Arkwright Rd	020 7472 5500	66
Cartoon Museum	35 Little Russell St	020 7580 8155	4
Chelsea FC Museum and Stadium Tour	Stamford Bridge	087 1984 1955	43
Chelsea Physic Garden	66 Royal Hospital Rd	020 7352 5646	45
Churchill Museum and Cabinet War Rooms	King Charles Street	020 7930 6961	24
Clink Prison Museum	1 Clink St	020 7403 0900	106
Clockmakers' Museum	Aldermanbury	020 7332 1868	16
Cuming Museum	151 Walworth Rd	020 7525 2332	113
Dennis Severs' House	18 Folgate St	020 7247 4013	91
Design Museum	Shad Thames	020 7403 6933	107
The Dickens House Museum	48 Doughty St	020 7405 2127	5
Dr Johnson's House	17 Gough Square	020 7353 3745	15
Fan Museum	12 Croom's Hill	020 8305 1441	120
Fashion and Textile Museum	83 Bermondsey St	020 7407 8664	107
Florence Nightingale Museum	2 Lambeth Palace Rd	020 7620 0374	131
Flowers	82 Kingsland Rd	020 7920 7777	91
Foundling Museum	40 Brunswick Square	020 7841 3600	5
Freud Museum	20 Maresfield Gardens	020 7435 2002	66
Geffrye Museum	136 Kingsland Rd	020 7739 9893	88
Grant Museum of Zoology	Malet Place	020 7679 2647	4
Guards Museum	Birdcage Walk	020 7414 3428	22
Hampstead Museum	New End Square	020 7431 0144	56
Handel House Museum	25 Brook St	020 7495 1685	2
Haunch of Venison	6 Burlington Gardens	020 7495 5050	10
Hayward Gallery	Belvedere Rd	0871 663 2501	104
Horniman Museum & Gardens	100 London Rd	020 8699 1872	n/a
Hunterian Museum	35 Lincoln's Inn Fields	020 7869 6560	14
Imperial War Museum	Lambeth Road	020 7416 5000	104
Jewish Museum	129 Albert St	020 7284 7384	71
Kinetica Place Gallery	90 York Way	020 7520 1485	79
Kirkaldy Testing Museum	99 Southwark St	013 2233 2195	105
Leighton House Museum	12 Holland Park Rd	020 7602 3316	34
The Library and Museum of Freemasonry	60 Great Queen St	020 7395 9251	13
Linley Sambourne House	18 Stafford Terrace	020 7602 3316	35
London Canal Museum	12 New Wharf Rd	020 7713 0836	79
London Dungeon	29 Tooley St	020 7403 7221	106
London Fire Brigade Museum	94 Southwark Bridge Rd	020 8555 1200	106

Museums & Galleries	Address	Phone	Map
London Sewing Machine Museum	293 Balham High Rd	020 8767 4724	151
London Transport Museum	Covent Garden Piazza	020 7379 6344	24
Marylebone Cricket Club Museum	St John's Wood Rd	020 7616 8656	76
Messum	8 Cork St	020 7437 5545	10
Museum in Docklands	Hertsmere Road	020 7001 9844	100
Museum of Brands, Packaging and Advertising	2 Colville Mews	020 7908 0880	29
Museum Of Childhood	Cambridge Heath Road	020 8983 5200	92
Museum of Fulham Palace	Bishops Avenue	020 7736 3233	48
Museum of Garden History	Lambeth Palace Road	020 7401 8865	131
Museum of London	150 London Wall	020 7001 9844	7
Museum of Methodism & Wesley's Chapel	49 City Rd	020 7253 2262	7
Museum of the Order of St John	26 St John's Ln	020 7324 4005	15
Museum of the Royal Pharmaceutical Society	1 Lambeth High St	020 7572 2210	131
National Army Museum	Royal Hospital Road	020 7881 2455	46
National Gallery	Trafalgar Square	020 7747 2885	24
National Maritime Museum	Park Row	020 8312 6565	n/a
National Portrait Gallery	St Martin's Place	020 7306 0055	24
Natural History Museum	Cromwell Rd	020 7942 5460	36
The Old Operating Theatre, Museum & Herb Garret Venue	9 St Thomas St	020 7188 2679	106
Petrie Museum of Egyptian Archaeology	Gower St	020 7679 2884	4
Pollock's Toy Museum	1 Scala St	020 7636 3452	3
Ragged School Museum	46 Copperfield Rd	020 8980 6405	98
Riflemaker Gallery	74 Beak St	020 7439 0000	10
Rootstein Hopkins Parade Ground	16 John Islip St	020 7514 8514	21
Rotherhithe Picture Research Library	82 Marychurch St	020 7237 2010	109
Royal Academy of Music Museum	Marylebone Rd	020 7873 7373	2
Saatchi Gallery	King's Road	020 7823 2332	46
Science Museum	Exhibition Rd	087 0870 4868	36
Serpentine Gallery	Kensington Gardens	020 7402 6075	30
Sherlock Holmes Museum	221 Baker St	020 7224 3688	76
Sikorski Museum	20 Princes Gate	020 7589 9249	37
Sir John Soane's Museum	13 Lincoln's Inn Fields	020 7440 4263	14
Smythson Stationery Museum	40 New Bond St	020 7629 8558	10
South London Gallery	65 Peckham Rd	020 7703 6120	122
Spencer House	27 St James's Pl	020 7499 8620	23
St Bartholomew's Hospital Museum	West Smithfield	020 7601 8152	15
Tate Britain	Millbank	020 7887 8888	21
Tate Modern	Bankside	020 7887 8888	105
Tower Bridge Exhibition	Tower Bridge	020 7403 3761	107
Victoria & Albert Museum	Cromwell Rd & Thurloe Pl	020 7942 2000	37
Victoria Miro Gallery	16 S Wharf Rd	020 7336 8109	31
Wallace Collection	Manchester Square	020 7563 9500	2
Wellcome Collection	183 Euston Rd	020 7611 2222	4
Westminster Abbey	Parliament Square	020 7222 5152	22
White Cube	26 Mason's Yard	020 7930 5373	23
White Cube	48 Hoxton Square	020 7930 5373	84
White Cube	144 Bermondsey St	020 7930 5373	107

Overview

Stumbling out teary-eyed into the light, pallid skin wrecked by long hours in darkness and surrounded by strangers, it's hard to believe that this time last year we were counting out our coppers and begging our friends to buy us another drink. Okay, so we're not completely in the red and London's cash registers may not be overflowing with moolah as they once were but we've managed to open new bars, forget about old ones, sing ourselves raw in amateur karaoke sessions, break a few bones dancing in scary clubs we shouldn't be in—you know, the usual. What is scary though is how fast the night-time landscape is changing around us. These days walking around Soho is like picking your way through a war zone; with The Astoria and its surrounding area now bulldozed, it sometimes feels the heart of London's soul has been ripped out by greedy developers. Maybe it has, but we're not dwelling on all those bad vibes: we're too busy digging amateur folk in Stokey, or quaffing luxurious cocktails in the depths of Old Street, or down the front at some dingy gig hellhole in the depths of Brixton having the time of our sorry little lives. As you may have gathered by now, London's options are as endlessly varied as her tastes. And being children of the post-modern age (or is that post-post-modern age?) we've given up caring about tribalism and consistency and have dived head-first into everything at once. Economy, what economy?

Local Pubs for Local People

North to South, East to West, whether in Zone 1 or Zone 6 the London 'local' encapsulates the city itself. That calm beating heart of the old geezer talking of times gone by in Limehouse or the adrenaline-fuelled racing heart of the City's next 'big' thing in Farringdon—all echoing around a city that tells its stories, shares its woes and gets itself together over a pint of 'Pride' in the local boozer. The cavernous bowels of Dickens' favourite local **Ye Olde Cheshire Cheese (Map 15)** now provide tourist-free shelter for City folk. Borough's **George Inn (Map 106)**, with a dazzling selection of ales, is as ancient as boozy gets. **The Lamb (Map 14)** is where to go after your office job if you want to pretend you're a writer, while the Grade-II-listed **Princess Louise (Map 4)** is sparkling with old man-ness but in the heart of London. In Hampstead, you want to be the pretty, and pretty hidden, **Holly Bush (Map 56)**. And while it's been gentrified since

it was run by the Kray's mum, **The Carpenter's Arms (Map 91)**, is still a great, tiny little foreign beer-heaven. Modern rot has yet to set in at Highgate's old-school **The Winchester (Map 52)** and you can eyeball woodworm in the brilliant **The Compton Arms (Map 80)**. The old-timers in Rotherhithe's dream-of-your-dad **The Mayflower (Map 109)**, and Brixton's **The Effra (Map 150)** will have never heard of the 'Inter-web', never mind Facebook. Way out west, **The Dove (Map 40)** draws the local collective with its cosy fire, relaxed chatter and river spectacular.

Keep-It-Real Ale

The Carling brigade can take a hike, this town takes Price (sic) in its real brews. **The Wenlock Arms (Map 83)** proves we can do down-to-earth ale-enthusiast and **The Jerusalem Tavern (Map 3)** shows we can do fake ye olde times with amazing beer selection as well as any Lancashire local. Borough's **Market Porter (Map 106)** has a great selection, and is full of market traders counting their cash. Lovers of the Belgian stuff (and trendy Hackney-ites) will feel at home in **The Dove (Map 89)** and those after an even greater selection of European ales without the pretentiousness should head to **Quinns (Map 71)** in Camden. Too fancy? For great ale selections, there's **The Royal Oak (Map 106)** also in Borough, where the taps come courtesy of the Harveys brewery. Pitfield, Freedom and St Peter's, meanwhile, supply Islington's **Duke of Cambridge (Map 83)** with organic beer, if you like that kind of stuff. In Parson's Green **The White Horse (Map 49)** is a Victorian gem and the **Roebuck (Map 38)** provides Chiswick with an ever changing selection of local and national brews.

Good Mixers

While our ale keeps us down to earth, it's the lure of the cocktail that causes us to show off. Shaken or stirred, it doesn't matter. It's all about looking good with a long glass of the colourful sugary stuff dressed to the nines, glace cherry 'n all. For aesthetic hedonism we love **Loungelover (Map 91)** and **Lounge Bohemia (Map 8)**. Martinis? You'll find us at the **Charlotte Street Hotel (Map 3)**. At **5th View (Map 9)** there's vistas of Big Ben with your Kir Royal and the secretive speak-easy mood of **Milk & Honey (Map 10)** comes

with eight handy house rules, including "no star fucking." See also the plush Art Deco heaven that is **Claridge's Bar (Map 2)**, while **Montgomery Place (Map 29)** serves Notting Hill a bit of old world cool. If you find yourself on Clapham High Street then you could do a lot worse than heading to **The Loft (Map 143)**—a modern, lush escape. One can feel studious while nursing a punch bowl at **The Cinnamon Club (Map 22)**, nestled perfectly inside the old serenity of the Old Westminster Library. On the contrary, vivacious **Buena Vista (Map 143)** brings a bit of Havana to the streets of Clapham and is the perfect spot for a mojito.

Weirdos

Let's face it, sometimes the booze just isn't enough to keep you entertained. Destroying your internal organs with the stuff is just sometimes a little boring, right? **Jamboree at Cable Street Studios (Map 97)** is an artist-run warehouse space that does hipster rave-offs. **The Windmill (Map 150)** of Brixton is a handmade weirdo magnet and **The Battersea Barge (Map 134)** is a friendly old pub—on a very thin barge. **The Coronet (Map 74)** in Holloway has a desolate, nostalgic charm as does perhaps the weirdest pub of them all, the **Palm Tree (Map 93)**, a celebration of British antiquity with crooners of a certain age most nights.

Smoker-Friendly

If the merciless prohibition regime of 2007 hasn't resulted in reluctant surrender, don't despair: from provisionally erected patios to all-year beer gardens to secret backdoors, London's ban-bashing creativity knows no boundaries. Great fag spots include the terrace at **Proud (Map 71)**, overlooking Camden's roofs, the barbeque-and-beer-can courtyard of **93 Feet East (Map 91)** and the tree-shaded garden of the **Edinboro Castle (Map 77)**. Hang out in front of Highgate favourite **The Flask (Map 51)** or combine a late-night joint with a rollie in the backyard of the **The Dolphin (Map 89)**. For clubbing, consider **Egg (Map 79)**, where you're allowed to smoke in the massive garden. **The Owl & Pussycat (Map 91)** is not just a surprisingly pleasant pub in Shoreditch, it's also got a surprisingly nice garden, where smoking is not just allowed, dear friends, but encouraged.

We're Raving, We're Raving

While the fierce bass from the basement at **Plastic People (Map 84)** reverberates around Shoreditch, over at superclub **Fabric (Map 15)** the cool kids of the capital are bringing down the house with ... er, a bit of House music. For the groovier seeking a smaller joint try **Guanabara (Map 13)**. The ever-so-eclectic **Notting Hill Arts Club (Map 29)** continues to come up with exhilarating and inventive nights, as does Brick Lane's 93 **Feet East (Map 91)** and **333 (Map 84)**. **Cargo (Map 84)** is for those who like a deep seated couch with their DJ while **Madame Jojo's (Map 11)** provides exactly the kind of decadence we demand from Soho clubbing. As long as lip fuzz is still trendy there's always the **Moustache Bar (Map 86)** and for quirky, artsy fartsery head to **Passing Clouds (Map 88)**, both in Dalston, natch. For serious rockabilly, find **Ye Olde Axe (Map 91)** gentlemen's club on Hackney Road, where the rock 'n' roll starts as soon as the last naked girl has disappeared behind the big-mirrored wall.

Great Bars

George Orwell's ideal pub was all about "draught stout, open fires, cheap meals, motherly barmaids and no radio." These days we'd maybe add music straight from a blog, handmade decor and a dangerous vibe. For some if not all of these try up-beat **Jaguar Shoes (Map 91)**. **Freud (Map 13)** or the French House **(Map 11)** in the West End are also solid contenders for boho schlock. But there's so much more: crawl from **Barrio North's (Map 80)** caravan to the country-house of **Lost Society (Map 142)**, from the **Island Queen (Map 83)** to the Moijto-fuelled **Mau Mau (Map 29)**. We like standing next to (would-be) artists at the **ICA Bar (Map 23)** and actor types on the terrace of **The Cut Bar (Map 104)**. Or in front of a movie screen, at **Roxy Bar and Screen (Map 106)**. Later on, you'll find us nibbling cheese in Dalston's **Jazz Bar (Map 82)**, dancing to trashy music at **Da Vinci's (Map 104)**.

Best of the Rest

Want to feel exclusive? Members-only clubs are not only becoming ever more popular, but also ever more accessible. So there. Escape Shoreditch's terrifying hordes to the rooftop swimming pool of **Shoreditch House (Map 91)** or the boredom of Shepherd's Bush to the

underground ex-toilets that have become **Ginglik (Map 33)**. Of course, most of those in the know will drag you to the various warehouse raves that fire up every weekend. People like **Real Gold** (http://wearerealgold.com) are a good place to start if you fancy some of this awfulness. Remember it's not who you know but, oh wait, it is who you know.

To create your own entertainment and/or embarrass yourself, **Lucky Voice (Maps 10, 80)** is one of many joints offering private karaoke booths for you and some people who will most probably cease to be your friends after they hear you massacre 'Time After Time.' Shoreditch's exposed brick joint **The Book Club (Map 8)** has a list of 'Social Athletics' on the bill—ping pong, old chap? If relying on that notoriously joke-cracking ex-friend of a friend for your evening's amusement sounds a bit risky, consider these alternatives: The standard-setting **Comedy Store (Map 11)** (book in advance) and **Covent Garden Comedy Club (Map 24)**, or, at the pub end of things, **The Bedford (Map 148)** and the **Camden Head (Map 78)**. If you think that YOU should in fact provide the evening's amusement, well, the **Poetry Café (Map 13)** gives you the stage. Or stay at home and talk to yourself; it's cheaper.

Music, Sweet Music

London's veins are pumped by its mellifluous melodies, the driving sound of grime, the sneers of angry young men and the coos of sweet maidens. Whether you're dub-stepping in the dark or jamming along at folk night there'll be something to hear at any given time of the week.

Strummin' Mental

This city's music scene is in a constant state of flux with bands, venues and styles falling in and out of cool lists quicker than a Ramones song. What never changes though is that there always is a scene and with that scene comes the venue. The good news is that there are so many great places to do this in. Yes we've got our share of corporate megaliths (that means you **O2**) but for every church of Carling there are two or three brilliant dives like the punky **Grosvenor (Map 145)** or the ever-mobbed **Stag's Head (Map 84)**.

For the sweatily inclined there are infinite choices. Bethnal Green's **Star of Bethnal**

Green (Map 92)** (formerly the Pleasure Unit), Highgate's **Buffalo Bar (Map 80)** and Angel's **Lexington (Map 79)** are as pant-wettingly indie as they come but if you like harder or weirder stuff the **Camden Underworld (Map 71)** does all the metals while **Cafe Oto (Map 86)** handles experimental and improv. **The MacBeth (Map 84)** is very popular yet somehow suffers from a fun bypass but **Monto Water Rats (Map 5)** is an unshakeable legend. The refurbished **Old Blue Last (Map 84)** or Vice Magazine party HQ has surfed to the crest of the trend wave fueled by young kids attempting to be sexually harassed by older men like in their favourite adverts for American Apparel. Mid-sized venues for mid-fame bands? The **Scala (Map 78)** is a brilliant converted cinema. The now legal **Barden's Boudoir (Map 86)** has come a long way since it was a dingy dive run by gangsters and of course the **ICA (Map 23)** is the 'art-space' par excellence for all artistes who insist on that 'e' at the end of 'artist.' The **Amersham Arms (Map 126)** is a good place to watch some twonks you've been told to like by Dazed. The city's electronic music scene generally piggy-backs the guitars, but check out **Cable (Map 107)** and **Lightbox (Map 134)**.

As for the classics, the **Shepherd's Bush Empire (Map 33)** and the breathtakingly beautiful **Bush Hall (Map 32)** remain west London's finest, while Camden stalwart **Koko (Map 71)** keeps rocking in the free world. The north London show is being stolen by **Roundhouse (Map 71)**, though, boasting a healthy "I am Legend"-attitude and some bloody horrible Anthony Gormley statues waiting to jump from the top. **Brixton Academy (Map 145)** might be slightly overrated, but its sky-like ceiling remains awesome. If you have to do stadium-size, do stadium-size in style and get your seat in the **Royal Albert Hall (Map 36)**, which is increasingly luring good non-classical acts. The refurbishment of the **Royal Festival Hall (Map 104)**, meanwhile, has kick-started more pop-oriented programming on the South Bank.

A World of Jazz and Blues

Camden's intimate **Jazz Café (Map 71)** seems to have no intention of stopping its relentless stream of first-rate jazz performances, getting in more soul, funk and pop at the same time, while **Ronnie Scott's Jazz Club (Map 12)**, London's undisputed grandaddy of jazz original continues to offer up an eclectic programme of past and present. For some of the freshest jazz, alongside great contemporary folk and world music, head to Dalston, where the plush **Vortex (Map 82)** is a-buzz with free-spirited legends. On the other side of town, Fulham's small but perfectly formed **606 Club (Map 50)** sets the tone with crammed, small tables within slobbering distance from the saxes. Catch excellent blues and singer/songwriter stuff every night of the week at **Ain't Nothing But**

The Blues Bar (Map 10), or Denmark Street's **12 Bar Club (Map 12)**. Latin jazz breezes through the air at Archway's **Caipirinha Jazz Bar (Map 52)**. For world music, the **Barbican Centre (Map 7)** leads the pack, but is easily beaten in atmosphere stakes by the **Union Chapel (Map 80)**, an Islington church doubling as one of London's most beautiful venues and in scummy stakes by **Dingwalls (Map 71)** who continue to expand their programming. The home of folk is the brilliant **Cecil Sharp House (Map 70)**. If classical music floats your boat, look beyond the obvious venues and settle amid the great acoustics of Chelsea's **Cadogan Hall (Map 19)**, the historical brilliance of Hackney's **Sutton House (Map 87)** or the magnificent **Wigmore Hall (Map 2)**, in Mayfair.

Map 1 • Marylebone (West)

Duke of York	45 Harrowby St	020 7262 9129	The ideal local.

Map 2 • Marylebone (East)

Claridge's Bar	55 Brook St	020 7629 8860	Posh and plush and Art Deco. More champagne!
Gunmakers	33 Aybrook St	020 7487 4937	Nice boozer on quiet street.
Inn 1888	21 Devonshire St	020 7486 7420	Quiet pint perfection.
The Phoenix	37 Cavendish Sq	020 7493 8003	A quirky gem amidst an ocean of crappy chain bars.
Purl	50-54 Blandford St	020 7935 0835	Victorian themed experimental cocktail bar.

Map 3 • Fitzrovia

100 Club	100 Oxford St	020 7636 0933	Ancient club that's seen off Nazi bombs and Sex Pistols.
The Albany	240 Great Portland St	020 7387 0221	Swanky, but nice. And the music's good.
Bourne & Hollingsworth	28 Rathbone Pl	020 7636 8228	Fine Fitzrovian basement boutique.
Bradley's Spanish Bar	42 Hanway St	020 7636 0359	60's rock joint with awesome jukebox and disgusting toilets.
Bricklayers Arms	31 Gresse St	020 7636 5593	Advertising types fake no-nonsense boozing.
Charlotte Street Hotel	15 Charlotte St	020 7806 2000	Dirty gossip over dirty martinis.
The Cock	27 Great Portland St	087 2107 7077	Cheap, cheerful and central.
The Fitzroy Tavern	16 Charlotte St	020 7580 3714	Sam Smith's, anyone?
Hakkasan	8 Hanway St	020 7927 7000	Sleek, blue-lit boutique. For saketinis and rose petal martinis.
The Jerusalem Tavern	55 Britton St	020 7490 4281	A tiny old wooden gem of a pub. And organic ale.
Market Place	11 Market Pl	020 7079 2020	Warm buzz. Hot crowd. Cool prices.
The Northumberland Arms	43 Goodge St	020 7580 7975	Cosy, old-style bar with a local feel.
The Remedy	124 Cleveland St	020 3489 3800	Deep dive into wine, with food pairings, too.
Rising Sun	46 Tottenham Ct Rd	020 7636 6530	Bordering studentland and Fitzrovia; pretty name, less pretty pub.
The Roxy	3 Rathbone Pl	020 7255 1098	Hip subterranean hangout. More chicks than dicks.
Shochu Lounge	37 Charlotte St	020 7580 6464	Japanese-styled cocktails underneath Roka restaurant.
The Social	5 Little Portland St	020 7636 4992	Fab music, nonchalant surroundings and plenty of trendsetters.
Yorkshire Grey	46 Langham St	020 7636 4788	Upstairs is perfect when Oxford Street's pissing you off.

Map 4 • Bloomsbury (West)

All Star Lanes	Bloomsbury Pl	020 7025 2676	You'll be bowled over. Oh yes you will.
Bloomsbury Bowling Lanes	Bedford Way	020 7183 1979	As cool as bowling gets.
Marquis Cornwallis	31 Marchmont St	020 7278 8355	Chilled couches.
The Old Crown Public House	33 New Oxford St	020 7836 9121	After-work bar that takes itself very seriously.
The Plough	27 Museum St	020 7636 7964	Fancy a bite? London Vampyre Society meetings held here monthly.
The Princess Louise	208 High Holborn	020 7405 8816	Victorian gin palace now serving cheap but good lager.
ULU	Malet St	020 7664 2000	Student union, student prices, student bands.

Map 5 • Bloomsbury (East)

06 Chad's Place	6 St Chad's Pl	020 7278 3355	Stylish wine bar with plastic chairs? SOOO avant-garde, dahhhling!
The Blue Lion	133 Grays Inn Rd	020 7405 4422	Pool table!
Calthorpe Arms	252 Gray's Inn Rd	020 7278 4732	Impressive old man pub.
The Clerk & Well	156 Clerkenwell Rd	020 7837 8548	You and a hundred cycle couriers.
Mosto	328 Grays Inn Rd	020 3589 5983	No rats here, only the best up-and-coming bands.
The Perseverance	63 Lamb's Conduit St	020 7405 8278	Bustling, young and semi-trendy.
Pi Shuei	59 Mount Pleasant		Kung fu-themed bar.
S hy's	15 Leeke St	020 7278 5949	Our lunchtime to late-night-wind-down friend.

Map 6 • Clerkenwell

19	19 Great Sutton St	020 7253 1920	Classic American pool hall with occasional DJ events.
Bar stand Busking	Northampton Square		Free acoustic gigs in summer. Dreamy.
The Betsey Trotwood	56 Farringdon Rd	020 7253 4285	Thoroughly likable Shepherd Neame pub renowned for live music.
Caf Kick	43 Exmouth Market	020 7837 8077	Creaky, Latin American table football cafe.
The Dovetail	9 Jerusalem Passage	020 7490 7321	Small, but perfectly formed Clerkenwell sister to Broadway Market's The Dove.
The Harlequin	27 Arlington Way	079 7565 2669	Livingroom boozer.
Old Red Lion	418 St. John St	020 7833 3053	Theatre pub legend.
The Slaughtered Lamb	34 Great Sutton St	020 7253 1516	Dimly-lit pub that's still packing in the Clerkenwell crowd.
The Three Kings	7 Clerkenwell Close	020 7253 0483	Quirky pub that dies on weekends.
The Wilmington Arms	69 Rosebery Ave	020 7837 1384	Staff have 'arsehole' tattooed on their foreheads.

Map 7 • Barbican / City Road (South)

Ni tjar	129 City Rd	020 7253 4101	Like Fat Sam's Grand Slam.
The Two Brewers	121 Whitecross St	020 7819 9539	Traditional English pub with a young hip crowd.

Map 8 • Liverpool Street / Broadgate

The Book Club	100 Leonard St	020 7684 8618	All day food and drink venue with outdoor space and basement club.
Cal oh Callay	65 Rivington St	020 7739 4781	Not-so-secret cocktail bar in The City; enter through a wardrobe.
Cas a	5 Ravey St	020 7729 7230	Gorgeous cocktails and entertaining bar staff.
Lou ge Bohemia	1 Great Eastern St	077 2070 7000	Vintage martinis make up for neo-avant-garde pretenses.
Red Lion	1 Eldon St0	20 7247 5381	Drinkers near Moorgate can't be choosers. So there.
Wo ship Street Whistling Shop	63 Worship St	020 7247 0015	Wet your whistle.
XO D	32 Cowper St	020 7354 9993	Concrete music bunker with quality acts and a buzzing vibe.

Map 9 • Mayfair / Green Park

17 Wine Bar	181 Piccadilly	020 7734 8040	Empty Fortnum & Mason's wine cellar.
bbe	43 Buckingham Palace Rd	020 7958 7000	Get drunk behind Elizabeth's back.
Fur ky Buddha	15 Berkeley St	020 7495 2596	Overpriced, overrated, tacky Z-list haunt. Apart from that, it's great!
Ma iki	1 Dover St	020 7493 9529	Crushingly tropical cocktail bar. Pineapples a-go-go.
Shepherd's Tavern	50 Hertford St	020 7499 3017	For drinking within Shepherd's Market.
Wh sky Mist	35 Hertford St	020 7208 4067	High-end hotel bar with a huge selection of whiskies.

Map 10 • Piccadilly / Soho (West)

5th iew	203 Piccadilly	020 7851 2433	Spill Bloody Marys over books in full view of Big Ben.
Ain Nothing But...	20 Kingly St	020 7287 0514	Bracingly raw music in a tiny frontroom.
The Blind Pig	58 Poland St	020 7993 3251	Challenging cocktails above Social Eating House.
Cou house Bar	19 Great Marlborough St	020 7297 5555	Drink where Oscar Wilde was in the dock.
The John Snow	39 Broadwick St	020 7437 1344	Yet another cheap, old school boozer from Samuel Smith Brewery.
Luc y Voice	52 Poland St	020 7439 3660	Why is this London's best karaoke bar? The dress up box.
Mil & Honey	61 Poland St	020 7065 6800	Sister to the New York members' bar.
The Red Lion	14 Kingly St	020 7734 4985	Amazingly cheap for such a central spot.
Stra wberry Moons	15 Heddon St	020 7437 7300	Dig the cheese, with your new squeeze.
The Windmill	6 Mill St	020 7491 8050	Fab beers on tap but you come here for the pies.

Map 11 • Soho (Central)

Blu Posts	22 Berwick St	020 7437 5008	Unreformed, scuzzy boozer.
The Blue Posts	28 Rupert St	020 7437 1415	Hey, a decent pub in Soho.
The Comedy Store	1 Oxendon St	084 4847 1728	It ain't world famous for no reason, chuckles.

Arts & Entertainment • **Nightlife**

De Hems	11 Macclesfield St	020 7437 2494	Dutch bar with brain-cell-annihilatingly strong beer. Hic!
Experimental Cocktail Club	13 Gerrard St		The modern-day speakeasy: reservation by email only.
Freedom	66 Wardour St	020 7734 0071	Neon green cocktail kitsch.
The French House	49 Dean St	020 7437 2799	Boho Soho hang-out for eccentrics.
The Lyric	37 Great Windmill St	020 7434 0604	Charming Victorian pub with many draughts.
Old Tom & English	187 Wardour St	020 7287 7347	Sleek cocktails in mid-century modern atmosphere.
The Shadow Lounge	5 Brewer St	020 7317 9270	Gay chi chi lounge.
Village	81 Wardour St	020 7478 0530	Tacky, flirtatious Soho gay bar.

Map 12 • Soho (East)

68 and Boston	5 Greek St	020 7287 3713	68's wine is on ground floor; Boston's cocktails live above.
Ape & Bird	142 Shaftesbury Ave	020 7836 3119	Italian-focused beverages from folks behind Polpo.
Bar Termini	7 Old Compton St	07860 945018	Italian coffee and cocktails; efficiently scheduled.
The Borderline	Orange Yard	020 7734 5547	Cool basement club, bizarrely got up in Tex-Mex decor.
Cafe Boheme	13 Old Compton St	020 7734 0623	Beautiful bar to prop up and people watch.
Comptons	53 Old Compton St	020 3238 0163	Crammed gay pub.
The Crobar	17 Manette St	020 7439 0831	Heavy metal and cheap bourbon. Be a man for once.
G-A-Y Bar	30 Old Compton St	020 7494 2756	Poptastic gay bunker.
G-A-Y Late	5 Goslett Yard	020 7734 9858	Cheap drinks and pop videos wipe out brain functions 'til 3am.
Garlic & Shots	14 Frith St	020 7734 9505	Drunken vampires beware.
Green Carnation	5 Greek St	020 8616 8087	Sexy, Oskar Wilde-inspired lounge that Oskar would have approved of.
Jazz After Dark	9 Greek St	020 7734 0545	Tunes and cheap drinks, until LATE.
Karaoke Box	18 Frith St	020 7494 3878	A bit gritty but one of London's cheaper karaoke bars.
Ku	30 Lisle St	020 7437 4303	Newly relocated gay bar for the young and clueless.
LAB Bar	12 Old Compton St	020 7437 7820	London Academy of Bartending—they know how to make martinis.
The Montagu Pyke	105 Charing Cross Rd	020 7287 6039	Cheap beer—in the West End.
Ronnie Scott's	47 Frith St	020 7439 0747	Original, and still the best.
The Royal George	133 Charing Cross Rd	020 7734 8837	Busy, but the crowd's nice. Board games and food.
The Three Greyhounds	25 Greek St	020 7494 0953	Recall glory days of Soho hunting grounds with real ale.
The Toucan	19 Carlisle St	020 7437 4123	Small and snug central bolthole for Guinness.

Map 13 • Covent Garden

Compagnie Des Vins Surnaturels	8-10 Neal's Yard	020 7734 7737	Encyclopedic wine bar with French-Italian focus.
The Cross Keys	31 Endell St	020 7836 5185	Tiny old-school boozer.
Freud	198 Shaftesbury Ave	020 7240 9933	Intimate basement bar that used to be Alex of Blur's living room. Literally.
Guanabara	Parker St	020 7242 8600	Brasil. But in Holborn.
Lamb and Flag	33 Rose St	020 7497 9504	Cobbled lane leads to a crowded but gloriously timeless inn.
Poetry Cafe	22 Betterton St	020 7420 9888	Eat, drink, write, listen or, yes, PERFORM!

Map 14 • Holborn / Temple

Bar Polski	11 Little Turnstile	020 7831 9679	With 50 types of vodka, even beetroot soup tastes good.
Bounce	121 Holborn	020 3657 6525	Anyone for (table) tennis?
Cittie of Yorke	22 High Holborn	020 7242 7670	Soe olde its name has extra e's. A marvellouse pube.
The Craft Beer Co.	82 Leather Ln		Beer drinkers heaven, albeit with a scramble to get served.
The Enterprise	38 Red Lion St	020 7404 8461	More Captain Cook than Captain Kirk.
The Lamb	94 Lamb's Conduit St	020 7405 0713	Legendary little place with Victorian touches.
The Seven Stars	53 Carey St	020 7242 8521	Tiny, slightly dusty bar frequented by barristers.
Volupte	9 Norwich St	020 7831 1622	They call it burlesque, we call it strippers with tassles.

Map 15 • Blackfriars / Farringdon

The Cocktail Trading Co.	50-52 Long Ln	020 7427 6097	Mixologically compelling drinks; fun attitude.
Fabric	77 Charterhouse St	020 7336 8898	Debauched club mecca for gurners of all persuasions.
Fox and Anchor	115 Charterhouse St	020 7250 1300	Amazing interior and the tankards make up for the wankers.
The Hat and Tun	3 Hatton Wall	020 7242 4747	Home of the original politically incorrect 100 shooter list.
Ye Olde Cheshire Cheese	145 Fleet St	020 7353 6170	Get tanked up where Dickens used to. Historic.
Ye Olde Mitre	1 Ely Pl	020 7405 4751	Elizabeth I used to dance here, don't you know?!

Map 16 • Square Mile (West)

The Hatchet	28 Garlick Hill	020 7236 0720	Lost in the City? Escape here.
Planet of the Grapes	74 Queen Victoria St	020 7248 1892	The clue is in the name.
The Samuel Pepys	Stew Ln	020 7489 1871	Find it and be rewarded with Thames views.
Ye Olde Watling	29 Watling St	020 7248 8935	Squeeze in.

Map 17 • Square Mile (East)

The Counting House	50 Cornhill	020 7283 7123	A truly magnificent (former) bank. That sells beer now.
Royal Exchange Grand Café and Restaurant Sauterelle	Royal Exchange	020 7618 2480	The courtyard of the Royal Exchange. Fancy, eh?

Map 18 • Tower Hill / Aldgate

Dion	52 Leadenhall St	020 7702 9111	Veuve Clicquot La Grande Dame Rose, anyone?
Kenza	10 Devonshire Sq	020 7929 5533	Belly-dancers, cocktails & couscous.
Mary Janes	124 Minories	020 7481 8195	Inconspicuous perspex floor catches out the knickeries.
The Minories	64 Minories	020 7702 1658	Cavernous boozer by day, thumping disco by night.
Revolution	140 Leadenhall St	020 7621 9955	Vodka-drenched, vault-like DJ bar that couldn't care less about the revolution.

Map 19 • Belgravia

The Blue Bar	Wilton Pl	020 7235 6000	It's blue. Mindbogglingly so.
The Nag's Head	53 Kinnerton St	020 7235 1135	No mobiles allowed. Says it all.
The Plumber's Arms	14 Lower Belgrave St	020 7730 4067	Tradesman's pub from days of yore. Ask about Lord Lucan.
The Wilton Arms	71 Kinnerton St	020 7235 4854	A Shepherd Neame pub? In Belgravia?

Map 20 • Victoria / Pimlico (West)

The Cask & Glass	39 Palace St	020 7834 7630	Teeny tiny, English country garden-esque drinking hole. Flower-festoned fortitude, real ale.
The Warwick	25 Warwick Way	020 7834 4987	Gastropub with fine selection of booze.
Windsor Castle	23 Francis St	020 7834 7260	Easier to like than to find.

Map 21 • Pimlico (East)

Morpeth Arms	58 Millbank	020 7834 6442	Where Millbank prisoners used to escape to.

Map 22 • Westminster

The Albert	52 Victoria St	020 7222 5577	Distinguished, well-preserved period pub. Tourist haunt but rightly so.
The Cinnamon Club	30 Great Smith St	020 7222 2555	Cocktail classiness inside the Old Westminster Library. Try finding it.
The Speaker	46 Great Peter St	020 7222 1749	Good after-worker with guest ales.
St. Stephen's Tavern	10 Bridge St	020 7925 2286	Tiny pub with character, despite being on tourist trail.
Two Chairmen	39 Dartmouth St	020 7222 8694	Public servants galore! Decent pub for this area though.

Map 23 • St. James's

Aura	48 St James's St	020 7499 9999	If you ain't on the list, you ain't coming in. Seriously.
Dukes Hotel	35 St James's St	020 7491 4840	Channel 007 and have a martini at Ian Fleming's haunt.
Institute of Contemporary Arts	The Mall	020 7930 3647	Cutting edge arts complex/bar, weirdly stuck on the upper-crust Mall.

Map 24 • Trafalgar Square / The Strand

Asia de Cuba	45 St Martin's Lane	020 7300 5588	For rum-drinking with the jet set.
BYOC	28 Bedfordbury	020 7240 7810	Underneath Juice Bar. Bring Your Own Cocktails to this intimate den.
The Chandos	29 St Martin's Ln	020 7836 1401	All Trafalgar Square pubs tourist traps? Think again.
The Coal Hole	91 Strand	020 7379 9883	Genuine old style.
Covent Garden Comedy Club	The Arches	079 6007 1340	Good acts play to a friendly crowd drinking awful beer.
Gordon's Wine Bar	47 Villiers St	020 7930 1408	Candle-lit vaults. Romantic perfection.
The Harp	47 Chandos Pl	020 7836 0291	Covent Garden's secret spot for sausage and a good brew.
Heaven	The Arches	020 7930 2020	Epicentre of London's late night gay scene.
Maple Leaf	41 Maiden Ln	020 7240 2843	Just don't ask which State they're from.
Punch & Judy	The Covent Garden Piazza	020 7379 0923	Naff, naff, naff. 'Nuff said?
Retro Bar	2 George St	020 7839 8760	Chilled gay bar, hiding from Charing Cross in a small alley.
Roadhouse	The Covent Garden Piazza	020 7240 6001	"You're the one that I want, ooh-ooh-ooh"
The Sherlock Holmes	10 Northumberland St	020 7930 2644	Unintentionally sinister, must-see Holmes waxwork upstairs. Expect bad dreams.
The Ship and Shovell	1 Craven Passage	020 7839 1311	A pub made of two pubs, both obsessed with Sherlock Holmes.
Terroirs	5 William IV St	020 7036 0660	Non-pretentious wine bar with good eats too.
Zoo Bar & Club	13 Bear St	020 7839 4188	Wake up with someone new.

Map 26 • Maida Hill

The Union Tavern	45 Woodfield Rd	020 7286 1886	A pub that bakes its own bread! Oh, and it's canal side...

Arts & Entertainment · **Nightlife**

Map 27 · Maida Vale

The Bridge House	13 Westbourne Terrace Rd	020 7266 4326	Canal views and comedy. Lovely.
The Warwick Castle	6 Warwick Pl	020 7266 0921	Down-to-earth drinking in Maida Vale. Indeed.
The Waterway	54 Formosa St	020 7266 3557	Try not to fall into the canal.

Map 28 · Ladbroke Grove / Notting Hill (West)

Julie's Restaurant & Champagne Bar	135 Portland Rd	020 7229 8331	Pleasantly posh wine bar full of pleasantly posh ladies.

Map 29 · Notting Hill Gate

Mau Mau	265 Portobello Rd	020 7229 8528	Ace mojitos and Thursdays open-mic. Wear your dancing shoes.
Notting Hill Arts Club	21 Notting Hill Gate	020 7460 4459	Indie cave with bands, lurid projections and teenagers.
Sun in Splendour	7 Portobello Rd	020 7792 0914	Notting Hill denizens' choice.
Trailer Happiness	177 Portobello Rd	020 7313 4644	Step back in time.
Uxbridge Arms	13 Uxbridge St	020 7727 7326	Warm little place full of eccentric old toffs.
Windsor Castle	114 Campden Hill Rd	020 7243 8797	A wood-panelled piece of pub history.

Map 30 · Bayswater

All Star Lanes	6 Porchester Gardens	020 7313 8363	Glitzy bowling madness.
The Cow	89 Westbourne Park Rd	020 7221 0021	Lovely pub. Let down by braying trustafarians.

Map 31 · Paddington

Royal Exchange	26 Sale Pl	020 7723 3781	Salt beef sarnies and hot and cold Guinness.
The Victoria	10 Strathearn Pl	020 7724 1191	British pub straight from a Richard Curtis film. Simply perfect.

Map 32 · Shepherd's Bush (West)

Bush Hall	310 Uxbridge Rd	020 8222 6955	The red carpet, the ornate walls...the sheer beauty!
The Queen Adelaide	412 Uxbridge Rd	020 8746 2573	Chic gastropub serving the West Bush.
White Horse	31 Uxbridge Rd	020 8723 4531	Did you call my pint a slag? Outside, now!

Map 33 · Shepherd's Bush

Albertine	1 Wood Lane	020 8743 9593	Drink wine with the Beep set.
The Defector's Weld	170 Uxbridge Rd	020 8749 0008	Tarted up boozer.
O2 Shepherd's Bush Empire	Shepherd's Bush Green	020 8354 3300	Still among London venueland's finest.

Map 34 · West Kensington / Olympia

The Cumberland Arms	29 North End Rd	020 7371 6806	Where long hard days become good again.
Famous 3 Kings (F3K) Bar	171 North End Rd	020 7603 6071	Brilliant atmosphere for big matches especially rugby. Pool tables too.
Society Bar	380 Kensington High St	020 7603 3333	Dying for a drink in Kensington? Well there.

Map 35 · Kensington

The Builders Arms	1 Kensington Ct Pl	020 7937 6213	Boozy haven from High Street Kensington's shopping madness.
The Devonshire Arms	37 Marloes Rd	020 7937 0710	Warm and cosy for a roast on a rainy Sunday.

Map 36 · South Kensington / Gloucester Rd

Boujis	43 Thurloe St	020 7584 2000	If you want to see the two princes drunk. And only then.
The Queen's Arms	30 Queen's Gate Mews	020 7823 9293	South Ken's secret drinking spot. Close to the Royal Albert Hall.

Map 38 · Chiswick

Carvosso's	210 Chiswick High Rd	020 8995 9121	For a glass of wine before dinner.
George IV	185 Chiswick High Rd	020 8994 4624	Fullers pies, real ale and a comedy club on the High Road? Sweet.
Packhorse & Talbot	145 Chiswick High Rd	020 8994 0360	A Chiswick institution. Proper British pub...with live jazz?! Truly.
The Roebuck	122 Chiswick High Rd	020 8995 4392	Best pub in West London. Unpretentious charm, killer Sunday roast.

Map 39 · Stamford Brook

The Raven	375 Goldhawk Rd	020 8748 6977	A bit grubby on the outside but £4 handmade pies are part of the appeal.

Map 40 · Goldhawk Rd / Ravenscourt Park

The Dove	19 Upper Mall	020 8748 9474	So perfect for dates that Charles II brought Nell Gwynne here.

Map 41 · Hammersmith

Brook Green	170 Shepherd's Bush Rd	020 7603 2516	Lost between Hammersmith and Shepherd's Bush? Fear not.
The Distillers	64 Fulham Palace Rd	020 8748 2834	Chandelier clad pub-bar with ace live music and comedy in The Regal Room.
Hammersmith Apollo	45 Queen Caroline St	020 8563 3800	Still West London's best music venue.
The Hampshire Hog	227 King St	020 8748 3391	Relaxing spot for a Pinot Noir after a hard day.
Lyric Hammersmith	King St	020 8741 6850	Hammersmith's hottest home of hentertainment.

Map 42 · Baron's Court

Colten Arms	187 Greyhound Rd	020 7385 6956	If you're not already a regular, you'll wish you were.
The Curtains Up	28 Comeragh Rd	020 7386 7543	Pub which keeps actors in the basement.
The Fulham Mitre	81 Dawes Rd	020 7386 8877	Young, trendy Fulhamites like it. We don't.
The Queen's Arms	171 Greyhound Rd	020 7823 9293	Relaxed and comfy local boozer with tip top Sunday roasts.

Map 43 · West Brompton / Fulham Broadway / Earls Court

The Blackbird	209 Earl's Court Rd	020 7835 1855	Proper London local amidst the chaos of Earl's Court Road.
Chair & Coffee	512 Fulham Rd	020 7018 1913	Friday is aperitivo night.
The King's Head	17 Hogarth Rd	020 7373 5239	Tucked away with British style tapas. Who knew!
Onboard Karaoke	8 Kenway Rd	020 7244 6850	Truly authentic Japanese karaoke at truly authentic London prices.
Prince Of Teck	161 Earl's Court Rd	020 7373 4291	Locals and tourists receive a friendly welcome in this pub.

Map 44 · Chelsea

Brinkley's	47 Hollywood Rd	020 7351 1683	Enter the cougar's lair.
The Drayton Arms	153 Old Brompton Rd	020 7835 2301	Low-lit Victorian pub with mismatched chairs and a great beer selection.
The Duke of Clarence	148 Old Brompton Rd	020 7373 1285	All leather seats and wooden floors. Cool spot for a drink after work.

Map 45 · Chelsea (East)

The Anglesea Arms	15 Selwood Terrace	020 7373 7960	4th Best Pub in the UK, says The Morning Advertiser Industry.
Chelsea Potter	119 Kings Rd	020 7352 9479	Chelsea old school.
The Pig's Ear	35 Old Church St	020 7352 2908	Relaxed, tasteful, friendly.

Map 47 · Fulham (West)

The Crabtree	Rainville Rd	020 7385 3929	The Thames view from the garden is reason alone to visit.

Map 49 · Parson's Green

Amuse Bouche	51 Parsons Green Ln	020 7371 8517	Fizzy fun.
Duke on the Green	235 New King's Rd	020 7736 2777	If only all pub food was this good (but half the price).
The White Horse	1 Parsons Green	020 7736 2115	Victorian pub and a beer drinker's heaven. Book a table.

Map 50 · Sand's End

606 Club	90 Lots Rd	020 7352 5953	Great jazz venue. If you like ten minute sax solos.

Map 51 · Highgate

The Angel Inn	37 Highgate High St	020 8341 5913	Lively local with board games and unusual beers.
The Boogaloo	312 Archway Rd	020 8340 2928	Not as cool as it thinks it is.
The Flask	77 Highgate West Hill	020 8348 7346	Great beers, great food, great place. Really, it is.
Prince of Wales	53 Highgate High St	020 8340 0445	Friendly local for posh Highgaters and their even posher dogs.
The Victoria	28 North Hill	020 8340 6091	Try to catch the Sunday sing-along sessions.
The Woodman	414 Archway Rd	020 8340 3016	Reformed fight club with gastropub intentions.
The Wrestlers	98 N Rd	020 8340 4297	Branded "best pub in Highgate" by residents.

Map 52 · Archway (North)

Caipirinha Bar	177 Archway Rd	020 8340 2321	Cosiness! Cocktails! Latin jazz! Sherpa required to find it!
The Winchester Pub Hotel	206 Archway Rd	020 8374 1690	Wonky-floored palace of boozy delight.

501

Arts & Entertainment · **Nightlife**

Map 53 · Crouch End

The Harringay Arms	153 Crouch Hill	020 8292 3624	No music, plenty of beer.
King's Head	2 Tottenham Ln	020 8340 1028	Plenty of funny business.
The Queens	26 Broadway Parade	020 8340 2031	God save the Queens.
The Shaftesbury	534 Hornsey Rd	020 7272 7950	Family-friendly local with hearty food menu.
Stapleton Tavern	2 Crouch Hill	020 7272 5395	Super laid-back local.

Map 54 · Hornsey

The Hope & Anchor	128 Tottenham Ln	020 8340 3051	Proper local.

Map 55 · Harringay

The Beaconsfield	359 Green Lanes	020 8800 2153	Friendly local. The footy's always on!
Bruhaha	501 Green Lanes	020 8348 8563	Friendly, laid back atmosphere and varied clientele.
Jam In A Jar	599 Green Lanes	079 5176 9981	Reliably good local watering hole.
The Salisbury	1 Green Lanes	020 7836 5863	A local's secret...no longer! Exceptional.

Map 56 · Hampstead Village

Duke of Hamilton	23 New End	020 7794 0258	Lovely local, nicely tucked away.
The Flask	14 Flask Walk	020 7435 4580	Hampstead alleyway classic that's been refitted. But nicely so.
The Freemasons Arms	32 Downshire Hill	020 7433 6811	Lovely beer garden.
The Holly Bush	22 Holly Mount	020 7435 2892	It's hidden. It's a gem. Really.
The Horseshoe	28 Heath St	020 7431 7206	Birthplace of Camden Town Brewery.

Map 57 · Hampstead Heath

The Garden Gate	14 S End Rd	020 7435 4938	Nice pub with garden for those sunny days. (yeah right)
Roebuck	15 Pond St	020 7435 7354	Somewhere between cosy pub and stylish bar. And good at it.
The White Horse	154 Fleet Rd	020 7485 2112	Yet another pub on the thai food bandwagon.

Map 58 · Parliament Hill / Dartmouth Park

The Bull and Last	168 Highgate Rd	020 7267 3641	Good place for a post-Heath pint.
The Southampton Arms	139 Highgate Rd	079 5878 0073	Best pub in the area. A real ale lover's dream.

Map 59 · Tufnell Park

Aces And Eights Saloon Bar	156 Fortress Rd	020 7485 4033	Rock n roll n pizza.
Boston Arms	178 Junction Rd	020 7272 8153	Ferociously scruffy but friendly Irish pub, with rock pit attached.
The Hideaway	114 Junction Rd	020 7561 0779	Beer, pizza, dancing. What else do you need?
The Lord Palmerston	33 Dartmouth Park Hill	020 7485 1578	Gone a bit plastic, but still worth it.
The Star	47 Chester Rd	020 7272 2863	It's a star.

Map 60 · Archway

Mother Red Cap	665 Holloway Rd	020 7263 7082	Begorra! Bejesus! Be better off going to another boozer!

Map 61 · Holloway (North)

The Quays	471 Holloway Rd	020 7272 3634	Into bad U2 cover bands? Then you'll love it here.
The Swimmer	13 Eburne Rd	020 7281 4632	No running, diving in the shallow end, or heavy petting.

Map 62 · Finsbury Park

Faltering Fullback	19 Perth Rd	020 7272 5834	Tardis-like local. Avoid match nights unless you're a Gooner.
The Old Dairy	1 Crouch Hill	020 7263 3337	Great food, great drink, great place.
The Silver Bullet	5 Station Pl	020 7619 3639	Mix-and-match music, edgy vibe, and very cheap drinks.
WB Yeats	20 Fonthill Rd	020 8617 3400	Good selection of craft beers.
The World's End	21 Stroud Green Rd	020 7281 8679	Football and live music, sometimes at the same time.

Map 63 · Manor House

The Brownswood	271 Green Lanes	020 8802 0494	Enter, before Manor House drives you mad.
The Happy Man	89 Woodberry Grove	020 8800 0074	Great sunny day spot, looks naff but never disappoints.

Map 64 · Stoke Newington

Auld Shillelagh	105 Stoke Newington Church St	020 7249 5951	The best Guinness in London; you won't leave standing up.
The Londesborough	36 Barbauld Rd	020 7254 5865	Stokey trendies on leather sofas.
The Rose and Crown	199 Stoke Newington Church St	020 7923 3337	Sunday roasts to die for and step-back-in-time décor.

Ruby's	76 Stoke Newington Rd		Underneath the cinema sign.
Ryan's Bar	181 Stoke Newington Church St	020 7275 7807	Boho cafe and venue with a noise limiter! Pussies.
The Shakespeare	57 Allen Rd	020 7254 4190	The Bard would be proud.
White Hart	69 Stoke Newington High St	020 7254 6626	Huge pub, huge beer garden—really it's huge.

Map 65 • West Hampstead

The Black Lion	274 Kilburn High Rd	020 7624 1424	Popular local since the 6th century.
Czech and Slovak Bar	74 West End Ln	020 7372 1193	Go Czech.
The Good Ship	289 Kilburn High Rd	079 4900 8253	Where Kilburn takes music seriously.

Map 66 • Finchley Road / Swiss Cottage

Ye Olde Swiss Cottage	98 Finchley Rd	020 7722 3487	What can we say.

Map 67 • Belsize Park

The Washington	50 England's Ln	020 7722 8842	Monday night is pub quiz night.

Map 68 • Kilburn High Road / Abbey Road

Love & Liquor	34 Kilburn High Rd	020 7625 7500	Niteclub evoking "Brooklyn, USA"; cocktails, bottle service.

Map 69 • St. John's Wood

The Star	38 St. John's Wood Terrace	020 7722 1051	Drink face-to-face with a huge Highland Terrier.

Map 70 • Primrose Hill

The Albert	11 Princess Rd	020 7722 1886	A local. Cosy and relaxed.
Cecil Sharp House	2 Regent's Park Rd	020 7485 2206	Sword dancing and Olde Stuffe.
The Lansdowne	90 Gloucester Ave	020 7483 0409	Home of the beautiful people.
The Princess of Wales	22 Chalcot Rd	020 7722 0354	Traditional pub with occasional jazz performances.
Sir Richard Steele	97 Haverstock Hill	020 7483 1261	Friendly local with quirky decor.

Map 71 • Camden Town / Chalk Farm / Kentish Town (West)

Bar Vinyl	6 Inverness St	020 7485 9318	DJ Bar. And good coffee.
Brewdog	113 Bayham St	020 7284 4626	Original London branch of the Fraserburgh craft beer renegades.
Camden Town Brewery Bar	55 Wilkin Street Mews	020 7485 1671	Where better for a pint of Camden Ink.
The Constitution	42 St Pancras Way	020 7387 4805	Proper boozer away from the madness of Camden Taaahn.
Dingwalls	Middle Yard	020 7428 5929	Camden Lock's guitar-smashing heartland.
The Dublin Castle	94 Parkway	020 7485 1773	Famous, small, LOUD.
Electric Ballroom	184 Camden High St	020 7485 9006	Scruffy but essential rock haunt, perennially threatened by developers.
The Enterprise	2 Haverstock Hill	020 7485 2659	Literary Irish pub with tiny indie venue upstairs.
Fiddler's Elbow	1 Malden Rd	020 7485 3269	Live music venue pub spits pretention.
The Good Mixer	30 Inverness St	020 7916 7929	Ah, remember those halcyon days of Britpop?
The Grafton	20 Prince of Wales Rd	020 7482 4466	Hosts regular DJs from renowned Dirty Water Club.
The Hawley Arms	2 Castlehaven Rd	020 7428 5979	The Hawley will rise from the ashes. Camden needs it.
The Jazz Cafe	5 Parkway 020 7485 6834	A relentless stream of excellent gigs.	
KOKO	1 Camden High St	087 0432 5527	From Charlie Chaplin to Lenny Kravitz, playing Koko still kicks ass.
The Lock Tavern	35 Chalk Farm Rd	020 7482 7163	Great gigs, Sunday roasts and (unpainfully) hip clientele
Oxford Arms	265 Camden High St	020 7267 4945	Theatre pub where you may stumble upon Amy Winehouse, stumbling.
Proud Camden	Stables Market	020 7482 3867	Oh-so-casual, trendy little bar. Fairy lights and arty types
Quinn's	65 Kentish Town Rd	020 7267 8240	More German beer than you can pronounce.
The Underworld	174 Camden High St	020 7482 1932	Throbbing pit of angry rock and even angrier metal.

Map 72 • Kentish Town

The Abbey Tavern	124 Kentish Town Rd	020 7267 9449	Fairy-lit, casual beer garden with talented DJs on Saturdays.
The Assembly House	292 Kentish Town Rd	020 7485 2031	Massive pub with friendly atmosphere.
Club Fandango @ The Bull & Gate	389 Kentish Town Rd	020 7704 0187	A gigging institution.
The Forum	9 Highgate Rd	020 7428 4099	Good venue for medium-sized bands.
Ladies and Gentlemen	2 Highgate Rd		Once a disused Victorian lav, now a gin palace.
The Lion & Unicorn	42 Gaisford St	020 7267 2304	Old school pub, with upstairs theatre space.
The Pineapple	51 Leverton St	020 7284 4631	Backstreet Victorian with good beers and Thai grub.
Rio's	239 Kentish Town Rd	020 7485 0607	Bored of your wife? Swap her here.

Arts & Entertainment • **Nightlife**

Map 73 • Holloway

The George Shillibeer	Carpenter's Mews	020 3218 0083	For relaxed drinking on comfy couches.
The Lord Stanley	51 Camden Park Rd	020 7428 9488	Dark wood, Edwardian interior, fireplace and secret wailed garden.
Shillibeer's Bar and Grill	1 Carpenter's Mews	020 3218 0083	Warehouse-style venue good for large groups.
The Unicorn	227 Camden Rd	020 7485 3073	Venue for the brilliant club Garageland.

Map 74 • Holloway Road / Arsenal

The Coronet	338 Holloway Rd	020 7609 5014	The smell of old men's piss is abound, but it's cheap!
The Garage	20 Highbury Corner	020 7619 6720	Bad sound and a guaranteed black hole in your evening.
Hen and Chickens	109 St. Paul's Rd	020 7704 2001	All the best pubs have theatres. Fact.
The Horatia	98 Holloway Rd	020 7682 4857	Forward thinking live music gem, packs a sexy crowd.

Map 75 • Highbury

The Alwyne Castle	83 St. Pauls Rd	020 7359 7351	Alright for a pint
Snooty Fox	75 Grosvenor Ave	020 7354 9532	Strangely empty—shame for such a great pub.

Map 76 • Edgware Road / Marylebone (North)

twotwentytwo	222 Marylebone Rd	020 7631 8000	Grand is the word.
The Volunteer	245 Baker St	020 7486 4091	Grand old Victorian taphouse great for a lively post-work pint.

Map 77 • Mornington Crescent / Regent's Park

The Crown & Anchor	137 Drummond St	020 7383 2681	A pub makeover masterpiece.
The Edinboro Castle	57 Mornington Terrace	020 7255 9651	Huge outdoors bit, great BBQ on summer weekends.
Euston Tap	190 Euston Rd	020 3137 8837	Post journey boozer with an award winning variety of beer.
Queen's Head & Artichoke	30 Albany St	020 7916 6206	The pinchos are addictive. We have warned, friends.

Map 78 • Euston

The Camden Head	100 Camden High St	020 7485 4019	Pre-gig/post gig boozer.
The Doric Arch	1 Eversholt St	020 7383 3359	Impressive range of all things ale.
Lincoln Lounge	52 York Way	020 7837 9339	Arty, quirky and cool. Does King's Cross proud.
The Purple Turtle	65 Crowndale Rd	020 7383 4976	Rock club that looks like a wacky goth spaceship.
Scala	275 Pentonville Rd	020 7833 2022	Historic venue with plush edges. If these walls could talk...
Searcys St Pancras Grand Brasserie	Pancras Rd	020 7870 9900	Miss your train!

Map 79 • King's Cross

The Big Chill House	257 Pentonville Rd	020 7427 2540	Allow staff 28 working days to process your drinks order.
Canal 125	125 Caledonian Rd	020 7837 1924	Upmarket local bar that draws a swanky crowd.
Central Station	37 Wharfdale Rd	020 7278 3294	Ominous looking cabaret bar-cum-cruise emporium. Check site first.
Drink, Shop & Do	9 Caledonian Rd	020 7278 4335	Perfect cocktails, art to buy, and lovely atmosphere.
EGG	200 York Way	020 7871 7111	Big club, big garden, big night out.
The Hemingford Arms	158 Hemingford Rd	020 7607 3303	Full of local aleheads.
The Lexington	96 Pentonville Rd	020 7837 5371	Come and support your boyfriend's shit band.
Simmons	32 Caledonian Rd	020 7278 5851	The bar Alice goes when Wonderland's closed.
Tarmon	270 Caledonian Rd	020 7607 3242	Character. Lots of character.

Map 80 • Angel / Upper St

'Round Midnight Jazz and Blues Bar	13 Liverpool Rd	020 7837 8758	Great music and a good atmosphere.
69 Colebrooke Row	69 Colebrooke Row	075 4052 8593	The kind of bar Hemingway would drink in.
The Angel	3 Islington High St	020 7837 2218	Students. The elderly. The unemployed.
The Angelic	57 Liverpool Rd	020 7278 8433	A sophisticated local.
Camden Head	2 Camden Walk	020 7359 0851	Comedians debut new gags upstairs. Cheap—and mostly cheerful.
The Castle	54 Pentonville Rd	020 7713 1858	Needs breaking in.
The Compton Arms	4 Compton Ave	020 7359 6883	Islington's only real pub—or so they say.
The Crown	116 Cloudesley Rd	020 7837 7107	Jovial spot for a quiet pint and Sunday roasts.
Dead Dolls House	181 Upper St	020 7288 1470	Sign up online and bring a bottle of the hard stuff.
The Drapers Arms	44 Barnsbury St	020 7619 0348	Celeb backlash against new CCTV. Big Brother really is watching.
Hope And Anchor	207 Upper St	020 7354 1312	Scuzzy pub with even scuzzier bands in the basement.
King's Head Theatre Pub	115 Upper St	020 7478 0160	Proper, good-time boozer.
Lucky Voice	173 Upper St	020 7354 6280	Singing in private? Like a bathroom with beer.
O2 Academy	16 Parkfield St	020 7288 4400	Grubby live music. Slap on some skinny jeans first.
Public House	54 Islington Park St	020 7359 6070	This boutique pub offers an escape from hedonistic Upper Street.
The Regent Pub	201 Liverpool Rd	020 7700 2725	Good news: it's finally starting to fray.
Union Chapel	Compton Terrace	020 7226 1686	God's favourite music venue. Hell, everyone's.

Arts & Entertainment • **Nightlife**

Map 81 • Canonbury

The Lord Clyde	342 Essex Rd	020 7288 9850	Like boozing in Land of Leather.
Marquess Tavern	32 Canonbury St	020 7359 4615	Scruffy locals live on, despite gastro revolution.
Myddleton Arms	52 Canonbury Rd	020 7226 4595	Don't those people have, y'know, jobs?

Map 82 • De Beauvoir Town / Kingsland

Dalston Boys Club	68 Boleyn Rd		Keep your eyes peeled for gigs at this place.
Dalston Jazz Bar	4 Bradbury St	020 7254 9728	Kitschy cool and not suffocatingly trendy, but no jazz, figure?
The Duke of Wellington	119 Ball's Pond Rd	020 7275 7640	Nice little boozer, as they say.
The Hunter S	194 Southgate Rd	020 7249 7191	As Hunter says, "Buy the ticket, take the ride."
The Northgate	113 Southgate Rd	020 7359 7392	Reliable local despite being—gasp!—a gastro.
Rosemary Branch Theatre	2 Shepperton Rd	020 7704 2730	Theatre pub with great selection of ales and hearty fare.
The Vortex	11 Gillett Sq	020 7254 4097	Dalston's only real jazz bar.

Map 83 • Angel (East) / City Rd (North)

Barrio North	45 Essex Rd	020 7749 3940	Groovy little bar with friendly international vibe. And a caravan!
The Duke of Cambridge	30 St. Peter's St	020 7359 3066	Feel self-righteous in the world's first organic pub.
The Earl of Essex	25 Danbury St	020 7424 5828	For drinking in the day. In the dark.
Island Queen	87 Noel Rd	020 7354 8741	Where NFT planned the London guide. Sweet.
The Mucky Pup	39 Queen's Head St	020 7226 2572	The dog's bollocks.
The Narrow Boat	119 St Peters St	020 7400 6003	Cheerful canal-side pub for lazy pints and people watching.
The Old Queen's Head and Kitchen	44 Essex Rd	020 7354 9993	Trendier than the name suggests.
The Wenlock Arms	26 Wenlock Rd	020 7608 3406	Threadbare, battered old boozer with a magnificent range of real ales.

Map 84 • Hoxton

333 Mother	333 Old St	020 7739 5949	Mama told you not to come, but you need it.
Cargo	83 Rivington St	020 7739 3440	Cavernous hole with bad sound but good gigs.
Charlie Wright's	45 Pitfield St	020 7490 8345	Does anyone turn up here sober?
Club Aquarium	256 Old St	020 7251 6136	After-hours swimming pool scuzzfest.
Electricity Showrooms	39 Hoxton Sq	020 7739 3939	Shark-infested waters.
Happiness Forgets	9 Hoxton Sq	020 7613 0325	No door policy just no wallies.
Howl at the Moon	178 Hoxton St	020 7739 9221	Chuffing good little pub serving burgers.
Hoxton Square Bar and Kitchen	2 Hoxton Sq	020 7613 0709	Snotty bands and doormen. Wear something uber.
The Macbeth	70 Hoxton St	020 7749 0600	Hot new bands love it. And so do we.
The Old Blue Last	38 Great Eastern St	020 7739 7033	Until the bass drum WILL bring down that pub ceiling.
PortSide Parlour	14 Rivington St	020 3662 6381	Friendly rum bar.
Red Lion	41 Hoxton St	020 7729 7920	Stay forever if you bag the chaise lounge...
The Stag's Head	55 Orsman Rd	020 7739 5186	Run down boozer currently being used for hip gigs.
Strongroom	120 Curtain Rd	020 7426 5103	Shoreditch's last stronghold of unpretentiousness?
Troy Bar	10 Hoxton St	079 5829 8607	A semi-hidden gem with soul and funk music most nights.
Zigfrid	11 Hoxton Sq	020 7613 1988	Cross between a club and an antique store.

Map 85 • Stoke Newington (East)

Blush	8 Cazenove Rd	020 7923 9202	Pink pint-parlour with poker and personable patrons (oh please!)
The Jolly Butchers	204 Stoke Newington High St	020 7249 9471	Revamped but unpretentious pub with great beer selection.
Royal Sovereign	64 Northwold Rd	020 8806 2449	Drink with the locals.

Map 86 • Dalston / Kingsland

The Alibi	91 Kingsland High St	020 7249 2733	The kids like it.
Bar 23	23 Stoke Newington Rd	020 7241 2060	A slice of weirdness with wacked out DJing and drinking.
Bardens Boudoir	36 Stoke Newington Rd	020 7923 9223	Anything can happen in this basement. The beating heart of Dalston's music shenanigans.
Cafe Oto	18 Ashwin St	020 7923 1231	Mysterious new venue importing music from the hinterlands of psychedelia.
Dalston Superstore	117 Kingsland High St	020 7254 2273	Uber hip polysexual squelch-a-thon.
Efes Pool Club & Bar	17 Stoke Newington Rd	020 7249 6040	Down some pints at this great spot to play pool.
The Haggerston	438 Kingsland Rd	020 7923 3206	Artist-run flea pit. Chaotic crowd surfing most nights.
Moustache Bar	58 Stoke Newington Rd	075 0715 2047	Follow the moustache (sticker) trail to this trendy/grimy subterranean bar.
The Nest	36 Stoke Newington Rd	020 7354 9993	Electronic dance club in basement.
Passion Social Club	251 Amhurst Rd	020 7254 3667	Tiny basement venue that hosts massive all-nighters.
The Prince George	40 Parkholme Rd	087 1934 1384	Buzzing local favourite. Renowned Monday quiz night, great jukebox.
Ridley Road Market Bar	49 Ridley Rd		A contender for best little bar in Dalston.
The Shacklewell Arms	71 Shacklewell Ln	020 7249 0810	Relive your punk youth.
Vogue Fabrics	66 Stoke Newington Rd	020 7249 2733	The latest place to Vogue.

Map 87 • Hackney Downs / Lower Clapton

Biddle Brothers	88 Lower Clapton Rd	020 8985 7052	Almost trendy oasis for the trendy in an eccentric neighbourhood.
The Crooked Billet	84 Upper Clapton Rd	020 3058 1166	Proof that Clapton can still be f***ing terrifying.
The Pembury Tavern	90 Amhurst Rd	020 8986 8597	Large selection of microbrews.
Star by Hackney Downs	35 Queenstown Rd	020 7458 4481	Fun, circus themed pub.

Map 88 • Haggerston / Queensbridge Rd

The Fox	372 Kingsland Rd	020 3215 2093	Half-way stop for Shoreditch-to-Dalston pub crawls.
Passing Clouds	1 Richmond Rd	020 7241 4889	Back alley arts collective and live venue.

Map 89 • London Fields / Hackney Central

Baxter's Court	282 Mare St	020 8525 9010	A chain pub, okay, okay. But check the ladies' toilets!
The Dolphin	165 Mare St	020 8985 3727	Pathos sodden karaoke occasionally ruined by post-opening art people.
The Dove	24 Broadway Market	020 7275 7617	Belgian beer paradise.
Draughts	337 Acton Mews	020 7254 1572	A library of 500 board games to choose from.
The Old Ship	2 Sylvester Path	084 4264 1444	Nicely refurbed ex-dive.
Pub on the Park	19 Martello St	020 7923 3398	Tap for London Fields.

Map 90 • Homerton / Victoria Park North

Chats Palace	42 Brooksby's Walk	020 8533 0227	Fantastic community arts venue—Hackney classic.
The Kenton	38 Kenton Rd	020 8533 5041	Local favourite.
The Lauriston	162 Victoria Park Rd	020 8985 5404	As vamped up as its would-be-village surroundings.
Royal Inn on the Park	111 Lauriston Rd	020 8985 3321	Victoria Park's prime boozer.

Map 91 • Shoreditch / Brick Lane / Spitalfields

93 Feet East	150 Brick Ln	020 7247 3293	Enthusiastic, trendy club (to impress out-of-towners).
The Archers	42 Osborn St	020 7247 3826	Nice ole pub that's resisted Shoreditchification. Perfect for pre-curry pints.
Bar Kick	127 Shoreditch High St	020 7739 8700	Lemon-yellow table football gaff.
Bar Music Hall	134-136 Curtain Rd	020 7729 7216	Nice wallpaper, free music. Who's complaining?
Bedroom Bar	62 Rivington St	020 7739 5706	Saturday's DJ'n'sax players mean dancing til dawn.
The Big Chill Bar	Dray Walk	020 7392 9180	Still among Brick Lane's better drinking spots.
The Birdcage	80 Columbia Rd	020 7739 0250	Karaoke! Til 3am!
Browns	1 Hackney Rd	020 7739 3970	Now really. What would your mother say?
Café 1001	91 Brick Ln	020 7247 6166	Like a house party. But one where cans cost £3.
The Carpenters Arms	73 Cheshire St	020 7739 6342	No longer run by the Kray twins' mother, still felonious fun.
Catch	22 Kingsland Rd	020 7729 6097	Reliable active dancefloor, reliable silly hats, reliable good fun.
The Cocktail Trading Co.	68 Bethnal Green Rd	020 7427 6097	Mixologically compelling drinks; fun attitude.
Comedy Cafe	68 Rivington St	020 7739 5706	Fun venue, but invariably a dud in the line-up.
The Commercial Tavern	142 Commercial St	020 7247 1888	Quirky Shoreditch traditional.
The Culpeper	40 Commercial St	020 7247 5371	Used to be The Princess Alice. Beautiful interior.
Danger of Death	202 Brick Ln	020 7065 6806	Naughty little speakeasy.
George & Dragon	2 Blackheath St	020 8691 3764	Witness the E2 gay clique rev up for imminent carnage.
Golden Heart	110 Commercial St	020 7247 2158	Has it all: fires, pints and a lazy resident dog.
Jaguar Shoes	32 Kingsland Rd	020 7729 5830	Happy hipsters behind wide windows.
Loungelover	1 Whitby St	020 7012 1234	Kitsch-colonial glitter-ball of a cocktail bar.
The Love Shake	5 Kingsland Rd	07850 383178	Chic media-café-cum-bar with mid Atlantic vibe.
The Old Shoreditch Station	1 Kingsland Rd	020 7729 5188	Used to be cool. When it was a train station.
The Owl & Pussycat	34 Redchurch St	020 3487 0088	Crooked little place, tucked in the folds of Shoreditch's blubber.
Prague	6 Kingsland Rd	020 7739 9110	The closest you'll ever get to a romantic bar in Shoreditch.
The Pride of Spitalfields	3 Heneage St	020 7247 8933	The only East End boozer left on Brick Lane
The Redchurch	107 Redchurch St	020 7739 3440	Late, loud DJ box.
The Royal Oak	73 Columbia Rd	020 7729 2220	Gentrifying, gentrifying...gentrified.
Sager + Wilde	193 Hackney Rd	020 8127 7330	Get yer wine on.
Shoreditch House	Ebor St	020 7739 5040	Last one in the rooftop pool buys the drinks!
The Ten Bells	84 Commercial St	075 3049 2986	Jack The Ripper's local. An oddly nice place for an evening drink.
Vibe Bar	91 Brick Ln	020 7247 3479	Bar in a brewery. Feel the vibe?
The Water Poet	9 Folgate St	020 7426 0495	Mismatched chairs, over-stuffed sofas, philosophy and beer.
Ye Olde Axe	69 Hackney Rd	020 7729 5137	Rockabilly-only weekends. That's right: rockabilly-only. Occasional gentleman's club.

Map 92 • Bethnal Green

The Albion	94 Goldsmiths Row	020 7739 0185	Friendly, footy-mad local. All welcome.
Bethnal Green Working Men's Club	44 Pollard Row	020 7739 7170	Saucy amateur burlesque that still confuses the resident Working Men.
The Florist Arms	255 Globe Rd	020 8981 1100	The Camel's naughty little sister.

Arts & Entertainment · **Nightlife**

Satan's Whiskers	343 Cambridge Heath Rd	020 7739 8362	Devilishly good cocktails.
Seabright Arms	31 Coate St	020 7729 0937	Meantime lager and Lucky Chip burgers.
The Star Of Bethnal Green	359 Bethnal Green Rd	020 7458 4480	Formerly the Pleasure Unit. Still Bethnal Green's live music best.

Map 93 · Globe Town / Mile End (North)

The Approach	47 Approach Rd	020 8983 3878	Great if you can tolerate the ironic haircuts crew.
Morgan Arms	43 Morgan St	020 8980 6389	Grab a pint with some gourmet food.
Palm Tree	Haverfield Rd	020 8980 2918	Brass walls and retired crooners! Amazingly old-fashioned boozer.
The Victoria	110 Grove Rd	020 8980 6609	Coolified old man's boozer turned hipster joint.

Map 94 · Bow

Coborn Arms	8 Coborn Rd	020 8980 3793	Nice ales, nice beer garden.
Lord Morpeth	402 Old Ford Rd	020 3022 5888	Bow boozing's best.
The Lord Tredegar	50 Lichfield Rd	020 8983 0130	Trusty local boozer.
Young Prince	448 Roman Rd	020 8980 1292	If on Roman Road...

Map 95 · Whitechapel (West) / St Katharine's Dock

The Dickens Inn	St Katharine's Way	020 7488 2208	Proof that an awesome location can conquer all.
Rhythm Factory	16 Whitechapel Rd	020 7375 3774	The Libertines' old haunt, with all the grimy 'chic' that implies.
Simmons	61 Mint St	020 7702 9481	Reliable good time place.

Map 96 · Whitechapel (East) / Shadwell (West) / Wapping

Captain Kidd	108 Wapping High St	020 7480 5759	Pub with nice Thames-side beer garden.
Indo	133 Whitechapel Rd	020 7247 4926	Very narrow and everything but narrow-minded.
Town of Ramsgate	62 Wapping High St	020 7481 8000	Get nautical.
Victualler	69 Garnet St	020 7481 9694	Natural, organic and biodynamic wines in shop setting.

Map 97 · Stepney / Shadwell (East)

Cable Street Studios	566 Cable St	020 7790 1309	'Artists.' 'Warehouse studios.' 'Parties.' It'll never work.
The George Tavern	373 Commercial Rd	020 7790 7335	Old men, hipsters and blue-collar poets in imperfect harmony.
The Prospect of Whitby	57 Wapping Wall	020 7481 1095	Ye olde pub(e) on ye Thames(e).
Troxy	490 Commercial Rd	020 7790 9000	Glorious art deco palace.

Map 98 · Mile End (South) / Limehouse

The Grapes	76 Narrow St	020 7987 4396	True to its roots East End boozer—natural survivor.

Map 100 · Poplar (West) / Canary Wharf (West)

Davy's	31 Canary Wharf	020 7363 6633	Traditional-style with fine ales, wine and food.
Via Fossa	18 Hertsmere Rd	020 7515 8549	Three floors of bankers...

Map 101 · Poplar (East) / Canary Wharf (East)

The Greenwich Pensioner	28 Bazely St	020 7987 4414	No pensioners and not in Greenwich.

Map 102 · Millwall

Hubbub	269 Westferry Rd	020 7515 5577	Oasis in Docklands desert.

Map 103 · Cubitt Town / Mudchute

The Ferry House	26 Ferry St	020 7537 9587	Beer-drenched docks time capsule.
The Lord Nelson	1 Manchester Rd	020 7987 1970	Can I have a half, Nelson?

Map 104 · South Bank / Waterloo / Lambeth North

The Anchor & Hope	36 The Cut	020 7928 9898	For that intellectual pre-theatre/dinner chat.
Benugo Bar & Kitchen	Belvedere Rd	020 7401 9000	Long tables, sofas, soft lighting. Sup cocktails, feel cultured.
Concrete	Southbank Centre	020 7921 0758	Restaurant/bar features Russian beer, food, absinthe.
Cubana	48 Lower Marsh	020 7928 8778	Still riding the mojito trend. But good at them.
The Cut Bar	66 The Cut	020 7928 4400	Enjoy the outdoor terrace with trendy media types and thesps.
Da Vinci's	6 Baylis Rd	020 7928 8099	Cheesy and bizarre late-night fun.
The Pit Bar	The Cut	020 7928 2975	Guzzle champagne with Kevin Spacey and friends.
Royal Festival Hall	Belvedere Rd	020 7960 4200	Increasingly exciting programming amid nicely refurbished surroundings.
Skylon	Belvedere Rd	020 7654 7800	Impress someone with the view, then split the bill.

Arts & Entertainment · **Nightlife**

Map 105 · Southwark / Bankside (West)

Albert Arms	1 Gladstone St	020 7401 2362	Where yuppies meet students meet blow-ins meet locals.
The Libertine	125 Great Suffolk St	020 7378 7877	Pizza and beer, what more do you want?
Lord Nelson	243 Union St	020 7207 2701	Like a student union.
Ministry of Sound	103 Gaunt St	087 0060 0010	The sound really IS amazing.
The Prince of Wales	51 St George's Rd	020 7582 9696	Cheap local with downright scary karaoke.

Map 106 · Bankside (East) / Borough / Newington

The Anchor	34 Park St	020 7407 1577	Did Samuel Johnson have to battle this many tourists?
Belushi's	161 Borough High St	020 7939 9710	Drunk Antipodeans. Karaoke. General carnage.
The Blue-Eyed Maid	173 Borough High St	020 7378 8259	It's never too late for a last drink in Borough.
Brew Wharf	Stoney St	020 7378 6601	Beer lovers' heaven.
The George Inn	77 Borough High St	020 7407 2056	Grab a home brew in the dazzlingly ancient George Inn.
The Globe	8 Bedale St	020 7407 0043	Bridget Jones' home? Do we care?
The Market Porter	9 Stoney St	020 7407 2495	Market traders and suits neck real ale. Smell the testosterone.
The Rake	14 Winchester Walk	020 7407 0557	Tiny place with a hundred different beers. Honestly, a hundred.
The Roebuck	50 Great Dover St	020 7357 7324	Backstreet boozer full of human oddities.
The Rose	123 Snowfields	020 7378 6660	Mingle with baby yuppies at the Roxy Bar & Screen.
Roxy	128 Borough High St	020 7407 4057	Mingle with baby yuppies at the Roxy Bar & Screen.
The Royal Oak	44 Tabard St	020 7357 7173	Possibly the friendliest landlords in London.
Southwark Tavern	22 Southwark St	020 7403 0257	Traditional ambience and ordinary fare in ye olde Southwark Tavern.
Wine Wharf	Stoney St	020 7940 8335	If you're as crazy about wine as they are.

Map 107 · Shad Thames

Cable	33 Bermondsey St	020 7403 7730	Get messed up in a dark tunnel. Again.
The Hide	39 Bermondsey St	020 7403 6655	Slightly odd vibe, but cracking drinks.
Hilton London Tower Bridge	5 More London Pl	020 3002 4300	Super-chilled, low lit relaxation zone for the wealthy.
Village East	171 Bermondsey St	020 7357 6082	Wine buffs and cocktail lovers will lap it up.
The Woolpack	98 Bermondsey St	020 7357 9269	Filling lunches, comfy sofas, great garden. Job done.

Map 109 · Southwark Park

The Ancient Foresters	282 Southwark Park Rd	020 7394 1633	Surprise charmer in an otherwise grimy area.
The Angel	101 Bermondsey Wall E	020 7394 3214	Sam Smith pub with great views across the river
The Mayflower	117 Rotherhithe St	020 7237 4088	Used to be The Shippe from whenst the Mayflower departed

Map 110 · Rotherhithe (West) / Canada Water

The Albion	20 Albion St	020 7237 0182	Only if three generations of your family drank here first.
Old Salt Quay	163 Rotherhithe St	020 7394 7108	Pub-by-numbers, but the riverside patio of dreams.
The Ship	39 St Marychurch St	020 7237 4103	Sunny day? Settle in with a beer and a sarnie.

Map 111 · Rotherhithe (East) Surrey Quays

The Blacksmith's Arms	257 Rotherhithe St	020 7064 4355	Good enough for the Queen Mum: good enough for us.
The Moby Dick	6 Russell Pl	020 7231 6719	Once here, hard to leave. Because it's really far from the tube.
The Ship & Whale	2 Gulliver St	020 7237 7072	So good we even come for breakfast.
Whelan's	11 Rotherhithe Old Rd	020 7237 9425	Looks rough around the edges, but you could do worse.
Wibbley Wobbley	Rope St	020 7232 2320	Great dinky boat-bar, for short people.

Map 112 · Kennington / Elephant and Castle

Brasserie Toulouse Lautrec	140 Newington Butts	020 7582 6800	Eclectic music venue in the Belle Epoque tradition.
Corsica Studios	5 Elephant Rd	020 7703 4760	Sweaty music venue with 'home-made' vibe.
The Dog House	293 Kennington Rd	020 7820 9310	Like your scruffy, unpretentious younger brother. Made for chill-axing.
The Doghouse	293 Kennington Rd	020 7820 9310	Solid local drinking hole.
The Old Red Lion	42 Kennington Park Rd	020 7735 4312	Best pub in the area.
Prince of Wales	Cleaver Sq	020 7735 9916	Stuart's favourite pub in Kennington.
South London Pacific	340 Kennington Rd	020 7820 9189	Step off Kennington Road into the heart of Honolulu.

Map 113 · Walworth

Banana's Bar	374 Walworth Rd	020 7703 3295	New party bar for excitable funsters.
The Beehive	60 Carter St	020 7703 4992	The local bit of nice.
Red Lion	407 Walworth Rd	020 7703 7075	They'll look at you funny, but you'll be welcome enough.

Map 118 · Deptford (Central)

Lord Palmerston	81 Childers St	020 8692 1575	Fewer brawls than your average Deptford pub.

Arts & Entertainment • **Nightlife**

Map 119 • Deptford (East)

The Bird's Nest	32 Deptford Church St	020 8692 1928	Hilarious 'locals vs. trendies' vibe. Go for monthly Flesh Dunce!
The Bunker Club	46 Deptford Broadway	020 8691 0000	The name tells all.
The Dog & Bell	116 Prince St	020 8692 5664	Now why can't ALL pubs in Deptford be like this?

Map 120 • Greenwich

The Greenwich Union	56 Royal Hill	020 8692 6258	Beers galore.
The O2	O2 Arena	020 8463 2000	The grandaddy of mainstream live music.
The Old Brewery	Pepys Building	020 3327 1280	Get the excellent range of Meantime beers direct from the source.
Up The Creek	302 Creek Rd	020 8858 4581	Comedy club (plus comedy dancing at the disco)

Map 121 • Camberwell (West)

The Joiners Arms	35 Denmark Hill	020 7701 1957	Friendly local with occasional Irish dancing.
The Sun of Camberwell	61-63 Coldharbour Ln	020 7737 5861	Same owners and decor as nearby Tiger. Great beer garden.

Map 122 • Camberwell (East)

The Flying Dutchman	156 Wells Wy		Old man's boozer given an outrageously camp revamp.
Grand Union	26 Camberwell Grove	020 3247 1001	By far the best of the Grand Union chain.
Hermit's Cave	28 Camberwell Church St	020 7703 3188	Log fire and Deuchars on the pump.
Stormbird	25 Camberwell Church St	020 7708 4460	Insane selection of beers makes the bland décor bearable.

Map 123 • Peckham

Bar Story	213 Blenheim Grove	020 7635 6643	Peckham's first and finest cocktail bar. Best when sunny.
Canavan's Peckham Pool Club	188 Rye Ln	075 6348 2439	Where art students meet alcoholics in late, late night harmony.
The CLF Art Cafe	133 Rye Ln	020 7732 5275	Ex-cricket bat factory hosting galleries, studios and anything goes raves.
Dead Dolls House	1 Clayton Rd	020 7732 2691	Apply for 'membership' on the website.
The Four Quarters	187 Rye Lane	020 3754 7622	Arcade games bar: Hadouken!
Frank's Cafe	95 Rye Ln	075 2860 0924	Cheap Campari cocktails in a multi-story car park. Pure class.
The Montpelier	43 Chomert Rd	020 7635 9483	Cosy pub with free regular and eclectic film nights.
Peckham Palais	1 Rye Ln		Sprawling old club recently given new hipster lease on life

Map 126 • New Cross

Amersham Arms	388 New Cross Rd	020 8469 1499	Art school hipdom in grimy New Cross's coolest venue.
Marquis of Granby	322 New Cross Rd	020 8692 3140	Lovely old corner pub with mix of students and oldtimers.
New Cross Inn	323 New Cross Rd	020 8355 4976	Someone's gotta keep "the scene" going.

Map 127 • Coldharbour Lane / Herne Hill (West)

The Commercial	212 Railton Rd	020 7733 8783	Roaring fire and mulled wine in winter. Fits like a glove.
The Florence	133 Dulwich Rd	020 7326 4987	Microbrewery on premises.
The Prince Regent	69 Dulwich Rd	020 7274 1567	Life drawing on Wednesdays to titillate posh diners.

129 • East Dulwich

East Dulwich Tavern	1 Lordship Ln	020 8693 1316	Jeremy Clarkson was once thrown out for nefarious activities.

Map 130 • Peckham Rye

The Gowlett	62 Gowlett Rd	020 7635 7048	Shabby local serving pizzas famous across the area.
The Rye	31 Peckham Rye	020 7639 5397	For lazy lunches on summer Sundays.

Map 131 • Vauxhall / Albert Embankment

Area	67 Albert Embankment	020 3242 0040	Another massive Vauxhall rave hole. Serious gay clientele.
Eagle London	349 Kennington Ln	020 7793 0903	Fur on tap throughout the week. Sundays recommended.
The Royal Vauxhall Tavern	372 Kennington Ln	020 7820 1222	Fun gay pub with trashy cabaret.
Zeitgeist at the Jolly Gardeners	49 Black Prince Rd	020 7840 0426	German gastropub with uber-extensive collection of beer and sausages.

Map 132 • Battersea (West)

Barrio	14 Battersea Sq	020 7801 9548	What balmy Sunday evenings were made for.
The Draft House	74 Battersea Bridge Rd	020 7228 6482	A great pub well worth the trek.
Le QuecumBar	42 Battersea High St	020 7787 2227	Gypsy jazz, honkytonk and frogs legs in bygone Parisian chic.
The Prince Albert	85 Albert Bridge Rd	020 7228 0923	Enjoy a regal roast with a view of the park.
The Woodman	60 Battersea High St	020 7228 2968	A nice Fire. Pint of Badger. Luverleee.

509

Arts & Entertainment · **Nightlife**

Map 133 · Battersea (East)

The Mason's Arms	169 Battersea Park Rd	020 7622 2007	Perfect local boozer with quality Sunday roasts.

Map 134 · South Lambeth

Bar Estrela	113 S Lambeth Rd	020 7793 1051	Portugal transplanted to South London. Beer, tapas and football.
The Battersea Barge	Nine Elms Ln	020 7498 0004	Bouncy, buoyant, thrilled to see you—the Labrador puppy of venues.
The Cavendish Arms	128 Hartington Rd	020 7498 7464	Shabby, unpretentious pub with comedy nights and a cool streak.
Fire	38 Parry St	020 7820 0550	Legendary gay terrordrome with LED ceiling.
The Hoist	47 S Lambeth Rd	020 7735 9972	Slap on some leather and get hoisted up.
Lightbox	6 S Lambeth Pl	020 3242 0040	15,000 LED lights. Enough to give us all seizures.
The Priory Arms	83 Lansdowne Way	020 7622 1884	Renowned for their excellent selection of proper, geeky real ales.
The Vauxhall Griffin	8 Wyvil Rd	020 7622 0222	Theme nights to knock your socks off

Map 135 · Oval

The Brown Derby	336 Kennington Park Rd	020 7735 5122	A ray of rock n' roll sunshine in South East's dubstep wastelands.
The Fentiman Arms	64 Fentiman Rd	020 7793 9796	The staff believe that smiles kill kittens.

Map 136 · Putney

The Boathouse	Brewhouse Ln	020 8789 0476	Riverside pub with loadsa outdoor space.
Duke's Head	8 Lower Richmond Rd	020 8788 2552	Typical gastro pub upstairs. Dark DJ bar downstairs.
The Jolly Gardeners	61 Lacy Rd	020 8789 2539	Like all good pubs. And sock monkey classes on Wednesdays.
Star & Garter	4 Lower Richmond Rd	020 8788 0345	Upscale Saturday night hotspot on the Thames.

Map 138 · Wandsworth (Central)

The Cat's Back	88 Point Pleasant	020 8874 7277	Atmospheric and busy with loadsa obscure decoration.
GJ's	89 Garratt Ln	020 8874 2271	Party with snow bunnies.

Map 139 · Wandsworth (East)

Powder Keg Diplomacy	147 St Johns Hill	020 7450 6457	Like stepping into a colonial Victorian plantation.
The Waterfront	Juniper Dr	020 7228 4297	No Marlon Brandos here. Not much of a view either.

Map 140 · Clapham Junction / Northcote Rd

B@1 Cocktail Bar	85 Battersea Rise	020 7978 6595	Be at one with a cocktail menu the size of a book.
Humble Grape	2 Battersea Rise	020 3620 2202	Unpretentious wine bar—hurray!

Map 141 · Battersea (South)

The Lost Angel	339 Battersea Park Rd	020 7622 2112	Put this in your pipe and smoke it, Shoreditch.

Map 142 · Clapham Old Town

Prince of Wales	38 Old Town	020 7622 3530	Eccentric, friendly. Run by a magpie.
Rose & Crown	2 The Polygon	020 7923 3337	For the CAMRA purists.
The Sun	47 Old Town	020 7622 4980	Nice pub. Ruined by surfeit of twats.

Map 143 · Clapham High Street

The Alexandra	14 Clapham Common South Side	020 7627 5102	Join an up-for-it crowd as multinational as the sport here.
Bread and Roses	68 Clapham Manor St	020 7498 1779	Surprisingly pleasant socialist boozer. Without Clapham tossers.
Buena Vista Cafe	19 Landor Rd	020 7326 0280	Sunday at this Cuban hangout features dirty mojitos and tunes.
The Clapham North	409 Clapham Rd	020 7274 2472	A bit 'Clapham', but pretty likable really.
The Coach and Horses	173 Clapham Park Road	020 7622 3815	Honest little boozer.
The Falcon	33 Bedford Rd	020 7274 2428	"I told Daddy, I've nowhere to even PARK a GTI!"
Infernos	146 Clapham High St	020 7720 7633	Oh God no.
Inn Clapham	15 The Pavement	020 7652 2948	Charmingly tatty and full of French people
The Left	67 Clapham High St	020 7627 0792	A welcome oasis from Clapham High Street.
The Railway Tavern	18 Clapham High St	020 7622 4077	Half-trendy, half-local, three-quarters cool.
Two Brewers	114 Clapham High St	020 7819 9539	Club nights, gay cabaret, lots of fu-un!

Map 144 • Stockwell / Brixton (West)

The Duke of Edinburgh	204 Ferndale Rd	020 7326 0301	Warm, traditional pub with massive beer garden.
Marquis of Lorne	49 Dalyell Rd	020 7771 9408	A dying breed.
Plan B	418 Brixton Rd	020 7733 0926	Has made a name for itself, but pretty lame really.
The Prince of Wales	469 Brixton Rd	020 7095 1978	Behind dealers chanting skunk lies a nothin' special pub.
The Queen's Head	144 Stockwell Rd	020 7737 3519	Bastion of true Brixton.
Seven at Brixton	7 Market Row	0207 998 3309	Cheap cocktails taken seriously with board games to boot.
The Swan	2 Stockwell Rd	020 7978 9778	Don't worry about spitting on the floor.

Map 145 • Stockwell / Brixton (East)

Brixton Academy	211 Stockwell Rd	020 7771 3000	Overrated, but still a tad awesome.
Jamm	261 Brixton Rd	020 7274 5537	The real deal a little way out.

Map 146 • Earlsfield

Bar 366	366 Garratt Ln	020 8944 9591	Chilled, lounge-type bar.
Halfway House	521 Garratt Ln	020 8946 2788	Slinky, chardonnay-swilling pub with terrific terrace.
Le Gothique	Windmill Rd & John Archer Wy	020 8870 6567	The answer to: "Open a bar! What could go wrong?"

Map 147 • Balham (West)

The Hope	1 Bellevue Rd	020 8672 8717	Consider nearby Wandsworth Common an extension of the beer garden.
The Nightingale	97 Nightingale Ln	020 8673 1637	Untrendified local. Long may it stay so.

Map 148 • Balham (East)

The Avalon	16 Balham Hill	020 8675 8613	Beer garden for lazy Sunday lunches and, er, Japanese whisky.
Balham Bowls Club	7 Ramsden Rd	020 8673 4700	A pub. In a bowling club circa 1950. Genius.
The Bedford	77 Bedford Hill	020 8682 8940	Music and comedy pub with great bands but crappy beer.
The Exhibit	12 Balham Station Rd	020 8772 6556	Bar with indie cinema attached
Hagen & Hyde	157 Balham High Rd	020 8772 0016	Popular boozer.

Map 150 • Brixton

The Dogstar	389 Coldharbour Ln	020 7733 7515	The burritos are great, but leave before the tunes get cheesy.
The Effra	38 Kellett Rd	020 7274 4180	A slice of the real Brixton.
Effra Social	89 Effra Rd	020 7737 6800	Retro pub in former Brixton Conservative Club.
Electric Brixton	Town Hall Parade	020 7274 2290	DJs and live music venue in former Fridge space.
Grand Union	123 Acre Ln	020 7274 8794	Come for the tiki shacks and burgers.
Gremio de Brixton	St. Matthew's Rd	020 7924 0660	Spanish tapas bar in church crypt.
Hootananny	95 Effra Rd	020 7737 7273	Great gigs—many for free
Prince Albert	418 Coldharbour Ln	020 7274 3771	It's charming, trust us. In a not too obvious kindaway.
Satay	447 Coldharbour Ln	084 4474 6080	Cocktails to suit the snobbiest of drinks connoisseurs
Upstairs at the Ritzy	Brixton Oval	020 7326 2627	Where Brixton sparkles. Cinema, bar, café and free live music.
The Windmill	22 Blenheim Gardens	020 8671 0700	Rough-edged weirdo magnet. Unique and brilliant.

Map 151 • Tooting Bec

The Bec Bar	26 Tooting Bec Rd	020 8672 2979	Pleasant enough. Go for sport.
The King's Head	84 Upper Tooting Rd	020 8767 6708	Former gin palace brings yesteryear flair to the wasteland.

Map 152 • Tooting Broadway

The Little Bar	145 Mitcham Rd	020 8672 7317	It's a bar and it's little
The Ramble Inn	223 Mitcham Rd	020 8767 4040	Irish/locals bullcrap-free boozer.
The Secret Bar	Totterdown St	07508 369 722	Convivial Portuguese bar.
Tooting Tram and Social	46 Mitcham Rd	020 8767 0278	Cavernous, funky and cool without trying.
Unwined	21 Tooting High St	020 3286 4631	Pop up turned permanent providing excellent wines.

British food and British chefs had a pretty bad reputation until fairly recently; greasy piles of stodge topped off with gravy was the general consensus for what to expect in a London restaurant. A couple of years back France's premier chef Alain Ducasse upped the ante for the London dining scene by declaring it the 'restaurant capital of the world.' While there are still numerous naff cafes around they're far outnumbered by brilliant bistros, bountiful brunch places, bodacious BBQs and boatloads of other badass eateries.

As one of the most multicultural cities in the world, London is packed with cuisine from around the world, with some areas dedicated to a signature cuisine. We've got Jewish, Indian, Peruvian, Mexican, Vietnamese, Moroccan, hell even Mongolian. Visitors don't even have to look at a Yorkshire pudding, roast beef, a full English, or fish & chips if there're not so inclined but anyone would be a fool to miss out on some of the better English places.

Foodie trends come and go in this dusty old town so if you really want be down with the urban gourmands you'll need to know what's hot right now. It would be terribly embarrassing to be caught nibbling on sushi when munching on king ribs is the thing. Then there's the staple and stable cool places that manage to keep the hungry masses happy no matter what's cool.

What you spend on food is as flexible as British weather too; street food provides some of London's most famed snacks while places like Hix's **Tramshed** dishes out minimalist done well, and old English favourites like **The Ritz** stick to the traditional-type menu its customers expect. For everyone else in between there's everything else in between. London even does Vegetarian, apparently.

Eating for Britain

In a country whose national dish is reportedly a Chicken Tikka Masala, pin-pointing what British cuisine actually is doesn't come easy. Taking a traditional approach we've got those archetypal dishes like the Sunday Roast, Full English, Fish & Chips, and Jellied Eels; if visitors believed every stereotypical image of the British it would stand to reason that these dishes make up our standard diet, along with bucket loads of builder's tea, of course.

Delve a little deeper though and you'll find a revolutionised British menu brought about by the demand of a newly sophisticated palate. We still do the soggy seaside favourite but you're just as likely to find grilled mackerel with potato salad on a chip-shop menu as you are a battered saveloy which is what you'll see at **Poppie's** in Spitalfields (Map 91). We still do Sunday lunch but you're more likely to be served the rarest of beef, a whole Poisson, or tenderloin pork than a leathery piece of gravied meat. Breakfast is a class of its own and though we're still to see a food revolution hit the East End pie shops, some things are best left as they are like the centuries-old **F.Cooke (Map 89)** on Broadway Market.

We're partial to a fusion, too; it's not unusual to see British tapas on a pub menu – expect things like mini toad-in-the-hole, bite sized beef wellington, and pork belly squares served with apple sauce. We're seeing things like whole Indian menus that are made entirely of British ingredients to keep the eco-warriors happy, and we're munching on American-style pulled pork that is smoked over English craft ales.

Our adopted second cuisine award goes to the Indian sub-continent whose spicy dishes us Brits consider to be synonymous with a night out on the tiles or a night in front of the telly. Samosas a snack, bhajis on the way home from work, and a five course special of a Sunday eve; it's all good.

Hold the Pesticides

You'd think that with all the smog the city creates, and the pollution that's pumped around this place that Londoners would have come to accept the pesticides and chemicals often found in food; you would, of course, be wrong. London loves a good farmer's market and all organic café, and a good serving of local produce and meat. Weekly farmer's markets like those in **Islington (Map 80)**, London Fields and **Borough (Map 106)** are credited with starting the trend for street food in London, a few years back. The vendors would cook each other's produce to sell to hungry shoppers which in turn created a demand for top end, tasty, chemical-free food.

Any café worth its salt uses free-range eggs, bacon from British pigs, lamb (from Wales not New Zealand), apples from Somerset orchards and oysters from Whitstable. There's certainly no crime in sticking to produce form British soils, serving misshapen tomatoes, and purple carrots, just be aware that more than a handful of organic' places like to charge over the odds for the pleasure of non-tainted meals.

Breakfast & Lunch—Brunch

Any good Londoner values their weekend days off like a dog loves his bone. The working week leaves time for no more than coffee and a croissant at breakfast time which is why we revel so much in a weekend brunch date. Be it with a lover, a group of rowdy friends, or visiting family members, we've developed the act of brunching into an art form in its own right.

You'll still see the off greasy spoon around, serving lukewarm baked beans, fatty bacon, and pebbly scrambled eggs but chances are that the dove grey (or Victorian green) painted shop two doors down will be packed to the proverbial rafters with a convivial young crowd of foodies and hipsters. There's a lot to be said for the Full English; it's a world-famous classic, and done well, it's the breakfast of kings. We've even branched out into providing grease-free breakfasts for the more delicate morning palate.

Nothing beats the Veggie Breakfast at the **Counter Café (Near Map 94)** in Hackney Wick, and **Pavilion Café (Map 93)** in Victoria Park is a close contender for feeding the east's foodies – kippers with potato cakes and poached eggs is a fantastic Irish classic. **Caravan (Map 6)** has enjoyed its time at the top for a City brunch and it looks set to stay in the number one spot for some time; the chefs here are renowned for mixing up exotic flavour and creating elixical hangover cures. For American treats **The Breakfast Club (Map 80)** is a firm favourite and with three locations there's a seat for everyone. **Dukes Brew and Que (Map 82)** is a sneaky American brekkie place vying for the winner's ribbon and Scandinavian-influenced **Cooper and Wolf (Near Map 87)** has some wholesome northern European options on offer for the more health conscious.

Street Is Sweet

Eating on the street might mean using a plastic fork and sitting on a kerb but it certainly doesn't mean dissecting your way through a soggy sarnie or pulling half-eaten burgers out of the bin. It does mean queuing for a while to eat at the best places, trying to decide which of the tempting street stalls to eat from, and possibly dripping mustard down your best top.

You can literally find everything on the streets of London; from cockroaches to sleeping people, dog shit and hypodermics. Quite delightfully you can also find the much more attractive options of food from all over the world – we've got Peruvian, Polish, Vietnamese, Mexican, French, and pretty much everything else you can think of.

The humble burger has enjoyed huge acclaim over the past year with stalls like **Lucky Chip** reinventing the British BBQ classic to resemble something much more palatable. **Bahn Mi** is a travelling Vietnamese baguette specialist that keeps chiming in reward for serving the best pork rolls in town, and the East.St collective have a permanent spot at Kings Cross where they present the baying public with things like **The Wild Game Co (Map 11)**, and **Engine** with its haute-gourmet Hot Dogs. Even city centre workers have taken the bait for their bait though there is a heavy lean towards superfood salads and sushi in the city, the current bento leader is also perfectly positioned for visitors; right outside of Liverpool Street Station, **Wasabi** has a stall where you can pick up a salad, a couple of bits of sushi, and a delicious miso soup for less than a fiver.

Camden Market food used to be famous for all the wrong reasons; overcooked noodles, oily fried chicken, watery curry and cardboard pizzas, there's still plenty of that around but a newer set of stalls also caters to more refined tastes. What's on offer can be interchangeable but there are a few stalwarts that are worth a go. There's a French stall that does mushrooms and sauté potatoes in a Roquefort sauce and there's no exceptions made just because the chefs are serving from a stall instead of inside a restaurant; these things are literally sit-down-white-table-cloth standard.

The absolute upside to street food stalls, which we've cleverly held back 'til last, is the ability to enjoy top-notch, amazing food for a fraction of the price that a restaurant would charge for the same dish. We're talking £5–6 a go for a main meal that might be paella, Moroccan tagine, Goan curry, or an Argentinian steak. A little cake for afters should knock you back a couple of quid and will round off your stand-up meal quite nicely —**Violet's (Map 89)** lemon drizzle cake makes the proverbial icing on your day.

Doffing Hats to a Trend

The London food scene can be a fickle thing. One day it's Gin and Venison that's the reigning king of the food world and the next it's knocked off its perch by a BBQ rib and a craft beer. See, once the masses have caught onto a top secret food trend, the gourmands move on to new pastures where The Guardian is yet to report, and a license is yet to be passed.

We've lately seen some foodie revolutions, the death of others, and the birthing of a few. While the burger has surely enjoyed its time, one of the new kids on the block, Peruvian, is sticking around for a while, and crawling across the city like a drunk crab – the **Last Days of Pisco** pops up in venues across the city which can be a bit pesky if you turn up the day after it has moved on but their ceviche is possibly one of London's best new additions. Out in the West, the aptly named **Ceviche (Map 12)** does more of the fish-cooked-with-citrus thing and complements each dish with lashing of Peruvian firewater, Pisco which comes on its own, in dessert, and as a range of cocktails.

Onto another trend which is set to stay; the French have hors d'oeuvres the Spanish have tapas, the Swedish have smorgasbord and now the British have small plates, and we love them. Russell Norman's **Polpo (Map 10)** restaurants will remain as popular as ever to serve up shareable small plates in a New York diner-style setting. Expect to see things like Anchovy & Chickpea Crostini, Spicy Pork & Fennel Meatballs, and Rabbit & Chicory Salad, all made in perfect proportions whether you're planning to take a couple for yourself or share a load with friends.

Yauatcha (Map 10) is Soho's answer to the small plate influx where head chef Tong Chee Whee is renowned for combining complicated flavours and adding delicate notes to create things like Venison Puffs. **Brawn (Map 91)** on Columbia Road is in a class of its own when it comes to creating meaty feasts; the restaurant shamelessly rejoices in all things pig and waives any requests for a veggie option. The menu is dependent on season and on what the chefs feel like cooking; you might find salted ox tongue, pork scratching, or pickled wild boar here and it will all be delicious and meaty.

Pop-Up, Pop-Down

Providing a location for these pop up restaurants and supper clubs can be a challenge, mainly because the very nature of them means that most don't stay in the same place for too long, instead choosing to change venues every 3-6 months, allowing each little part of insular London to enjoy the experience.

Some of the more business-inclined places choose to pop in the same place, say, once a month, which makes it easier to pinpoint them but harder to actually get a table. Other that started as a travelling-circus version of a restaurant have settled into grown-up, permanent accommodation, or at least rented a kitchen to become semi-perm tenants. The **Seagrass (Map 80)** in Islington is one of the second type – started as a pop-up and matured to a mainstay; they take over a pie & mash shop three nights a week to serve up a menu heavy on game and fish, you're also invited to bring your own booze.

Disappearing Dining Club follows a similar vein. Having started as a pop-up group offering tea dances and three course dinners, it recently moved out of its student digs into a parently home on Brick Lane where they're operating under the name of **Back in Five Minutes (Map 91)**. It's hidden behind a clothes shop, limited to thirty guests, and operates from Wednesday to Saturday.

Pay for What You Eat

It seems only sensible and fair that you should only pay for what you eat, right? Think about how much of your evening dining bill is often down to the sheer amount of booze you've put away though. Now imagine that you don't have to pay for that portion of the bill.

London has its fair share of bring your own bottle restaurants and the best part is that they're not all of one vein i.e Oriental, dingy, or in one place; even high-end Mayfair has BYOB bottle restaurants. There does seem to be a higher than normal number of BYOB eateries in the east but that's just because hipsters are skint, preferring to spend their cash on purple leggings and (il) legal highs.

By day **Hurwendeki (Map 92)** is a standard little coffee shop, tucked in a railway arch with a unique terrace, by night it is a Korean restaurant with perfect ambiance a brilliant, affordable menu and a BYOB policy. **Little Georgia (Map 92)** is a darling of a place; pretty pale green with a warm, inviting basement, and hearty portions of Georgian food is what to expect here. Kingsland Road is scattered with Vietnamese places where u can BYOB and while they're all fairly good **Mien Tay (Map 91)** is always packed out.

Key: £: Under £10 / ££: £10–£20 / £££: £20–£30 / ££££: £30–£40 / £££££: £40+
* : Does not accept credit cards / † : Accepts only American Express / †† : Accepts only Visa and Mastercard
Time listed refers to kitchen closing time on weekend nights

Map 1 · Marylebone (West)

Abu Ali	136 George St	020 7724 6338	£		Good cheap 'n cheerful Lebanese joint among many similar in the area!
Beirut Express	112 Edgware Rd	020 7724 2700	££	2 am	Chaotic, rude and the best Lebanese in town.
Daisy Green	20 Seymour Street	020 7723 3301	££		Aussie style easy eating.
Locanda Locatelli	8 Seymour St	020 7935 9088	££££	11.30 pm	Outstanding Italian food.
Maroush VI Express	68 Edgware Rd	020 7224 9339	££	12 am	Wax philosophical while smoking a hookah out front.
Twist	42 Crawford St	020 7723 3377	£££		Italian-focused small plates.

Map 2 · Marylebone (East)

Casa Becci	32 Paddington Street	020 7935 7031		11 pm	Cosy Lady and the Tramp-style Italian eaterie
Chiltern Firehouse	1 Chiltern St	020 7073 7676	£££	12 am	Delicious food and celeb-spotting.
Comptoir Libanais	65 Wigmore St	020 7935 1110	£	8 pm	Uncompromisingly cheap and cheerful mezes.
Diwana	31 Thayer St	020 7935 2445	££	11 pm	Lebanese gorge spot.
Fischers	50 Marylebone High St	020 7466 5501	£££		Pitch-perfect Viennese cafe.
Galvin Bistrot de Luxe	66 Baker St	020 7935 4007	£££	11 pm	Veloutés, ballantines, tartares and escargots. Delicieux? Mais oui.
The Golden Hind	73 Marylebone Ln	020 7486 3644	££	10 pm	Fish and chips from the top-drawer. Can do BYOB
Goodman Mayfair	24-26 Maddox St	020 7499 3776	£££££		London steak institution.
Hush Brasserie	8 Lancashire Ct	020 7659 1500	££££	11 pm	European food al fresco. Go on a lunch hour holiday.
Meat Liquor	74 Welbeck St	020 7224 4239	£	12 am	Best burgers and chilli cheese fries in town.
MEATliquor	74 Welbeck St	020 7224 4239	£		No reservations, queues round the block but it's worth it.
No. 5 Cavendish Square	5 Cavendish Sq	020 7079 5000	£££	11 pm	A No. 5 desperately trying to be as opulent as Chanel's.
Patisserie Valerie	105 Marylebone High St	020 7935 6240	£	9 pm	Boho coffee and pastry.
Patty & Bun	54 James St	020 7487 3188	£		Exactly what a burger should be. Be prepared to wait.
Pollen Street Social	8 Pollen St	020 7290 7600	£££££		The mighty Jason Atherton's flagship restaurant.
The Providores and Tapa Room	109 Marylebone High St	020 7935 6175	££	11 pm	Sip Rioja and gorge on tapas for the cognoscenti.
Royal China	24-26 Baker St	020 7487 4688	£££		Cantonese culinary powerhouse flagship; dim sum mandatory.
Royal China Club	40-42 Baker St	020 7486 3898	££££		More upscale iteration of Cantonese culinary powerhouse; dim sum mandatory.
Trishna	15 Blandford St	020 7935 5624	££££		Starred Indian cuisine highlighting the subcontinent's coastal regions.
Zoilo	9 Duke St	020 7486 9699	££££		Haute Argentine transcending beef-industrial complex.

Map 3 · Fitzrovia

Archipelago	53 Cleveland St	020 7383 3346	££££	10.30 pm	London's best, alright only, chocolate-covered scorpions and crocodile steaks.
Ask	48 Grafton Way	020 7388 8108	£	11.30 pm	...for pizza.
Bao	31 Windmill St		££		Scrumptious meat-filled buns.
Barnyard	18 Charlotte St	020 7580 3842	££		Muscular New British cuisine.

515

Key: £ : Under £10 / ££ : £10–£20 / £££ : £20–£30 / ££££ : £30–£40 / £££££: £40+
* : Does not accept credit cards./ † : Accepts only American Express./ ‡: Accepts only Visa and Mastercard
Time listed refers to kitchen closing time on weekend nights

Barrica	62 Goodge St	020 7436 9448	£££		Tapas and sherry-forward bar.
Berners Tavern	10 Berners St	020 7908 7979	£££	10:30 pm	One for special occasions.
Beyond Bread	2 Charlotte Pl	020 7636 7055	££		Breads and pastries made from alternative grains.
Bonnie Gull	21 Foley St	020 7436 0921	££	10 pm	Best fish and chips.
Boopshi's	31 Windmill St	020 3205 0072	££	10 pm	Schnitzel and every kind of Spritz.
Brazilian Gourmet	70 Cleveland St	020 7018 0879	£	6 pm	Authentic and friendly.
Carluccio's	8 Market Pl	020 7636 2228	££	11 pm	Pretty good for a chain. Have the espresso and ice cream.
Crazy Bear	26 Whitfield St	020 7631 0088	££££	10.30 pm	Thai deluxe. Where the media world feeds its clients.
Elena's L'Etoile	30 Charlotte St	020 7636 7189	£££££	11 pm	Old school French sophistication, politicians and journo's.
Gitane	60 Great Titchfield St	020 7631 5269	£	6 pm	Parisian meets Persian
Govinda's	10 Soho St	020 7440 5229	£*	8 pm	Cheap Krishna food. You know the deal.
Hakkasan	8 Hanway Pl	020 7927 7000	£££££	12 am	Soho's sexiest subterranean Chinese. China-chic dining for the beautiful people.
Honey & Co	25 Warren St	020 7388 6175	££	10:30 pm	Husband and wife run.
Iberica	195 Great Portland St	020 7636 8650	££	4 pm	Jamon Jamon
Italiano Coffee Co.	46 Goodge St	020 7580 9688	£	11 pm	Zen it is not—but who cares at £3.50 a pizza?
Kin Cafe	22 Foley St	020 7998 4720	£	5:30 pm	Father and son team cooking fresh and healthy.
Koba	11 Rathbone St	020 7580 8825	£		A Korean delight! Set lunch is a bargain.
Latium	21 Berners St	020 7323 9123	£££	10.30 pm	Romantic (and pricey) first date place.
Market Place	11 Market Pl	020 7079 2020	£	1 am	Warm buzz all day/night. Hot clientele/tepid Prices.
Navarro's	67 Charlotte St	020 7637 7713	£££	10 pm	Delicioso! Smells like Seville, tastes like Seville.
Nyonya	11 Warren St	020 7387 0300	£	7pm	Peranakan Chinese food!
Picture	110 Great Portland St	020 7637 7892	£	10:30 pm	Bistro fayre for sharing. Date night?
Portland	113 Great Portland St	020 7436 3261	££	11 pm	For when you want to impress the parents.
Ragam	57 Cleveland St	020 7636 9098	££	10.45 pm	Can't dis these dosas (potato crepes) at very decent prices.
The Riding House Cafe	43 Great Titchfield St	020 7927 0840	££		Ignore the stuffed squirrels and focus on the buttermilk pancakes.
Roka	37 Charlotte St	020 7580 6464	£££	11 pm	Dazzling Izakaya concept Japanese.
Salt Yard	54 Goodge St	020 7637 0657	££££	11 pm	Intimate and sexy. Take a date. Get laid. Possibly.
Sardo	45 Grafton Way	020 7387 2521	££	11 pm	Hit after hit. Try the crab pasta.
Stef's	3 Berners St	020 3073 1041	££	11 pm	You can't knock the gnocchi.
Thai Metro	38 Charlotte St	020 7436 4201	££	11 pm	Thai food, cooked well, served well, job done.
Villandry	170 Great Portland St	020 7631 3131	££		Hot, tasty, homemade food and very ready-to-eat.
Yalla Yalla	12 Winsley St	020 7637 4748	£	11:30 pm	Shawarma-rama.

Map 4 · Bloomsbury (West)

Alara	58 Marchmont St	020 7837 1172	£££	7 pm	Hardcore veggie/vegan mecca, surprisingly good.
Bi Won	24 Coptic St	020 7580 2660	£	10 pm	Manhandling staff but great food.
Hummus Bros	37 Southampton Row	020 7404 7079	£		Second branch of independent chain serving hummus and meze.
Savoir Faire	42 New Oxford St	020 7436 0707	££	10.30 pm	Sweet little rustic restaurant, a stroll from Soho.

Map 5 · Bloomsbury (East)

Banh Mi Bay	4-6 Theobalds Rd	020 7831 4079	£		One of the originator's of London's bahn mi craze.
Bea's of Bloomsbury	44 Theobald's Rd	020 7242 8330	£	6 pm	You can watch the chefs create artisan cupcake masterpieces here.
Ciao Bella	86 Lamb's Conduit St	020 7242 4119	££	11 pm	Authentic, rustic feel Italian complete with piano.
Cigala	54 Lamb's Conduit St	020 7405 1717	££	10.45 pm	Great service and gorgeous salty Spanish bread.
The Food Bazaar	59 Grays Inn Rd	020 7242 6578	£*	9 pm	Casual and friendly with great hot food selection.
Fryer's Delight	19 Theobald's Rd	020 7405 4114	£*	10 pm	No frills chippie; big portions of chunky, salty, greasy tastiness.

Arts & Entertainment · **Restaurants**

Itadaki Zen	139 King's Cross Rd	020 7278 3573	£	10 pm	Get your zen on.
The Lady Ottoline	11 Northington St	020 7831 0008	££		Great gastropub from owner's of Shoreditch's Princess.
Mary Ward Centre	42 Queen Sq	020 7269 6000	£*	5 pm	Hippy educational centre with a great organic cafe.
Pacina Snack Bar	181 King's Cross Rd	020 7278 8176	£*	10 pm	Grotty exterior disguises this diamond of cheerful authentic Thai.
The Perseverance	63 Lamb's Conduit St	020 7405 8278	££	10.30 pm	Good quality gastropub food.
You Me Sushi	180 Gray's Inn Rd	020 7278 8699	£££		Burgeoning sushi empire; good for takeout.

Map 6 · Clerkenwell

Bad Ibing	120 St. John St	020 7253 3723	£	4 pm	Excellent lunch joint. The toasted ciabattas are divine.
Caravan	11 Exmouth Market	020 7833 8115	£		Exceptional coffee and food.
Dans Le Noir	30 Clerkenwell Green	020 7253 1100	££££	9 pm	Blind waiters serve in pitch darkness: don't wear white.
The Eagle	159 Farringdon Rd	020 7837 1353	££	10.30 pm	London's first gastro pub—just look where they started.
Little Bay	171 Farringdon Rd	020 7278 1234	£	12 am	Posh-people food at pikey-people prices.
The Modern Pantry	47 St Johns Sq	020 7553 9210	££		From breakfast through brunch to lunch and dinner with a modern twist.
Morito	32 Exmouth Market	020 7278 7007	£££		Moro's tapas-mezze sister restaurant.
Moro	34 Exmouth Market	020 7833 8336	££££	11 pm	DO believe the hype.
Pham Sushi	159 Whitecross St	020 7251 6336	£££		Central independent sushi for great healthy lunch.
The Sandwich Man	23 Easton St	020 7833 9001	£*	2.30 pm	Office delivery returns. Gourmet—and just 65p. Best lunch in London.
Sushi Tetsu	12 Jerusalem Passage	020 7278 0421	££££		Tiny, unpretentious, and world class.

Map 7 · Barbican / City Road (South)

Bavarian Beerhouse	190 City Rd	084 4330 2005	££	11 pm	Unlace your lederhausen for some serious schnitzel madness.
Carnevale	135 Whitecross St	020 7250 3452	££	11 pm	Veggie on the cheap.
De Santis	11 Old St	020 7689 5626	££	9.30 pm	Like being in Milan; owner Enzo takes care of you
Nusa Kitchen	9 Old St	020 7253 3135	£*	5 pm	People queuing? For ages? For soup? Now I've seen everything.
Original Bagel Bakery	22 Goswell Rd	020 7251 5576	£		Try the halloumi and olive or peanut butter and jam.

Map 3 · Liverpool Street / Broadgate

Damascu Bite	21 Shoreditch High St	020 7247 0207	£*	1 am	It's the way they grill them from the outside.
Duck & Waffle	110 Bishopgate	020 3640 7310	£££		Remarkably good value for such an 'elevated' dining experience.
Eyre Brothers	70 Leonard St	020 7613 5346	££	10.45 pm	Great place run by the Eyre brothers—Jane no relation.
Gaucho Broadgate	5 Finsbury Ave	020 7256 6877	£££	11 pm	Divine, ohmigod, melt-in-your-mouth steak. Oops, drooling!
Hoxton Grill	81 Great Eastern St	020 7739 9111	£££		Very sexy. Very nice. Very expensive.
The Princess of Shoreditch	76 Paul St	020 7729 9270	££		Gastropub and drinking hole for city workers and slackers.

Map 9 · Mayfair / Green Park

Alain Ducasse at The Dorchester	Park Ln	020 7629 8866	££££	10 pm	Better known for its extortionate prices than michelin-starred food
Burger & Lobster	29 Clarges St	020 7409 1699	££		Burger or lobster or both? Greedy!
Citrus	112 Piccadilly	020 7499 6321	££££		High-end Italian at the Sheraton Park Lane.
Cookbook Cafe	1 Hamilton Pl	020 7318 8563	£££		A celebration of fresh produce from the market table.
Corrigan's	28 Upper Grosvenor St	020 7499 9943	£££££		When in Rome/ Mayfair...
El Pirata Mayfair	5 Down St	020 7491 3810	££	11.30 pm	Don't be put off by stuffy location—this is f'ing good tapas.
The English Tea Room at Brown's	Albemarle St	020 7518 4155	££££	11 pm	Ah, so that's what a £48 cup of tea tastes like.
Galvin at Windows	22 Park Ln	020 7208 4021	£££££	11 pm	Art Deco French overlooking Buckingham Palace. We're not worthy!
Gymkhana	42 Albemarle St	020 3011 5900	££££		Posh four-star Indian with slightly disarming colonial flourishes.

Key: £ : Under £10 / ££ : £10–£20 / £££ : £20–£30 / ££££ : £30–£40 / £££££ : £40+
* : Does not accept credit cards./ † : Accepts only American Express / ††: Accepts only Visa and Mastercard
Time listed refers to kitchen closing time on weekend nights

Kitty Fisher's	10 Shepherd Market	020 3302 1661	£££	Mediterranean-British in cozy digs.
L'Autre	5 Shepherd St	020 7499 4680	£££££	11 pm	Polish meets Mexican. Surprisingly well.
Momo	25 Heddon St	020 7434 4040	££	Tea, cous-cous, shisha, and tagines; perfectly Moroccan.
Nobu	19 Old Park Ln	020 7447 4747	£££££	12 am	Rob a bank on the way as it's bloody expensive!
The Ritz	150 Piccadilly	020 7493 8181	£££££	10 pm	High tea amidst ornaments and swank—resist temptation to swipe towels.
Theo Randall	1 Hamilton Pl	020 7318 8747	£££££	11 pm	Sincere and stylish cuisine unfortunately hidden behind a hotel façade.

Map 10 · Piccadilly / Soho (West)

Bao	53 Lexington St		££	Scrumptious meat-filled buns.
Bob Bob Ricard	1 Upper James St	020 3145 1000	£££	11.30 pm	Proper posh British diner serving Cornish crab cake and...Ribena.
Bodean's BBQ	10 Poland St	020 7287 7575		Resistance is futile. Soho Special—great way to end a night.
Brasserie Zedel	20 Sherwood St	020 7734 4888	£	Service so-so, atmosphere tres Parisian. Great value.
Cecconi's	5 Burlington Gardens	020 7434 1500	££££	11.15 pm	All day menu for the spoilt. Delicious breakfasts.
Cha Cha Moon	15 Ganton St	020 7297 9800	££	11 pm	Like Wagamamas but for Chinese.
Dehesa	25 Ganton St	020 7494 4170	£££	11 pm	Faux-rustic protein-rich tapas, sweetie.
Detox Kitchen	10 Kingly Street	0207 499 6417	££	6:30pm	Clean eating made simple.
Dishoom	22 Kingly St	020 7420 9322	££	All-day Parsi cafe straight outta Bombay.
Fernandez & Wells	73 Beak St	020 7287 8124	££	6 pm	Perfect pasteis de nata and locally made ice-cream. Delightfully friendly!
Fernandez & Wells	43 Lexington St	020 7734 1546	£	10 pm	European style eating and drinking.
Kulu Kulu	76 Brewer St	020 7734 7316	£	10 pm	Great, fresh, fast sushi for people on the go. Sit down is 45 minutes only.
Le Pain Quotidien	18 Great Marlborough St	020 7486 6154	£	10 pm	Feel like a right old tartine.
Mildred's	45 Lexington St	020 7494 1634	££	11pm	Even non-vegetarians are fans.
Nordic Bakery	14 Golden Sq	020 3230 1077	£	7 pm	Authentic sticky cinnamon buns, Karelian pies and smoked Moomin.
The Photographers' Gallery	16 Ramillies St	020 7087 9300	£*	5.30 pm	Artsy coffee spot with photos on view.
Ping Pong	45 Great Marlborough St	020 7851 6969	££	11 pm	Don't leave without trying a char sui bun!
Pitt Cue Co.	1 Newburgh St	020 7287 5578	£££	Best Southern BBQ this side of Austin, Texas.
Polpo	41 Beak St	020 7734 4479	£	Venetian-style bacaro.
San Carlo Cicchetti	215 Piccadily	020 7494 9435	£££	Seasonal Italian; fresh ingredients; all-day menu.
Sartoria	20 Saville Row	020 7534 7000	£££££	11 pm	The pick of the Conran restaurants.
Sketch	9 Conduit St	020 7659 4500	££££	1 am	Colossally trendy kitsch palace.
Social Eating House	58 Poland St	020 7993 3251	££££	Fun, creative cuisine with studiously low-key vibe.
Taro	61 Brewer St	020 7734 5826	£££	10.30 pm	Where London's Japanese locals eat sushi.
Ten Ten Tei	56 Brewer St	020 7287 1738	£££££	10pm	The Japanese restaurant Japanese people love.
Tibits	12 Heddon St	020 7758 4110	££	12 am	Buffet: sans meat, sold by weight. Genius!
Wagamama	10 Lexington St	020 7292 0990	£	11 pm	Reliable, speedy noodle chain.
Wild Honey	12 St George St	020 7758 9160	££	10.30 pm	This Michelin star's got skillz (and a damn good tête de veau).
Yauatcha	15 Broadwick St	020 7494 8888	£££££	11.45 pm	Traditional Chinese tea-house meets star-spangled media haunt.
Yoshino	3 Piccadilly Pl	020 7287 6622	££	10 pm	Back alley bentos so good you'll pretend they were your discovery.

Map 11 · Soho (Central)

Ba Shan	24 Romilly St	020 7287 3266	££	User-friendly Szechuan from Barshu folks.
Balans	60 Old Compton St	020 7439 2183	££	3 am	Share a 4am breakfast with the likes of Amy Winehouse.
Bar Bruno	101 Wardour St	020 7734 3750	£*	10 pm	Hidden Italian cafe gem. Authentically loud and friendly.
Blanchette	9 D'Arblay Street	020 7439 8100	££	Three French brothers bring modern bistro to Soho.
Bocca di Lupo	12 Archer St	020 7734 2223	£££	12 am	Italian for 'break a leg'; authentic fare gets your bocca watering.

Bone Daddies	31 Peter Street	020 7287 8581	£	11:30pm	Tonkotsu ramen, slurp.
Busaba Eathai	110 Wardour St	020 7255 8686	£££		Never mind the shared benches, the food's too yummy.
Café Espana	63 Old Compton St	020 7494 1271	££	11 pm	Highly recommended. 10% off for eating with castanets (possibly).
Copita	27 D'Arblay St	020 7287 7797	£££		Continually changing tapas menu and full bar.
Ember Yard	60 Berwick St	020 7439 8057	£££		Tapas-y charcoal-grilled meats and charcuterie via Spain & Italy.
Foxcroft & Ginger	3 Berwick Street		£	10 pm	Casual cafe eating all day.
The Full English	83 Wardour St		£££		Proper British comfort food at unbelievably reasonable prices.
Gelupo	7 Archer St	020 7287 5555	£		Grab a granita, close your eyes and you're in Sicily.
Grace	42 Great Windmill St	020 7851 0800	££££	10.30 pm	Wannabe a WAG? Get in 'ere!
Honest Burgers	4 Meard St	020 3609 9524	£		Why keeping it simple works. A+ reasonably priced burgers.
Hummus Bros	88 Wardour St	020 7734 1311	££	11 pm	Where hummus is the main dish.
Imli	167 Wardour St	020 7287 4243	££	11 pm	Tapas + curry. Fusion gone insane but somehow works.
Jazz Club	10 Dean St	084 5602 7017	£	11 pm	Surprisingly, jazz takes the mediocre chain up a notch.
Jerk City	189 Wardour St	020 7287 2878	£	10 pm	Jamaican fast food. In doubt? Go for ackee and saltfish.
Kirazu	47 Rupert St	020 7494 2248	£££		Artfully crafted Japanese tapas.
Leong's Legends	4 Macclesfield St	020 7287 0288	££	11 pm	A Taiwanese Chinatown legend.
Maoz	43 Old Compton St	020 7851 1586	£*	1 am	Falafeltastic!
Morada Brindisa Asador	18-20 Rupert St	020 7478 8758	££££		Wood-fired pig via Spain.
The Palomar	34 Rupert St	020 7439 8777	££££		Open-kitchen gastroexperimentation.
Paul	49 Old Compton St	020 7287 6261	£	10 pm	French cafe/bakery chain. Amazing baguettes!
Pizzeria Malletti	26 Noel St	020 7439 4096	£*	3 pm	Amazing! Use your mobile and you won't get served.
Princi	135 Wardour St	020 7478 8888	£		Italian deserts you didn't know existed. Tempting new pizzeria area.
Randall & Aubin	16 Brewer St	020 7287 4447	£££	11 pm	Over-indulgently carnal seafood delights which only call for champagne.
Snog	9 Brewer St	020 7494 3301	£*	12 am	If they had frozen yoghurt and not milk in Clockwork Orange.
Soho Joe	22 Dean St	075 3413 4398			Darn good pizza with the locals that won't break the bank.
Spuntino	61 Rupert St		£££	12 am	Hidden nameless bar serving up tasty b tes.
St Moritz	161 Wardour St	020 7734 3324	££££	11.30 pm	Swiss cheese heaven.
Thai Square	27 St. Annes Ct	020 7287 2000	££	11 pm	Thai with a good range. In set meals—go for starter NOT dessert.
Tokyo Diner	2 Leicester St	020 7287 8777	£		One of London's best for katsu curry. No tipping!
Wong Kei	41 Wardour St	020 7437 8408	££	10 pm	AKA Wonky's: institutionally rude service, cheap fast Chinese.
Yoshino Delicatessen	59 Shaftesbury Ave	020 7287 6622	£	10 pm	Cheap as chips but with sushi.

Map 12 • Soho (East)

10 Greek Street	10 Greek St	020 7734 4677	£££		Farm—and sea-to-table; courier font and slate.
Abeno Too	17 Great Newport St	020 7379 1160	££	11 pm	Addictive Okonomiyaki (pancakes) flipped and fried on the table.
Arbutus	63 Frith St	020 7734 4545	££	11 pm	Chocolate soup! Worth it for that alone.
Assa	53 St Giles High St	020 7240 8256	££	12 am	Cheerful eager-to-please Korean cafe
Baiwei	8 Little Newport St	020 7494 3605	££		Highly recommended Szechuan; encyclopedic menu.
Baozi Inn	26 Newport Court	020 7287 6877	£		No frills, quality Szechuan.
Bar Italia	22 Frith St	020 7437 4520	££	4.30 am	Soho institution; perfect for people watching at any hour.
Barrafina	54 Frith St	020 7813 8016	££	11 pm	Seriously, the best (and hippest) place for tapas.
Barshu	28 Frith St	020 7287 8822	£££		Hot 'n' heavy Szechuan in well-appointed digs.
Bi Bim Bap	11 Greek St	020 7287 3434			Cheap and healthy Korean rice bowls.
Bo Drake	6 Greek St	020 7439 9989	£££		Asian meets American barbecue.

Arts & Entertainment · **Restaurants**

Key: £ : Under £10 / ££ : £10–£20 / £££ : £20–£30 / ££££ : £30–£40 / £££££ : £40+
* : Does not accept credit cards / † : Accepts only American Express / †† : Accepts only Visa and Mastercard
Time listed refers to kitchen closing time on weekend nights

Boheme Kitchen and Bar	19 Old Compton St	020 7734 5656	£££	11.45 pm	You want frites with that? Deliciously snobby comfort food.
Ceviche	17 Frith St	020 7292 2040			Brining Peruvian to the perverted.
Corean Chilli	51 Charing Cross Rd	020 7734 6737	££	12 am	Karaoke and stir-fries with the Korean cool kids.
Ed's Easy Diner	12 Moor St	020 7434 4439	££	11 pm	It's like, you know? Soooo, like, American? You know?
The Friendly Inn	47 Gerrard St	020 7437 4170	£	1 am	Where Londoners go for Chinese in Soho.
Gaby's Deli	30 Charing Cross Rd	020 7836 4233	££	10 pm	High on tradition, low on frills. Authentically spartan.
Garlic & Shots	14 Frith St	020 7734 9505	££££	1 am	Garlic, garlic and more garlic. No-go zone for vampires.
Gay Hussar	2 Greek St	020 7437 0973	££	10.45 pm	Everything from strudel to cherry soup at this old-school Hungarian.
Haozhan	8 Gerrard St	020 7434 3838	£££	11 pm	Can't pick? This is the one.
Imperial China	25 Lisle St	020 7734 3388	££		Solid dim sum option.
The Ivy	1 West St	020 7836 4751	££££		Dining experience that will prove memorable.
Koya	49 Frith St	020 7434 4463	£		Blink and you'd miss London's worst-kept udon secret.
La Bodega Negra	16 Moor St	020 7758 4100	££		Shh, it's a secret! Mexican food underneath a Soho sex shop.
La Porchetta Pollo Bar	20 Old Compton St	020 7494 9368	£££	12 am	Cheap and cheerful Italian. In the West End? Well, exactly.
Le Beaujolais	25 Litchfield St	020 7836 2955	££	10 pm	Get insulted by a Frenchman here in London—Mai oui!
New World	1 Gerrard Pl	020 7434 2508	£	11.45 pm	Crispy duck, Dim Sum, custard dumplings... bring it on!
Pizza Express	20 Greek St	020 7734 7430	£		Pizza. Really fast.
Sartori	15 Great Newport St	020 7836 6308	££		Hit and miss service but all is forgiven with metre long pizzas.
Smoking Goat	7 Denmark St		£££		Stylish, adventurous full-service Thai restaurant.
Soho's Secret Tea Room	29 Greek St	020 7437 5920	£		Secret tea! Hoorah!
The Stockpot	18 Old Compton St	020 7287 1066	££*	12 am	Fantastically cheap stodge.
Taro	10 Old Compton St	020 7439 2275	££	10.30 pm	Like Taro Brewer Street. But gayer, obviously.
Yang Guang Supermarket	28-29 Newport Ct	020 8494 9222	£		Pork buns and coconut jam waffles from vendors outside.

Map 13 · Covent Garden

Battersea Pie	28 The Market	020 7240 9566	£	6 pm	Who ate all the pies?
Belgo Centraal	50 Earlham St	020 7813 2233	£££	11 pm	Thoroughly enjoyable moules et frites. And beer... mmm... beer.
Café Mode	57 Endell St	020 7240 8085	££	11.30 pm	Pizza, pasta, salad. No fuss.
Dishoom	12 Upper St Martin's Ln	020 7420 9320	£		A bustling Bombay brunch. One of the cafe rules—'no fighting.'
Flesh & Buns	41 Earlham St	020 7632 9500	££		Fun izakaya and bun spot from folks behind Bone Daddies.
Great Queen Street	32 Great Queen St	020 7242 0622	£££	11 pm	Affordable and might be London's best gastropub.
Jar Kitchen	176 Drury Ln	020 7405 4255	£££		Farm-to-table modern British.
Kulu Kulu Sushi	51 Shelton St	020 7240 5687	££	10 pm	Tiny conveyor belt sushi joint. Bang on the money.
Lima Floral	14 Garrick St	020 7240 5778	££££		Elegant Peruvian, the way it's meant to be.
Mon Plaisir	21 Monmouth St	020 7836 7243	£££	11.15 pm	Not up to typical Paris standards, but still tres bon!
Punjab	80 Neal St	020 7836 9787	£££	11.30 pm	Relive the days of the Raj in this old-school curry house.
Rock & Sole Plaice	47 Endell St	020 7836 3785	£££	11 pm	London's oldest chippie. Est. 1871. On-street, fairy-lit picnic benches. Huge portions.
Rossopomodoro	50 Monmouth St	020 7240 9095	£	12 am	Chain Italian with very tasty pies. Cutlery prohibited!
Sarastro	126 Drury Ln	020 7836 0101	££	11.30 pm	Hilarious over-the-top decor; includes fornicating cherubs.
Souk Medina	1 Shorts Gardens	020 7240 1796	££	11 pm	Atmospheric Morrocan joint. Free refills on mouthwatering £20 set menu.
Wild Food Cafe	14 Neal's Yard		££	10pm	Delicious, vibrant and healthy.

Arts & Entertainment · **Restaurants**

Map 14 · Holborn / Temple

Asadal	227 High Holborn	020 7430 9006	£££	10.30 pm	Go on—venture down those stairs—it's worth it.
Casanova's Treats	13 Lamb's Conduit Passage	020 7405 5505	£	4 pm	Come get seduced by this tasty Casanova.
Inc⊡go	1 Aldwych	020 7300 0400	£££	11 pm	Sunday brunch and a movie—all in the same place!
The MEATmarket	Jubilee Market Hall, Tavistock St	020 7240 4852	££		Try the hard shakes.

Map 15 · Blackfriars / Farringdon

Beppe's Sandwich Bar	23 W Smithfield	020 7236 7822	££	3 pm	As classically Italian as oversized sunglasses. Only much, much better.
Bleeding Heart	Bleeding Heart Yard	020 7242 2056	£££	10.30 pm	Historic, hard to find, eccentric beauty.
Foxlow	69-73 St John St	020 7014 8070	£££		Neighborhood-friendly meat-forward comfort cuisine.
Gaucho Smithfield	93 Charterhouse St	020 7490 1676	££	11 pm	Where cows would choose to be eaten.
Hix Oyster & Chop House	36 Cowcross St	020 7017 1930	££		Never tried beef and oyster pie?
Kurz + Lang	1 St. John St	020 7993 2923	£	11.30 pm	Ze German Bratwurst sausage at its zizzling best.
Le Cafe du Marche	22 Charterhouse Sq	020 7608 1609	£££	11 pm	Wonderful French cuisine in delightful venue. Tucked away in Charterhouse Square.
Pho	86 St. John St	020 7253 7624	£	10.30 pm	Steaming bowlfuls for hungry Clerkenwell workers. Specialises in street food.
Poncho8	11 Queens Head Passage	020 7248 6744	£		St. Paul's branch of the Mexican restaurant.
Portal	88 St John St	020 7253 6950	££££	10.15 pm	Astoundingly good Portuguese. Swanky but not stuffy.
Shoshan	64 Turnmill St	020 3805 2304	££££		Exquisite multi-level Anglo-Japanese cuisine.
Smiths of Smithfield	67 Charterhouse St	020 7251 7950	£££	10.45 pm	Overflowing with yuppies and trendy types; pricey but tasty.
St John	26 Saint John St	020 7251 0848	££	11 pm	Nose to tail eating.
St. John	26 St John St	020 7251 0848	£££	11 pm	This place is ALL about the offal.
Tinseltown	44 St. John St	020 7689 2424	£	24 hrs	Funky diner serving great late-night milkshakes.
Vivat Bacchus	47 Farringdon St	020 7353 2648	£££	9.30 pm	Three wine cellars and a cheeseroom. A ROOM of cheese.

Map 16 · Square Mile (West)

Barbecoa	20 New Change Passage	020 3005 8555	££££		Steak-y Jamie Oliver fire-cooked joint.
Planet of the Grapes	74 Queen Victoria St	020 7248 1892	££	12 am	Finally, a reason to go to the Square Mile.
Pull'd	61 Cannon St	020 3752 0326	£	9 pm	Pulled pork/beef/chicken.
Sweetings	39 Queen Victoria St	020 7248 3062	£££	4 pm	Old fashioned institution for nostalgia trips. Lunch only.

Map 17 · Square Mile (East)

Gaucho City	1 Bell Inn Yard	020 7626 5180	££££	11 pm	The best steakhouse in the city. Located in former gold vaults.
Jamie's Italian	38 Threadneedle St	020 3005 9445	£££		Slight ray of hope in city boy wasteland.
The Mercer	34 Threadneedle St	020 7628 0001	££	9.30 pm	Proper British grub in a light contemporary atmosphere.
Nusa Kitchen	2 Adams Ct	020 7628 1149	£	4 pm	Fresh soup made daily.
Simpson's Tavern	38 Ball Court Alley	020 7626 9985	££		Perfectly cooked classics in a pub full of history.
Wasabi	52 Old Broad St	020 7374 8337	£*	10 pm	Delicious sushi and bento for those in a rush.

Map 18 · Tower Hill / Aldgate

Jeff's Cafe	14 Brune St	020 7375 2230	£*	10 pm	Cheap as chips (which they serve here, incidentally).
La Pietra	54 Commercial St	020 7247 0988	£		Hey mambo, mambo Italiano.
Poncho 8	5 Steward St	020 7247 2008	£		Spitalfields branch of the Mexican restaurant.

Key: £ : Under £10 / ££ : £10–£20 / £££ : £20–£30 / ££££ : £30–£40 / £££££: £40+
* : Does not accept credit cards./ † : Accepts only American Express / †† : Accepts only Visa and Mastercard
Time listed refers to kitchen closing time on weekend nights

Map 19 · Belgravia

Amaya	Motcomb St	020 7823 1166	££££	11.30 pm Where the trendies go for their curry fix.
Boisdale	15 Eccleston St	020 7730 6922	£££££	11 pm Posh Scottish nosh. No deep-fried Mars Bars, sadly.
Noura	12 William St	020 7235 5900	££	11 pm Frequently orgiastic Lebanese pig-outs.
One-O-One	101 Knightsbridge	020 7290 7101	££££	10 pm One man's fish is another man's pleasure.
The Pantechnicon	10 Motcomb St	020 7730 6074	££££	To impress the parents.
Yo! Sushi	109 Knightsbridge	020 7841 0775	££	10 pm A London institution—we dream in sashimi on conveyor belts.

Map 20 · Victoria / Pimlico (West)

Grumbles	35 Churton St	020 7834 0149	££	11 pm Unfashionably unfussy Brit/French home-cooking. Gorgeous pies, no grumbles.
Pimlico Fresh	86 Wilton Rd	020 7932 0030	££	Best bet for a quality bite before your show.

Map 21 · Pimlico (East)

Regency Cafe	17 Regency St	020 7821 6596	£*	7 pm Proper British fry-ups and atmosphere in this 1940's cafe.
The Vincent Rooms	76 Vincent Sq	020 7802 8391	£££	7 pm Brilliant food served by awkward catering students.

Map 23 · St. James's

Inn The Park	St James' Park	020 7451 9999	££££	7.30 pm Watch the ducks watching you as you eat.
Laduree	71 Burlington Arcade	020 7491 9155	£££	10 pm Grande Dame of Parisian tearooms and purveyor of cult macaroons.
The Stockpot	38 Panton St	020 7839 5142	££*	10.45 pm Treacle pud & custard. Bish bash bosh.
The Wolseley	160 Piccadilly	020 7499 6996	££	12 am Step back in time for an elegant afternoon tea.

Map 24 · Trafalgar Square / The Strand

Cafe in the Crypt	6 St Martin's Pl	020 7766 1158	££	10 pm Spooky sandwiches and fruit crumble.
Gourmet Burger Kitchen	13 Maiden Ln	020 7240 9617	££	11 pm Go for the Kiwiburger. Don't question the ingredients.
Herman Ze German	19 Villiers St	020 7839 5264	£	Great currywurst for the brave, fab hot dogs for the rest!
India Club	143 The Strand	020 7836 4880	£	11 pm Quirky run-down BYOB eaterie; more character than Brick Lane equivalents.
J Sheekey	28 St. Martin's Ct	020 7240 2565	££££	11 pm Old-fashioned seafood haven that the celebs still love.
Portrait Restaurant	St Martin's Pl	020 7312 2490	£££	10.30 pm Exceptional view over London; dinner Thursday and Friday only.
R.S. Hispaniola	Victoria Embankment	020 7839 3011	££	10 pm Feel the bloat, on a boat.
Rules	35 Maiden Ln	020 7836 5314	£££££	10.30 pm London's oldest restaurant with old-fashioned comfort food to match.
Scott's Sandwich Bar	10 New Row	020 7240 0340	££	4 pm Gets very busy at lunch mainly for the salt beef.
Thai Pot	1 Bedfordbury	020 7379 4580	££	11 pm Busy but fast with fresh and generous helpings. Delicious Massaman curry.
Wahaca	66 Chandos Pl	020 7240 1883	£££	11 pm Tasty Mexican market food/tapas. Always busy.

Map 25 · Kensal Town

Boom Burger	272 Portobello Rd	020 8960 3533	££	11 pm Jamaican burgers, jerk chicken and red snapper. Irie.
Lowry and Baker	339 Portobello Rd	020 8960 8534	££	Top notch eggs benedict.
Santo	299 Portobello Rd	020 8968 4590	££	11.30 pm Fresh, frisky Mexican. Too bad about the resentful waiters.
Snaps + Rye	93 Golborne Road	020 8964 3004	££	6 pm London's only Danish restaurant.
Thai Rice	303 Portobello Rd	020 8968 2001	££	10.30 pm Jaw-dropping food in sterile, bland enviornment.
Yum Yum	312 Ladbroke Grove	020 8968 1477	£	Tasty Carribean baked goods and punches.

Arts & Entertainment · **Restaurants**

Map 26 · Maida Hill

Mosob	339 Harrow Rd	020 7266 2012	£ 11:30pm	Fresh, spicy home-cooked food.

Map 29 · Notting Hill Gate

Beach Blanket Babylon	45 Ledbury Rd	020 7229 2907	££££ 12 am	Maze of baroque nooks and crannies where celebs nibble discreetly.
Café Diana	5 Wellington Terrace	020 7792 9606	£ 10.30 pm	Creepy, kitsch shrine to Princess Diana with so-so food.
Crazy Homies	125 Westbourne Park Rd	020 7727 6771	££ 10.15 pm	Avoid first date awkwardness over quality Mexican at this lively get-up.
The Elgin	96 Ladbroke Grove	020 7229 5663	££	Gussied up pub classics.
Geales	2 Farmer St	020 7727 7528	£££ 10.30 pm	Feels ever-so-slightly like a front to appease visiting Americans.
Lucky 7	127 Westbourne Park Rd	020 7727 6771	£££ 10.30 pm	Atmospheric diner for wistful yuppies.
Manzara	24 Pembridge Rd	020 7727 3062	£ 10 pm	Burek Obama for president! Arf.
Nama	110 Talbot Rd	020 7313 4638	££ 10 pm	Raw food nirvana.
Osteria Basilico	29 Kensington Park Rd	020 7727 9957	£££ 11.30 pm	Quaint, buzzing and full of Italian rustic charm. A local hot spot.
The Rum Kitchen	6-8 All Saints Rd	020 7920 6479	££	Fun beach shack themed Jamaican joint.
The Shed	122 Palace Gardens Terr	020 7229 4024	£££	Best of British seasonal.
Taqueria	139 Westbourne Grove	020 7229 4734	££ 11 pm	Wash down these fresh mini-tacos with a good tequila.

Map 30 · Bayswater

Al Waha	75 Westbourne Grove	020 7229 0806	££	Highly regarded Lebanese.
The Cow	89 Westbourne Park Rd	020 7221 0021	£££ 9.45 pm	Top end bar food. Smart restaurant upstairs.
Royal China	13 Queensway	020 7221 2535	£££ 11.15 pm	Keep the Cantonese dim sum comin'!
Tiroler Hut	27 Westbourne Grove	020 7727 3981	££££ 1 am	Dementedly kitsch Austrian madhouse with lederhosen-clad waiters.

Map 31 · Paddington

Bonne Bouche	129 Praed St	020 7724 5784	£ 4.30 pm	Deli counter is popular with local workers for sandwiches.
Casa Malevo	23 Connaught St	020 7402 1988	££££	Warm, welcoming Argentine steakhouse.
Mandalay	444 Edgware Rd	020 7258 3696	£ 10.30 pm	Cheap treats await, despite the God awful situation.
Ranoush Juice Bar	43 Edgware Rd	020 7723 5929	£	Stalwart late night Lebanese cafe.

Map 32 · Shepherd's Bush (West)

Abu Zaad	29 Uxbridge Rd	020 8749 5107	£ 11 pm	A colourful Syrian welcome. Posh Kebabs.
Esarn Kheaw	314 Uxbridge Road	020 8743 8930	£ 11.30 pm	Outstanding Thai. Transport your taste buds to Bangkok.
Vine Leaves Taverna	71 Uxbridge Rd	020 8749 0325	£ 1 am	Friendly staff, traditional grub, huge portions.

Map 33 · Shepherd's Bush

Busaba Eathai	Westfield Shopping Centre	020 3249 1919	££	Westies can now chow down on great Mussaman closer to home.
Jasmine	16 Goldhawk Rd	020 8743 7920	££ 11 pm	Awesome Thai.
Kerbisher & Malt	164 Shepherd's Bush Rd	020 3556 0228	£	Making fish and chips contemporary, ketchup 'n all.
Mr Falafel	Units T4-T5, New Shepherd's Bush Market	077 9890 6668	£	Contender for best falafel in the city.
Patio Restaurant	5 Goldhawk Rd	020 8743 5194	££	Highly regarded home-style Polish.
Piansu	39 Bulwer St	020 8740 4546	£	Steam rising, Nihao at the door. China right here in SheBu.
Popeseye	108 Blythe Rd	020 7610 4578	££££ 10.30 pm	London's ONLY member of the Aberdeen Angus Society.

Map 34 · West Kensington / Olympia

Belvedere	Abbotsbury Rd	020 7602 1238	£££ 11 pm	Sublime setting—the same cannot always be said for the service.

Arts & Entertainment · **Restaurants**

Map 35 · Kensington

Bone Daddies	63-97 Kensington High St	020 7368 4575	££		Rock 'n' roll ramen.
Byron	222 Kensington High St	020 7361 1717	££	10 pm	London's best burger? Locals in the know say so.
Cable Bar and Cafe	8 Brixton Rd	020 8617 9629	£		Charming 50s style hangout. Cocktails at night.
Clarke's	124 Kensington Church St	020 7221 9225	££	10 pm	Elegant, English fine dining. Perfect brunch spot if feeling refined.
Maggie Jones's	6 Old Court Pl	020 7937 6462	£££	10.30 pm	A British culinary time warp, but we like it anyway.
The Roof Gardens & Babylon Restaurant	99 Kensington High St	020 7368 3993	££££	1 am	Truly spectacular roof gardens and devine restaurant 100 foot above HS Ken.
Yashin	1 Argyll Rd	020 7938 1536	£££		Sushi that's Japanese fresh, venue that's London cool.

Map 36 · South Kensington / Gloucester Rd

Caffe Forum	146 Gloucester Rd	020 7259 2322	£*	11 pm	Strange proverbs about cows on the wall and £3.75 pizza. Student digs.
Cremerie Creperie	2 Exhibition Rd	020 7589 8947	£*	11 pm	The best sweet and savoury crepes in London.
Da Mario	15 Gloucester Rd	020 7584 9078	£££	11.30 pm	Apparently Princess Di's local Italian Pizzeria. Affordable and A+ pizza.
Jakobs	20 Gloucester Rd	020 7581 9292	££	10 pm	Brave the slow service for delicious veggie dishes and fresh juices.
Little Japan	32 Thurloe St	020 7591 0207	£*	11.30 pm	Wowzers: bento for a fiver? Suspicious and delicious.
Oddono's	14 Bute St	020 7052 0732	£	11 pm	Gelato fix for homesick Italians and ice-cream freaks alike.
Zack's Deli	115 Gloucester Rd	020 7373 2221	£		More cafe than deli but has tasty home-cooked food.

Map 37 · Knightsbridge

Bar Boulud	66 Knightsbridge	020 7201 3899	££		Best burger in town.
Daquise	20 Thurloe Square	020 7589 6117	£££		Haute Polish cuisine.
Ognisko	55 Prince's Gate	020 7589 0101	£££		Schmancy Polish.
Zuma	5 Raphael St	020 7584 1010	£££	12 am	If your gal likes sushi, ideal for a romantic night out.

Map 38 · Chiswick

Boys Authentic Thai	95 Chiswick High Rd	020 8995 7991	££	10.30 pm	The staff are as funky and fresh as the food.
Chris' Fish Bar	19 Turnham Green Terrace	020 8995 2367	£*	12 am	It's all British-ness wrapped in warm, greasy paper.
Foubert's	2 Turnham Green Terrace	020 8994 5202	£	11 pm	Little Italian owned cafe. Excellent ice cream and gelato.
Franco Manca	144 Chiswick High Rd	020 8747 4822	££	10 pm	London's best pizza with longer opening hours.
High Road Brasserie	162 Chiswick High Rd	020 8742 7474	££	11 pm	As good as it looks. The continent comes to the High Road.
Kalamari	4 Chiswick High Rd	020 8994 4727	££	12 am	For those with a feta fetish.
La Trompette	5 Devonshire Rd	020 8747 1836	£££	10.30 pm	Unpretentious French restaurant with excellent service and set menus.
Le Pain Quotidien	214 Chiswick High Rd	020 3657 6933	£		Lacks the charm of its W11 cousin but delivers fine pastries.
Maison Blanc	26 Turnham Green Terrace	020 8995 7220	£		Windows full of divine cupcakes; wait until you get inside.
Union Jacks	217 Chiswick High Rd	020 3640 7086	££		Mr Oliver's fused British and Italian. Flats and Perry! Genius.
Zizzi	235 Chiswick High Rd	020 8747 9400	££	11.30 pm	Skip the mains—cut straight to the heavenly Apple Crumble.

Map 39 · Stamford Brook

Azou	375 King St	020 8563 7266	££	11 pm	Chilled, candle lit place in amongst a heap of other places. Great tagines.
The Carpenter's Arms	89 Black Lion Ln	020 8741 8386	£££	11 pm	As gastropub as it gets.
Lola & Simon	278 King St	020 8563 0300	££		Cosy and welcoming Kiwi-Argentine eatery serving a great brunch.
Saigon Saigon	313 King St	020 8748 6887	££		Inside and outside are charming, the pho and welcome authentic.
Tosa	332 King St	020 8748 0002	£	10 pm	Low-key authentic yakitori (fried skewered meat) joint. Easy on the wallet.
Upsy Daisy Bakery	387 King St	020 0011 3387			Like your Mum's front room but with nicer cakes. Friendly staff.

Map 40 · Goldhawk Rd / Ravenscourt Park

Mahdi	215 King St	020 8563 7007	££	12 am	Truly authentic, unpretentious Iranian place—menu in Arabic 'n all. Tasty!
Sagar	157 King St	020 8741 8563	££	11 pm	Yummy South Indian veggie food at a great price.
Zippy Diner	42 Goldhawk Rd	020 8740 5473	£		Local greasy spoon diner from the old school. Hearty breakfasts.

Map 41 · Hammersmith

The Gate	51 Queen Caroline St	020 8748 6932	££££	10 pm	Light and airy by day, cosy at night. Lovely food.

Map 42 · Baron's Court

Best Mangal	104 North End Rd	020 7610 1050	££	1 am	Proper good kebabs with heeeeaps of nosh. Can sit in too—a rarity.
The Malt House	17 Vanston Pl	020 7084 6888	££		Vogue Livingesque interiors with the poshest pork scratchings money can buy.

Map 43 · West Brompton / Fulham Broadway / Earls Court

Bodean's BBQ	4 Broadway Chambers	020 7610 0440	£££	11 pm	Stuff yourself on BBQ pulled-pork sandwiches. Yee haw!
Cafe Brazil	511 Fulham Rd	020 7385 2244	£	10:30pm	Brazilian pizza and other delights.
Chutney Mary	535 King's Rd	020 7351 3113	££££	11.30 pm	Get coddled over a curry (at a price).
The Harwood Arms	Walham Grove	020 7386 1847	£££		Michelin-starred cheese and Guinness on toast and a pint!
Megan's Deli & Restaurant	571 King's Rd	020 7348 7139	£		Boiled eggs in the calm and beautiful courtyard. Ah, bliss...
Pizza@Home	350 Old Brompton Rd	020 7244 8080	£*	10 pm	Maybe London's most authentic Italian pizza. Fast and cheap as chips!!
Vingt-Quatre	325 Fulham Rd	020 7376 7224	£	24 hrs	24 hour booze! Incidentally, the food is very good.

Map 44 · Chelsea

Bluebird Chelsea	350 King's Rd	020 7559 1000	£££	10.30 pm	So it seems you can get a bacon butty and look cool on the Kings Road.
Eight Over Eight	392 King's Rd	020 7349 9934	££££	11 pm	Exotic and dripping with celebs.
Haché	329 Fulham Rd	020 7823 3515	£		Top notch gourmet burgers—check out the £1 lunch voucher!

Map 45 · Chelsea (East)

Big Easy	332-334 King's Rd	020 7352 4071	££		Tuesdays are all you can eat shrimp, Louisiana style.
The Chelsea Kitchen	451 Fulham Rd	020 3055 0088	£	11 pm	New place, same affordable stodge. A Winner.
Four o Nine	409 Clapham Rd	020 7737 0722	££££	10.30 pm	Inviting and intimate, it's nice.
Made In Italy	249 King's Rd	020 7352 1880	££	11 pm	"Food Mama used to Make." Unless you're not Italian, obviously.
My Old Dutch Pancake House	221 King's Rd	020 7376 5650	£	11.30 pm	Sweet or savory pancakey goodness in the heart of Chelsea.
The Pig's Ear	35 Old Church St	020 7352 2908	££	10 pm	Quirky, restored boozer. Deep fried pigs ear anyone? Seriously.
Tom's Kitchen	27 Cale St	020 7349 0202	££££	11 pm	Crush-worthy (maybe just us?) Tom Aiken's British brasserie masterpiece.

Arts & Entertainment · **Restaurants**

Map 46 · Sloane Square

The Admiral Codrington	17 Mossop St	020 7581 0005	£££	10.30 pm	Go for simplicity here. Even the chips they get exactly right.
Bibendum Restaurant & Oyster Bar	81 Fulham Rd	020 7581 5817	£££££	11 pm	French institution with a cool (literally) oyster bar.
Foxtrot Oscar	79 Royal Hospital Rd	020 7352 4448	££	10 pm	Tango Alpha Sierra Tango Yankee.
The Good Life Eatery	59 Sloane Ave	020 7052 9388	££		Seriously good, yah.
Restaurant Gordon Ramsay	68 Royal Hospital Rd	020 7352 4441	£££££	11 pm	Mmmmm...debt...

Map 47 · Fulham (West)

The River Café	Rainville Rd	020 7386 4200	£££	11 pm	Fine dining by the Thames for champagne socialists.

Map 48 · Fulham

The Drawing Room Cafe	Bishop's Ave	020 7610 7160	£	5 pm	A historical and elegant spot for a cup of Earl Grey and a scone.
Fisher's Fish & Chips	19 Fulham High St	020 7371 5555	£	10 pm	Quality chips AND quality punning. It's why Britain's Great.
Royal China	805 Fulham Rd	020 7731 0081	£££		Cantonese culinary powerhouse; dim sum mandatory.

Map 49 · Parson's Green

Little H	267 New Kings Rd	020 3417 8228	£		Cali-style eating in Parson's Green. Perfecto!
Tendido Cuatro	108 New King's Rd	020 7371 5147	£££	12 am	Mouth watering iberico jamon, buzzing and friendly Spanish staff.

Map 50 · Sand's End

Blue Elephant	The Boulevard	020 7751 3111	££££	11:30 pm	A classy new location but still damn fine Thai food.
The Sands End	135 Stephendale Rd	020 7731 7823	£££	10 pm	Hearty, rustic Irish fare. Nowt much else around but makes the grade.

Map 51 · Highgate

The Bull	13 N Hill Ave	020 8341 0510	£££	12 am	Chic eatery with perfectly positioned front terrace.
Cafe Rouge	6 S Grove	020 8342 9797	££	11 pm	Decent French restaurant and cafe chain.
Papa Del's	347 Archway Rd	020 8347 9797	££	11 pm	Nice place. Good cookies. £3 pizzas after 9pm!
The Red Lion & Sun	25 North Rd	020 8340 1780	££££	10 pm	Excellent Sunday roasts.

Map 52 · Archway (North)

Bengal Berties	172 Archway Rd	020 8348 1648	££	11 pm	Spit and sawdust venue with excellent nosh.
Fish Fish	179 Archway Rd	020 8348 3121	££	11 pm	Outstanding fresh fish joint flies beneath radar.

Map 53 · Crouch End

Hot Pepper Jelly	11 Broadway Parade	020 8340 4318	££*	5 pm	Pepperphobes probably shouldn't come to this culinary wonder.
Jai Krishna	161 Stroud Green Rd	020 8340 4539	£	11pm	Super delicious vegetarian Indian food.
Wow Simply Japanese	18 Crouch End Hill				Naff name, good food.

Map 54 · Hornsey

Ridge Cafe	97 Tottenham Ln	077 3305 0375	£		Good place for quick lunch or just a caffeine boast.

Map 55 • Harringay

Antepliler	46 Grand Parade, Green Lanes	020 8802 5588	££		Turkish pide pizzas and grilled meat. Lots of it.
Autograf Grill	499 Green Lanes	020 8347 7788	££		Colorless gut-busting cuisine. And delicious.
Blend	587 Green Lanes	020 8341 2939	£		Cafe and seasonal dishes.
Bun & Bar	553 Green Lanes	020 8348 5111	££		Burgers & live music.
Cafe Moka	5 Wightman Rd	020 8340 8664			Oasis in area somewhat of a culinary desert.
Deniran	485 Green Lanes	020 8340 2288	£	2 am	Complementary baklava (if you have any room left!)
Fogo Vivo	Harringay Green Lanes Station	078 7707 4062	£		Hearty Brazilian home cooking and great caipirinhas.
Gokyuzu	26-27 Grand Parade, Green Lanes	020 8211 8406	££		Wear stretchy trousers.
Hala	29 Grand Parade	020 8802 4883	£	2am	Delicious Turkish breakfast.

Map 56 • Hampstead Village

Carluccio's	32 Rosslyn Hill	020 7794 2184	£££	11 pm	Deli by day, diner by night.
Jin Kich	73 Heath St	020 7794 6158			Great range of reasonably priced Japanese favourites.
La Crepe de Hampstead	77 Hampstead High St	020 7445 6767	£*	11 pm	No crap crepes at this sublime French street stall.
Louis Patisserie	32 Heath St	020 7435 9908		6 pm	Tea and gorgeous cakes beloved of elderly Eastern European gentlemen.
Tinseltown	104 Heath St	020 7435 2396	£	3 am	Welcome to milkshake heaven!

Map 57 • Hampstead Heath

Mimo La Bufala	45 South End Rd	020 7435 7814	£££		Charming neighborhood Italian.
Paradise	49 S End Rd	020 7794 6314	£££		Excellent Indian with a modern twist.
Polly's	55 S End Rd	020 7431 7947	£	5 pm	Sometimes you just fancy a sarnie and a cuppa.

Map 58 • Parliament Hill / Dartmouth Park

Al Parco	2 Highgate West Hill	020 8340 5900	£	10 pm	Probably the best pizza in London.
Bistro Laz	1 Highgate West Hill	020 8342 8355	£	11 pm	Lovely meze. Or order in pizza if next door's full.
Carob Tree	15 Highgate Rd	020 7267 9880	£££	11 pm	Swanky Greek place with nice terrace in summer.
Lalibela	137 Fortress Rd	020 7284 0600	££		Steaming pots of Ethiopian stew mopped up with injera.
Stingray Cafe	135 Fortess Rd	020 7482 4855	£	11 pm	Another reason why Tufnell Park rocks: great place!

Map 59 • Tufnell Park

Nuraghe Trattoria	12 Dartmouth Park Hill	020 7263 4560	££		Stylish urban Italian joint with a quirky atmosphere.
Rustique Cafe	142 Fortess Rd	020 7692 5590	££	8 pm	Damn those tasty tasty cookies for being so small.
The Spice	161 Fortess Rd	020 7482 2700	££	11.30 pm	Top-notch curries

Map 60 • Archway

500 Restaurant	782 Holloway Rd	020 7272 3406	££		Excellent homemade gnocchi.
Il Molo Mosaic	24 Junction Rd	020 7272 3569	££	10.30 pm	Head for the back garden sun-trap in Summer.
Junction Café	61 Junction Rd	020 7263 2036	£*	10 pm	Greasy. Spoon.
Nid Ting	533 Holloway Rd	020 7263 0506	£££	11.15 pm	Bigger, meatier portions than most Thai restaurants.
St John's Tavern	91 Junction Rd	020 7272 1587	££££	11 pm	Gastro pub oasis stranded among the pound-shops of Archway.

Map 61 • Holloway (North)

El Molino	3.9 Holloway Rd	020 7700 4312	£	11 pm	One of those, and those, and that..oh and that!
The Landseer	37 Landseer Rd	020 7263 4658	££	9.30 pm	Gastropub extraordinaire.
North Nineteen	19 Sussex Way	020 7281 2786	££		A bright spark in an area of surrounding darkness.

Key: £ : Under £10 / ££ : £10–£20 / £££ : £20–£30 / ££££ : £30–£40 / £££££: £40+
* : Does not accept credit cards./ † : Accepts only American Express / ††: Accepts only Visa and Mastercard
Time listed refers to kitchen closing time on weekend nights

Map 62 · Finsbury Park

Dudley's Pancake House	119 Stroud Green Rd	020 8447 3966	££		Damn good pancakes.
Exeter Street Bakery	Morris Pl	020 7272 8266	££	9:30 pm	Italian-inspired cafe.
Fassika	152 Seven Sisters Rd	020 7272 7572	££	12 am	Intimate with lovely food. Distinctly flirty waitresses though...
Girasole	150 Seven Sisters Rd	07870607959	£		Parmigiana like mama used to make.
Hana Sushi	150 Seven Sisters Rd	020 8964 3333	££	11pm	Authentic sushi.
Le Rif	172 Seven Sisters Rd	020 7263 1891	£*	10 pm	Essential for all your banter and microwaved Tagine needs.
Lulu's Caribbean Cuisine	84 Stroud Green Rd	020 7263 9690	££	11 pm	Caribbean food done just right. Irie.
N4 Street Burger & Burrito	8 Clifton Terrace	020 7502 7741	£	11 pm	Gourmet junk food comes to N4.
Osteria Tufo	67 Fonthill Rd	020 7272 2911		11 pm	Delicious authentic Italian.
Petek	96 Stroud Green Rd	020 7619 3933	£	10.45 pm	Classy but cheap Turkish.
Pizzeria Pappagone	131 Stroud Green Rd	020 7263 2114	££		Has NFT's very own Italian seal of approval.
Season	53 Stroud Green Rd	02072635500	££	10:30 pm	Delicious seasonal food.

Map 63 · Manor House

Fink's Salt & Sweet	70 Mountgrove Rd	020 7684 7189	££	11 pm	Restaurant/deli/wine/coffee/everything you could want.
Il Bacio	178 Blackstock Rd	020 7226 3339	££	11 pm	Friendly, reliable and huge portions.
New River Cafe	271 Stoke Newington Church St	020 7923 9842	£	11 pm	Steamy windows and top hangover cure fry-ups.

Map 64 · Stoke Newington

Anglo-Asian Tandoori	60 Stoke Newington Church St	020 7254 3633	££	11.30 pm	Classic curry house right down to the free sherry.
The Blue Legume	101 Stoke Newington Church St	020 7923 1303	£	11 pm	Dreamy eggs benedict, served under a giant aubergine.
El Olivo	24 Stoke Newington Church St	020 7254 7897			Welcome Spanish addition to areas Turkish foodie landscape.
Fifty Six	56 Newington Green	020 7359 6377	££	11.30 pm	Bring a date.
Foxlow	71-73 Church St	020 7481 6377	£££		Neighborhood-friendly meat-forward comfort cuisine.
Homa	71-73 Stoke Newington Church St	020 7254 2072	£££		Upmarket Italian catering to Stokeys buggy parade.
Rasa N16	55 Stoke Newington Church St	020 7249 0344	££	11.30 pm	Vegetarian-style Indian cooking at its mouth-watering best.
Yum Yum	187 Stoke Newington High St Mussaman.	020 7254 6751	£££	11 pm	Tasty tasty, Thai Thai. Go for the Kang

Map 65 · West Hampstead

Barraco Cafe	10 Kingsgate Place	020 7604 4664	£	11 pm	Boteca bar frequented by Brazilians.
Small & Beautiful	351 Kilburn High Rd	020 7328 2637	£		Small and beautiful indeed, as is the bill.

Map 66 · Finchley Road / Swiss Cottage

Bradleys	25 Winchester Rd	020 7722 3457	£££	11 pm	Your friendly face in the neighbourhood that loves wine.
Camden Arts Centre	Arkwright Rd	020 7472 5500	£	6 pm	Excellent food in buzzing artistic setting.
Loft Coffee Company	4 Canfield Gardens				Simple, tidy cafe, with brilliant coffee.
Singapore Garden	83 Fairfax Rd	020 7328 5314	££	11 pm	Surprising flavours make a welcome alternative on a night out.

Map 67 · Belsize Park

Artigiano	12 Belsize Terrace	020 7794 4288	£££	11 pm	Fancy some fancy pasta?
Ginger & White	2 England's Ln	020 7722 9944	£	5:30 pm	All-day breakfasts and lunch specials.
Paradiso	36 England's Ln	020 7586 9001	££	11.30 pm	For those on a carbs, cheese and cream diet.
Retsina	48 Belsize Ln	020 7431 5855	£££	11 pm	Lively Greek—grilled meat galore!
Violette Cafe	2 England's Ln	020 7586 4326	£	6.30 pm	Cakey goodness.

Map 68 · Kilburn High Road / Abbey Road

Little Bay	228 Belsize Rd	020 7372 4699	££*	11 pm	Crazy cheap. Crazy cute!
Tamada	122 Boundary Rd	020 7372 2882	£££		Proper Georgian winter food.

Arts & Entertainment · **Restaurants**

Map 70 · Primrose Hill

The Hill	94 Haverstock Hill	020 7267 0033	£££	11 pm	The Hill is an ideal place to meet friends before heading off to a show.
J Restaurant	148 Regent's Park Rd	020 7586 9100	££	11 pm	Excellent food, especially brunch. Tempestuous service.
The Regal Cafe	81 Haverstock Hill	020 7586 7412	£	6 pm	Great coffee, good food and wifi: a pleasant working environment.
Lemonia	89 Regent's Park Rd	020 7586 7454	£££	11.30 pm	Fancy a real Greek meal?
Manna	4 Erskine Rd	020 7722 8028	££	11.30 pm	Aesthetically gorgeous veggie restaurant, serving scrumptious food.
Melrose and Morgan	42 Gloucester Ave	020 7722 0011	£	8 pm	Scrumptious food and coffee. Good for solo snacks.
Odette's	130 Regent's Park Rd	020 7586 8569	£££	1 am	Delectably dainty restaurant, high-class service.
Primrose Bakery	69 Gloucester Ave	020 7483 4222	£	6 pm	A delectably dinky bakery. These cakes can't be missed.
Tandis	73 Haverstock Hill	020 7586 8079	££		Iranian food with a touch of elegance.

Map 71 · Camden Town / Chalk Farm / Kentish Town (West)

Andy's Taverna	81 Bayham St	020 7485 9718	££	11 pm	Big Greek restaurant with a garden.
Anima e Cuore	129 Kentish Town Rd	020 7267 2410	££		BYOB affordable fan-favorite Italian.
Arancini Factory Cafe	115 Kentish Town Rd	020 3583 2242	£	5 pm	Aussie guys making risotto balls.
Bar Gansa	2 Inverness St	020 7267 8909	££	12 am	More buzzing and pleasurable than a Rampant Rabbit.
Bento Cafe	9 Parkway	020 7482 3990	££	11 pm	Exquisite Japanese food at very reasonable prices.
Cafe Chula	89 Camden Lock Pl	020 7284 1890	££		Mexican, for brunch?! Si, si si! A+ Huevos Rancheros.
Cottons	55 Chalk Farm Rd	020 7485 8388	££	10 pm	No hustle and bustle, just chill Jamaican style.
Falla and Mosaer	82 Parkway	020 7428 7586	£		Great cakes and snacks.
Haché	24 Inverness St	020 7485 9100	££	10.30 pm	Burger heaven for both vegetarians and carnivores.
Kim's Vietnamese Food Hut	Stables Market		£*	11 pm	Once you pass the Spanish Inqusition, some excellent slop.
Marathon Kebab House	87 Chalk Farm Rd	020 7485 3814	£*	4 am	Legendary late-night venue serving kebabs, chips and beer.
Marine Ices	8 Haverstock Hill	020 7482 9003	£		Fantastic ice cream restaurant with '70s decor and autographed photos.
Market	43 Parkway	020 7267 9700	£££	11 pm	The only restaurant in Camden deserving of the name.
Muang Thai	71 Chalk Farm Rd	020 7916 0653	£	11 pm	Quiet vibe, tinkly music, reliably decent food.
My Village	37 Chalk Farm Rd	020 7485 4996	£	9 pm	Cute ethnic organic shop serving food, tea and coffee.
Q Grill	29-33 Chalk Farm Rd	020 7267 2678	£££		Fun, festive New World-themed barbecue.
Thanh Binh	14 Chalk Farm Rd	020 7267 9820	£	10 pm	Excellent Vietnamese with very friendly and chatty staff.
Viet-Anh Cafe	41 Parkway	020 7284 4082	£	11 pm	Surly service, cheap plentiful food. Would it hurt to smile?
Woody Grill	1 Camden Rd	020 7485 7774	£*	12 am	Late night post-alcohol food without salmonella poisoning.
Yumchaa	91 Camden Lock Pl	020 7209 9641	£*	6 pm	The carrot cake...oh mama!
Zorya Imperial Vodka Room	48 Chalk Farm Rd	020 7485 8484	££	12 am	Vodka, vodka and more vodka. Oh ...and gorgeous food too.

Map 72 · Kentish Town

Bengal Lancer	253 Kentish Town Rd	020 7485 6688	£££		The best (and priciest) indian in the area.
Cafe Renoir	244 Kentish Town Rd	020 7485 7186	£		Nice and bright with simple food and decent coffee.
Dirty Burger	79 Highgate Rd	020 3310 2010		12 am	Burgers that are dirty.
Itta	225 Kentish Town Rd	020 7267 5622	£	10 pm	Awesome pizza for those on a budget.
Mario's Cafe	6 Kelly St	020 7284 2066	£*	10 pm	Saint Etienne's local greasy spoon.
The Oxford	256 Kentish Town Rd	020 7485 3521	££	9.45 pm	Smug comfort eating.
Pane Vino	323 Kentish Town Rd	020 7267 3879	££	10.30 pm	Staff can be Italian. Food can be fantastic.
Phoenicia	186 Kentish Town Rd	020 7267 1267	£	10 pm	Coffee 'n baclava, falafel, meze. All a steal.

Arts & Entertainment • **Restaurants**

Key: £ : Under £10 / ££ : £10–£20 / £££ : £20–£30 / ££££ : £30–£40 / £££££ : £40+
* : Does not accept credit cards./ † : Accepts only American Express / †† : Accepts only Visa and Mastercard
Time listed refers to kitchen closing time on weekend nights

Map 74 • Holloway Road / Arsenal

El Rincon Quiteno	235 Holloway Rd	020 7700 3670	££		A ray of South American sunshine on bleak Holloway Road.
Kokeb	45 Roman Way	020 7609 9832	£	10 pm	Getenesh will look after you.
Wolkite Kifto	82 Hornsey Road	020 7700 3055	£	11 pm	Good veggie options as well as kitfo.

Map 75 • Highbury

Firezza	276 St. Paul's Rd	020 7359 7400	£		Up market-esque stone baked pizza joint.
Highbury Arts Club	73 Highbury Park	07826 899499	££	11 pm	Cosy space with live events.
Prawn on the Lawn	220 Saint Paul's Rd	020 3302 8668	£££	12 am	As fresh as it gets.
Primeur	116 Petherton Rd	020 7226 5271	£££		Fun, fresh European menu with French focus.
San Daniele Del Friuli	72 Highbury Park	020 7226 1609	£££	12 am	Like mama used to make—well someone had to say it.
Trullo	300-302 St Paul's Rd	020 7226 2733	£££		Well-done rustic seasonal Italian.
Ustun Lahmacun	107 Green Lanes	020 7704 0360	£*	10 pm	Very nice lamachun.

Map 76 • Edgware Road / Marylebone (North)

The Sea Shell Lisson Grove	49 Lisson Grove	020 7224 9000	££	10.30 pm	Pescatarians will love this place—sorry, carnivores!

Map 77 • Mornington Crescent / Regent's Park

Chutneys	124 Drummond St	020 7388 0604	££	11.30 pm	Flavoursome, no-frills, fill-yer-boots affair. Bargainous buffet colossal.
Diwana Bhel Poori House	121 Drummond St	020 7387 5556	££	11 pm	South-Indian veggie with tasty dosai and puris.
Mestizo	103 Hampstead Rd	020 7387 4064	£££	11 pm	Great. The margarita is made by the devil himself.
York & Albany	127 Parkway	020 7388 3344	£££	11 pm	Gordo on a budget.

Map 78 • Euston

Asakusa	265 Eversholt St	020 7388 8533	£££	11.30 pm	Authentic Japanese.
Banger Bros.	Euston Station	020 7387 6958	£	7.30 pm	Sing it: It's a small world (of sausages) after all!
The Booking Office	St Pancras Renaissance London Hotel, Euston Rd	020 7841 3566	££		Where the lucky few have pre Eurostar cocktails and snacks.
Camino Cruz del Rey	3 Varnisher's Yard	020 7841 7330	£££	12 am	Sophisticated Spanish restaurant in Kings Cross. Seems wrong, somehow.
Caravan	1 Granary Building	020 7101 7661	££	11:30 pm	Industrial space serving food and awesome coffee.
Chop Chop Noodle Bar	1 Euston Rd	020 7833 1773	£	11 pm	Great for a quick and cheap meal. Massive portions.
Dishoom	5 Stable St	020 7420 9321			All-day Parsi cafe straight outta Bombay.
El Parador	245 Eversholt St	020 7387 2789	££	11 pm	Great tapas. A little ray of sunshine in your mouth.
Grain Store	1-3 Stable St	020 7324 4466	££		United Nations of food; good vegan and vegetarian options.
Great Nepalese	48 Eversholt St	020 7388 6737	££	11 pm	Really the only option in the area.
Kerb	Kings Blvd		£		Ever changing market showcasing best in London street food.
Kitchin N1	8 Caledonia St	020 7713 8777	££	11 pm	Round-the-world all-you-can-eat. Vile and great.
Rodon Live	Pratt St	020 7267 8088	£££	11 pm	Friendly rotund owner masks just above average food.
The Somers Town Coffee House	60 Chalton St	020 7387 7377	££	10 pm	Bistro food in grade II listed pub. Excellent set menu.

Map 79 · King's Cross

Addis	42 Caledonian Rd	020 7278 0679	££	11 pm	Lovely food with convivial sloth-like service.
Cafe Oz	53 Caledonian Rd	020 7278 9650	£*	10 pm	Unusually well-kept greasy spoon.
Euro Café	299 Caledonian Rd	020 7607 5362	£	10 pm	Loveable caff with some unusual specials.
Marathon	196 Caledonian Rd	020 7837 4499	££	12 am	Raw meat, ritualistic coffee and crazed dancing.
New Didar	347 Caledonian Rd	020 7700 3496	£	12 am	Friendly staff willing to strike deals. Haggling gets you everywhere.
Yum Yum	48 Caledonian Rd	020 7278 4737	£	11 pm	Super-cheap Chinese that may even remain in your stomach.

Map 80 · Angel / Upper St

Afghan Kitchen	35 Islington Green	020 7359 8019	£££*	10.45 pm	Only a few tables; Islington's smallest—and biggest—Afghan place.
The Albion	10 Thornhill Rd	020 7607 7450	££	10 pm	How many places offer whole suckling pigs? Not enough.
Alpino	97 Chapel Market	020 7837 8330	£	4 pm	This, guv'nor, is a proper tea'n'two slices caff. Alright?
The Breakfast Club	31 Camden Passage	020 7226 5454	££	9.30 pm	Not just breakfast, not a club. But just so gooood.
Candid Café & Courtyard	3 Torrens St	020 7278 9368	£	10 pm	Laid-back, arty cafe for dreamy types. Candle-lit. Perfect for lingering.
Dead Dolls House	181 Upper St	020 7288 1470	££	11 pm	Hand illustrated walls using marker pen.
Desperados	67 Upper St	020 7226 5055	££	11.30 pm	Garish. More like the Mexico of MTV than the real world.
The Elk in the Woods	39 Camden Passage	020 7226 3535	££	10.30 pm	Laid-back, hunting-themed eatery.
Fig and Olive	151 Upper St	020 7354 2605	££	11 pm	Incredibly busy at weekends which can affect service and quality.
Fredericks	Camden Passage	020 7359 2888	££	11 pm	Swanky Euro-flash bistro.
Gem	265 Upper St	020 7359 0405	£££	4 am	A good vibe is precious.
Indian Veg Bhelpoori House	93 Chapel Market	020 7833 1167	£	10 pm	Honest all-you-can-eat Indian. Veggie propaganda on walls.
Isarn	119 Upper St	020 7424 5153	££	11 pm	Pretty, flower-adorned food, green curry cooked to perfection. Candle-lit courtyard.
La Forchetta	73 Upper St	020 7226 6879	££	11.30 pm	Unpretentious, cheap pizza. Eat fast, then leg it.
La Porchetta	141 Upper St	020 7288 2488	£££	11 pm	This little pig says yes to good cheap pizza.
Le Mercury	140 Upper St	020 7354 4088	££	1 am	This place will seduce you AND your mother.
Masala Zone	80 Upper St	020 7359 3399	££	11 pm	Cheap, good thalis served on metal trays.
Mem & Laz	8 Theberton St	020 7704 9089	££	11 pm	Mediterranean chaos by candlelight.
Oldroyd	344 Upper St	020 8617 9010	£££		Ever-changing pan-European menus using seasonal ingredients.
Ottolenghi	287 Upper St	020 7288 1454	££	10 pm	Staff you'll want to take home to meet your mum.
Pera	170 Upper St	020 7704 6888	££		It's all about the Turkish brunch in this friendly joint!
Pizzeria Oregano	19 St. Alban's Pl	020 7288 1123	££	11 pm	Great pizza and lentil soup. Delicious odd couple.
Rodizio Rico	77 Upper St	020 7354 1076	£££	11 pm	Meat. And lots of it.
The Seagress	74 Chapel Market	079 0201 5200	££		Authentic 19th century décor, cockney culture, pie and mash perfection.
Tortilla	13 Islington High St	020 7833 3103	£	10 pm	Damn good burritos!
Zaffrani	47 Cross St	020 7226 5522	££	11 pm	Thinking man's curry.

Map 81 · Canonbury

Raab's Bakery	136 Essex Rd	020 7226 2830	£	6 pm	Use your loaf sunshine.

Map 82 · De Beauvoir Town / Kingsland

De La Panza	105 Southgate Rd	020 7226 0334	£££	12 am	Bodegon-style eating.
Duke's Brew & Que	33 Downham Rd	020 3006 0795	£		Whatchoo want to eat? Ribs.
Mother Earth	101 Newington Green Rd	020 7359 7353	£	8 pm	Wholesome cafe food.
Peppers and Spice	40 Balls Pond Rd	020 7275 9818	£*	10.30 pm	The real deal: jerk, oxtail, festival, plantain, ackee. Everything irie.
Pond	3 Gillett St	020 3772 6727	££	11pm	Hawaiian, anyone?
Vietnamese Canteen Huong Viet	12 Englefield Rd	020 7249 0877	££	11 pm	A crumbling old bath house? Look again.

Arts & Entertainment · Restaurants

Key: £ : Under £10 / ££ : £10–£20 / £££ : £20–£30 / ££££ : £30–£40 / £££££ : £40+
*: Does not accept credit cards./ † : Accepts only American Express / †† : Accepts only Visa and Mastercard
Time listed refers to kitchen closing time on weekend nights

Map 83 · Angel (East) / City Rd (North)

The Shepherdess	221 City Rd	020 7253 2463	£	5 pm	Cafe offering no-frills traditional English fare.
William IV	7 Shepherdess Walk	020 3119 3012	££	12 am	Lovely gastropub, off the beaten track and with delicious food.

Map 84 · Hoxton

8 Hoxton Square	8 Hoxton Sq	020 7729 4232	£££		Eponymously named farm-to-table simplicity, with good drinks.
The Barrel Boulangerie	110 Hoxton St	020 7683 0353	£	10 pm	Local favourite spot for pizza.
Big Apple Hot Dogs	239 Old St	079 8938 7441	£		Offers a gourmet British twist on a classic American treat.
The Clove Club	380 Old St	020 7729 6496	££££		Nu British tasting menus in grand setting.
Cream	31 New Inn Yard	020 7247 3999	££	5 pm	Chef earned his stripes at Rooftop Cafe.
The Diner	128 Curtain Rd	020 7729 4452	£££	10.30 pm	Door-stopper burgers that should come with health warnings.
F. Cooke's Pie & Mash	150 Hoxton St	020 7729 7718	£	8 pm	Pies, Liquor, Eels... British culinary retardation at its finest.
Jamie Oliver's Fifteen	15 Westland Pl	020 3375 1515	£££££	10 pm	Lots of Jamie Oliver. Lots of great, expensive food.
The Jones Family Project	78 Great Eastern St	020 7739 1740	££		Excellent steak and fish dishes.
Meat Mission	15 Hoxton Market	020 7739 8212	£	12 am	Sister restaurant to Meat Liquor.
MEATmission	14-15 Hoxton Market	020 7739 8212	££		Make sure to try the Peckham dip.
Rivington Grill	28 Rivington St	020 7729 7053	££	11 pm	Emin on the walls, meat in the buns.
Tramshed	32 Rivington St	020 7749 0478	££		A.K.A The Cow and Chicken.

Map 85 · Stoke Newington (East)

19 Numara Bos Cirrik	34 Stoke Newington Rd	020 7249 0400	££	10 pm	Meat, meat, meat—oh and onion, pomegranate and turnip salad.
Addie's Thai Cafe	3 Northwold Rd	020 7249 2618	££		Deceptively pokey, unimaginatively named, yet brilliant.
The Bagel House	2 Stoke Newington High St	020 7249 3908	£*		Bagels to rival Brick Lane and without the queues.
Cafe Z Bar	58 Stoke Newington High St	020 7275 7523	£*	11 pm	Popular grease-shop/hangover center for Stokey Lefties.
Tatreez Cafe	188 Stoke Newington High St	020 8616 5434	££		Charming Palestinian restaurant; beer and wine available.
Testi	38 Stoke Newington High St	020 7249 7151	£££	12 am	It's the dog's bollocks.
The Three Crowns	175 Stoke Newington High St	020 7241 5511	££		Impressive Victorian pub that's undergone gastropubification.

Map 86 · Dalston / Kingsland

A Little Of What You Fancy	464 Kingsland Rd	020 7275 0060	££		A bit like being in a friend's kitchen/dining room.
Arancini Brothers	592 Kingsland Rd	020 3583 7303	£	10 pm	This is how you do fast food (and coffee).
The Best Turkish Kebab	125 Stoke Newington Rd	020 7254 7642	£*	12 am	Feed your soul. Always buzzing.
Dalston Eastern Curve Garden	13 Dalston Lane		£	11pm	Check website for days when food is served.
Evin	115 Kingsland High St	020 7254 5634	££	11 pm	Fantastic Turkish place without the grease factor. Speciality is gozleme.
Mangal 1	10 Arcola St	020 7275 8981	£*	12 am	May the grill's smoke guide you, meat-loving friends.
Mangal 2	4 Stoke Newington Rd	020 7254 7888	££	12 am	Gilbert & George aren't the only ones loving this one.
The Russet	Amhurst Terrace	020 3095 9731	£		Hanging out with the creatives.
Shanghai	41 Kingsland High St	020 7254 2878	££	10.30 pm	Tasty, good-value Chinese hiding behind the facade of a dingy old Kaff.
Somine	131 Kingsland High St	020 7254 7384	£*	24-hrs	Reanimating your lentil soup, Turkish style. Around the clock.
Stone Cave	111 Kingsland High St	020 7241 4911	££	12 am	Cave look and cave feel. Up-scale(ish) Turkish. And great.
The Tea Rooms	155 Stoke Newington Rd	020 7923 1870	£	10 pm	Stokey in a tea-cup. Pleasant...
Voodoo Ray's	117 Kingsland High St	020 7254 2273	£		All American late night pizza from folk behind Dalston Superstore.

Arts & Entertainment · **Restaurants**

Map 87 · Hackney Downs / Lower Clapton

India Gate	75 Lower Clapton Rd	020 8986 0505	£*	11 pm	Very, very cheap, pretty cheerful and a little rank.
Mess Café	38 Amhurst Rd	020 8985 3194	£*	5 pm	All manner of breakfast all the time.

Map 88 · Haggerston / Queensbridge Rd

Beagle	397 Geffrye St	020 7613 2967	£££		Tasteful Modern British cuisine plus cocktails and all-day coffee.
Berber & Q	Arch 338, Acton Mews		£££		BBQ meets mezze under railroad arches.
Chicken Sours	390 Kingsland Rd		££	10:30pm	Fried chicken and cocktails. Of course.
Fabrique Bakery	385 Geffrye St	020 7033 0268	£		Great Nordic bakery and café.
Faulkners	424 Kingsland Rd	020 7254 6152	£	10 pm	Legendary and traditional with traditional opening times.
Hackney City Farm	1 Goldsmith's Row	020 7729 6381	£	4.30 pm	Animals! In Hackney! And some overpriced fry-up.
Song Que	134 Kingsland Rd	020 7613 3222	£	11 pm	Still Little Vietnam's queen. An authentic, no-nonsense affair.
Uludag	398 Kingsland Rd	020 7241 1923	£		Great falafels and a bit of a nutter hub to boot.
Viet Hoa Cafe	70 Kingsland Rd	020 7729 8293	£	11.30 pm	Bland looking cafe hides gorgeous delicacies.

Map 89 · London Fields / Hackney Central

Buen Ayre	50 Broadway Market	020 7275 9900	££££	10.30 pm	Vegetarians take note—run for the hills.
Cafe Bohemia	2 Bohemia Pl	020 8986 4325	£	11 pm	Feeling Bohemian? Quirky cafe with live blues/jazz/world Saturday nights.
The Cat and Mutton	76 Broadway Market	020 7254 5599	££	10 pm	Gastropub without the gastropub nastiness.
The Corner Deli	121 Mare St	020 8986 0031	£	9 pm	Nice spot for brunch away from the bustle of Broadway Market.
Hai Ha	206 Mare St	020 8985 5388	££*	11 pm	Brilliant BYO Vietnamese cafe.
Ombra	1 Vyner St	020 8981 5150	£		Neighbourhood Italian, good honest food.
Pidgin	52 Wilton Wy	020 7254 8311	£££		Ever-changing seasonal set menus, charming digs.
The Spurstowe Arms	68 Greenwood Rd	020 7249 2500	££	11 pm	Suntrap beer garden, good wine selection and gamey menu. Marvellous.

Map 90 · Homerton / Victoria Park North

Eat 17	64-66 Brooksby's Walk	020 8986 6242	££		Convenience store, burger bar, restaurant, florist, bakery, off licence, etc.
The Empress	130 Lauriston Rd	020 8533 5123	£££	10 pm	Spiffy menu from brekkie through to dinner in Hackney Village.
Fish House	126 Lauriston Rd	020 8533 3327	££	9.45 pm	Not as cheap as chips but still very good.
Machete	91 Lauriston Rd	020 8533 3100	££	11:30 pm	Great cocktails too.
Well Street Kitchen	203 Well St	020 8533 6275	£	5 pm	Good honest caff food.

Map 91 · Shoreditch / Brick Lane / Spitalfields

Andina	1 Redchurch St	020 7920 6499	££		Fun Peruvian beyond the usual.
Back in 5 Minutes	222 Brick Ln	075 0775 4318			Pop in a pop up for shopping and a 3 course.
Beigel Shop	155 Brick Ln	020 7729 0826	£*	24 hrs	For 3am cravings: salted beef bagel from the Beigel Shop.
Boundary	2 Boundary St	020 7729 1051	£££	10.30 pm	Warehouse conversion, great view, some major boxes being ticked here.
Brawn	49 Columbia Rd	020 7729 5692			No pig left unturned.
Cafe Bangla	128 Brick Ln	020 7247 8981	£	12 am	Popular Bangladeshi adorned with psychedelic and surreal fantasy art.
Chez Elles	45 Brick Ln	020 7247 9699	££		Out-Frenches most actual French bistros, and does it deliciously.
Clipper Bangladeshi Cusine	104 Brick Ln	020 7377 0022	££	12 am	For less spice-oriented connoisseurs, Bengali Clipper's exceptional lamb korma.
The Culpeper	40 Commercial St	020 7247 5371	££	2 am	Seasonal and local food.
Dishoom	7 Boundary St	020 7420 9324	££		All-day Parsi cafe straight outta Bombay.
The Drunken Monkey	222 Shoreditch High St	020 7392 9606	££	12 am	Debauched, dimly-lit dim-sum drinking hole. Chinese lanterns and lethal mojitos.
Ethiopian Food Stall	Brick Ln		£*		One of many great food stalls, get Brazilian desert after!
Frizzante	1 Goldsmith's Row	020 7739 2266	££		All the Italians go to Agriturismo night (Thurs) just sayin'.
Gourmet San	261 Bethnal Green Rd	020 7729 8388	£*	11 pm	Whole crabs and minimal English.

Arts & Entertainment • Restaurants

Hanoi Cafe	98 Kingsland Rd	020 7729 5610	££	11 pm	Cosy Viet joint, where the whole family's around.
Hawksmoor	157 Commercial St	020 7426 4850	£££	10.30 pm	France and America forget their differences over some serious steakage.
Les Trois Garcons	1 Club Row	020 7613 1924	££££	11 pm	Kitch décor/slick service/fantastic grub.
Lyle's	56 Shoreditch High St	020 3011 5911	££££		Modern British.
Marksman Public House	254 Hackney Rd	020 7739 7393	£££		Cut-above pub grub.
Mien Tay	122 Kingsland Rd	020 7729 3074			Kingsland's supreme Vietnamese.
Mr Buckley's	277 Hackney Rd	020 3664 0033			Uber hip without falling into usual cliches.
Noodle King	185 Bethnal Green Rd	020 7613 3131	£*	11.30 pm	Half the normal price; double the normal portions. Come hungry.
Poppies	6 Hanbury St	020 7247 0892	£		The Great British dish served '50's style.
The Premises	209 Hackney Rd	020 7729 7593	££	11 pm	Bistro swarming with musicians thanks to next door's recording studio.
Que Viet	102 Kingsland Rd	020 7033 0588	££	11 pm	So du jour—even Marc Jacobs munches noodles here.
Rosa's	12 Hanbury St	020 7247 1093	££	11 pm	Quirky, warm little Thai place.
St. John Bread and Wine	94 Commercial St	020 7251 0848	£££		Minimalist and meaty. Anyone for deep-fried pig's head?
Taberna do Mercado	107 Commercial St	020 7375 0649	£££		Stylish, tasty Portuguese.
Tay Do	65 Kingsland Rd	020 7729 7223	£	11 pm	Squish 'em in, feed 'em quick variety of cheap & filling Vietnamese cuisine.
Troy Cafe	124 Kingsland Rd	020 7033 9514	£	7 pm	Delicious lunchtime buffet.
Viet Grill	58 Kingsland Rd	020 7739 6686	££	11 pm	Eccentric but tasty. Non edible tropical fish as decor...

Map 92 • Bethnal Green

Bistrotheque	23 Wadeson St	020 8983 7900	££	11 pm	Brunch, burlesque and pianist playing Smells Like Teen Spirit. Fabulous.
E. Pellicci	332 Bethnal Green Rd	020 7739 4873	£	4.30 pm	Challenge your hangover to survive their fry-ups.
The Gallery Cafe	21 Old Ford Rd	020 8980 2092	£	9 pm	Veggie/vegan haven.
Little Georgia	87 Goldsmiths Row	020 7739 8154	££	10 pm	Hearty fayre from the former Soviet State. No drinks licence.
Mission	250 Paradise Row	020 7613 0478	£££	12 am	Californian high-end drinking and eating.

Map 93 • Globe Town / Mile End (North)

Greedy Cow Burgers & Steaks	2 Grove Rd	020 8983 3304	$$		Burger and exotic meat taste explosion.
Morgan Arms	43 Morgan St	020 8980 6389	£££	12 am	Which joker invented the term "gastropub"? This is one of them.

Map 94 • Bow

Chicchi	516 Roman Rd	020 8141 4190	£*	7 pm	The Italians reclaim Roman Road
G. Kelly Noted Eel & Pie Shop	526 Roman Rd	020 8980 3165	£	7 pm	Servin' 'ot 'ome-made pies, jellied eels 'n mash since 1937.
Pavilion Victoria Park	Old Ford Rd	020 8980 0030			Kippery breakfast with a view

Map 95 • Whitechapel (West) / St Katharine's Dock

Cafe Spice Namaste	16 Prescot St	020 7488 9242	££	10.30 pm	Open-minded Indian that strays far from run of the mill.
The Empress	141 Leman St	020 7265 0745	£	11.45 pm	Forget Brick Lane. This is where it's at.

Map 96 • Whitechapel (East) / Shadwell (West) / Wapping

Lahore Kebab House	2-10 Umberston St	020 7488 2551	$		Pakistani grub gives new insight to 'eyes bigger than stomach'.
Needoo Grill	87 New Rd	020 7247 0648	£		For when Tayyabs queue is just too long.
Tayyabs	83 Fieldgate St	020 7247 6400	£	12 am	Lipsmacking seekh kebabs alone are worth the queues.

Arts & Entertainment • **Restaurants**

Map 97 • Stepney / Shadwell (East)

Dirt Burger	27 Mile End Rd	020 3727 6165	£	11 pm	East London outpost of this gourmet fast food fave.
Foxcroft & Ginger	69 Mile End Rd		£	10 pm	Sister to popular Soho cafe.

Map 98 • Mile End (South) / Limehouse

The Narrow	44 Narrow St	020 7592 7950	£££	11 pm	Gordon Ramsay's nod to gastropubs—cracking views.
The Orange Room	63 Burdett Rd	020 8980 7336	£££	11.30 pm	Tasty, fresh Lebanese food in a wasteland of stodgy takeaways.

Map 100 • Poplar (West) / Canary Wharf (West)

Brownn	Hertsmere Rd	020 7987 9777	£££	11 pm	Always reliable.
Nicola	1 Canada Sq	020 7512 9092	££	10.30 pm	Micro French restaurant and vintners in one.
Plateau	Canada Pl	020 7715 7100	££££	10.30 pm	Striking views and truffle gnocchi.
Royal China	30 Westferry Circus	020 7719 0888	£££		Cantonese culinary powerhouse; dim sum mandatory.

Map 101 • Poplar (East) / Canary Wharf (East)

The Gun	27 Coldharbour	020 7515 5222	£££	11 pm	Enjoyed by 18th century dockers and city workers alike.
Jamie's Italian	2 Churchill Pl	020 3002 5252	£££	11 pm	Bang-on Jamie O on the cheap.

Map 103 • Cubitt Town / Mudchute

Mudchute Kitchen	Pier St	020 3069 9290	££	5 pm	Food companion to the farm bit. Chi chi children.

Map 104 • South Bank / Waterloo / Lambeth North

The Anchor & Hope	36 The Cut	020 7928 9898	££££	10.30 pm	A British gastro-pub obsession, long waits though.
Canteen	Belvedere Rd	084 5686 1122	££	10.30 pm	A menu that sums up the best of British food with aplomb.
Concrete	Southbank Centre	020 7921 0758	£	1 am	Restaurant/bar features Russian beer, food, absinthe.
The Cut Bar	66 The Cut	020 7928 4400	£££	11 pm	Brilliant chips. A cut above the rest.
Giraffe	Riverside	020 7928 2004	££	10.45 pm	Good crowd pleaser. Though too much world music and balloons.
Marie's Cafe	90 Lower Marsh	020 7928 1050	£	10.30 pm	Greasy spoon by day, a no-frills, super-yum BYO thai by night.
OXO Tower Wharf	Barge House St	020 7803 3888	££££	11 pm	You might have to rob a bank, but the view's amazing.
RSJ	33 Coin St	020 7928 4554	££	11 pm	Forget about those crappy South Bank chains. Go here.
Skylon	Belvedere Rd	020 7654 7800	££££	10.45 pm	Expensive but staffs' uniforms and view make up for it.
Studio 6	56 Upper Ground	020 7928 6243	££	11 pm	Service with a reluctant grunt doesn't stop the crowds.
Tas	33 The Cut	020 7928 2111	££	11.30 pm	Blink and you'll miss it. Buzzing Turkish cafe—best hummous in London.

Map 105 • Southwark / Bankside (West)

Baltic	74 Blackfriars Rd	020 7928 1111	££££	10.30 pm	Try Polish Hunters stew: made with real Polish Hunters. Probably.
El Vergel	132 Webber St	020 7401 2308	£*	10 pm	It's Latin breakfast: Oh. My. God. Soooooo good.
Restaurant at Tate Modern	Bankside	020 7887 8888	££	6 pm	Stunning views, crap food, clueless staff.
The Table	83 Southwark St	020 7401 2760	£*	10.30 pm	Go and find out why we're all obsessed.
Terry's Cafe	158 Great Suffolk St	020 7407 9358	£	2 pm	Mom & Pop British fare including mushy peas.

Arts & Entertainment · **Restaurants**

Key: £ : Under £10 : ££ : £10–£20 : £££ : £20–£30 : ££££ : £30–£40 : £££££ : £40+
* : Does not accept credit cards./ † : Accepts only American Express / †† : Accepts only Visa and Mastercard
Time listed refers to kitchen closing time on weekend nights

Map 106 · Bankside (East) / Borough / Newington

Arabica Bar & Kitchen	3 Rochester Walk	020 3011 5151	££		Fresh, fun, game-upping Middle Eastern cuisine.
The Boot and Flogger	10 Redcross Way	020 7407 1184	££	8 pm	Splendidly gentleman's club-esque—all savile row suits and chesterfield sofas.
Brew Wharf	Stoney St	020 7378 6601	££	11 pm	Unusual comfort food and tasty home brews.
Champor-Champor	62 Weston St	020 7403 4600	£££	10.15pm	Jaw-droppingly inspired high-end Malaysian cuisine. Totally impressive.
Elliot's Cafe	12 Stoney St	020 7403 7436	£££		Rumoured by some to serve London's best burgers.
Feng Sushi	13 Stoney St	020 7407 8744	££	10 pm	The best sushi in London and available to takeaway. Dangerous!
Fish!	Cathedral St	020 7407 3803	££	10.30 pm	Great fish. Simple. Let it have its exclamation mark.
Hing Loong	159 Borough High St	020 7378 8100	£	11 am	Stupidly cheap. Very cheerful. The duck rocks.
Nando's	225 Clink St	020 7357 8662	££	11 pm	Peri-peri madness underneath the arches.
Roast	Stoney St	084 5034 7300	££	9.30 pm	Meat, glorious meat. High-end food. Fab location.
Silka	6 Southwark St	020 7378 6161	£££	11.30 pm	Curry house that won't damage your arse in the morning.
Tapas Brindisa	18 Southwark St	020 7357 8880	££	11 pm	If you can bear the crowds; lovely market-bordering eaterie.
Tas	72 Borough High St	020 7403 7200	££	11 pm	Reduce your carbon footprint: come here and feel 1000 miles away.
Wright Bros Oyster & Porter House	11 Stoney St	020 7403 9554	£££	10.30 pm	Tastebuds say no, but libido says YES.

Map 107 · Shad Thames

Butlers Wharf Chop House	36 Shad Thames	020 7403 3403	£££	11 pm	What better place for British best than under Tower Bridge?
Casse-Croute	109 Bermondsey St	020 7407 2140	£££		Fun French bistro with chalkboard menu.
Jose	104 Bermondsey St	020 7403 4902	£££		Sister sherry bar and restaurant to nearby Pizarro. More casual.
Le Pont de la Tour	36 Shad Thames	020 7403 8403	£££££	11 pm	Blair & Clinton's rendezvous. Posh but gosh!
M. Manze Pie and Mash	87 Tower Bridge Rd	020 7407 2985	£	2.30 pm	As English as it gets. Try it once.
Magdalen	152 Tooley St	020 7403 1342	££££	10.30 pm	Forever fascinating Franco-Spanish cuisine.
Pizarro	194 Bermondsey St	020 7378 9455	£££		A slice of Spain south of the river, top Menu del Dia.
Pizarro Tapas	104 Bermondsey St	020 7256 5333	£££	10:15 pm	The real deal for tapas.
Village East	171 Bermondsey St	020 7357 6082	£££	11 pm	Superior food. Slick surroundings.

Map 108 · Bermondsey

Poppy Hana	168 Jamaica Rd	020 7237 9416	£	11 pm	Cute as a button Japanese. Don't be put off by the food sculptures.
Tentazioni	2 Mill St	020 7237 1100	££	10.45 pm	Stunningly sophisticated for a neighbourhood eaterie.

Map 109 · Southwark Park

The Mayflower	117 Rotherhithe St	020 7237 4088	£££	The pub Sunday Lunch was invented for.

Map 110 · Rotherhithe (West) / Canada Water

Café Silka	30 Albion St	020 7237 2122	££		Wishes it were somewhere else, but nicely done.
Rainbow	33 Brunel Rd	020 7231 0028	£££	11 pm	Will make you happily plump.
Simplicity	1 Tunnel Rd	020 7232 5174	££	10:30 pm	Boldly goes where no restaurant has gone before: Rotherhithe.

Arts & Entertainment • **Restaurants**

Map 111 • Rotherhithe (East) Surrey Quays

Cafe East	100 Redriff Rd	020 7252 1212	££		Best Vietnamese pho this side of the Kingsland Road.

Map 112 • Kennington / Elephant and Castle

Brasserie Tolouse Lautrec	140 Newington Bts	020 7582 6800	££££		French cuisine as excellent as the owners are eccentric.
Brasserie Toulouse Lautrec	140 Newington Butts	020 7582 6800	££	12 am	French brasserie and bar.
Chatkhara	84 Walworth Rd	020 7701 8899	£		Possibly the best value lunch deal in the city.
Dragon Castle	100 Walworth Rd	020 7277 3388	££	11 pm	Odd locale for such a curious pocket of culinary authenticity.
La Bodeguita	Elephant & Castle Shopping Centre	020 7701 9166	££		Colombian home cooking and salsa parties. Whats not to like?
The Lobster Pot	3 Kennington Ln	020 7582 5556	£££	10.30 pm	Dine to a soundtrack of seagull caws. We don't kid.
Mamuska	233 Elephant & Castle Shopping Centre	020 3602 1898	£		Hearty polish grub to stave off winter blues.

Map 113 • Walworth

Aobaba and Longdan Express	128-132 Walworth Rd	020 7701 2566			Canteen serving proper bahn mi, with adjoining oriental supermarket.
Bage King	280 Walworth Rd	020 7277 4060	£		Refuge in the night.
La Luna	380 Walworth Rd	020 7277 1991	££	11 pm	Ignore exterior. It's the garlic bread inside that counts.

Map 114 • Old Kent Road (West) / Burgess Park

Shu Castle	194-202 Old Kent Rd	020 7703 9797	£££		£££

Map 115 • Old Kent Road (East)

Roma Café	21 Peckham Park Rd	020 7639 7730	£	10 pm	Escape Peckham and enjoy a good fry-up here.

Map 119 • Deptford (East)

The Big Red Pizza Bus	30 Deptford Church St	020 3490 8346	£	11 pm	It's a bus. Where you can get pizza!
Chacunia	26 Deptford High St	020 8692 8815	£		Lip-tingling rotis made by the Trinidadian version of your Granny.
Pand Panda	8 Deptford Broadway	020 8616 6922	£		Bahn mi and other Vietnamese treats.
The Waiting Room	142 Deptford High St	079 6803 6562	£	7 pm	Veggie and vegan heaven

Map 120 • Greenwich

Craft London	1 Greenwich Place	020 8465 5910	£££	10:30 pm	Stevie Parle and Tom Dixon collaboration celebrating British fayre.
Goddards at Greenwich	22 King William Walk	020 8305 9612	£	6 pm	Pie n' mash n' eels. Only at the weekend.
Greenwich Tavern	1 King William Walk	020 8858 8791	£££	10 pm	Kobe steak burgers. Nuff said.
The Hill	89 Royal Hill	020 8691 3626	£££	10 pm	Bistro food. Local favourite.
The Longos Company	5 Greenwich Market	075 2586 1964	£		Deep fried flatbread like no other.
Piano Restaurant	131 Greenwich High Rd	020 8853 3020	£££££	2 am	Fish swim in the chandeliers. Get the idea?
Rivinton	178 Greenwich High Rd	020 8293 9270	£££	11 pm	Good for brekkie or dinner before a Picturehouse movie

Map 121 • Camberwell (West)

Kazan Kyrgyz	158 Camberwell Rd	020 7871 9963	££	1 am	Unsuspectingly tantalising Central Asian cuisine—belly dancer included
New Dewaniam	225 Camberwell New Rd	020 7703 9318	£	12 am	Mouth-watering Indian takeaway for a tenner.
Rocksteady Eddie's	2 Coldharbour Ln		£		Where Elvis would eat if he was born in King's College.
Viet Cafe	75 Denmark Hill	020 7703 2531	£		One of the original and more upmarket banh mi cafes.
Zeret Kitchen	216 Camberwell Rd	020 7701 8587	£	11 pm	Order the special to try a bit of everything.

Map 122 • Camberwell (East)

Angels & Gypsies	33 Camberwell Church St	020 7703 5984	££		Like some kind of Dali-Almodovar fantasy.
Caravaggio	47 Camberwell Church St	020 7207 1612	£	11 pm	Cheap Italian with impressive fare. Stands out from the rest.
Crooked Well	16 Grove Ln	020 7252 7798	££££		A damn fine taste of the genteel side of Camberwell.
Falafel	27 Camberwell Church St	020 7277 2573	£		Better bet for an evening snack than stale friend chicken.
FM Mangal	54 Camberwell Church St	020 7701 6677	££		Book a taxi because the monstrous portions seriously hinder mobility.
Silk Road	49 Camberwell Church St	020 7703 4832	££		As far away from chicken chow mein as Chinese gets.
Wuli Wuli	15 Camberwell Church St	020 7708 5024	££		Go for the regional Sichuan dishes.

Map 123 • Peckham

Agrobeso African Cuisine	139 Peckham High St	020 7501 8792	£		For anyone mad enough to try honeycomb tripe.
The Begging Bowl	168 Bellenden Rd	020 7635 2627	£££		Great food, outstanding cocktails.
Dead Dolls House	1 Clayton Rd	020 7732 2691	££	3 am	Enjoy a bacon sarnie in opulent surroundings.
Ganapati	38 Holly Grove	020 7277 2928	£	10:30 pm	Influenced by street food of South India.
M. Manze Pie and Mash	105 Peckham High St	020 7277 6181	£		One of the only remaining original pie and mash shops.
Miss Tapas	45 Choumert Rd	07838 821 836	£		Andalucian fare.
Obalende Suya Express	43 Peckham High St	020 7703 7033	£		Nigeria's answer to a kebab shop.
Peckham Refreshment Rooms	12 Blenheim Grove	020 7639 1106	£	12 am	Mediterranean influenced eats in New York style surrounds.

Map 124 • Peckham East (Queen's Road)

805	805 Old Kent Rd	020 7639 0808	£££	12 am	West African oasis. In Peckham.
Tops Carribean Takeaway	173 Queens Rd	020 7732 7557	£		Eat incredible fried dumplings under a massive Obama mural.

Map 125 • New Cross Gate

Hong Kong City	43 New Cross Rd	020 7252 9888	££		Tastes like it's in a much better part of town.
Smokey Jerky	158 New Cross Rd	020 7639 6204	£		Some of the best, messiest jerk in South London.

Map 126 • New Cross

Birdie Num Nums	11 Lewisham Way	020 8692 7223	£	7 pm	Smashing cafe with occasional evening events.
The London Peculiar	399 New Cross Rd	020 8692 6149	£		Quaint little cafe.

Map 127 • Coldharbour Lane / Herne Hill (West)

Beanery	Coldharbour Ln	077 3431 9081	£		Good strong coffee to perk you up before your train.
Café Prov	2 Half Moon Ln	020 7978 9228	£££	10 pm	Local art (for sale) decorates this relaxed restaurant/bar/ cafe.
Ichiban Sushi	58 Atlantic Rd	020 7738 7006	£	11 pm	The bee's knees.
Naughty Piglets	28 Brixton Water Ln	020 7274 7796	££		Nouveau bohemian French cafe-inflected menu.
New Fujiyama	5 Vining St	020 7737 6583	£	10.30 pm	This place blows Wagamama's out of the water.

Map 128 • Denmark Hill / Herne Hill (East)

Lombok	17 Half Moon Ln	020 7733 7131	£££	10.30 pm	From Stir-fries to curries, a no-fuss pan-Asian standby.
Number 22	22 Half Moon Ln	020 7095 9922	££££	10.30 pm	Gorge yourself on Spanish wine, sherry and loads of brilliant tapas.

Map 129 • East Dulwich

Anderson & co	139 Bellenden Rd	020 7469 7078	££	10:30 pm	Fresh and delicious.
The Palmerston	91 Lordship Ln	020 8693 9662	££££	10 pm	Gastropub that's a lot more gastro than pub.

Map 130 · Peckham Rye

Artusi	161 Bellenden Rd	020 3302 8200	££	10 pm	Italian-inspired seasonal menu.
Pedler	58 Peckham Rye	£	11pm	Vibrant neighbourhood eatery.
Thai Corner Cafe	44 North Cross Rd	020 8299 4041	££*	11 pm	Tiny, laidback neighbourhood cafe.

Map 132 · Battersea (West)

Ransome's Dock	35 Parkgate Rd	020 7223 1611		11 pm	Friendly, stylish, likes wine and children.

Map 134 · South Lambeth

A Toca	343 Wandsworth Rd	020 7627 2919	£££		Football on numerous screens, as if you were in Lisbon!
Bar Estrela	113 S Lambeth Rd	020 7793 1051	£	11 pm	Like mama used to make. Probably.
Brunswick House	30 Wandsworth Rd	020 7394 2100	££	12 am	Opulent setting.
Canton Arms	177 S Lambeth Rd	020 7582 8710	££	10 pm	Recently acquired by Anchor & Hope folks. Bring on the yuppies.
Hot Stuff on Wheels	19 Wilcox Rd	020 7720 1480	£	10 pm	Hard to find. Slightly dinghy. Mental Staff. Amazing food.
O Moinho	355 Wandsworth Rd	020 7498 6333	£££		Well-done traditional Portuguese.
Tia Maria	126 South Lambeth Rd	020 7622 3602	£	1 am	Known for its tapioca wraps.

Map 135 · Oval

Adulis	44 Brixton Rd	020 7587 0055	£	11 pm	C'mon, it's yummmy and cheap. And we can't cook Eritrean.
Bonnington Café	11 Vauxhall Grove	Check Website	£*	10.30 pm	Wonderful vegetarian meals in a communified (ex-squat) environment.
Oval Kebab	32 Clapham Rd	020 7820 8846	£*	10 pm	Fancy a doner kebab? Go nowhere else.

Map 136 · Putney

Enoteca Turi	28 Putney High St	020 8785 4449	£££		Aperol Spritz followed by some homemade ravioli?
Ma Goa	242 Upper Richmond Rd	020 8780 1767	££	11 pm	Amazing regional Goan cuisine.
Talad Thai	320 Upper Richmond Rd	020 8789 8084	££	10.30 pm	Thai-ny, family-run restaurant with Thai supermarket, cooking classes and Thai regulars.

Map 137 · Wandsworth (West)

Miraj	123 Putney Bridge Rd	020 8875 0799	£	10 pm	Curry in a hurry? Cheap, tasty take away joint.

Map 138 · Wandsworth (Central)

Brady's	Smugglers Way	020 8877 9599	££	11 pm	Up-market fish and chip cafe and take-away.
Kathmandu Valley	5 West Hill	020 8871 0240	££	11.45 pm	Nepalese is the new black (read: curry).

Map 139 · Wandsworth (East)

The Fish Club	189 St. John's Hill	020 7978 7115	££	10 pm	The thinking man's chippie.
Gazette	79 Chatfield Rd	020 7223 0999	£££		Unpretentious French brasserie fare that is tres sophisticue.

Map 140 · Clapham Junction / Northcote Rd

Gail's Bread	64 Northcote Rd	020 7924 6330			Clapham branch of North London artisanal chain.
Jack's At The Junction	252 Lavender Hill	020 7228 9111	£		There's only one rule here—be a very hungry Jack.
Mien Tay	180 Lavender Hill	020 7350 0721			Kingsland Road stalwart brough to Lavender Hill.
Parisienne	225 Lavender Hill	020 7924 5523	£	5 pm	Massive sarnies and baked potatoes.
Pizza Metro	64 Battersea Rise	020 7228 3812	£££		Pizza by the metre!

Map 141 · Battersea (South)

The Lavender	171 Lavender Hill	020 7978 5242	££	11 pm	Rustic European eclectic—stellar cassoulets.

Map 142 · Clapham Old Town

Nardullis Ice Cream	29 The Pavement	020 7627 1515	£		Real Italian gelato to smear over your chops.
Trinity	4 The Polygon	020 7622 1199	£££	10.30 pm	How to do local dining really quite fantastically well.

Map 143 · Clapham High Street

Brickwood	16 Clapham Common South Side	020 7819 9614	£	6.30 pm	Top brunch.
The Dairy	15 The Pavement	020 7622 4165	£££		Charming seasonal British cuisine.
Gastro	67 Venn St	020 7627 0222	££	12 am	Low-lit gallic bistro extraordinaire
The Pepper Tree	19 Clapham Common South Side	020 7622 1758	£*	11 pm	Speedy Thai with soul.
Roti Joupa	12 Clapham High St	020 7627 8637	£	11 pm	Pick up some real Trinidadian food and enjoy it on the common.
San Marco Pizzeria	126 Clapham High St	020 7622 0452	££~	11.30 pm	Arguably the best pizza outside Italy—take that New York!
Tsunami	5 Voltaire Rd	020 7978 1610	££££	10.30 pm	The new Nobu. Unbelievable. Unfortunate name.

Map 144 · Stockwell / Brixton (West)

Agile Rabbit	24-25 Coldharbour Ln	020 7738 7646	££*		Tough contender with Franco Manca. Plus live music.
Bellantoni's	81 Granville Arcade	078 7294 5675	££		Artisan homemade pasta for date night at Brixton Village.
Breads Etcetera	88 Brixton Village Market	077 1764 2812	££		DIY toast comes to Brixton.
Brixton Cornercopia	65 Coldharbour Ln	079 1954 2233	££		Ultra-local fare with a changeable menu to match.
Casa Morita	9 Market Row	020 8127 5170	£££		Try-hard and pricey taqueria. Decent tacos; less decent guacamole.
Falafel Van	Station Rd		£		Tasty falafel from a man with a nice Muhammad Ali portrait.
Honest Burgers	12 Brixton Village	020 7733 7963	££		Best British burgers in Brixton. Not gonna lie.
Jeff the Chef	Station Rd				Proper oil drunk jerk and fresh coconuts.
Mama Lan	18 Brixton Village Market		£		Slap-up corner joint selling nom noodle soups and dumplings.
SW9 Bar	11 Dorrell Pl	020 7738 3116	£	9 pm	Great hangover curing breakfasts (and hangover causing booze).

Map 146 · Earlsfield

Amaranth	346 Garratt Ln	020 8874 9036	££*	10 pm	Rarefied, bustling restaurant with tacked-on takeout element.
Cah Chi	394 Garratt Ln	020 8946 8811			Pick of the areas many Korean joints. Try the pa jeon.
Carluccio's	537 Garratt Ln	020 8947 4651	££	11.30 pm	Sensational pasta dishes and optional curbside setting

Map 147 · Balham (West)

Chez Bruce	2 Bellevue Rd	020 8672 0114	££££	10.30 pm	Worth its fancy-pants (read Michelin) star.

Map 148 · Balham (East)

Brickwood	11 Hildreth Street		£	6 pm	Top brunch.
The Exhibit	12 Balham Station Rd	020 8772 6556	£££	2 am	Cool event space: friendly, laid back vibe.
Hagen & Hyde	157 Balham High Rd	020 8772 0016	££	2 am	Modern British pub food.
Harrison's	15 Bedford Hill	020 8675 6900	££	10.30 pm	Great food if you can tolerate the 'look at me!' crowd.

Map 149 • Clapham Park

Bistro Union	40 Abbeville Rd	020 7042 6400	£££		All-day bistro featuring well-crafted modern fare.

Map 150 • Brixton

Asmara	386 Coldharbour Ln	020 7737 4144	££	11.15 pm	Disconcerting but delicious curry with pancakes to mop it up.
Boqueria	192 Acre Ln	020 7733 4408	£££		Insanely good croquetas de jamon. Excellent value too.
Curry Ono	14 Market Row	020 7326 1399	£££		Katsu that makes Wagamama's taste like a crying shame.
Duck Egg Cafe	424 Coldharbour Ln	020 7274 8972	££		Unassuming brunch. Go duck eggs, ginger beer and hash browns.
Elephant	55 Granville Arcade	075 9038 9684	£	10 pm	Hip, understated and authentic Pakistani street food. Go thali.
Franco Manca	4 Market Row	020 7738 3021	££	10 pm	London's best pizza? Eclectic concoctions of sour dough goodness comes west.
KaoSarn	Coldharbour Ln	020 7095 8922	££		The beating heart of Brixton Village. Half-chicken or bust.
Khan's of Brixton	24 Brixton Water Ln	020 7326 4460	££	11 pm	Great curry, and BYO to boot. Have it!
Lounge	56 Atlantic Rd	020 7733 5229	£	10 pm	A local favourite for breakfast, recovery and hanging on weekends.
Negril	132 Brixton Hill	020 8674 8798	£	10 pm	Tasty Carribean with veg options (which are joy).
Opus Café	89 Acre Ln	020 7737 1414	£	6 pm	Cakes and coffee. Niceness.
The Phoenix	441 Coldharbour Ln				Old school institution. Good bubble and squeak.
Refill	500 Brixton Rd	020 7274 5559	£		24 hour with suprisingly good patties and jerk sandwiches.
Yum D	14 Market Row	020 7274 8824	£		Thai deli that makes tasty beef salads to order.

Map 151 • Tooting Bec

Al Mirage	215 Upper Tooting Rd	020 8772 4422	££	10.30 pm	Better than Mirch Masala? We think so.
The French Cafe	16-18 Ritherton Rd	020 8767 2660	££		Extraordinarily good value set deals.
Masaledar Kitchen	121 Upper Tooting Rd	020 8767 7676	££	11 pm	Last word in top-notch Indian cuisine
Mirca Masala	213 Upper Tooting Rd	020 8672 7500	£	12 am	Cheap, no frills, award-winning curries. Sublime.
Spice Village	32 Upper Tooting Rd	020 8672 0710	£	11 pm	Go for grilled.

Map 152 • Tooting Broadway

Dosa n Chutny	68 Tooting High St	020 8767 9200	£		Breakfast, South Indian style. Amazing.
Jaffna House	90 Tooting High St	020 8672 7786	£	12 am	Mediocre curry fare beneath flourescent bulbs.
Radha Krishna Bhavan	86 Tooting High St	020 8682 0969	££	11.30 pm	Busy, buzzing, bhavan of South Indian curry.
Rick's Restaurant	122 Mitcham Rd	020 8767 5219	£££	11 pm	Tooting's best kept culinary secret

So are we still in the Recession? Who knows? Who cares? We're getting used to this boom and bust cycle but we've cut up all our credit cards. When it comes to retail, people will always spend whether money or no (that's how we got in this fine mess remember Stanley?), it's just that with little of the stuff about, people are more discerning about what they spend their hard earned cash/State Benefits on. And of course if we didn't spend we would never collectively crawl out of this endless dirge of gloom. As the well-observed slogan on the reusable eco-shopping bag from Modern Toss (available at **Magma, Maps 5, 12**) says, "Buy More Shit Or We're All Fucked". Indeed. But if the economic crisis is teaching us anything it's to be more picky about what we purchase and for retailers not just to deliver the goods but also all the extras that we, as polite English people, so foolishly see as just "extras". Primarily what we mean is, that intangible thing that contributes to a satisfying shopping experience and brings a customer back to the same store again and again: excellent service—helpfulness, genuine smiles and interest in the product and the customer. Beautiful packaging, loyalty cards, discounts, samples, invites to in-store events all help, too. In an adverse way, consumers have never had more power than now to demand what they want or—as important—don't want. So just make sure you buy more cool shit as opposed to any old shit.

The British High Street is certainly changing and support for independent shops is growing. A leaning towards handmade items and crafts which support local designers and artisans—Columbia Road and Cheshire Street are hotspots for this kind of thing. Yes there are a lot of these shops cropping up that purely sell "beautiful things" like **Of Cabbages And Kings (Map 64)** and (if it's a beauty of a decaying kind you're looking for) **Viktor Wynd's Shop of Horrors (Map 87)** to name just a couple (and we like them). But when it comes to fashion we also like to know that a little bit of love has been sprinkled into the making of an item. Special mention here must go to Amy Anderson of **Comfort Station (Map 91)** who produces the most thoughtful and whimsical pieces of jewellery and **Vivien of Holloway (Map 74)** who has built a real niche following but whose fabulous 1950s tailoring would make any gal feel like a doll. Both have gorgeous, well-fitted, unique shop spaces, too.

For blokes, **Folk (Map 5)** are renowned for their limited collections, particularly shoes which are hand-stitched (hence the price tag).

Part of this trend is Pop-Up Shops which are installed for a few months at a time sometimes displaying the work of a single designer/company or else a co-operative of independent designers. Not only is this a thrifty way of setting up shop in these uncertain times, it also provides a showcase for new young things so always worth a look. These tend to appear around Carnaby Street and Spitalfields, especially in the summer.

The Big Boys

When it comes to department stores, **Selfridges (Map 2)** is without a doubt the daddy of them all—arguably, (and the emphasis is on that word depending on your budget) you can just get everything you need from here but if you're strapped, at least go and marvel at the window displays. **Harvey Nics (Map 37)** and **Harrods (Map 37)** are very much for ladies who lunch, and the Knightsbridge set use them like corner shops—that's not to say they don't have their uses. For a more personal touch, **Fenwick (Map 2)** and **Liberty (Map 10)** are wonderful British institutions which take you far from the madding crowd. If all these close-quarters encounters get up your nose head to **Whiteleys (Map 30)** or the Behemoth that is **Westfield Shopping Centre (Map 33)**.

Haute Et High Street

For flexing that plastic, Bond Street has always been the place to spend but Bruton Street, which branches off the main drag, is setting quite a precedent with **Matthew Williamson (Map 9)**, **Stella McCartney (Map 9)** and **Diane Von Furstenburg (Map 9)** all in residence. Always one to mix things up and throw us off track, **Marc Jacobs (Map 9)** London store is to be found on Mount Street—check out the Marc for Marc Jacobs range for affordable designer garb—by which we mean £3 and upwards. Yes, really. If you want to feel like Alice down the rabbit hole, make a trip to **Dover Street Market (Map 9)**, owned by Rei Kawakubo of Comme Des Garçons—a real experience even if you're not buying. Throwing down the gauntlet when it comes to experiential retail is **LN-CC (Map**

86). For those of us in the real world, **Topshop** (Map 3) is the grand kahuna of high street shopping—seventh heaven on three floors for fashionistas. For super-slick, sharp ready-to-wear you can't beat Spanish stores, **Zara (Map 2)** and **Mango (Map 3)** which both do high street with an edge and turnover is pretty quick to ensure their stock remains covetable. New contenders for higher end high-street include **Cos (Map 10)** and **Hoss Intropia (Map 10)**, and let's not forget our Stateside cousins who have sent ripples of excitement through the fash pack by opening flagship stores of **Anthropologie**, **Banana Republic**, and **Abercrombie & Fitch (Map 10)** all in the big smoke. There are also little shopping oases to be found in the capital. St Christopher's Place is hidden behind the hustle and bustle of Oxford Street and houses cool European brands like **Marimekko (Map 2)** alongside more familiar fare. Kingly Court (behind Carnaby Street—itself a great shopping space for trend-led labels) has independent boutiques. The area around Seven Dials in Covent Garden which includes Neal's Yard is eclectic with high-end boutiques like **Orla Kiely (Map 1)** on Monmouth and skatewear at **Slam City Skates (Map 13)** and **Superdry (Map 13)** on Earlham. Edgy fashion abounds out East: head to **Good Hood (Map 84)** to start your shopping crawl.

Back to the Future

'Vintage' seems to be the term for anything over five years old nowadays but London's vintage (and secondhand) scene is thriving. Some of the best-known, best-loved shops include **Rellik (Map 25)** in Portobello, **Annie's (Map 80)** in Islington (a favourite of La Moss), **Beyond Retro (Map 91)** and **Absolute Vintage (Map 91)** in Shoreditch (famous hunting ground for stylists). If you want to hear what the young, stylish and clueless get up to head to **Rokit (Maps 13, 71)** and eavesdrop on the staff's mindnumbing conversations. For genuine thrift, the turnover of goods in our charity shops is mind-boggling. **Oxfam Dalston (Map 86)** is renowned for being a good rummage: it's hit and miss but then that's the nature of the thrifting beast. Most hardy shoppers will happily tread the city twice over for good charity shop finds but if you want some certainty of finding designer threads you can't beat the **British Red Cross (Map 45)** where you will discover the likes of Ralph Lauren, Armani and pairs of Manolos amongst the usual flotsam and jetsam. The **Octavia Foundation Charity Shop (Map 35)** is also a reliable source of local celebrities' cast-offs from like, yesterday. For all you true vintage fashion fiends who want to mingle with like-minded souls and find genuine vintage togs (i.e. pre-1980s) the **Frock Me! Vintage Fashion Fair (Map 45)** and **Anita's Vintage Fashion Fair (Map 135)** are unequalled for choice and variety. Wake up and smell the mould.

Keep on Running, Cycling, Skating Etc.

Lillywhite's (Map 10) is the obvious place to go for cheap sportswear—it has earned a bit of a bargain basement tag where once it was prestigious (the Lillywhites were instrumental in the game of cricket during the 19th century) but it doesn't stop the shoppers pouring in, and tourists buying their favourite London football team shirts. A good indie chain is **Runners Need (Map 20)**. If it's sweatshop-made kit you're after head to **Niketown (Map 2)**, which is as scary as the name suggests. Though we're no Amsterdam, the economic shitstorm has inspired many Londoners to don skintight clothes and take to two wheels. If you're after a battered old charmer of a bike, **Recycling (Map 112)** does a fab job at selling secondhand wheels. If you've had your designer bike nicked, head down to Brick Lane at the weekend and buy it off some dodgy geezer. **Slam City Skates (Map 13)** is the only dedicated place for Southbank skaters to get their duds.

Home Sweet Home

John Lewis (Map 2) is a British standard (read: very sensible) and has been the store of choice for middle-class couples' wedding lists for decades. With fantastic staff (who all get a share of the profits) and well-made stuff, their maxim is "never knowingly undersold." **Twentytwentyone (Map 80)** is a designer's wet dream selling originals as well as new items. So impressive is their collection that they often lend out furniture to film companies who want the authentic look of an era on set. **SCP**

(Maps 30, 84) is perfect for unnecessary-yet-tasteful knick-knacks. The wonderfully named **Timorous Beasties (Map 6)** make wickedly amusing wallpapers—their most famous being a toile de jouy design for modern days (spot the alcopop-drinking chavs and the Gherkin in the background). **Labour and Wait (Map 91)** does the retro home stuff better than most. If you want personable, "Where can I find one of these?" type of service try **Russell's Hardware & DIY (Map 151)** in Tooting or **KTS The Corner (Map 86)** in Dalston.

Electricity for You and Me

Apple have done a very good job at monopolising our lives and getting everyone to 'Think Different', so why you'd need to go anywhere other than the **Apple Store (Map 10)** we're not sure. However, traditionally, Tottenham Court Road is the hideout for the anally retentive hi-fi nut and the nerdoid pirate radio enthusiast a-like. The area positively thrums with electricity. In all cases it's best to shop around, play prices against each other and barter until you get the lowest price—often cash payment will get you well below the RRP. **Computer Exchange (Map 3)** is the one-stop shop for gaming, DVDs, computing and phones, which—as the name suggests—will part-exchange and knock money off for cash transactions. **Richer Sounds (Map 106)** is a trusted chain, and if we're talking electronics in the purist sense, **Maplin (Map 3)** is geek central. Whether you'll get anyone who knows what they're talking about is another matter. Photography enthusiasts should check out the **London Camera Exchange (Map 24)** for old-school SLRs and digital cameras and **Red Dot Cameras for Leicas (Map 7)**.

Food for Thought

We like our food in London and the more diverse the better. Whether it's chowing down on burgers from Lucky Chip and Vietnamese baguettes from Banh Mi 11 down **Broadway Market (Map 89)** or fresh scallops and some raclette down Borough Market (Map 106) before moseying on down to **Maltby Street Market (Map 107)** for gelato, we're not afraid to say, "Please Sir, I want some more" (mainly because we're paying for it). **Whitecross Street (Map 7)** also has an impressive selection of foodie

stalls. We have New York (and in particular, the Magnolia Bakery) to thank for the invasion of cupcake stores but the original and best is the **Hummingbird Bakery (Maps 29, 45)** which makes Red Velvet cupcakes that taste like little pieces of baked orgasm. Just try and restrain yourself from licking the last morsels of frosting from the paper. Nostalgia for old style sweetie shops can be bought at **Mrs. Kibble's Olde Sweet Shop (Map 10)** whether your fetish is for cola cubes, sherbet flying saucers or Wham bars. Numerous Italian delis can be found around the city selling cured meats, buffalo mozzarella, biscotti and everything else that Mama used to make—**I Camisa & Son (Map 11)** is small but crammed full of delicacies, while **Spiazzo (Map 53)** is bigger and sparklier. Organic freaks can bypass the rather average Whole Foods chain and head to local independent places like **The Grocery (Map 91)** or **Mother Earth (Map 75)**. For the cheapest and best coffee-to-go in Soho try the **Algerian Coffee Stores (Map 11)**. Looking for Unicum? Look no further than **Gerry's Spirits Shop (Map 11)** where you can find obscure liquors like Zubrowka Bison Grass Vodka and good quality Cachaça.

Art and Craft Supplies

Crafty types and closet Van Goghs can pick up supplies at **Cass Art's (Map 80)** three-storey flagship store in Islington. There's everything here for aspiring Manga cartoonists and weekend watercolourists alike, and lots of fun bits and pieces for school holiday/rainy day projects in the basement. Much of the high quality stock can be found at cut-price throughout the year—stock up on Moleskine note and sketchbooks which are frequently marked down. The **London Graphic Centre (Map 13)** has more design-led stock as well as fine art material attracting architects and graphic designers. Known for its greeting cards and stationery, **Paperchase (Map 3)** on Tottenham Court Road also has—true to its name—an astonishing array of handmade papers on its top floor—from flocked designs to fibrous papers made with dried flowers. You've got to love **Blade Rubber (Map 4)** just for its name, and for keeping sketches, photos, and memories intact. **Wyvern Bindery (Map 6)** is one of few of its kind to offer book-making services.

Axes, Saxes, Drums, Strums…

Traditionally, Tin Pan Alley (real name: Denmark Street) has always been the hub of musical creativity in the city. Back in the day when rents were affordable, a community grew up around this little side street which went on to see Jimi Hendrix and The Beatles record in the basement, and a young Elton John sitting on the rooftops penning "Your Song". Nowadays you may spot Jack White trying out a Digitech Whammy or Jonny Greenwood looking for some new toy to replace his Marshall Shred Master. If we had to choose a couple, we'd bug **Macari's (Map 12)** for cheapness and **Wunjos (Map 12)** for friendliness. There are plenty of independent music stores to be found in London's boroughs, and often they are specialists, happy to have a natter about what exactly it is that you're looking for and what the weather's like. Try **Top Wind (Map 104)** for all your flute needs, Duke of Uke **(Map 91)** for banjo and ukulele-lovers, though the staff are a little arsey, and **Phil Parker (Map 1)** for all you jazz cats needing a hand with your brass. For the medieval troubadour in your life, **Hobgoblin (Map 3)** has its own luthier who makes lutes. Try **Ray Man (Map 71)** in Camden for unusual ethnic instruments and drone boxes. For the largest collection of sheet music in Europe, **Chappell of Bond Street (Map 11)** (now on Wardour Street but they've kept the name) is your destination. One thing though, will you instrument shop assistants please stop jamming while you're talking to us?

Music Nonstop

The slow, painful death of the CD can be seen in almost every indie music store in London, and it coincides with the financial doom and gloom that has befallen Virgin Records, Zavvi and Sanctuary (thankfully we still have one branch of **Fopp (Map 12)** left. Bizarrely, the death march of the traditional record shop has become a moonwalk: more and more boutique record shops are springing up selling new and used wax. The Berwick Street vinyl epicenter may have been drained of late, but other parts of London have become haunts for us of haunched posture and good taste. **Sister Ray (Map 11)** is forever teetering on the edge, but

Reckless Records (Map 11) seems here to stay. If you find yourself on the Essex Road, have a gander at **Flashback (Maps 53, 83)** and **Haggle Vinyl (Map 83)**: you're sure to find something to please and appeal in the former and appall in the latter. The **Music & Video Exchange (Map 29)** in Notting Hill was way ahead of its time and has been the swapshop of choice for years, it's still the king as far as we're concerned. When south of the river, do as Camberwellians do and drop in at **Rat Records (Map 121)**. To guarantee a withering look from a record shop lifer go and discuss the use of naivety in Legowelt's output at **Phonica (Map 10)** in Soho. Many a muso's all-round fave, **Sounds of the Universe (Map 11)** is owned by the **Soul Jazz** label.

Antiques and Bric-A-Brac, Flea Markets and Stalls

There may have been a time, dear reader, when markets sold fleas. And brics and bracs. Perhaps we used to know what these elusive words meant. Frankly, we numbskulls at NFT don't care about etymology unless it's secondhand and collectable. First stop on many shoppers' lists—both serious collectors and weekend browsers—are **Alfie's Antique Market (Map 76)** and **Gray's Antique Market (Map 2)**. Here you'll find art, antiques, jewellery, vintage clothing and rare books all housed under one roof.

Once the centre of the Britpop phenomenon in the '90s and a thriving mini-metropolis for vintage and antique stalls, Camden is now rather anaesthetised, but packs of German and French kids on school trips still rifle through the emo and goth gear that overfloweth. There is some gold to be found in shops like **Episode (Map 71)** and **Rokit (Map 71)**, and **Aldo Liquidation (Map 71)** is good for a bargain (or practising your rugby tackle). Certainly the place still has atmosphere.

Well-known to scavengers, **Camden Passage (Map 80)** in Angel rather confusingly, is a welcome retreat from the mallrat-filled N1 centre across the road in Islington. The Mall and also Pierrepoint Arcade (tucked away behind the passage) offer a cornucopia of clothing, jewelry, military paraphernalia, homewares, prints, and a host of other bits and bobs. On

Saturdays, market stalls set up in the street and surprises like original Givenchy earrings from 1978 (4 quid!) can be salvaged from amongst the knick-knacks. This is another brilliant little vintage bazaar continually threatened by chains and redevelopment. Go protest by buying any old crap.

Brick Lane (Map 91) also opens up on Sunday and in the summer there is a real carnival feel with fruit and veg, plumbing and DIY bits and pieces, electricals, toiletries, furniture (dentist's chair anyone?), clothes, DVDs lining the lane and spilling into Sclater Street. Watch your bags and all the silly haircuts. Brick Lane also has the added advantage of having many a watering hole and curry house where you can stop and people-watch if it all makes you want to go all 'Falling Down' on their asses. If that's not your thing, (Up)Market is held in the **Truman Brewery (Map 91)** every Sunday and showcases new designers as well as housing some vinyl, vintage and gourmet street food. **Spitalfields Market (Map 91)** has been tarted up to be a

sanitized precinct of chain stores but there are still some unusual boutiques and independent shops.

The triumvirate of hipster markets consists of **Columbia Road Market (Map 91)**, **Broadway Market (Map 89)**, and Chatsworth Road Market (just north of Map 90). Also in the East is **Roman Road Market (Map 94)**. It's proper gorblimey, lor' love a duck cockerney territory but you may find yourself soaking up the atmosphere more than finding anything of real interest. If Lady Luck is stroking your inner thigh you get some great bargains Sarf of the river at **Deptford Market (Map 119)**.

Though certainly not as bountiful in treasure as the car boot sales of other parts of the country, London does have some. The best in Zone 2 is definitely the **Battersea Car Boot Sale (Map 141)**, a sprawling mess that kicks off around midday is a godsend to all us alcoholics and narcoleptics.

Map 1 · Marylebone (West)

Maroush Deli	45 Edgware Rd	020 7723 3666	Lebanese food emporium—fresh coffee, ice-creams and best houmous in town.
Phil Parker	106 Crawford St	020 7486 8206	Brass-o-rama.
Primark	499 Oxford St	020 7495 0420	Enter the scrum.
Spymaster	3 Portman Sq	020 7486 3885	Stab-proof vests, in house P.I., you know, the usual.
Totally Swedish	32 Crawford St	020 7224 9300	Salt liquorice and Plopp bars for scandiphiles.

Map 2 · Marylebone (East)

Browns	24 S Molton St	020 7514 0016	Sleep with someone rich, then bring them here.
The Button Queen	76 Marylebone Ln	020 7935 1505	Antique buttons galore for budding fashionistas.
Content Beauty & Wellbeing	14 Bulstrode St	020 3075 1006	Exceptional selection of organic beauty products.
Daunt Books	83 Marylebone High St	020 7224 2295	Almost intimidatingly beautiful book shop.
Divertimenti	33 Marylebone High St	020 7486 8020	Go and pretend you need a £500 coffee machine.
Fenwick	63 New Bond St	020 7629 9161	A welcome escape from Oxford Street for those in the know.
French Sole	61 Marylebone Ln	020 7486 0021	Spendy but these pumps can withstand London's terrible pavements.
Gray's Antique Market	58 Davies St	020 7629 7034	A world of bygone beauty a skip away from Bond Street.
John Lewis	300 Oxford St	020 7629 7711	Where John Betjeman would have gone if the world exploded.
Monocle	2 George St	020 7486 8770	Super stylish travel gear from the folks behind the magazine.
Niketown	236 Oxford St	020 7612 0800	Like a real town! Owned by Nike! But without sweatshops.
Paul Smith	38 Marylebone High St	020 7935 5384	Kitsch and dolls from the fashion designer. Don't ask why.
Postcard Teas	9 Dering St	020 7629 3654	Taste tea. Send tea. Love tea. Right here.
Selfridges & Co.	400 Oxford St	080 0123 400	A Mecca for the shopping elite who want everything.
Skandium	86 Marylebone High St	020 7935 2077	Ikea for grown-ups.
VV Rouleaux	102 Marylebone Ln	020 7224 5179	Trimmings and ribbons like you've never seen.
The Widescreen Centre	47 Dorset St	020 7935 2580	Telescopes, binoculars, projectors, screens, film cameras & virtual reality.
Zara	242 Oxford St	020 7318 2700	Spiffy suits and cute casualwear from the Balearic brand.

Map 3 · Fitzrovia

The Aquatic Design Centre	107 Great Portland St	020 7580 6764	You will want an aquarium after visiting this place.
Ben's House	64 Grafton Way	020 7388 0850	Impeccable curation of delectable treats.
Computer Exchange	32 Rathbone Pl	084 5345 1664	Good selection of secondhand DVDs, games and gadgets.
Harmony	103 Oxford St	020 7734 5969	Also known as Butt Plugs R Us.
Hobgoblin Music	24 Rathbone Pl	020 7323 9040	Folky paradise; impressive/amusing collection of alternative instruments.
Mango	225 Oxford St	020 7534 3505	Let's go Mango!

Maplin	218 Tottenham Court Rd	084 3227 7353	A whole world of technical geeketry to immerse yourself in.
Paperchase	213 Tottenham Court Rd	020 7467 6200	More than meets the eye to this high street card shop.
Scandinavian Kitchen	61 Great Titchfield St	020 7580 7161	Smorgasbord!
Stargreen Box Office	21 Argyll St	020 7734 8932	Try here for tickets to sold-out gigs.
Topshop	216 Oxford St	020 7927 7634	Kate Moss still loves it. We do too.
Topshop	36 Great Castle St	084 4848 7487	Clothing for the New Generation.
Trimmings	14 Great Titchfield Street		Treasure trove for craftsy folk.
Urban Outfitters	200 Oxford St	020 7907 0800	Heaps of streetwear and crazy things for your house.

Map 4 · Bloomsbury (West)

Aperture	44 Museum St	020 7242 8681	Specialists in new and vintage cameras.
Blade Rubber Stamps	12 Bury Pl	020 7831 4123	Scrapbooking materials plus traditional and made-to-order rubber stamps.
Gosh!	1 Berwick St	020 7636 1011	A Japanese school boy's wet dream. Comics galore!
James Smith & Sons	53 New Oxford St	020 7836 4731	Umbrella shop—because you might just need one.
London Review Bookshop	14 Bury Pl	020 7269 9030	Big books, big name personal appearances—and cake!
York Cameras	18 Bury Pl	020 7242 7182	New and secondhand, specializing in Canon.

Map 5 · Bloomsbury (East)

Antoni & Alison	43 Rosebery Ave	020 7833 2141	Home of "bonkers" fashion duo.
Biba Hair and Beauty	72 Marchmont St	020 7837 9555	Lovely, friendly hair salon, excellent prices, 15% student discount
The Brunswick	Hunter St	020 7833 6066	Brutalist shopping centre pushing the utopian/dystopian envelope.
The Flash Centre	68 Brunswick Centre	020 7837 5649	Studio lighting specialists.
Foli	49 Lamb's Conduit St	020 7404 6458	Great clothes, even better shoes.
Gay's the Word	66 Marchmont St	020 7278 7654	Britain's only dedicated Gay & Lesbian book store.
International Magic	89 Clerkenwell Rd	020 7405 7324	When you need some tricks up your sleeve.
JOY	22 Brunswick Centre	020 7833 3307	Funky Urban Outfitters type stuff, but cheaper.
Magma	117 Clerkenwell Rd	020 7242 9503	Funky book & novelty shop.

Map 6 · Clerkenwell

EC One	41 Exmouth Market	020 7713 6185	Gorgeous sparkly fings.
The Family Business Tattoo Shop	58 Exmouth Market	020 7278 9526	Tatts for all the family.
London Tattoo	332 Goswell Rd	020 7833 5996	Was on the telly. Caused quite a buzz.
M E R Meats	399 St. John St	020 7837 1781	So meat-savvy they'll even know the best cut on you.
Metro Imaging	32 Great Sutton St	020 7865 0000	Photo processing.
Timorous Beasties	46 Amwell St	020 7833 5010	Outlandish prints for the daringly tasteless home.
The Wyvern Bindery	56 Clerkenwell Rd	020 7490 7899	Book binding for theses, portfolios and presentations. Repairs and restoration.

Map 7 · Barbican / City Road (South)

Red Dot Cameras	68 Old St	020 7490 8444	Like yer Leica.
Whitecross Market	Whitecross St		Street food central.

Map 9 · Mayfair / Green Park

Diane Von Furstenberg	25 Bruton St	020 7499 0886	Forget the LBD, every girl needs a DVF.
Dover Street Market	17 Dover St	020 7518 0680	Serious designer wear for people with serious money.
Marc Jacobs	24 Mount St	020 7399 1690	Never out of fashion.
Matthew Williamson	28 Bruton St	020 7629 6200	The boy who knows how to dress real girls.
Stella McCartney	30 Bruton St	020 7518 3100	Stella's star keeps rising despite initial doubts in Fahionland.

Map 10 · Piccadilly / Soho (West)

Abercrombie & Fitch	7 Burlington Gardens	084 4412 5750	Like GAP but more expensive.
American Apparel	3 Carnaby St	020 7734 4477	25% off all sexual harrassment lawsuits.
Anthropologie	158 Regent St	020 7529 9800	Go check out the innovative window dressing if nothing else.
Apple Store	235 Regent St	020 7153 9000	Get your hardware here so you can buy NFT apps
Banana Republic	224 Regent St	020 7758 3550	Your Stateside buddies don't need to ship over your clothes anymore
Beyond Retro	58 Great Marlborough St	020 7434 1406	Biggest, original, live-bands-on-Saturday vintage.
Burlington Arcade	Piccadilly	020 7493 1764	Welcoming shoppers since 1819.
COS	222 Regent St	020 7478 0400	COS you can. See what I did there?
The European Bookshop	5 Warwick St	020 7734 5259	For when you get sick of English.
Fortnum & Mason	181 Piccadilly	020 7734 8040	The world's poshest marmalades.
Figgo	27 Swallow St	020 7287 9506	Argentinean ice cream for insomniacs. About freakin' time.
Hamley's	188 Regent St	087 1704 1977	World's biggest toy store. Terrifying just before Christmas.
Hatchards Bookshop	187 Piccadilly	020 7439 9921	Still musty, floors still creak, despite being owned by The Man.
Hoss Intropia	211 Regent St	020 7287 3569	High-end high street.
Lazy Oaf	2 Ganton St	020 7287 2060	Rockin good little design shop with the emphasis on illustration.

Liberty	214 Regent St	020 7734 1234	Splendid wood-panelled department store. Beautiful and obscure scents and perfumes.
Lillywhites	24 Regent St	084 4332 5602	Good if you know exactly what you're looking for.
Muji	41 Carnaby St	020 7287 7323	Japanese chain hits London—simple, minimalist goods but great quality.
Phonica	51 Poland St	020 7025 6070	Cutting edge vinyl/CD shop; alas, no Michael Bolton in stock.
Richard James	29 Savile Row	020 7434 0605	Bespoke contemporary Savile Row tailoring.
Rigby & Peller	22 Conduit St	020 7491 2200	Furnishers of the Queen's basement.
Vin Mag Shop	39 Brewer St	020 7439 8525	Yellowing magazines and a million student classic posters.

Map 11 • Soho (Central)

Algerian Coffee Store	52 Old Compton St	020 7437 2480	Pick up some Blue Mountain beans and a 95p cappu-to-go.
Calumet Photographic	175 Wardour St	020 7434 1848	Cameras and accessories.
Chappell of Bond Street	152 Wardour St	020 7432 4400	Which is actually on Wardour Street.
Gerry's	74 Old Compton St	020 7734 2053	A veritable alcoholic's Utopia.
I. Camisa & Son	61 Old Compton St	020 7437 7610	The best Italian deli outside of Italy.
Reckless Records	30 Berwick St	020 7437 4271	Sickly phoenix risen from the ashes of Reckless Records.
Sister Ray	34 Berwick St	020 7734 3297	Alternative vinyl, CDs and DVDs.
Snog	9 Brewer St	020 7494 3301	Healthy dessert!
Sounds of the Universe	7 Broadwick St	020 7734 3430	Blow your friends' minds with obscure African vinyl.

Map 12 • Soho (East)

Angels Fancy Dress	119 Shaftesbury Ave	020 7836 5678	Chock full of fancy dress outfits.
Fopp	1 Earlham St	020 7845 9770	May Fopp never, ever die again. Long live the music bargain!
Forbidden Planet	179 Shaftesbury Ave	020 7420 3666	Cult/film/TV memorabilia shop that will leave Star Wars fans salivating.
Foyles	113 Charing Cross Rd	020 7437 5660	Convivial shop/cafe. Essential for Americana and, uh, jazz!
Kokon to Zai	57 Greek St	020 3601 1414	Mad fashion laboratory providing competition for The Pineal Eye.
Macari's	92 Charing Cross Rd	020 7836 2856	Family run instrument shop with historic roots.
Magma	16 Earlham St	020 7240 7571	Super-cool housewares and knick-knacks from the Magma gods.
Porselli Dancewear	9 West St	020 7836 2862	Before American Apparel...when only dancers wore dancewear.
Quinto Bookshop	72 Charing Cross Rd	020 7379 7669	Pretend you're a character in Black Books.
Rockers	5 Denmark St	020 7240 2610	Quiffs, picks, riffs and licks. Sick.
Wunjo Guitars	20 Denmark St	020 7379 0737	Mind-bendingly friendly Scot selling lovely vintage gear...

Map 13 • Covent Garden

Artbox	29 Earlham St	020 7240 0097	Hello Kitty overload.
The Astrology Shop	78 Neal St	016 2482 7000	For people who believe that shit—and people who don't.
Beadworks	21 Tower St	020 7240 0931	Great resource for amateur beaders and professional designers
Ben's Cookies	13 The Piazza	020 7240 6123	Cookie chain good. Chips in dough yum.
Blackout II	51 Endell St	020 7240 5006	Vintage heaven.
Cath Kidston	28 Shelton St	020 7240 8324	Kitsch at its most chic, and vice-versa.
Coco de Mer	23 Monmouth St	020 7836 8882	High-class, kinky fun.
Cybercandy	3 Garrick St	084 5838 0958	For when a plain old Mars bar just won't cut it.
David and Goliath	4 The Market	020 7240 3640	Droll, funky t-shirts and other fun stuff.
Libiden at Liberation	49 Shelton St	020 7836 5894	Caters for all your kinks. Yes, even that one.
London Graphic Centre	16 Shelton St	020 7759 4500	One stop shop for graphics geeks.
Neal's Yard Dairy	17 Shorts Gardens	020 7240 5700	Follow your nose to very fine cheeses.
Nigel Hall	18 Floral St	0207 836 8223	Where to get business casualed well.
Octopus	54 Neal St	020 7836 2911	Makes the everyday so much more fun.
Orla Kiely	31 Monmouth St	020 7240 4022	Trademark cutesy prints from the Irish designer.
Pop Boutique	6 Monmouth St	020 7497 5262	Retrotastic!
Rokit	42 Shelton St	020 7836 6547	Vast array of vintage clothing.
Scoop	40 Shorts Gardens	020 7240 7086	Queues out the door for freshly made gelato. Fragola rocks.
Slam City Skates	16 Neal's Yard	020 7240 0928	Rambunctious skate shop.
Stanfords	12 Long Acre	020 7836 1321	Treasure trove of maps, travel books and accessories.
Superdry	24 Earlham St	020 7240 9437	Super funky pseudo-Japanese urbanwear. Friendly staff.
Tabio	66 Neal St	020 7836 3713	Only the Japanese could create such an array of socks.
Urban Outfitters	42 Earlham St	020 7759 6390	Heaps of streetwear and crazy things for your house.

Map 14 • Holborn / Temple

Konditor & Cook	46 Grays Inn Rd	084 4854 9365	Unusual location to find K&C's famous Magic Cakes.
Topshop	60 The Strand	020 7839 4144	Clothing for the New Generation.

Map 16 • Square Mile (West)

Church's	90 Cheapside	020 7606 1587	An English shoe institution.
Space NK Apothecary	145 Cheapside	020 7726 2060	Skincare heaven.

Map 17 • Square Mile (East)

Lulu Guinness	23 Royal Exchange	020 7626 5391	Eccentric yet stylish bags and purses.
Paul A. Young Fine Chocolates	20 Royal Exchange	020 7929 7007	"Everytime you go away..." you take a piece of chocolate.
Pretty Ballerinas	30 Royal Exchange	020 7929 6994	Find rich banker, take to fabulous shoe shop.

Map 18 • Tower Hill / Aldgate

A. Gold	42 Brushfield St	020 7247 2487	Perfect for impressive picnic supplies. But smells like a sock.
Montezuma's	51 Brushfield St	020 7539 9208	Chocolate you'd leave your boyfriend for.
Petticoat Lane Market	Middlesex St		No petticoats here love, but look for the FCUK stall.
Precious	16 Artillery Passage	020 7377 6668	One of few independent boutiques left standing.

Map 19 • Belgravia

Daylesford Organic Farmshop and Cafe	44 Pimlico Rd	020 7881 8060	Fresh as you can get ingredients from their Gloucestershire farm.
Mungo & Maud	79 Elizabeth St	020 7467 0823	Real dogs don't wear clothes! Chihuahuas do though...and pugs.

Map 20 • Victoria / Pimlico (West)

Capital Carboot Sale	Lupus St	084 5094 3871	We love a rummage through other people's rubbish.
Grays of Westminster	40 Churton St	020 7828 4925	Charming period shop specializing in Nikon.
La Bella Sicilia	23 Warwick Way	020 7630 5914	Old-skool deli with cheery old owners and pasta aplenty.
Rippon Cheese Stores	26 Upper Tachbrook St	020 7931 0628	A world of cheese.
Runners Need	24 Palace St	020 7630 5056	Place for all you joggers "who go round and round."
Topshop	18 Victoria St	020 7828 6139	Clothing for the New Generation.

Map 21 • Pimlico (East)

Black Rose	112 Belgrave Rd	020 8279 2014	Gothic. Very, very gothic.

Map 22 • Westminster

Haelen Centre	41 Broadway	020 8340 4258	All your hippy, wholemeal, organic needs under one roof.

Map 23 • St. James's

Richard Caplan	60 Pall Mall	020 7807 9990	New and used equipment, specializing in Leica.

Map 24 • Trafalgar Square / The Strand

Austin Kaye	425 The Strand	020 7240 1888	Vintage watches. Don't expect e-bay prices.
London Camera Exchange	98 Strand	020 7379 0200	My lens is longer than yours.
Stanley Gibbons	399 Strand	020 7836 8444	World's leading stamp dealer attracts collectors, investors and the curious.

Map 25 • Kensal Town

Honest Jon's	278 Portobello Rd	020 8969 9822	Obscure and rare Jazz, Funk, Reggae and Hip-Hop.
Rellik	8 Golborne Rd	020 8962 0089	Opposite the Trellik Tower—geddit? Specialises in Queen Viv (Westwood).
What Katie Did	281 Portobello Rd	084 5430 8743	Fabulous 1940s-inspired boudoir boutique for rib-crushing corsets, stockings and pointy bras.

Map 28 • Ladbroke Grove / Notting Hill (West)

Cowshed	119 Portland Rd	020 7078 1944	Express mani-pedis for women who have places to go etc.
The Cross	141 Portland Rd	020 7727 6760	The original London boutique, still going.
Gelato Mio	138 Holland Park Ave		Get ice-cream, head to park.
Jeroboams	96 Holland Park Ave	020 7727 9359	London's largest independent wine merchant.
Virginia	98 Portland Rd	020 7727 9908	If money is no object, what you want is here.

Map 29 • Notting Hill Gate

Boda	36 Ledbury Rd	020 7727 5063	Everyday underwear that gives M&S a run for its money.
Clark's	124 Kensington Church St	020 7221 9225	All-butter brioche and honey loaves for Harvey Nicks, Selfridges—and you.
Diane Von Furstenberg	83 Ledbury Rd	020 7221 1120	High end wear for those who can afford it.
The Grocer on Elgin	6 Elgin Crescent	020 7221 3844	Restaurant standard ready-meals for lazy people.
The Hummingbird Bakery	133 Portobello Rd	020 7851 1795	Takeaway cupcakes reminiscent of New York's Magnolia Bakery.
Melt Chocolates	59 Ledbury Rd	020 7727 5030	Posh chocs made before your bulging eyes.
Mr Christian's Delicatessen	11 Elgin Crescent	020 7229 0501	Great little deli with non-Portobello Rd prices.
Music & Video Exchange	38 Notting Hill Gate	020 7243 8573	Invented second hand record shops. Best in London.

Negozio Classica	283 Westbourne Grove	020 7034 0005	Half bar, half store selling high-end Italian kitchen goods.
Portobello Road Market	Portobello Rd	020 7727 7684	The Notting Hill institution.
R. Garcia and Sons	246 Portobello Rd	020 7221 6119	Overwhelming selection of Spanish groceries.
Retro Man	34 Pembridge Rd	020 7792 1715	Vintage fixes for modern men. And men only.
Retro Woman	32 Pembridge Rd	020 7598 2233	Exclusive vintage ware that's worth it.
Rough Trade West	130 Talbot Rd	020 7229 8541	More character and better records than the soulless East Branch.

Map 30 · Bayswater

Al Saqi Bookshop	26 Westbourne Grove	020 7229 8543	Specialist book shop for anything and everything Middle Eastern.
Planet Organic	42 Westbourne Grove	020 7727 2227	Organic heaven.
Porchester Gate Spa	Queensway & Porchester Rd £25!	020 7792 3980	Proper old school art deco Turkish baths and spa for less than
SCP	87 Westbourne Grove	020 7229 3612	Design-led homeware.
Whiteleys Shopping Centre	Queensway	020 7229 8844	Slightly more soulful than Smithfields.

Map 32 · Shepherd's Bush (West)

| Damas Gate | 81 Uxbridge Rd | 020 8743 5116 | Incredible range of Middle Eastern food. |
| Nut Case | 352 Uxbridge Rd | 020 8743 0336 | About time nuts got some respect. |

Map 33 · Shepherd's Bush

| Westfield Centre | Ariel Way | 020 3371 2300 | Very likable shopping center. Really. |

Map 34 · West Kensington / Olympia

| Homebase | 195 Warwick Rd | 084 5640 7062 | So much stuff that you never knew you needed. |

Map 35 · Kensington

Ben's Cookies	12 Kensington High St	020 7376 0559	Chunky cookies in wonderous flavours. Hidden in High Street Ken station.
Octavia Foundation Charity Shop	57 Kensington Church St	020 7937 5274	There's gold in them thar (clothes) hills.
Trailfinders	194 Kensington High St	020 7938 3939	Personable one-stop shop for travel bookings, advice and services.
Urban Outfitters	36 Kensington High St	020 7761 1001	Heaps of streetwear and crazy things for your house.
Whole Foods Market	63 Kensington High St	020 7368 4500	Overwhelming selection of organic exotica.

Map 36 · South Kensington / Gloucester Rd

Maitre Choux	15 Harrington Rd	020 3583 4561	Pimp your choux!
Partridges	17 Gloucester Rd	020 7581 0535	Family run mega-deli to the queen.
Snog	32 Thurloe Pl	020 7584 4926	Crazy frozen yoghurt joint with an interior mad enough to be in Tokyo.

Map 37 · Knightsbridge

Burberry	2 Brompton Rd	020 7980 8426	Flagship store of the classic British brand.
Divertimenti	227 Brompton Rd	020 7581 8065	Go and pretend you need a £500 coffee machine.
Harrods	87 Brompton Rd	020 7730 1234	Arch conspiracy theorist Mr Al-Fayed's still classy department store.
Harvey Nichols	109 Knightsbridge	020 7201 8081	Not sure who really shops here.
Rigby & Peller	2 Hans Rd	020 7225 4760	Sexy lingerie fit for a queen...for THE Queen?
Skandium	247 Brompton Rd	020 7584 2066	For lottery winners who can't shake their love of Ikea.
Space NK Apothecary	307 Brompton Rd	020 7589 8250	Skincare heaven.

Map 38 · Chiswick

As Nature Intended	201 Chiswick High Rd	020 8742 8838	Main store from organic food company. Pricey but worth the trek.
The Bread Shop	296 Chiswick High Rd	020 8747 8443	Bloomin' marvellous bread! Great selection and they even do spelt loaves.
Chiswick Health & Wellness Spa	300 Chiswick High Rd	020 8995 2293	A calming oasis hidden on the High Road. Fantastic products.
Gail's Bread	282 Chiswick High Rd	020 8995 2266	Enough artisan pastries to tempt you for seconds. Busy weekends.
Mortimer & Bennett	33 Turnham Green Terrace	020 8995 4145	Gourmet deli that is guaranteed to get you excited about pickled asparagus.
Outsider Tart	83 Chiswick High Rd	020 7096 1609	Two American dudes start a US baked goods revolution—cupcakes!
Oxfam Books	90 Turnham Green Terrace	020 8995 6059	Fantastic fiction selection—the rich read too!
Wheelers Flowers	Turnham Green Terrace	020 8747 9505	Last chance station for forgotten occasions next to Turnham Green tube.

Map 39 · Stamford Brook

Mac's Cameras	262 King St	020 8846 9853	Used and hard-to-find gear. Heaven for photography nerds.
Thai Smile	287 King St	020 8846 9960	Heaven for those who love Asian cooking. For the rest it's just intriguing.

Map 40 · Goldhawk Rd / Ravenscourt Park

Bushwacker Wholefoods	132 King St	020 8748 2061	Small and friendly organic and health food shop. Booja Booja ice-cream!
Patisserie Sainte-Anne	204 King St	020 8563 2046	Heavenly Parisian cakes, breads, and pastries.

Map 41 · Hammersmith

Bakehaus	71 King St	020 3490 3231	Traditional German baking through and through, Bratwurst roll an' all.

Map 43 · West Brompton / Fulham Broadway / Earl's Court

Vagabond Wines	18-22 Vanston Pl	020 7381 1717	Try before you buy wine.

Map 44 · Chelsea

The Furniture Cave	533 Kings Rd	077 6771 3314	Swanky. Huge. Quintessentially Kings Road.
Richer Sounds	258 Fulham Rd	033 3900 0027	Chain selling all things electronic, technologic, and so forth.
The Shop At Bluebird	350 Kings Rd	020 7351 3873	Spend a fortune here and become an "edgy" individual.
Worlds End	430 King's Rd	020 7352 6551	Ever changin outlet of Dame Viv.

Map 45 · Chelsea (East)

Ad Hoc	153 King's Rd	020 7376 8829	Gold sequin knickers—what more do you want?
British Red Cross	69 Old Church St	020 7376 7300	Known locally as La Croix Rouge Boutique.
Frock Me! Vintage Fashion Fair	Kings Rd	020 7254 4054	Held every couple of months, "pre-war" tearoom refreshes shopping casualties.
The Hummingbird Bakery	47 Old Brompton Rd	020 7851 1795	Notting Hill's big brother with seating to devour Red Velvets and lattes.
Nomad Books	781 Fulham Rd	020 7736 4000	Glorious little place with added coffee shop.
Sweaty Betty	125 King's Rd	020 7349 7597	Clothes for you to stretch in, Gretchen.

Map 46 · Sloane Square

Partridges	2 Duke of York Sq	020 7730 0651	Family run mega-deli to the queen.
Rigby & Peller	13 Kings Rd	020 7824 1844	Sexy lingerie fit for a queen...the queen?
Space NK Apothecary	307 King's Rd	020 7351 7209	The Superdrug for the Sloane Square ladies who lunch.

Map 48 · Fulham

Hurlingham Books	91 Fulham High St	020 7736 4363	More stacked than Arnie was in the 70s.

Map 51 · Highgate

The Corner Shop	88 Highgate High St	020 8340 1118	Locals' favourite fending off the advance of Tesco's.
Highgate Butchers	76 Highgate High St	020 8340 9817	Reassuringly expensive meat. Them cows must have lived like kings.
Hops & Pops	389 Archway Rd	020 8348 0624	Great selection for all budgets.
Le Chocolatier	78 Highgate High St	020 8348 1110	Essential at Easter—not just eggs but whole chocolate chickens.
Mind	329 Archway Rd	020 8341 1188	Great selection for skint book worms.
Oxfam	80 Highgate High St	020 8340 3888	Musty bookstore with some cracking titles.
Wild Guitars	393 Archway Rd	020 8340 7766	Get your retro gear in this brilliant guitar shop.

Map 52 · Archway (North)

The Green Room	192 Archway Rd	079 6144 1722	Amazing selection of weird things you probably don't need.
Pax Guns	166 Archway Rd	020 8340 3039	Errm..."best" gun shop in the area?

Map 53 · Crouch End

Flashback	144 Crouch Hill	020 8342 9633	2nd hand vinyl and DVD goldmine.
Italian Farmers	186 Stroud Green Rd	020 3719 6525	Gorgeous produce direct from Italian farmers.
Organic Food	196 Stroud Green Rd	020 7281 1115	Well-stocked local shop.
Riley Bee Cream Cafe	32 The Broadway	020 8347 7825	Particularly creamy and good ice cream.
Soup Dragon	27 Topsfield Parade	020 8809 6123	Paradise for yummy mummies and their tots.
Walter Purkis And Sons	17 The Broadway	020 8340 6281	Proof that fish don't need their tasty batter skins.

Arts & Entertainment · **Shopping**

Map 54 · Hornsey

Micycle N4	8 Ferme Park Rd	020 8347 9180	Friendly bike repairs and cafe.

Map 55 · Harringay

Beans and Barley	595 Green Lanes		Organic emporium.
Harringay Local Stores	581 Green Lanes	020 8347 6070	Hipsters do their grocery shopping.
Yasar Halim	495 Green Lanes	020 8340 8090	Amazing Turkish grocery store.

Map 56 · Hampstead Village

Happy Returns	36 Rosslyn Hill	020 7435 2431	Boring posh toys...and some cool stuff for normal kids.
Keith Fawkes	1 Flask Walk	020 7435 0614	Books, books, books. A glorious mess of a shop.
Mystical Fairies	12 Flask Walk	020 7431 1888	It's a fairy shop. Really.

Map 57 · Hampstead Heath

Daunt Books	51 S End Rd	020 7794 8206	A right daunty little shop.
Giocobazzi's Delicatessen	150 Fleet Rd	020 7267 7222	The taste of posh Italy.

Map 58 · Parliament Hill / Dartmouth Park

Baba	11 Swain's Ln	020 8442 9111	Quirky kitchenware and gifts.
Corks	9 Swain's Ln	020 8340 4781	Superb selection of interesting wines and beers.
Forks	7 Swain's Ln	020 8340 1695	Friendly, well-stocked deli. Fresh crepes in summer!

Map 59 · Tufnell Park

The Hornsey Trust Charity Shop	124 Fortess Rd	020 7267 2338	Eccentric staff? Check. Affluent, moth-eaten cast offs? Check.
North London Adoption Centre	135 Junction Rd	020 7272 6048	Need a cat? Of course you do! Miaow!

Map 60 · Archway

Second Chance	7 St John's Way	020 7281 5449	Heaps of rubbish and the occasional incredible find.
Super Perla	621 Holloway Rd	020 7272 2665	Very proud little shop specializing in Iranian sweets.

Map 61 · Holloway (North)

Holloway Car Boot	Opposite Odeon Cinema	019 9271 7198	Scavenge with North London's finest.
Michael's Fruiterers	56 Seven Sisters Rd	020 7700 1334	Fruit n veg fest. Nowhere's fresher.

Map 62 · Finsbury Park

The Deli at 80	80 Stroud Green Rd	020 7272 6622	Epicurean delights.
Exeter Street Bakery	Morris Pl	020 7272 8266	Fantastic sourdoughs.
The Happening Bagel Bakery	284 Seven Sisters Rd	020 8809 1519	Another Haringey gem, with some delicious pastries too!
Hettie Holland	19 Charter Court	020 7272 2002	Gorgeous gifts and homewares.

Map 63 · Manor House

Bennet & Brown	84 Mountgrove Rd	020 7704 9200	Secondhand furniture and interesting things.
Cafe Vintage	88 Mountgrove Rd	07903 875 750	Super cute vintage fashion shop.
Sargent & Co.	74 Mountgrove Rd	020 7359 7642	Passionate about bike building and bespoke.
Simply Organique	316 Green Lanes	020 8800 4668	Local organic store.
Sylvanian Families	68 Mountgrove Rd	020 7226 1329	It is indeed a shop that solely sells Sylvanian Families.

Map 64 · Stoke Newington

The Ark	161 Stoke Newington Rd	020 7275 9311	Cute little interiors and gift shop.
Beaucatcher Salon	44 Stoke Newington Church St	020 7923 2522	Hairdressers and community hub.
Belle Epoque Patisserie	37 Newington Green	020 7249 2222	Fancy schmancy, delicious pastries.
Bridgewood & Neitzert	146 Stoke Newington Church St	020 7249 9398	Renowned string section repair, exchange and sales.
Church Street Bookshop	142 Stoke Newington Church St	020 7241 5411	Great shack with out-of-print books and shite records.
Metal Crumble	13 Stoke Newington Church St	020 7249 0487	Affordable, flippin' gorgeous, jewellery made on site.
Of Cabbages & Kings	127 Stoke Newington High St	020 7998 3282	Another of those crafty little shops that keep popping up.
Pelicans & Parrots	81 Stoke Newington Rd	020 7249 9177	Boutique hipster fashion joint which mixes oddness with elegance.
Ribbons and Taylor	157 Stoke Newington Church St	020 7254 4735	Long-standing vintage clothes shop—Stokey original.
Rosa Lingerie	3 Church Walk	020 7254 3467	The oldest knickers in Stokey.

Route 7 Kids	92 Stoke Newington Church St	020 7923 7873	Bus inspired toy shop.
S'Graffiti	172 Stoke Newington Church St	020 7254 7961	You've been framed.
Sacred Art Tattoos	148 Albion Rd	020 7254 2223	(Needles + Ink + Skin) x Pain = Art.
The Spence Bakery & Cafe	161 Stoke Newington Church St	020 7249 4927	Bread elevated to an art form.
Stoke Newington Farmers' Market	Stoke Newington High St	020 7502 7588	Overpriced, organic, natural, hea... Zzzzzzzz

Map 65 • West Hampstead

Party Party	206 Kilburn High Rd	020 7624 4295	Party Party Stuff Stuff!

Map 67 • Belsize Park

Belsize Village Delicatessen	39 Belsize Ln	020 7794 4258	For a truly international picnic basket.
Lotus and Frog	32 England's Ln	020 7586 3931	Quirky gifts for young and old.

Map 70 • Primrose Hill

Nicola	67 Regent's Park Rd	020 7722 8576	A wide range of wines, including some cheap ones.
Press	3 Erskine Rd	020 7449 0081	Impressive array of brands for a boutique. Good sales.
Primrose Hill Books	134 Regent's Park Rd	020 7586 2022	Fabulously curated selection of new books.
Primrose Hill Pets	132 Regent's Park Rd	020 7483 2023	Everything your handbag mutt could need.
Primrose Newsagent	91 Regent's Park Rd	020 7722 0402	Newsagent, stationers, post office, drycleaners and internet cafe.
Richard Dare	93 Regent's Park Rd	020 7722 9428	Quite lovely kitchen/cooking products.
Shepherd Foods	59 Regent's Park Rd	020 7586 4592	Highly priced but quaint local deli.
Shikasuki	67 Gloucester Ave	020 7722 4442	Affordable vintage and modern design.
Sweet Pea	77 Gloucester Ave	020 7449 9292	Unusual handmade jewelry.
Tann Rokka	123 Regent's Park Rd	020 7722 3999	Wildly expensive "lifestyle store" in old Primrose Hill train station.

Map 71 • Camden Town / Chalk Farm / Kentish Town (West)

AcuMedic	105 Camden High St	020 7388 6704	Chinese medicine centre offering acupuncture AKA polite masochism.
Aldo Outlet	231 Camden High St	020 7284 1982	If you find shoes that fit they're free. Not really.
Cyberdog	Stables Market	020 7482 2842	Enormous sci-fi set displaying PVC, neon, and leather clubbing gear.
Escapade	45 Chalk Farm Rd	020 7485 7384	Dress up as Wonder Woman! Also caters for females.
Eye Contacts	10 Chalk Farm Rd	020 7482 1701	Opticians that sells uber-trendy spectacles.
General Eyewear	Chalk Farm Rd & Castlehaven Rd	077 9010 2204	Those film kids get their vintage eyewear here.
Graham and Green	164 Regent's Park Rd	020 7586 2960	Wonderfully dinky yet scarily pricey shop.
Proud Camden	Stables Market	020 7482 3867	Stock up on contemporary photography.
Ray Man Music	54 Chalk Farm Rd	020 7692 6261	Wonderful shop full of exotic instruments. Bavarian noseflute, anyone?
Rokit	225 Camden High St	020 7267 3046	Secondhand, sorry, vintage clothing store to the stars.
Three Amigos Skateboard Shop	118 Camden High St	020 7284 4515	Skater owned, skater run. Best in London.
TRAID	154 Camden High St	020 7485 5253	Characterful recycled clothes. Touch of wank, but sti l we like.
Village Games	65 Camden Lock Pl	020 7485 0653	Huge selection of boardgames.
Whole Foods Market	49 Parkway	020 7428 7575	Organic and wholefood oasis with eat-in possibilities.

Map 72 • Kentish Town

Phoenicia	186 Kentish Town Rd	020 7267 1267	Olives, just-roasted nuts, baclava, ice-cream bar. Meze heaven. Ditch Sainsburys.
Ruby Violet	118 Fortress Rd	020 7609 0444	Housemade ice cream with bold, inventive flavours.

Map 73 • Holloway

Bumblebee Natural Foods	33 Brecknock Rd	020 7284 1314	Hot veggie lunches, lush cakes. Organic fruitopia over the road.

Map 74 • Holloway Road / Arsenal

Vivien of Holloway	294 Holloway Rd	020 7609 8754	Want to dress like Joan from Mad Men?

Map 75 • Highbury

Cassies Delight Autospares Car Parts	9 Green Lanes	020 7226 1692	21,000 car parts and 21 years experience.
Highbury Vintners	71 Highbury Park	020 7226 1347	Discount when you buy 6 or 12 bottles.
La Fromagerie	30 Highbury Park	020 7359 7440	Blow your inheritance on some Abbaye De Trois Va ux.
Mother Earth	282 St. Paul's Rd	020 7354 9897	Unfortunate New Age name, decent little shop.
Prawn on the Lawn	220 Saint Paul's Rd	020 3302 8668	Ethically and sustainably sourced fish.

Map 76 · Edgware Road / Marylebone (North)

Alfie's Antiques Market	25 Church St	020 7723 6066	Kitsch oddball sanctuary for vintage treats.
Archive Bookstore	83 Bell St	020 7402 8212	Old and unusual books.
London Beatles Store	231 Baker St	020 7935 4464	All you need is love, and no taste.
Lord's Cricket Store	Lisson Grove	020 7616 8570	They won't even ask you want a cricket bat.

Map 77 · Mornington Crescent / Regent's Park

Calumet Photographic	93 Drummond St	020 7380 1144	Cameras and accessories.

Map 78 · Euston

All Ages Records	27 Pratt St	020 7267 0303	Truly independent punk & hardcore record shop. F*** the system!
Housman's Bookshop	5 Caledonian Rd	020 7837 4473	Bookshop for progressive peaceniks and radical revolutionaries.
Peyton & Byrne	Pancras Rd	020 7278 6707	Cupcake perfection.
Transformation	52 Eversholt St	020 7388 0627	The world's largest shop for transvestites and transexuals. Seriously.

Map 79 · King's Cross

Cosmo Cornelio	182 Caledonian Rd	020 7278 3947	Old-skool, moustache trimming Italian barbers.

Map 80 · Angel / Upper St

After Noah	121 Upper St	020 7359 4281	Stuff your Nintendo Wiis—these are proper toys, retro-style.
Annie's Vintage Costume and Textiles	12 Camden Passage	020 7359 0796	Proper vintage—1900s to 1940s.
Camden Passage	Camden Passage		Thingamebobs, whatsits and doodahs aplenty.
Cass Art	66 Colebrooke Row	020 7354 2999	Large, neat-as-a-pin, extremely pleasing art supply shop.
Gill Wing Cook Shop	190 Upper St	020 7226 5392	Splendid array of kitchen gadgetry to keep foodies amused.
Little Paris	262 Upper St	020 7704 9970	A Francophile's paradise.
Micycle N1	47 Barnsbury St	020 7684 0671	Friendly and knowledgeable. With cafe!
Monte's Italian Deli	23 Canonbury Ln	020 7354 4335	Tasty, but look elsewhere if you need a hearty meal.
Paul A. Young Fine Chocolates	33 Camden Passage	020 7424 5750	"Everytime you go away..." you take a piece of chocolate.
twentytwentyone	274 Upper St	020 7288 1996	Bauhaus to Boontje and beyond.

Map 81 · Canonbury

Get Stuffed	105 Essex Rd	020 7226 1364	Polar bear for the living room, anyone? Taxidermy emporium.
HG Lockey & Sons	8 Halton Cross St	020 7226 7044	For all your er, coal and smokeless fuel needs.
James Elliott Butchers	96 Essex Rd	020 7226 3658	So much choice they'd probably stock human if they could.
Planet Organic	64 Essex Rd	020 7288 9460	Organic heaven.
Sew Fantastic	107 Essex Rd	020 7226 2725	If you'd thought it up, you'd have opened it too.
Steve Hatt	88 Essex Rd	020 7226 3963	A fishmonger's so good, people queue to get in.

Map 82 · De Beauvoir Town / Kingsland

2&4	4 Southgate Rd	020 7254 5202	Independent shop selling furniture but coffee too.
Mother Earth	101 Newington Green Rd	020 7359 7353	Organic, vegan and raw produce.
North One Garden Centre	25 Englefield Rd	020 7923 3553	Dinky little garden centre catering for dinky little London gardens.

Map 83 · Angel (East) / City Rd (North)

Flashback	50 Essex Rd	020 7354 9356	Don't come in whistling Barbie Girl.

Map 84 · Hoxton

Good Hood	41 Coronet St	020 7729 3600	Like American Apparel before it got shit.
Hoxton Street Monster Supplies	159 Hoxton St	020 7729 4159	World's only grocer for monsters, don't forget your fang floss.
SCP	135 Curtain Rd	020 7739 1869	Design-led homeware.
Sh!	57 Hoxton Sq	020 7613 5458	Dildo-tastic! Guys must come (ahem) accompanied by a galpal.
Tord Boontje Shop	23 Charlotte Rd	020 7717 5398	Whimsical, magical things.

Map 85 · **Stoke Newington (East)**

Bargain Bookshop	153 Stoke Newington High St	020 7249 8983	Books! Bargains! AH!
Hamdy	167 Stoke Newington High St	020 7254 0681	Porn-free newsagents run by stubborn maverick.
Rouge	158 Stoke Newington High St	020 7275 0887	Cool Chinese housewares. Via Belgium of course.
Stoke Newington Bookshop	159 Stoke Newington High St	020 7249 2808	Long-standing local stellar indie bookshop.

Map 86 · **Dalston / Kingsland**

Centre Supermarket	588 Kingsland Rd	020 7241 4472	Beers from all corners of the globe.
Dalston Mill Fabrics	69 Ridley Rd	020 7249 4129	Veritable treasure trove for budding Vivienne Westwoods and John Gallianos.
Healthy Stuff	168 Dalston Ln	020 7812 9604	Fresh health foods and organic goods in Hackney.
LN-CC	18 Shacklewell Ln	020 7275 7265	Appointment only darling.
Oxfam	514 Kingsland Rd	020 7254 5318	Flagship charity shop. Go find treasures!
Party Party	9 Ridley Rd	020 7254 5168	Fancy dress and party supplies plus an outstanding cake decorating department.
Ridley Road Market	Ridley Rd	084 4657 4634	Giant (live!) snails, Nigerian DVDs, fresh fish, 'taters, "Pound a bowl!"
St Vincent's	484 Kingsland Rd	020 7249 3511	Christian charity shop. Jesus galore.
Turkish Food Centre	89 Ridley Rd	020 7254 6754	Olives and feta galore, bakery onsite, plus other fresh groceries.

Map 87 · **Hackney Downs / Lower Clapton**

Kate Sheridan	112 Lower Clapton Rd	020 8985 7500	Covetable prints.
Palm 2	152 Lower Clapton Rd	020 8533 1787	Legendarily friendly corner shop beloved of bloggers.
The Pet Shop	40 Amhurst Rd	020 3330 2520	Brilliant local pet shop.
Salvation Army Clapton	122 Lower Clapton Rd	020 8985 3902	Come all ye unfaithful...
Umit & Son	35 Lower Clapton Rd	020 8985 1766	Crazed film buff selling vintage porn, super 8 and crisps?!
Viktor Wynd's Little Shop of Horrors	11 Mare St	020 7998 3617	Macabre and marvellous shop and gallery.
X Marks The Bokship	44 Copperfield Rd		Interesting bookshop specialising in independent publishers and small presses.

Map 88 · **Haggerston / Queensbridge Rd**

KTS The Corner	415 Kingsland Rd	020 7249 3199	Helpful DIY store if you can't do it yourself.

Map 89 · **London Fields / Hackney Central**

Broadway Market	Broadway Market		Yummy mummies and Guardian-reading couples peruse.
Burberry Factory Shop	29 Chatham Pl	020 8985 3344	Ever wondered how Burberry became associated with chavs?
Candle Factory	184 Mare St	020 8986 6356	Well-made, well-priced candles.
E5 Bakehouse	395 Mentmore Terrace	020 8525 2890	Sour dough to make you happy.
L'eau à la Bouche	35 Broadway Market	020 7923 0600	Cute French delicatessen shop.

Map 90 · **Homerton / Victoria Park North**

Eat 17	64-66 Brooksby's Walk	020 8986 6242	A bit like a farmers' market but you don't have to wait for the weekend.
The Ginger Pig	99 Lauriston Rd	020 8986 6911	Brilliant butcher bequeathing beef to the Borough.
Perlie Bides	137 Well St	020 8525 5694	Need a Dick Van Dyke? (Bike)
Sublime	225 Victoria Park Rd	020 8986 7243	Boudoir-like boutique selling select and independent labels.
Work Shop	77 Lauriston Rd	020 8986 9585	Beautiful handmade pottery for home and kitchen by Caroline Bousfield Gregory.

Arts & Entertainment · **Shopping**

Map 91 · Shoreditch / Brick Lane / Spitalfields

A Child of the Jago	10 Great Eastern St	020 7377 8694	Slapdash assortment of otherworldy vintage.
A Portuguese Love Affair	142 Columbia Rd	020 7613 1482	Wonderfully curated collection of beautifully packaged items from Portugal.
Absolute Vintage	15 Hanbury St	020 7247 3883	If Imelda Marcos ran a misanthropic clothes shop.
Bangla City	86 Brick Ln	020 7456 1000	Breaks the rule saying you should avoid smelly supermarkets.
Bernstock Speirs	234 Brick Ln	020 7739 7385	Look no further if you're searching for a signature titfer.
Beyond Retro	112 Cheshire St	020 7613 3636	The Daddy of all jumble sales.
Blackman's Shoes	42 Cheshire St	078 5088 3505	Chaotic hole-in-the-wall selling £5 plimsolls.
Caravan	5 Ravenscroft St	020 7033 3532	Quirky interiors shop with items new and old on offer.
Comfort Station	22 Cheshire St	020 7033 9099	Quirky and comforting collection of handmade jewellery.
Duke of Uke	88 Cheshire St	020 3583 9728	For all your many ukelele and banjo needs.
Dum Dum Donutterie	2-4 Bethnal Green Rd	020 7426 0436	Baked not fried, with a patissier's craftsmanship.
Fairy Goth Mother	72 Commercial St	020 7377 0370	Not entirely "Goth"—a Dita Von Teese of a shop.
The Grocery	54 Kingsland Rd	020 7729 6855	Selling the good life to lower Kingsland Road.
Junky Styling	91 Brick Ln	020 7247 1883	Bespoke tailoring from old rags. But posher.
Labour And Wait	85 Redchurch St	020 7729 6253	Brilliant wee shop selling old and old-looking goods.
The Laden Showroom	103 Brick Ln	020 7247 2431	Eclectic bazaar of small labels scavenged by stylists and starlets.
Lily Vanilli	6 Ezra St		Cult bakery.
Luna and Curious	24 Calvert Ave	020 3222 0034	Curiouser and curiouser..lovely local artists' and designers' co-operative.
Mast Brothers	19 Redchurch St	020 7739 1236	Bearded brothers from Brooklyn set up in Shoreditch.
Peloton & Co	4 Market St	020 7183 5530	Get off your face on coffee before buying some cycling gear.
Present	140 Shoreditch High St	020 7033 0500	Fashionable designer menswear shop with a coffee bar.
Rough Trade East	91 Brick Ln	020 7392 7788	East London outpost of the absurdly cool Rough Trade Records.
Ryantown	126 Columbia Rd	020 7613 1510	Home of the ever popular paper cutter Rob Ryan.
Sunday (Up)Market	91 Brick Ln	020 7770 6028	Great Sunday market with lots of food and cool clothes.
Taj Stores	112 Brick Ln	020 7377 0061	Weird and wonderful Eastern food.
Tatty Devine	236 Brick Ln	020 7739 9191	Bonkers jewellery loved by celebs, fashionistas and hipsters.
Taylor Taylor	12 Cheshire St	020 7033 0330	Salon for the indulgent customer.
Taylor Taylor	137 Commercial St	020 7377 2737	French boudoir-style hairdressers with free cocktail bar. Feel like a princess.
Treacle	110 Columbia Rd	020 7729 0538	Dreamy cupcakes. Don't ask for coffee—this is a TEAshop!

Map 92 · Bethnal Green

AP Fitzpatrick Fine Art Materials	142 Cambridge Heath Rd	020 7790 0884	Art supplies and expert advice.

Map 94 · Bow

Roman Road Market	Roman Rd	020 7364 1717	Big, colourful, cheap as chips—bargain tat hawked by lively east-end traders.
Sew Amazing	80 St Stephens Rd	020 8980 8898	Long established sewing machine shop. Repairs and recycling service provided.
South Molton Drug Store	583 Roman Rd	020 8981 5040	Branded cosmetics and toiletries at knock-down prices.

Map 95 · Whitechapel (West) / St Katharine's Dock

Freedom Press	84 Whitechapel High St	020 7247 9249	Long running bastion of radical thinking.

Map 97 · Stepney / Shadwell (East)

East End Thrift Store	1 Assembly Passage	020 7423 9700	Come on Thursday nights for the in-store parties.
John Lester Wigs	32 Globe Rd	020 7790 2278	Need a syrup?

Map 101 · Poplar (East) / Canary Wharf (East)

Billingsgate Fish Market	Trafalgar Way	020 7987 1118	Slice of real London in the shadow of Canary Wharf.

Map 104 · South Bank / Waterloo / Lambeth North

Calder Bookshop & Theatre	51 The Cut	020 7620 2900	Enduringly fashionable hub for the unfashionably literate.
Greensmiths	27 Lower Marsh	020 7921 2970	Old skool greengrocer's and fine foods.
I Knit London	106 Lower Marsh	020 7261 1338	The UK's only knitting shop with a licensed bar. Wool is cool.
Konditor & Cook	22 Cornwall Rd	084 4854 9361	Yummy scrummy choccies and cake.
The Oasis	84 Lower Marsh	020 7401 7074	Friendly independent salon for massages, waxing, facials and pedicures.
Radio Days	87 Lower Marsh	020 7928 0800	Cave of vintage wonders.
ScooterCaffe	132 Lower Marsh	020 7620 1421	Scooter shop has superb coffee. Word spreads. Becomes café too.
Southbank Centre Book Market	Belvedere Rd	087 1663 2501	Fun little scribe's market in brilliant surroundings.
Top Wind	2 Lower Marsh	020 7401 8787	Serious flute worship.
What The Butler Wore	131 Lower Marsh	020 7261 1968	60s, 70s vintage boutique—retro-glam party garments plus resident moggy, Binky.

Map 105 · Southwark / Bankside (West)

Elephant & Castle Shopping Centre	Elephant & Castle	020 7703 5678	An anti-Portobello Road Market...slightly dodgy but dirt-cheap.
Silverprint	120 London Rd	020 7620 0169	Photographic retailer specialising in analogue and alternative photography.

Map 106 · Bankside (East) / Borough / Newington

Borough Market	8 Southwark St	020 7407 1002	Go on an empty stomach and feast on samples.
Brindisa Shop	Borough Market	020 7407 1036	Chorizo, salchichon, Serrano ham—famed importers Brindisa have it all.
Paul Smith	13 Park St	020 7403 1678	Kitsch and dolls from the fashion designer. Don't ask why.
Richer Sounds	2 London Bridge Walk	033 3900 0021	The original store of this small chain offering low prices.
Vinopolis	1 Bank End	020 7940 8300	Wine tasting and buying megastore. Spitting optional.

Map 107 · Shad Thames

Design Museum Shop	28 Shad Thames	020 7940 8775	Stuff you wish you'd thought of.
Fine Foods	218 Long Ln	020 7403 7513	Little, local Italian deli to coo over.
Maltby Street Market	Maltby St		Snapping at the ankles of Borough Market.

Map 108 · Bermondsey

The Kernel Brewery	11 Dockley Road Industrial Estate	020 7231 4516	Open on Saturdays for brewskis.

Map 111 · Rotherhithe (East) Surrey Quays

Decathlon	Surrey Quays Rd	020 7394 2000	The Daddy of sports & outdoors shops.

Map 112 · Kennington / Elephant and Castle

Pricebusters	311 Elephant & Castle	020 7703 8244	Impressively cheap, friendly staff and an amusing collection of bric-a-brac.
Recycling	110 Elephant Rd	020 7703 7001	They sell'em bikes, they fix'em bikes. Secondhand.

Map 113 · Walworth

Threadneedleman	187 Walworth Rd	020 7701 9181	Outfitter to Suggs, David Haye and countless other suave gentlemen.
Walworth Surplus Stores	211 Walworth Rd	020 7703 4759	Decades worth of dust and grumpiness to boot.

Map 119 · Deptford (East)

Deptford Market	Deptford High St		Cheap, busy, eclectic: Proof that there IS life in Deptford.

Map 120 · Greenwich

The Beehive	320-322 Creek Rd	020 8858 1964	Greenwich's quirky vinyl-vintage cohabitation.
Black Vanilla	5 College Approach	020 8858 3283	Good gelato south of the river.
Bullfrogs	22 Greenwich Church St	020 8305 2404	Strange name, decent shop. Independent boutique.
The Cheeseboard	26 Royal Hill	020 8305 0401	Buy your cheese then head to Theatre of Wine.
Johnny Rocket	10 College Approach	020 8269 1814	One-stop jewelery shop for when you're seeking a gem.
The Junkshop	9 Greenwich South St	020 8305 1666	Voodoo masks, Guiness mugs and everything in between.
Meet Bernard	23 Nelson Rd	020 8858 4047	Dapper gents outfitters.
Mr Humbug	Greenwich Market	020 7871 4944	Infinitissimal old-fashioned sweets to relive your childhood sugar buzzes.
Music & Video Exchange	23 Greenwich Church St	020 8858 8898	Greenwich branch of the second hand empire.

Map 121 · Camberwell (West)

Butterfly Walk	Denmark Hill		The usual attractions.
Men's Traditional Shoes	171 Camberwell Rd	020 7703 4179	Visit Fred "The Shoe" Harris for classic mod footwear.
Pesh Flowers	31 Denmark Hill	020 7703 9124	Freshest daisies for miles around.
Rat Records	348 Camberwell New Rd	077 9542 4575	Ramshackle and friendly. There's bargains if you've got superhuman patience.

Map 122 · Camberwell (East)

Architectural Rescue	1-3 Southampton Way	020 7277 0081	Dig through the architectural salvage of South London's past.
Cowling and Wilcox	8-12 Orpheus St	020 7703 1342	Suppliers to the local art school hordes.

Map 123 · Peckham

Persepolis	30 Peckham High St	020 7639 8007	Can a deli change your life? Yes. Yes, it can.
Primark	51 Rye Lane	020 7639 9655	More of a chance of scoring that 'it' item at this branch.

Map 127 • Coldharbour Lane / Herne Hill (West)

Blackbird Bakery	208 Railton Rd	020 7095 8800	London needs more lovely independent bakeries (like this).

Map 128 • Denmark Hill / Herne Hill (East)

Tales on Moon Lane	25 Half Moon Ln	020 7274 5759	Cute children's bookshop (as if there were any other kind!).

Map 130 • Peckham Rye

Flock and Herd	155 Bellenden Rd	020 7635 7733	Posho butchers for Peckhams new residents. Good sausages.

Map 133 • Battersea (East)

London Recumbents	Battersea Park	020 7498 6543	Much more fun in theory than in practice.

Map 134 • South Lambeth

Fetish Freak	76 Bolton Crescent	020 7091 0031	Witness the wall of dildos.
LASSCO	30 Wandsworth Rd	020 7394 2100	Homebase for the unique, antique, or eccentric.
New Covent Garden Market	New Covent Garden Market	020 7720 2211	Known as London's Larder. Nowhere near Covent Garden
The Nine Elms Sunday Market	New Covent Garden		Challenge yourself to think of something this place doesn't sell.

Map 139 • Wandsworth (East)

Cake Boy	2 Kingfisher House	020 7978 5555	Cookery school and cake emporium extraordinaire.

Map 140 • Clapham Junction / Northcote Rd

Anita's Vintage Fashion Fair	Battersea Arts Centre	077 6834 6999	Hardcore collectors, designers, and students find inspiration amongst the rails.
The Hive Honey Shop	93 Northcote Rd	020 7924 6233	Every kind of honey you could want.
Huttons	29 Northcote Rd	020 7223 5523	Eclectic mix of unusual clothes, furniture and gifts.
Party Superstores	268 Lavender Hill	020 7924 3210	The queues on Halloween will scare you to death.
Russ	101 Battersea Rise	020 7228 6319	Model specialist—trains, boats, planes and more.
Space NK Apothecary	46 Northcote Rd	020 7228 7563	Skincare specialist.
Sweaty Betty	136 Northcote Rd	020 7978 5444	Look like a total Betty, like, even when you're sweaty.
TK Maxx	St John's Rd & Barnard Rd	020 7228 8072	The best bargains in town.
TRAID	28 St John's Rd	020 7924 3065	Characterful recycled clothes. Touch of wank, but still we like.
Whole Foods Market	305 Lavender Hill	020 7585 1488	Overwhelming selection of organic exotica.

Map 141 • Battersea (South)

Battersea Boot	401 Battersea Park Rd	079 4138 3588	Yeah! A huge, tumultuous boot sale that starts mid afternoon!
Comet Miniatures	44 Lavender Hill	020 7228 3702	Get your Airfix fix. Model shop and sci-fi.
Get A Grip Bicycle Workshop	19 Lavender Hill	020 7223 4888	These people know their stuff.

Map 142 • Clapham Old Town

M. Moen & Sons	24 The Pavement	020 7622 1624	Butcher for the bourgeoisie, incredibly good, massively expensive.
Puppet Planet	787 Wandsworth Rd	020 7627 0111	Not great if you're pupaphobic but otherwise rather charming.

Map 143 • Clapham High Street

Apex Cycles	40 Clapham High St	020 7622 1334	Bikes fixed, bikes sold.
Esca	160 Clapham High St	020 7622 2288	Your Clapham Common picnic starts here.
Today's Living Health Store	92 Clapham High St	020 7622 1772	Health foods, herbal remedies and other jiggery pokery.

Map 144 • Stockwell / Brixton (West)

A & C Co. Continental Grocers	3 Atlantic Rd	020 7733 3766	Portuguese-owned institution, famous for pestos, chorizo and mamma's tortilla.
Brixi	7 Second Ave	079 1916 2428	A look inside an eccentric's closet.
Funchal Bakery	141-143 Stockwell Rd	020 7733 3134	Portuguese grocery with good coffee and better pastel de nata.
Lisa Stickley London	74 Landor Rd	020 7737 8067	Dotty 1940s-inspired handbags to tea-towels. Cath Kidston but better.
The Old Post Office Bakery	76 Landor Rd	020 7326 4408	Disused P.O turned artisan baker's. Local loaf? The Brixton Rye.

Map 147 · Balham (West)

Bon Vivant	59 Nightingale Ln	020 8675 6314	Great local deli.

Map 148 · Balham (East)

Moxon's Fishmongers	Westbury Parade	020 8675 2468	Fresh fish for foodies with deep pockets. Knowledgeable staff.

Map 149 · Clapham Park

Macfarlane's	48 Abbeville Rd	020 8673 5373	Gourmet goodness galore.

Map 150 · Brixton

Bookmongers	439 Coldharbour Ln	020 7738 4225	Truly great local bookshop with friendly staff and dog.
Lab G	6 Granville Arcade	078 0392 2616	End your Brixton night right here with salted caramel gelato.
Ms. Cupcake	408 Coldharbour Ln	020 7733 9438	A lactose-intolerant 1950s housewife's wet dream (ir 120 flavours).
Selectors Music Emporium	100 Brixton Hill	020 7771 2011	Black music specialist.
Supertone Records	110 Acre Ln	020 7737 7761	Legendary reggae shop.
Tasty Rich Bakery	Brixton Village Market		Spicy lamb patties like you've never had before.
TRAID	2 Acre Ln	020 7326 4330	Characterful recycled clothes. Touch of wank, but sti l we like.

Map 151 · Tooting Bec

Crazy Horse Bike Workshop	275 Balham High Rd	020 8767 5614	Bikes and bike repairs.
Russell's Trade & DIY	46 Upper Tooting Rd	020 8672 1576	DIY treasure chest. Friendly, helpful owners.
Wandsworth Oasis HIV/AIDS Charity Shop	40 Trinity Rd	020 8767 7555	Thrift store treasure trove.

Map 152 · Tooting Broadway

Tooting Market	21 Tooting High St	020 8672 4760	Quaint indoor labyrinth worth nosing about.

MapMovies get ACTION

Quickmap makes very special maps for clients around the world.
See our map of London Buses in this London Not for Tourist guide.
Quickmap makes MapMovies **MM**s too. Here buses run around their London routes on screen. **MM**s are Information Entertainment.
MMs get the viewer's attention and change behaviour.

Quickmap has made **MM**s for sport venues such as Wembley National Stadium in the UK, major shopping centres and many new office or commercial developments that show how visitors can travel to that new location.
MMs can show environmentally friendly walking, cycling and transit routes to schools, town centers, airports, national parks and leisure destinations.

MM = more visitors

by animating your existing maps (send sample for costing) or develop new maps as MapMovies **MM** online.
Search for **Quickmap MapMovies** on the web.

Quickmap Limited
The Hat Factory
65-67 Bute Street
Luton
Bedfordshire
LU1 2EY
United Kingdom

44 (0)20 7813 3397
info@quickmap.com
www.quickmap.com

Quickmap ®

Street Index

Street Index

Street Index

Street Index

Street Index

Street	Page	Grid
Chertsey Street	151	B1
Cheryls Close	50	A1
Chesham Close	19	A2
Chesham Mews	19	A1
Chesham Place	19	A1/A2
Chesham Street	19	A2
Cheshire Close	126	B1/B2
Cheshire Street	91	A2/B2
Cheshire Street	91	A2/B2
Street Market		
Chesholm Road	64	B2
Chesilton Road	48	A2
Chesney Street	141	A1
Chesson Road	42	A2/B1
Chester Close	19	A2
Chester Close North	77	B1
Chester Close South	77	B1
Chester Cottages	19	B2
Chester Court	77	B1
Chester Crescent	86	B2
Chester Gate	77	B1
Chester Mews	19	A2
Chester Place	77	B1
Chester Road	59	A1
	77	B1
Chester Row	19	B2
Chester Square	19	A2/B2
Chester Square Mews	19	A2
Chester Street	19	A2
	91	B2
	92	B2
Chester Terrace	77	B1
Chester Way	112	A1
Chesterfield Gardens	9	A1
	55	B2
	120	B2
Chesterfield Grove	129	B2
Chesterfield Hill	9	A1/A2
Chesterfield Mews	55	B2
Chesterfield Street	9	A1
Chesterfield Way	124	A2
Chesterford Gardens	66	A2
Chesterton Close	138	B1
Chesterton Road	25	B1
	28	A1/A2
Chestnut Alley	42	B2
Chestnut Close	64	A1
	126	B2
Chestnut Court	42	B2
Chestnut Grove	147	B2
	148	B1
Chettle Court	54	B2
Chetwode Road	151	A1
Chetwynd Road	58	B1/B2
Cheval Place	37	B1/B2
Cheval Street	102	A1
Cheverton Road	52	B2
Cheyne Court	45	B2
Cheyne Gardens	45	B2
Cheyne Mews	45	B2
Cheyne Row	45	B1
Cheyne Walk	44	B2
	45	B1/B2
Chichele Street	104	A1
Chichester Road	30	A2
Chichester Street	20	B2
	21	B1
Chichester Way	103	A2
Chicksand Street	91	B1/B2
Chiddingstone Street	49	A1
Chigwell Hill	96	B1
Chilcot Close	99	B2
Child's Place	43	A1
Child's Street	35	A1
Childbert Road	148	B1
Childeric Road	126	A1
Childerley Street	47	B2
Childers Street	118	B1/B2
Chillington Drive	139	A1
Chillingworth Road	74	B1
Chiltern Road	99	A2
Chiltern Street	2	A1
Chilton Grove	117	A2
Chilton Street	91	A2
Chilworth Mews	31	B1
Chilworth Street	30	B2
	31	B2
China Hall Mews	110	B2
Ching Court	13	B1
Chipka Street	103	A1
Chipley Street	118	B1
Chippenham Gardens	26	A2
Chippenham Mews	26	B2
Chippenham Road	26	A2/B1/B2
Chipstead Street	49	A2
Chisenhale Road	93	A2
	94	A1
Chiswell Street	7	B2
Chiswick Common Road	38	A1/A2
Chiswick High Road	38	A1/A2
	39	B1
Chiswick Lane	38	A2/B2
Chiswick Lane South	38	B2
Chiswick Mall	38	B2
	39	B1
Chiswick Square	38	B2
Chiswick Wharf	38	B2
Chitty Street	3	A2/B2
Chivalry Road	140	B1
Cholmeley Crescent	51	B2
Cholmeley Park	51	B2
	52	A1/B1
Choppins Court	96	B1
Choumert Grove	123	B2
Choumert Mews	123	B1
Choumert Road	123	B1/B2
Chow Square	86	A1
Chrisp Street	99	B2
Christchurch Avenue	65	A1
Christchurch Hill	56	B2
Christchurch Road	53	A1
Christchurch Square	89	B2
Christchurch Street	45	B2
	46	B1
Christchurch Terrace	46	B1
Christchurch Way	103	B2
Christian Street	95	A2/B2
Christie Road	90	B2
Christina Square	63	A1
Christina Street	8	A2
Christopher Close	110	A2
Christopher Place	78	B1
Christopher Street	8	B1/B2
Chryssell Road	135	B2
Chubworthy Street	125	A2
Chudleigh Street	97	A2/B2
Chumleigh Street	114	B1
Church Avenue	71	B2
Church Crescent	90	B1
Church Gate	48	B1
Church Lane	54	A2
	151	B1/B2
	152	A2
Church Road	51	A2
	81	A2
Church Row	56	B1
Church Street	31	A2
	38	B2
	76	B1
Church Terrace	143	A2
Church Walk	64	B1
Churchcroft Close	147	B2
Churchfields	120	A2
Churchill Gardens Road	20	B2
Churchill Place	101	B1
Churchill Road	58	B2
Churchill Walk	90	A1
Churchway	78	B1
Churchwell Path	89	A2
Churchyard Row	112	A2
Churton Place	20	A2
Churton Street	20	A2/B2
Chusan Place	100	A1
Cicada Road	139	B1
	146	A1
Cicely Road	123	A2/B2
Cinnamon Close	123	A1
Cinnamon Row	139	B1
Cinnamon Street	96	B1
Circus Mews	1	A2
Circus Place	8	B1
Circus Road	68	B1/B2
Circus Street	120	A1/B2
Cirencester Street	30	A1
Citadel Place	131	B1
Citizen Road	74	A1
City Garden Row	83	B1
City Road	7	A2
	8	A1/B1
	80	B1
	83	B1/B2
	84	B1
Clabon Mews	37	B2
Clack Street	110	B1
Claire Place	102	A1
Clancarty Road	49	B1/B2
Clanricarde Gardens	29	B2
Clapham Common North Side	140	A2
	141	B1/B2
	142	B1/B2
Clapham Common South Side	143	B1
	148	A2
	149	A1
Clapham Common West Side	140	A2/B2
	147	A2
	148	A1
Clapham Crescent	143	B1
Clapham High Street	143	A2/B1/B2
Clapham Manor Street	143	A1/B1
Clapham Park Road	143	B1/B2
Clapham Road	135	A2/B1/B2/B2
	143	B2
	144	A1
Clapton Common	86	A1

Street Index

Street Index

Street Index

Street Index

Street Index

Street Index

Street Index

Street Index

Street Index

Street Index

Street Index

Street Index

Street Index

Street Index

Street Index

Street Index

Street Index

Street Index

Street Index

Street Index

Street Index

Street Index

Departures

anythink™

A REVOLUTION OF RANGEVIEW LIBRARIES

0506

Tired of your own city?

You buy the ticket, we'll be the guide.

Customize your NFT.

We can put **your organization's logo or message** on NFT using custom foil stamps of your (or our) design. Not For Tourists Guidebooks make **great gifts** for employees, clients, and promotional events.

For more information, visit
www.notfortourists.com/corporatesales.aspx